MOROCCO

the collected traveler

Also in the series by Barrie Kerper

CENTRAL ITALY
The Collected Traveler

PARIS
The Collected Traveler

PROVENCE
The Collected Traveler

MOROCCO

the collected traveler

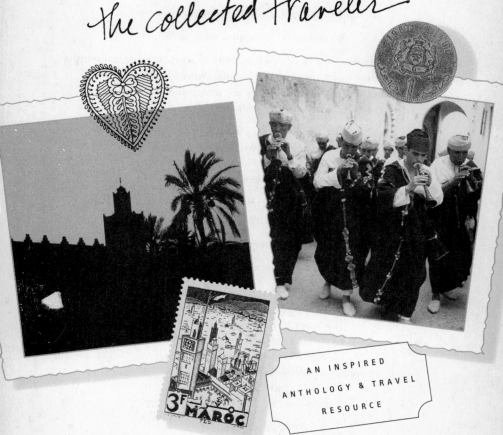

AN INSPIRED
ANTHOLOGY & TRAVEL
RESOURCE

Collected by Barrie Kerper

Three Rivers Press / NEW YORK

Anthology copyright © 2001 by Barrie Kerper

Additional credits appear on page 591.

Published by Three Rivers Press, New York, New York.
Member of the Crown Publishing Group.
Random House, Inc. New York, Toronto, London, Sydney, Auckland
www.randomhouse.com

THREE RIVERS PRESS is a registered trademark and the Three Rivers Press colophon is a trademark of Random House, Inc.

Printed in the United States of America

DESIGN BY LYNNE AMFT

Library of Congress Cataloging-in-Publication Data
Morocco: an inspired anthology and travel resource /
collected by Barrie Kerper.—1st ed.
(The collected traveler)
Includes bibliographical references.
1. Morocco—Guidebooks.   I. Kerper, Barrie.   II. Series.
DT304 .M6515 2001
916.404′5—dc21   2001027982

ISBN 0-609-80859-1

10 9 8 7 6 5 4 3 2 1

First Edition

*Once again, for my mother, Phyllis,
who always believed my boxes of files
held something of value.*

acknowledgments

For a variety of reasons, this edition in the series has been the hardest to pull together, and so I am especially grateful to the following friends, colleagues, and Morocco enthusiasts for all their assistance, support, and expertise: Al Adams, Alison Gross, Amy Myer, Andrea Rosen, Audrey Bekany, Becky Cabaza, Cara Brozenich, Cherie Nutting, Craig Young, Dave Garber, Doug Jones, Florence Porrino, Holly Clarfield, James Perry, Jill Flaxman, Joan DeMayo, Kathy Burke, Lauren Shakely, Linda Loewenthal, Margaret Hathaway, Murray Berman, Patty Flynn, Philip Patrick, Rachel Kahan, Rebecca Strong, Rich Romano, Roberto Diaz, Roy Finamore, Stacy Laufer, Susan Ralston, Teresa Nicholas, Teryn Johnson, and Vivian Fong. Once again, special thanks are due to the art and production team of Amy Boorstein, Derek McNally, Lauren Dong, Lynne Amft, Mark McCauslin, and Whitney Cookman for their patience, talent, and ability to work miracles. I extend my heartfelt thanks and deep gratitude to Farid Najjar, Samira Najjar, Katherine Dietzen, and Nadia Nassif, as well as to Benjaafar Marrakchi and Amar Hynd of the Moroccan National Tourist Office in New York. *Merci beaucoup* to Dr. Mark Fialk of the Scarsdale Medical Group. I remain in awe of the knowledge imparted to me on Islam by Bradley Clough and Jonathan Brockopp, both assistant professors of religion at Bard College, and Maha Khalil, and on Moroccan history and literature by Mohamed Ben Madani and Mohamed El Mansour. They are founts of knowledge all. As before, extra special thanks are due to each of the individual writers, agents, and permissions representatives for various publishers and periodicals—especially Leigh Montville of The Condé Nast Publications, Rose Cervino of *The New York Times,* and Steven McChesney of the William Morris Agency—without whose generosity and understanding there would be nothing to publish; to Shaye Areheart, my amazing editor and friend who can solve any manuscript problem; to Chip Gibson, my boss, for displaying great reserves of calm on those occasions when a manuscript is due and there is a maelstrom outside his office; and to my great friends and travelers, Lorraine and Luc Paillard. Lastly, big hugs and kisses to my husband, Jeffrey, and daughter, Alyssa. There is not a road or medina alley in Morocco that is too difficult for Jeff to navigate, and I hope we have the opportunity to take Alyssa with us next time.

contents

Au Delà des Villes

Saveurs et Tables Marocaines

Les Personalités

Des Belles Choses

MOROCCO

the collected traveler

La Maison Bleue
Maison d'Hôtes &
Restaurant Gastronomique

Mehdi El Abbadi
Directeur Général

Introduction

"A traveller without knowledge is a bird without wings."
—Sa'di, *Gulistan* (1258)

Some years ago my husband and I fulfilled a dream we'd had since we first met: we put all our belongings in storage and traveled around the countries bordering the Mediterranean Sea for a year. In preparation for this journey, I did what I always do in advance of a trip, which is to consult my home archives, a library of books and periodicals. I have been an obsessive clipper since I was very young, and by the time I was preparing for this trip, I had amassed an enormous number of articles from a wide variety of periodicals. After a year of reading and organizing all this material, I then created a package of articles and notes for each destination and mailed them ahead to friends we'd be staying with as well as appropriate American Express offices—although we had no schedule to speak of, we knew we would spend no less than six weeks in each place.

My husband wasted no time informing me that my research efforts were perhaps a bit over the top. He shares my passion for travel (my mother-in-law told me that when he was little, he would announce to the family exactly how many months, weeks, days, hours, minutes, and seconds it was before the annual summer vacation) but not necessarily for clipping. (He has accused me of being too much like the anal-retentive fisherman from an old *Saturday Night Live* skit, the one where the guy neatly puts his bait, extra line, snacks, hand towels, etc., into individual sandwich bags. In my defense, I'm not *quite* that bad (although I *am* guilty of trying to improve upon pocket organizers, and I do have a wooden rack for drying rinsed plastic bags in my kitchen).

While we were traveling that year, we would occasionally meet other Americans, and I was continually amazed at how ill-prepared some of them were. Information, in so many different forms, is in such abundance in the twenty-first century that it was nearly inconceivable to me that people had not taken advantage of the resources available to them. Some people we met didn't even seem to be having a very good time; they appeared to be ignorant of various customs and observances and were generally unimpressed with their experience because they had missed the significance of what they were seeing and doing. Therefore, I was surprised again when these same people—and they were of varying ages with varying wallet sizes— were genuinely interested in my little packages of notes and articles. Some people even offered to *pay* me for them, and I began to think that my collected research would perhaps appeal to other travelers. I also realized that even the most well-intentioned people were overwhelmed by trip planning or didn't have the time to put it all together. Later, friends and colleagues told me they really appreciated the packages I prepared for them, and somewhere along the line I was being referred to as a "modern-day hunter-gatherer," a sort of "one-stop information source." Each book in *The Collected Traveler* series provides resources and information to travelers—people I define as inquisitive, individualistic, and indefatigable in their eagerness to explore—or informs them of where they may look further to find it.

While there is much to be said for a freewheeling approach to travel—I am not an advocate of sticking to rigid schedules—I do believe that, as with most things in life, what you get out of a trip is equal only to what you put into it. James Pope-Hennessy, in his wonderful book *Aspects of Provence,* notes that "if one is to get

M o r o c c o

best value out of places visited, some skeletal knowledge of their history is necessary. . . . Sight-seeing is by no means the only object of a journey, but it is as unintelligent as it is lazy not to equip ourselves to understand the sights we see." I feel that learning about a place is part of the excitement of travel, and I wouldn't dream of venturing anywhere without first poring over a mountain of maps, books, and periodicals. I include cookbooks in my reading (some cookbooks reveal much historical detail as well as prepare you for the food and drink you will most likely encounter), and I also like to watch movies before I leave that have something to do with where I'm going. Additionally, I buy a blank journal and fill it with all sorts of notes, reminders, and entire passages from books I'm not bringing along. In other words, I completely immerse myself in my destination before I leave. It's the most enjoyable homework assignment I could ever give myself.

Every destination, new or familiar, merits some attention. I don't endorse the extreme—spending all your time in a hotel room reading books—but it most definitely pays to know something about your destination before you go—just leave some room for the chance encounter or unpredictable surprise. The reward for your efforts is that you'll acquire a deeper understanding and appreciation of the place and the people who live there, and not surprisingly, you'll have more fun.

"Every land has its own special rhythm, and unless the traveler takes the time to learn the rhythm, he or she will remain an outsider there always."

—Juliette de Bairicli Levy,
English writer, b. 1937

Occasionally I meet people who are more interested in how many countries I've been to than in those I might know well or particularly like. If *well-traveled* is defined only by the number of places I've been, then I suppose I'm not. But I feel I *really know* and have *really seen* the places I've visited, which is how *I* define *well-traveled*. I travel to see how people live in other parts of the world—not to check countries off a list—and doing that requires immediately adapting to the local pace and rhythm and (hopefully) sticking around for more than a few days. Certainly any place you decide is worthy of your time and effort is worthy of more than a day, but you don't always need an indefinite period of time to immerse yourself in the local culture or establish a routine that allows you to get to know the merchants and residents of your adopted neighborhood. One of the fastest ways to adjust to daily life in Morocco is to abandon whatever schedule you observe at home and eat when the Moroccans eat. Mealtimes in Morocco are not as strictly established as in France, for example, but—especially in the summer—if you have not bought provisions for a picnic or found a place to eat by one o'clock, most shops will be closed for the afternoon siesta, and restaurants—which aren't numerous in Morocco—will be full. Likewise, dinner is not typically served at six P.M., an hour that is entirely too early for anyone in a Mediterranean country to even contemplate eating a meal. The earliest Moroccans sit down to dinner is about eight P.M., after the evening *paseo* (stroll). Adjust your schedule, and you'll be on Moroccan time, doing things when the Moroccans do them, eliminating possible disappointment and frustration. I would add that it's also rewarding to rise early in Morocco. It may be difficult to convince holiday travelers who like to sleep late to get out of bed a few hours earlier, but if you sleep in every day, you will most definitely miss much of the local rhythm. By nine A.M. in Morocco—and in any Mediterranean country—much has already happened, and besides, you can always look forward to a delicious afternoon nap.

About fifteen years ago the former Paris bureau chief for *The*

New York Times, John Vinocur, wrote a piece for the travel section entitled "Discovering the Hidden Paris." In it, he noted that the French have a word, *dépaysement,* which he translated into English as meaning "the feeling of not being assaulted by the familiarity of things, a change in surroundings where there is no immediate point of reference." He went on to quote a French journalist who once said that "Americans don't travel to be *dépaysés,* but to find a home away from home." This is unfortunate, but too often true. These tourists can travel all around the world if they desire, but their unwillingness to adapt ensures they will never really leave home. As Alain D'Hooghe notes in the wonderful book *The Magic of Morocco,* "To appreciate all its riches, one must approach Morocco while accepting from the very outset all its differences, without trying at any cost to find the comfort of familiarity or reassuring landmarks. The journey, with no certainties to mark its course, will be all the more fascinating and our encounters all the more delightful." Similarly, Paul Bowles wrote in *Their Heads Are Green and Their Hands Are Blue,* "Each time I go to a place I have not seen before, I hope it will be as different as possible from the places I already know. I assume it is natural for a traveler to seek diversity, and that it is the human element which makes him most aware of difference. If people and their manner of living were alike everywhere, there would not be much point in moving from one place to another."

Diverse is the single word I would use to best describe Morocco, not only in reference to its physical attributes but to its population. Barnaby Rogerson, author of the commendable *Cadogan Morocco Guide,* notes that "Moroccan landscape and the country's regional cultures are all extraordinarily diverse, but ultimately it is its people that prove most fascinating. In any one Moroccan there may lurk a turbulent and diverse ancestry: of slaves brought across the Saharan wastes to serve as concubines or warriors; of Andalucian refugees who came from the ancient Muslim and Jewish cities of southern

Spain, and of Bedouin Arabs from the tribes that fought their way along the North African shore. All these peoples have mingled with the indigenous Berbers, who have continuously occupied the land since the Stone Age." Similarly, Fatima Mernissi, in her wonderful book *Dreams of Trespass*, describes a time in the 1940s when she was a young girl in Fez and the Americans had recently landed in Casablanca. All the women in her extended family were wondering why the American white men were so very white and the blacks so very black. They were then informed that Americans didn't intermarry. "We had a good laugh about that up there on the terrace, because anyone who wanted to separate people according to their skin color in Morocco was going to run into severe difficulties. People had mixed together so much that they came in hues of honey, almond, café au lait, and so many, many shades of chocolate. In fact, there often were both blue-eyed and dark-skinned brothers and sisters in the same family." Morocco may actually be the most diverse country bordering the Mediterranean Sea, and it is certainly one of the most diverse in the world.

Similar to the *dépaysés*-phobic are those who endorse "adventure travel," words that make me cringe as they seem to imply that unless one partakes in kayaking, mountain climbing, biking, rock

climbing, or some other physical endeavor, a travel experience is somehow invalid or unadventurous. *All* travel is an adventure, and unless adventure travel allows for plenty of time to adapt to the local rhythm, the so-called adventure is really just a physically strenuous—albeit memorable—outdoor achievement. Occasionally I hear descriptions of a biking excursion, for example, where the participants spend the majority of each day making biking the priority instead of incorporating biking into the local cadence of daily life. When I ask if they joined the locals at the café for a morning *thé à la menthe,* shopped at the souk, went to a local *musée,* or people-watched in the Djemaa el Fna, the answer is invariably no. They might have had an amazing bike trip, but they didn't get to know Morocco—one has to get off the bike a bit more often to do that—and if a biking experience alone is what they were seeking, they certainly didn't need to fly to Morocco: there are plenty of challenging and beautiful places to bike in the United States.

I believe that *every* place in the world offers *something* of interest. In her magnificent book *Black Lamb and Grey Falcon,* Rebecca West recounts how in the 1930s she passed through Skopje, in what was then Yugoslavia (and is now the Republic of Macedonia), by train twice, without stopping, because friends had told her the town wasn't worth visiting. A third time through she did stop, and she met two wonderful people who became lasting friends. She wrote, "Now, when I go through a town of which I know nothing, a town which appears to be a waste land of uniform streets wholly without quality, I look on it in wonder and hope, since it may hold a Mehmed, a Militsa." I, too, have been richly rewarded by pausing in places (Skopje included) that at first appeared quite limiting.

There are any number of Moroccan towns and villages that, at first glance, seem limiting and downright dreary. In many developing nations—and in plenty of first world countries as well—*le style cement block* is all the rage, and it doesn't get more drab than cement block gray. But the Moroccans, who tend to build new apartments and businesses of this same cement block, have had the good sense to smooth out the surface and paint it over in the bright colors of the *sud marocain*. As Jeffrey Becom has noted in *Mediterranean Color*, this practice is most likely a method of averting the evil eye, prevalent throughout the Mediterranean: "One morning I watched a man confidently painting his shop an auspicious, buoyant blue. Even I thought it looked reassuring, something like the shade at the bottom of a swimming pool. With a long-handled, round-bristle brush, he slapped on the paint. After splashing saturated pink across his counter, he stenciled rows of Nile-green hands and lemon-yellow stars around his door until he was sure to be safe and prosperous, surrounded by his fresh bouquet of color." The evil eye aside, I admit I like to think that such festive colors also have an uplifting effect upon the inhabitants. But even without the colors, don't let a rather run-down Moroccan town deceive you: Moroccan hospitality is not limited to the country's imperial cities.

"Travel is fatal to prejudice, bigotry, and narrow-mindedness."
—Mark Twain

"Travel across foreign nations, leave your homeland behind. In the effort and exhaustion of travel, you will find the savor of life."

—Al-Imam Al-Shafi'

I am assuming, if you've read this far, that something compelled you to pick up this book, and that you feel travel is an essential part of life. I would add to Mark Twain's quote above one by Benjamin Disraeli (1804–81): "Travel teaches toleration." People who travel with an open mind and are receptive to the ways of others cannot help but return with more tolerance for people and situations at home, at work, and in their cities and communities. James Ferguson, a nineteenth-century Scottish architect, observed this perfectly when he wrote, "Travel is more than a visitor seeing sights; it is the profound changing—the deep and permanent changing—of that visitor's perspective of the world, and of his own place in it." I find that travel also ensures I will not be quite the same person I was before I left. After a trip, I typically have a lot of renewed energy and bring new perspectives to my job. At home, I ask myself how I can incorporate attributes or traits I observed while traveling into my own life and share them with my husband and daughter.

The anthologies in *The Collected Traveler* series offer a record of people's achievements and shortcomings. It may be a lofty goal to expect that they may also offer us an opportunity to measure our own deeds and flaws as Americans, so that we can realize that, despite cultural differences between us and our hosts in *any* country, we have much more in common than not. It is a sincere goal, however, and one that I hope readers and travelers will embrace.

About This Series

The Collected Traveler editions are not guidebooks in the traditional sense. In another sense, however, they *may* be considered guidebooks in that they are books that guide readers to other sources. Each book is really the first book you should turn to when planning a trip. If you think of the individual volumes as a sort of planning package, you've got the right idea. To borrow a phrase from a reviewer who was writing about the Lonely Planet Travel Survival Kit series years ago, *The Collected Traveler* is for people who know how to get their luggage off the carousel. If you enjoy acquiring knowledge about where you're going—whether you're planning a trip independently or with a like-minded tour organization—this series is for you. If you're looking for a guide that simply informs you of exact prices, hours, and highlights, you probably won't be interested in the depth this book offers. (That is not meant to offend, merely to say you've got the wrong book.)

A few words about me may also help you determine if this series is for you: I travel somewhat frugally, not out of necessity but more because I choose to. I respect money and its value, and I'm not convinced that if I spent $600 a night on a hotel room, for example, it would represent a good value or I would have a better trip. I've been to some of the world's finest hotels, mostly to visit friends who were staying there or to have a drink in the hotel bar. With a few notable exceptions, it seems to me that the majority of these places are all alike, meant to conform to a code of sameness and predictability. There's nothing about them that is particularly Moroccan or French or Italian or Turkish—you could be *anywhere*. The cheapest of the cheap accommodations don't represent good value, either. I look for places to stay that are usually old, possibly historic, and have lots of charm and character. I do not mind if my room is small; I do not need a television, telephone, or hair dryer; and I most definitely do not care for an American-style buffet breakfast, which is hardly what the locals eat. I also prefer to make my own plans, send my own letters and faxes, place my own telephone calls, and make my own transportation arrangements. Not because I think I can do it better than a professional agent (whose expertise I admire), but because I enjoy it and learn a lot in the process. Finally, lest readers think I do not appreciate elegance, allow me to state that I think you'll quickly ascertain that I do indeed enjoy many of life's little luxuries, when I perceive them to be of good value to me.

The Collected Traveler focuses on one corner of the world, the countries bordering the Mediterranean Sea. I find the Mediterranean endlessly fascinating; the first time I saw the sea, in 1979, I understood perfectly Samuel Johnson's observation, "The grand object of travelling is to see the shores of the Mediterranean." The sea itself is the world's largest, the region is one of the world's ancient crossroads, and as it stretches from Asia to the Atlantic, it is home to the most diverse humanity. As Paul Theroux has noted in his excellent book *The Pillars of Hercules,* "The Mediterranean, this simple almost tideless sea, the size of thirty Lake Superiors, had everything: prosperity, poverty, tourism, terrorism, several wars in progress, ethnic strife, fascists, pollution, drift nets, private islands owned by billionaires, Gypsies, seventeen countries, fifty languages, oil drilling platforms, sponge fishermen, religious fanatics, drug smuggling, fine art, and warfare. It had Christians, Muslims, Jews; it had the Druzes, who are a strange farrago of all three religions; it had heathens, Zoroastrians and Copts and Baha'is." Diversity aside, the great explorers in the service of Spain and Portugal departed from Mediterranean ports to discover so much of the rest of the world. "This sea," writes Lisa Lovatt-Smith in her beautiful book *Mediterranean Living,* "whose shores have hosted the main currents in civilization, creates its own homogenous culture, end-lessly absorbing newcomers and their ideas . . . and is the one I con-sider my own." I, too, consider the sea my own, even though I live thousands of miles away from it.

As readers of my previous three books know, this series typically focuses on individual cities and regions rather than entire countries. This book, however, on *all* of Morocco, is a departure from my strongly held view of staying longer within a smaller area. I found that it did not make a shred of sense to divide Morocco up into regions or cities. Gavin Maxwell, in *Lords of the Atlas,* noted, "There have been many attempts to divide Morocco into convenient sections for discussion, but most of them appear unnecessarily complex; it is easier to consider an inner Morocco and an outer Morocco, the two being divided by the whole mass of the Atlas Mountains running from the south-west to the north-east of the country, and the Rif mountains which turn at right angles to these and form the Mediterranean wall." I had originally thought to put together two books, one on northern Morocco and another on southern Morocco. There are, after all, fundamental differences between the country south of the High Atlas and the fertile hills around Meknes and Fez—with regard not only to topography but to climate, language, and customs. But I realized that, aside from its natural features like the desert, mountains, and oases, the main reason to visit Morocco is to see its four Imperial Cities—Rabat, Meknes, Fez, and Marrakesh—and seeing these remarkable cities takes travelers from the north Atlantic coast over to the Middle Atlas and south toward the desert. Repeat visitors to Morocco often choose just one region or corner of the country to see, but first-time visitors want to—and should—see the diversity that is Morocco. Eventually, I think I *would* like to present two separate books on Morocco, but my current goal is simply to entice North Americans to get on the next Royal Air Maroc flight departing for Casablanca and see, smell, and experience this extraordinary country!

My friend Peter A. still teases me for making a comment—now fifteen years ago—that if one couldn't stay in a place for at least a month, one might as well not go. Morocco can easily be dubbed a one-month country, not least because getting around takes more time than is immediately apparent. If you look at a map of Morocco, driving the distance between Casablanca and Essaouira (351 kilometers), for example, would seem to take much less than the five to six hours the tourist office said it would; but indeed it took us five hours by car, with one brief stop in Safi. The drive from Marrakesh to Fez takes nearly a full day. If one took the train, it would take even longer, as the route cannot cut through the Middle Atlas Mountains, so one must first travel west over to Casablanca and then east again to Fez. (If you take the bus, you'll need *two* months in Morocco.) Flying, via Royal Air Maroc, is obviously a faster method of getting from place to place, but some flights are offered only two or three times a week, and when you fly, you miss much of the magnificent Moroccan landscape. The first piece of advice I would give to anyone bound for Morocco is to allow plenty of time to plan your itinerary, because you will most likely have to change it a number of times. I recognize that most readers probably do not have the luxury of one month to set aside and see Morocco. I have found that the best way to see the country in a short period of time is to make use of the train, a car, and internal RAM flights. But the *very* best way is to get around by car for the entire time and stay longer. Barnaby Rogerson, again in his Cadogan guide, offers some related advice for visitors: "It is a mistake to move too quickly around Morocco. Far too many visitors visit a city, suffer all the initial hassle and leave before they are relaxed enough to explore beyond the well-trodden list of major tourist sites. The frenetic energy, noisy animation, odours and ceaseless babble of the Moroccan street initially threaten to overwhelm a visitor. In Morocco, however, do as the Moroccans do. Take things slowly, and catch the afternoon siesta in order to be fresh for the evening *paseo*."

Each section of this book features a selection of articles from various periodicals and an annotated bibliography relevant to the theme of each section. (The *Renseignements Pratiques* section is a bit different, with the books being a part of the A–Z listings.) The articles and books were chosen from my own files and home library, which I've maintained for over two decades. The selected writings reflect the culture, politics, history, current social issues, religion, cuisine, and arts of the people you'll be visiting. They also represent the observations and opinions of a wide variety of novelists, travel writers, and journalists. These writers are authorities on Morocco, or a particular part of Morocco, or are extremely passionate about Morocco in general; they either live there (as permanent or part-time residents) or visit there often for business or pleasure. I'm very discriminating in seeking opinions and recommendations, and I am not interested in the remarks of unobservant wanderers. I am not implying that first-time visitors to Morocco have nothing noteworthy or interesting to share—they very often do and are often very keen observers; conversely, frequent travelers are very often jaded and apt to miss the finer details that make Morocco the exceptional place it is. I am interested in the opinions of people who want to *know* Morocco, not just *see* it.

I've included numerous older articles (even though some of the specific information regarding prices, hours, and the like is no longer accurate) because they were either particularly well written, thought-provoking, or unique in some way, and because the authors' views stand as a valuable record of a certain time in history. Often, even with the passage of many years, you may share the same emotions and opinions of the writer, and equally as often, *plus ça change, plus c'est la même chose.* I have many more articles in my files than I was able to reprint here. Though there are a few pieces whose absence I very much regret, I believe the anthology you're holding is very good.

A word about the transliteration of Arabic spellings: Readers will notice a variety of spellings for place names and words as they read each piece, such as Fez versus Fes, or *djellebah* versus *jellaba*. I decided to retain the variety, as visitors will encounter this in their own travels, not just in Morocco but in any country with a different alphabet. This decision has, let me assure you, driven my copy editor nearly to the brink, but I think it's important for readers to understand that there is no direct translation from alphabet to alphabet, which I explain more fully in the language entry in *Renseignments Pratiques.*

The annotated bibliography for each section is one of the most important features of this book. Reading about travel in the days before trans-Atlantic flights, I always marvel at the number of steamer trunks and baggage people were accustomed to taking. If it were me traveling then, however, my bags would be filled with books, not clothes. Although I travel light and seldom check bags, I have been known to fill an entire suitcase with books, secure in the knowledge that I could have them all with me for the duration of my trip. Each *Bibliothèque,* or list of books, features titles I feel are the best available, most worth your time. I realize that "best" is subjective; readers will simply have to trust me that I have been extremely thorough in deciding which books to recommend. (I own and have read them all, by the way, with the exception of a few I borrowed.) If the lists seem long, they are, but the more I read, the more I realize there is to know, and there are an awful lot of really good books out there! I'm not suggesting you read them *all,* but I do hope you will not be content with just one. I have identified some

books as *de rigueur,* meaning that I consider them required reading; but I sincerely believe that *all* the books I've mentioned are important, helpful, well written, or all three. There are surely some books I've not seen, so if some of your favorites aren't included here, please write and tell me about them.

I have not hesitated to list out-of-print titles because some very excellent books are declared out of print (and deserve to be returned to print!), and because many out-of-print books can be found, through individuals who specialize in out-of-print books, booksellers, libraries, and on-line searches. I should also mention that I believe the companion reading you bring along should be related in some way to where you're going. (Anne Fadiman, in her great little book *Ex Libris,* calls this "You-Are-There Reading, the practice of reading books in the places they describe.") Therefore, the books listed in *Des Belles Choses* are novels and nonfiction titles that feature characters or settings in Morocco, or aspects of Morocco and the Moroccans (such as *The Sheltering Sky, The Arabian Nights, Arts and Crafts of Morocco,* and *The Sand Child*). Biographies represent the bulk of the books in the *Les Personalités* section. The selection isn't meant to be comprehensive—although truthfully, I don't believe there are a great many others—but I separated them from books about artists, for example, who lived or worked in Morocco. (Some of these titles are catalogs from museum exhibits and feature many reproductions of artworks.)

Together, the articles and books lead you on and off the beaten path and present a reality check of sorts. Will you learn of some nontouristy things to see and do? Yes. Will you also learn more about the better-known aspects of Morocco? Yes. Ait-Benhaddou, the Bab Boujeloud in Fez, and staying with a Berber family in the High Atlas are equally representative of Morocco. Seeing them *all* is what makes for a memorable visit, and no one, by the way, should make you feel guilty for wanting to see some famous sites. They have become famous for a reason: they are really something to see, Ait-Benhaddou included. Readers will have no trouble finding a multitude of other travel titles offering plenty of noncontroversial viewpoints. This is my attempt at presenting a more balanced picture. Ultimately, this is also the compendium of information that I wish I'd had between two covers years ago. I admit it isn't the "perfect" book; for that, I envision a waterproof jacket and pockets inside the front and back covers, pages and pages of accompanying maps, lots of blank pages for notes, a bookmark, photos and beautiful drawings, mileage and size conversion charts . . . in other words, something so encyclopedic—in both weight and size—that positively no one, my editor assures me, would want to read it. That said, I am exceedingly happy with *The Collected Traveler,* and I believe it will prove helpful in heightening the anticipation of your upcoming journey; in the enjoyment of your trip while it's happening; and in the remembrance of it when you're back home.

It may seem impossible today that a country on the south shore of the Mediterranean only nine miles from Spain could still be referred to as "exotic," but in fact Morocco *is* exotic—in fact, it serves so many helpings of exoticism that it can make your head spin. This remains true partly because some areas of the country were long closed to outsiders. In the mid-1800s, very few Europeans had ever set foot in Morocco, let alone cross the High Atlas Mountains to the Sahara. Gavin Maxwell notes in *Lords of the Atlas* that Morocco, "despite its geographical position as a neighbour to Europe, remained as unknown as Tibet. . . . In fact, Morocco at the end of the last century was little different in any external respect from what it had been at the end of the century before—or, indeed, the end of any other century for a thousand years or more." I have a copy of the 1904 *Macmillan's Guide to the Western Mediterranean* that contains more than a few references to sites or entire towns that were off-limits to non-Muslims. 1904 is not so very long ago, and in 1918, when Edith Wharton wrote *In Morocco,* there were a number of places that were even then just welcoming foreigners. (When she was in Marrakesh, no travelers before her had as yet been admitted to the Saadian tombs, discovered just a year earlier when the sultan's government privately informed Marshal Hubert Lyautey that an "unsuspected treasure of Moroccan art was falling into ruin.") By the 1920s, the French had big plans for the development of Morocco, but the country still appeared antique to French author André Chevrillon, who wrote in *Marrakesh dans les Palmes,* "Without doubt, Morocco, with one or two of the kingdoms of Asia, represents the last surviving example of a civilization of the ancient world. . . . That it has survived until our own times, that we can see it, we can touch it, mix with its people, is a miracle that never ceases to astonish." In a beautifully printed album I have dated from the 1920s (I think; no copyright is provided)—complete with watercolor aquarelles, woodblock prints, and photographs—that was published by the Protectorate of the French Republic at Morocco, the unidentified author says, "You must be quick and visit Morocco if you wish to see, elsewhere than at exhibitions, the Middle Ages rubbing shoulders with modern civilization. The country is changing from month to month, almost from day to day. A port is opened, a railway station which only yesterday appeared to you to be a rather pretentious construction, now seems hardly able to contain the number of passengers; a street blossoms forth in all the splendour of lighted shop-windows. Where else in all the world is so much work being done, so much energy spent, as in this sunny, prosperous land? Ten years ago, the main road from Rabat to Casablanca was a dusty mule track, crossing endless plains of shrub and dwarf palm. Today, avenues of trees are beginning to shade it, thriving farms provide landmarks, crops and vineyards are to be seen everywhere." Morocco hasn't *entirely* remained in the Middle Ages (though sometimes, when I'm wan-

dering around Fes-el-Bali, I wonder), but it is a place I encourage you to see sooner rather than later. Fortunately, the French presence in the country—though undeniably annoying, harsh, and ultimately quite *grave*—was not of such duration as to destroy the pride and soul of Moroccans or the unique and picturesque qualities of the land.

Morocco has changed and is still changing. The beginning of the twenty-first century is an exciting time to visit, as dramatic shifts are occurring at every level of society. Sometimes those shifts are nothing less than a collision: a donkey slowly navigating a narrow street in the medina is transporting small television sets; a young Moroccan woman wearing tight jeans, stiletto heels, and a skimpy shirt that doesn't quite reach her hips runs to a car where her family is waiting, the mother almost completely covered, the father donning *djellaba* and skullcap; a donkey pulls a cart heavy with green cuttings from a nearby field, while women in head scarves and flowing skirts walk behind—and together they walk across the overpass on the *péage* superhighway between Rabat and Casablanca. My friend Audrey, who lives in Fez, says these scenes are positively surreal, but they are to be expected in a nation trying to catch up to the twenty-first century.

Morocco has gotten under my skin, so to speak, and is one of the most extraordinary places I've ever seen. Surprisingly, while it is a popular destination for many Europeans, I have not encountered many Americans there; our Canadian neighbors to the north seem to be much more aware and appreciative of Morocco. I use the word *surprisingly* because, much as I am tempted to keep it free of hordes of American tourists, Morocco has too much going for it to remain a secret. I cannot, in good conscience, refrain from promoting such an astonishing country. We all have lasting impressions of a place, and for me, when I imagine Morocco, I am walking through a souk, one minute smelling spices, rose petals, jasmine, and mint, the next smelling something strong, pungent, unidentifiable, and unpleasant. Then I am being jostled by Moroccan housewives all a-gaggle over some new clothing being hawked by a merchant, and a few steps later I am in the middle of a quiet *fondouk,* with the sun shining in the middle of the courtyard and some cats playing in the corner. Morocco is shadow and light, old and modern, hot and cold, rich and poor, beautiful and run-down, all rolled into one big, giant *kefta* (meatball). Like its cuisine, the entire nation of Morocco can be said to be a balance of sweet and sour.

Morocco is only a six-and-a-half-hour flight from New York, the same as flying to much of Europe; the Atlas Mountains and the Sahara serve to separate Morocco from the rest of Africa, effectively creating an island of civilization in the corner of the continent; it is exotic, the closest Muslim nation to North America; the government, under the leadership of Mohammed VI, is attempting reforms in many areas, and they are doing an admirable job at keeping extremism at bay; Morocco is home to six World Heritage Sites (Fez medina, Marrakesh medina, Ait-Benhaddou, Meknes, Volubilis, and Tetouan medina), which encompass 630 natural and cultural sites "of outstanding value to humanity." It is the most varied and scenic of any North African nation (visitors can, in a single day, be among snow-capped mountain peaks and the sand dunes of Merzouga), with a greater network of good roads and transportation and a more varied cuisine. King Hassan II was famous for comparing Morocco with the desert palm, "rooted in Africa, watered by Islam, and rustled by the winds of Europe."

Herbert Ypma provides an excellent parting snapshot of Maroc in his beautiful book *Morocco Modern:* "It is a country of donkeys and mules and motorbikes and Renaults, where the cry of the *muezzin* calling the faithful to prayer still wafts across the labyrinth-like medina of the old city, while the sophisticated young population make calls on their cellular phones from café terraces in the *ville nouvelle.* Traditional *djellabas* and *haiks,* in impossibly bright shades of blue, purple, pink and yellow, mingle with smart suits, couture fashion and jeans. Colourfully ethnic and stylishly urban, Morocco is, above all, a visually sophisticated nation. Its landscapes and culture have a distinctive beauty which has impressed artists and travellers alike over the ages."

Bon voyage et bonne chance! / Inshallah and *fursa sa'eeda!*

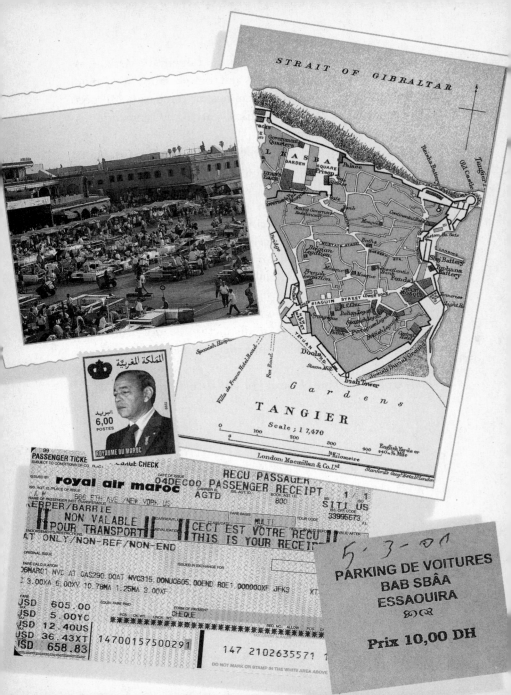

Renseignements Pratiques
(Practical Information)

"We shall never apprehend all the subtleties of Morocco, any more than we shall eventually succeed in understanding its profound reality. Too many things there are different from what seems to us natural, logical and commonsensical. Geography, as though deliberately capricious, compounds the paradox: no more than a few nautical miles separate Europe from the Kingdom of Morocco, but that narrow corridor of sea between Algesiras and Tangier, which a boat can cross in under two hours, marks the passage from one world to another."

—Alain D'Hooghe, from
"WITH DESIRE AS THE SOLE GUIDE,"
THE MAGIC OF MOROCCO

A–Z Renseignements Pratiques

Accommodations

Generally speaking, it is not much of a problem to travel around Morocco without reservations, except during the summer months of June, July, and August. Just as in Europe, August is the absolute worst time, as most all of Morocco—including Moroccans living abroad—is *en vacances*. I maintain, however, that unless you're traveling for an indefinite period of time, it's a good idea to make reservations. Many wonderful inns, hotels, and *chambres d'hôtes* (bed and breakfasts) are quite small with only a few rooms, and they can fill up fast, even in the off-season. It can be very time consuming, not to mention frustrating, to go from place to place and find no vacancy. But, if you do arrive without a room, the staff at the local tourist offices will typically be happy to assist you in finding a place. The offices in the larger cities and towns are perhaps better with this kind of assistance, but it has been my experience that the staff at even the smallest office in the smallest village is willing to help—after all, Moroccans want to be accommodating, and they will go to great lengths to make sure visitors are properly installed. Tourist office staff will not always place telephone calls for you or make the actual reservations, but they will, at the least, tell you what choices there are and give directions. Some offices may charge a fee for booking services.

If you're traveling around all or part of the country by train, you're in luck because the Ibis Moussafir chain has had the brilliant idea of situating its hotels just opposite train stations—and by *just opposite,* I mean they really are right there: travelers will never have to walk more than the equivalent of a city block. Moussafir hotels receive consistently high marks from business and pleasure travelers, and I'm a big fan of the chain. It's not considered budget but is not expensive and is very good value for the level of service, convenience, and quality. The Ibis chain is actually owned by the Accor hotel group—which also owns Etap, Formule 1, Mercure, Novotel, Sofitel, and Motel 6 and Red Roof Inn in the U.S.—and to research locations or make reservations, browse either www.accor.com or www.accorhotels.com.

As readers of my previous books know, I prefer to consult the experts when it comes to accommodations, but unfortunately, I have been unable to find a single book devoted to Moroccan hotels, inns, or *chambres d'hôtes* of any kind. It's possible that there is such a book in French, although I have looked in Morocco and at the Librairie de France here in New York and have never seen one. I believe that one reason a guide has not been published is that there really are not that many places to stay in Morocco, in the same way that there is no restaurant guide for the country, either. My advice is to spend some time selecting the right guidebook(s) and trust the author's recommendations. You'll find that most of the worthwhile places are featured in nearly every book anyway, and for what it's worth, I mention some of my own favorite places to stay in the section *Des Belles Choses*. It is completely unnecessary to continue seeking information on the places you've chosen to stay. Trying to "validate" your choices by searching the Web, for example, serves no good purpose: remember, *you don't know the people who are writing reviews, and you have no idea if the same things that are important to you are important to them*. The authors of the books you've chosen have shared their standards with you and explained their criteria in rating accommodations. Stick with them, and move on to the next step in planning your trip. Following are brief descriptions of the various types of accommodations you'll find throughout Morocco.

Auberges de jeunesses (youth hostels) are the premier choice for those seeking budget accommodations (and keep in mind that hostels are not just for the under-thirty crowd). I would take back in a minute my summer of vagabonding around Europe, meeting young people from all over the world, and feeling that my life was one big endless possibility. I now prefer to share a room with my husband rather than five twenty-somethings, but hosteling remains a fun and exciting experience for young and old alike. Younger budget travelers need no convincing that hosteling is the way to go, but older budget travelers should bear in mind that although some hostels offer individual rooms (mostly for couples), comparing costs reveals that they are often the same price as a room in a real (albeit inexpensive) hotel, where you can reserve a room in advance and comfortably keep your luggage. (You must pack up your luggage every day when hosteling, and you can't make a reservation.) Additionally, most hostels have an eleven P.M. curfew. Petty theft—of the T-shirts-stolen-off-the-clothesline variety—seems to be more prevalent than it once was, and it would be wise to sleep and shower with your money belt close at hand. For a complete list of hostels in Morocco, contact the Moroccan tourist offices (here or abroad) or the national headquarters of Hostelling International here in the United States (733 15th Street N.W., Suite 840, Washington, D.C. 20005; 202-783-6161; fax: -6171; www.hiayh.org; hours 8:00 A.M.–5:00 P.M. Eastern Standard Time, with customer service staff available until 7:00 P.M.). In fact, while there are no age limits or advance bookings, many of the hostels require membership in HI. A membership card is free for anyone up to his or her eighteenth birthday. Annual fees are $25 for anyone over eighteen and $15 for anyone over fifty-five. HI also publishes several guidebooks, one of which is *Europe and the Mediterranean*, which includes Morocco. The price is $13.95, and books can be purchased from the main office or one of the council affiliates. (HI staff have addresses and phone numbers for affiliates nearest you.)

Camping (known simply as *camping* or sometimes *campings municipaux*) is an option in Morocco, but visitors should know that most of the sites are not well maintained. Camping out is not a very popular concept among Moroccans, and most visitors—including Europeans, who love to camp—come not to camp but to stay in some of Morocco's unique old palaces and restored private homes. If you're dead set on camping around the country (which I do not recommend, because you'll miss out on some truly memorable places to stay, and I think you may have some truly dreadful nights at some campgrounds), inquire at the Moroccan National Tourist Office for more detailed information, and consult some of the guidebooks I recommend below under G.

Chambres d'hôtes or *maisons d'hôte* (bed and breakfast accommodations) do not exist in the same way we know them in the United States. Taking in paying overnight guests is just not a fast-developing concept in Morocco, although it seems to be better accepted among Berber families in the mountains. However, the *chambres d'hôtes* concept is alive and well and growing in buildings that are not private homes (see hotels entry below).

Home exchange might be an appealing option, although I cannot confirm that many Moroccans participate in this practice. I've read wildly enthusiastic reports from people who've swapped apartments or houses, and it's usually always an economical alternative. Interested readers will have to investigate and report back. One service to contact is Intervac (30 Corte San Fernando, Tiburon, California 94920; 800-756-4663 or 415-435-3497; www.intervacus.com). Intervac is one of the oldest (over fifty years) and largest exchange clubs and has the largest database of home exchange offers in the world. Intervac clients consistently report "superlative" vacation experiences. Other services include HomeLink International (another leading agency, which publishes multiple directories each year; P.O. Box 650, Key West, Florida 33041; 800-638-3841 phone/fax; www.homelink.org); Trading Homes International (P.O. Box 787, Hermosa Beach, California 90254; 800-877-8723; www.trading-homes.com); and Worldwide Home Exchange Club (806 Branford Avenue, Silver Spring, Maryland 20904; 301-680-8950). A general home exchange website is www.webhomeexchange.com. A good but out-of-print book to read is *Trading Places: The Wonderful World of Vacation Home Exchanging* (Bill and Mary Barbour, Rutledge Hill Press, Nashville, Tennessee, 1991).

Hotels. As I stated in the introduction, I seek hotels that are distinctive but not over-the-top. Architecture critic Paul Goldberger has written, "A good hotel is a place, a town, a city, a world unto itself, and the aura it exudes has almost nothing to do with its rooms and almost everything to do with everything else—the lobby, the bar, the restaurants, the façade, the signs, even the corridors and the elevators." This applies to hotels large and small, expensive and not. The first fact to establish about hotels in Morocco is that they are either classified or unclassified. Classified lodgings are those that meet certain criteria by the government, and as such are assigned a star rating. Unclassified hotels are just that: they do not meet the governmental criteria, and I do not hesitate to say that most readers would not want to stay at any of them (you do not have to take my word for this, obviously, but a quick read in a few guidebooks will confirm it). I once did not mind staying in rather funky, perhaps even seedy, accommodations, but I have never enjoyed staying at places described with phrases like "best to bring your own sheets," "communal bathroom should be used only in an emergency," and "relatively safe." I will add, however, that I would stay in unclassified hotels if faced with the choice of going or not going to Morocco. True budget travelers should read these hotels' descriptions in the guidebooks carefully and plan as far in advance as possible in order to secure the best lodgings. Regarding classified hotels, readers should be aware that, just as with any star-rating system, the rankings are rather unreliable, and very often a modest two-star can be more beautiful and charming than a four-star establishment, or a three-star can be more expensive than a four-star. Again, readers should compare descriptions carefully in a variety of guidebooks before deciding on a particular place. One of the most amazing aspects of traveling throughout Morocco to me is the opportunity to stay in an old palace or mansion, referred to in Morocco as a *dar* or *riad* (see individual entries for both of these below). Originally built as private homes for the well-to-do, these magnificent *maisons* are now experiencing a revival as many modern Moroccans prefer to live in more contemporary apartments and complexes. Based on the success of La Maison Arabe in Marrakesh and La Maison Bleue in Fez—both former palace restaurants—Moroccan and foreign entrepreneurs are stepping in to renovate others. I cannot say enough about the experience of staying at one (or more!) of these fabulous places (see "The Riad Thing" in *Des Belles Choses* for some good recommendations); it is an experience unique to Morocco, and is also a good value when compared with similar establishments in, say, France, Italy, or Spain. These palaces are so appealing that it is tempting to stay at them exclusively; but as my colleague Lauren pointed out, that could easily result in a trip to a Third World country becoming the most expensive trip you've ever planned. I think, as Barnaby Rogerson suggests in his Cadogan guide, that the best way to travel around Morocco is to stay in a variety of places. As I have noted previously, there is no single guide to accommodations in Morocco that I know of, so you will have to rely on guidebooks, the piece on riads in *Des Belles Choses,* and other articles you may find.

Relais & Chateaux is an association of over 400 independently owned hotels (and restaurants) of charm and prestige in over 40 countries around the world. R&C properties offer a perfect balance of exceptional service, food, comfort, and surroundings, with an emphasis on charm rather than luxury. The annual R&C guide features color photos, maps, and all details about each property. Currently there is only one R&C property in Morocco, La Villa des Orangers in Marrakesh. As this is the only one, I will share some details with you: the residence—which is entirely enclosed with two Andalusian-style patios—is located at the end of an avenue of orange trees, and dates from the early twentieth century. There are four rooms and twelve suites, and there is a rooftop swimming pool and solarium with a smashing view. Reservations can be made directly with each hotel, through the central reservations department (U.S. number is 800-735-2478), via the Internet (www.relaischateaux.com/orangers), or by a travel agent.

Renting an apartment or villa might be a suitable choice depending on how long you'll be in the area and the number of people traveling together. I like the idea of renting because it's a quick way to feel a part of the local routine—you have daily chores to accomplish just like everyone else (except that I would hardly call going to pick up provisions at the souk or *marché* a chore). Though the tasks are mixed in with lots of little pleasures and trips, you somehow avoid the too-much-to-do rut. What to eat for dinner suddenly looms as the most important question of the day, the same question that all the local Moroccan mothers are trying to answer. Renting, therefore, forces you to take an active part in the culture rather than catch a glimpse of it. While a great number of organizations will arrange short- and long-term rentals for countries like France and Italy, Morocco is not a country that has such an established tradition of renting to foreigners. As with the other books in my series, it is not my intent here to provide a comprehensive listing of rental organizations; and as it is, I have learned of only a few in Morocco and would welcome hearing from you if you can recommend others: Barclay International Group (3 School Street, Glen Cove, New York 11542; 516-759-5100 or 800-845-6636; fax: 516-609-0000; e-mail: information@barclayweb.com; www.barclayweb.com) is a well-established company offering rentals in the Caribbean, Europe, and Mexico, which obviously doesn't include Morocco, but it's a good idea to contact Barclay anyway because it's the sort of company that can accomplish just about anything (its website encourages browsers to send an e-mail about destinations it doesn't currently offer). It also reserves car rentals, sight-seeing tours, rail passes, cellular phones, and laptop computer rentals. Marrakech Ryads (44.38.58.58 and 61.16.36.30; fax: 44.04.38.57.08), contact Abdellatif Ben Abdallah. Marrakech Medina (102, Dar El Bacha, Medina, 44.42.91.33 or 44.44.45.32; fax: 44.39.10.71; www.marrakech-medina.com) has properties in the medina that, depending on the level of comfort and luxury one is seeking, are ranked by *palmiers,* four being *luxe* and one being simple but very tasteful and comfortable. This company can also arrange rentals in the mountains or by the sea and also offers a full range of services—see its website for more details. Morocco Made to Measure (CLM Morocco, 69 Knightsbridge, London, SW1X 7RA; 011.44.207.235.0123/fax: 207.235.3851). This British company is actually a full-service tour operator, but arranges rentals as well. Villas and Apartments Abroad (1270 Avenue of the Americas, 15th floor, New York, New York 10020; 800-433-3020 or 212-897-5045; fax: -5039; www.ideal-villas.com), which is more than twenty-five years old, informs its clients that "Morocco is not another vacation destination—it is an experience!" and I couldn't agree more. VAA offers a variety of villas, some with a complete staff, while others less *luxe* in the heart of the medina; the staff will also organize customized tours within Morocco. Additionally, check some of the guidebooks for rental suggestions, and do not overlook the classified ads in magazines and newspapers. By renting directly from an owner, you avoid paying a middleman fee, and there are plenty of places to rent that are every bit as nice as those represented by agencies.

General accommodation notes to keep in mind: ~Ask for reservation confirmation in writing. Though I may place an initial call to an inn or hotel, I prefer that communication be by fax or e-mail. This allows for any language errors to be corrected in case my French—or their English—was faulty and serves as an official document. While a fax alone does not guarantee something won't go wrong, it certainly helps to produce one at check-in. If you arrive at your lodging and the staff cannot honor your reservation, be polite but firm in asking for a better room elsewhere in the hotel (at the same price) or a comparable room at another lodging. You could also push the envelope here and ask that they pay for your first night. The hotel is obligated to find you comparable alternative lodgings—not to pay for your first night someplace else—but I figure this is part of a bargaining process in arriving at a solution. You should also ask for them to pay for your transportation to the other location, which they should not hesitate to do. ~Moroccan cities and towns can be noisy, even at night. Though some streets may be limited or closed to cars, scooters are usually permitted, so select rooms accordingly. ~If your lodgings are located in a medina, ask the proprietor for the name of the closest *bab* (gate) so you can at least be reasonably close by when you enter the medina. It's best to ask if the hotel can send someone to meet you at the *bab* because truthfully, even if you have an excellent sense of direction, it's truly difficult to find your way since there are no maps that are detailed enough. Fortunately, most of the better known places are signposted, but you can't rely on signs exclusively. Alternatively, you could also offer a few *dirhams* to a young boy in exchange for showing you the way. ~When you first arrive at your hotel, ask to see your room first. This is a common practice in most countries (apart from the U.S.), and it is understood that if a room is not to your liking, you may request a different one. This is also your opportunity to ask for a room upgrade; if the hotel is not fully booked (and it rarely will be during low season), you may end up with a significantly nicer room at the same rate. It never hurts to ask. ~Speaking of fully booked: if you've been told that you can't get a room, call again between four and six P.M. Morocco time and double-check. This is the time of day when many establishments cancel the reservations of guests who haven't shown up. ~If a hotel you choose also has a reservations office in the United States (usually an 800 number), call both numbers. It is entirely possible that you will be quoted different rates. Also, some of the more expensive hotels offer a rate that must be prepaid in full, in U.S. dollars, but that is lower than the local rack rate. ~No matter what type of lodging you choose, *always* inquire if there is a lower rate. Reservationists—and even the owners of small inns—always hope the rate they quote will be accepted, and if you don't ask about other possibilities, they will not volunteer any. In addition, ask if there are corporate rates; special rates for seniors, students, or government and military employees; weekend rates (this usually only applies to city hotels, as business travelers will have checked out by Friday); and even special prices for newlyweds. Hotels and inns large and small all want to fill their rooms, and if you'll be staying four nights or longer, you may also be able to negotiate a better rate. Most important, ask how long the rate you're quoted is available and how many rooms at that price are left. In smaller places especially, a day can mean the difference between securing a reservation or losing it. ~Be aware, even if no one on the staff mentions it, that plumbing in Morocco can be problematic, even in top-quality hotels. If something is not working properly with your toilet, this is not occasion for you to get angry with the manager or demand a discount; rather, this is the moment you should remember you are not in Kansas anymore. Discreetly tell someone on staff that your toilet *ne marche pas* (doesn't work). ~Useful vocabulary: *oreiller* (pillow); *clef* (key); *draps* (sheets); *couverture* (blanket); *serviette de toilette* (hand or face towel); *serviette de bain* (bath towel); *l'eau chaud* (hot water); *compris* (included, as in, "Is breakfast included in the price?").

Airfares and Airlines

We all know that not everyone pays the same price for seats on an airplane. One of the reasons is that seats do not hold the same value at all times of the year, month, or even day of the week. Recently, I was researching some fares to Paris for a long weekend. One of my calls produced a particularly helpful representative who proceeded to detail all available fares for the entire month of September. There were approximately fifteen different prices—based on a seemingly endless number of variables—within that month alone. The best way, therefore, to get the best deal to accommodate your needs is to check a variety of sources and be flexible. Flexibility is, and has always been, the key to low-cost travel, and you should be prepared to slightly alter the dates of your proposed trip to take advantage of those airline seats that hold less value. If you think all the best deals are to be found on the Internet, you're mistaken: airlines, consolidators, and other discounters offer plenty of good fares over the telephone and through advertisements. In order to know with certainty that you've got a good deal, you need to compare fares, which requires checking more than one source. I believe that on any day of the week, the lowest fares can be found equally among websites, wholesalers, airlines, charters, tour operators, travel agents, and sky auctions—you don't know until you inquire.

I like flying a country's own airline whenever possible, and Morocco's official airline is Royal Air Maroc. RAM was founded in 1957 and is the largest airline in North Africa. It has service to sixty-four destinations in thirty-two countries on four continents, and its domestic network links fourteen cities within Morocco. RAM is the only carrier that offers nonstop service to Morocco, and as I write this, RAM offers four direct flights a week from New York to Casablanca (on Tuesday, Thursday, Friday, and Saturday) and two a week direct from Montreal (on Wednesday and Sunday; it used to be that Montreal passengers first had to fly to New York before continuing to Casablanca). Beginning in early spring of 2002, RAM will begin daily service from New York, while Montreal will have dedicated service three or four times a week. Delta Airlines has a code-share agreement with RAM, broadening the scope of RAM's service to U.S. passengers. Travelers can fly out of eight major cities via Delta to New York, connecting with RAM's flight to Casablanca. I went into detail about the value of seats on an airplane in the previous paragraph because I think readers should understand one of the basic economic principles of airline travel. But as there isn't another airline that flies nonstop from North America to Morocco, much of the airfare information in my previous books does not apply to Morocco. Royal Air Maroc dominates the market, and in my experience, when I compared fares between the airline itself, some of the Internet companies, and a consolidator, the fares were identical, *and* they were all via RAM. I have no problem with RAM's dominance: I think it's a fine airline that offers a variety of fares throughout the calendar year. You should certainly do some research on your own, but I think you'll find that you cannot better the schedules and fares of Royal Air Maroc. In addition to some good fares offered during the low season, the RAM website (www.royalairmaroc.com) periodically offers special fares, valid for a limited time and only via the Internet. Travelers should remember to check the website frequently, as RAM's advertising and promotional efforts do not always mention the special fares. Royal Air Maroc's U.S. headquarters are in New York City at 55 East 59th Street, Suite 17B, New York 10022; 212-750-5115 or 800-344-6726 for reservations.

In my previous three books, I shared the sources I typically consult before I purchase any airline ticket. As I feel it would be a disservice to readers not to include them in this edition, I am doing so, but only as sources for you to check off on a list because, as I noted above, I think you'll find that nothing will beat Royal Air Maroc. Note that some of these have corresponding websites mentioned below, but I typically prefer calling 800-AIRFARE (800-247-3273); 800-FLY-CHEAP; Cheap Tickets, 800-377-1000; Lowestfare.com, 888-777-2222; 800-FLY4-LESS; 800-CHEAP-AIR; STA Travel (Student Travel Association but plans trips for "generations X, Y and Z"; 800-777-0112 or www.statravel.com); Council Travel (known as "America's Student Travel Leader," this fifty-three-year-old company also offers good fares for adults and a host of useful stuff for students and teachers; 800-2COUNCIL or counciltravel.com); and the travel section of *The New York Times* (my local daily newspaper), which I scan for ads of all the area agencies offering low prices. Many of these ads typically reveal the same low fares by one or two particular airlines. The airlines are almost always smaller foreign lines currently trying to expand their business in the United States. So, for example, a few years ago all the agencies I called were featuring cheap flights to Paris on Pakistan International Air. I bought a round-trip ticket for under $400 on a flight that was destined for Karachi via Paris. (Note that if you do fly on an airline of a Muslim country, there will not usually be alcohol served; Royal Air Maroc does, however, serve alcohol, as does Air Saudia, which employs non-Muslim flight attendants.) Booking travel on the Web works best for people with simple requirements and lots of flexibility. In fact, if you can leave on *really* short notice, some great deals may be in store for you: a website specializing in just such spur-of-the-moment travel is lastminutetravel.com, which offers last-minute fares from a number of airlines, and the carriers then have the opportunity to reduce fares if seats aren't selling. Another site is 11thhourvacations.com. With both, make sure to check their fares against the airlines' to ensure you're really getting a last-minute bargain. If you have a lot of questions (as I always do), you can't get them answered when arranging travel on the Web and are setting yourself up for potential headaches. And in my experience with sky auctions, I never seem to be able to find a flight scenario that works with my schedule, and I don't like that I can't more finely narrow the criteria when submitting my initial bid— what *time* of day I fly is just as important as the date. The time it takes to continue submitting bids (my initial bid is never accepted) seems wasteful to me, time I could be spending getting concrete information from other sources. Additionally, I have read that the idea of submitting your own price for a ticket is illusory; in fact, the Internet firms buy discounted seats from the airlines but sell only those seats at fares above an established level. Bids below that level are rejected. Also, travelers seldom have control over which airlines they'll fly or which cities they'll stop in if it's a connecting flight. And most don't allow you to earn mileage points. But if you have no parameters to work around and are just looking for a good fare, here are some web sites to check: www.airfare.com; www.cheaptickets.com; www.economytravel.com; www.expedia.com; www.hotwire.com; www.itn.com; www.lowestfare.com; www.priceline.com; www.sidestep.com; www.skyauction.com; www.thefarebusters.com; www.travelocity.com; www.travelscape.com; and www.TRIP.com. (Most of these began their Internet life as search engines for airfares only but now offer rental cars and hotel accommodations, too.)

In the controversy over paper tickets versus e-tickets, I'm for old-fashioned paper. Currently, if an airline has to route passengers on another flight or another carrier, holders of paper tickets are ahead of the game because computers between airlines can't communicate with each other, so e-tickets are impossible to verify. Airline representatives will serve holders of paper tickets first, while e-ticket holders have to wait in line to have their e-tickets converted into paper, and then wait in *another* line to be confirmed on another flight. As travel guru Peter Greenberg notes, "The e-ticket is NOT your friend."

Readers who don't live near New York may want to investigate flying to a European city—Paris or London, for example—since you can't fly nonstop to Morocco anyway, and there is a greater selection of flights available into a wider variety of Moroccan cities. The flexibility this extra choice provides may solve an itinerary problem. London, especially, is a city filled with consolidators (known as bucket shops), and there are many flights from Paris to accommodate the great number of business and holiday travelers.

A word about travel agents: though it was perhaps inevitable that a great number of travel agencies would close due to the arrival of the Internet, do not underestimate what a quality agent can do for you. Readers who have one already know this: good travel agents are indispensable, worth their weight in gold. Resourceful travelers will often be able to put a detailed trip together on their own equally as well as an average agent, but even the most resourceful and determined travelers will not be able to match the savvy of top-notch agents. I believe that at the end of the day, the Internet is a great resource tool, but it's not a human being watching over every last detail for you. The more specialized or complicated your trip is, the more reason you should employ the services of an experienced agent. To read more about exactly what good agents are capable of, see "Miracles Are Us" by Wendy Perrin (*Condé Nast Traveler,* June 2000). Perrin identified seventy travel consultants described as "better connected than the Internet, faster than a T3 line, able to book the unbookable." Of the seventy, sixty-three of them are members of the Virtuoso network, which specializes in leisure travel for discerning clients. Less than 1 percent of consultants in the Americas are accepted for membership in Virtuoso, which utilizes a worldwide network of four hundred cruise, tour, adventure, property, and ground operator partners in sixty countries. Contact Virtuoso at 800-401-4274 or www.virtuoso.com).

Don't be afraid of reputable consolidators, but recognize that their lower fares come with more restrictions. If there are flight cancellations or delays, you have no recourse with the airline since it didn't sell you the ticket directly. (This holds true with tickets purchased through discount Internet companies as well.) If you want to make any changes, you have to pay a penalty. The question to ask of a consolidator is, "Do you accept credit cards?" The rule of thumb is, if it doesn't, go elsewhere; but I will tell you that on two occasions I purchased tickets with cash and had absolutely no problems.

Reputable charter flights, too, should not be feared. I've had three good experiences on charter flights and encourage you to investigate them. The limitations are that most charters offer only coach class and tend to be completely full—in fact, a charter operator is legally allowed to cancel a flight up to ten days before departure if it doesn't fill enough seats. I wouldn't, therefore, travel with children or plan a honeymoon on a charter flight. Although I did not experience any problems on my charter flights, I understand that delays are common, and—as with consolidators—passengers don't have any recourse. But operators who organize charter flights are required to place passengers' flight payments in an escrow account, so if the flight is canceled or if the operator doesn't abide by its agreement, you receive a refund. A publication called *Jax Fax Travel Marketing Magazine* lists more than five thousand scheduled charter flights to more than one hundred destinations worldwide. Previously available only to industry folks, the general public can now subscribe. Contact Jax Fax at 48 Wellington Road, Milford, Connecticut 06460; 800-9-JAXFAX or 203-301-0255; fax: -0250; www.jaxfax.com. A single issue can be purchased for about $5 as well as a one- or two-year subscription.

Flying as a courier is no longer the amazing deal it once was, but can still be a good deal if you're a light packer. (Luggage is usually limited to one carry-on bag.) Couriers also can't usually reserve a seat for more than one person, although your traveling companion could purchase a ticket on the same flight. Air couriers are cogs in international commerce; they are completely legal and legitimate, and demand for them exceeds the supply. They are a necessity simply because companies doing international business send a large number of documents overseas, and those documents can get held up in customs unless accompanied by a person. Couriers are responsible for chaperoning documents through customs and then hand-delivering them to a person waiting outside the customs area. There are several companies that arrange courier flights in the United States, but the one I'm most familiar with is Now Voyager (74 Varick Street, New York, New York 10013; 212-431-1616). To review more options, consider joining the International Association of Air Travel Couriers (P.O. Box 1349, Lake Worth, Florida 33460; 561-582-8320). Members receive a regular bulletin with a variety of international routes being offered by air courier companies departing from several U.S. cities. Reservation phone numbers are included so you can make inquiries and schedule your trip yourself. I have seen some *incredible* bargains, and some fares were valid for several months.

If you're making arrangements directly with an airline, ask if your flight is a "code-share." Code-sharing (mentioned above in connection with Delta and Royal Air Maroc) is complicated, to say the least. (Betsy Wade of *The New York Times* says that "the general theory of relativity is not too much more complex" than the code-sharing network.) In a very small nutshell, code-sharing is an agreement between airline partners that allows them to share routes, but what it means for the consumer is that each airline sharing a code may offer a different price for the same trip. Find out which other airline(s) is in on the code, and compare prices.

Note that airlines are not required to offer much to passengers due to flight delays or cancellations. If you have visions of free meals, hotel rooms, and flights, you may be in for a disappointment. Each airline has its own Conditions of

Carriage—known in airline lingo as "Rule 240"—which you can request from an airline's ticket office or public relations department, but the legalese is not identical from airline to airline. From what I can tell, the employees who stand at the gates are the ones who have the authority to grant passengers amenities, so if you *don't* ask them for something (a seat on the next flight, a long-distance phone call, a meal, whatever), you *definitely* won't get it.

Technically, airlines no longer allow passengers to fly standby at a discount, but I've been told that seats are occasionally sold at reduced prices for flights that aren't full. There is, however, an official standby service offered by Whole Earth Travel Airhitch (two U.S. offices: 2641 Broadway, 3rd floor, New York, New York 10025; 800-326-2009 or 212-864-2000; fax: -5489, and 13470 Washington Boulevard, Suite 205, Marina del Rey, California 90292; 800-834-9192; fax: 310-574-0054; www. 4cheapair.com). Very affordable flights are available for worldwide destinations, but you must be flexible, seeing that Airhitch selects the date you travel based on a five-day range, which you provide. Similar to a consolidator, Airhitch offers seats on commercial airlines that are about to be left empty, and the company's philosophy is one akin to *The Collected Traveler:* "The experience of travel is a benefit that should be available to everyone. It is through travel that we each learn to accept the differences in others while realizing the similarity in our common goals. We believe travel is the best road to peace and understanding, and it's a whole lotta fun!" Airhitch also offers an option called Target Flights: you supply the dates of travel and desired destination, plus the best quote you've obtained, and Airhitch will respond in twenty-four hours if it can buy a similar ticket at a cheaper price. (When I checked, this feature wasn't yet available on its website, but travelers can call the New York office at 800-326-2009 for details.) I've also been told that one of the best days of the year to show up at the airport without a ticket is Christmas Day. I can't personally confirm this, and it's doubtful an airline employee can, either. Perhaps this is either a very well-kept secret or a myth, but if you're able to be that flexible, it would be worth trying.

Airports

Besides Casablanca, the other airports in Morocco are in Rabat-Sale, Tangier, Oujda, Fez, Al Hoceima, Marrakesh, Agadir, Ouarzazate, and Laayoune. A good book to consult is *Salk International's Airport Transit Guide* (Ron Salk, editor-in-chief, Millennium Edition, Salk International Travel Premiums, Sunset Beach, California), a handy, pocket-sized paperback that is indispensable for frequent business and pleasure travelers and an awfully great resource for everyone else. The book has been published annually for twenty years, and includes ground transportation information for 447 airports worldwide. As stated in its introduction, "In the air, others worry about getting you safely from point A to point B. But on the ground you're on your own. And unless you're returning home or being met by a welcoming committee, getting from the airport to point C may require information you don't have. That's what this book is for." The Mohammed V Airport in Casablanca entry details bus, train, and taxi transportation to downtown Casablanca, twenty-two miles away. This book is a little hard to find—I used to see it frequently in bookstores, but now I rarely do. I ordered mine from Magellan's mail-order catalog (800-962-4943), but you can also call Salk directly at 714-893-0812 or visit its website: www.airporttransitguide.com. The book also features a world time zones map at the back.

Alcohol

The word *alcohol* is derived from the Arabic word *al-kuhl,* meaning "the powdered antimony, the distillate." The Koran, of course, forbids the consumption of alcohol, so neither beer nor wine is given much preference in Morocco. Morocco is, however, rather liberal as Muslim countries go, and beer, wine, and harder alcohol can be obtained with little effort. (You will find the names of shops and supermarkets that sell alcohol in all the guidebooks, and you're sure to run across a few on your own.) At some cafés, you'll find men drinking alcohol in the back rooms, out of view from passersby on the street. My friend Audrey, an American who lives in Fez, told me that she has seen Moroccan men drink alcohol from time to time, but never has she seen a woman take a drink (even at parties Audrey and her housemates have given at their house in the medina). Whether Moroccan women occasionally take a drink in the privacy of their own homes, we'll never know; but since my husband and I were out to dinner with our Moroccan friend Samira at restaurant Yacout in Marrakesh. Our waiter came to pour wine into our glasses, and Samira indicated that she did not want any. Later in the meal, however, he returned to the table, and while we were deep in conversation, he inadvertently filled all three of our glasses. Samira, thinking it was water, picked up her glass, sipped, and immediately recognized that it was wine. Horrified, she discreetly leaned behind my chair and spit it out. (Our table was against a wall, and therefore her action was not observed by anyone.) She told us that that was the only time she had ever had alcohol in her life and that in all likelihood it would be the last.

Architecture

The key examples of Moroccan architecture can be easily divided into four groups: the fortress (*kasbah*), the mosque, the Islamic university college (*medersa,* singular; *medersat,* plural), and the private home. Of these, *kasbah* requires a bit of an explanation: a *kasbah* is a fort or citadel and often the administrative center of a palace. The word has also been used to refer to the walled residential quarter surrounding the medina or the citadel, or even the whole medina. Just to confuse things further, forts and fortified villages in the south of Morocco are referred to as *ksour* (singular is *ksar*). *Kasbah* is, not surprisingly, the root of the Spanish word *alcazar*. Regarding Moroccan mosques, their most significant trait is the square minaret, which is prevalent throughout the Maghreb. The slender spires we so associate with minarets of mosques in other Muslim countries do not appear in Morocco.

B

Bargaining

Bargaining, for goods and services, is one of the most important topics in this book, as it is the accepted way of doing business in Morocco. But it makes many North American visitors uncomfortable, because, I've found, they do not take the time to understand and appreciate the art of bargaining and hence have some of the most backward and wrong opinions about it, usually stemming from the idea that they're surely being taken to the cleaners. To appreciate and get the most out of Morocco, you must first appreciate bargaining. Bargaining is fun, interesting, and revealing of national character. It isn't something you do in a hurry, and it's not an antagonistic game of Stratego—it does incorporate strategy, but it isn't battleships being sunk, it's goods or services on offer that you do or do not have to purchase.

In an old issue of *Horizon* magazine, I found an interesting piece excerpted from a book entitled *Silent Language* by Edward T. Hall (Doubleday, 1959). It emphasizes the subtle ways in which people communicate by means other than words—always of great import in Morocco! At the time the book was published, Hall, an anthropologist, was director of the State Department's Point Four Training Program as well as president of Overseas Training and Research, a company that advised American corporations with business overseas. Though Hall refers only to the Middle East in this passage, one can easily substitute the word *Morocco:*

Throughout the Middle East bargaining is an underlying pattern which is significantly different from the activity which goes under that name in our culture. Yet what is perceived on the surface (i.e., Arab methods of bargaining) looks familiar and is assumed to be the same. Nothing could be farther from the truth.

The American asks, "What percentage of the asking price shall I give as my first offer?" What he doesn't know is that there are several asking prices. Like the Eskimo who has many different words for snow, the Arab has many different asking prices, each with a different meaning. . . . The American pattern of bargaining is predicated on the assumption that each party has a high and a low point that is hidden (what he would like to get and what he will settle for). The function of the bargaining is to discover, if possible, what the opponent's points are without revealing one's own. The American in the Middle East, projecting his own unconscious pattern, will ask, "What percentage of the asking price do I give?" That is, "If he's asking ten pounds, will he settle for five?" This procedure is not only wrong but can end in trouble. The principle to be remembered is that instead of each party having a high and a low there is really only *one* principal point, which lies somewhere in the middle. Much like our latest stock market quotation, this point is determined, not by the two parties, but by the market or the situation. An important isolate in this pattern is that the price is never determined by the person or his wishes but always by some set of circumstances which are known to both parties. If they are not known it is assumed that they could be. Negotiation, therefore, swings around a central pivot. Ignorance of the position of the pivot opens one up to the worst type of exploitation, as well as loss of face. It doesn't matter whether it is a squash in the bazaar or a hydroelectric dam in the international market. The pattern remains constant. Above and below the central point there is a series of points which indicate what the two parties feel as they enter the field.

Here is how an Arab from Damascus described this process. The pivotal point was six piasters, the price of squash on the day he described. Above and below this there were four points. Any one of the lower four represents the first offer made by the prospective buyer. The hidden or implicit meaning of this code is given opposite each step on the scale below. This meaning is not exact but represents a clue as to the attitudes of the two parties as they enter the bargaining process.

PIASTERS

12 or more	complete ignorance on the part of the seller	
10	an insult, arguments and fights ensue, seller doesn't want to sell	SELLER'S ASKING PRICES
8	will sell, but let's continue bargaining	
7	will sell under the market	
6	MARKET PRICE (THE PIVOT)	
5	buyer really wants the squash, will pay over the market	
4	will buy	
2	arguments and fighting, buyer doesn't want to buy	BUYER'S OFFERING PRICES
1	ignorance of the value of the item on the part of the buyer	

Considering the difference of meaning which is carried by a variation of one piaster, the question, "What percentage of the asking price do I give?" seems meaningless. Which asking price? The let's-do-business one, the let's-not-do-business one, or the let's-fight asking price? Other variations on this pattern have as many as five or six points above and below the line, each with its own meaning.

One cannot underestimate the importance of such patterns and the hold they have on people at all levels. In discussing our stand in Egypt during and directly following the Aswan Dam fiasco and before our position in the Middle East had deteriorated so badly, an Arab sympathetic to our cause expressed it this way. "If you don't give a little in bargaining, the other fellow will back up. If he gives two steps, you have to give two steps. If you don't, he will back up four." We didn't give our two steps and Nasser backed up four.
—From SILENT LANGUAGE by Edward T. Hall, copyright © 1959, 1981 by Edward T. Hall. Used by permission of Doubleday, a division of Random House, Inc.

As interesting as all this is, I caution you against placing too much emphasis on the deal itself. There are few absolutes in the art of bargaining—each merchant is different, and the particulars of each transaction are different, and you will not be awarded a medal at the end of your visit for driving hard bargains all over Morocco, especially if you accumulate things you don't really want. More important than any of my tips that follow is that you do not lose sight of the fact that what you want is something that appeals to you in some special way that you bargained for in the accepted manner. Does it really matter, at the end of the day, that you *might* have gotten it for twenty or fifty *dirhams* less? If you end up with a purchase that you love and every time you look at it or wear it you have a warm feeling about your trip to Morocco, it definitely does not matter what you paid for it. There is a difference between savvy bargaining and obsessive bargaining, and I don't know about you, but when I'm on vacation, obsessing about mercantile matters is the equivalent of postponing joy.

Here are some well-practiced and worthwhile tips that have worked well for me in Morocco, Egypt, Turkey, and France:

~Educate yourself on the items you're interested in, which I presume, for most readers, will be the arts and crafts of Morocco. If you have been able to learn how much these items sell for here in the States before you leave home, this is also useful information as you'll know how much (or how little) savings are being offered. I know it's tempting to head right for the souks, but it will be time (and money) well spent if you first head for the local government-run arts and crafts center. Prices here are fixed, so you will have an idea of what the highest price should be for any given item as well as the skill and effort that went into making it. It's also a good idea to visit the traditional house museums—Dar Si Said and the Bert Flint in Marrakesh, Dar Batha in Fez, and the Dar El Makhzen in Tangier, for example—to see first-rate examples of a wide variety of Moroccan crafts. If you rush to the souks without really knowing what you're looking for, you run the risk not only of overpaying but of purchasing items you may later regret buying, when you see things you *really* like and recognize as being of better quality—and therefore of better value.

~Walk around the entire souk first and survey the scene—do not purchase a thing. If you have decided to skip my advice above, this is the next best thing you can do to educate yourself. It doesn't take very long to see that a lot of vendors sell identical merchandise, much of it kitschy and probably of interest only as gifts for children and wacky friends. Look for distinctive items, and identify those vendors you want to revisit. If prices are not marked, ask what they are for the items you're interested in, but don't linger and explain that you're just looking. What you're trying to do is ascertain the average going rate for certain items, because if you don't have any idea what the general price range is, you won't have any idea if you're paying a fair price or too much.

~If you do spy an item you're particularly interested in, try not to reveal your interest; act as nonchalant as you possibly can, and remember to be ready to start walking away.

~It's considered rude to begin serious bargaining if you're not interested in making a purchase. This doesn't mean you should refrain from asking the price on an item, but to then begin naming numbers is an indication to the vendor that you're a serious customer and that a sale will likely be made.

~Politeness goes a long way in the souks. Vendors appreciate being treated with respect, and they don't at all mind answering questions from interested browsers. Strike up a conversation while you're looking at the wares; ask about the vendor's family, share pictures of yours, or ask for a recommendation of a good local restaurant. Establishing a rapport also shows that you are reasonable, and that you are willing to make a purchase at the right (reasonable) price.

~If you don't want to be hassled by vendors as you walk through a souk, make sure any previous purchases you may have made are hidden from view. To a vendor, anyone who walks through the souk is a potential customer, but someone who has already spent money is even better. From a vendor's perspective, customers who have already parted with their money are interested in parting with more, if only they are shown something else they like. If you have purchased a rug and you decline an offer to look at some more by another merchant by saying you've already bought one, you may think you're saying, "No, thank you, I've already bought a rug and don't need another," but the vendor doesn't translate it the same way. He will (correctly) assume that you like rugs and will definitely be interested in purchasing another if he has an opportunity to show you some. A rug is hard to hide, but I always carry a canvas tote bag or buy one of those striped bags sold in all the souks for carrying whatever I've accumulated. Perfume bottles, jewelry, small pieces of pottery, soap, henna, and spices all fit easily in the bag, and no one but you knows they're there.

~Occasionally, I feign interest in one particular item when it's a different item I *really* want. The tactic here is to begin the bargaining process and let the vendor think I'm about to make a deal. Then I pretend to get cold feet and indicate that the price is just too much for me. The vendor thinks all is lost, and at that moment I point to the item I've wanted all along, sigh, and say I'll take that one, naming the lowest price from my previous negotiation. Usually, the vendor will immediately agree to it, as it means a done deal.

~Other times I will plead poverty and say to the vendor that I had *so* wanted to bring back a gift for my mother from "your beautiful country—won't you please reconsider?" This, too, usually works.

~If you're traveling with a companion, you can work together: one of you plays the role of the designated "bad guy," scoffing at each price quoted, while the other plays the role of the demure friend or spouse who hopes to make a purchase but really must have the approval of the "bad guy."

~If you discover a flaw in an item, point it out and use it as a bargaining chip. I do this at home as well, and I have never been unsuccessful at convincing the clerk to take some money off the price. A few times I've bought the display sample—the only one remaining in my size, for example—and wasn't charged the sales tax.

~You'll always get the best price if you pay with cash, and in fact many vendors accept only cash. I prepare an assortment of paper *dirhams* and coins in advance so I can always pull them out and indicate that it's all I have. It doesn't seem right to bargain hard for something that's 100 *dirhams* and pay for it with a 500-*dirham* note.

~Remember that a deal is supposed to end with both parties satisfied. If, after much back-and-forth, you encounter a vendor who won't budge below a certain price, it's likely that it's not posturing but a way of letting you know that anything lower will no longer be advantageous to him or her. If you feel you're stuck and have reached an impasse, try asking the vendor once more, "Is this your very best price?" If he or she has spent a considerable amount of time with you, this is the moment when it would be advantageous to compromise, or all that time will have been wasted.

~Pay attention when a merchant wraps up your purchase—dishonest vendors may try to switch the merchandise. Though this has never happened to me, I read a lot of letters from people who didn't know they were had until they got home.

~If you're a real shopaholic and plan to ship large items home, remember that rates are based on cubic measurement, not weight. The shipping minimum is one cubic meter, which translates to about $400 on top of fees for packing, insurance, and U.S. customs. Therefore, make sure the savings you receive at the souks are truly significant to justify the shipping home.

~If you're interested in buying antiques—or making large purchases of any kind—it would be worthwhile to get a copy of the "Know Before You Go" brochure from the U.S. Customs Service. You can write for a free copy (1300 Pennsylvania Avenue N.W., Washington, D.C. 20229) or view it on-line at www. customs.ustreas.gov/travel/kbygo.htm. (First click on "Traveler Information," and then select "Know Before You Go.") Dull as it may sound, I found this document to be incredibly interesting, and of special interest here are the details on What You Must Declare, Duty-Free Exemption, $200 Exemption, $400 Exemption, Gifts, Household Effects, Paying Duty, Sending Goods to the United States, Freight Shipments, Duty-Free Shops, and Cultural Artifacts and Cultural Property.

~Useful vocabulary: *une tranche* or *deux tranches* (one slice, two slices); *j'en voudrais trois* (I would like three of them); *la moitié de ça* (half that much); *encore un peu* (a little more); *ça c'est parfait* or *suffit* (that's perfect, sufficient/enough); *une bonne poignée* (a good-sized bunch/handful); *trop cher* (too expensive); *c'est pour offrir* or *c'est un cadeau* (it's a gift); *pouvez-vous l'emballer?* (could you wrap it up?).

Bars and Cafés

There are bars in Morocco and cafés aplenty, but neither is especially welcoming to women, as both have long been the domain of men. Single local women in bars are thought to be prostitutes; foreign women, too, are immediately summed up as such or are at the least considered disrespectful—no good can come from hanging out in a bar if you are female, and while a café is somewhat more acceptable, women may still be stared at or receive unwanted attention. (Exceptions to this are bars in Westernized hotels.) I frankly never became accustomed to this situation, even though I was with my husband. There are few pleasures greater to me than taking a morning coffee or an afternoon aperitif at a bar or café—sometimes alone—especially in as lively a spot as the Djemaa el Fna in Marrakesh, for example, which has to be the world's premier people-watching spot. While I have never been made to feel unwelcome, with my husband, at cafés in Morocco, I nonetheless was conscious of often being the only female—or one of only three or four—and I

began to prefer buying a bottle of local wine and drinking it in the privacy of my hotel room. Over an extended period of time, I would probably no longer notice that this pleasure was being denied me, but it definitely began to bother me that, at the end of an amazing but exhausting day, I could not just plop myself down in a café chair and order a beer.

Beer
The national brand of beer most always on offer is Flag Speciale (I've read of another, called La Cigogne, but I've never seen it), and it's quite tasty, if not always served very cold.

Berbers
"Berbers live in Earth's extreme places. Their lands are beautiful, but they are harsh. From snow-blasted mountain to wind-scoured sand dunes, the Berbers have been forced by their history to inhabit the barely habitable." To those words by writer Geraldine Brooks, which she contributed to the book *Imazighen,* I would add that Berbers are mysterious. Mysterious because even today, scholars are not in complete agreement about their origins. Most scholars seem to accept that Berbers originally came from the Middle East, but this is not conclusive. What *is* agreed upon is that the Berbers speak in three dialects—Tarift, Tamazight, and Shulha—and that all three are spoken, not written. Furthermore, Berbers from the south often cannot comprehend the speech of Berbers from the north. Unless you are living or working in a remote village where no one knows any dialect except Berber, it is probably not worth the effort to learn the language. Apparently, there are no good learning materials, let alone a standardized writing system, and Berber is not related to any other languages with which one is commonly familiar. Just as their speech cannot easily be defined, neither can their appearance: Berbers have both dark hair and blond hair, straight and curly, and black eyes and blue eyes, with fair and darker complexions. What is incontestably true of Berbers is that they are great in number in Morocco. As Mary Cross notes in her book *Morocco: Sahara to the Sea,* "Anthropologists speculate that after a thousand years of intermarriage at least 85 percent of all Moroccans have some Berber blood."

In reading about Berbers it is not uncommon to run across the Tuaregs, who are Berber- or Hamitic-speaking members of the Muslim nomads of the Sahara. *Tuareg* is also the word for the language of the Tuaregs, and is considered a Berber language of the Afro-Asiatic family. However, as Susan Searight points out in her *Maverick Guide to Morocco,* no Tuaregs live in Morocco, even though visitors will see signs advertising Tuareg goods in the south (this is because the camel-owning Tuaregs today live even farther south, mostly in Mali and Niger). Generally speaking—again according to Searight—Berbers live in the Rif and Middle and High Atlas Mountains; Berbers who are also known as Chleu inhabit the Anti-Atlas; Berbers or Arabs who are also known as Haratin live in the southern oases, and Saharaoui (people who do not define themselves as either Berber or Arab) live along the desert fringes of Morocco.

Biking
Biking for pleasure is rare among Moroccans, but the country is a rewarding one for those who wish to spend part—hopefully not all—of their visit on two wheels. Mountain biking especially has become popular, due in part to the great number of *pistes* (dirt trails in the mountainous areas of the country). I have read of some hazards—kids throwing stones, angry dogs that bite—and I think I would prefer to join an organized tour for a few days (see "Tours" for some suggestions). Useful vocabulary: *velo tout terrain* (VTT) is an all-terrain bike.

Bismallah
Besides being my favorite word in the song "Bohemian Rhapsody" by the rock band Queen (from the album *A Night at the Opera*), this oft-heard Arabic word roughly translates as "through the grace of God." It's used to give thanks and is often said before the start of a meal.

Le Bisou
French for "the kiss," from the verb *baiser*. Actually, *le bisou* is a social kiss, as opposed to *le baiser,* which is a much more passionate kiss between lovers. You'll notice that Moroccans kiss each other in greeting. The established practice is to kiss first the left cheek and then the right, but sometimes people kiss three or even four times—two kisses on each cheek—always beginning with the left cheek. Moroccans of the same sex hold hands often as well, and this should not be considered a sign of homosexuality or lesbianism.

Bled el Makhzen and Bled es Siba
These two key Moroccan Arabic phrases, which you will encounter in nearly every book about Morocco, are essential to understanding much about the history of the country. *Bled el makhzen* means "land of government," while *bled es siba* means "land of lawlessness." The *bled es siba* covered—and still does to a certain degree—an infinitely greater territory. As Gavin Maxwell noted in *Lords of the Atlas,* "It was from the *bled es siba,* and more especially the land of desert and palm oasis lying to the east of the Atlas, that almost every new dynasty of Sultans rose to conquer and replace the last."

Bookstores

Like Moroccans and Europeans, I prefer to buy whatever goods and services I need from specialists. One-stop shopping is a nice idea in theory, but it has not been very appealing to me, as convenience seems to be its only virtue. Therefore I buy fish from a fishmonger, flowers from a florist, cheese from a real cheese shop, and so on. And when I'm looking for travel books, I shop at travel bookstores or independent bookstores with strong travel sections. The staff in these stores are nearly always well traveled, well read, very helpful, and knowledgeable. An aspect I don't like about nationwide chain stores is that travel guides tend to be shelved separately from travel writing and related history books, implying that guidebooks are all a traveler needs or wants. Stores specializing in travel take a wider view, understanding that travel incorporates many different dimensions. Following is a list of stores in the United States that offer exceptional travel book departments. (I've also included a few stores specializing in art books and cookbooks, as some of these titles are mentioned throughout the book.) Note that all of them accept mail orders, and some publish catalogs and/or newsletters.

CALIFORNIA

Black Oak Books
1491 Shattuck Avenue, Berkeley
510-486-0698

Bon Voyage Travel Books & Maps
2069 West Bullard, Fresno
800-995-9716
www.bon-voyage-travel.com

Book Passage
51 Tamal Vista Boulevard,
Corte Madera
800-999-7909 or 415-927-0960 (locally)
www.bookpassage.com

The Cook's Library
8373 West Third Street, Los Angeles
323-655-3141

Distant Lands
56 South Raymond Avenue, Pasadena
626-449-3220 or 800-310-3220
(California only)
www.distantlands.com

The Literate Traveller
8306 Wilshire Boulevard, Suite 591,
Beverly Hills
800-850-2665 or 310-398-8781
fax: 310-398-5151
www.literatetraveller.com
~In addition to its regular catalog,
The Literate Traveller publishes
Around the World in 80+ Mysteries.

Pacific Travellers Supply
12 West Anapamu Street,
Santa Barbara
888-PAC-TRAV
www.pactrav.com

Phileas Fogg's Books, Maps & More
240 Stanford Shopping Center,

Palo Alto
800-533-3644
www.foggs.com

Rizzoli (five locations):
2 Rodeo Drive, Beverly Hills
310-278-2247
South Coast Plaza, Costa Mesa
714-957-3331
1 Colorado Boulevard, Pasadena
626-564-1300
117 Post, San Francisco
415-984-0225
332 Santa Monica Boulevard,
Santa Monica
310-393-0101
Rizzoli catalog orders:
800-52-BOOKS

Traveler's Bookcase
8375 West Third Street, Los Angeles
323-655-0575
www.travelbooks.com

COLORADO

Tattered Cover
2955 East First Avenue, Denver
303-322-7727

CONNECTICUT

R. J. Julia Booksellers
768 Post Road, Madison
203-245-3959

WASHINGTON, D.C.

AIA/Rizzoli
1735 New York Avenue, N.W.

202-626-7541
catalog orders: 800-52-BOOKS

Travel Books & Language Center
4437 Wisconsin Avenue, N.W.
202-237-1322 / fax: -6022
800-220-2665 (mail orders)
e-mail: travelbks@aol.com

FLORIDA

Andrea's Bookstore, Inc.
308 Highway 19 South, Palatka
904-325-2141 / fax: -8352

GEORGIA

The Civilized Traveller (two locations):
Phipps Plaza, Atlanta
404-264-1252
Perimeter Mall, Atlanta
770-673-0111
www.civilizedtraveller.com
~Not exclusively a bookstore, its
focus is more on globes, luggage, and
travel accessories. But the guidebooks
selection is thorough. See the sister
stores in New York and Virginia
below.

ILLINOIS

The Book Stall at Chestnut Court
811 Elm Street, Winnetka
847-446-8880 / fax: -2894

The Savvy Traveler
310 Michigan Avenue, Chicago
888-666-6200
www.savvytraveler.com

Rizzoli
Water Tower Place, Chicago
312-642-3500
catalog orders: 800-52-BOOKS

LOUISIANA

Beaucoup Books
5414 Magazine Street, New Orleans
504-895-2663 / fax: -9778

MASSACHUSETTS

*Globe Corner Bookstore (two
locations):*
500 Boylston Street, Boston
800-358-6013 / 617-859-8008
28 Church Street, Harvard Square,
Cambridge
617-497-6277

Brattle Book Shop
9 West Street, Boston
617-542-0210 / fax: 617-338-1467
800-447-9595 (mail orders)
~Brattle's specialty is art books, but it
also stocks more than 250,000 used,
rare, and out-of-print books.

Rizzoli
Copley Place, Boston
617-437-0700

MINNESOTA

Books for Travel, Etc.
857 Grand Avenue, St. Paul
888-668-8006

NEW HAMPSHIRE

Magellan Travel Books
53 South Main Street, Suite 211,
Hanover
800-303-0011 or 603-643-6100
fax: -6014
www.magellantravelbooks.com

NEW YORK

Archivia
944 Madison Avenue, New York
212-439-9194
~Beautiful store with a beautiful
selection of decorating, garden, style,
history, and art titles, some in French.

Bonnie Slotnick Cookbooks
163 West 10th Street, New York
212-989-8962
~Bonnie deals almost exclusively with
out-of-print cookbooks.

*The Civilized Traveller (two
locations):*
864 Lexington Avenue (at 65th
Street), New York
212-288-9190
2003 Broadway (at 68th Street),
New York
212-875-8809
www.civilizedtraveller.com

The Complete Traveller
199 Madison Avenue (35th Street),
New York
212-685-9007
~In addition to a great selection of
current books, a separate room is
reserved for rare and out-of-print
travel books. Owners Harriet and

Arnold Greenberg and their superb
staff will do their very best to track
down your most obscure request.

Hacker Art Books
45 West 57th Street, New York
212-688-7600 / fax: 754-2554
e-mail: hackerartbooks@
infohouse.com
www.hackerartbooks.com
~John Russell, former art critic of
The New York Times, has written of
Hacker, "For an all-round art bookstore, this one is something near
to ideal."

Kitchen Arts & Letters
1435 Lexington Avenue (between 93rd
and 94th), New York
212-876-5550 / fax: -3584

Posman Books
Grand Central Terminal, New York
212-533-2665 / fax: 983-1849
1 University Place, New York
212-533-2665 / fax: -2681
e-mail: posmanbook@aol.com

Strand Book Store
828 Broadway (at 12th Street),
New York
212-473-1452 / fax: -2591
800-366-3664 (mail orders)
e-mail: strand@strandbooks.com

Strand Book Annex
95 Fulton Street, New York
212-732-6070 / fax: 406-1654

Rizzoli (four locations):
Manhattan:
31 West 57th Street
212-759-2424
3 World Financial Center
212-385-1400
454 West Broadway
212-674-1616
Manhasset:
The Americana
516-365-9393
Rizzoli catalog orders:
800-52-BOOKS

NORTH CAROLINA

Blue Planet Map Company
487 West King Street, Boone
828-264-5400 / fax: -5400

Omni Resources
10004 South Mebane Street,
Burlington
800-742-2677
www.omnimap.com

OKLAHOMA

Traveler's Pack, LTD
9427 North May Avenue,
Oklahoma City
405-755-2924 / fax: -0257
www.travelerspack.com

OREGON

Book Mark
856 Olive Street, Eugene
541-484-0512 / fax: 686-2957

Powell's City of Books
1005 West Burnside, Portland
800-878-7323 / 503-228-4651 (locally)
www.powells.portland.or.us

Powell's Travel Store
701 Southwest Sixth Avenue, Portland
800-546-5025
www.powells.com

PENNSYLVANIA

Franklin Maps
333 South Henderson Road,
King of Prussia
610-265-6277 / fax: 337-1575
~Extraordinary selection of foreign
and domestic maps as well as books.
One journalist wrote, "What travelers
will find at the 15,000-square-feet
Franklin Map store are maps, charts,
and books covering almost every
square inch of earth and universe."

VERMONT

Adventurous Traveler Bookstore
P.O. Box 64769 (for mail orders)
245 South Champlain Street (for
visiting), Burlington
800-282-3963 or 802-860-6776
fax: -6667
www.adventuroustraveler.com

VIRGINIA

The Civilized Traveller
Tysons Galleria, Fairfax
703-917-9535
www.civilizedtraveller.com

Rizzoli
Merchants Square, Williamsburg
757-229-9821

WASHINGTON

Wide World Books & Maps
4411A Wallingford Avenue North,
Seattle
206-634-3453 / fax: -0558
www.travelbooksandmaps.com

And because some books I recommend
are British publications, I include four
excellent stores in London: The Travel
Bookshop (13–15 Blenheim Crescent,
W11 2EE, 44.171.229.5260; fax: 243.
1552; www.thetravelbookshop.co.uk);
Books for Cooks (a few doors down
from The Travel Bookshop at 4
Blenheim Crescent, 44.171.221.1992;
fax: 221.1517); Stanford's International
Map Centre (12–14 Long Acre, 020.
7730.1354); and The Maghreb Book-
shop/Librairie due Maghreb (45
Burton Street, London, WC1H 9AL;
phone/fax: 011.44.207.388.1840). The
Maghreb is probably the single best
source for any books on Morocco you
may be searching for. The owner,
Mohamed Ben Madani, is also the editor of *The Maghreb Review* and is a
fount of information about all things
Maghrebi. He stocks new, rare, and
out-of-print books on all aspects of
North Africa, the Arab world, and
Islam.

Additionally, I must mention two
favorite mail-order book catalogs: *A
Common Reader* and *Bas Bleu*. Both

are issued monthly and offer a most excellent selection of travel writing, biographies, history, cookbooks, and general fiction and nonfiction books for adults as well as selected books for children. *ACR's* selection is more extensive, but this does not make *Bas Bleu's* offerings any less appealing. James Mustich Jr. is the man behind the *ACR* venture, and his reviews are of the sort that wander here and there and make you want to read every single book in the catalog. (His writing has been an inspiration to me for the annotated bibliographies in *The Collected Traveler*.) Not content simply to offer new books, Mustich even arranges to bring out-of-print books back into print by publishing them under his own Common Reader Editions imprint. To add your name to these catalog mailing lists, contact *A Common Reader* (141 Tompkins Avenue, Pleasantville, New York 10570; 800-832-7323; fax: 914-747-0778; www.commonreader.com) and *Bas Bleu* (515 Means Street N.W., Atlanta, Georgia 30318; 404-577-9463; fax: -6626; www.basbleu.com).

If your favorite bookseller can't find an out-of-print title you're looking for, try contacting members of Book Sense, a network of more than eleven hundred independent booksellers around the country (888-BOOKSENSE or www.BookSense.com), or search one of the following websites: ~www.longitudebooks.com is a wonderful source for travel books—which they define as comprehensively as I do, including travel narratives, art, archaeology, novels, essays, guidebooks, etc.—and maps. When you select a destination, you can view an Essential Reading list plus an accompanying map). ~www.travelbooksclub.com (Traveler's Book Club) features more than fifteen thousand available travel titles in prin t by North American publishers plus thousands of others by foreign distributors. TBC guarantees some of the lowest prices for travel guidebooks on the planet—new books are priced 15 to 30 percent below retail, and clearance titles are as low as 75 percent off. There are also regular specials throughout the year, and the company offers maps and language sets as well. TBC can also be contacted by regular mail at P.O. Box 191554, Atlanta, Georgia 31119. ~www.abebooks.com (American Book Exchange) I like because you purchase books directly from independent booksellers. ~www.alibris.com, www.bookfinder.com, www.elephantbooks.com deal in rare and collectible books. For books in French—including some otherwise hard-to-find titles on Morocco—perhaps the best store in the United States is Librairie de France (Rockefeller Center Promenade, 610 Fifth Avenue, New York, New York 10020; 212-581-8810; fax: 265-1094; www.Frencheuropean.com). Books on food, wine, fiction, and travel are all available, as well as dictionaries, Michelin maps, and gifts. Mail orders are happily accepted. Also, browse www.chapitre.com—"*votre librairie sur internet*"—for the vast selection offered by this Paris store.

English-language bookstores in Morocco include:

The American Language Center and Bookstore, 4 rue Tangier, Rabat; this little shop (on the street-level floor, straight back and to your left) is generally considered to be the best English-language bookstore in Morocco. Of all the bookstores I have visited, I think it is easily the best, with a very good selection of fiction and nonfiction titles on all aspects of Morocco, plus a fairly extensive selection of recent American fiction. The staff is very helpful, too.

The English Bookshop, 7 Zankat Alyamama, Rabat; selection of mostly used novels (British and American) plus some Moroccan guidebooks and language books.

La Mamounia Bookshop, La Mamounia hotel, Avenue Bab Jdid, Marrakesh; this small gift shop in the front of the hotel's entrance stocks a number of travel, cooking, and fiction titles in English (other languages are represented as well). This shop is also the only place I found packaged sets of old Moroccan stamps.

Librairie des Colonnes, 54 boulevard Pasteur, Tangier; though mostly a French-language store, there is a pretty good assortment of books in English.

Buses

I admit I have never been a passenger on a Moroccan bus. The ONCF (Office National des Chemins de Fer) train network is generally efficient, pleasant, and comfortable, so I simply have had little incentive to take the bus. I also admit that I have been a bus passenger elsewhere in Africa—Egypt and Kenya—and so "experiencing" bus travel is something I have done and may not ever do again in Africa. My opinion aside, you may decide to travel by bus in Morocco (and in some cases, the train lines don't take you all the way to your destination, so you'll have to take the connecting bus anyway), so you should know that the national line is called the Compagnie de Transports Marocains (CTM) and that it is the most extensive line in the country. You can obtain schedule and fare information from the Moroccan National Tourist Board here in the United States, and most guidebooks provide details as well. From what I've read and heard, I recommend making a seat reservation whenever possible. Also, if it's a long trip, bring your own food, with enough to share with your fellow passengers.

C

Calendar

Islam, like Judaism, follows a lunar calendar, and in Morocco—just as in other Muslim countries—events are dated from the year of the *hadj,* when Muhammad moved to Medina. So add 622 to all dates you see—in museums, for example—to arrive at the proper century.

Car Rental

Driving around Morocco at the time of the First World War, Edith Wharton noted, "If one loses one's way in Morocco, civilization vanishes as though it were a magic carpet rolled up by a *Djinn.*" After some car trouble early on in her journey, she added, "It is a good thing to begin with such a mishap, not only because it develops the fatalism necessary to the enjoyment of Africa, but because it lets one at once into the mysterious heart of the country: a country so deeply conditioned by its miles and miles of uncitied wilderness that until one has known the wilderness one cannot begin to understand the cities." Renting a car or hiring a driver for one today isn't quite the ordeal it was for Wharton, but it is important to rent the newest car available, inspect it carefully before driving off the lot, and be especially alert when driving. (Mountain roads are seriously windy, goats cross the road often, and the roads in and out of Marrakesh, for example, are shared with more donkeys than perhaps one is used to.) The desert is a whole other driving experience: be certain you have provisions, both for the vehicle and yourself. I highly recommend seeing at least part of Morocco by car. For one thing, the train service

(ONCF), while good and reliable, isn't as extensive as it could be if the Atlas and Rif ranges weren't in the way. The bus? Forget about it, unless you're desperate. You can simply see much, much more of the country with a car. My colleague, Dave, swears by hiring a car and driver, or just a driver if you want to arrange the rental of the car separately. He feels that with a driver along, visitors will be hassled less—or not at all—by locals wanting to help you park the car, watch it, or show you around. I think investigating this is worthwhile (and Dave thinks that $200 a day is a reasonable and worthwhile fee), although I admit that my husband and I have not had problems when we rented a car on our own. Perhaps a good compromise would be to experience driving on your own but hire a driver for a particular day trip or longer journey.

My favorite feature of travel publications is the section featuring reader's letters. I have probably learned more from these letters than any other source, and the largest number of complaints seem to be about problems encountered when renting a car. No matter what you read, hear, or assume, the only word that counts is the one from your policy administrator, be it a credit card or an insurance company. If you have any questions about renting a car overseas and what is and isn't covered on your existing policy (including collision damage waiver), contact your provider in advance. Request documentation in writing, if necessary. It is your responsibility to learn about your coverage *before* you rent a car. I have never encountered any rental car problems, but then again I make it a habit to state to the company representative, "When I return the car to you, I will not pay anything more than this amount" while pointing to the total on my receipt.

Some general points to keep in mind: ~You should get an International Driver's License for driving in Morocco. I don't recommend it for many other countries in the world, but it's a good idea to have one in Morocco. ~Reserve a car *before* you arrive in Morocco. Anytime you see ads announcing special rates, those rates apply to those customers who reserve in advance. Also, rental cars are limited, and you want to avoid a scenario where there are no cars available, at any price. ~Hertz offers a competitive rate with its prepaid car rental voucher. The conditions are that you prepay in U.S. dollars in advance of your trip, and the vouchers are typically faxed to a U.S. fax number or mailed to a U.S. address. The prepaid rate does not include such things as drop charges, car seats, collision damage waiver, or gas, and these must be paid for in local currency at the time you pick up the car. ~It's helpful to begin thinking in kilometers instead of miles. I jot down sample distances to use as a ready reference: 1 mile = 1.6 kilometers, so 12 km = 7$^{1}/_{2}$ miles; 16 km = 10 miles; 40 km = 25 miles; 80 km = 50 miles; 160 km = 100 miles; 320 km = 200 miles, etc.

~Road maps and atlases obviously employ route numbers for large and small roads, but the signs you'll see typically indicate a city or town rather than a road number, and sometimes that city or town will be quite far away. (Initially this threw me off and reminded me of a sign I used to see years ago just outside of

Philadelphia for a restaurant at the New Jersey shore; the sign advertised that the restaurant was "minutes away" but was in fact two *hours* away.) Begin thinking in terms of *direction* rather than road number, and consult your map(s) often—you'll find that it's quite a sensible way of getting around, and it forces you to be better versed in geography. ~Driving in the fast lane on Moroccan highways can be a bit disconcerting as any car suddenly looming up behind you is closing in at a *much* faster speed than we're accustomed to in the United States. (The official speed limit on the *autoroutes* is approximately 74 mph, but drivers typically push this to eighty.) These drivers usually have no patience for your slowness and will tailgate you and flash their lights until you get out of the way. So if you're going to pass, step on the gas and go, and return quickly to the right lane. ~There is no nation-wide road assistance organization. ~I've read conflicting advice on parking tickets, so I would not recommend taking a chance if you're in doubt. Rental agencies do have your credit card number, and it seems to me they can eventually bill you for any tickets you've received and add a service charge if they're so inclined. ~Note that the blue signs with white lettering indicate the *péage* or *autoroute* highways; white signs with blue lettering indicate nonpay roads often running parallel to the *péage* route. Make sure you choose the right one. ~Gas prices in Morocco are quite high, and tolls, too, are very expensive. Gas is available twenty-four hours a day, seven days a week, on the *autoroutes,* but on other roads, gas stations are typically closed on Sunday and/or Monday. If you'll be driving in mountainous areas or in the desert, be aware that gas stations are few and far between, so plan accordingly or bring along a can of gas. ~As all gas stations are full service, attendants do not necessarily expect a tip; but it's proper to give two or three *dirhams* for checking the oil, windows, and tires. ~One of the guidebooks I read emphasized that there are two rules of the road in Morocco: *priorité à droite* (giving way to traffic coming from the right) and every man for himself, both of which I also endorse.

~A note if you are returning a rental car at Mohammed V Airport: the rental agencies are all located on the lower level in the arrivals section. It might seem logical to drive up to the departures section, but there are no staff or services on the upper level for the return of rentals. The signs are a little confusing, and you may, like my husband and I, drive around the airport a few times before you figure it out. The airport is not really so big, but if you are in a hurry, this could be just the sort of annoyance to make you hit the roof, a very un-Moroccan reaction.

~Drivers will encounter lots of police roadblocks throughout Morocco. It is essential to slow down and stop at all of them—it doesn't hurt to smile and wave, either—and it is unlikely you will ever be asked to show your papers. I have heard that if driving in the Rif, you are more likely to be pulled over as officials assume you may be involved in the *kif* (hash) trade. If you are asked to open your trunk, be sure to watch the officials carefully: it is not unheard of for *kif* to be planted in the cars of tourists.

~Be sure to receive proper paperwork from the firm you rent a car from if you will be driving into Ceuta or Melilla, the Spanish-controlled enclaves of Morocco. Technically, these are another country, and border officials will need to see authorization.

Useful vocabulary: *location de voitures* (car rental agency); *essence* (regular, lower octane leaded gas); *sans plomb* (unleaded gas); *super* is the kind of gas most commonly used in both local and tourist cars, and is premium petrol; *un bon* (gas station receipt); *gasoil* (diesel); *défense d'entrer* (no entry); *défense de stationner* (no parking); *sortie* (exit); *vous n'avez pas la priorité* (you don't have the right of way—seen mostly at traffic circles, where you give way to traffic already in the circle coming from your left); *passage protégé* (yellow diamond-shaped road signs on main roads indicating that you have priority over traffic on any minor side roads; priority on Moroccan roads, just as in France, is always given to vehicles approaching from the right—*priorité à droite*—unless indicated otherwise); *cédez le passage* (give way to traffic); *serrez à droite* (keep to the right); *déviation* or *route deviée* (diversion); *péage* (toll); *dépannage* (breakdown); *tout droit* (straight ahead—not to be confused with *à droit*, which means "to the right"; *à gauche*, by the way, is "to the left"); *rappel* (reminder of the speed limit); *aire de repos* (rest area, sometimes with a view); *près* (near); and *loin* (far).

Children

A few months before my daughter was born, I was feeling anxious that my life as a mother was going to drastically alter my ability to travel. My colleague and friend Bruce helped me snap out of this funk by pointing out that my husband and I might travel *differently* than we did before, but we would indeed still travel, because we love it. As Bruce is both a parent and a world traveler, he advised us not to over-think the situation, because then we would find a million reasons *not* to travel. The way I see it, parents can make the decision never to go anywhere and deprive both their children and themselves of a priceless experience, but I believe that children have as much to teach us as we do them, especially when traveling—their curiosity and imagination make even familiar destinations seem new.

All this said, I have reservations about traveling with young children in Morocco. It's not that it can't be accomplished, or that you wouldn't have an amazing time doing it, but I think it is hard enough keeping myself healthy without the added worry of diarrhea or dehydration (or worse) in a small child. I have seen some foreigners in Morocco with babies and children under the age of five, and they looked like they were having an okay time. It is not a decision I will endorse, though a bit of a compromise would be to stay at the Club Med in Agadir, which accepts children, and make day trips from there. If you are determined to bring the kids along, read on with my best wishes for a safe and happy trip for everyone.

I have been unable to find a book devoted exclusively to traveling with children in Morocco, but some guidebooks—including many of those mentioned in the entry for Guidebooks—offer excellent suggestions for things to see and do with kids. A way to build excitement in advance of a trip is to involve children in the planning, showing them maps and books and talking about the things you'll see and do. Give them a blank book so they can start creating a journal, or buy a ready-made one such as *How to Draw a Clam: A Wonderful Vacation Planner* (Joy Sikorski, Clarkson Potter, 2000); and buy them an inexpensive aim-and-shoot camera: they'll show more interest in things if they can take their own pictures, and they can include the photos in their trip journal. Something parents will be sure to notice: in Morocco—as in most other Mediterranean countries—young children stay up late at night, even at restaurants and cafés. Do not be surprised if it's eleven P.M. and there are lots of kids running around. I've never seen the children looking unhappy or tired, and it seems to make sense in a region with an afternoon siesta tradition. There is not an abundance of books available on traveling with children (although this seems to be a growing area of publishing), but two good volumes are *Have Kid, Will Travel: 101 Survival Strategies for Vacationing with Babies and Young Children* (Claire Tristram with Lucille Tristram, Andrews McMeel Publishing, Kansas City, Missouri, 1997; this is loaded with good, concrete suggestions and tips: Tristram has visited all fifty U.S. states and thirty countries, and Lucille, her daughter, has been named "the best baby in the world" by several strangers sitting next to her on long-distance flights—a great recommendation for reading this book! Among the best words of advice: "Above all, don't let a bad moment become a bad day, and don't let a bad day become a bad week.") and *Travel with Your Baby: Experts Share Their Secrets for Trips with Your Under-4-Year-Old* (Fodor's Travel Publications, 2001; readers around the country contributed their real-life travel stories and tips to this small, pocket-sized edition. There are good checklists, and I think the best overall suggestion is KTWF—Keep Them Well Fed). None of the tips in either of these books, however, prepares parents for a situation like the one my friend Katie found herself in. She, her husband, and their one-year-old son, Jack, were on an airline terminal van at the Nice airport when Jack suddenly and inexplicably projectile vomited all over anyone who was on either side of the van. After they hastily apologized and tried their best to clean everyone off with pieces of their own clothing, Jack repeated the performance. They did their best once again to wipe everyone off, but by now they had determined there was probably something wrong with Jack and they had to find the resident doctor at the airport. (It all ended up fine, though it didn't help that their flight was delayed three hours.) There are just some things you can't prepare for, and some situations when you really need a sense of humor.

Clothing

It's impossible to address clothing without also talking about packing, but I have included a separate Packing entry below. In general, I pack light, and unless I have plans to be at fancy places, I pack double-duty items (stuff that can go from daytime to evening) in low-key colors that also mix and match so I can wear garments more than once. I also tend to bring items that aren't my favorites, figuring that if someone does snatch my suitcase or rummage through my hotel room, at least I won't lose the things I love the most. When visiting a country like Morocco, where there are so many beautiful *objets,* I like to know that if I need more room in my bags for souvenirs, I can leave some clothing behind. Morocco presents travelers, both male and female, with some etiquette issues, and it is significantly more time consuming to pack for Morocco than it is for, say, France or Italy. Keep in mind that a person's appearance counts for a lot with Moroccans; the hippie look and the *schlump* look (my made-up Yiddish-sounding phrase, indicating a rumpled, baggy-sweatshirt-with-American-college-name-on-the-front-and-backward-baseball-cap appearance) will not endear you to the locals. Generally speaking, Morocco is a nation of informal dress, but Moroccans do tend to dress up a bit more than Americans. Blue jeans are relatively rare. Men mostly wear cotton or wool slacks, and only very modern Moroccan women wear jeans, usually not skin-tight. Jeans are definitely not welcome in Morocco's palace restaurants—or any fine dining venue—so I don't find them particularly versatile. The American predilection for color-coordinated jogging suits, complete with sneakers, is probably somewhat puzzling to Moroccans—it's not like they haven't seen them, but like the French, they believe that jogging attire is worn *only* when engaging in that activity and is not a fashion statement.

For both men and women, dressing on the conservative side is always a good idea. Visitors staying at one of the country's Mediterranean or Atlantic coastal resorts have a little more flexibility in terms of how much skin to show, but outside of the resorts it is still important to dress modestly. Non-Muslims are not permitted to visit mosques in Morocco (with the exception of four: Grande Mosquee Hassan II in Casablanca, the ruined mosque at Chellah in Rabat, Tin Mal in the High Atlas, and the Spanish mosque near Chefchaoun), so the clothing you bring isn't for visiting religious houses of worship but for the very public streets of cities and villages. Visitors will earn respect and goodwill by following a few guidelines, difficult as they may be in hot weather. Men should refrain from wearing shorts, except at the beach or at a hotel's pool. (You'll quickly notice that Moroccan men, like Asian men, just do not wear shorts.) Suits and ties are necessary only at the very finest establishments (even at some of the country's famous palace restaurants, diners wear *nice* clothes but not finery), while polo shirts, khaki and other cotton pants, and cotton sweaters are welcome throughout the country.

Women, obviously, have a bit more difficulty. In my opinion, the best way to describe a conservative Muslim woman's appearance is frumpy. Modern Moroccan women wear very contemporary clothes, so the trick for a visitor is to strike some sort of respectful balance. I feel that for myself, a trip to Morocco is not about looking my best every day. There are some outfits I've worn that I would *never* consider wearing at home, but I sure was glad I had them in Morocco. A lot of Moroccan women wear pants, but usually of the very loose variety. Tight pants are a no-no as they leave nothing to the imagination, but comfortable pants with some flare in the legs work just fine. I found skirts to be a much better option, although these should always be long, to the ankle. Short skirts are never acceptable, and even those that fall at the knee will raise some eyebrows. A word of warning: I once wore an ankle-length skirt in a taupe color (good for not showing dirt very quickly) that was a wrap-around variety; but I did not anticipate that even a slight wind would render the skirt virtually useless, despite all its other attributes. Sleeveless shirts, too, are unacceptable, unless they are worn underneath a cardigan or blazer. (I had great success with this sort of layering, by the way.) Long-sleeved shirts are naturally a better choice than short-sleeved, especially since one can roll the sleeves up or down, although short-sleeved is certainly better than no sleeves. Scarves are great, too, for covering your neck if you're wearing a V-neck shirt or just to wear every day—they somehow give an impression of propriety. Muslim women readers who wear a head scarf in the United States or Canada will be quite at home in Morocco, but head scarves aren't required or necessary for non-Muslim women visitors (and note that there are very few completely veiled women in Morocco).

Although comfortable shoes are of the utmost importance, I never, ever bring sneakers—and I positively forbid my husband to bring them—and you might not either once you realize that they scream "American." I prefer Arche, a line of French walking shoes and sandals for men and women, but there are several other lines available (Mephisto, for example, another French line for men and women) that are also stylish *and* comfortable. Sandals, by the way, are not the ideal footwear for walking in the medina, unless they are of the closed-toe variety.

I recently discovered a unique shoe line just for women: "à propos . . . conversations." I loved the shoes right away when I read they were "influenced by European women whose fashion sense does not include white athletic shoes outside of sports." All the shoes—which are soft and flexible and easily fold down to handbag or briefcase size—are limited editions and sport such names as Liquid Lemons, Peacock Punch, Linen Sands, African Sun, and Khaki Krunch. There are over a dozen styles offered in two collections a year, and many styles are available two ways: with one solid center elastic band or two cross straps of elastic. "Like a scarf for your feet" is how they're trademarked, and you can view the styles on-line at www.conversationshoes.com or call 800-746-3724 for a catalog.

The following mail-order catalogs offer some practical clothes, shoes, packing accessories, and gadgets for travelers. At L. L. Bean Traveler (800-221-4221; www.llbean.com/traveler), some of the items I like best are its personal organizers, which are sized for from one to five days, come in eight cool colors, and have hooks so you can hang them up on a shower or closet rod; and its Burt's Bees travel kit, which contains eleven products all sized for travel. Good for Morocco-bound women are the "easy-comfort travel pants," which are comfortable and loose-fitting, and for men, the "equator zip-off pants," which are casual pants with a hidden zipper at the knee, allowing one to create shorts for visits by the pool—it's like packing one item but bringing two. At Magellan's (800-962-4943; www.magellans.com), I especially like the Travel Toilet Tissue, Toothettes, and microfiber towels. At TravelSmith (800-950-1600; www.travelsmith.com), besides its famous packable microfiber raincoats, I like the "guaranteed not to wrinkle" items and pack-it system cubes; also— and I know readers may be surprised by this since I just grumbled about sneakers—the stretch canvas sneakers are terrific! I like them because they're stylish in a European way, weigh only twenty-two ounces, are incredibly comfy, and make locals think twice before summing the wearer up as American. The Territory Ahead (888-233-9954; www.territoryahead.com) offers the most stylish clothing of the bunch, and I'm especially fond of its footwear and shorts—unfortunately not appropriate for Morocco but great for other Mediterranean trips.

Club Méditerranée (Club Med)

I have never been an advocate of a Club Med vacation in a foreign country because its all-inclusive package makes it tempting to never leave the compound, ensuring you never experience anything of the local culture. But it offers one of the few opportunities in the world for a family vacation that allows parents to have time to themselves—at an affordable price. The Club Med package includes airfare, three meals a day, unlimited wine or beer with meals, accommodations for seven nights, and unlimited sports and activities. Although, as my friend Lorraine says, you still have to sleep with your kids and deal with middle-of-the-night and early awakenings, parents can drop their kids off in the morning and pick them up again in the late afternoon. There are seven Club Med properties in Morocco, at least one of which—at Agadir—accepts children from age two. Though Club Med rates are not prohibitively expensive at any time of year, the company has slower periods, and during these times—early April, Thanksgiving, and early to mid December are typically periods when its properties are undersold—you can often take advantage of even lower rates. As an aside, if you'd like to stay on in Morocco for a while and work, you could apply for a position as a Club Med *Gentil Organisateur* (GO). For details on all of the above, call Club Med direct at (800)-CLUB-MED or view its website (www.clubmed.com). Travel agents, too, can make Club Med reservations for you.

Coins

If you have leftover *dirhams* in the form of coins, you can always save them for a future trip, but perhaps a better idea is to give them to a great cause: UNICEF's Change for Good program. A number of airlines pass out envelopes to passengers on flights back to the United States, but if you've never received one and want to contribute, contact the U.S. Committee for UNICEF (333 East 38th Street, 6th floor, New York, New York 10016; 212-824-6972; fax: 824-6969).

Cooking Schools

The best single source for cooking schools in Morocco—and the entire world—is the *Shaw Guide to Cooking Schools: Cooking Schools, Courses, Vacations, Apprenticeships, and Wine Instruction Throughout the World* (ShawGuides, New York). Cooking school opportunities in Morocco are not abundant, but interest for more, on the part of residents and visitors alike, seems to be growing—so stay tuned! (And of course, Morocco being Morocco, where almost any request can be satisfied, I'm sure if you told the *patron* or *concierge* where you're staying that you're interested in Moroccan cuisine and would like to be an observer in a restaurant or home kitchen, it could be arranged.) In addition to the annual *Shaw Guide,* interested food lovers can also view updates at its website: www.shawguides.com.

~Not exactly a cooking school but very popular nonetheless is cookbook author Kitty Morse's annual "Come With Me to the Kasbah!" culinary tour of Morocco. Morse takes fourteen travelers all over the country with stops at local *marchés,* private homes, and restaurants. The trip in early summer of 2001 was fifteen days in length and included La Mamounia and Palais Jamai hotels. For information on next year's trip, contact Natalie Tuomi, Carefree Vacations, 2727 Roosevelt Street, Suite B, Carlsbad, California 92008; 800-533-2779 or 760-729-3454; fax: -2482; e-mail: ntuomi@sdtg.com; website: www.kittymorse.com.

Cuisine

Author Mort Rosenblum, in his book *Olives,* notes, "In Morocco, cooks use every spice that ever found its way across the desert or the Mediterranean." A walk around the souk and a multicourse meal at a grand palace restaurant will bear this out and then some. Cookbook author Paula Wolfert, in her outstanding book *Couscous and Other Good Food from Morocco,* outlines some key spices and herbs to recognize and become familiar with in Moroccan cuisine. The ten important spices are cinnamon, cumin, saffron, turmeric, ginger, black pepper, cayenne, paprika, aniseed, and sesame seeds. The nine secondary aromatics are allspice, caraway, cloves, coriander seeds, gum Arabic, fenugreek, licorice, honey dates, and orrisroot (also known as *amber el door*). A most unusual spice mixture—and a good thing to buy because it is rarely as good in the United States and is more expensive—is *ras el hanout* (meaning "top of the shop"). It's even a little pricey in Morocco, and it will always cost significantly more than other spices you may purchase. According to Wolfert, *ras el hanout* is a very old mixture of many spices, sometimes ten, sometimes nineteen, sometimes twenty-four. Some mixtures of *ras el hanout* are apparently better than others, and Wolfert notes that "the aphrodisiacs (Spanish fly, ash berries, and monk's pepper) that appear in most formulae seem to be the reason why the mere mention of this mixture will put a gleam into a Moroccan cook's eye." Here are the possible ingredients of *ras el hanout:* allspice, ash berries, belladonna leaves, black cumin seeds, black peppercorns, cantharis (Spanish fly), cardamom pods, wild cardamom pods, cayenne, cassia cinnamon, Ceylon cinnamon, cloves, coriander seed, cubebe pepper, earth almonds (used to make the Spanish drink *horchata*), galingale, ginger, *Gouza el asnab* (a kind of nut), grains of paradise, long pepper, lavender, mace, monk's pepper, nutmeg, orrisroot, and turmeric. The nine important herbs in Moroccan cooking are onions, garlic, parsley, green coriander, basil, marjoram, grey verbena, mint, and za'atar. The fragrant orange and rose waters, plus the spicy salsa *harissa,* preserved lemons, and olives, round out the list of Moroccan flavors 101.

Customs

There seems to be a lot of confusion over what items can and positively cannot be brought into the United States—and not only on the part of travelers but customs agents, too. The rules, apparently, are not as confusing as they might seem, but sometimes neither customs staff nor travelers are up to date on what they are. Some examples of what's legal and what's not include: olive oil, yes, but olives, no (unless they're vacuum-packed); fruit jams and preserves, yes, but fresh fruit, no; hard cheeses, yes, but soft, runny cheeses, no; commercially canned meat, yes (if the inspector can determine that the meat was cooked in the can after it was sealed), but fresh and dried meats and meat products, no; nuts, yes, but chestnuts and acorns, no; coffee, yes, but roasted beans only; dried spices, yes, but not curry leaves; fresh and dried flowers, yes, but not eucalyptus or any variety with roots. If you think all this is unnecessary bother, remember that it was quite likely a tourist who carried in the wormy fruit that brought the Mediterranean fruit fly to California in 1979. Fighting this pest cost more than $100 million. For more details, call the U.S. Department of Agriculture's Animal and Plant Health Inspection Service at 301-734-8645, or visit its website www.aphis.usda.gov (click on "Travelers' Tips").

Dar

Simply put, a *dar* is a type of Moroccan house. More precisely, a *dar* (plural *diour*) is a house with a patio whose central space (*wast ed-dar*) does not typically have any plants and is open to the sky. In the center of the patio is often a fountain. A garden in the center of a house naturally requires more space, so *riads* are typically larger than *diour,* which is why a dense neighborhood like a medina has more *diour* than *riads.* These are not hard and fast descriptions, however: note that the lovely Riad Enija in Marrakesh is quite large and is in the thick of the medina, while the Dar al Assad, in the same quarter, has a garden with palm trees in the middle of its courtyard. As a visitor, it really doesn't matter which one you have the opportunity to visit or call home for a few days: they are each stunningly beautiful, and you will find yourself wishing you could knock one down *zellige* by *zellige* and reconstruct it fully in your hometown.

E

El-Hamdu Lillah
This widely used phrase (although I heard it more frequently in Egypt) translates as "Praise be to God." Like *bismillah,* it's an expression of thanks, but it is used in the way we might say "Thank God!" with relief that a catastrophe has been averted.

Elderly Travel
The two best-known organizations for elderly travelers are Elderhostel (75 Federal Street, 3rd floor, Boston, Massachusetts 02110; 877-426-8056; fax: -2166) and Interhostel (University of New Hampshire, 6 Garrison Avenue, Durham, New Hampshire 03824; 800-733-9753; fax: 603-862-1113; www.learn.unh.edu). I've listed them here instead of under Tours because I wanted them to stand apart from the more general travel companies. For some good articles about these two educational companies and others, see "Senior Classes" and "Catering to Older Travelers," both of which appeared in *The New York Times* travel section, August 25, 1991.

F

Faire le Pont
This French expression is the equivalent of our *long weekend* in English. When a holiday falls on a Thursday or a Tuesday, for example, the Moroccans like to "bridge" (*pont*) the holiday by also taking off on Friday and/or Monday. Note, however, that the Moroccans are a bit more liberal with the *pont* than the French. If a holiday falls on a Monday or Tuesday, for example, you can count on no one being back at work for the remainder of the week. This is useful to keep in mind if there is a scheduled holiday during your trip, as stores and businesses may be closed for all or part of the time, and the plumber you need to fix a major problem with the pipes at the *riad* you've rented may be unavailable.

Fantasia

Simply speaking, a *fantasia* is a Berber equestrian display, but it is much more of an extravaganza than that. Though I haven't yet had the chance to attend one, I've been told a fantasia is quite impressive, even if it is primarily for tourists. For more details, inquire at the tourist office or your hotel.

Film

I'm aware the FAA maintains that film less than 1,000-speed sent through X-ray scanners won't harm picture developing; but my friend Peggy, a freelance photographer, maintains that multiple trips through the scanner will indeed harm the film. Also, if you pack your film in checked bags, the scanners that inspect them are stronger than those for carry-on bags and should definitely be avoided.

~I always keep rolls of film—no matter what speed—accessible and hand them to the security inspectors before I walk through the scanner. (Remember to retrieve them after you pass, however!)

~If you take a lot of photos, you might want to buy some lead-lined pouches from a camera store. They're inexpensive and will protect film even in checked bags.

~Professional film (which is very sensitive and must be kept refrigerated until used and developed a day later) aside, a general guideline for us amateurs is that the higher the film speed, the faster the film—and fast film requires less light. So think about the situations in which you anticipate taking pictures: if it's off-season and overcast, select 200; if it's spring or summer with bright sunlight, select 400; for indoor gatherings in restaurants, try 800 or higher (unless you want to employ the flash); for approaching dusk and sunsets, select 400.

~I happen to be very fond of black-and-white photos, so I always include a roll or two in my bag.

Frequent-Flier Miles

From what I've read, it seems the airlines wish they'd never created mileage award programs. There are now fewer and fewer seats reserved for frequent fliers, and you need even more miles to earn these seats. Should you happen to have enough miles and want to fly to Morocco, plan to redeem those miles about six months to a year ahead *or* plan to fly in the off-season. (It's also possible that airlines will reduce the miles needed for the off-season flight.) Don't immediately give up if your initial request can't be confirmed. Apparently, the airlines tinker with frequent-flier seats every day as they monitor the demand for paying customers. If the number of paying travelers is low as the departure date approaches, more frequent-flier awards may be honored. Also, check to see if your accrued miles have expired before you try to redeem them. All airlines have expiration dates on frequent-flier miles, but they don't all adhere to strict enforcement of those deadlines. Try to reserve your valid mileage for expensive flights rather than those that you can get for a good price anytime.

G

General Travel

Here are some good books to consult about trip planning in general. *The Travel Detective: How to Get the Best Service and the Best Deals From Airlines, Hotels, Cruise Ships, and Car Rental Agencies* (Peter Greenberg, Villard, New York, 2001): As long as the title is, it could be even longer, as Greenberg covers—and uncovers—so much indispensable information on all aspects of travel. If I could have, I would have excerpted nearly every entry in Greenberg's book in my own. You want to read this book. It's remarkably interesting, and *de rigueur*. *The New York Times Practical Traveler Handbook: An A–Z Guide to Getting There and Back* (Betsy Wade, Times Books, New York, 1994) and *Wendy Perrin's Secrets Every Smart Traveler Should Know: Condé Nast Traveler's Consumer Travel Expert Tells All* (Fodor's Travel Publications, 1997): It might seem like these two books cover the same ground, but in fact there is very little overlap, and I refer to both of them all the time. The Practical Traveler book is really an A–Z guide, organized alphabetically and covering such topics as airline code-sharing, customs, hotel tipping, and closing up the house. Perrin's book is divided into eight sections plus an appendix, and the anecdotes featured were all previously published in the "Ombudsman" column of the magazine. She covers the fine art of complaining; what to do if your luggage is damaged or pilfered; travel agents and tour operators, car rentals, shopping and cruises, and so on, as well as the ten commandments of trouble-free travel, which I think should be given to every traveler before he or she boards the plane. In a similar but different vein, I highly recommend *Traveler's Tool Kit: How to Travel Absolutely Anywhere!* (Rob Sangster, Menasha Ridge Press, Birmingham, Alabama, 1999). "Tool kit" is really the best description of this travel bible, which addresses *everything* having to do with planning, packing, and departing. Who is this book for? Everyone really, or at least people who are curious about the rest of the world; people who are thinking about their very first foreign trip; budget travelers; business travelers; people who want to travel more independently; and people who know "that life offers more than a two-week vacation once a year." It's a *great* book, with lots of great ideas, tips, and advice. I've found Sangster's checklists at the back of the book particularly helpful, and his bibliography is the most extensive I've seen aside from my own.

Gifts

It is not necessary or expected that you bring gifts to Morocco. Certainly the best thing you can do if you want to give something back is to donate medical supplies or money to a clinic or an organization that supports medical efforts. (The ratio of doctors to residents in Morocco is not sufficient.) But there is also nothing wrong with bringing small items for the sons or daughters of your guide, young boys who watch your car or show you around the souk, and so on. I like to bring items that are representative of America, or New York, where I live, so those floaty pens that have the Statue of Liberty floating down the center, magnets, keychains, and pencils—airports usually have at least one shop selling this stuff—are all welcome little trinkets.

Gilbert Grandval

In my opinion, there were only two good Frenchmen in Morocco before independence: Marshal Hubert Lyautey, who served as resident-general of Morocco from 1912 to 1925, and Gilbert Grandval, who replaced Francis Lacoste as resident-general on June 22, 1955 (by which time, it should be noted, Charles de Gaulle expressed the opinion that there was only one solution left to the Moroccan problem: to restore Sultan Mohammed V to the throne). As Gavin Maxwell noted in *Lords of the Atlas,* "Among the French viceroys in Morocco Grandval towers head and shoulders above them all—greater even than Lyautey, for he was that great rarity, a truly civilized human being who was against violence and repression." Grandval, after trying desperately to avert disaster, "left Morocco, secretly, on the afternoon of 26 August, 1955, letting it be known that he was paying a brief visit to France, and would return in forty-eight hours. The Moroccan people did not mourn his departure—he was just another Frenchman gone, and good riddance. In Morocco now there should be some monument to this honest man who was so grossly exploited and deceived by his own country."

Golf

It may seem unlikely that Morocco is a country with golfing opportunities, but in fact golf was first introduced into Morocco at the beginning of the twentieth century and has become a national passion. It helped that King Hassan II loved golf, which you may not find exceptional, but to quote David Lamb in *The Arabs* (Vintage, 1988), "An Arab monarch who likes to chip out of bunkers with a nine-iron is unique. With the exception of President Mubarak, a squash enthusiast, I never knew another Arab leader who exercised, let alone partook in sports. King Fahd of Saudi Arabia, who had the elevators installed in his private jet and his Kuwait residence, doesn't even like to *walk.*" There are about thirty gorgeous golf courses in Morocco. If you look at a map of Morocco and draw an imaginary line across the country from Agadir to Ouarzazate, you will find that all the golf courses are north of this line. The Moroccan National Tourist Office publishes a brochure on golf in Morocco that includes telephone and fax numbers, addresses, and number of holes for each course. All the clubs described in the brochure are open to the public even if access is sometimes limited to players holding a handicap card. Greens fees vary, usually from 100 to 500 *dirhams,* and most courses offer caddies and electric carts. Some courses are closed one day a week. Additionally, interested enthusiasts may contact the Royal Moroccan Golf Federation, The Royal Dar Es-Salam Golf Club, Rabat, 07.75.59.60; fax: 07.75.10.26.

Guidebooks

Choosing which guidebooks to use can be bewildering and overwhelming. I have yet to find the perfect book that offers all the features I need and want, so I consult a variety of books, gleaning tips and advice from each. Then I buy a blank journal and fill it with notes from all these books (leaving some pages blank) and end up with what is, for me, the perfect package: the journal plus two or three guidebooks I determine to be indispensable. (I don't carry them around at the same time.) In the end, the right guidebook is the one that speaks to you. Go to the Morocco section in the travel department of a bookstore, and take some time to read through the various guides. If you feel the author shares a certain sensibility with you, and you think his or her credentials are respectable, then you're probably holding the right book. Recommendations from friends and colleagues are fine only if they travel in the same way you do and seek the same qualities as you in a guidebook. Also, if you discover an older guide that appeals to you, don't immediately dismiss it. Background information doesn't change—use it in combination with an updated guide to create your own perfect package. Keep in mind, too, that guidebooks within the same series are not always consistent, as they aren't always written by the same authors. Listed below are the guides I consult before heading to Morocco. They appear alphabetically, not in any order of preference. I have, however, noted which features I find particularly helpful in each book, and I've indicated those that I consider to be "bring-alongs." (I use some books for very specific reasons but don't consider them thorough enough to bring them along in my suitcase.)

Blue Guide: Morocco (Jane Holliday, A & C Black Publishers, London; published in the United States by W.W. Norton, New York). Perhaps because it is so authoritative, like Baedeker, I always feel like I *have* to check in with the Blue Guide. In fact, the Blue Guide series has been around since 1918, and the original founders were the editors of Baedeker's English-language editions. Blue Guides are very straightforward and practical with a no-nonsense approach that sets the series apart from so many others. The author of this Morocco edition lived in the country—and traveled all around it—for four years, when she was married to a senior diplomat. (She's still a regular visitor.) One very specific reason I like this guide is that Holliday seems to have more experience in traveling by car through Morocco, and therefore her advice and descriptive information about road conditions and the like is more detailed than in any other guide. Personally, while I hold the Blue Guide series in high regard, I do not consider this edition a bring-along. But, I would not set off for Morocco without consulting it, and I did record a fair amount of practical tips from its pages into my blank book, and—shhhh!—I also photocopied some chapters on particular destinations that I then glued into my book.

Cadogan: Morocco (Barnaby Rogerson, Cadogan Books plc, London; distributed in the United States by Globe Pequot Press, Old Saybrook, Connecticut). Cadogan (rhymes with *toboggan*) Guides are almost all written by Dana Facaros and Michael Pauls (they've written more than twenty now), but a few titles in the series are authored by other, equally talented and exacting folks. I consider Cadogan Guides to be of the bring-along variety. They're discriminating without being snooty, as well as honest, witty, and interesting. All the authors—not just the Facaros-Pauls team—are difficult to impress, so when they enthuse about something, I pay attention. In fact, I occasionally find them too jaded, which can be refreshing in a sea of books that only gush with sentimentality. This Morocco edition weighs in at six hundred pages, but I wouldn't dream of leaving it behind even if it were twice the size. My husband and I have taken to referring to Barnaby Rogerson as "Mr. Morocco" because not only is he an authority as an author but a number of Moroccans know him and like him. In addition to the overall quality and detail of this guide, I'm especially fond of the "Moroccan Themes" section, covering Moorish decorative arts, geology, Jewish Morocco, rural souks, Sufi brotherhoods, and more, as well as the "History" section and bibliography. Rogerson has also compiled a "Best of Morocco" list, which appears on the inside front flap, containing the best beaches, cities, hotels, landscapes, restaurants, towns, and villages.

~Cadogan's *Marrakesh Fez Rabat* is also a very good guide, also authored by Rogerson, and obviously it just covers these Imperial Cities. (It weighs a good deal less than the whole Morocco edition.) Both titles are *de rigueur* bring-alongs.

Fodor's Morocco (Fodor's Travel Publications). I typically crave more information than Fodor's guides seek to provide, but I think the entire line of Fodor's guides gets better and better every year. I *always* read them before I go and *always* discover a handful of useful tips. Of the seven writers who collectively authored this Morocco edition, six have lived and/or worked or do live and/or work in Morocco. (The seventh writer is a Barcelona-based journalist who has visited and written about Morocco for about a decade.) Features I found helpful were the "Smart Travel Tips A to Z" in the front of the book (though most entries are more detailed in other guides); the "Need a Break?" suggestions throughout the book; and the "Destination: Morocco" section immediately following it, which includes the "Fodor's Choice" list of architecture, the outdoors, shopping, people-watching, and lodging. Also, the "Islam: Five Steps to a Life of Peace" essay at the back is quite good. Not a bring-along, but a good source to consult before you go.

Footprint Morocco Handbook (Justin McGuinness, Footprint Handbooks, Bath, England; published in the United States by Passport Books, a division of NTC/Contemporary Publishing Group, Lincolnwood, Illinois). My first and only experience with a Footprint guide was some years ago, when the series was published solely in hardcover. Then the Morocco handbook was by far the best book of its kind I'd ever seen, and launching it into a paperback edition was wise as it weighs less, is less expensive, and will hopefully find a wider audience. This and the Cadogan Morocco guide are my two favorite guidebooks. Justin McGuinness, like Cadogan author Barnaby Rogerson, is a true authority: he is widely traveled in North Africa (he's also the author of the *Footprint Tunisia Handbook*) and studied Arabic at Cambridge. He has taught at the University of Tunis, where he lives, and his interest in Morocco was inspired by a research project on architecture of the medinas. I love this guide for the quality and depth of the writing, especially the essays, which are marked with an icon of a pointing finger.

Insight Guide: Morocco (Apa Publications, Singapore; distributed in the United States by Langenscheidt). I have been an enormous fan of the Insight Guides for years. When they first appeared, about twenty years ago, they were the only books to provide outstanding color photographs matched with perceptive text. The guiding philosophy of the series has been to provide genuine insight into the history, culture, institutions, and people of a particular place. The editors search for writers with a firm knowledge of each city or region who are also experts in their fields. I do not think the recent editions are quite as good as they used to be, but, as I mentioned above, some guidebooks in a series are better than others, and I think this Morocco edition is very much worth perusing. I like the introductory section best of all (it's always been the best section, in my opinion, in *all* the books), a series of magazine-style essays on architecture, food, markets, the people, history, the arts, and politics. Some of the essays in this book are "Morocco Bound," "The Essence of Architecture," "A Feast of Flavors," "Islam and the Dynasties," and "A Woman's Place." Typically for Insight, the selection of hotels and restaurants is not very helpful unless you have deep pockets, though there is some information on camping, Club Med properties, and youth hostels. I especially like the assorted tips sprinkled throughout the book. This edition is also one of the few guides to alert readers that they must cross the Mellah River before reaching the kasbah of Ait-Benhaddou, near Ouarzazate. This may not seem particularly important, since at most times of the year the river is low and it's a simple matter to negotiate the well-placed stepping stones; but still, fording a river requires some thought of footwear, and what one thinks appropriate for a nice hike through a kasbah may not at all be the right thing for crossing a river and possibly getting your feet wet. Insight is recommended for advance reading, not a bring-along.

~*Knopf Guides: Morocco* (Alfred A. Knopf, originally published in France by Nouveaux-Loisirs, a subsidiary of Gallimard, Paris). I'm fond of the Knopf Guides in general, and the Morocco edition is no exception. Just as I'm crazy for the time-lines and bird's-eye maps in Eyewitness Guides, I'm a bit nuts for the visually entic-ing layout and graphics in the Knopf Guides. I'm most fond of the Morocco edition's initial sections on nature; history and language; art and tradition; archi-tecture; and Morocco as seen by painters and writers. The architecture section is especially good for seeing cross-sections of *medersat* and medinas, and there are lots of visual details of kasbahs, nomads' tents, coastal fortifications, ramparts, gateways, minarets, and mosques. This architecture section and the history outline proved to be, for me, one the best preparations for Morocco, because I was trying to establish clear differences between the dynasties—the way I do before any trip—and I was having difficulty. As wonderful as Richard Parker's work on Moroccan architecture is, I was looking for a sort of pictorial timeline, on one or two pages, of architectural styles and developments matched up with the proper rulers and dates. But unlike the Paris Knopf Guide, for example, the Morocco guide does not have page after page of architectural styles, such as Romanesque, Gothic, Renaissance, and Art Nouveau. It's true that a few significant architectural ele-ments were introduced during different dynasties in Morocco, but they were not always so obvious or numerous, and because most architecture was of a religious nature, there could never have been a tradition like that which existed in France. So with the help of the Knopf Guide's illustrations and timelines, I memorized the major dynasties (Idrissid, Almoravid, Almohad, Merinid, Saadian, Alaouite) and was able to grasp a better overall picture of the nation's history. The gray-colored practical-information pages at the back of this book are helpful in ways other guides aren't, and I especially like "Profile of a Country," "A Weekend in Marrakesh," "Morocco in a Week," and "Alternative Morocco." As visually appealing and chunky as Knopf Guides are, they are actually surprisingly short on in-depth information. I wouldn't use this Morocco edition exclusively, but it's a great companion to a more substantial guidebook.

~*Let's Go: Spain, Portugal & Morocco* (edited by Bruce F. McKinnon, St. Martin's Press). "The World's Bestselling Budget Travel Series" is the Let's Go slo-gan, which is hardly debatable. This is the only multiple-country book mentioned here because Let's Go is still the bible, and there is still not yet a separate edition on Morocco. If you haven't looked at a copy since your salad days, you might be surprised: now each edition contains color maps, advertisements, and an appendix that features a wealth of great practical information. A team of Harvard student interns still offers the same thorough coverage of places to eat and sleep, and things to see and do, and true to Let's Go tradition, rock-bottom budget travelers can find suggestions for places to sleep under $10 a night (sometimes it's the roof), and trav-elers with more means can find clean, cozy, and sometimes downright fancy accom-modations. I think the presentation of facts and history is quite substantive in Let's Go—better, in fact, than in many more so-called sophisticated guides—and I would eagerly press a copy into the hands of anyone under a certain age (thirty-five?) bound for Morocco. Definitely a bring-along if you're traveling with a backpack, sleeping bag, and a desire to meet other travelers seeing the country in the same way.

Lonely Planet: Morocco (Frances Linzee Gordon, Dorinda Talbot, and Damien Simonis). Lonely Planet Guides have been among my most favorite for many years. Tony and Maureen Wheeler founded the series in Australia in 1973. Originally the series focused solely on Asia, but about a dozen years ago they realized that the Lonely Planet approach to travel was not exclusive to any particular geographic area of the world. The series is aimed at independent travelers, and each book is organized by chapters such as "Facts for the Visitor" (covering everything from health and gay and lesbian travelers, to pickpockets and legal matters), "Getting Around," "Things to See & Do," "Places to Stay," "Places to Eat," and so on. I am fondest of the opening chapters covering history, politics, ecology, religion, economy, and practical facts: the information on sites to see, however, is not nearly detailed enough. I like that hotels and restaurants are presented from least expensive to most expensive, and I like the candid opinions of the contributing authors. A percentage of each book's income is donated to various causes such as Greenpeace's efforts to stop French nuclear testing in the Pacific, Amnesty International, and agricultural projects in Central America. Travelers can also check the website: www.lonelyplanet.com. Definitely a bring-along.

Maverick Guide to Morocco (by Susan Searight, Pelican, Gretna, Louisiana). Before going to Morocco, I had never used a Maverick Guide. The series is mostly known for its books on Hawaii, the South Pacific, and Southeast Asia, and Morocco is the series' first Mediterranean destination. At the front of each book are several definitions of *maverick:* "a person not labeled as belonging to any one faction, group, etc. who acts independently"; "one who moves in a different direction than the rest of the herd—often a nonconformist"; and "a person using individual judgment, even when it runs against majority opinion." Maverick Guides definitely stand apart, though they are not of the highest quality in terms of printing. (In fact, the photos are so poor that I think they should be eliminated since they add nothing to the otherwise well-written text.) Searight has lived in Morocco for more than twenty-five years, in Casablanca, and she works as a researcher in prehistory, so she has spent time in a number of places around the country "where there are no hotels or restaurants." I like that she is honest enough to admit, therefore, that "I have not stayed in *all* the hotels (there are 532 classified and a host of unclassified) nor have I eaten in *all* the restaurants (there are too many to count) . . . but I have tried out many and I confess I have relied on trustworthy friends to give me information on others." This book has all the usual features of any other good guide—maps, accommodation listings, practical tips, bibliography, and so on—but it is simply the author's warmth and style of writing that appeal to me. The chapters "Who Are the Moroccans?" and "The Land and Life of Morocco" are particularly good. It was from Searight that I learned of the excellent and indispensable book *A Practical Guide to Islamic Monuments in Morocco* by Richard Parker (see the *Des Belles Choses bibliothèque* for details). And in her chapter on Fez, Searight provides a very good itinerary based on one Parker provides in his book. In fact, I thought her itinerary was so good—and better than those in other books—that I photocopied the pages and gave them to our guide, Rashid, who followed it to the letter. Ultimately, I don't recommend this book as a bring-along, but I like it very much, and there are portions of it that are essential.

~*The Green Guide: Morocco,* Michelin. A Michelin guide might be more trustworthy than your best friend. Its famous star-rating system and "worth a detour" slogan may have become a bit too formulaic, but it's a formula that works. The series was created in 1900 by André Michelin, who compiled a little red book of hotels and restaurants that today is the Michelin Red Guide, famous for the stars it awards to restaurants. The green tourist guides first made their appearance in 1926. Each guide is jam-packed with information and is easy to pack. It will come as no surprise to readers that I prefer even more detail than Michelin offers, but I find it an excellent series, and each guide I've used has proven to be exceptionally helpful. Each Michelin guide is complemented by a Michelin map, of course, and the Morocco edition is meant to be used in conjunction with maps. I am fond of the touring programs in each book, as well as the introductory information, which includes topics such as traditional rural architecture. A new route-planner service, which I happen to think takes much of the joy out of trip planning, is available by visiting www.michelin-travel.com. Viewers type in start and finish points and are provided with a suggested route, travel time, distances, road numbers, and any tolls. A bring-along, especially if you'll be renting a car.

~*The Rough Guide: Morocco* (Mark Ellingham, Shaun McVeigh, Don Grisbrook; distributed in the United States by Penguin Books). When the Rough Guides first appeared, in the early 1980s, they had limited distribution in the United States. Then the guides were sort-of-but-not-quite the British equivalent of Let's Go. I sought them out because I found the British viewpoint refreshing and felt the writers imparted more knowledge about a place than was currently available in U.S. guidebooks. Mark Ellingham was inspired to create the Rough Guides series because at the time current guidebooks were all lacking in some way: they were, for instance, either strong on ruins and museums but short on bars, clubs, and inexpensive eating places, or so conscious of the need to save money that they lost sight of things of cultural and historical significance. None of the books mentioned anything about contemporary life, politics, culture, or the people and how they lived. Now, since the series opened a New York office in the late 1990s, the series has evolved into one that is broader-based but still appealing to independent-minded travelers who appreciate the Rough Guides' honest assessments, and historical and political backgrounds. (These last are found in the "Contexts" section of each guide, and my only complaint is that I think this section should appear at the beginning of each book instead of at the end.) In the "Basics" section readers will find specifics on working and studying, gay and lesbian life, accommodations, food and drink, health and insurance, culture and festivals, and the like. After "Contexts," this "Basics" section is my favorite feature of the Morocco guide; it contains an essay entitled "From a Woman's Perspective," which is *great,* and the Rough Guide is the only guide not only to feature such an entry but even to then share another woman's (slightly different) perspective in a footnote. I also simply enjoy the descriptive writing in the "The Guide" portion of the book, and I really like the boxed essays on a variety of topics, such as *kif,* the Sultan Moulay Ismail, kasbah maintenance and destruction, and so on. The music listings and bibliography—including excerpts from works by Mohammed Mrabet, Abdeslam Boulaich, Mohamed Choukri, Budgett Meakin, Walter Harris, Elias Canetti, and Paul Bowles—are fantastic and are excellent resources on their own. On-line updates to the Rough Guides can be found at www.roughguides.com for those who feel this is essential. All in all, each edition in the Rough Guides series is dependable and informative. Definitely a bring-along.

Guides

After bargaining, I think arranging for a guide is the thing that perplexes visitors to Morocco the most. There are guides who specialize in individual cities and others who are national guides, who know the entire country intimately. Most guides today are official, meaning that they have passed an exam and are approved by the tourist office. Guides are mostly male, although sometimes they are female. And most guides are good, taking you where you want to go and protecting you from potential hassle. You can find a guide through the assistance of the local Moroccan tourist office or your hotel. (You may even want to ask for their assistance in advance of your visit, depending upon what you want to see and do or how specialized your interests are; the U.S. Moroccan tourist offices can provide you with the phone and fax numbers of tourist offices throughout Morocco.) A guide can literally make or break your trip, so make an effort to select one you think will be accommodating to your desires. Certainly if you are traveling with an organized tour, ask about the quality of the tour operator's guides. I have heard of a few unpleasant experiences where guides simply did not take visitors where they requested, and it seems to me that the guides are really what you're paying for and what ultimately separate one tour company from another; after all, you could easily make hotel, restaurant, and travel arrangements yourself, but it is more difficult to find a good guide.

You'll find that all the guidebooks say not to buy anything in the souks in the presence of your guide or you will overpay, since it is assumed the guide will receive a percentage of the price. But none of the guidebooks suggests what you should do with your guide if you run across a vendor you want to purchase something from. I think the unwritten assumption is that you should return the following day without a guide; but what if one is leaving the next day? Or what if you can't find the vendor the next day? In a particular case with Rashid, my guide in Fez, the opposite occurred: he helped me negotiate a lower price with a vendor, and I'm sure I would not have been offered that lower price even with persistent haggling. My advice here is that which I offered under "Bargaining": if you feel you're paying a fair price for the object in question, buy it and feel good about it and forget about whether or not the guide is receiving a cut. Alternatively, if you are really hung up on the middleman cut, you could ask the concierge at your hotel to buy the goods for you. He or she will also factor in a cut, but there is a good chance it will be less than that paid to a guide in the presence of a foreigner. A few pointers: remember to agree on a price for the guide in advance of starting out. As a general rule, the quoted price for a full day is about $30, and guides are typically employed for a half or full day. I believe in tipping generously as I think the services of a good guide are indispensable. Remember, too, that it is customary to invite your guide to join you if you stop for a meal or a mint tea. He or she may decline, but it is polite to extend the invitation.

H

Halal or Hallal

An Arabic word meaning "lawful" or "permissible." It is most commonly used in reference to an animal or its meat slaughtered or prepared in a manner prescribed by Islamic law. Think of it as equivalent to *kosher*: there are *halal* butchers just as there are kosher butchers, and there is *halal* meat and kosher meat.

Hamsa or Khamsa

This is the Berber word for "the symbol of an open human hand," which visitors will see absolutely everywhere. The most common explanation for the hand is that it represents the hand of Fatima, Mohammad's favorite daughter. But in fact, according to Geraldine Brooks in *Imazighen,* "the motif predates Islam, and is a visual representation of the gesture and chant 'Five in your eye,' swiftly made by anyone who felt they may have been victimized by someone giving them the evil eye." The symbol is believed essentially to offer protection against the evil eye and the *djinn* (geni, evil spirit), and the number five is thought to have magical properties that protect people from the forces of evil. Interestingly, the *hamsa* is also an important and ubiquitous symbol for Moroccan Jews: when the Phoenicians sailed to Africa, in the ninth century before the birth of Christ, they brought with them an amulet in the form of a hand, which was known among Jews as *hamsa* (meaning "five") and among Muslims as the Hand of Fatima.

Harem

Another Arabic word familiar to nearly everybody, commonly used to denote the part of a Muslim palace or house reserved for women or all female household members. *Harem* is a variation of the word *haram* (meaning "forbidden" or "proscribed") and is quite the opposite of *halal,* above. As Fatima Mernissi explains in her wonderful book *Dreams of Trespass,* the truer definition of the word is much broader: "Harem was the place where a man sheltered his family, his wife or wives, and children and relatives. It could be a house or a tent, and it referred both to the space and to the people who lived within it. One said 'Sidi So-and-So's harem,' referring both to his family members and to his physical home. One thing that helped me see this more clearly was when Yasmina explained that Mecca, the holy city, was also called Haram. Mecca was a space where behavior was strictly codified. The moment you stepped inside, you were bound by many laws and regulations. People who entered Mecca had to be pure: they had to perform purification rituals, and refrain from lying, cheating, and doing harmful deeds. The city belonged to Allah and you had to obey his *shari'a,* or sacred law, if you entered his territory. The same thing applied to a harem when it was a house belonging to a man. No other men could enter it without the owner's permission, and when they did they had to obey his rules. A harem was about private space and the rules regulating it."

It is Ottoman royal harems, however, that fascinated (and seemingly obsessed) the Western imagination. All those Orientalist painters were first and foremost inspired by Turkish harems, especially the most famous one of all in the Topkapi Palace in Istanbul. Mernissi opines that one reason for this popularity may be the Ottomans' spectacular conquest (under Mehmet the Conquerer) of Constantinople in 1453 and their subsequent occupation of some European cities. Once the Byzantine Empire had collapsed, present-day Turkey, with Istanbul as its new capital, was the West's most threatening neighbor. By comparison, ordinary domestic harems were rather dull. A good book to consult for those interested in reading more is *Harem: The World Behind the Veil* (Alev Lytle Croutier, Abbeville Press, 1989). The author was born in Istanbul and came to the United States when she was eighteen. Her grandmother and grandmother's sister were brought up in a harem; they were also among the last women who lived in one, as in 1909 harems were declared illegal. The only reference in this book to Morocco is for an 1879 painting entitled *A Morocco Terrace, Evening* by Jean-Joseph Benjamin-Constant. Nonetheless, it's a great read, profusely illustrated with both color and black-and-white illustrations and photos.

Hassan II

There are far too many thoroughfares in Morocco named after King Hassan II for a visitor to not have at least some idea who he was and why he was significant. First of all, it was his great-great-great-great-great-grandfather who initiated the still-valid U.S.–Moroccan Treaty of Friendship in 1778, making Morocco the first country in the world to recognize the existence of the United States. (The treaty is, by the way, the longest uninterrupted accord in American history.) Mohammed V— who also has a preponderance of streets named after him—was Hassan's father. Hassan's family legacy reaches back seventeen generations in Morocco, and Hassan himself is a direct descendant of Muhammad. Among Hassan's many milestones are his organization of the Marche Verte (see the Polisario entry for more details) and his role in arranging secret meetings between the Egyptians and the Israelis, which resulted in Anwar Sadat visiting Jerusalem in 1977. He then led the campaign to allow Egypt back into the Organization of the Islamic Conference, which had expelled Egypt after it made peace with Israel. It has been speculated that Hassan was able to look to the West so often—indeed, embrace so many Western ideals—and take so many risks because his family's credentials are impeccable and the Maghreb is many miles away from problematic places in the Arab world like the Middle East, Baghdad, and fundamentalist corners of Egypt. Politically savvy Hassan was also known as the "Great Unifier," but for all his modernity, Hassan also ruled in much the same way as kings and sultans before him. In describing some of the savageries of Sultan Moulay Ismael and Moulay Hafid, Gavin Maxwell, in his book *Lords of the Atlas,* reminds readers that these were not in any way a departure from tradition that was many centuries old. "They were unjust, they were terrible; but, a learned Moroccan pointed out to me, they could not be compared in scope or numbers to the atrocities of the Holy Wars of France during the crusading days, or of the Spanish Inquisition. I protested that he was going back centuries to find parallels, but he replied, 'Consider, my friend; you are speaking of Moulay Hafid. His reign ended two years before the First World War, when an unthinkable number of Europeans died in circumstances of horror. Then, only twenty-one years later, came the Second World War, the famous concentration camps, and the new refinements of torture invented by Germans, Russians—and, for all I know, Englishmen and Frenchmen. And then the Algerian War, in which the French tried hard to surpass the most terrible acts that any nation, Eastern or Western, had ever committed. The Algerians tried to rival them, but without success. No, my friend, be reasonable; these things were not only the tradition of North Africa, they are the tradition of all mankind." If it's difficult to assess Hassan II in this context, remember that he imprisoned the wife and six children of General Mohammed Oufkir—the powerful Moroccan minister of defense who led a failed coup against Hassan in 1972—for twenty years. Oufkir's oldest daughter, Malika, wrote a book about the horrific ordeal (published as *La Prisonnière* in France and as *Stolen Lives: Twenty Years in a Desert Jail* in the United States by Talk Miramax Books, 2001). According to Amnesty International, political prisoners in Morocco number in the hundreds, and the Moroccan government admitted that between the years 1960 and 1980, fifty-six political prisoners died in Moroccan jails.

Health

Staying healthy while in Morocco can be a challenge, but it does not have to be an especially big one. The first issue to address is vaccinations. It's important to know the difference between *required* and *recommended* vaccines. According to a very good article in *Consumer Reports Travel Letter* ("Healthy Travels: Tips for Wellness Abroad," February 2001; to request this back issue, send $5 to CRTL, 101 Truman Avenue, Yonkers, New York 10703-1057), "vaccines are *required* to protect a country from a disease travelers may import into it; they are *recommended* to protect a traveler from getting an illness." All the guidebooks provide information about vaccinations, some more thoroughly than others, but you should not rely solely on this information—check with your primary doctor. (Alternatively, the *Consumer Reports* article features a two-page chart provided by the Centers for Disease Control and Prevention, which is a common source that doctors around the nation use.) Guidebook authors, friends, family, and colleagues all seem to approach vaccines in different ways: some have not a single shot, others just a few, still others leave no stone unturned and have the full array. Similarly, they all have had different experiences: some got so ill they had to seek medical help while in Morocco, some had severe diarrhea for days, and others had not a moment of poor health. Which is why I recommend you go to your doctor for the final word. He or she may recommend more vaccinations than you feel comfortable with, but it's a doctor's job to give you the complete picture, not just half of it. I chose a plan of attack that erred on the side of caution, but I did not agree to have every vaccination—or fill every prescription—my doctor recommended. As *Consumer Reports* noted, "In much of the world, the two great scourges are poor sanitation and the mosquito." In Morocco one need be concerned with mosquitoes only in a very few remote and rural areas, areas that are not generally frequented by visitors. (Your doctor can show you a map.) But poor sanitation and water quality are of major daily concern and, combined, are the second issue to address when visiting Morocco.

I believe that water, more than the handling of food, is the big danger in Morocco. The fresh vegetables and fruit I saw in the souks and *marchés,* and at the stalls in the Place Djemaa el Fna in Marrakesh, were all of excellent quality and appeared to be cooked with care and be quickly eaten, not left to sit for very long.

The sausages and cuts of meat, too, appeared to be freshly prepared, as well as the fried fish and soups. But tap water can all too easily find its way into your bowl or on your silverware, onto your lettuce in that delicious-looking salad or in that glass of *thé à la menthe*. (Did the water reach a full boil?) The primary precaution of every visitor should be the water, and for those who have never visited a country with poor water before, here are some tips: ~Do not brush your teeth with tap water, even if you are at a luxury hotel. ~Do not order a drink with ice in it, even if you are at a luxury hotel. ~If you are at a café or restaurant and silverware is brought to you with water drops on it, wipe the water off. (In addition to the obvious reason, this is another reason you will want to carry toilet paper with you each day.) Silverware that has been rinsed and then dried will not make you sick, but eating from just-washed cutlery definitely carries risk. The same goes for plates or glasses; either wipe them off or ask for dry ones. ~If you are contemplating eating at a food stall, like those at the Djemaa el Fna, for example, review the scene carefully before settling on one. The escargots smell and look delicious, but the bowls they're ladled into are wet, making the venture off-limits. The fresh-squeezed orange juice? *Harira?* Both no, because the glasses and bowls are being rinsed in a big tub with tap water by a young boy right before our eyes. Good choices are fried fish served on paper plates, and grilled meat served inside bread—no utensils are provided for either one. Grilled eggplant is delicious and safe, as are the peppers and olives; but no rinsed greens or tomatoes. The mountains of couscous that look so good *are* good, if you eat them in a bowl or a plate that you are sure isn't wet. Not surprisingly, the stalls that are the most crowded are usually the ones held in high regard with the locals, and they are often serving food that you eat with your hands or with bread.

~Do not even think of setting foot in Morocco without a prescription for Lomotil, or the over-the-counter Imodium AD. You may never use it, but you'll be mighty glad you have it if you do come down with traveler's diarrhea. And a word of advice if you do get it: begin taking the pills right away—and continue taking them. I once made the mistake of taking one pill, and I felt so much better (they really do work quickly) that I thought I could stop. After all, it really isn't healthy to remain on drugs of this sort, as they kill not only the nasty stuff inside but the good stuff, too. (Diarrhea remedies don't "cure" you, they just stop you from having to look for a toilet every fifteen minutes.) So I was under the mistaken impression that I must be better and promptly stopped taking the pills. I didn't take any the next day, with only a minor incident, but by the third day I had a major rumbly in my tumbly (to borrow a phrase from Winnie the Pooh), so I started taking them again. But it was too late: by the time I arrived home two days later, I had blood in my stool, and my doctor confirmed I had contracted shigella. (You'll have to look it up; I didn't know what it was, and I'm not going to go into detail here.) ~Plain yogurt (and yogurt pills) are good aids in helping to prevent traveler's diarrhea, and truly delicious yogurt is widely available in Morocco. (For yogurt pills, consult your doctor about a prescription or possible over-the-counter brand.)

Not related to traveling in Morocco but related to flying to and from is deep vein thrombosis (DVT), sometimes called coach-class thrombosis or economy-class syndrome. Visitors flying from the East Coast of the United States or Canada to Morocco are probably not at great risk for DVT, as the flight is only six and a half hours in length; but travelers flying from other parts of North America are prime candidates for this condition, in which prolonged periods of sitting in one position cause blood clots in the leg veins that can travel to the lungs and get stuck there, causing death. Though long plane flights are not the only cause of DVT—sitting for long periods at an office desk, on a train or bus or in a car are equally bad— it's important to remember to get up and walk up and down the plane's aisles while en route. My chiropractor tells me I should never sit for more than twenty minutes at a stretch because I have lower-back problems. Now I have another reason for getting up and moving about. Concerned travelers should contact the Aerospace Medical Association, 320 South Henry Street, Alexandria, Virginia 22314; 703-739-2240; www.asma.org. ~I haven't investigated these yet, but Hyland's makes homeopathic tablets for leg cramps. An active ingredient is quinine, and they are 100 percent natural and do not interact with other medications. Perhaps they would be helpful for long flights. Call 800-624-9659 for details.

A good, small-enough-to-pack general reference book is *The Rough Guide to Travel Health* (Dr. Nick Jones, Rough Guides, distributed by the Penguin Group, 2001). In addition to an A–Z listing of diseases and health risks, it provides good coverage on being prepared (including homeopathic suggestions) as well as summaries of potential health concerns region by region around the world. Travelers with special needs—asthma, diabetes, epilepsy, HIV, disability, pregnancy, and so on—are also addressed, and a very thorough directory with a wide range of resources is found at the back of the book. Another good book is *Travelers' Health: How to Stay Healthy All Over the World* (Richard Dawood, M.D., former medical editor for *Condé Nast Traveler,* foreword by Paul Theroux, Random House, 1994). This thick, 600-plus-page book isn't for bringing along—it's for reading before you go. In addition to Dr. Dawood, sixty-seven other medical experts contributed to this volume, which covers everything from insect bites, water filters, and sun effects on the skin to gynecological problems, altitude sickness, children abroad, immunizations, and the diabetic traveler. It also features essays on such topics as "The Economy-Class Syndrome" and "Being an Expatriate." Travelers with diabetes might want to refer to *The Diabetes Travel Guide* (American Diabetes Association, 2000), which is filled with good tips and info.

~One website to consult is www.cdc.gov/travel, which is the on-line site for the federal Centers for Disease Control in Atlanta. The content on the website is from the CDC's *Yellow Book: Health Information for International Travel.* Travel

Medicine Inc.'s site is www.travelmed.com, which complements *The International Travel Health Guide* by Dr. Stuart Rose (Chronimed Publishing). The very best site, in my opinion, is www.tripprep.com. When I clicked on Morocco, up came more thorough information than in my favorite guidebooks, as well as information about crime, entry and exit requirements, traffic safety and road conditions, and medical insurance. Links to food and beverage precautions and traveler's diarrhea were particularly helpful. ~Another site, www.medicinePlanet.com, is good for names of local health care providers and general recommendations. ~To find English-speaking doctors, you can contact the International Association for Medical Assistance to Travelers (417 Center Street, Lewiston, New York 14092; 716-754-4883), which provides a directory of English-speaking doctors around the world. IAMAT is a nonprofit organization, and while membership is free, donations are greatly appreciated. In addition to the directory, IAMAT mails members other material on malaria, immunizations, and so on, as well as a membership card, which entitles you to member rates should you have to pay for medical help. Travelers can also always contact the closest American embassy or local U.S. military installation for a list of local physicians and their areas of expertise. Additionally, some credit cards offer assistance: American Express's Global Assist program is available to all cardholders at no extra fee. It's a full-service program offering everything from doctor and hospital referrals to emergency cash wires, translation assistance, lost item search, legal assistance, and daily monitoring of your health condition. When abroad, travelers can call cardmember services at 800-528-4800; international collect at 1-336-393-1111; or the local American Express office.

Henna

It won't take long for visitors to Morocco to notice henna designs, either faded or newly painted, on the hands, feet, or ankles of Moroccan women. Henna paste is applied for various celebrations and observances in a woman's life, including marriage, pregnancy, and death, while Berbers believe that the henna plant is a mother lode of *baraka* (see entry for Islam). The application and display of henna patterns is essentially women's work. Female visitors who wish to have some designs applied need look only as far as the Place Djemaa el Fna in Marrakesh, for example, where local women advertise their skills. (Negotiate the fee before they begin painting.) In addition, the concierge at your hotel can assist you in finding a henna artist, as well as merchants in the souks who sell henna stencils. Two good books (both paperback) to consult on the subject are *Traditional Mehndi Designs: A Treasury of Henna Body Art* (Dorine van den Beukel, Shambhala Publications, Boston, 2000), which contains a few color photographs and more than five hundred traditional Indian motifs; and *Mehndi: The Art of Henna Body Painting* (Carine

Fabius, Three Rivers Press, 1998), a smaller book with black-and-white photographs throughout and a list of Mehndi artists, salons, and suppliers, by state, at the back.

Hiking

There are some wonderful opportunities for hiking in Morocco, although the country lacks the extensive trail and footpath networks that traditionally exist in Europe. I believe that whether you hike or walk, spending some time getting around via your own two feet makes you feel a part of Morocco in a special way. The High Atlas range is one of the least spoiled in the world, and what hikers give up in terms of an extensive trail network they gain in more pristine conditions and significantly less human development. Walking or hiking in the Middle Atlas, Anti-Atlas, or in the Rif is also rewarding, but walkers will encounter more small villages and roads and, in other words, less of a wilderness experience. In addition to long-distance Atlas routes—including a Grand Traverse of the entire range—there are shorter routes to walk, and it's very possible to arrange day trips that allow for you to be back at your hotel in time for dinner. ~Good resources—and there aren't many— you should consult include *Atlas Mountains Morocco* (Robin Collomb, West Col Productions, U.K., 1987), a mountaineering and climbing guide that includes trail maps, but they're not topographical. Author Collomb provides information on obtaining the topo maps and gives route descriptions and photos with route overlays throughout the book. "The Great Trek Through the Moroccan Atlas" and "Morocco: Mountains and Valleys" are both brochures published by the Tourist Office. The first is the one you *really* need, as it includes a list of agencies and mountain escorts (you'll be glad to have it, as available maps are poor, except for the official topo maps from a government office in Rabat, and it seems permission is rarely given for distribution of the maps), mountain refuges, other accommodations, services, first aid, and the like.

~What I most recommend is that you contact Hamish Brown in the U.K. He contributed the High Atlas chapter to the Rough Guide and is absolutely *the* person you want to guide you through the Atlas. I very much enjoy hiking and rambling on my own, and ordinarily it would never occur to me to hire someone to lead me on a hiking journey; but good, detailed maps of the mountains of Morocco are not easy to come by, and there aren't a great number of good books, either. Brown heads up the Atlas Mountain Information Services agency, and leads customized walking tours, treks, climbing trips, and occasional trips focusing on birds and wildflowers. It is fair to state that Brown knows the Atlas ranges like the back of his hand, and you could not find a better guide at any price. Contact him at AMIS, 26 Kirkcaldy Road, Burntisland, Fife, KY3 9HQ, Scotland, 011.1592.873546. At the very least, interested walkers should contact Brown for survey maps and briefing sheets. ~A company called Kasbah du Toubkal, winner of a Green Globe Award for sustainable tourism, offers an exclusive, one-day excursion to Toubkal National Park in the High Atlas, about 60 kilometers from Marrakesh. I haven't done it myself, but I've heard it's an unforgettable experience, and overnight accommodation can also be arranged in the kasbah, which formerly belonged to the Glaoui brothers (visitors may stay longer than one night if they wish). Contact Kasbah du Toubkal in the U.K. at Discover Ltd, Timbers, Oxted Road, Godstone, Surrey, England, RH9 8AD; 011.44.1883.744392; fax: .744913; www.kasbahdutoubkal.com.

Hours

Opening and closing hours in Morocco follow the same general pattern as in other Mediterranean countries. As I mentioned in my introduction, visitors should as quickly as possible embrace a schedule that allows for rather early risings, pauses for an afternoon siesta, and dinner no earlier than 8:00 to allow for an evening *paseo*. The majority of shops and businesses are open by about 8:30 in the morning until about 11:30 to 1:00. They reopen again at about 3:00 or 4:00 and close at about 7:00 or 8:00. Banks, however, tend to honor slightly different hours and stick to them more stringently than other businesses in the country. While banks may keep similar morning hours as other businesses (8:30 to 11:30), they are only open again in the afternoon for a short time, typically from about 3:00 to 4:00. During the summer and the month of Ramadan, however, banks tend to stay open uninterrupted from about 8:30 to 2:00. It is always best to do your bank chores first thing in the morning, when there is the likeliest possibility the bank will be open with plenty of time to make transactions or solve any financial problems. Hours at post offices are also slightly different than regular shops. Usually they are open continuously from about 8:00 or 8:30 to about 3:00, but in the summer months they may keep a siesta schedule of about 8:00 to noon and then again from about 3:00 to 6:00 or 6:30.

Do not forget that Friday is the day of communal prayer in mosques all over the country. This means that if you are thinking of visiting the Hassan II mosque in Casablanca, one of the few mosques in Morocco that non-Muslims can visit, you must plan to see it on any day of the week except Friday, when it is closed to visitors entirely. It also means that a *medersa* you hoped to see might not be open the full day.

Before I had spent much time in the Mediterranean, I was frustrated by how (seemingly) little I was able to accomplish in the course of a day, since I did not live in a culture where the lunch break was much longer than an hour. It's easy to lose sight of the fact that there really is plenty of time to see and do what you want by adapting to the siesta schedule. Much can still be accomplished in the hours between 4:00 and 7:00 P.M.

Imazighen
This is the Berber word for "free men." Its singular form is *amazigh*.

Independence
Moroccan Independence Day is March 2, 1956, a key date to know in Moroccan history.

Inshallah
Probably the Arabic word most frequently uttered in all Muslim countries, *inshallah* translates as "if God wills." Visitors will hear it constantly, especially since it can also be used to indicate an array of nuances between the words *yes* and *no*, such as *perhaps, maybe, of course, absolutely,* and *why not?* Interestingly, I read in the *Insight Guide: Morocco* that in the early 1970s, the state television network began forecasting the weather, but the Ulema (council of professors of Islamic law) strongly reprimanded the network because its broadcasters did not say *inshallah* after stating it was going to rain. Now, *all* weather predictions end with *inshallah*.

The best passages I have read about this essential Islamic word are from Peter Mayne's wonderful book *A Year in Marrakesh.* Early on during his stay, Mayne relates that "the air is vibrant with *Insha'Allah.* Wherever I go it is on men's lips, this phrase which admits the omnipotence of God. *Insha'Allah*—if God wills—I will do so-and-so; *Insha'Allah,* it will rain; *Insha'Allah,* Mohamed will return my packet of 'Casa Sport' cigarettes. Resignation to the will of God and to what He may decide shall become of you is the very essence of Islam. It is no good making plans as if you were a free agent in the matter. No Muslim would consider trying. Any references to the future require that *Insha'Allah* should be added, and if the speaker forgets (which is unthinkable) somebody else must say it for him. This does not mean that a simple repetition of the formula will secure whatever it is that you are hoping for, but not to say it involves serious risk of failure." Later, he admits to an even greater understanding of the concept. He says that it is one step to utter the phrase, but that it is the next step that troubles the Western mind (although it no longer troubles his at this point). This next step, as he explains, depends entirely upon whether you need to do the thing referred to, whether it will have a distinct advantage for you: "If the thing has no importance—which is taken to mean that it has no real bearing upon your personal prosperity or pleasure—you may quite easily find that something outside your control prevents your doing whatever it was. Perhaps on the way to this engagement, for example, you meet a friend and the friend is thirsty and needs mint-tea. He obliges you to sit with him in a teashop. Or something else unforeseeable happens. Anyway, there it is, the appointment has been missed. . . . Naturally you have to agree at the time to whatever is suggested, *Insha'Allah,* for it would be exceedingly rude to say 'no' to anything. Yet to agree certainly smacks of presumption, of an attempt to interfere with the workings of fate. The past is past: the present is living evidence of God's wishes, but the future is in His hands. How can you foretell what He has in mind for you when you are making your plans? Anyone can see that the very fact of failure to carry out such plans shows that He never intended that you should."

My colleague Toinette, after a few days in Morocco, decided that a better translation of *inshallah* is "fat chance."

Internet Access

I'm including this here only for business travelers. If you're traveling for pleasure and feel you need to surf the Web, perhaps you should save your money and stay home. I take the view that vacations are for removing yourself from your daily grind; if you're dying to log on to the Internet, you're not on vacation, and you need to read *Turn It Off* (Gil Gordon, Three Rivers Press, 2001). Visiting another country is about doing *different* things and putting yourself in unfamiliar situations. Overseas telephone services are generally not as reliable as those in the United States, ensuring that connecting to the Internet is also not as easy or inexpensive. Business travelers who need to check in with the office via e-mail should consider what it will cost for a laptop, power adapter, disk, and/or CD-ROM drives, plus any other related accessories, as well as how heavy it will be to carry. You may conclude that cybercafés (or Internet cafés) are more economical (and easier on your back). Cybercafé fees for access to the Internet vary, but when you compare a hotel's charges for the same access (often at slower speeds), cybercafés represent good value. I found cybercafés in Afourar, Rabat, Al Hoceima, Essaouira, Marrakesh, Fez, Tangier, Tetuan, and Zagora (some cities had more than one café) by searching www.cybercaptive.com, www.netcafeguide.com, and www.net-cafes.com. Two other sources are *The Internet Café Guide* (by Ernst Larsen) and *Cybercafés: A Worldwide Guide for Travelers* (cyberkath@traveltales.com, Ten Speed Press, 1989), both of which feature a comprehensive list of the world's Internet cafés. I personally like the idea of keeping my business tasks separate from my hotel room, but those who can't stand the thought of leaving the hotel premises may be happy to know that hotels are definitely improving their Internet services. Most of the world's major hotel chains are leading the way on this front, and some also have at least one technologically savvy employee on hand to assist guests with problems. Additionally, I've noticed recently that many public telephone booths, including those at airports and in hotel lobbies, are now equipped for Internet access.

Islam

Without a basic understanding of Islam, visitors will never comprehend Morocco. Though I am admittedly not an Islamic scholar, and a scholarly study of Islam is outside the scope of this book, I do have friends who are scholars and/or Muslims, and I am grateful to them for their advice on this entry. First, the word *Islam* means "surrender" to the will of God. Second, it is considered essential to know the five pillars of Islam: *shahada* (professing that "There is no god but Allah and Muhammad is his prophet"); *sala* (praying five times daily); *zakah* (giving alms to the needy; welfare contribution); *sawm* (observing Ramadan); and *hadj* (making a pilgrimage to Mecca at least once in one's lifetime). Third, it is helpful to know that Morocco is a Sunni Muslim nation and what that means. The two great religious divisions of Islam are Sunnism and Shiism. *Sunniis* (or *Sunnites*) regard the first four caliphs as legitimate successors of Muhammad. (The first four caliphs were Abu Bakr, Umar ibn al-Khattab, Uthman ibn Affan, and Ali ibn Abi Talib; they were friends and immediate successors of Muhammad.) *Shiis* (or *Shiites*) regard Ali—the same Ali ibn Abi Talib, son-in-law of Muhammad—as the legitimate successor of Muhammad, and they disregard the first three caliphs who succeeded him. Shiis take their name from Shiah i-Ali, the Partisans of Ali. (Ali was murdered in 661 by the Kharajites, who felt that the ruler of the Islamic community must be the most committed Muslim, not the most powerful.) Sunnis take their name from the word *sunnah*, meaning "custom" or, in the words of author Karen Armstrong, "the habits and religious practice of the Prophet Muhammed, which were recorded for posterity by his companions and family and are regarded as the ideal Islamic norm." Sunnis stress the importance of *sunnah* as a basis for law. The majority of Muslims in the world today are Sunni, and according to Armstrong, the difference between Shiites and Sunnis is now purely political.

Morocco is not as strictly observant as, say, Saudi Arabia, and has even incorporated a few concepts that are unique to Moroccan Islam, which probably represent a compromise between pre-existing Berber beliefs and the Islam that the Arabs originally brought to Morocco in 683. The two most notable aspects are *baraka* and *murabitin*. It's easy to understand them because you can't talk about one without talking about the other. *Baraka,* which will be familiar to readers who have visited other Muslim nations, translates as "blessing" or "grace." It is believed to be granted to individuals by Allah, Muhammad being the ultimate grantee. It is also believed that *baraka* begets *baraka,* so being associated with someone who is thought to have an especially large share of *baraka* may mean that some will find its way to you. The most common way, however, to get *baraka* is out of one's control, as it is handed down—"inherited" is perhaps a better way of looking at it— by males, and by males only. In Morocco, men who have been so fortunate are known as *murabitin* (similar to saints in the Judeo-Christian tradition). When *murabitin* pass away, they are believed to retain great spiritual power and so are carefully placed in a special shrine known as *marabout*. Visitors will see a great number of these small white domed temples throughout the country, mostly in rural areas. Men and women both make pilgrimages to *marabouts* for a number of reasons, mostly to seek good fortune. (Think of it as desperately seeking *baraka* in some cases, such as when a woman is trying to have a baby.) The obsession with *baraka* and the belief that *murabitin* have almost supernatural powers would be considered heretical in other Muslim countries, as the Koran forbids a "tangible link or intermediary between God and man."

If you've never read the Koran (more properly Qur'an), or haven't since your comparative religions class in college, I encourage you to seize the day and pick up a copy. Becoming more familiar with this great spiritual (and literary) work is an enriching experience and is perfect companion reading for a trip to Morocco. Muslims believe that the words of the Koran were directly revealed from God to Muhammad, his messenger. Because of this role as messenger, Muhammad enjoys a place of centrality in Islam and is regarded as the "ideal" Muslim. Very strict Muslims hold that the Koran is untranslatable, which is why the art of translation is always an act of interpretation, and why a great number of translations are available. One edition you may want to examine, which was recommended to me by two professors of Eastern religion, is *The Koran Interpreted* (translated by H.A. Arberry, Macmillan, 1955), a standard edition in colleges and universities. Most scholars feel Arberry has struck a nice balance between a literal translation and one that captures the spirit of the text. Note the word *Interpreted* in the title, the author's nod of respect for the Koran and an indication of the personal nature of translation. A former professor of Islamic studies at Harvard, Wilfred Cantwell Smith, said of this Arberry edition that it is "certainly the most beautiful English version, and among those by non-Muslim translators the one that comes closest to conveying the impression made on Muslims by the original." Another popular but controversial edition is *The Meaning of the Glorious Koran: An Explanatory Translation* (translated by Marmaduke Pickthall, first published by Knopf in 1930; reprinted by Everyman's Library in 1992). According to William Montgomery Watt, a former professor of Arabic and Islamic studies at the University of Edinburgh, who wrote the introduction to this edition, Pickthall was an Englishman who became Muslim and worked for the Muslim ruler of Hyderabad, the nizam. He was granted a two-year leave of absence to write this translation and spent time in Egypt with a number of authorities, including Sheykh al-Azhar, traditional head of al-Azhar University, the oldest in the world. It might be said therefore that Pickthall had official approval among the most respected sources; but many scholars today feel that Pickthall strays too far from the literal and that he is ultimately misleading.

Some other excellent and related books that come highly recommended are

Islam (Fazlur Rahman, University of Chicago Press, 1979); *Islam Observed: Religious Development in Morocco and Indonesia* (by Clifford Geertz, University of Chicago Press, 1971); *Muhammad* (by Michael Cook, Past Masters series, Oxford University Press, New York, 1983); *Muslims: Their Religious Beliefs and Practices* (in two volumes, Andrew Rippin, Rutledge, 1994); *Textual Sources for the Study of Islam* (an anthology edited by Andrew Rippin and Jan Knappert, University of Chicago Press, 1986). Three of my favorites are *The World of Islam: Faith, People, Culture* (Bernard Lewis, W.W. Norton, 1992); *Islam: A Short History* (Karen Armstrong, Modern Library Chronicles, 2000); and *A History of God: The 4,000-Year Quest of Judaism, Christianity and Islam* (also Karen Armstrong, Alfred A. Knopf, 1993). Both of these books explore a number of themes central to Islam that I feel are essential; I'm not sure if my scholar friends would consider them so, but as parting thoughts, I would like to share two of them. One, which is so often overlooked and misunderstood in the West, is that the religion of Islam cannot be separated from society or politics. Western societies, especially the United States, have long believed in the separation of church and state. The thinkers of Europe's Enlightenment believed this separation freed religion from the inevitable corruption of affairs of state. But "in Islam," writes Armstrong, "Muslims have looked for God in history. Their sacred scripture, the Quran, gave them a historical mission. Their chief duty was to create a just community in which all members, even the most weak and vulnerable, were treated with absolute respect. The experience of building such a society and living in it would give them intimations of the divine, because they would be living in accordance with God's will. A Muslim had to redeem history, and that meant that state affairs were not a distraction from spirituality but the stuff of religion itself." Second, fundamentalism is not unique to Islam, and fundamentalists come in nearly every religious stripe (the word was first used by American Protestants, in fact), and it is a false stereotype to believe that Muslims are filled with hatred of the West. (It isn't difficult, however, to understand why some Muslims might be.) As Armstrong has noted, "On the eve of the second Christian millennium, the Crusaders massacred some thirty thousand Jews and Muslims in Jerusalem, turning the thriving Islamic holy city into a stinking charnel house." Until this time, the three religions of Abraham had coexisted relatively well in that great city for almost five hundred years. In our own times, Muslims worldwide admire the efficiency and technology of the West, as well as some of our democratic ideals. In fact, what many Muslims dream of is a balance between modernism and Islamic traditions. In her book *Islam,* Armstrong quotes Yusuf Abdallah al-Qaradawi, an al-Azhar graduate and director of the Centre for Sunnah and Sirah at the University of Qatar, as saying, "It is better for the West that Muslims should be religious, hold to their religion, and try to be moral." Armstrong herself writes, "Western people must become aware that it is in their interests too that Islam remains healthy and strong. The West has not been wholly responsible for the extreme forms of Islam, which have cultivated a violence that violates the most sacred canons of religion. But the West has certainly contributed to this development and, to assuage the fear and despair that lies at the root of all fundamentalist vision, should cultivate a more accurate appreciation of Islam in the third Christian millennium."

J

Jet Lag

I have read about a number of methods to reduce jet lag that involve diet and the amount of sunlight one receives during the days leading up to departure. (An interesting article to read is "A Cure for Jet Lag?" *Condé Nast Traveler,* April 2000, which details new research into the use of melatonin.) Now an overwhelming number of books, regimens, and potions—both chemical and homeopathic—claim to offer jet-lag solutions. Frankly, it all seems a lot of bother, and I would rather spend my time in advance of a trip doing other things. I also have no incentive to try any of these so-called solutions, because I've always had success with simply adjusting to local time upon my arrival. If I land in the morning (and all Royal Air Maroc flights from New York to Casablanca arrive in the morning), no matter how tired I might be, I do not take a nap. (I might possibly consider taking one if it was after lunch, but only then, and for no longer than one hour.) On that first night, I turn in rather early—by nine or ten—to get a very full night's sleep, and I do not sleep late the next morning. If I am fortunate enough to have a bathtub, I do not miss the opportunity to fill it with aromatic *bain moussant* (bubble bath) and get in for a soothing soak—this is actually a good activity for the early afternoon, when many merchants have gone home for lunch and museums and monuments are closed for a few hours. (As an aside, I'm loyal to two brands of *bain moussant* when traveling: Kiehl's (a New York family business since 1851, now owned by L'Oréal, with another store in San Francisco) and l'Occitane (a Provençal company with a number of outposts in the United States); both offer products for men and women in plastic bottles good for traveling. From Kiehl's I like the Lavender Foaming-Relaxing Bath with Sea Salts and Aloe Vera and the Mineral Muscle Soak Foaming-Relaxing Bath with Sea Salts and Aloe Vera, while from l'Occitane, I'm particularly fond of the restorative balm and relaxing essential oils in its Aromachologie line (Kiehl's 800-543-4571 and l'Occitane 888-623-2880 or 212-696-9098; www.loccitane.com). I know all the health experts and seasoned travelers say to refrain from alcoholic drinks on the flight, but I always have a glass of wine with my meal, and the result of all of the above is that I have never had a problem with jet lag. About naps: I cannot overstate the importance, pleasure, and restorative powers of a daily afternoon nap while in Morocco. Not only do most businesses and sites close for a few hours in the middle of the day anyway, but you'll feel refreshed and more alert after a brief rest. As Jane Brody noted in one of her "Personal Health" columns in *The New York Times,* naps "are far better than caffeine as a pick-me-up."

Jewish History in Morocco

Though scholars are unable to pinpoint exactly when Jewish communities were established in Morocco, it is believed that they date from the time of the destruction of the Temple in Jerusalem in 587 B.C. The lovely town of Ifrane, in the Middle Atlas, was home to the oldest continuously existing Jewish community in Morocco, where Jews lived until the 1960s. There once were more than two hundred Jewish communities in the country, the largest principally in Essaouira, Casablanca, Fez, and Marrakesh. Morocco has the largest Jewish community in the Arab world, and has the distinction of being one country in the world where Jews and Arabs have, until recently, lived together tolerably well. Jews were protected by the sultans over the centuries, though they were forced to live in their own quarter known as a *mellah,* which was always located close to the palace. They also had to dig deep into their pockets on occasion for the privilege of being left alone, a situation Edith Wharton referred to as "unrestricted extortion." Jews became moneylenders throughout the Maghreb, as the Koran forbids charging interest, and they distinguished themselves as master jewelers as well. But Islamic law does not recognize the oath of a Jew to be valid, and so the true status of Jews in Morocco has long been rather ambiguous. That said, when the Vichy government approached Mohammed V during World War II and asked for a list of Morocco's Jews and their assets, the king's famous reply was, "We have no Jews in Morocco, only Moroccan citizens." He is to be commended for deciding their status at a time when it really mattered.

Moroccan Jewry, like Italian Jewry, is unique, with its own traditions, customs, and food. In parts of the country where Spanish Jews settled (after their expulsion from Spain), they were known in Hebrew as the *megorashim* (those expelled) in order to differentiate them from native Jews, who were often called the *toshavim* (residents). A uniquely Moroccan Jewish custom is called *mimouna,* a day of outdoor celebration following Passover. *Mimouna* symbolizes a reintegration into society of sorts, following eight days of restricted eating. Muslims believe that the reintegrated Jews bring a bountiful year in nature, and to mark this return, Muslim neighbors bring food to their Jewish friends. *Mimouna* was brought to Israel by Moroccan *émigrés,* where it has been transformed into a celebration of ethnic diversity.

Casablanca was home to the largest Jewish community in the country by 1952, and it remains the largest today. By the early 1950s, the Jewish population of the city was almost 75,000, about 10 percent of the total. The creation of Israel in 1948 encouraged the first major wave of emigration to that country, and by 1955, only a year before Moroccan and Tunisian independence, North African Jews represented 87 percent of Israel's new immigrants. Moroccan independence and the Suez Canal crisis, both in 1956, prompted later waves of Jewish emigration to Israel (including a number of *pieds noirs*). In 1995 there were estimated to be about 6,000 Jews left in Morocco, but according to data from the American Jewish Year Book and the American Jewish Joint Distribution Committee, that number now hovers around 2,000. So one of the most ancient Jewish communities in the world literally vanished in less than a decade. In Israel today, Jews of Moroccan origin (including those born to Moroccan parents) number almost half a million.

Though Moroccan Jews were clearly in an unenviable position during the times of crisis noted above, they were made to feel unwelcome more than they were persecuted, which is no doubt why some did not emigrate and chose to remain in a land where they *had* been (relatively) welcome since antiquity. Historic upsets like civil war or the creation of a new country are obvious explanations for people of any nation to panic or flee, but it was not until I read *The Spider's House* by Paul Bowles that I fully grasped the more subtle yet significant explanation for the Moroccan Muslim impulse to create a new sort of terror: "Listening, Amar could not help hearing again the potter's words of only a few short hours ago: 'Sins are finished.' In some hideous, perverse fashion the two statements coincided. If there were no sins, then everything was necessarily a sin, which was what his father meant by the end of Islam. He felt the imperative and desperate need for action, but there was no action which could possibly lead to victory, because this was a time of defeat. Then the important thing was to see that you did not go down to defeat alone—the Jews and the Nazarenes must go, too. The circle was closed; now he understood the Wattanine whom the French called *les terrorists* and *les assassins*. He understood why they were willing to risk dying in order to derail a train or burn a cinema or blow up a post office. It was not independence they wanted, it was a satisfaction much more immediate than that: the pleasure of seeing others undergo the humiliation of suffering and dying, and the knowledge that they had at least the small amount of power necessary to bring about that humiliation. If you could not have freedom you could still have vengeance, and that was all anyone really wanted now."

For further reading, an excellent book is *Morocco: Jews and Art in a Muslim Land* (edited by Vivian Mann, Merrell Publishers, London, 2000; distributed in the United States by Rizzoli through St. Martin's Press). The book was published on the occasion of the exhibition of the same name at The Jewish Museum, New York, September 24, 2000–February 11, 2001. This exhibit, one of the best I've ever seen, paid tribute to "one of the most remarkable experiences of tolerance of our time," to quote from the introductory statement by *Sa Majesté le Roi du Maroc,* Mohammed VI. The book features chapters on topics such as the Jewish communities of Morocco, customs of the Jews of Morocco, and the Kabbalah in Morocco, as well as personal memoirs. I especially like "Esther and I: From Shore to Shore" by Oumana Aouad Lahrech, a teacher at the University of Rabat. In her essay she writes, "In my travels, I have had the opportunity to meet with members of the Jewish Moroccan diaspora, and I have seen how faithful they remain to their Moroccan origins. I will not forget the warmth of my meeting with North African Jews in Caracas in 1987. I need not say how moved I was when I saw how strongly Moroccan these men and women still felt after twenty or thirty years. For an outsider, such loyalty to one's Moroccan roots, and the profound brotherly feeling among Moroccans—probably unique in all of the Judeo-Muslim world—are difficult to understand. Indeed, they seem to resurface with national events, such as King Hassan's recent death. The transmission of that attachment to new generations of Jews who have never lived in Morocco is also remarkable. This should be seen not as an idealized nostalgia, but as a kind of mutual loyalty, the result of a fundamentally happy common history, despite the recent travails." Paintings, clothing, jewelry, ceremonial art, works on paper and parchment, photographs, and textiles are highlighted, with descriptive text, after the essays. It is an important and fascinating work that, due to such a long period of coexistence, should be of interest to all readers of any faith. ~Another significant work, especially valuable due to the time period it represents, is *Travels in North Africa* (Nahum Slouschz, The Jewish Publication Society of America, Philadelphia, 1927). "The Jews of Morocco" is the fifth and final section of this out-of-print book, which includes an especially interesting chapter on customs and traditions. At the time of the author's travels to Marrakesh (1912), it was still referred to as the city of "Morocco."

L

Laayoune and the Western Sahara
I do not have any articles in my files about this contested part of Morocco, which is not surprising as it has been the site of armed conflict between government forces and the Polisario (see the Polisario entry for more details). Some guidebook writers have written that they experienced a little trouble with Moroccan authorities when they were carrying maps that did not clearly indicate that this portion of the country was part of Morocco. The official Moroccan position is that this land is incontestably part of the country, and though there has been a cease-fire in effect since 1991, travel to this area remains restricted. Interested visitors should inquire about possible clearance requirements from the Moroccan embassy before setting off. (If you plan to continue farther south to Mauritania by road, you will definitely need appropriate visas and a *laisser-passer* from the local police; you will also have to be escorted by the Moroccan military to La Gouera, at the border, where you'll then be met by Mauritanian troops, who will escort you to Nouadhibou.) I have not yet ventured into this part of the country, but I have read that it is rewarding.

There are few tourists, and one would have an opportunity to witness daily life as it's lived by people who are not in any way connected to the tourist trade. Laayoune is the provincial capital of this region and is, as Justin McGuinness describes in his Footprint guide, "a strangely calm place, and not unpleasant to stay in." The legendary city of Smara is probably more interesting (to me, at least), although McGuinness says it is situated "in one of the most inhospitable regions of southern Morocco." Dakhla, almost on the Tropic of Cancer, is, again according to McGuinness, in a beautiful location with nice beaches.

Lalla

An Arabic word that visitors may occasionally encounter, a title of respect for women of some importance. *Sidi* is the same title of respect given for men.

Language

The language totem pole in Morocco puts Moroccan Arabic at the top (or Berber in certain villages), followed by French, Spanish, and finally English. My friend Mohamed El Mansour, who is on the Faculty of Letters at the University of Rabat, has told me the pecking order on this totem pole is (slowly) changing, and that more and more Moroccans entering the university do speak English and that they are learning it at a younger age. Moroccan Arabic is a dialect of Modern Standard Arabic, which is considered to be "classical" Arabic and is the Arabic spoken in Egypt. Modern Standard Arabic (MSA) is also the "official" language of Morocco, which means that it is the Arabic used by the media and employed in official speeches. Moroccan Arabic is considered to be less pure than the Arabic spoken by its neighbors to the east (partly because of Berber influence), and while someone from Casablanca would be understood in Algiers, he or she might run into communication problems in Libya or Egypt. Moroccan Arabic is, however, the spoken dialect of the country, and as author Orin Hargraves notes in his Culture Shock! Guide, "it is the single most useful language for a foreigner in Morocco to know. The practical benefits of mastering Moroccan dialect cannot be overemphasized."

Arabic in any dialect is, of course, a Semitic language, and like Hebrew, it is written from right to left. It is naturally difficult to learn because some of its sounds have no precise equivalent in English (or French or Spanish, either), and there aren't many vowels, adding to the difficulty. Serious presentation of either MSA or Moroccan Arabic is beyond the scope of this book and my abilities, and I understand from foreigners living in Morocco that the way to learn Arabic is to enroll in a language class; indeed, the advice given in the Culture Shock! Guide is the same. (Hiring a tutor is another suggestion.) Resources for those who want to embark on serious comprehension and pronunciation should consult the Culture Shock! edition and guidebooks for suggestions. But for those who want a more casual relationship with Moroccan Arabic, I am able to offer some guidance. The first point readers should remember is that Moroccan Arabic is a spoken language only, and therefore one word may have a number of different spellings, all of which could be called correct. Two of the more common examples of this that visitors frequently encounter are: the famous pigeon dish of Fez, *b'stilla,* is also written as *bisteeya, bstila, pasteeya, pastilla, pastela,* and *bastela;* and the word for mountain, *jbl,* is also transliterated as *djebel, jebel, jabal, dzhabel, giabel,* and *giebel.* If you listen closely to Moroccans in conversation, they will often switch back and forth between Moroccan Arabic and French, even within a single sentence. This is not surprising, since the average Moroccan speaks at least two languages fluently. This hybrid language, known as *l'arancia,* is spoken, not written, and visitors to Morocco would not be expected to understand it.

Readers of my other books know that for learning a language on your own, the best course is Living Language. There are certainly others, but Living Language has been around longer (since 1946), the courses are continually updated and revised, and in terms of variety, practicality, and originality, I prefer it. Though the Living Language "Fast & Easy" Arabic course is MSA, I found it very helpful to listen to the cassette tape and learn how to pronounce some key words and letters. (Some basic greetings and polite expressions are the same as or very similar to Moroccan Arabic.) And, after comparing the language sections of all the guidebooks I consulted, the Lonely Planet Guide—and its Moroccan Arabic Phrasebook—proved the best companion to the Living Language cassette. The clearest example I can give is that Lonely Planet is the only guide to fully elaborate on consonants and to transcribe one of the most important ones—the letter *h*—by capitalizing it when it should be pronounced like a strong whisper. The everyday phrase "good morning," for example, is written in Lonely Planet as *sabaH-al-kher,* and that is exactly how it sounds on the Living Language cassette. (In other words, the capital *H* serves as kind of a breathy pause, making the phrase almost five syllables instead of four.) As an aside, some readers may want to know that the Footprint guidebook is the only one to include Arabic script for the alphabet, streets, sites, services, and city names (not that this helps much with pronunciation, but it is interesting nonetheless). In case you're wondering if learning a few words of Moroccan Arabic is worth the effort, rest assured that it most definitely is. Besides one's attire, there is no better way to show your respect for Moroccans and their country than by attempting to use courteous expressions and greetings.

French is without question the second language of the country, and Moroccans will automatically speak to you in French even if they don't have any idea what nationality you are. All business documents are in French, and French appears side by side with Arabic on such things as restaurant menus, store signs, advertisments, road signs, and packaging for a wide variety of products. Again, readers familiar with my other books know how useful I believe French to be, not just in Morocco:

French is still a nearly universal language. It has been my experience that *someone* always speaks French, even in such seemingly unlikely countries as Egypt, Portugal, Turkey, Greece, and Croatia. Spanish may be the second language in the United States, but it won't serve you very well outside of Mexico, Central and South America, Spain, and the Philippines. A multitude of French words and phrases have made their way into English, and it would never be a bad investment of your time to either brush up on your high school French or begin learning for the first time. Living Language offers courses for beginner, intermediate, and advanced levels, in either audiocassette or CD editions. The "Fast & Easy" course (referred to as "virtually foolproof" by the New York *Daily News*) is for beginner business or leisure travelers and is a sixty-minute survival program with a cassette and pocket-sized pronunciation guide. The "Ultimate Course" is for serious language learners and is the equivalent of two years of college-level study. In a copublishing venture with Fodor's, Living Language also offers the pocket-size *French for Travelers,* which is a handy book/cassette reference designed for business and leisure travelers, with words and phrases for dozens of situations, including exchanging money, using ATMs, and finding a hotel room. It also includes a two-way dictionary. To help build excitement for young children coming along, Living Language offers the *Learn in the Kitchen* and *Learn Together: For the Car* series. These book/cassette kits are for children ages four to eight and include a sixty-minute bilingual tape; sixteen songs, games, and activities; a forty-eight-page illustrated activity book with color stickers; and tips for parents on how to vary the activities for repeated use. If you prefer learning by videotapes, a respected course is "French in Action." Call 800-LEARNER for additional information, and see the September 1999 issue of *Paris Notes* for the article "Paris 'In Action'" (Ellen Williams) about this series.

~Another related language book to consult is *501 French Verbs* (Barron's). In addition to providing really good descriptions of the various tenses, this book allots a full page to each verb, showing all the tenses fully conjugated, plus the definition and a useful selection of "Words and Expressions Related to This Verb" at the bottom of each page. As if this weren't enough, it also has chapters on "Verbs Used in Idiomatic Expressions," "Verbs with Prepositions," "Verbs Used in Weather Expressions," "Thirty Practical Situations for Tourists and Popular Phrases," and "Words and Expressions for Tourists." If you're serious about learning or brushing up on French, I really can't see doing it without this essential book. ~*Fodor's to Go: French for Travelers* (Fodor's Travel Publications, 2000) is not a book but a nifty credit card–size, fold-out magnet that you can conveniently keep in your pocket and unobtrusively retrieve when you need to look up a word or phrase. It is great for pretrip quizzing: you can keep it in your kitchen on the refrigerator at eye level and, while holding a glass of wine, for example, in one hand, unfold the magnet with the other and test your memory. Note, however, that as this is a magnet, you have to make sure it doesn't touch your credit cards or any other data storage items. ~*Insiders' French: Beyond the Dictionary* (Eleanor Levieux and Michel Levieux, The University of Chicago Press, 1999) is a smart and infinitely useful book. Much more than a dictionary, it includes terms and phrases that virtually did not exist before 1990. The authors describe the book as an attempt to present a verbal snapshot of France in the mid to late nineties. They acknowledge (happily) that some classic images and phrases still exist, "but today there are other Frances as well: a France of high unemployment, a France that is hooked on fast food but ambivalent about the country where it originated, a France that is about to experience the European single currency but is not at all certain what being part of Europe is going to entail, a France with a substantial and ever more controversial immigrant population, a France with a much diminished Communist Party and a provocative extreme Right, a France that cannot agree on what nationality and cultural identity mean." Brilliant. ~*Champs-Élyseés* (P.O. Box 158067, Nashville, Tennessee 37215; 800-824-0829; www.champs-elysees.com) is not a book but a monthly audiomagazine for intermediate and advanced students of French. Each cassette or CD is a monthly hour-long program accompanied by a complete transcript, with a French-English glossary. The programs include current events, music, cuisine, culture, and business news of France. I have found them interesting, well produced, and good preparation for a trip. Also, they're great to listen to while cleaning up around the house! Subscriptions are available for one year or five months. ~*Le Mot Juste: A Dictionary of Classical and Foreign Words and Phrases* (Vintage Books, 1991) includes French, Italian, German, Spanish, and a smattering of other languages (Arabic included) around the world. It's a great reference book that I use all the time. ~*Les Bons Mots: How to Amaze Tout le Monde with Everyday French* (by Eugene Ehrlich, Henry Holt, 1997) is not a dictionary but rather an alphabetical listing of idiomatic phrases, many of which have found their way into English. If you always wanted to know how to say the equivalent of "don't judge by appearances" (*l'habit ne fait pas le moine*), "seize the moment" (*il faut vivre dans l'instant*), "I couldn't care less" (*je m'en fous*), or simply "hangover" (*guele de bois*), you need this book. ~*Je Ne Sais What?: A Guide to de Rigueur Frenglish for Readers, Writers, and Speakers* (Jon Winokur, Plume, 1996) is about "Frenglish" (not to be confused with "Franglais"), or grammatically correct *French* that enriches the *English* language. This book is a collection of French expressions, maxims, and literary phrases that have found their way into our vocabulary. So one will find *nouvelle cuisine, mauvais goût, enfant terrible*, and *tant pis* and their definitions and related quotations. As Winokur states in the introduction, "Much of our political, military, artistic, and culinary vocabulary originated in France."

Luggage

I've read of a syndrome—really—called BSA (Baggage Separation Anxiety), which you may at first be inclined to laugh at, but as reports of lost luggage have escalated in the last few years, I'm not at all surprised that fear of losing luggage is now a syndrome. (All the more reason, I say, not to check bags, and *definitely* the reason to pack at least some essentials in a carry-on bag.) Essentials, by the way, don't add up to much: it's remarkable how little one truly "needs." Recently, one of my bags did not turn up, and the airline representative was honest enough to tell me that when flights are full, sometimes not all the bags are loaded onto the plane—intentionally (#&!). Distressing as this is, at least it explains part of the problem and is one more reason to keep essentials with you. Even if you are the sort of traveler who cannot lighten your load, you will still probably bring a carry-on. As I write this, the standard limit for carry-on luggage, for most airlines (including Royal Air Maroc), is 9 by 14 by 22 inches, otherwise known as 45 linear inches. The problem, as I understand it, is the 22-inch bags. Some airlines will accept these as legitimate carry-on luggage, while others will not. To be safe, however, make sure you have a 20-inch bag, and you will never have to worry. It seems simple to me, and it seems foolish not to comply—storage space is limited, and less baggage means more on-time schedules and better passenger safety. Some airlines have even installed size templates at the security X-ray machines, so if your bag doesn't fit, you don't walk through (or rather, *you* can walk through, but you can't bring your bag). Many luggage manufacturers, including Tumi and Samsonite, have responded, turning out a variety of bags at varying prices that are meant to hold enough stuff for about three days of traveling—about the time it takes for a misrouted bag to show up, assuming it isn't lost altogether!

The ubiquitous—and always black—suitcase on wheels has taken a beating of late. Some travelers complain that it's too heavy to lift in and out of the overhead bins without hitting someone on the head, and trying to find one at the baggage claim is like Harry the dog trying to find his family's umbrella at the beach in the children's book *Harry by the Sea*. Plus, they've become decidedly unhip: a writer for *The Wall Street Journal* claimed that "the wheelie has become a fashion faux pas—the suitcase equivalent of a pin-striped suit on a casual Friday." I may be the lone voice in the wilderness, but the wheelie is essential for those of us with back problems. (I am extremely happy with my Dakota 20-inch wheelie, and it's forest green, by the way. The entire Dakota line is one of the better-kept secrets in the luggage world: "the hardest working bags in the business" are a division of Tumi and are equally as well made, for about half the price.) Also, I like the freedom of not having to depend on only one type of ground transportation. With a wheelie, I don't need a porter or a luggage cart, and I can choose from all forms of public (and private) transportation. ~Now that I have said all of this in defense of the 20-inch wheelie, I do want to share an experience I had with Royal Air Maroc: I was boarding a very full flight, and by the time my row was called, an attendant informed me that I had to check my bag. When I pointed out that I did not have any checked luggage whatsoever and that my 45-linear-inches bag was decreed acceptable by RAM, it didn't matter. You will see when you fly RAM that, in both directions, a lot of Moroccans are carrying *a lot of very large bags,* both checked and carry-on. The staff had let all those other people on the plane ahead of me, with all of their gigantic bags that they just had to have, and I was being penalized for following the airline's directions. So while I do recommend that you stick with carry-on bags (after all, in the words of Antoine de Saint-Exupéry, "He who would travel happily must travel light,"), do not have a cow if you are told you must check it. Remember: it's Morocco, and you need to adjust accordingly, and you might as well start now.

Marshal Hubert Lyautey

As I stated earlier, the only two good Frenchmen in Morocco before independence were Gilbert Grandval and Hubert Lyautey, who served as resident-general of Morocco from 1912 to 1925. Readers will repeatedly come across references to Lyautey, and with good reason. Edith Wharton opened the chapter on Lyautey in her wonderful book, *In Morocco,* with this praise: "It is not too much to say that General Lyautey has twice saved Morocco from destruction: once in 1912, when the inertia and double-dealing of Abd-el-Hafid abandoned the country to the rebellious tribes who had attacked him in Fez, and the second time in August, 1914, when Germany declared war on France." Lyautey is also responsible for coining the phrase "Morocco is a cold country with a hot sun." John Gunther, in *Inside Africa,* said of Lyautey, "He was one of the authentic creators of modern Africa. He was indisputably a great man. Also he was a prima donna and a fuss-pot. He loved negotiation, to which he addressed himself with supple finesse, and hated battle." In addition to the great works he achieved in Morocco (amply detailed in Wharton's book), he is best known for establishing the *villes nouvelles* in the imperial cities (which preserved their medinas) and for his famous reply to his home government when war broke out in 1914. France requested that Lyautey send all available troops to France, abandoning every part of the country except the coastal towns. Lyautey knew that if he followed orders, this would be tantamount to giving France's richest colonies to Germany, since what the colonies could supply— "meat and wheat"—was what Germany needed most; plus, it would be only a matter of time before the loss of Morocco would lead to the loss of all of French North Africa. So Lyautey decided to "empty the egg without breaking the shell," according to Wharton. His answer was "I will give you all the troops you ask, but instead of abandoning the interior of the country I will hold what we have already taken, and fortify and enlarge our boundaries." Lyautey knew, even if the rest of France didn't, that Germany coveted North Africa, at least for the duration of the war, and he was determined to prove the worth of Morocco. After he gave France nearly all his troops, he asked for an "agricultural and industrial army," or specialists who could help develop Morocco. As a result, for every battle fought, a road was built; for every fortress shelled, a factory was built, a harbor dug, or farmland plowed and sown. Again to quote Wharton, "It will not seem an exaggeration to speak of General Lyautey's achievement during the first year of the war as the 'Miracle of Morocco' if one considers the immense importance of doing what he did at the moment when he did it. And to understand this it is only needful to reckon what Germany could have drawn in supplies and men from a German North Africa, and what would have been the situation of France during the war with a powerful German colony in control of the western Mediterranean." It is tragically unfortunate, especially in light of what was to come, that such a talented, progressive man eventually lost his job precisely because he defied orders one too many times, but Morocco is fortunate that it was the beneficiary of his wise if short-lived policy, which was to create an administration that developed the best native aspirations, as opposed to one that applied French ideals to African reality. Lyautey's grave was for a number of years in Rabat; though his tombstone read, "Profoundly respectful of the ancient traditions and of the Moslem religion preserved and practiced by the People of the Maghreb amongst whom he has desired to rest in this land which he has loved so well," he is now interred at Les Invalides in Paris, where no less a personage than Napoleon is also buried.

M

El Maghreb El Aksa

"The Land Farthest West," or the westernmost portion of the Islamic world. The term *Maghreb,* as it's used today, refers to Morocco, Algeria, Tunisia, and part of Libya (in other words, nearly all of North Africa except Egypt). But many travel accounts of the 1800s and early 1900s use the word in reference to Morocco only; both are correct. Almost all of the population of the Maghreb is Sunni Muslim, and according to author David Lamb, "the preamble to Morocco's constitution defines Moroccan identity as being, in order, Maghreb, Arabic, Islamic and African." But apart from religion, the Maghreb is not as unified as might be assumed, and attempts at creating (or forcing) unity among the countries have mostly failed due to the real differences among them.

Maps

Getting lost is usually a part of everyone's travels, but it isn't always a bonus. Inexplicably, there is no truly great map of Morocco, or at least I've not yet come across one. I do not seem to be alone in holding this opinion, either. The only good map from the Moroccan tourist office is the general road map of the country. It's a pretty good map, and it's available free, but it isn't sufficiently detailed for travel off the main roads or approaching major cities. The individual city maps available at the tourist offices in Morocco are barely acceptable, and a special trip for them is certainly not worthwhile. The Reise & Verkehrsverlag relief map of Morocco is interesting and can keep one occupied for hours, but it is really only helpful as a reminder that the Atlas and Rif Mountains ensure that distances are always greater than they seem. ~For *individual cities and towns:* I used the city maps provided in the Cadogan, Footprint, and Lonely Planet Guides, and I thought they were, by using them all together, just fine. What one guidebook's map lacked, another had, so I was able to get around. ~For *driving:* If someone forced me to pick one, I would have to say Michelin, but even with the trusty tubby guy, I would always revert to the guidebooks' maps as we were approaching a city or town because they had better details on the incoming roads. I did see a few road maps for sale in Morocco that looked as if they might have been worthy. I regret now that I did not buy them and give them a try so I could report back to you. You certainly have nothing to lose, so if you do see one and it turns out to be a winner, I hope you'll write and let me know.

Medina

To quote from *Insight Guide: Morocco,* "All Arab cities with some history have their medina. The Prophet Mohammed founded the first Islamic community in a city named Medina, second only to Mecca in importance, and it quickly became the prototype for other towns in the Arab world." *Medina* simply means "city," but has now come to stand for the original Arab part of any Moroccan town. Lyautey, who recognized immediately the uniqueness of Morocco's medinas, decreed that the French would live in areas—known as *villes nouvelles*—set apart in order that the medinas would be preserved. This significant decision was undoubtedly the right one, but it hasn't been without consequences, especially in our modern times. Inevitably, the medinas have lost the administrative and political importance they once had to the *villes nouvelles.* At independence, the wealthier families of the medinas moved to the more modern new towns, replacing the French, leaving the poor and the very poor—who are unfortunately much greater in number—behind. ~A note about finding one's way around the medina: it's not that difficult. Reading the guidebooks will sometimes make it sound as if, without a guide, *you will get lost and never get out.* Certainly a medina is confusing, with winding and narrow passageways, lots of people and animals, noise, and unfamiliar smells, but anyone with a good sense of direction will not find it hard to leave the medina, although one may not exit from the same place one entered.

Menzeh

This is an Arabic word you'll see often, typically as the name of a hotel or restaurant. It refers to a pavilion in a garden with a view, so you can see why it's an appealing name for a hotel or restaurant.

Money

The best way to travel is with a combination of local cash, American Express traveler's checks (other types are not universally accepted), and credit cards. If you have all three, you will *never* have a problem. (You should not rely on wide acceptance of credit cards in the more remote areas of Morocco.) How you divide these up depends on how long you'll be traveling and on what day of the week you arrive— banks, which of course offer the best exchange rate, aren't generally open on the weekends, and most aren't open all day during the week. If you rely solely on your ATM card and you encounter a problem, you can't fix it until Monday, when the banks reopen (often not until the afternoon). Though savvy travelers always arrive with some local currency in their possession, Moroccan currency is legally not permitted to circulate outside of Morocco, making it difficult to obtain any in advance. Still, it is sometimes possible to buy *dirhams* from certain American Express offices (a few branches have what are referred to as "exotic" currencies) and banks (again, some branches just happen to have some on hand occasionally). Make several calls before you give up. Given this limitation, you may have no choice but to arrive in Morocco empty-handed and will then have to buy some *dirhams* at the airport, as you'll need some to pay for your transportation to your hotel and to tip porters. Be sure to allow for extra time to accomplish this, as everyone else on your flight will be doing the same thing, and lines can be long. Some pointers: ~ATM cash machines are sometimes out of order, or out of cash. Then customers are forced to make their transactions by going into the bank, where the lines are usually very, very long, turning a five-minute task into one that may take an hour. Once I even had the admittedly unusual experience of going directly to a large bank in a capital city only to find a posted sign stating that the bank was closed because it had *run out of money!* This is why you should not count on them exclusively.

~Overseas ATMs may limit the number of daily transactions you can make, as well as place a ceiling on the total amount you can withdraw. Since you are charged a surcharge each time you use the ATM, keep your transactions to a minimum: make larger, fewer withdrawals. Call your home bank and inquire about the exact fees for withdrawals, and ask if there is an additional fee for overseas transactions. (I've read that it can range from $1.50 to $5 per transaction.) Make sure you can withdraw money from both your checking and savings accounts or from only one, and ask if you can transfer money between accounts. ~Make sure your ATM password is compatible with Moroccan ATMs (if you have too many digits, you'll have to change it), and if, like me, you have memorized your password as a series of letters rather than numbers, write down the numerical equivalent before you leave. Most Moroccan (and European) cash machines do not display letters, and even if they did, they do not always appear in the same sequence as we know it in the United States. ~Check the business section of your local daily newspaper for current exchange rates, or check the websites www.xe.net and www.oanda.com. ~The major banks of Morocco include BMCE (Banque Marocaine du Commerce Exterieur) and Banque Credit du Maroc. You don't usually have to look very far to find one, and most are located in the *villes nouvelles*, almost always on the main street, which is almost always named Avenue (or Boulevard) Mohammed V or Hassan II. ~Though I think this is a bit anal-retentive, even for me, it's possible to view in advance the exact street locations of ATM machines in Morocco on-line. To see where Plus systems are, check www.visa.com; for the Cirrus network, go to www.mastercard.com/atm. Once in, select "ATM Locator," and you'll be given an opportunity to select a country, city, street address, and postal code. (For best results, enter cross streets and a city.)

~American Express traveler's checks can also be purchased from the American Automobile Association (AAA). Members may purchase either traditional AmEx traveler's checks or Cheques for Two in denominations of $20, $50, and $100 and are fee-free. (There is usually a one percent service fee.) The checks can be purchased at any AAA branch office or by mail (although by mail there is a $500 minimum and a $3,000 maximum; also, allow for first class mail delivery within fourteen business days). AAA members who also hold a Visa card can purchase traveler's checks by telephone. The checks are delivered to your home, and there is no transaction fee or postage, shipping, or handling charges. Call 800-374-1258 for more information and to find out the AAA office nearest to you. ~Refrain from wearing one of those ubiquitous waist bags, or as my friend Carl says, "Make our country proud, and don't wear one of those fanny packs!" A tourist plus a fanny pack equals a magnet for pickpockets. I know of more people who've had valuables stolen from these pouches than I can count (not to mention that one looks incredibly ridiculous wearing one). Keep large bills, credit cards, and passport hidden from view in a money belt worn under your clothes, in a pouch that hangs from your neck, or in an interior coat or blazer pocket. My husband had great success in Morocco with a money belt worn around his leg, underneath his pants. This obviously won't work with shorts, but since men shouldn't be wearing shorts in Morocco anyway, it's quite a good solution and very practical. ~If possible, don't keep everything in the same place, and keep a separate piece of paper with telephone numbers of companies to contact in case of emergency. ~Useful vocabulary: *des pièces* (coins); *d'argent* (money); *billets* (bank notes); *chèques de voyages* (traveler's checks).

Monuments and Museums

The *medersat* and decorative arts museums in Morocco are truly beautiful—and in some cases extraordinary—works of art and architecture. But visitors should not expect them to be maintained in quite the same way as museums and monuments in Europe or America, for example. There are some portions of the structures that are in need of repair, and they are dusty, and there are no brightly lit bookstores with postcard reproductions and posters that we're so used to seeing in our mercantile societies. Moroccans may not have caught on yet to the vast merchandising opportunities that could be available to them, but they are very proud of their *patrimoine* (patrimony), as the French refer to it, even if that *patrimoine* is a bit tattered around the edges. It is easy, however, to begin to feel as if everything looks the same, especially if you're moving too quickly from place to place. As Edith Wharton noted in *In Morocco,* "it is difficult, in describing the architecture of Morocco, to avoid producing an impression of monotony. The ground-plan of mosques and Medersas is always practically the same; and the same elements, few in number and endlessly repeated, make up the materials and the form of the ornament. The effect upon the eye is not monotonous, for a patient art has infinitely varied the combinations of pattern and the juxtapositions of color; while the depth of undercutting of the stucco, and the treatment of the bronze doors and of the carved cedar corbels, necessarily varies with the periods which produced them." It is essential for me to emphasize again that you should move slowly throughout Morocco, and pay attention to the details, or you will indeed never comprehend what is unique about each monument, city, or craft. And if you feel you keep running into the same foreigners and that your itinerary in each place you visit is the same, it's not an accident; this isn't a fact to regret, but it also isn't unique to Morocco, as readers who've visited Egypt, for example, already know. In a country where you most likely do not know the language (and therefore cannot sit down at a café and get to know the locals) and where you most likely don't share the same religion (and cannot enter a mosque or comfortably drink alcohol in public), there are only so many sites and activities accessible to foreigners (even at the beach, for example, one must be modest, unless you are at an established resort). In this sense, I think Morocco is not the same kind of holiday as a trip to Italy, for example; and I think if visitors know this in advance, they will approach Morocco in such a way as to get the most out of it, and find that it is indeed kaleidoscopic in ways never imagined.

Moors

I suspect that the first time most of us heard of the Moors was in either a history or a Spanish class, since the Moors invaded Andalucia 711 years after the birth of Christ. (These Moors were actually Berbers led by Tariq Ibn Ziryab.) However, as John Gunther stated in *Inside Africa,* the words *Muslim, Arab,* and *Moor* are not synonyms; *Muslim* is a religious term, and *Arab* is ethnic or linguistic. The simplest definition of a Moor, according to Gunther, is geographical. "A Moor is any African living in Morocco, no matter what race or religion. Folk in Algeria and Tunisia are not Moors, properly speaking, though they may have Moorish background and characteristics." Further, he notes that a Moor cannot be defined simply as a *Muslim* inhabitant of Morocco, since there are also Christian and Jewish Moors; yet *most* Moors (Arabs and Berbers) *are* Muslim. Additionally, *Moors* is purely a European term—it is not a word used by Moroccans themselves.

Moucharabieh or Moushrabya

This Arabic word refers to a carved wooden window of sorts, but it can only be seen *out* of, not *into*. *Moucharabieh* does not appear to a great degree in contemporary Moroccan houses, but its purpose was for the women of fairly well-to-do households to be able to discreetly see who was outside the dwelling. Windows, balconies, and walkways reserved for women all would have been protected by *moucharabieh*. Often the *moucharabieh* is strategically placed within view of the main entrance to the house, so that if there is an unexpected knock at the door, the women can see who it is without running the risk of being seen, especially if the caller is a man. (The main door, by the way, typically will have two knockers, one at a lower level for children and another at a higher level for adults. The women, of course, are able to recognize the sound of the different knockers and know immediately if a knock means the children are home from school or a visitor has arrived.) *Moucharabieh* is not unique to Morocco, and readers may have seen similar examples in other Muslim countries. I remember seeing particularly fine and intricate versions in Egypt, where the unique aspect of *moucharabieh* is that each piece is carved from a single piece of wood.

Moussem

A *moussem* is a festival, usually religious but not always, and if you are in Morocco at the time of one, you should not miss the opportunity to attend—it will be an experience you'll never forget. The majority of *moussems* are religious and are usually days-long festivals where the pilgrims gather in celebration and honor of a particular saint. These are held at or near the appropriate *marabout* (see entry for Islam), and there is feasting, music, and dancing into all hours of the night. *Moussems* are also an opportunity for family and friends who may not see each other often to spend time together; there is even a marriage *moussem,* where prospective men and women turn out to hopefully meet a mate. All the *moussems* and festivals are listed in most guidebooks, so there is no need for me to outline them here. Some are annual events with fixed dates, while others may occur during a particular season or month. When attending either a *moussem* or a festival, remember to respect the occasion and dress conservatively; if the occasion for the *moussem* is religious, do not approach the *marabout;* and make arrangements in advance—as many of these festivities are not held in Morocco's major cities, finding accommodations can be next to impossible if you haven't.

Movies

Before you leave, plan a meal from one or more of the cookbooks mentioned in the *Saveurs Marocains Bibliothèque,* and invite some friends and family over for dinner and a movie. Some suggestions: *Casablanca, Hideous Kinky, Jesus of Nazareth, The Jewel of the Nile, Lawrence of Arabia, The Man Who Knew Too Much, The Man Who Would Be King, Othello,* and *The Sheltering Sky.* Not all of these are necessarily *about* Morocco, or even—in the case of *Casablanca*—*filmed* in Morocco, but who cares? They are all worthwhile viewing. The documentary *Night Waltz: The Music of Paul Bowles* focuses on Bowles's life as a composer and includes footage of him during his last years in Tangier. I don't know if this documentary is widely available, but it's directed by Owsley Brown and was released in January 2001. And while you're cooking, get in the mood by listening to some appropriate music, like the album *A Mediterranean Odyssey: Cairo to Casablanca* (Putumayo World Music, featuring ten great cuts; though only one is technically Moroccan, this is a most enjoyable odyssey), or see the suggestions just below. (Okay, I admit it: I love "Marrakesh Express" by Crosby, Stills, Nash, and Young.) All are great choices that will have you ready to say *à votre santé!* (to your health/cheers!) when your guests arrive. (I do not believe that there is an Arabic expression for "cheers!")

Muhammad V

As with Hassan II, visitors will encounter a lot of major thoroughfares and other things named after the sultan who helped forge the way to Moroccan independence in 1956. Muhammad is especially revered because the French exiled him and his family (which included young Hassan II) to Corsica and then to Madagascar in 1953 to diffuse the Moroccans' aspirations for independence. After increased acts of violence and massive rioting, the French were forced to release the royal family and allow them to return to Morocco in 1955.

Muhammad VI

Morocco's current king, who came into power upon the death of his father, Hassan II, who reigned for thirty-eight years until July 1999. Thirty-eight-year-old Muhammad VI has, in a short time, already taken steps to democratize the country's political system and liberalize its economy. He made headlines by announcing he would allow the return of Morocco's best-known political exiles, and he established a fund equivalent to four million dollars to compensate victims of political torture. Muhammad VI is also much more public than his father—he attended Moroccan schools rather than studying abroad, and he reportedly genuinely enjoys meeting the people. A *Time* cover story dubbed him "The King of Cool," after his visit to Washington in June 2000, and the interviewer described him as "hip, charming, and mod."

Music

In "Letter from Morocco," an article that appeared in the December 22, 1956, issue of *The Nation*, Paul Bowles wrote, "The most important single element in Morocco's folk culture is its music. Since it always has been a land where illiteracy is the general rule, its production of written literature is negligible. . . . At the same time, the very illiteracy which through the centuries has precluded the possibility of literature has abetted the development of music: the entire history and mythology of the people is clothed in song." Bowles then traveled all around Morocco in 1959 with the intention of recording—and thus preserving—every single major musical genre found in the country. The Moroccan government was cooperative at first but later let him know in no uncertain terms that he was to halt the recordings and that it would no longer assist him in any way. Thankfully, he had already recorded an enormous body of work, and the recordings are now intact in the American Folk Life Center at the Library of Congress. A cassette has been issued from The Paul Bowles Moroccan Music Collection entitled *Music of Morocco,* which can be ordered by mail directly from the Library of Congress. (Send a check or money order for $17.90 to American Folklife Center, Library of Congress, MBRS Division, 101 Independence Avenue S.E., Washington, D.C. 20540; or visit www.loc.gov/folklife for details.) Seriously interested audiophiles may come to the library Monday through Friday, 8:30 to 5:00, and listen to the original recordings (first come, first served, no appointments taken; two listening stations are available). The phone number at the Folk Archive reference desk is 202-707-5510, and the woman I spoke with, who was extremely knowledgeable and helpful, told me the Paul Bowles recordings were her favorite in the entire archive. Also, Rounder Records has recently issued *Sacred Music of the Moroccan Jews* from the Paul Bowles Collection, a compact disk that can be ordered directly from Rounder (www.rounder.com).

It's obvious by the number of pages devoted to it in the guidebooks that Moroccan music is something special. Due to its unique position in the far western corner of Africa and its proximity to Europe, Morocco has long been a musical crossroads, welcoming and incorporating styles and instruments from Andalucia, sub-Saharan Africa, and Arabia, as well as its own Berber, Sufi brotherhood, and Moroccan Jewish music. Whatever readers may think of rock music, perhaps one of the greatest tributes paid to the rich tradition of Moroccan music was the interest shown in it by the Rolling Stones, Led Zeppelin, and Jimi Hendrix. The Rolling Stones, in fact, recorded an album with the Master Musicians of Jajouka (*Brian Jones Presents the Pipes of Pan at Jajouka,* 1969). I am rather ashamed to admit— since I do love music, especially African music—that I do not seem to have an ear for distinguishing the styles of Moroccan music, with the exception of Gnaoua, which has a *very* distinctive sound. (The word comes from the West African nation of Guinea.) Pop music, too, heard blaring from radios and tape players in cafés and shops all over Morocco, I can't seem to grasp—it all sounds the same to me, which is not to say I don't enjoy it, but I often have the feeling everyone is listening to variations of the same song all day long. Interested readers with better acoustical ears than mine should consult the music pages in both the Cadogan and the Rough Guides (there are even some recommendations for further listening) and should run right out to buy the compact-disk-and-book package *Morocco: Crossroads of Time,* which is so wonderful (music compiled by Randall Barnwell and Bill Lawrence, text written, translated, and compiled by Lawrence and Barnwell, Ellipsis Arts, Roslyn, New York). I wish there were one of these packages for every country bordering the Mediterranean. A dozen tracks present the full array of the music tradition in Morocco, and these include ambient sounds of the Fez and Marrakesh medinas; Gnaoua, Berber, Andalucian, and Moroccan Jewish selections; and one selection by Nouamane Lahlou, a pop star in Morocco. Two of the cuts were recorded by Paul Bowles. The accompanying booklet features some very good essays on Paul Bowles and Tangier, Islam and life in Morocco, women and Islam, hospitality, and recipes for *harira* and mint tea. It's really brilliant and *de rigueur* for anyone interested in a good introduction to Moroccan musical styles. I tried searching for Moroccan Jewish music selections at www.jewishmusic.com, but when I entered *Moroccan,* no results came up; there are a great number of Sephardic selections to browse, however, and some may very well include Moroccan choices.

O

Office National de Chemin de Fer (ONCF)

ONCF is the Moroccan national railway, which offers good, reliable service to most parts of the country. Passengers can also buy a through ticket covering the bus portion of a trip (heading far south, for example, or to Agadir). There are both first-class and second-class seats, but first class is such a good value and is so affordable that I don't see any reason to buy second class. The website (in French) is www.oncf.org.ma and you can obtain a copy of the schedule from the Moroccan Tourist Board offices in the United States. Remember that about 70 percent of the country is mountainous, which means that it takes a half or a full day to reach some destinations (not because it's slow going through the mountains, but because there *are* no tracks through the mountains, so the ride from Marrakesh to Fez, for example, takes you first over to Casablanca and Rabat before heading east to Fez). Just as on trains in other parts of the world, including the United States, a supplement is charged if you purchase your tickets on board the train. Don't discard your ticket, as inspectors check while en route, and tickets are then collected upon arrival. Overnight service in a *couchette* is available from Tangier to Marrakesh and Tangier to Ougda.

Packing

Most people, whether they travel for business or pleasure, view packing as a stressful chore. It doesn't have to be, and a great book filled with excellent suggestions and tips is *How to Pack: Experts Share Their Secrets* (Laurel Cardone, Fodor's Travel Publications, 1997). You might think it silly to consult a book on how to pack a suitcase, but this is eminently practical and worthwhile. Cardone is a travel journalist who's on the road a lot, and she meets a lot of fellow travelers with plenty of packing wisdom to share. How to buy luggage, how to fill almost any suitcase, how to fold nearly crease-free, how to choose the right wardrobe for the right trip, and how to pack for the way back home are all thoroughly covered. Also, some of the best tips from the book are compiled in *Fodor's to Go: How to Pack,* a credit card–size fold-out magnet. Some pointers that work for me include: ~Select clothing that isn't prone to wrinkling, like cotton and wool knits; when I *am* concerned about limiting wrinkles, I lay out a large plastic dry-cleaning bag, place the garment on top of it, place *another* bag on top of that, and fold the item up between the two bags. The key here is that the plastic must be layered in with the clothing; otherwise it doesn't really work. ~If I'm packing items with buttons, I button them up before I fold them—the same with zippers and snaps. ~If I'm carrying a bag with more than one separate compartment, I use one for shoes; otherwise I put shoes at the bottom (or back) of the bag opposite the handle, so they'll remain there while I'm carrying the bag. ~Transfer shampoo and lotions to travel-size plastic bottles, which can be purchased at pharmacies, and then put these inside a sealed plastic bag to prevent against leaks. (The plastic bag is then also useful for storing a wet bathing suit.) ~Don't skimp on underwear—it's lightweight, it takes up next to no room in your bag, and it's never a mistake to have more than you think you need. ~Belts can be either rolled up and stuffed into shoes or fastened together along the inside edge of your suitcase. ~Ties should be rolled, not folded, and also stuffed into shoes or pockets.

~Some handy things to bring along that are often overlooked: a pocket flashlight for looking into ill-lit corners of old buildings, reading in bed at night (the lights are often not bright enough), and for navigating the dark hallways of hotels at night (the light is usually on a timer and always runs out before you've made it to either end of the hallway); binoculars, for looking up at architectural details; a small travel umbrella; a penknife/corkscrew; if I'm camping, plastic shoes— referred to in the United States as jellies, which the Europeans have been wearing on some of their rocky *plages* (beaches) for years and years—for campground showers; an empty lightweight duffel bag, which I fold up and pack and then use as a carry-on bag for gifts and breakable items on the way home; copies of any current prescriptions, in case I need to have one refilled; and photocopies of my passport and airline tickets (which should also be left with someone at home).

Passports

For last-minute crises, it *is* possible to obtain a new passport, renew an old one, or get necessary visas (not required for Morocco). Two companies that can meet the challenge: Travisa (2122 P Street N.W., Washington, D.C. 20037; 800-222-2589) and Express Visa Service (353 Lexington Avenue, Suite 1200, New York, New York 10016; 212-679-5650; fax: -4691)

Periodicals

Following are some newsletters and periodicals, a few of which are not available at newsstands, that you may want to consider subscribing to in advance of your trip—or upon your return, if you decide you want to keep up with goings-on in Maroc:

GEO: I include this French magazine here for a special edition published in January 2001, "Maroc 2001," which featured excellent articles covering history, society, development, economics, women, and so on, with color photos and a pull-out map. Intermediate-level readers of French will be able to understand this issue without much difficulty—they may have to consult the dictionary a few times, *mais pas grave*. To inquire about buying this back issue (about $10.95), contact the magazine at its U.S. office: Express Magazine, P.O. Box 2769, Plattsburg, New York 12901; 877-363-1310.

Journal Français: Again, I include this entry for those who read French or want to improve their French. This is perhaps the best and most pleasant way to feel connected with all that's happening in France and the Francophone world. The *Journal* is a monthly, covering all the topics of a daily newspaper—politics, business, travel, features, and the like. It is published by France Press, 1051 Divisadero, San Francisco, California 94115; 415-921-5100; fax: -0213; www.francepress.com.

Maisons Côté Sud: This bimonthly magazine, which is one of my favorite periodicals, is devoted to southern latitudes around the world but is mainly the leading magazine of Mediterranean culture. The editorial staff is based in Mougins on the Côte d'Azur and doesn't miss a beat on cultural, design, or decorating topics. The text is in French, and it's the sort of writing you dream about, thoroughly transporting readers to the table set under the olive trees or the sleeping couch by the sea. Morocco is often featured in its pages. To subscribe, contact Express Mag, 8155 Larrey Anjou, Quebec H1J 2L5, Canada; 800-363-1310; www.expressmag.com.

North Africa Travel Collected Essays: At about the same time as this book appears, the British company North Africa Travel will be issuing its first collection of travel essays. Cadogan Guide author Barnaby Rogerson is spearheading this new periodical, and though I haven't yet seen it, I am anticipating that it will be great. Rogerson suggests that readers contact him at North Africa Travel (3 Inglebert Street, Clerkenwell, London EC1R 1XR, England; barnaby@inglebert.demon.co.uk) for details on subscribing or becoming a member of NAT.

Photography

I would rather have one great photo of a place than a dozen mediocre shots, so I like to page through photography books for ideas and suggestions on maximizing my picture-taking efforts. One book I've particularly enjoyed is *The Traveler's Eye: A Guide to Still and Video Travel Photography* (Lisl Dennis, Clarkson Potter, 1996). Dennis, who began her career in photography at *The Boston Globe,* is also the photographer for *Morocco: Design from Casablanca to Marrakesh* (Clarkson Potter, 1992). I like her sensitive approach to travel photography and find her images and suggestions in this book inspiring. After chapters covering such topics as travel photojournalism, shooting special events, and landscape photography, she provides an especially useful chapter on technical considerations, with advice on equipment, film, packing, the ethics of tipping, and outsmarting airport X-ray machines. *Focus on Travel: Photographing Memorable Pictures of Journeys to New Places* (Anne Millman and Allen Rokach, photographs by Allen Rokach, Abbeville Press, 1992) is more of a tome than *The Traveler's Eye,* although it doesn't cover video cameras. The authors offer much more information on lenses, filters, films, and accessories, and there are separate chapters on photographing architecture, shooting subjects in action, and taking pictures in a variety of weather conditions. The appendix covers selecting and preparing your photos after the trip, fill-in flash guidelines, a color-correction chart, and a page-by-page reference to all the photos in the book. Unlike these books, which should be consulted before you go, *Kodak Guide to Shooting Great Travel Pictures: Easy Tips and Foolproof Ideas from the Pros* (Jeff Wignall, Fodor's Travel Publications, 2000) is a very handy, small paperback good for bringing along as a reference. Seven chapters present more than 250 color photos, ninety expert tips, and specific photographic challenges—such as city vistas, digital photography, close-ups of faces, mountain scenery, motion, lights at night, silhouettes, and black-and-white images—and each is dealt with in one page with accompanying photos. It's important to note that this guide is meant for experienced *and* point-and-shoot photographers, and many of the images featured in the book are from the Eastman Kodak archives, a great number of which were taken by amateurs. The final chapter is devoted to creating a travel journal.

These good books aside, it's important to note that a camera is not an object taken lightly in Morocco, especially in mountainous areas. Berbers believe that a camera will steal your soul, so remember never to take someone's photograph without asking permission first. In Morocco's big cities, charging *dirhams* for the privilege of taking someone's picture can be big business. You shouldn't begrudge your subject's request, but if you tire of handing out *dirhams,* stop taking photos for a day or two. And regarding what type of camera to bring, I recommend one with a zoom lens attachment. Morocco is all about the details—intricately carved tiles, a graceful stucco archway, perfect pyramids of spices in the souk, a smile on a young girl's face, Arabic calligraphy on a marble stone. If you don't have a zoom lens and don't want to invest in one, don't bring a camera and buy one of the books I recommend in the *Le Kiosque—Maroc Bibliothèque* instead.

Pieds Noirs

Pieds noirs (black feet) is a term you will run across frequently in readings on North Africa. It is an expression the Arabs used to describe French soldiers landing in North Africa wearing clunky black military boots. This attire may seem unremarkable, but in paintings by Delacroix, who was in Morocco in the 1830s with a French delegation, all the North Africans depicted seem to be wearing sandals or *babouche*-type footwear, so big black boots must have seemed a novelty. The immigrants who came in the wake of the soldiers were not exclusively French: Italians came (and mostly settled in Tunisia), Spaniards came (and mostly settled in northern Morocco and western Algeria), and nonmilitary French men and women came and spread out across all three countries. "The result," notes Aline Benayoun in the introduction to her book *Casablanca Cuisine,* "was the creation, out of this melting pot, of a new breed of Frenchman—the *pied noir*—a Frenchman who, in many cases, had never been to France." Sephardic Jews, originally from Spain and Portugal, also called North Africa home, with the largest communities in Fez, Marrakesh, and Mogador (now known as Essaouira). As the Jews in Morocco had long been protected and separated from the Muslim society in which they coexisted, they felt a natural affinity with the European immigrants. Remaining in Morocco after independence didn't necessarily mean certain death for the *pieds noirs,* but they were not made to feel welcome, so Benayoun and her family "returned" to France, which to her was hardly more than a place to visit on school holidays.

Pisé

Pisé is sun-dried earth, often mixed with lime or straw, used in building kasbahs and *ksours* in the south of Morocco, in the countryside bordering the Sahara. Its closest equivalent is adobe, common in the southwestern United States.

Piste

An Arabic word designating an old caravan trail from the south.

Les Plages (Beaches)

Bordering both the Atlantic and the Mediterranean, Morocco has miles and miles of coastline, and in theory, beach lovers should have no difficulty in finding a nice spot to greet the sea. But due to pollution in some areas, rocky shores in others, and a culture that doesn't hold beach frolicking in skimpy attire as an admirable pastime, beaches are not a reason to visit Morocco. I do not mean to imply that *some* of the country's beaches are less than magnificent, or that the pleasures of beach towns such as Essaouira are anything but fabulous; but I do not feel the beaches of the north Atlantic are anything to write home about—and certainly should be avoided in July, August, and early September, when Moroccans working abroad crowd the resorts for their annual four-to-six-week holiday. Although the Mediterranean is no longer the healthy and bountiful sea it once was, it is still gorgeous, and the beaches here are a little less crowded and, correspondingly, a little less developed.

Polisario

Polisario is an acronym for the Popular Front for the Liberation of Saquia el Hamra and Rio de Oro, which are the Spanish names for the two regions of the Western Sahara (formerly known as Spanish Sahara). The front was formed in 1968 and is based in Tindouf, just over the Algerian border. Like most conflicts, it is complicated, but here is a very basic explanation. Shortly after Franco's death in 1975, the Spanish decided they were no longer interested in maintaining a presence in that part of Morocco. (They have remained in northeastern Morocco, notably in Ceuta and Melilla; in fact, the sovereign communities of Spain maintain Spanish telephone codes, so if you're in Morocco and want to call Ceuta, you must dial the number as if it were an international call.) Spain had initially been interested in the Western Sahara in the late 1800s, when it was looking for a security base for the Canary Islands. But other than being phosphate-rich, the area doesn't offer much in the way of attributes. So when Spain announced it wanted to leave, Morocco and Mauretania both claimed sovereignty over the region, and Algeria—for reasons not entirely clear to me, other than to be a bully—announced it must be a part of any negotiations. King Hassan II then organized the famous Marche Verte (Green March), where 350,000 Moroccan civilians walked to Spanish Sahara in support of incorporating the Western Sahara into Morocco. Hassan then shrewdly made sure to fill up the region with settlers loyal to him and the cause, and for years he poured money into schools and housing there. Spain then swiftly got out and ceded the northern two-thirds of the Western Sahara to Morocco and the southern one-third to Mauretania, and it let the Algerians know in no uncertain terms that they had no proper role in the affair. Mauretania then decided that it didn't really want the land after all, but the Polisario (Algerian-backed Muslim guerrillas) decided the fight had only just begun. The Polisario wants to create a separate state for the native Saharans, to be called The Saharan Arab Democratic Republic. It appealed to The Arab League for help, but the league decided it wanted nothing to do with the conflict, conveniently referring to it as an "African" problem and therefore outside the realm of its interests. The Organization of African Unity admitted the Polisario as a member in 1982, and Morocco promptly rescinded its own membership. Since then there have been numerous proposals for an internationally supervised referendum, but it has yet to be scheduled. King Hassan II used to say that there are only two things that aren't negotiable: the flag and the stamp.

Politesse (Politeness)

A few words from the Fodor's guide bear repeating: "Everyone is polite in Morocco, even to their sworn enemies. Moroccans shake hands with each other every time they meet. Nothing can happen without politeness: if you have a problem and you lose your temper you give up hope of solving it. A combination of courtesy and persistence is the best approach. Open transactions with the proper greetings before getting down to business, and remember that people come first; the actions to be accomplished are secondary." Likewise, as stated in the Rough Guide, "If you want to get the most from a trip to Morocco, it is vital not to start assuming anyone who approaches or talks to you is a hustler. Too many tourists do, and end making little contact with what must be one of the most hospitable peoples in the world." It's important to keep in mind that Moroccans also do not always say what they mean. This is perhaps not entirely unique to Moroccans; ask directions of an Italian and, eager to help you out, he or she will point any which way regardless of whether he or she has any idea where you're going. However, the concept of duality *is* unique to Moroccans, and is explained well in this passage from Orin Hargraves's Culture Shock! guide: "Moroccans live with contrasts in every sphere of life, and they have a very high tolerance for dualities of all kinds. Consistency of behavior is very much context-driven, and contexts change a lot in Morocco. Moroccans are thus quite masterful at adapting to different contexts, even those which are polar opposites. Hand in hand with this ability comes a talent for reconciling conflicts, for finding a happy medium between the diverse forces and ideas that influence them. In a culture as rich in contrast as Morocco's, this is not only an admirable trait, it is a survival skill."

Public Life Versus Private Life

The difference between public and private life in Morocco is an essential concept that extends to other Arab countries as well. The two lives oppose each other to the strongest degree, representing one of the greatest contrasts you'll ever encounter. In a tiny nutshell, public life refers to how one acts and behaves in the street, while private life refers to the home. It may seem paradoxical that Arabs, who are famous for their hospitality, behave in a way we in the West consider to be quite rude in the streets of their own cities. According to Orin Hargraves, author of the *Culture Shock! Morocco* guide, "In Morocco, the street is the street. It belongs to no one and to everyone. Without the matrix of family relationships, or those between guest and host that prevail in the home, there is virtually no protocol for the street. People fend for themselves." Conversely, private life is extremely private, far more so than we define it in the West. This public/private concept extends to the architecture of Morocco's medinas. If you are not staying in a *dar* or *riyad* in a medina, this may not be immediately apparent; but a key feature of the architecture of a medina is that residential facades look alike and are typically unassuming. Passersby never know what wealth or poverty lies behind each door; indeed, the rich live side by side with the poor in Morocco's medinas. The Marrakesh medina is the best one for observing this, probably because it has the greatest number of *dars* and *riyads,* and visitors will quickly see that there are few windows at street level (and if there are any, they are covered). Even in the Gueliz neighborhood, outside the center of Marrakesh, private homes are hidden behind high walls with flowering plants cascading over them, revealing nothing of the spaciousness or beauty within. With all this in mind, you may understand better how fortunate you would be to receive an invitation to a Moroccan home. A private home is the only place where everyone, women included, can truly be themselves.

R

Riad or Riyad

A *riad* (plural *roud*) is, like a *dar,* a type of Moroccan house, usually belonging to a fairly wealthy family. A *riad* can be described as any type of house whose central space contains trees, and like a *dar,* it is open to the sky and also usually contains a fountain.

Ribat

This Arabic word refers to a fortresslike structure that was intended to shelter soldiers (and other defenders of the faith) at the time of any holy war. The structure had not only simple quarters for the soldiers but also a prayer room, meeting rooms, stores, and stables. A *ribat* was built along the Islamic border regions, where such wars were typically fought.

S

Sahara

In Arabic the word *sahara* means "emptiness" or "nothing." Appropriately, John Gunther's chapter on the desert in *Inside Africa* is entitled "Inside Nowhere—the Sahara." Though the Sahara cuts across only a small portion of Morocco, it is approximately the size of the entire United States, and it has shaped the history of Morocco in many ways. It pays to know something about its contradictions and beauty. Gunther noted that "I had always been told that the Sahara was notable for being flat, hot, and full of sand. Around Tamanrasset it is about as flat as Switzerland and, in winter, cold as a cadaver. As for sand, it was several days before we found any, but when we did there was plenty." Paul Bowles, in *Their Heads Are Green and Their Hands Are Blue,* wrote, "You leave the gate of the fort or the town behind, pass the camels lying outside, go up into the dunes, or out onto the hard, stony plain and stand awhile, alone. Presently, you will either shiver and hurry back inside the walls, or you will go on standing there and let something very peculiar happen to you, something that everyone who lives there has undergone and which the French call *le baptême de la solitude.* It is a unique sensation, and it has nothing to do with loneliness, for loneliness presupposes memory. Here, in this wholly mineral landscape lighted by stars like flares, even memory disappears; nothing is left but your own breathing and the sound of your heart beating. A strange, and by no means pleasant, process of reintegration begins inside you, and you have the choice of fighting against it, and insisting on remaining the person you have always been, or letting it take its course. For no one who has stayed in the Sahara for a while is quite the same as when he came." I think, however, that the best writing on the desert is by William Langewiesche, author of one of my favorite books, *Sahara Unveiled* (Pantheon, 1996, hardcover; Vintage, 1997, paperback). "There is no place," writes Langewiesche, "as dry and hot and hostile. There are few places as huge and as wild." He opened my eyes to many realities about the Sahara, among them that we should not view the desert "simply as some faraway place of little rain. There are many forms of thirst." I don't know about you, but I had always believed that human beings lived on the *edges* of the Sahara, not actually *within* it. I once thought it would be groovy to cross the Sahara by camel caravan, but now I'm not at all sure. There is, remarkably, something called the Trans-Saharan, which, according to Langewiesche, "is shown on maps in bold ink, as if it were an established highway. You might expect gas stations and the occasional motel. But the maps reflect ambitions that have never been realized. A road from north to south across the Sahara would have to cross 2,000 miles of the most tormented land on earth, conquering drought and flash flood, canyon and mountain, salt, sand, mud, rock, and war. And then it would have to be maintained." I will never think about the Sahara the same way again, and I loved this book. I think you will, too.

Sidi Ali and Sidi Harazem

These are the two most popular brands of bottled water in Morocco. Connoisseurs can tell the difference between them; I cannot, and because Sidi Ali rolls off the tongue more easily, it's my water of choice.

Single Travelers

Those traveling alone (not necessarily looking for romance) might be interested in reading *Traveling Solo: Advice and Ideas for More Than 250 Great Vacations* (Eleanor Berman, Globe Pequot Press, Old Saybrook, Connecticut, 1997). Berman offers the names of tour operators for different age groups and different types of trips and asks all the right questions in determining if a proposed vacation is right for you. ~Female *and* male solo travelers should beware of revealing too many personal details about your travels. If you admit that you're traveling for an indefinite period of time, for example, the perception is that you are probably carrying a lot of money. I met an Australian man who had the bulk of his money stolen from a youth hostel safe, and he was certain it was taken by a fellow hosteler he had befriended, but who had disappeared by the time the discovery was made. ~A few Internet sites that assist single travelers in finding a compatible travel mate are www.travelchums.com; www.whytravelalone.com; and www.cstn.org. (This last is the site for Connecting: Solo Travel Network.)

Le Soleil (The Sun)

The sun is legendary, of course, in the Sahara and the southern half of Morocco, but it is also strong around the Mediterranean, in winter as well as summer. Even if you will not be partaking in hiking, biking, or sunbathing at the beach, bring some protective lotion and use it—liberally. Many people do not realize that for sunscreen to work, you have to apply it copiously, about thirty minutes *before* you go into the sun. Some doctors recommend applying sunscreen even if you're just running errands around town; this would apply to sight-seeing and visiting outdoor markets as well. Women who wear makeup should consider selecting a brand with UV (ultraviolet) protection, and *everyone* should note that by *not* using protective lotion, you are exposing your skin to a lot of irreversible damage, even if you don't develop a sunburn. According to recent reports, skin cancer rates are on the rise around the world, not to mention that overexposure to the sun is dangerous to your eyes, potentially causing the development of cataracts. Lotions with the ingredient known as Parsol 1789 (avobenzone) have recently been touted as offering the best UV protection on the market. But my searches have not revealed many sunscreens that have it, and I admit that on the three occasions I used one with Parsol, I developed a red bumpy rash. (Other people I know did not.) It's probably more important to be vigilant with whatever product you use and mindful of the benefits of wearing a hat and good sunglasses. Remember: there is no such thing as a healthy tan, and according to the Skin Cancer Foundation, more than 80 percent of lifetime sun exposure happens before the age of eighteen. Log on to www.skincancer.org for more information.

Souks and Marchés (markets)

Souks and *marchés* are synonyms, though it is generally understood that a souk (usually partially or fully covered) is in the medina and a *marché* is in the *ville nouvelle*. They are one of the unrivaled pleasures of Morocco. Even if you have no intention of purchasing anything, you should not miss walking around at least one souk—it is an integral part of Moroccan life. A visit to the market should not be an activity you try and do in a hurry. (See the entry for Bargaining.) Take your time, remember to stop for something to eat or drink so your stomach (or companion) doesn't grumble, and enjoy searching for a unique souvenir or soaking up the atmosphere.

Stendhal Syndrome

Named for the sick, physical feeling which afflicted French novelist Stendhal after he visited Santa Croce in Florence, this syndrome is synonymous with being completely overwhelmed by your surroundings (my translation: seeing and doing way too much). Visitors to Morocco who arrive with too long a list of must-sees are prime candidates for the syndrome. My advice is to organize your days, factor in how long it takes to get from place to place, and see only what you want. Go forth with confidence, feel good about the way your spend your days, and do not feel guilty about missing a particular site or event. There will be no quiz.

Storage

If you plan on traveling around Morocco (or beyond) for extended periods of time (say, a month or longer) and want to store some baggage or other belongings, you should first investigate the facilities (*consigne automatique*) at ONCF train stations. A locker at one of the stations may prove to be the ideal storage location if you'll be traveling on by train anyway. However, only locked luggage is accepted, not backpacks. Otherwise, check with the tourist office and ask for recommendations of storage companies.

Studying in Morocco

There aren't a great many American colleges and universities that have reciprocal schools or exchange programs in Morocco, but a good guide to get to find out what's available is the *Directory of French Schools and Universities* (Michael Giammarella, EMI International, P.O. Box 640713, Oakland Gardens, New York 11364-0713; 718-631-0096; fax: -0316). This annual guide ($19.95 plus $3.00 for first-class shipping) details a wide variety of programs, not just language, at schools in the broader Francophone world, including Morocco, Quebec, Switzerland, and the Caribbean. Giammarella handles the bookings for the programs and also publishes directories for Spain and Italy. ~Though I didn't find anything in Morocco when I searched, things change all the time, so interested readers should check in with www.collegeclub.com under the Study Abroad field. ~A company called Gateway2 Morocco (www.gateway2morocco.com) specializes in tour services to students (and corporations, organizations, and individuals) and might very well be a good resource for study opportunities. ~The Moroccan Tourist Offices here in the States may be able to refer you to language and cultural programs in Morocco—and not just for twenty-somethings. ~Don't forget about the Peace Corps if you're in a position to make a two-year commitment. I met several Americans who were working for the Peace Corps in Morocco teaching English, and there are other Peace Corps projects as well.

T

Telephones

Morocco is five hours ahead of Eastern Standard Time, six ahead of Central Time, seven ahead of Mountain Time, and eight hours ahead of Pacific Standard. Morocco observes Greenwich Mean Time year round, so that in the summer, when the United States, the United Kingdom, and continental Europe are observing daylight savings time, Morocco is four hours ahead of Eastern Standard Time, one hour behind the U.K., and two hours behind continental Europe. All of this means that if you're flying via London, and it isn't summer, you're already on the same time; if you're flying via Paris or another city on the continent, remember that Morocco is one hour behind. To call Morocco from the United States, dial 011 + 212 + eight-digit local number. (011 is the overseas line, 212 is the country code for Morocco, and the local number includes the appropriate provincial and/or city code.) The local city code for Casablanca is 02, Fez and Meknes are 05, Laayoune and Agadir are 08, Marrakesh and Safi are 04, Oujda and Sefrou are 06, Rabat, Sale, and Kenitra are 07, and Tangier and Tetouan are 09. Note that when calling any city or town in Morocco from the United States, you omit the initial 0 from the local number. When dialing a number within Morocco, you must include the 0. All the phone numbers in this book include the 0 because travelers may want to place calls after they've arrived in Morocco. Double- and triple-check Moroccan phone and fax numbers: the entire telephone system has been completely renovated over the last few years, and even guidebooks dated 2001 do not all have the correct (expanded) numbers. The first way to tell if a number you have is potentially correct is to see if it has eight digits after the 212 country code. Fewer than eight digits means the number is old, and probably a digit needs to be added to the city/provincial code. But in other cases, the entire number may simply be wrong. (This applies even to major hotel and restaurant establishments.) As Barnaby

Rogerson notes in his Cadogan Guide, "In practice, Moroccan telephone numbers are constantly being changed [and] there is no authoritative listing of numbers in any part of the country." As in France, phone numbers are given as a series of three two-digit numbers, so while we offer our phone numbers as individual single digits, a Moroccan phone number of, for example, 48.99.65, would be given as forty-eight, ninety-nine, sixty-five. To call the United States from Morocco, dial 00 + 1 + area code + number. To dial Canada, dial 00 + 1 + number. To reach directory assistance, dial 16 from anywhere in Morocco—operators all speak French, and some will speak English. In an emergency (the equivalent of 911 in the United States), dial 113.

~Everyone knows that making calls from a hotel room is an expensive venture. Even if some hotels don't exactly gouge you, all of them charge significantly more than it would cost for you to place the call by any other method. AT&T, Sprint, and MCI all offer access numbers that automatically connect you with a U.S. dial tone. (Hotels still usually charge you for even this, but at least they can't charge you for the length of the call.) You enter the number you're calling, followed by your personal ID number, and the call is then billed to your home address and appears on your regular phone bill. These access numbers can be obtained by calling the companies directly or viewing their websites. (AT&T is at 800-CALL-ATT; www.att.com; Sprint is at 800-877-4646; www.sprint.com; and MCI is at 800-444-3333; www.mci.com.) Frequent international business travelers (and those with family or friends overseas) may want to investigate other options offered by Sprint, MCI, and other long-distance services; some monthly plans offer low rates that are appealing to those who regularly make overseas calls. ~The best and most affordable way to make a call, local or long distance—short of having someone call you at your hotel—is to do what the Moroccans do: buy a *télécarte* (phone card) and place the call yourself. (You can also use a *télécarte* to connect with an AT&T operator.) Just as in France, the majority of public telephones no longer accept coins or *jetons,* and *télécartes* are definitely the wave of the future. They're available in three denominations—20, 40, and 100 units—and can be purchased at shops, newsstands, train and bus stations, or the post office, as well as at *téléboutiques,* where you also go to make your calls. *Téléboutiques* are practically everywhere in Morocco, but for international calls, you can also go to the main branches of the PTT (Poste, Telephone, Telegraphique, now mostly known as La Poste), where you give an attendant the number and then wait for your turn in an individual cabin. You pay after you make the call. Some of the larger PTT branches in the country also have rows of international phone booths outside, where, with a *télécarte,* you can dial the number direct. Note that although the international phone room of a PTT may keep longer hours than the regular post office, it will always be closed on a holiday. The only catch with *télécartes* is that if you have units remaining on the card, you can't get reimbursed, so try to purchase the *carte* you're sure you'll use. ~Useful vocabulary: *annuaire* (telephone directory); *un coup de téléphone* (a telephone call); *ne quittez pas* (hold on, don't hang up); *téléphoner en PCV* (reverse-charge or collect call).

Thé à la Menthe

Mint tea is the national drink, jokingly called the "whiskey of Morocco." It is so ubiquitous that one might assume tea had been around forever in Morocco, but in fact it was introduced to the country only in 1854 when, due to the Crimean War, the British were casting about for new ports of call for their goods. Happily, the Moroccans liked it and added their personal touch (of fresh mint and lots of sugar), allowing us all to share in the pleasure of drinking it. Robert Carrier, in *Taste of Morocco,* notes, "It has been said that Morocco is a land that yields its meaning only to those who are able to take the time to draw water and make a pot of tea," a statement that is utterly, positively true. It's considered polite to drink at least three glasses before taking your leave, and it's correct to drink it at *any* time of day—before a meal, after a meal, and anytime in between; *thé à la menthe* is also an excellent digestive. Served properly, *thé à la menthe* arrives at your table in a teapot with a small tea glass and some sugar cubes. Sugar should already have been added to the pot, but you'll have to taste it to see. Moroccans take their tea quite sweet, but you can add as much or as little sugar as you like. At lesser establishments, the tea arrives in an individual tea glass, with a fistful of mint in it. This is never as good as it is in a teapot, but you'll have to accept it. If you like it as much as I do and want to try making it at home, you'll find recipes in most of the cookbooks (and some guidebooks) recommended in the *Saveurs et Tables Marocains Bibliothèque.* They are all nearly identical, and all are quite sweet. The two most important points to remember are: you must use very fresh mint, and you must put the sugar directly into the teapot (this according to Aline Benayoun, author of *Casablanca Cuisine*). Not for nothing is *thé à la menthe* referred to as "a gift of Allah."

Theft

Whether of the pickpocket variety or something more serious, theft can happen anywhere, in a fine neighborhood, at a souk, in a park, on a street corner. Morocco, especially Tangier, has had a reputation for petty theft over the years, but I think some of it is undeserved and exaggerated, and it's been my experience that alert travelers who wander about with their valuables hidden are not attractive to potential thieves. It bears repeating not to wear a waist pack, which is nothing but a neon magnet for a dishonest person who is sizing up opportunities. (Note to women readers: I've had the best success with interior money belts worn around my waist, but they work best when I'm wearing skirts. Underneath pants, unless the pants are jeans, the belt is often too revealing and lumpy, making one look as ridiculous as wearing a fanny pack. The same with pouches that hang around my neck: with certain types of shirts, they're fine, but with others, they're too obvious and funny-looking. As my husband had such success with the leg money belt, I think I will try that next time.) A lot of incidents could so easily have been avoided. In 1998 I read a lengthy piece in the travel section of *The Philadelphia Inquirer* about a husband and wife traveling in France whose pouch, with all their valuables in it, was stolen. What made this story remarkable was that they were shocked that the pouch was stolen. *I* was shocked reading their tale because they seemed to think it was a good idea to *strap their pouch under the driver's seat of their rental car*. This couple had apparently traveled all over Europe and North America every year for twelve years, so they weren't exactly novices. I think it's a miracle that they hadn't been robbed earlier.

Some pointers: ~Do not leave your passport, money, credit cards, important documents, or expensive camera equipment in your room. (Yes, American passports are still very much a hot commodity.) The hotel safe? If the letters I read are any indication, leaving your belongings in a hotel safe—whether in your room or in the main office—is only slightly more reliable than leaving them out in plain view. Sometimes I hear that valuable jewelry was taken from a hotel safe, which I find baffling, as there really is only one safe place for valuable jewelry: your home. No occasion, meeting, or celebration, no matter how important or festive, requires bringing valuable jewelry. I happen to also find it offensive to display such wealth. ~If possible, don't keep everything of value in the same place, and keep a separate piece of paper with telephone numbers of companies to contact in case of emergency. ~Rental cars are easily identified by their license plates and other markings that may not be so obvious to you and me but signify pay dirt to thieves. Do not leave anything, anything at all, in the car, even if you're parking it in a secure garage. My husband and I strictly follow one rule when we rent a car, which is that we never even put items in the trunk unless we're immediately getting in the car and driving away, as anyone watching us will then know there's something of value there. Also, hatchback-type cars are good to rent because you can back into a spot against a wall or tree, making it impossible to open the trunk.

~Pickpockets employ a number of tactics to prey on unaware travelers. Even if you travel often, live in a big city, and think you're savvy, professional thieves can usually pick you out immediately. (They'll also identify you as American if you're wearing the trademark sneakers and fanny pack.) Beware the breast-feeding mother who begs you for money (while her other children surround you looking for a way into your pockets), the arguing couple who make a scene (while their accomplices work the crowd of onlookers), the tap on your shoulder at the baggage security checkpoint (when you turn around, someone's made off with your bags after they've passed through the X-ray machine)—anything at all that looks or feels like a setup. For a look at some common tricks, you might want to see *Traveler Beware!,* a video directed by a seventeen-year undercover cop, Kevin Coffey. This is a real eye-opening program with all the scams used to target business and holiday travelers. Coffey was founder of the Airport Crimes Detail and investigated literally thousands of crimes against tourists. He's been a guest on *The Oprah Show* and *20/20* and has been featured in *The Wall Street Journal* and *USA Today.* The seventy-minute cassette is available from Penton Overseas (800-748-5804; e-mail: info@pentonoverseas.com) and costs $14.95. ~If, despite your best efforts, your valuables are stolen, go to the local police. You'll have to fill out an official police report, but this is what helps later when you need to prove you were really robbed, and reporting thefts to the police alerts them that there is a persistent problem. You will also need to call your credit card companies (which is why you have written down these numbers in a separate place), make a trip to the American Express office if you've purchased traveler's checks, and go to the U.S. embassy to replace your passport.

Tipping

Tipping in Morocco is not the mystery some people perceive it to be. First of all, most restaurants and hotels include the service charge (*service compris*) and tax in the bill. But it is customary to leave a little extra for waiters—about 10 percent of the total bill—and they will usually work hard to receive it. At cafés, leave one to two *dirhams* per person for the waiter. Male travelers who join the local Moroccan men at a bar should leave an additional one or two *dirhams,* just as at a café. Male or female visitors who are having a drink at a fancy hotel bar should leave two or three *dirhams,* and if you end up in a deep conversation about vintages or fine spirits with the bartender, it is proper to leave more, about three to four *dirhams* extra. At Morocco's palace restaurants, wine is typically included in the *prix-fixe* meal and is preselected, so an additional tip for whoever pours the wine isn't necessary; but if you're dining at another top-quality restaurant and the *sommelier* has chosen a special wine for you, it's considered appropriate to give him 10 percent of the price of the bottle. Generally speaking, if you receive exceptional service at any establishment, or are on a plan where you're taking all your meals at the hotel, or you simply want to return and be remembered, you should of course feel comfortable leaving a larger tip.

Other tipping guidelines: Taxi drivers—they are not usually tipped by locals, and if they are not using the meter, you can assume that the price you agree on leaves something left over for them. If they do use the meter, I like to add a *dirham* or two, depending on their friendliness, and because, as Barnaby Rogerson says, "I like to reward them for their honesty." ~Bathroom attendants—one or two *dirhams,* depending on the type of establishment and its cleanliness. Cloakroom attendants—one *dirham* per coat. Porters—five to ten *dirhams* per bag, depending on how heavy they are and how far the porter has to carry them. (I don't skimp on carrying bags, as it is one of the services I appreciate the most.) Parking attendants who watch your car—about two *dirhams* per hour, or about ten *dirhams* per day. (It's never a bad idea to negotiate the fee in advance.) Barbers and hairdressers— two or three *dirhams.* Movie ushers—one *dirham.* Museum attendants—two or three *dirhams.* Gas station attendants—two or three *dirhams.* Housekeeping services at a rented villa—a general guideline is 10 percent of the rental fee, but certainly if the staff is exceptional you should feel free to give more. Conversely, if a housekeeper is coming in for five hours a day and the cost of your rental is $10,000 a week, leaving 10 percent of the fee would be excessive. ~For any of the above estimates relating to hotels, double the amounts if you're in a very expensive place, on a par with, say, La Mamounia. ~Be prepared to tip by putting some small change in your pocket *in advance,* before you set out each day. I cannot overstate this. Until you are accustomed to it, it is remarkable how often you will be expected to tip. If you need coins, exchange some paper notes at the bank or your hotel. Don't be without any, however, as it is truly embarrassing to be empty-handed and not be prepared to give a little something that means so very much to the recipient. I recommend getting some money at the airport upon arrival in Morocco so you will have some coins in your pocket for the porter both at the airport and your hotel.

Toilets and Toilet Paper

Never set out each day without stuffing some toilet paper in your pockets or your bag. Public toilets—and even those in some of the nicest places—can be abominable and often do not have toilet paper, which is called *papier hygiénique* in French. I have always found good American-style toilet paper in the bathrooms at American Express offices, which are unfortunately usually located in the *villes nouvelles* and not the medinas, where you will likely spend most of your time. Nine times out of ten, the toilets you will encounter when you're out and about are of the squat variety, sometimes referred to as Turkish toilets. Though this topic is not the most pleasant of entries in this book, it is, in my opinion, perhaps the most important after that for health. None of the guidebooks I have read provided enough detail on toilet etiquette and what to expect, and so I am going to offer you some tips that I wish had been offered to me (forgive me in advance for any discomfort you may feel in reading this): first of all, there is no reason to fear squat toilets; in fact, relieving oneself in this fashion is actually healthier than our fashion of sitting on a toilet seat. However, handicapped visitors or anyone of any age who has difficulty squatting and standing up again will positively not be able to navigate a Turkish toilet, as there is nothing to hold on to. As I noted above, it is highly unlikely that you will find toilet paper inside individual stalls of squat toilets. This is also true in other Muslim countries, although I have run across single rolls of toilet paper on the floor occasionally in Turkey. At some establishments, you will enter the washroom and there will be a few rolls of toilet paper on a stool outside of the individual stalls. You may take from these rolls, but better, of course, is to use the paper you've remembered to bring along in your pocket, in case you need more than what you've taken from the roll. Inside some stalls, there will be a small faucet coming out of the wall, and sometimes there will be a small plastic bucket on the floor. The bucket is for toilet paper—do not put toilet paper in the toilet itself due to the country's poor plumbing facilities—and the faucet is for water with which to wash your left hand. This is actually a best-case scenario. In most cases, there is no bucket for the toilet paper, and you are faced with the dilemma of what to do with the paper. I have absolutely no idea what other people do with the paper, but I have a system whereby I always have a fat wad of toilet paper in one pocket and the other pocket is left empty for, you guessed it, my soiled toilet paper. I simply manage to neatly and cleanly fold the paper up, stick it in my pocket, and then remove it and deposit it in the trash basket in the washroom. (There usually is one, and for those times there is not, I just throw it out the next time I see one.) I no longer remember when I devised this system, but it seems to work reasonably well (I would welcome any of your suggestions, however, so please don't hold back if you have another method).

The next hurdle to overcome is that though there is a sink in most washrooms, most of the time with running water, there is rarely a towel of any kind with which to dry your hands, which is why I always carry those packaged towelettes (these are also handy in general, as Morocco can be quite dusty). And you'll also have your toilet paper. If there is a bathroom attendant, he or she will leave you in privacy and there will be a small dish set aside for you to place a few *dirhams*. When you walk out, the attendant quickly reappears to clean the stall and collect the coins.

You may sometimes encounter a type of Turkish toilet that actually flushes. Typically you pull down on a cord or chain, but remember not to flush your toilet paper down the drain. Some of these flushing varieties produce quite a wave, with the water coming up over the basin (and your feet). Guard against this possibility by not flushing until you're ready to step away, then flush as you simultaneously open the door of the stall.

I would like to add two final notes to female readers: if you can at all avoid visiting Morocco during the time you're menstruating, you will be happier and infinitely more comfortable. Additionally, I recently read, in the "It Came in the Mail" column of *The Washington Post* travel section, of an item called the TravelMate. I'm not necessarily endorsing it, and I haven't tried it, but it's a "discreet, mobile 'toilet' that lets a woman relieve herself like a man." I'm not making this up. Use your imagination. It's supposedly aimed at "Turkish toilet phobics," so if you're one of those, you can find out more by visiting www.travelmateinfo.com.

Tourist (as in, Being One)

Whether you travel often for business or are making a trip for the first time, let's face it: we're all tourists, and there's nothing shameful about that fact. Yes, it's true that one feels a real part of *la vie quotidienne* when you blend in and are mistaken for a native; but since that's not likely to happen unless you live there, it's far better just to get on with it and have a good time. Most likely, you'll stick out like a sore thumb anyway in Morocco, so why try to be something you're not? Do your best to respect the customs of the country, smile a lot, try speaking some local greetings and words, and relax.

Tourist Office (Moroccan National Tourist Office)

I cannot stress enough how helpful it is to contact the Moroccan National Tourist Office as soon as you learn you're going to Morocco. Think of it as the ultimate resource: all the information you need is there, or the staff will know how to direct you elsewhere. At the New York office, I have never stumped anyone with my questions or requests, and I think readers have observed that I ask a lot of questions about a lot of little details. A word of advice for dealing with tourist offices in general: it is not very helpful to say you're going to Morocco and would like "some information." Allow the staff to help you by providing them with as many details about your visit as you can: Is it your first trip? Do you need information only about hotels? Are you looking for tour operators? In my experience, the Moroccan tourist offices do not have quite as much printed information as the French or Italian tourist offices, for example, but the staff members are walking fountains of information and can help you greatly if you let them. If it is your first trip to Morocco, you may simply want to request the Morocco Pocket Guide, a road map (it's a pretty good one), a mileage chart, the ONCF schedule, a schedule of the main souks of Morocco, a ferry schedule from Algeciras to Tangier if you are coming from Spain, and individual color brochures on destinations you think you'd like to visit. These large brochures are quite beautiful, and though they don't contain much practical information, they are very enticing and feature quite good color maps on the back page. There are three tourist offices in North America: 2001 rue Université, Suite 1460, Montreal, Canada; 514-842-8111; fax: -5316; 20 East 46th Street, Suite 1201, New York, New York; 212-557-2520; fax: 949-8148; and ONMT, P.O. Box 2263, Lake Buena Vista, Florida 32830; 407-827-5337 or 827-5335; fax: -5129.

There are about twenty-five tourist offices throughout Morocco, and the staffs there are happy to help visitors in any way they can—no request is too unusual.

It may not be immediately apparent, but the resources and contacts these local and regional offices have are vast in number, yet probably visitors do not often take advantage of the assistance these offices can provide. This may be in part because in the Imperial Cities, the tourist office is located in the *ville nouvelle,* and if one is staying in the medina, the fifteen or twenty minutes it takes to get to the *ville nouvelle* may seem not worth the effort. I do not view the distance as so great, but you should keep tourist offices in mind if you are looking for a reputable guide, need some questions answered, or are trying to form a group for a particular excursion.

Tours

A list of full-service tour companies offering trips to Morocco could fill a separate book, and it is not my intent to promote only one company or one type of trip. Frankly, while I do enthusiastically recommend the organizations listed below, I'm bothered by the fact that too many of them focus on luxury meals and accommodations. I believe there are a great number of people who are seeking the personalized service and knowledgeable guides these companies offer but do not need or desire five-star elegance every step of the way. Today, in the popular restored *roud* and *diour,* Morocco has a number of distinctive, moderately priced lodgings that individuals can arrange for themselves, and as the country does not have an overwhelming number of restaurants, there aren't many well-kept secrets that determined travelers could not learn about on their own. So I often wonder if the luxury-oriented companies aren't missing the boat in reaching even more clients. That said, the combination of experience, insider's knowledge, and savvy guides that these companies offer is most definitely not found by searching the Web, and organizing trips like these requires a substantial amount of research and attention to detail, which some travelers do not always have the time or inclination to do (and for which they are willing to pay a great deal). Also, organized package tours now offer travelers more free time than in years past, as well as more choice in meals and excursions. If you do decide to join a tour, be prepared for the possibility of encountering some "unpleasant co-adventurers," in the words of Jey Burrows, a fellow passionate about Morocco who maintains an excellent website for visitors (see entry for websites). Burrows notes that "there is a type of tourist who does not wish to see Africa, but to *have seen* Africa, the experience of the trip being merely a tedious formality in order to collect brag-points and photographs for those back home—those who have been unfortunate to spend a few weeks with such virtual tourists have reported it an excruciatingly frustrating and irritating experience. However, it is practically unheard of for such sad human beings to buy a *Rough Guide,* stuff a ruck-sack, take some buses or even hire a Renault 4, this being the guarantee of avoiding them." Following are some companies that appealed to me and offer an authentic experience:

Amelia International (176 Woodbury Road, Hicksville, New York 11801; 800-742-4591; www.ameliainternational.com). "The Connoisseur's Mediterranean" is Amelia's slogan, and it offers distinctive trips to Morocco and most of the Mediterranean. Amelia arranges escorted bus tours, culinary holidays, and Sahara adventures, as well as trips for independent travelers.

Archaeological Tours (271 Madison Avenue, Suite 904, New York, New York 10016; 212-986-054; e-mail: archtours@aol.com). This quality company has been offering expert-led trips around the world for twenty-eight years. Each tour features distinguished scholars who emphasize the historical, anthropological, and archaeological aspects of the areas visited, and the Morocco trip is no exception. It's one of my favorite trips listed here, both for the fifteen-day duration and for the credentials of the scholar, who holds an M.A. and Ph.D. and is a specialist on the Islamic Middle Ages and whose research focuses on Islam, North Africa, architecture, and archaeology. The tour begins in Casablanca and continues to Rabat, Meknes, Fez, Erfoud, Tinerhir, Zagora, Ouarzazate, and Marrakesh. As the company explains, the word *scholar* should not be intimidating: "All our lecturers are carefully selected not only for qualities of scholarly excellence, but for their ability to communicate their willingness to share the experience of discovery. We believe that our tours should be both memorable and joyful." This trip is pricey, but I'm not sure it could be improved upon, except by making it longer!

The Best of Morocco (Seend Park, High Street, Seend, Melksham, Wilts, SN12 6NZ, England; 011.44.1380.828533 / fax: .828630; www.morocco-travel.com). If anyone is an expert on Morocco, it's the folks at Best of Morocco. I read so many superlative statements about this company that I had to find out for myself if they were truly true, and I'm happy to say they are. "Best of" has been managed by Chris Lawrence since 1967, and his son Max holds down the fort full time in Marrakesh, a clear sign of its seriousness. As Chris says in the brochure, "We are very passionate about Morocco and try to urge potential visitors to share and enjoy our sense of adventure and creativity. When I first started arranging holidays, most of our clients were traveling to Morocco for the first time, and it became a destination that people visited perhaps once every four or five years. I am now pleased to say that it is not uncommon for many of our clients to visit Morocco every year and in some cases twice a year." "Best of" is widely considered to be one of the leading specialist tour operators to Morocco.

Breakaway Adventures (1312 18th Street N.W., Suite 401, Washington, D.C. 20036; 800-567-6286; 202-293-2974 / fax: -0483; www.breakaway-adventures.com). Breakaway offers a variety of walking, cycling, and trekking journeys around the world. Within the Mediterranean region, it offers five different trips within Morocco, including to Jbel Toubkal, Jbel Sahro in the Dades Valley, Mgoun Massif in the High Atlas, a combination of the Sahara and the Atlas Mountains, and one to the Atlas Mountains alone. Groups are small, none of the walking is strenuous, and the staff is willing to adapt the itineraries depending on how people are reacting to the temperature and altitude.

Butterfield & Robinson (70 Bond Street, Toronto, Ontario, Canada M5B 1X3; 800-678-1147 or 416-864-1354; fax: -0541; www.butterfield.com). B&R is the leader in luxury active travel around the world, specializing in biking and walking, and it offers about ninety-five trips on six continents. A few lines from its beautiful catalog sum up the B&R philosophy: "We love exploring new places. We think biking and walking are the best way to see a region's people, history and culture. And at the end of each day, we like to treat ourselves well with a great meal and a great hotel. So that's what B&R does." For Morocco, it offers three biking trips, one walking trip, and two bike-and-walk trips to choose from.

Country Walkers (P.O. Box 180, Waterbury, Vermont 05676; 800-464-9255 or 802-244-1387; fax: -5661; www.countrywalkers.com). This group—whose motto is "Explore the world . . . one step at a time"—celebrates its twenty-second anniversary this year and believes that "to experience a region and its culture, you must see it at your own pace with a small group and a knowledgeable guide." "Medinas and Mountains" is the itinerary offered in Morocco, and the journey includes visits to Fez and Marrakesh; a sunrise Saharan camel trek; a tented desert camp; easy, moderate, and some challenging terrain averaging five to nine miles per day. "Each day," the group notes, "is an exotic feast for the senses," a phrase I think accurately describes Morocco.

Heritage Tours (216 West 18th Street, Suite 1001, New York, New York 10011; 800-378-4555 or 212-206-8400; fax: -9101; www.heritagetoursONLINE.com). Heritage has been one of the leading tour organizations to Morocco for many years. (It also specializes in travel to Spain, Turkey, and South Africa.) I like that Heritage grew out of the firsthand experience of Fulbright scholar, architect, and author Joel Zack, who has been working in Morocco in cultural tourism and historic preservation since 1985. As one of its (quite lovely) brochures states, "We are specialty travel professionals—and travelers ourselves—motivated by a profound understanding of and love for the countries we serve. The journey, we believe, is just as important as the destination." Zack is often asked what Spain, Turkey, and Morocco have in common and how he got into the business of organizing tours to these destinations. He replies, "Each of these countries, at a certain point in its history, developed a flourishing civilization based on a foundation of a constructive Jewish-Muslim coexistence (and in the case of Spain, Muslim-Christian-Jewish coexistence). A personal love for the history of the Jewish people and for the enthralling beauty of Moorish and Islamic civilization have bound me to these countries." Specializing in itineraries combining the legendary sites and the little-known, Heritage offers a variety of trips to all corners of the country, as well as Jewish Heritage tours and "adventure travel" tours.

Oussaden Tours (8 West 38th Street, 10th floor, New York, New York 10018;

800-206-5049 or 212-382-1436; fax: -3588; and Place de l'Atlas, 12 rue Omar Benjelloun, Appt. 21, Fez, V.N. 3000, Morocco; 05.93.03.70; fax: 05.93.04.21; www.morocco-oussaden-tours.com). Oussaden is one of the premier tour operators to Morocco, and is a family-owned-and-operated company. As its promotional material states, "We can guarantee you not only the best in quality, service, and price, but also the best in personal attention. We do not rely on strangers to handle our guests." Travelers can choose from one of ten different trips: Imperial Cities, Southern Cities, VIP Private, Trek Morocco, Golf Morocco, Jewish Heritage, A Taste of Morocco, Fez Festival, Sacred Music, and Morocco, Gibraltar, and Spain. Oussaden also arranges itineraries for independent travelers with a private guide.

Sarah Tours (1803 Belleview Boulevard, no. A-1, Alexandria, Virginia 22307; 703-765-5114; fax: -7809; e-mail: sarahtur@erols.com; www.morocco-fezfestival. com). Sarah is another well-respected company whose president, Hamid Mernissi, is gracious and passionate about his home country. The company's brochure is quite nice and details a dozen different itineraries to Morocco. (Sarah also arranges trips to Spain, but as I am not a fan of visiting both Spain and Morocco on the same trip unless one has a few months in which to do it, I focus only on Morocco here.) Sarah is perhaps best known for its annual trips to Fez for the World Sacred Music Festival, now in its seventh year. (Dates vary, but this festival is usually held in June or July.)

Smithsonian Study Tours (1100 Jefferson Drive S.W., Washington, D.C. 20560, 877-EDU-TOUR or 202-357-4700; www.SmithsonianStudyTours.org). This Smithsonian tour is one of my favorite Morocco tours because it includes the best all-around itinerary (except Essaouira, which doesn't seem to be included on anyone's tour). This trip begins in Casablanca and continues to Rabat-Sale, Tangier, Volubilis, Meknes, Fez, Erfoud, and Ouarzazate and then ends in Marrakesh. The study leaders—one has lived and studied in Morocco and specializes in politics, religion, and anthropology; the other is a frequent traveler to North Africa and specializes in the history of North Africa, Islamic civilization, and U.S. relations with the Middle East—are really what separate the Smithsonian's trips from others. Travelers are completely immersed in Moroccan life and receive a comprehensive introduction to Moroccan history, culture, and society through insightful lectures, specially arranged excursions, and private visits. This Morocco trip is pricey, but its combination of a great itinerary, excellent leaders, and high ratio of staff to participants make it a good value.

~If you do select a tour operator, ask a lot of questions so you get what you expect. For starters, ask if the operator employs its own staff or if it contracts with another company to run its trips. Remember, however, that standards differ around the world, and operators don't have control over every detail. For example, many beautiful old villas and inns do not have screens in the windows, and many first-class hotels don't have air conditioning. The price you pay for accommodations may not be the same as the posted rates, but you have to accept that you're paying for the convenience of someone else booking your trip. Tour operators also reserve the right to change itineraries, thus changing modes of transportation as well as hotels. If you have special needs, talk about them with the company in advance.

Travel Insurance

I have never purchased travel insurance because I have never determined that I need it, but it's worth considering if you think the risks to you are greater without it. Ask yourself what it would cost if you needed to cancel or interrupt your trip, and how expensive it would be to replace any stolen possessions. If you have a medical condition or if a relative is ill, insurance might be a wise investment. First, check to see if your existing health or homeowner's policies offer some protection, and if that protection is extended overseas. If you decide you need to purchase additional insurance, read all the fine print and make sure you understand it; compare deductibles; ask how your provider defines *preexisting condition,* and inquire if there are situations in which it would be waived; and check to see if the ceiling on medical expenses is adequate for your needs. *Emergency* medical insurance may be something to consider if you're planning on extended backpacking in the High Atlas or long stays in the Sahara, or if you have a medical condition that could quickly put you at serious risk. Elderly travelers may want to consider it in any event, and they should be aware that Medicare does not cover expenses incurred outside the United States.

W

Weather

Most people I meet think Morocco is hot as blazes year round, and they think nearly all of it is the Sahara. But aside from the desert and pre-desert areas, the weather in Morocco is not as hot as many people think it is. It is also colder than most people realize. Morocco's weather is defined by its four mountain ranges, the Rif, Middle Atlas, High Atlas, and Anti-Atlas; its position next to the Atlantic Ocean and the Mediterranean Sea; and its proximity to the Sahara in the bottom southeast corner. As with many countries around the Mediterranean, spring and fall are ideal times to visit Morocco. But picking the "perfect" time of year is subjective; when it's rainy and cold in Fez in February, airfares are great and the desert is warm. Summer is the time to hike in the High Atlas, as every other season of the year may mean closed passes and poor visibility. For skiing enthusiasts, winter is obviously the best time of year. Visitors may want to avoid traveling to Morocco during Ramadan, or at least make sure only part of their trip falls during this holiday, as most restaurants will be closed during the day, and it can be difficult to find something to eat outside of hotel restaurants. In general, go when you have the opportunity, and that will be your experience, your Morocco. It's true that peak season means higher prices and more people, but if you've determined you want to be in Fez for the music festival in June, then the cost and the crowds don't matter. If you're a weather maven, you'll love *Fodor's World Weather Guide* (E. A. Pierce and C. G. Smith, Fodor's Travel Publications, 1998; published in Great Britain as *The Hutchinson World Weather Guide, New Edition,* Helicon Publishing, Oxford). As frequent business or pleasure travelers know, average daily temperatures are only a small part of what you need to know about the weather. It is not helpful to know average monthly temperatures without also knowing the average number of rainy days. This guide features weather specifics for more than two hundred countries and territories and a map of the world's climate regions; humidity and wind chill charts; a centigrade and Fahrenheit conversion table; a rainfall conversion table; and a bibliography pointing interested readers to other sources.

Websites
Personally, I don't find there to be anything on the World Wide Web about Morocco that can compare with appropriate books or an especially helpful staff member at the tourist office. The Internet is only one resource among many—travelers who rely solely on it will be insufficiently informed indeed. But a few sites do offer some good features and are worth a browse:

www.arab.net/morocco—The arab.net site represents twenty-two countries of the Arab world. Click on the flag of the country you want to know about, then select a topic such as Government, History, Transport, Business, Culture, or Geography. Not all of the topics for Morocco are thorough, at least when I last checked: for "Transport," the page simply read, "Morocco has an outstanding network (59,198 km/36,786 miles) of paved roads which extend throughout the country, even into the Sahara." When I clicked on "Moroccan Pottery" under "Culture," however, a much more complete page came up. With patience, it's worth browsing.

www.geocities.com/TheTropics/4896/morocco.html—This is one of the best websites I've encountered, of any kind. The Rough Guide says the site "should be your first port of call," an assessment with which I wholeheartedly agree. A dedicated individual, Jey Burrows, has maintained the site—with input from travelers around the world—since 1992. An excellent "Frequently Asked Questions" section is particularly helpful and provides an opportunity for viewers to query Burrows directly about anything related to Morocco. I have found Burrows's suggestions for related books and music very comprehensive. His summaries of the Imperial Cities, though brief, are revealing. Burrows is a little too critical of the Rough Guide and Lonely Planet guidebooks—he remarks often on their information that is outdated or incorrect. (I think this is a bit unfair, as guidebooks are not meant to be perfect documents, and anyway that's what a website is good for: providing up-to-the-minute information.) But I believe he genuinely appreciates the value of quality guidebooks and related readings. There are lots of Web-wide links from this great resource.

www.jewishglobe.com/Morocco—This good Sephardic Morocco site gives you opportunities to click on "Synagogues," "Music" (you must subscribe to RealPlayer to hear the selections), "Culture," "Cooking," "Halacha," "Rabbanim," a Sephardic genealogy database, and more. *Les Affinités Recouvrées* (Recovered Affinities) is an animated, computerized video art project of three minutes down a street in Morocco, complete with music. The visual elements refer to historical sites and artifacts from both the Moroccan Jewish community and Islamic culture. Though it wasn't working quite right when I tried it, I encourage readers to open it up (it's under "Culture") because it's a great sensory trip. Viewers can also purchase Moroccan Sephardic Torah tapes and a variety of *hamsas,* or good-luck charms in the shape of a hand that are ubiquitous in Morocco, as they ward off evil for both Muslims and Jews.

www.maroc-hebdo.press.ma/—In French, this is the site for *Maroc Hebdo* (*hebdomadaire* meaning "weekly" in French), a newsmagazine strong on political and economic coverage. Viewers can subscribe on-line.

www.maroc.net/kiosque—*La Maison du Maroc* (The House of Morocco), this site—in English—features daily newsfeeds from a variety of sources, including *Le Matin du Sahara, Maroc Hebdo, Morocco Today, North Africa Journal,* and Radio Casablanca. Viewers can receive a weekly e-mail from the *North Africa Journal,* which, along with the *Maghreb Weekly Monitor,* has a U.S. office in Boston. (I am a subscriber and find the weekly missive interesting; the news is divided into two sections: economy, business, and industry; and politics and human relations and affairs. Most of the contents do not appear to be reported in the daily newspaper.) The site's archives are also available from September 1997. When I clicked on the "Books" box of *Morocco Today,* up popped the cover of *King Mohammed VI and Morocco Today* by H. B. Qounin, with the *Mission Impossible* theme playing in the background(?). The Radio Casablanca page is particularly great, as viewers can learn of current music and film personalities (and read reviews) as well as current periodicals, such as *Medina, Femmes du Maroc, Nissa Al Maghrib,* and *Maroc Business.*

www.mincom.gov.ma—This is one of the better sites, with information on the history of Morocco, the dynasties, important events, political parties and trade unions, handicrafts (did you know that the handicrafts sector holds a significant position in the Moroccan economy, second only to agriculture?), Moroccan music, and more. Definitely worth a browse.

www.morocco.com—This is a good site with home, business, community, travel, culture, news, sport, and shopping channels and Club Morocco, an international network of Morocco enthusiasts (users can select English or French dialogue). There are lots of links to other related sites—including Lonely Planet and a travel advisory from the U.S. State Department—as well as a dating board.

Wine

The vineyards in Morocco are all a legacy of the French, and though the majority of Moroccans do not drink the fruit of the vine, they have no conflict with producing and distributing it. In Jancis Robinson's seminal book *The Oxford Companion to Wine,* the entry on Morocco is less than a page. As she notes, "in 1990 more than 50 percent of Morocco's vines, many of them virused, were more than 30 years old (and therefore uneconomically unproductive)." There are actually five Appellation d'Origine Garantie (AOG) zones: the East, Meknes/Fez, Gharb, Rabat, and Casablanca. From what I have read, with a lot of work—and special attention to modernization, investment, and foreign expertise—Morocco has the potential to produce consistently good wines. Certainly the wines I've tasted have all been quite suitable partners for Moroccan food, and though none may stand out as stellar, more than a few were memorable. (A few were also, I admit, undrinkable.) Generally, the wines from the Meknes/Fez zone are held in highest regard, and Morocco's red wines are considered to be of finer quality than its whites. In light of this fact, I have to say that in my experience Moroccan white and rosé wines have been surprisingly good and were actually better, to my taste, than some established reds. Now, having said that, I need to emphasize that in warmer weather I tend to prefer lighter foods like chicken, fish, and vegetable dishes, all of which pair best with lighter wine. So I suppose it's no accident that the dry, crisp Moroccan whites I tried seemed so agreeable; still, they could easily have been dreadful. I encourage you to try a variety and decide for yourself. Some reputable rosés include Gris de Guerrouane, Gris de Boulaouane, and Oustalet; reputable whites include Valpierre blanc de blancs; and some reputable reds are Cabernet Président, Rabbi Jacob, and Guerrouane. Though I haven't yet had the chance to try them, the rosé, *vin rouge,* and chardonnay produced under a de Siroua/Martini & Rossi Maroc partnership would be worth tasting. As I noted in the entry for Alcohol, travelers will not have to make many detours to find a little shop or supermarket that sells alcohol, and in my experience they typically have a good selection of red, white, and rosé as well as kosher wines. On the other hand, bars, cafés, and restaurants that offer alcohol are nearly always located in the *villes nouvelles* of larger cities and towns as the medinas are typically alcohol-free.

Women Travelers

Whether traveling solo or not, lots of great advice is offered in *Travelers' Tales: Gutsy Women, Travel Tips, and Wisdom for the Road* (by Marybeth Bond, Travelers' Tales, San Francisco, 1996). This packable little book is filled with dozens of useful tips for women of all ages who want to travel or already travel a lot. Bond has traveled all over the world, much of it alone, and she shares advice from her own journeys as well as that of other female travelers. Chapters address safety and security; health and hygiene; romance and unwelcome advances; money, bargaining, and tipping; traveling solo; mother-daughter travel; travel with children, and more. ~The Women's Travel Club (800-480-4448; e-mail: Womantrip@aol.com; www.womenstravelclub.com) may also be of interest. Founded by Phyllis Stoller, this organization plans numerous domestic and international trips a year and guarantees everyone a roommate. Its great list of travel safety tips was featured on NBC's *Today* as well as in *Travel & Leisure* (August 1999). Membership is $35 a year, and members receive a newsletter.

Y

Yacoub El Mansour

Yacoub-el-Mansour's name means "Yacoub the victorious," and he is known firstly for continuing to spread Almohad rule throughout Spain in the late 1100s (the Almohads were the new "true believers" who were warring against the Almoravids) and secondly for his spectacular victory over Christian forces under Alfonso VIII of Castilla in 1195 at Alarcos. This was, however, a Pyrrhic victory since, according to Juan Lalaguna in *A Traveller's History of Spain*, "the Almohads could not follow it up and the terrified Christians from all over Europe came to the rescue, compounding their differences at least long enough to save Christian Spain from the clutches of the Almohads." He was described by Wharton as "the Victor of Alarcos, the soldier who subdued the north of Spain, dreamed a great dream of art. His ambition was to bestow on his three capitals, Seville, Rabat and Marrakesh, the three most beautiful towers the world had ever seen; and if the tower of Rabat had been completed, and that of Seville had not been injured by Spanish embellishments, his dream would have been realized."

Magic Carpets

BY SUZY GERSHMAN

~

editor's note

As I emphasized earlier, in Morocco bargaining, for just about everything, is an important aspect of life, whether as a visitor or a resident. There
are few people whose opinions on bargaining I trust more than Suzy
Gershman, to whom I often refer as the "queen of good value." In an interview with a reporter from *USA Today*, Gershman was asked, "What's the
best advice for successful bargaining?" Her reply: "Knowing the right price
that the item sells for is the key to successful bargaining. You can't know
that without having done that research in museums, seeing what locals are
paying for it by asking concierges and taxi drivers and people you run into.
Because the more foreign the country—if your skin is a different color, if you
don't speak the language—there's always going to be what I call a 'gringo
tax.' If you're an outsider and you could afford to get to that country, it's
open season on your purse. Sometimes 10 percent of the asking price is the
right price. It depends on understanding the local customs, the real value of
the merchandise, and then how to communicate with the merchant."

SUZY GERSHMAN, who lives in Paris, is the author of the popular and
indispensable Born to Shop Guides, published by Frommer's, as well as *Best
Dressed: The Born to Shop Lady's Secrets for Building a Wardrobe*
(Clarkson Potter, 1999). She worked as a correspondent for *Time* and has
contributed to a number of other magazines, including *Travel Holiday,
Luxe, McCall's,* and Neiman Marcus's *The Book*. Visitors to Paris may be
interested to know that the Hotel Meurice offers a custom shopping service
with Gershman (the fee is approximately $500 and up for two, which
includes lunch).

So what will you offer me for this carpet?" asks Abriz, my third
Moroccan carpet salesman of the day named Abriz.

"It's too big for my room," I say. "I don't like it enough to make
an offer."

"If you were going to make an offer, what would you pay?"

I can play this game, too: "I can't make a decision like this without my husband."

The tension explodes. "You come into my shop, you drink my Coca-Cola, you let me show you this carpet, and now, how much you pay? We make deal without your husband, then you bring him back to pay. Today is the day for the deal—what is your Golden Deal price?"

In the souks of Marrakech, every day is the day for a deal. Carpets are the principal souvenir of Morocco, perhaps because they reflect the country's spiritual and cultural heritage—or perhaps just because they make a fabulous addition to any living room. Either way, buying one is your best opportunity to experience the delights and drama of this city.

But no matter what trophy you bring home, chances are you will question your bargaining skills, the quality of your purchase, and even your sanity. You'll feel triumphant one minute, and then wake up in the middle of the night, convinced you were cheated. But as I discovered on my personal carpet quest, arming yourself with a little bit of knowledge and a lot of nerve is the crucial down payment on your own Golden Deal.

If These Floors Could Talk

Some of the first carpets, featuring a cartouche or medallion that could be faced toward Mecca, were made to cushion the knees of the devout when they prayed. Eleventh-century Crusaders brought the elaborate pieces back to Europe from the Middle East. Over the centuries, design influences from Persia, the Orient, India—even from America's Navajos—crept in. By the middle of this century, the craft of carpet making became a giant commercial enterprise. Today carpets are sold everywhere except the airport and your hotel lobby.

For the most part, the pieces are hand-knotted and feature pile. They are made on a loom by women who, after warping the loom, tie the knots with their left hands while slicing the wool with tiny machetes. Sometimes, two women work the loom and meet in the middle of the carpet. Because the carpets are made without patterns, no two are alike.

The value of any carpet depends on several factors: the number of knots per foot (don't try to count them, but know that about twenty thousand is good), the fiber, the dyes (natural, please), the age, and the condition. New carpets are easy to spot because they are too clean, with no sense of soul. Antiques, however, usually cost thousands of dollars, so I decided to focus my search on used carpets (twenty to fifty years old). The colors are slightly faded but subtler, and the wool feels softer to the touch.

You may want to read up on the different styles beforehand, but even if you don't, you'll find that by your second day of rug shopping, you'll have a handle on them. You'll recognize a formal, central medallion as Rabat style, or that dark blood red with black stripes as a member of the Berber family. And after a few "demonstrations" at selling venues, you'll be able to announce, with some authority, which styles you want to see, so that you're spared the endless unfurling of Rabat carpets when what you're really looking for are the highly graphic Middle Atlas Zemmours.

Souk and You Shall Find

Just as Djemaa el-Fna, the main square of Marrakech, boasts snake charmers and belly dancers, its medina (or marketplace, also known as the souk) is filled with its own kind of entertainers—salesmen who offer as many sales techniques as they do kinds of merchandise.

Most people get to a specific carpet shop through a guide (your hotel can arrange one for you). If you travel the medina unescorted, you'll get plenty of offers from earnest guides, but don't trust any who can't show an identification badge. Expect to pay a guide about 200 *dirham* ($25) a day, plus a tip. The best thing about having a guide is that it scares off other guides, though you can buy a carpet without one.

While making carpets is women's work, selling them is a sport for men. They display a constantly changing parade of emotions and enticements, ranging from reassuring lies ("This is a superior-grade carpet made with cashmere wool") to reassuring nonsense ("It's not the money spent—it's the money saved"). If the pitch is failing, the actor-salesman will switch methods, going from soft, manipulative tones to screaming, arm waving, and terrifying theatrics.

Salesmen admit that if they can get you in the door, they expect you will buy. Because guilt and obligation are Western sensibilities, salesmen will ply you with countless glasses of free mint tea, Coca-Cola, and mineral water to make you appreciate Moroccan hospitality—and to wear down your resistance.

"Morocco means not to hurry," one salesman explains to me. "It means drink tea, think about it, talk about it."

It's all part of the show.

At one store, I inquire about a carpet with a border featuring teapots and camels. It's charming, but I'm leery of the carpet's quality, since Muslim law forbids the depiction of any life forms in art.

"Oh, no," says the salesman. "Camels are okay." Sure.

This nonsense was reason enough for me to flee the medina and go to a dealer in downtown Marrakech (called Gueliz, and just minutes away by taxi). The head concierge at my hotel recommended El Badii, a hotshot dealer that moved out of the souk, supposedly to undercut the prices charged there. I am cautious at first, but within seconds the salesman passes my most important test.

I have yet to mention I'm interested in a carpet—the store sells all kinds of decorative arts—when I ask a simple question about a textile on exhibit. Immediately, I'm inundated with a barrage of details on this particular art form. When a dealer offers up so much information based on his love of the piece, chances are he won't cheat you. By the time I begin my first glass of mint tea, I trust this dealer.

He shows me books describing every style of carpet I admire, educating me to be a good consumer. But when I get serious about a carpet and bemoan the price, the dealer says, "Sorry, madame, but we don't negotiate."

It doesn't matter anymore. I now have enough confidence to return to the souk.

Back among the stalls, I find several shops with excellent merchandise and prices equal to El Badii's. Of course, price is hard to compare, since negotiations are always carpet-specific and involve a ballet of precision. What's more, they're led by a knowing partner who is more than happy to keep you stumbling.

First, after a pile of carpets is displayed, you will be asked to separate the group into yes, no, and maybe. One salesman taught me the words for "no" and "maybe"—I was not yet interested in yes—in Arabic, and insisted I use them as two different piles were built: *la* for no; *mounkine* for maybe.

The *la*s are removed, the maybes reappraised. I group my maybes by school of design, since it's like apples and oranges to choose between an Ouaouzquite and a Boujad.

Now you're ready to make your deal. Prices are quoted in *dirham,* which converts to dollars at roughly eight to one. Most salesmen refuse to quote price when you are merely curious, and, of course, the opening price is all but meaningless. At a dealer, a piece offered for 12,000 *dirham* will likely sell for 8,000 ($1,000). I found that in the 6-foot-by-9-foot to 8-foot-by-10-foot range, good carpets generally cost this much.

When bargaining in the souk, forget the Western notion that you should counter with half the opening price and settle somewhere in between. In my experience, half the opening price is the price the seller will happily take—and smugly brag about later. An opening bid of 25 percent of the asking price and a settlement at 40 percent (of, not off, the price) is about right. In the souk, a carpet with an asking price of 13,000 *dirham* should sell for about 5,000.

When I do my actual buying, my four maybes (all of them Ouaouzquites) are laid out on a clean floor. I find three to be of similar quality, and the fourth superior to them all. I toy with a $500 carpet—it's within my budget and I love it—but in the end I choose a carpet that is more classical and more expensive. I figure that once I've gone to this much trouble, I owe it to my family to come home with the better piece. In the end, I vote with my head, not my heart.

The decision haunts me after I get home. I toss and turn at night, worrying that I've been had. Finally, I summon the courage to take my carpet for an appraisal.

"You were smart not to buy a new carpet," says Vojtech Blau, one of Manhattan's leading antique carpet dealers. Although I had estimated my carpet to be about fifty years old, Blau suggests seventy to eighty years. "If you bought it for $1,000," he adds, "you have a fine eye and got a good bargain."

Phew! I had paid $750.

This makes me feel even better about how I spent my last day—and *dirham*—in Marrakech. I had returned to a dealer I'd found in the Souk du Tapis, the specialized carpet market hall. He sold far more unusual wares than any other dealer—such as kilims, woven mats with embroidery—and we spoke a happy jumble of English and French while he wrote down one particular style for me—Hasira—in French and in Arabic.

I bought two small carpets from him: an embroidered Hasira and a junky cotton fragment whose odd colors spoke to me. He asked $100 for the second piece, but I hesitated. It wasn't worth it.

"Okay, as good souvenir of the souk, 400 *dirham*."

I took it without hesitation.

A quirky mix of turquoise, pink, and orange, it's not a valuable piece, but it matches my bathroom and makes me laugh. Along with my six silver teapots and the bangle bracelet decorated with camels and the Hand of Fatima, it's the perfect souvenir of my time spent with the flying carpets.

Points de Vue—Maroc
(Points of View—Morocco)

"To say that Morocco is visually beautiful is to say nothing. In a single day's drive, the traveler can experience landscapes that range from high mountain peaks capped with snow to hot, rolling sand dunes."
—Mary Cross, MOROCCO: SAHARA TO THE SEA

"Morocco is a country where the problem of remaining alive is the principal preoccupation. The faces of the rustic population, weathered by wind, sun and constant hardship, show what life is like. It is a raw land where necessities are not plentiful and where living is difficult."
—Paul Bowles, from the Preface to
MOROCCO: SAHARA TO THE SEA

Late Nineteenth-Century Morocco Through Foreign Eyes

BY F. V. PARSONS

editor's note

Here is a very good and succinct—if rather academic—view of the late nineteenth century in Morocco, a time that I believe set the tone for the entire twentieth century there.

FREDERICK V. PARSONS is a specialist in Islamic studies and is the author of *The Origins of the Morocco Question, 1880–1900* (Michael Brett, London, 1968). He has contributed numerous articles to *The Maghreb Review*, where this piece originally appeared.

Marocco, as it was still often spelt in English into the 1880s, evoked conflicting responses from late nineteenth-century outside observers. To Walter B. Harris, subsequently a well-known correspondent of *The Times,* it was "an almost unknown country" when he began to report in 1887.[1] Apart from a few coastal towns, indeed, it could be seen as a land which still offered promising prospects for the intrepid explorer.[2] At the other extreme, especially to resident diplomatic and consular agents, and to the men who had to take into account their dispatches, the northwest corner of Africa was a possible, even probable, source of international discord. In 1891 a Spanish minister of state was surprised to note "with what facility everyone preoccupied themselves with the interests of the Sherifian Empire." By 1893, commenting on the attitude of other powers from the comparatively neutral atmosphere of Vienna, a responsible statesman similarly concluded that there was "almost more jealousy . . . about . . . Morocco than about any other subject which mutually concerns them."[3] Almost all commentators, however, agreed that the affairs of the area under discussion could not easily be ignored.

The Western Question

The society with which comparisons were most frequently made was the Ottoman Empire. Just as, measured at least by a simple military and naval yardstick, Turkey had long seemed to be in decline, Morocco was also deemed to be a "question," the Western as opposed to the more familiar Eastern one.[4] (China too was often cited as a parallel case of an ancient community doing its best to ignore "the monster innovation" and exclude all outside influence.)[5] Certainly France and Spain had been victorious in conflicts of 1844–1845 and 1859–1860. The cessation of levying payment for exemption from Moroccan raids on shipping was similarly symbolic. In practice al-Maghreb al-Akas, the Far West, was to keep free of foreign control longer than other Islamic communities around the Mediterranean. Many predictions, such as that of a United States consul in 1880, that "it can not last much longer," or that the anticipated death of the Sultan Moulay Hassan (1873–94) must automatically be followed by the loss of independence, only illustrated, with something like regularity, the dangers of expert opinion. Nevertheless, the prospect of a power vacuum in a key strategic area, with control of the southern shore of the Strait of Gibraltar and also an Atlantic coastline and important links with other parts of Africa, was one which almost inevitably aroused fears and, in a few instances, hopes. The existence of a "Sick Man of the West" was increasingly apparent. Even a Moroccan functionary was quoted, in 1871, as agreeing that another conflict with Spain could not be risked: "Morocco is like a threadbare garment, if the slightest force is used it will be rent and go to pieces."

The elements of decline which attracted most attention from observers, apart from direct military ones, were those connected with Morocco's government or, as usually described, misgovernment. Comment was basically critical. It was not an uncommon view, among individuals with experience of several continents, that the Moorish administration was "the worst in the world." Sir Arthur Nicolson, British representative from 1895–1905, had "been in most Oriental countries" but had "never seen such complete darkness as reigns here."[6] (The word *Oriental,* as noun or adjective, was much too loosely used in varying contexts.) What is meant by administration is, of course, open to question. One opinion, Nicolson's again, was that there was "merely a machine for raising money."

Local governors, like almost all officials, bought their unpaid posts and, whatever the theory of taxation, extracted as much as possible from the people of their district, while perforce sending a generous share of the spoils to the imperial treasury. It was not wise to show signs of ostentatious wealth; one would think, noted Harry Maclean, the ex–British army officer who arrived in 1887 to instruct the Moorish infantry, "there is not a man in the place who had a shilling." His sherifian majesty, the sultan, to whom credentials were addressed as ruler of the kingdoms of Morocco, Fes, and Sus, Meknes and Tafilalet, was generally recognized as spiritual lord of the inhabitants, although the existence of various confraternities was a complication. But in practice control of his nominal subjects was strictly limited. His own life was a peripatetic one as, accompanied by court, officials, and none too reliable troops, he journeyed between his capitals in what appeared as an endless series of military campaigns. On some occasions there was submission, or prudential evasion by the imperial forces. At other times burning villages and crops were the main signs of a royal progress, as territory was, in the contemporary phrase, "eaten up." The words *extortion, bribery,* and *pillage* often appeared in reports. Cruelty in the treatment of prisoners and flogging of offenders, sometimes fatally, were also noted, as was justice and police—or lack of them.

Governmental policy was often described as "divide and rule." But there was hardly need to play one tribe off against another, as rivalry and hostility seemed to be endemic. Nor in the more remote areas, in the Rif, the Sus provinces on the Atlantic, and in the Atlas Mountains, rarely penetrated by the Sultan's entourage, was there much rule of any type. Berber tribes "had long been free of any of the inconveniences of government," wrote Herbert White, a long-term British consular official (1882–1921). With no fixed law of succession, the death of a ruler was particularly liable to a period of civil disorder. "Insurrection and rebellion," indeed, according to Sir John Drummond Hay, who acquired a great knowledge of the country in his long service there from 1845 to 1886, was "the normal state of Morocco." Nowhere was Moulay Hassan the last "strong" sultan pictured in retrospect, and the contrast between a controlled *bled el-makhzan* under governmental authority and an unsubmitted *bled el-siba* was an oversimplified one. Life in the whole land of the Moors, where men habitually went armed, was in fact held cheaply. Not infrequent plague and famine, coupled with poor or nonexistent medical and sanitary standards, were even, indeed much more, destructive. A third of the population is estimated to have died in a period of bad harvests, drought, and cholera from 1878 to 1884. "You see very few old men in Morocco" was the verdict of Maclean.

Some observers found kinder things to say. Slavery, which led to much complaint from outside, was, in the words of Jules Patenôtre (French minister at Tangier, 1889–91), of the mildest domestic type. It was doubtful if negroes imported from the Sudan would consent "to exchange their situation for that of European workers." Also, reported Patenôtre, there was no color prejudice—although not everyone agreed on this. Casualties in tribal warfare were relatively light, and heads, whose exposure on city walls led to much adverse comment, were only removed after death. Capital punishment was rare. Administration was as corrupt in China and Persia, fanaticism as strong in Afghanistan. As against constant criticisms of Moorish policy of "passive resistance" and systematic obstruction, delay was, here as elsewhere, "part of the means of defence of diplomacy." Dilatoriness in correspondence, according to Sir Ernest Satow (at Tangier, 1893–95), no worse than in South American republics. Morocco, moreover, in the opinion of Sir Joseph West Ridgeway in a report of 1893, was "an advanced democracy. All men are equal except those who inherit sanctity. Every Moor considers himself to be as good as another, and far superior to any European." As regards military strength, although Moroccan forces were currently no match for more modern ones, their potential as a guerrilla force, notable in resistance down to 1934, was foreseen by British and French army officers. On the individual side, Moulay Hassan, often accused of misrepresentation and allied faults, was found, again by Patenôtre, to be "faithful to his given word," as well as, by others, dignified, "most gracious," "perfectly charming," and courteous.

Some few diplomats, notably Sir John Drummond Hay—still commemorated in a Tangier street name—acquired a notable understanding of and sympathy with the land and its language, the latter "half the battle" in any negotiation. Although frequently critical of the *makhzan*, the Moorish people, considered Hay, were "a hardy and intelligent race" who had "led the van in art and science" and "taught the world literature . . . and warfare"; they could become "a great nation" again if "under a good government" with "security for life and property" to provide an incentive. (Hay also spoke favorably of the Berbers, "a far superior race to their conquerors, the Arabs." There was, however, perhaps unavoidably, little consensus on the precise differentiation between Berber and Arab, and Moor.) Charles Féraud, the representative of France from 1885 to 1888, was an Arabic poet, and an affiliate of the Tijani confraternity. Like Sir John, he stressed that it was the long-oppressed peasant, not the slave, who was most deserving of sympathy and assistance. Nevertheless both these talented men, though differing on policies to be pursued, eventually, and independently, used the word *stagnant* to describe the society in which they were residing.

Difficulties of Observation

Whether foreign observers were correct in their varying conclusions is, understandably, debatable. Certainly the task of the diplomat was no easy one. He perforce resided at Tangier, apart from occasional visits to the elusive court, at the mercy of the numerous wild rumors which reached that city. (It was already of dubious reputation, principally as a refuge of adventurers, even if not the "Sodom in Africa" as described by another United States consul.) The sultan meanwhile was at days' or weeks' distance away. Nor was there any assistance from the *makhzan,* for example, of a statistical or cartographical kind. Wildly varying estimates of the total population, from approximately two to a decidedly exaggerated ten million, illustrated this problem. Language was another difficulty; too many representatives were dependent on interpreters, a considerable number of whom acquired both personal wealth and a dubious reputation. There was not even agreement on what constituted "Morocco." The sultan did not acknowledge any supremacy of the Khalifa at Constantinople and claimed dominion over all lands where his name was mentioned "in the prayers of the inhabitants." In 1879 and 1889 these lands were officially cited as those stretching from Guinea and Senegal to Egypt, Kordofan, and the Nile, representing a spiritual as opposed to territorial basis of sovereignty which brought obvious complications, still apparent in disputes involving Morocco's borders today. The fact that many of the people concerned were nomads did not help either. Nor did the Moroccan ruler's dilemma, to accept responsibility for the actions of nominal subjects over whom he had no real control, or to withdraw his territorial claims.

Other factors added to the task of getting an accurate picture. Analysis of Moroccan policy was not aided by any apparent recorded major literary or intellectual debate, such as was prompted by the current technological and scientific advancements. The press that appeared in Tangier from 1883 was in European languages, and the *makhzan* provided no parliamentary debates or white papers. There were present, however, a shrewd instinctive awareness of what had happened, for example, in Tunis and Egypt, not to mention Algeria. Moulay Hassan, wisely, as a visiting British army captain noted, "kept his own counsel. But if he did not reveal his innermost thoughts," let alone write them down, he had concluded by 1892, according to an Italian interpreter, that the sultan of Turkey had "ruined his Empire by cultivating relations with foreign Powers." There were signs that he himself had attempted, very tentatively, the difficult task of borrowing anything that might be useful, notably arms and military techniques, together with any changes that might create the necessary revenue to pay for them, while basically preserving Moroccan society; but any innovations became less in evidence with the years. The sympathetic Patenôtre considered that Hassan was conscious of the current trend of international events, and was resigned to postponing the evil day of foreign control for as long as possible. Féraud, like his compatriot the artillery instructor Jules Erckmann, took the view that the needs of the Moors were almost nil, that they could survive for a long time as they were; they held their independence and primitive customs more dearly than any material advantage from connection with the rest of the world. Such an interpretation was probably much nearer the mark than one which stressed an urgent desire to escape from existing intolerable conditions. But a determination to remain in as complete isolation as possible helped to keep Morocco a not too well-known land.

The diplomatic observer had to take into account too what may be termed outside pressures, viewpoints not necessarily their own. The existence of slavery and slave markets, the state of the non-salubrious Moorish prisons, and the treatment of the Jews were only amongst the most notable features of Moroccan society which prompted humanitarian pressure-groups to try to get their own governments to act on the *makhzan*. (British representatives considered they were more open to the effects, often unfortunate ones, of this sort of opinion than those of other states, such as France.) Diplomatic and consular agents also had legal obligations toward their own nationals, even if warnings were often given that travelers proceeded "at their own risk and peril." A special example of irritation was the system of protection, an equivalent of the Capitulations in the Ottoman Empire, whereby Moors could be withdrawn from their own jurisdiction and, in practice, from taxation and military obligations. Like any form of diplomatic immunity, it could be abused; and it was, increasingly, as, in an age of improved transport and greater movement, the small number of foreign residents grew. The chief culprits were not serious commercial interests—the half-dozen larger British firms who carried on most British trade rarely bothered official circles—or even genuine citizens of European states or the U.S.A., but the adventurers or worse who figured prominently among the few thousand non-Moroccan residents. It was individuals without capital, but in search of it, often willing virtually to sell protection illegally, who exacerbated relations. (On the other side it can only be said that Moroccan subjects, whether Muslim or from the small minority of Jews who were much involved with the myriad abuses of protection, were only too willing to buy the status of a *protégé;* no one would have been keen to pay the often high price demanded if there had been any security for life and property under the existing régime.) Allied with this development was the prevalent view that Morocco was, as described by a Swedish consul in 1838, the "Promised Land," of El Dorado qualities.[7]

Economic Prospects

Morocco seemed obviously a country whose full potential had not been developed, and there was no lack of recommendation, from outside, that changes be made. The richness of the soil, or some areas of it, was often emphasized, with suitable references to northwest Africa having been "the granary of the Roman Empire." (Few lands around the Mediterranean escaped this retrospective description at some time or another.) Forests could be exploited, in the best sense of the word. Alleged great untapped mineral wealth was additionally a subject of frequent comment, embracing almost everything except the later profitable phosphates. In practice, however, the only mode of production that still really counted was the traditional one, the harvest. Imports and exports, as they could be measured, varied according to good or lean years. The amount of total trade did show an overall increase, but only from approximately £2,000,000 in 1856 to £3,100,000 in 1891, before decreasing again until 1900. Indeed Europe found that grain and wool, regularly recommended as the main items for more exportation, could more easily be obtained, with improved communications, from farther afield. Humble commodities like almonds and beans were in certain years the principal items sent abroad. Some imports were acceptable, and not only the illegal arms often coveted by Moors, but tea and sugar which tended to become more of a necessity than a luxury, despite the very low standard of living. Simple contributions to an easier existence such as candles and sewing machines, and cheap cotton manufactures, also found some willing customers.

There was, however, no massive foreign encroachment, no fundamental disruption of Moroccan life, favorably or unfavorably. The most vocal and strident advocates of the "modernization" of Morocco tended to be those with vague proposals, energy, and ambition rather than resources to invest. Too many interested so-called "companies" had more prospectus than capital. Major business concerns and "high finance" were liable to be unwilling to take the risks involved.

Attitude of Foreign Governments

Above all, for many decades, governments who had to view Morocco from a distance were not convinced of the need, or in several respects were unable, to take any major initiative. Political authorities did have a natural interest in increasing commercial exchanges and not being surpassed by rivals, but they were by no means at the mercy of economics of financial pressure-groups. At times diplomats on the spot did voice criticisms of the inefficiency or apathy of their compatriots. Patenôtre found fault with French firms who expected him to do their work for them; Féraud regretted that there were only five or six genuine French merchants who could be relied on for honesty and punctuality. Germans in official positions had great difficulty in getting shipping lines to make regular calls; our "banks all strike immediately one mentions Morocco," complained state-secretary von Richtofen at Berlin. Similarly Cantagalli (at Tangier, 1888–95) bemoaned the lack of interest of Italian industrial and financial interests. But the many powers concerned, and the sheer number of them helped make Morocco a "question," had other things to bear in mind than direct commercial returns. The primary Italian objective was negative, to prevent France repeating the "Tunis coup." In Spain there was a vocal body of opinion that saw the land of the Moors as its natural heritage; but there was no repeat of the war of 1859–60. German policy can best be interpreted as a failure to decide what was wanted; what is ascertainable is that, despite much publicity as to the role Morocco might play in the future, no specific demands for territorial cessions were made, and that Germany's commerce with Morocco, as with other states, was only a minute proportion of her total world trade. Governments in the United Kingdom, Morocco's main customer and provider of goods, did want a revision of its commercial convention of 1856, itself an improvement on the eighteenth-century practice when the *makhzan* could arbitrarily impose bans and alterations in import and export duties. But though it approved of attempts, in the outcome unsuccessful, to get a lowering of tariffs, by ministers such as Kirby Green (1886–91) and Euan-Smith (1891–93), there was no support when they called for stronger action, whatever that might imply. As for France, although backing was given to enterprises of its own nationals, the view that prevailed was that of, in Féraud's own phrase, *le chien du jardinier,* the dog-in-the-manger. The security of Algeria took priority. It was realized that economic factors cannot be divorced from others involving political power, strategy, and prestige, and it was better to see Morocco remain in its existing condition than have other states establish greater influence there. Many words were spilt and written over the need for a Trans-Sahara railway, possibly crossing disputed Moroccan territory. But no such line was ever built. Apart from the cost, which the French taxpayer was certainly not prepared to bear, there was a reluctance to take action which might precipitate events. Prudence and caution, in fact, plus fear and endemic suspicion of what other powers might do, were the dominant features in the overall attitude of governments who, conscious of possible international dangers, kept a watchful eye on northwest Africa.

Morocco consequently survived the death of Moulay Hassan in 1894 and in the next six years, under Bu Ahmed as virtual regent, seemed to retreat even further into noncontact with the West. The Sherifian Empire still had no railways. Mining for suspected riches was similarly practically nonexistent. Also, a fact of great importance, the *makhzan* had no external debt. Borrowing from abroad was another subject on which there was much more talk than action. To pay an indemnity to Spain, a loan was obtained in London in 1861—though it was *not,* as was often said, "guaranteed" by the British Government—but it had been paid off by 1883. It was not until after Abd el-Aziz (1894–1908) had assumed personal control in 1900 that the climax came. The well-intentioned attempt of the new ruler to introduce the sort of reforms that had long been recommended as the cure for Morocco's ills accentuated internal unrest and at last drove a major power to take action.

It was at Paris that observation of Morocco had the greatest effect. It was considered, incorrectly, that the country was passing under control of Great Britain, a few of whose nationals were advising the young sultan. Well-entrenched fears of danger to Algeria and France's Mediterranean position from "les anglais," and others, plus traditional arguments of security and the prestige of France as a Muslim power, combined with the *mission civilisatrice* attitude of mind, prominent in a small but influential group in military, diplomatic, and intellectual circles. (It was publicists, journalists, academics, and geographers, rather than businessmen, who predominated in the minority "colonial" organizations.) With a foreign minister, Delcassé, who agreed that if Morocco must modernize, it must be under French auspices, and who was also able to make use of the financial group that eventually provided a key loan in 1904, steps were taken to deal with possible future eventualities. The way was open for the advance which, despite its provoking greater Moroccan opposition as military forces were increasingly active on the borders, had by 1912 led to the protectorate which heralded Morocco's brief period under foreign supervision.

The view of many foreign commentators that the Sherifian Empire was in decline and destined to lose its independence can accordingly be seen as a prophetic one, even if the "Sick Man of the West" had survived a good deal longer than often anticipated. The recovery of Morocco, and the short length of time outside control would endure, had not been foreseen with equal acuity. Expectations of economic gains, especially immediate ones, had been very extravagant; development of resources was to prove a very slow and arduous process. Apprehension that Morocco would provide the focus of dangerous confrontations in international relationships, however, was only too justified in the period 1904–11. European governments did not go to war on this issue, nor indeed on any other extra-European one. When conflict did come in 1914, it was over what were considered life-or-death matters, much nearer home. But individuals as distinguished as Bismarck and the Third Marquis of Salisbury had foreseen the complications of a "Western Question." In this respect at least foreign observers were not entirely off the mark. Perhaps the quite extensive body of information on Morocco that has been accumulated and recorded as a result of their efforts, however much it has to be criticized and modified in the light of later knowledge, will also prove to be useful to the twentieth-century student of the Maghreb.

Notes

1. *Morocco That Was* (Edinburgh and London, 1921), p. 2.
2. E.g., Charles De Foucauld, *Reconnaissance au Maroc en 1883–1884* (Paris, 1888).
3. F. V. Parsons, *The Origins of the Morocco Question, 1880–1900* (London, 1968), pp. 390, 3–4, quoting the duke of Tetuan and Count Kalnoky. Material cited is from this study of diplomatic history, unless otherwise stated.

4. Earl F. Cruickshank, *Morocco at the Parting of the Ways* (Philadelphia, 1935), p. 206, cites an article on *"la question du Maroc"* of 1859.
5. John H. Drummond Hay, *Western Barbary* (London, 1844), p. 122.
6. Harold Nicolson, *Sir Arthur Nicolson, Bart, First Lord Carnock* (London, 1930), pp. 118–19.
7. Jean-Louis Miége, *Le Maroc et l'Europe, 1830–1894*, vol. 2 (Paris, 1961), p. 126.

Bibliography

Brooks, L. A. E. *A Memoir of Sir John Drummond Hay*. London, 1896.
Conring, Adolf von. *Morocco das Land und die Leute*. Berlin, 1880.
Cruickshank, Earl F. *Morocco at the Parting of the Ways: The Story of Native Protection to 1885*. Philadelphia, 1935.
Erckmann, Jules. *Le Maroc Moderne*. Paris, 1885.
Frisch, Cdt. R. J. *Le Maroc: Geographie, organisation, politique*. Paris, 1895.
Guillen, Pierre. *L'Allemagne et le Maroc de 1870 à 1905*. Paris, 1967.
Harris, Walter B. *Land of an African Sultan*. London, 1889.
Meakin, Budgett. *The Moorish Empire*. London, 1899.
Miége, Jean-Louis. *Le Maroc et l'Europe, 1830–1894*, vols. 1–4. Paris, 1961–1963.
Parsons, F. V. *The Origins of the Morocco Question, 1880–1900*. London, 1968.
Patenôtre, Jules. *Souvenirs d'un diplomate*. Paris, 1913.

Last Refuge of the Tall Tasseled Ottoman Hat

BY CHRIS HEDGES

~~

editor's note

··

I knew that the fez had been banned in Turkey under Ataturk, but I did not realize it was *ever* worn in Morocco, since the Ottoman Empire never had Morocco in its fold; nor did I realize that the name is believed to have originated in the city of Fez. I rather like the funny-looking hat but can appreciate its recent negative associations.

CHRIS HEDGES is a reporter for the "Metro" section of *The New York Times*.

In the Middle East it still matters what you wear on your head. The Sudanese have floppy turbans, the Palestinians red and black checkered *kafiyehs,* and the Saudis the white *ghutra.* But the maroon brimless fez, once the epitome of Old World courtesy and taste, has become, for most Muslims, politically incorrect.

"It's a hat of the oppressors," said twenty-six-year-old Abdel Jouad. "This is why no one wears it anymore."

Only the Moroccan royal court has resisted the Muslim world's onslaught against the fez. King Hassan II is the only Arab leader to wear it. And cabinet ministers, the royal guard, and the palace staff all favor the fez, although the staff members wear a floppy, conical-shaped fez that denotes their status.

Any socially ambitious Moroccan man, hoping for an invitation to one of the king's dozen lavish palaces, would not dare show up bareheaded at the gate. And in the narrow cobblestone alleys of Fez one can still see men, often in immaculate suits, made a few inches taller by the bucket-shaped, dark red hat with the black silk tassel.

"In Morocco the fez was seen as a form of protest against the French occupation," said Chakib Laroussi, the director of the Ministry of Information. "To put on a fez was to make a statement that one was a nationalist. The fez has, for generations, been a symbol of the royal palace and part of our national dress."

The origins of the fez, which Moroccans call the *tarboosh,* is disputed.

The design may have come from ancient Greece or the Balkans. It gained wide acceptance in the early nineteenth century, when the Ottoman rulers, who actually never controlled Morocco, moved to modernize traditional costumes. The brimless hat did not get in the way of a Muslim's daily prayers and was cleaner, and less cumbersome, than the folds of cloth wound into a turban. The name *fez* is believed to come from this city, which once produced the dye, made from crimson berries, to color the hat.

But the fez fell on hard times after World War I with the dissolution of the Ottoman Empire. Ataturk outlawed the fez in 1925 as part of his drive to turn Turkey into a modern Westernized state.

Men who wore the hat were imprisoned. The military officers who overthrew the monarchies in Iraq, Egypt, and Libya condemned the fez as a royalist symbol. And Western fashions, which dropped the bowler and the fedora, left the chic in the Muslim world, like the chic in Europe, bareheaded.

The decline in the fez's popularity had its effect in Morocco. It is rare to see a young man, unless he is a member of the court or has dressed for a wedding or a funeral, wearing a fez. But enough Moroccans still need the hat to keep alive the small fez workshops, with their wheezing steam ventilators and bronze presses.

The Barrera Brothers Vox workshop, on Mohammed El Hayani Street, occupies three small rooms with low ceilings behind Fez's main vegetable market.

The company has been producing the fez for the royal court for almost one hundred years. Fifty years ago, at its height, it employed dozens of people in workshops that lined the narrow Derb al-Barka Street in Fez's old city. Today the company has fewer than a dozen employees.

The cramped workshop has rows of bronze molds and presses to shape the wool, which is imported from South Africa and Australia, into the hats.

The workers cut the brim of the fez by hand. One man sews in the leather hatbands on a machine. And workers lick their fingers to rub off any spots on the finished product before brushing the fez and wrapping it in white tissue paper.

"We make three grades," said Bachir Berrada, one of the owners. "We make one for everyday use, one for more formal occasions, and one that is worn to special events, such as the court. It takes two days to finish a fez."

Hamid Ginoon, wearing a soiled gray work coat, stood over a pyramid-shaped tin cone that had steam rushing out of dozens of small holes. He was straightening the black silk tassels over the steam before sewing them by hand on the top of the hats.

"The hardest part is when we place the wool over the inside pile," said Mr. Ginoon, who has worked here for more than twenty years. "You have to make sure there are no creases or bubbles between the wool and the lining. Otherwise the fez is ruined."

Amor Abdel Haman, a fifty-seven-year-old clerk, sat under the arches of an old stone arcade later that day, squinting into the sunlight. He wore a black suit coat, a tie, gray slacks, polished brown shoes, and a fez. "I have worn the fez every day since I was a boy of twelve," he said. "It is part of my identity."

When it came time to leave, he stood and bowed slightly, letting his right hand rest gently on his heart.

"It is sad, monsieur," he said, "but the fez is dying out, even among my generation. Dying out like elegance itself."

The Indices of Fate:
How Moroccan Time Works

BY ROGER JOSEPH

∼

editor's note

The Moroccans believe that a person without time is a dead person, a good adage to remember for all of your endeavors in Morocco.

Author ROGER JOSEPH specializes in Islamic studies and has contributed frequently to *The Maghreb Review*, where this piece originally appeared.

Anthropology is beset by the problem of defining concepts which are deeply embedded in differing cultural contexts, the translatability of which eludes us. Two of the most difficult concepts to translate are time and space. I have addressed some comments on space elsewhere (Joseph 1981 and 1984). Here I wish to discuss the properties of time.

Time is a cultural concept; its meaning is generated within specific contexts. We may qualify such a definition by recognizing that astronomical time exists independent of our wills; the earth rotates on its axis without reference to human activity. However, our interpretation of that rotation is a cultural construct. Concepts of temporality are cultural signs that reveal a society's notions about sequences. The cultural structuration of time is a problem of human categories of past, present, and future. We usually take our notion of time for granted. When other cultures do not share our concept of time, they are believed to have a dysfunctional apprehension of temporality. Anthropologists have attempted to puncture this Eurocentric notion starting at least as far back as Evans-Pritchard's account of Nuer time (1940), and including various studies by Bourdieu (1963), Bohannan (1967), Eickelman (1977), Middleton (1967), Pocock (1967), and others.

If human time (as opposed to astronomical time) is fictitious, in the sense that it is culturally arbitrary and interpretive, then what are the implications for a cultural investigation of time? How can we express the idea of an expectation? Can we argue that all cultures recognize the potentialities of past and future? May we assert that every people addresses the possibility of successive events? If events are successive, can we consider such temporality historical; or does time, alternatively, reside in cyclical, repetitive events? Does every society separate what we label history as opposed to myth? Can, in fact, an individual have potentialities in the future (not encumbered with past identification): or is each individual simply a representative figure for a collective? Alternatively, can we assert that communities have a memory, and if so, memory of what and to what purposes?

There is, of course, the simple idea that time is a measurement; a record, so to speak, of what occurred earlier and what came later. In many ways a benchmarking chronicle is derivative from textbook notions of history. Sequences are part of the classroom experience which lies behind our abstract notion of time, tacit conclusions we make about a very complex concept. As Leach stated more than two decades ago, "The regularity of time is not an intrinsic part of nature; it is a man-made notion which we have projected into our environment for our own particular purposes" (1961:133).

The cultural construction of time is, like all human products, a system which we assert and arrange. Its modeling is analogous to a system of distributing economic goods. In many ways, the two systems are parallel. Both goods and temporality can be arranged in any arbitrary manner. In fact, the manner that material goods are distributed is heavily influenced by the way society distributes time. Indeed, it is concepts of past, present, and future that are the more profound systems, legitimizing the framework of the exchange of material commodities.

One of the most interesting theorists of time is Pierre Bourdieu. Because he addresses the concept of time among Berber tribesmen, the subject of my essay, I believe it is useful to briefly review his work. According to Bourdieu, "Nothing is more foreign to the precapitalistic economy than the representation of the future as a field of possibilities to be explored and mastered by calculation" (1979:8). Bourdieu suggests that the economic formation associated with peasantry has a different calculus, indeed a different practical notion of temporality, than exists in the sort of society which is driven and motivated by capitalistic gain. To understand his argument, one must recall that capitalism is a particular historical configuration, one that "works" only after certain economic figurations realize themselves. One can only plan for the future when one can conceptualize the notion of the future. One can only calculate, if one believes in the power of prediction. One goes about doing these things for oneself if there exists the possibility of an individual, separate from the multiple pulls of clan, community, and family. Bourdieu argues that the Algerian peasant does not have the same "predictive" attitude toward economic calculation, and hence the future, that characterizes capitalistic modes of rationality.

Every society experiences repetitions and changes. Bourdieu's argument is that the context of perception differs; therefore repetitions and their sociological representations are different. As an anthropologist, I lived among rural Berber tribesmen in the Rif Mountains of Morocco for some eighteen months. I was invited, by the nature of my inquiry, to discuss time in a number of practical contexts: the hour of an interview, the day of a ceremony, the time to purchase a sheep, when Ramadan would start, on what date a rebellion against the French began, and so forth. Time constantly intruded itself as a category in which both Moroccans and I had enough agreement to sort out most of our mutually impinging affairs. But when we discussed time not as benchmarks to arrange our calendars but as systems of meaning, it was clear that my concepts of time were different from theirs. Indeed, the more we talked about such matters, the clearer it became that the landscape of our discourse was dotted with mutual misapprehensions.

Moroccan tribesmen invited me to think about their nature of temporality and my own; they compelled me to consider the problem of fate.

Fate has to do with the future. In Islamic cultures, fate is semantically interwoven with two central concepts: *maktub* and *in sha Allah*. Both notions have been inadequately glossed. I shall try to improve upon their definition.

Consider the Western notion of fate: it is a concept intimately coupled with time. It does not exist unless there is a suggestion of expectation. The idea of expectation can only exist if a culture has a notion of the future. In order to have a notion about the future, a culture must believe in its potentialities, accompanying beliefs in goals, and successive events toward outcomes.

The members of a culture must have a foreshadowing of possible events or, at least, the potentiality for expectations and disappointments. Events must be distributed in some manner and be, at least nominally, less than accidental. There must be some people who believe that the curve of coincidence is predictive and want to know how the curve will turn out.

The prediction of time must be judged by a set of cultural rules. These rules must represent a notion of discrete units along a temporal spectrum of events (beginnings, middles, and ends), which are ruled by a particular set of dispositions, matters which vary from one culture to another.

Everyone in the Rif Mountains, Morocco, and North Africa is quite aware of the notion of past, present, and future. There are, however, interesting footnotes to these tenses and their cultural translatability. I am especially interested in the future tense because I believe it speaks to the issue of fate. Bourdieu makes a distinction between Maghrebi ideas of foresight (*prévoyance*) and forecasting (*prévision*). His point is that humans can have foresight but that only God has the knowledge of forecasting (1963:61). To predict the future in the sense of calculating possibilities is within the human realm; to declare knowledge about the future is to intrude on God's ability (*'ilm Allah*). Events have a likelihood of occurring; whether they will or not is dependent upon calculations outside human knowledge. Moroccans acknowledge their own limitations and of the provisionality of God's activity (cf. Eickelman 1977:46–7).

Time is thus divided into twos: one time for those matters that humans can ascertain, the other for temporality outside of the reach of humans. There are two expressions which can help us with the latter. One of these is *1-maktub;* the other is *in sha Allah*. Both terms are used in Morocco and throughout the Middle East, although *in sha Allah* is used much more frequently, indeed is a commonplace. Both expressions are related to the concept of time and of the future. What sort of sense can we make of them?

Both terms are jointed with a social world. *Maktub* is translatable as "all which happens is written in the book." It argues that everything which is about to happen has been preordained. As Eickelman puts it, the expression "attenuates metaphysical speculation on the outcome of events" (1977:47). To attach the commentary *maktub* to an event, either in the past, present, or future, suggests that the occurrence is outside the volition of the human community. Westerners have glossed this term as a rejection of human volition and accompanying moral responsibility. Their argument runs that if God foreordains all things, human mediation is irrelevant. The indigenous meaning is, however, much more complex. The phrase has often become a rhetorical device, but behind it is a debate related to complex theological issues present in Judaism, Christianity, and Islam. The problem issues from whether all human action stems from God.

In the Qur'ān, as in the Old and New Testaments, there is a mixture of predestination and free will. Qur'ānic scholars have suggested that the universe is guided by a single, all-knowing entity; on the other hand, they have acknowledged that man is judged by his actions and hence there is a freedom of volition and an accompanying moral responsibility. There is, in Islam as in Christianity, a view that all action stems from God, whether for good or evil. The major proponent of this idea is the Umayyid philosopher Jahm bin Safwan, who founded the Jabria School which, from a theological point of view, could be compared with Calvinism (see, for example, Ameer Ali 1965).

In every school of Muslim philosophy, the fact that God is the dispenser of action, enlightenment, and human will never negates the reasoning ability of human beings. God has the supreme capacity to reason successfully, but humans have personal will and thus may reason correctly or incorrectly, according to the signs of God. The major difference between God and man is that God's reason is always correct; man's is mortal, arbitrary, and capable of error.

In Islam, human action is limited; its limitation is derived from its concept of time. But no society is free of time and its limitations. As one of the best North African scholars has stated in another context, "Societies exist in time [but the ways they conceive time] differ a good deal. The way in which time and its horizons are conceived is generally connected with the way the society understands and justifies itself" (Gellner 1964:1). What divorces Islamic notions of time, at least as they are represented in Morocco, from Occidental perceptions of temporality? The answer is complicated and reducible to neither sociological analysis nor axioms. The Occident has viewed the expression *maktub* as an attribute of God's will, often on an *ex post facto* basis. This attitude is, however, a recent attribution to Arabic theology. Prior to the eighteenth century, the West would have been uncomfortable with any differentiation between its own notions of God's will and man's capacity to influence events. Indeed, only in the past two hundred years has Europe rejected *maktub* in its own rhetoric, declining the possibility that any sign or significant event did *not* arise from God's proceedings. Both West and East would have agreed until fairly recently that time and circumstances were immutable and human potentiality preordained. In their mutual past, both Christians and Muslims were dependent upon divine will.

What do Moroccans mean by time, and how do they mean it? Moroccan cosmology never suggests that personal or collective goals are arbitrary and therefore pointless. Action moves toward outcome, although no one can guarantee the results. Moroccan tribesmen believed that the universe was guided by a supreme entity; yet at the same time they wanted to be judged by their actions. No act was free of comment, whether by God or other human beings. Nobody could live in the future free of the charge of the past. Indeed the past, not as a sequence of events but as a cast of characters, weighed heavily on everyone's consciousness in a world populated by saints, shrines, and *baraka*.

The time "behind" the tribesmen was cluttered by the relics of an earlier era, one dominated by holy men or *marabouts* whose heroic attributes were as mythic as they were historic. Indeed to be a *marabout* was to be part of the past; to possess *baraka* was to "belong to history." To possess a quality such as *baraka* places one in the past, but past in what chronological order? Few tribesmen worried about how far in the past the *baraka* was, and indeed, chronology was waived in favor of great saints and insignificant saints, the latter who could be "earlier" in chronological time than the former.

If some Moroccans believed in free will and prejudgment, others conceived of a universe of chance, accident, and individual responsibility. Resigned neither to the will of God nor to the hopelessness of preordained existence, many Moroccans, especially the young, kicked against the pricks of destiny. Many young men were receiving a secular education, even in the mountains. Others were acquiring passports and migrating to Europe. Both groups of Moroccans were acquiring, either formally or informally, a different kind of education and a shift in the reality notion of time.

For those who have received a Western-style education, the future is still rhetorically spoken of as God's will. But there is a special, bracketed category of activity that allows for the planning of budgets, works, lessons for schoolteachers, and other projects that "date" the future and presume a knowledge of its shape, just as written history to some extent fixed the patterns of the past (Eickelman 1977:53).

Does this education free Moroccans from judging their action, their honor, and their moral responsibility for their deeds? All Moroccans are subject to God, the conditioner of human will. This reality poses a question to both the Western and the Muslim educated students. Man cannot be excused from incorrectly interpreting the will of God. Humans may want to follow the correct path selected by God's superior knowledge; the problem is, how can they when human ways are arbitrary and capable of error?

The answer to this question is *in sha Allah*. Eickelman has suggested that the expression signifies "Men are free to take the world as it is and to determine action on the bases of their empirical observations. God's will attenuates speculation on why particular projects succeed or fail and blocks metaphysical speculation on the fate of the individual in this world" (1981:180). *In sha Allah* is part of a social contract in which time is part of a collective and at the same time individualistic contract between Moroccans. That is, time is both a collective promise and a withdrawal, on personal grounds, from that promise. *In sha Allah* is a double promise, both pledging and at the same time withdrawing its commitments. It is, of course, a promise of intent. But the enunciator, at the very moment of pledge, qualifies all promises with the restraint "if God so wills." Thus, the message conveys, on the one hand, "I will fulfill that which I have undertaken to assure you." But at the same time, the speaker announces an alternative consequence: "I will forfeit my obligations if divine providence intercedes." In the days of a strong source of social collectiveness this expression meant that I stood behind my promises to my allies, but I also announced that, in a competitive or contestational society, I must always seek my own way. I have made a contract but the world is uneasy and things change; the future is problematic.

No one, in their right mind, would make a stronger claim to prediction. The strategies of time utilized by the expression *in sha Allah* are not altogether different from Occidental categories of time, although the metaphor is somewhat different. The expression seeks to communicate that "if things don't work out, I'm not to blame." There is thus, within the same rhetorical strategy, both a commitment and a withdrawal.

Time, in Morocco, as everywhere else, is constrained by cultural limits. The expression *in sha Allah* means that the enunciator qualifies to undertake some act, presumably for the benefit of both speaker and listener. Yet at the same time, the speaker notationally withdraws his commitment, insisting in his verbal stroke that factors may intercede. The idiom of *in sha Allah* serves as an ontological critique to every endeavor, whether individual or collective. It both grants and cancels its promise. It concedes to the future any and all possibilities, while at the same time it restricts the bonds of obligation (*haqq*).

Time is conditional insofar as Moroccans conceptualize its properties on a cultural basis. The world of people and nature is superseded by irregularities outside human control. The language that one uses and the way one thinks about the language are continually expressed by the gulf between harmony and danger, between an old world of *baraka* and a new world of economic jeopardy. Each Moroccan places himself in the time machine: a world fraught with possibilities and disruptures between competing individuals, nature, and God. Within such possibilities, Moroccans seek to understand their indices of fate. They seek what unity they can; they avoid violence when possible. Neither of these possibilities eclipses the other; both are part of the potential which structures their notion of time, hope and fate.

References

Ameer Ali, Syed. 1965. *The Spirit of Islam*. London: Methuen.

Bohannan, Paul. 1967. "Concepts of Time Among the Tiv of Nigeria." In *Myth and Cosmos*, ed. John Middleton, New York.

Bourdieu, Pierre. 1963. "The Attitude of the Algerian Peasant Toward Time." *Mediterranean Countrymen*, ed. Julian Pitt-Rivers. Paris and The Hague.

———. 1979. "The Disenchantment of the World." In *Algeria 1960*. Cambridge: Cambridge University Press.

Eickelman, Dale. 1977. "Time in a Complex Society: A Moroccan Example." *Ethnology*, vol. 16, no. 1.

———. 1981. *The Middle East, An Anthropological Approach*. Prentice-Hall.

Evans-Pritchard, E. E. 1940. *The Nuer*. Oxford.

Gellner, Ernest. 1964. *Thought and Change*. Chicago.

Joseph, Roger. 1981. "The Semiotics of the Islamic Mosque." *Arab Studies Quarterly*, vol. 3, no. 3.

————. 1984. "The Symbolic Significance of the Moroccan City." In *Connaissances du Maghreb*. Paris.

Leach, Edmund. 1961. "Two Essays Concerning the Symbolic Representation of Time." In *Rethinking Anthropology*. London.

Middleton, John. 1967. "Some Social Aspects of Lugbara Myth." In *Myth and Cosmos*, ed. John Middleton. New York.

Pocock, D. F. 1967. "The Anthropology of Time-Reckoning." In *Myth and Cosmos*, ed. John Middleton. New York.

Encountering Morocco Head-On

By Ty Ahmad-Taylor

∽

editor's note

There's a lesson in this piece, I think (Be cautious when driving in Morocco?), but the reason I kept the article when I first read it seven years ago is that I liked the writer's tone and ability to tell the story of the accident and the subsequent trip to the hospital in true Moroccan fashion—that is, patiently, excluding no details, and leaving the listener in no doubt about the severity of the situation, but without undue exaggeration.

At the time he made this trip, TY AHMAD-TAYLOR was a graphics editor at *The New York Times,* where he has also worked as a news reporter covering such major stories as the Oklahoma City bombing, the siege in Waco, Texas, and the growth and inception of the World Wide Web. He holds a master's degree in journalism from Columbia University, and has studied French and French cuisine. Currently, he is the chief design architect for MetaTV, an interactive television firm based in Sausalito, California.

I was driving a rented Fiat Uno through the Atlas Mountains of Morocco in the rain when, coming over a hill, I saw the intercity bus sitting forty yards in front of me. But I didn't have time to brake. I could see the front of the car collapse as I hit the front of the bus, a little off-center to the right.

Coming to, I recognized the same bus bumper as it sat inside the car, holding the steering wheel against my chest, and heard an irate bus driver yelling at me in Arabic, presumably about the damage. But the most disconcerting thing was the blood coming from indeterminate places on my body. Two friends who had been riding in the car with me were unconscious, and I pulled them out.

Dazed and bleeding, I started collecting my belongings from the road. The bus driver wanted pictures of the interlocked vehicles, to show that I was in the wrong. The Fiat did not actually look like a car so much as a boulder at this point, its front wheels splayed out horizontally. Although I ignored the bus driver's request, I did take several pictures for posterity. Two women on the bus used a scarf to clean my wounds, including my right knee, which I discovered was open to the bone.

Later, two gendarmes—equivalent to our state police—climbed the steps of the bus with a certain imperiousness, their attitude suggesting they were there to lend order. The narrow road was cluttered with debris, and vehicles had to drive slowly on the shoulder to get by. In a country where radio brings most information and few people have television, the crash was the big news along the mountain road.

The gendarmes did not trouble themselves with details like traffic, instead focusing on the nuances of my employment. When I entered the country I had followed a friend's advice that I not identify myself as a journalist to avoid any possible bureaucratic snags. I was presenting myself as an *artiste,* which is not far off the mark, but Morocco's finest wanted a little more. My French is on the level of being able to order baguettes with jam or chicken—that is, enough to eat and get yelled at by native speakers of the language. So I became an *artiste diagrammatique*. The gendarmes wrote down the information dutifully.

Some two hours after the crash, an ambulance came, and the three of us were loaded into it. They placed me on a stretcher, as they had my friends, and drove like madmen for forty-five minutes to the nearest hospital, in Khénifra, in the Atlas foothills between Fez and Marrakesh.

After asking me questions that I did not wholly understand, and taking down my answers, which I suspect they did not understand at all, the hospital staff hustled me into the operating room. A Dr. Khaled anesthetized the knee and began sewing. Apparently not one to give up personal vices in the workplace and no doubt wanting to insure a steady hand, he lighted a cigarette.

Dr. Khaled was methodical. He would stitch three times, let the needle dangle, pick up his cigarette, take a puff, then resume stitching. Since he wore no surgical mask, he could inhale easily.

The door to the operating room was open, and through my delirium I noticed movement around the operating table. Yellow and brown stray cats roamed freely.

When the doctor was finished, he left a somewhat haphazard crescent-shaped pattern on my knee. He swathed it in bandages and then began to apply a small plaster cast.

Dr. Khaled lighted another cigarette while he finished the wrapping. I sat on the table wearing a T-shirt, button-down shirt, sweater and pullover on my upper body, and red thermal underwear from the waist down. I worried about how much blood I had lost; it was hard to determine what red was clothing and what was my blood.

Once upstairs, where I rejoined my friends, I received two injections in the rear as well as painkiller and tetanus shots. Smaller wounds on my hand and head were not cleaned. (I would need two more operations after I got home, one on my knee and another to remove glass from my body.)

We picked at a meal of steak, bread, and fruit after two more rounds of interrogation by another set of gendarmes and the local police. The hospital staff found me quite intriguing, as I had an Arabic surname but could not speak Arabic. My mother is a first-generation American, her father an Arab immigrant from Yemen, her mother a Jewish immigrant from Czechoslovakia.

That evening, I realized that no one in the States knew of the crash. The gendarmes told me they would contact the United States Embassy in Casablanca, but little things like the destroyed car and the hospital bills began to gnaw at me.

I told the orderly that I needed to use the telephone. X-rays had shown that my right leg was broken, and another orderly had earlier applied a full leg cast. The orderly agreed to my phone request and let me get out of bed by myself, walk down the hall-way and out of the building to the nearest pay phone, roughly one hundred yards away. This was at midnight, or six P.M. Eastern time. I waited while he went down the block to buy a telephone credit card for me.

Passersby kept staring. I was puzzled until I looked at my reflection in the metal of the phone booth: my face was streaked with blood, and I was standing at a phone booth in the middle of the night in red long johns with socks on and a leg cast in forty-five-degree weather.

I called my Aunt Shahara in New York and told her, with all the medical nuance at my disposal, that I had broken my leg and knocked my kneecap off. At least, that is what I could determine from the doctor's broken English and my bad French.

Morning came, after a fitful night's sleep. My friends were up and about, though under observation. Ismail, a man on the bus who had translated some French for me, stopped off to check on us. His cousin, Fatna, a large woman with big, soft hands, visited us that day and the days thereafter until we left. She did not know me, but communicated her relief that I had not died. Twice a day, she brought tea, fruit, and sweets and was a comforting presence though we couldn't speak to one another directly.

On my last day in the hospital I played an adult version of telephone. I asked an English-French speaker to tell Fatna "Thank you from the bottom of my heart," and the English-French speaker then had to tell a French-Arabic speaker what I had said to translate it for Fatna. The French-Arabic speaker gave up after the second word and said something to the effect of "You don't have to thank her, this is your country."

The day of departure from Khénifra for Casablanca dragged on endlessly into evening as my friends and I sought clearance from both the gendarmes and the local police before we could obtain our passports and go. Morocco's system of socialized medicine, it turned out, covered my hospital bills.

The agent from whom I rented the car, Said, came from Marrakesh to drive me to Casablanca for my flight back to the United States. He brought a little Peugeot 405; I am six feet two inches tall. The orderlies crammed me with my leg cast into the front seat; my rear was off the seat and my foot was jammed into the floor.

For the next five hours, I knew hell on earth. Said drove furiously. Each time he hit a bump, the fracture in my leg would compress, sending a raw pain shooting up my leg. We flew through the night, passing cars on narrow roads, hitting bumps randomly, as he flicked his high beams on and off incessantly, passing cars and trucks on the road's gravel shoulders.

The next day I was greatly relieved to board the airplane.

I was carted off the plane, in the same clothes I had been wearing during the accident, some three days after the fact and more than a little worse for wear.

I was still covered in patches of blood from head to toe, and the hole they had cut in the cast for my knee to "breathe" looked sickly. The customs official waved me through quickly. My father and aunt met me at the airport with an ambulance.

My aunt, who is also my godmother, was carrying a Harrods bag from London when she met me. As the paramedic affixed the blood pressure pad to my arm, I remembered my first vision of Fatna in the hospital in Morocco, and how she had also brought a Harrods bag on each and every visit.

The pictures I had taken of the wreck never came out.

A Moroccan Paradise Regained

By Michael Mewshaw

~

editor's note

I have a number of articles in my files about travelers returning to Morocco after some years hoping to find it exactly as they left it. Few places in the world change not at all, and it is undoubtedly foolish and selfish for us to want developing nations to remain in a time warp. It is not to be lamented that the area of the country the French called *Le Maroc utile*—the land with rich soil in the northeastern plains—now supports abundant fruit and vegetable crops (agriculture now accounts for one-fifth of Morocco's gross domestic product and provides 50 percent of jobs), or that Morocco's natural resources—petroleum, phosphates, iron ore, lead, zinc, manganese, fish, lead, and salt—contribute significantly to a healthy economy. The task, not an enviable one, is to find a balance. Perhaps, as Tahar Ben Jelloun has noted, "Morocco will achieve the perfect marriage between the most viable traditions and the most essential innovations. This opportunity depends on men, and not on the heavens. To bring together in one place all the contrasts of a civilization leaning towards Europe while remaining firmly rooted in its past and its history—that is the challenge the country faces every day." The happy news, as this writer and others like him found, is that even with an explosion of growth, Morocco is still seductive.

MICHAEL MEWSHAW writes often about travel for a wide variety of periodicals and is the author of numerous books, including *Playing Away: Roman Holidays and Other Mediterranean Encounters* (Atheneum, 1988) and *Ladies of the Court: Grace and Disgrace on the Women's Tennis Tour* (Crown, 1993).

More than two decades ago, not quite thirty and greatly under the sway of Lawrence Durrell's lush prose and Paul Bowles's lurid exoticism, I spent a winter larking around Morocco convinced I had discovered paradise. Now I was eager to regain it. But arriving in Marrakesh, I quickly realized that it had changed as much as I had. Condos and golf courses had cropped up in the palm grove. Guides mobbed luxury hotels and pounced on perplexed tourists like an NBA team in a last-gasp, full-court press. And while the square called Jemaa el Fna, the throbbing heart and vivid soul of the city, was still an authentic stronghold of native dancers, snake charmers, acrobats, and storytellers, everyone had developed an uncanny ability to switch gears at the sight of a foreigner. "Hey, Tokyo," a fortuneteller shouted at a Japanese tourist, "give me yen."

Deep in the meandering streets of the souk, however, things looked much as I remembered them. Sunlight slashed through reed awnings, zebra-striping merchants who hawked Berber carpets, ornate brass trays, and antique jewelry. Amid the pungent scent of incense, there were the riper odors of frying fish, animal skins curing in uric acid, vegetables slowly deliquescing in the heat. In the meat market, camel heads hung from rusty hooks. Below them, on the ground, their amputated feet stood lined up in the manner of shoes outside a mosque.

Yet even here the modern world had intruded. Vying with the raucous cries of vendors was the jackhammer beat of rap. Hustlers peddled pirated cassettes, "I ❤ Marrakesh" T-shirts, and what they swore was "dynamite hash." Next to a video rental outlet, a fellow in a spice shop shouted that he had just the elixir a man my age needed. Unplugging an odoriferous vial, he offered me an aphrodisiac. "One drop, and it's 'banzai!' all night."

Clearly, if I hoped to recapture the Morocco of my youth, I would have to leave Marrakesh.

The next day, I rented a car and drove across the High Atlas Mountains, south toward the town of Tafraoute, a miniature Shangri-La tucked away in a remote valley in the Anti-Atlas range. My spirits lifted immediately—as did the landscape, which surged into snow-capped peaks. Clear streams crackled down hillsides to irrigate patches of vegetation where oleanders flourished. In spots, the water had carved wide riverbeds whose sandy banks were lined with tree trunks peeled of bark and polished the silver-gray of beautifully grained marble.

As the road zigzagged higher, I had the exhilarating sensation of having the countryside to myself. There was just an occasional village, timeless and troglodytic, tucked away on a stony ledge from which it had been quarried. For miles, the silence was disturbed only by the hum of my tires on the black ribbon of asphalt.

When that hum was replaced by a loud slapping sound, I knew I had a flat and eased to a stop. Removing the jack, I tried to remember the rental agent's instructions. To get to the Peugeot's spare tire, you had to loosen a bolt. But I had no luck until a fellow ambled out of the wilderness. He was followed by others, and eventually a noisy quorum gathered around the car shouting encouragement in

French, Arabic, and Berber. A teenage boy and an old man went to work, moving with the speed of a pit crew at Indianapolis.

Afterward, I tipped them a few dollars and the old man dropped to his knees and kissed my hand. Embarrassed as I was, poised there like a sultan accepting obeisance from his subject, it did dawn on me that, in the space of an hour, I had traveled light-years from Marrakesh.

I had hoped to reach Tafraoute in a day's drive, but because of the delay, I stopped in Taroudant, the commercial and administrative center of the Sous valley. Reputed to have the best food in southern Morocco, Taroudant also offers two of the country's finest hotels—the celebrated Gazelle d'Or, an astonishingly luxurious and astonishingly expensive cluster of bungalows on a manicured estate, and the Palais Salam, a former palace set within the fortifications of the casbah. In the past, I had stayed in both places and preferred the Palais Salam, whose rooms opened onto courtyards canopied by banana plants and draped in bright swags of bougainvillea. On one visit, I had had the hotel to myself and sat in solitary splendor beside the pool eating a sumptuous meal.

But on this trip, a phalanx of tour buses nosed against Taroudant's crenelated walls, and the Palais Salam's restaurant was crowded with polyglot groups. At a table near mine, ruddy Finns waved sparklers and sang choruses of "Happy Birthday" as waiters wheeled out a cake.

I wheeled out to the front desk and attempted to telephone the Hotel des Amandiers in Tafraoute to book a room for the next day. That my repeated efforts failed to get a response didn't disappoint me. In fact, I was delighted by the thought of a hotel with a one-digit phone number that couldn't be bothered to answer.

Although Tafraoute lies fewer than one hundred miles from Taroudant, you'd have to be a bird or mountain goat to reach it by the most direct route. The road follows a circuitous course through the

Sous valley—west toward Agadir, south to Tiznit, then east into the thorny promontories of the Anti-Atlas. According to guidebooks, the Sous valley is a verdant flatland famed for olive and citrus groves and for argan trees full of foraging goats. The image that remained in my own mind from twenty years ago was of windfallen oranges rolling across the asphalt and being pulped to sweet ooze by passing cars.

But a prolonged drought has scorched the Sous to cinders. Although irrigated citrus groves have survived, the cactus hedges that once surrounded them now resemble puddles of melted candle wax. Outside the walled garrison town of Tiznit, the landscape looked as if it had been sandblasted, and for miles I drove over sun-bleached gravel that reminded me of those meticulously raked pebbles that pave the walkways in French parks.

Beyond Tirhmi, the countryside broke into canyons and towering cliffs, and the road swerved upward past unfenced abysses. For ten minutes, I made grueling progress behind a man on a bike. He had a long sheaf of reeds strapped to his rear fender and might have been an enormous insect with flapping wings. When I passed him, however, he looked weary and all too human.

At the crest of Col du Kerdous, at an elevation of 3,500 feet, stood the Hotel Kerdous, a starkly new structure with salmon pink walls and white-trimmed parapets. This area had been the impregnable redoubt of El Hiba, the Blue Sultan, whose troops battled the French until his death in 1918. (His younger brother continued the fight until 1926.) A forbidding moonscape of splintered rock, the mountains are a perfect rebel fortress, but beyond them lies the more clement territory of the Ammeln tribe, a division of the Chleuh Berbers, best known for financial acumen, not bellicosity. The Ammeln run grocery stores throughout Morocco, yet remain strongly attached to Tafraoute and its surrounding villages and return for weddings and religious feast days. Many have built modern villas in their birthplaces and intend to retire to them.

Lining the foothills around Tafraoute, strewn across valleys, stacked amid cultivated fields, and smack in the middle of towns are thousands of massive boulders. Paul Bowles has described the region as "the badlands of South Dakota writ on a grand scale." These rocks—outcroppings of igneous red lava that cooled thousands of years ago—are remarkable both for their shape and color. Some are phantasmagorical; others have the familiar contours of animals and humans. During the course of the day, they change from rose-tinted to terra-cotta to ocher, mauve, and aquamarine.

The boulders are more than merely picturesque. Many serve a practical purpose as the foundations and walls of houses. Constructed of hand-molded mud called *pisé,* painted delicate pastel shades, the houses cling to the rocks, their sharp-edged geometry describing misleading perspectives among the sensually curved stones.

Between the boulders, beside streams and irrigation ditches, almond trees grow, and in their shade, small plots of grain shimmer like cool green ponds. Wielding hoes and sickles, women cultivate the crops, wading through fields in robes shot through with gold and silver thread. Although 50 percent of the almond trees have died during the drought, February still transforms the area into a pointillist painting in which each blossom is a subtle brush stroke. When the wind blows, it unleashes a blizzard of pink and white petals.

Yet for all its beauty, Tafraoute will never be mistaken for a conventional resort; this is no country for sybarites. Rooms at the Hotel des Amandiers, the town's best accommodation, might most politely be described as basic. The hotel has a pool, but not enough water to fill it. During my stay, the electricity died every night at six P.M., then blinked back on at ten P.M., and the heat never came on that I noticed. Although winter days are mild in the high desert, it can be frigid after dark, and in summer the sun has the weight of molten lead.

The hotel does, however, have its quirky charms and unforgettable views. Seen from the window of my room, Tafraoute's monumental stones were burnished a rich gold, as were the mosques, minarets and houses of nearby hamlets. As evening advanced, the gold was slowly transmuted into baser metals, and when the sun slid behind the mountains, the landscape turned into a submarine world where palm fronds were transformed into swaying sea fans and casbahs appeared to be elaborate sand castles.

In a pen beneath my balcony a pile of spiny brush bounded up and trotted around. It was a wild boar with tusks the size of ivory letter openers. At the front desk, Dehbi Abdel-kader, the *chef de réception,* laughed and said, yes, he knew there was *un sanglier* out back. He had rescued it as a baby on the road to Tiznit and was raising it as a pet. Some of his French guests suggested he serve it up in a red wine sauce, but he wouldn't hear of that.

Wasn't a wild boar a dangerous pet? I asked.

"*Pas du tout,*" said Mr. Abdel-kader. "*Elle n'est pas méchante.* The bad ones are bad, but this one is good and cute."

Mr. Abdel-kader was a dependable fount of information about the area, and at his urging I made daily excursions. The first was a three-mile hike to the town of Agard Oudad, whose peach-colored cubistic structures lay scattered at the base of the Chapeau de Napoléon. A steeple of rocks over a hundred feet high, Napoleon's Hat casts a long shadow over the town's cumin-scented alleys.

On the return trip I passed a creek where women crouched washing clothes. The rocks behind them were a colorful collage of shirts, underpants, and socks, as the women kneaded the laundry, beat it against the stones, flung it into the air, then spread it out to dry.

Wednesday is market day in Tafraoute, and although the occasion can't compare with the commercial extravaganzas in Fez and

Marrakesh, the vendors are charmingly low-key and focus their attention on local trade instead of foreigners. I was free to stroll about, enjoying the ritualistic bargaining. In the shade of tattered umbrellas, merchants sold mounds of fly-ridden meat, buckets of olives, and pyramids of dates and figs. An itinerant dentist lounged next to a table littered with false teeth and did a brisk business— far better, at any rate, than the fellow who roosted behind dogeared, out-of-date magazines from France, Germany, and Spain. Cleaning their covers with a feather duster, he preserved the slick periodicals as if they were priceless icons.

North of Tafraoute, a necklace of towns adorns the base of Djebel el Kest, a jagged rooster comb of mountains. Starting at Oumesnat, one can walk for miles through a patchwork of culti- vated fields, palm groves, and fruit orchards. In the hills, just beyond the arable land, villages rise on terraces in the form of ancient amphitheaters. Constructed of mud and stone, the houses seem designed for defense, with slotlike windows, fortified towers, and heavy wooden doors. Over each lintel a palm print had been pressed into the clay as protection against the evil eye. Yet as formidable and secure as the houses appear to be, they are water-soluble, and after a few hard rains, they are always in danger of crumbling into the earth from which they have been built.

Until late in my trip, I delayed visiting an attraction everyone had recommended—the Painted Rocks. Sometime between 1980 and 1986 (sources vary), Jean Verame (or Veram or Varan, or maybe Derain), a Belgian (or French) artist, received permission to paint several acres of the landscape just off the road south of Agard Oudad. As described in guidebooks, the project sounded sopho- moric, but one could never have imagined the dramatic impact of Mr. Verame's work.

Giant monoliths, painted black, dotted an arid plain that glit- tered with specks of mica. Oval rocks, aqua in color, gargantuan in scale, lay heaped in piles; isolated boulders, sculptured by wind, resembled bluebirds about to take wing. An enormous cross formed by red and black stones loomed above a boulder in Easter egg stripes.

The natural setting was an essential ingredient of this marvelous mineral garden. Drywashes of pale sand banked by fig trees and wild sprays of jasmine sluiced among the stones. And over everything arched an enormous blue bowl of sky—a sky so clear that a passing jet left contrails like the score of a diamond on a pane of glass. The silence, too, was like glass—crystalline and easily shattered.

As I was departing, I heard the roar of two motorcyclists arriving and thought how lucky I had been to have the place to myself, to have had a last chance to luxuriate in the lovely, lonely expanses of Morocco. Then suddenly I realized I could come back—this evening, tomorrow morning, ten years from now. Of course, every return carries the risk of disappointment and ruined memories. But there's always the hope that remote places will remain the same— or, as in this case, that the artful application of a few buckets of paint will make them even better.

Moroccan Oases

Taroudant

Palais Salam Hotel (telephone: 048.85.25.01; fax: 048.85.26.54). "Crowded though it was on my visit," Michael Mewshaw writes, "the Palais Salam is still a lovely spot. The rooms are all on two levels, with a small sitting area and bathroom downstairs and a sleeping loft upstairs. The walls and ceilings have been painted with arabesque designs like those on local carpets."

Just outside town, the luxurious **Gazelle d'Or** has flower-filled gardens, a swimming pool, and tennis courts. Closed July and August.

Tafraoute

Hotel des Amandiers (telephone: 048.80.00.08; fax: 048.80.03.43). "In addition to being the best hotel in the area, the Amandiers has the best food and the largest selection of Moroccan wines," Mr. Mewshaw reports.

The **Restaurant l'Étoile du Sud** has an outdoor café that is a pleasant place during the day. At night, in cold weather, food is served indoors. In milder weather, meals can be taken in a huge tent. In both cases, there is Berber music (not bad) and dancing (a pale imitation of what one might see at feasts in mountain villages)."

Into the Arabesque:
On the Road in Morocco

BY BARBARA GRIZZUTI HARRISON

⁓

editor's note

This was the article that deeply, desperately consumed me with the overwhelming desire to go to Morocco. It originally appeared in the October 1991 issue of *Condé Nast Traveler*.

BARBARA GRIZZUTI HARRISON writes often about travel for a variety of periodicals and is the author of *The Islands of Italy* (Ticknor and

Fields, 1991), *The Astonishing World* (Ticknor and Fields, 1992), *An Accidental Autobiography* (Houghton Mifflin, 1996 in hardcover and 1997 in paperback); and *Italian Days* (Ticknor and Fields, 1989), which was honored with the American Book Award.

In the exotic and at the same time startlingly familiar landscape of dreams—in which the impossible is the inevitable—rivers run through deserts, paths where seductive dangers lurk give onto gardens of paradise, and houses are caves through which the unconscious searches and stumbles. Objects and events telescope and melt into a disorienting unity. And from this land no one returns undisturbed.

Driving through Morocco—sixteen kaleidoscopic days, from sea to desert sands, through high mountain passes and over stingy scrub, from the imperial cities to mud villages—I feel as if I am hurtling through a museum of Impressionist and Cubist paintings. I never feel quite relaxed. (One is never so alert as in a dream.) I am in the midst of dazzling confusion: rivers do run through deserts; in casbahs, or fortified castles, streets are underground tunnels; and within the textural, visual newness—the total otherness and strangeness of Morocco—I detect hints, not easy to decipher and decode, of things I have apprehended before . . . in art or in dreams. An alien culture through which threads of the familiar are woven rushes by me at sixty miles an hour.

Many travelers, whether of wholesome disposition like Edith Wharton or of decadent disposition like Paul Bowles, have perceived and described Morocco in terms of dreams. To Wharton, Morocco appeared to exist in its very own light, a light of "preternatural purity which gives a foretaste of mirage . . . the light in which magic becomes real, and which helps to understand how, to people living in such an atmosphere, the boundary between fact and dream perpetually fluctuates." For Bowles, who rejoiced in decay, Morocco came as a gift: he woke from a sleeping dream to enter a living dream; walking in the late afternoon North African sunlight "through complex and tunneled streets," he "realized with a jolt that the magic city really existed."

It comes as a surprise to me, now that I have been to Morocco, that dreams are not permeated with palpable fragrance, the sense of smell being, we are told, the most evocative of all the senses. Morocco smells better than any place I have ever been. It also smells worse.

One sometimes wonders what discernible mark the French—whose "protectorate" Morocco was between 1912 and 1956—had on this country placed between the desert and the sea. They left behind a language and a taste for sleazy satin; and they created a network of superbly serviceable roads. There were no modern roads in Morocco as late as the first decade of the present century. That was the time when, as Edith Wharton wrote, "the 'Christian' might enjoy the transient joy of wandering unmolested in cities of ancient mystery and hostility, whose inhabitants seemed hardly aware of his intrusion." The road that the photographer Philip-Lorca ("P.L.") diCorcia and I take through the fertile lowlands, from Casablanca, where our plane landed, to the Imperial City of Fez, is narrow but splendid. And the men and women sitting on their haunches along the roadside, among ancient wells and hand plows, seem hardly aware of our intrusion. Four men in long white cotton gowns sit, with biblical simplicity and intensity, under a date palm, turbans wound around their heads. A young girl carrying reeds and sweet grasses emerges from the shadow of a glade, papyrus rustling; a glance at us, and she is gone with the grace of a gazelle, leaving us to wonder if she was ever there.

I spot a profusion of red poppies, vivid and frail, among the green wheat. Carpets of wildflowers—gentian, violet, purple, pale buttercup yellow, acid lemon yellow—alternate with tidy fields of grasshopper green lined with neat rows of olive trees. A woman dressed in black, friendly and candid, next to an ancient Berber-painted bridge, waves to me (a coolie's conical hat, Cleopatra's face); more poppies, swaying among onions whose long, slender stalks culminate in many-headed white blossoms emerging from vellum jackets. The astringent smell of onions is added to the mint-scented air, and yeasty-smelling milk is sold in orange plastic buckets under eucalyptus trees in the heat of day.

In this purified, translucent light, soft and fresh, and in these luminous shadows, Matisse, who spent two winters in Morocco and claimed to have found paradise there, learned to reconcile abstraction and decoration with realism, and his paintings became tender, fluid—"fire," as one of his critics said, "filtered through water"; the red of Fauvism yielding to sap green and cameo pink, pale ocher, periwinkle, all as cool "as a freshly opened almond."

A viaduct of warm red-gold stone carries a train over a sluggish brown river in which an orange truck and a black Mercedes are being washed and little girls bathe. Sheep's wool, not pretty and white, as in fairy tales, but oily and brown, waits for its river bath among squatters' huts and cypresses and palm trees and a square of watered and manicured lawn ringed with century plants, their stalks like giant asparagus. Sheep wander on the banks. Dogs wallow like pigs in the swampy water. An old man in a silver *djellaba* stands on the viaduct to survey the scene; raggedy children chatter and touch.

Boys along the side of the road hold up strange artifacts—a hairy turtle?—for sale. And all the while our car is going so fast it startles the birds.

We stop in a village, at a generic café along a street of yellow-white, dirty arcades. Carcasses of animals, their tails and feet and privates intact, hang from hooks above the wooden tables where we sit, and from these unrecognizable animals, meat is carelessly hacked and placed on a brazier fanned with cardboard. We eat our succulent charred lamb with mint tea, a garden in a glass. There are no women in the café; there never are. (Men are superior to women, says the Koran, and wiser.)

In the dry hills above the old city of Fez, children romp among Merinid tombs, the detritus of a golden age of indigenous Berber kings who ruled Morocco from the thirteenth century to the fifteenth. (So far as anyone can tell, Berbers were always here; Arabs are relative newcomers—seventh- and eighth-century arrivals.) The hills are dun-colored; the houses and terraces, the ramparts and fortresses of the medina, the old walled Arab quarter that stretches below my hotel balcony, are a dull dun gloss on a tawny plateau, tumbling toward a brown river but frozen in their fall, as if arrested by a god who saw them in the pearly haze of dawn, when they take on the elegant, enameled look of a Persian miniature. Fez, the oldest Islamic medieval city in the world, home of the world's oldest Islamic university, was the prototype of the just and ordered city that communally minded Muslims aspire to create. It is dirty now, it crumbles; but it is alive, and its thrills are not vestigial. Pale mountains surround and cradle it.

Fez's medina is a labyrinth within an enclosure, impossible to map: its narrow streets twist and tangle obscurely, without apparent reason or comprehensible design, like a calligraphic arabesque in a foreign script. For a stranger it is a physical closure without a psychological one—an unsettling maze. It is impossible to walk through the winding streets of the medina without a guide; if you do not hire a guide, young men, old men, and ragamuffins will attach themselves to you offering their services—in either case, you are never ever alone. No experience in the medina—in any medina of Morocco, in any bazaar—is unmediated by another human being.

"Honey sweetheart darling madam," my guide calls me. His name is Ismail. He is unctuous, bossy, full of veiled but risible contempt. *Balak! Balak!* the donkey herders cry—beware! One donkey and his burden and a pedestrian in any threadlike street of the medina create a traffic jam. In blank facades, beautiful iron-embossed doors tantalize. That there are gorgeous gardens behind these endless tall walls one must take on faith; there is nothing visibly flowery here. In fact, the approaching stench suggests dead meat. Dead skins. We are nearing the medina's tanneries. Ismail says, unanswerably, "If you had a tannery in your country, darling madam, it would smell even more, I am sure." In round pits of dried earth, animal skins are washed and dyed. Cows' urine and excrement are integral to the process. Men, their skirts hiked above their knees, are trampling in the brilliant colors of the dye. Ismail grabs my hand and hauls me up deep steps to a rooftop observation post. On a terrace above the pits I wander among skins dyed poppy red and skins dyed indigo. "The soul is a newly skinned hide," writes Jalaluddin Rumi, the thirteenth-century scholar, poet, and theologian of the mystical Sufi brotherhood of Islam. "Work on it with manual discipline and the bitter tanning-acid of grief, and you'll become lovely, and *very* strong." Garbage burns on the river, which is an oily rainbow of vegetable dyes and animal and toxic wastes. Sheep and goats meander. This place, Ismail appears to believe, is the epiphany of a walk through Fez.

At my importuning we stop at the gate of the great ninth-century Karaouyine mosque, closed, as are nearly all mosques in Morocco, to non-Muslims "because," Ismail says, "the French soldiers broke beer bottles in our mosques, honey madam, and pissed"—for which French sin I can find no historical evidence. The mosque, its walls encrusted with shops and stalls, is the largest building in Fez, but elusive: you know you're approaching one of its four main gates only by the sweet smell of nougat, heaps of which are sold at every holy place. Above the mosque is a triptych of golden balls representing bread, water, and salt, the necessities of the desert, according to one explanation; talismanic protection against rats, scorpions, and serpents, according to another. I stop at one of the mosque's fourteen doors, and through it I glimpse rush matting, men abluting at a fountain, jute-covered white columns, green pitched roofs.

All my impressions are confused. There are more than two hundred quarters, or neighborhoods, in the medina, each with its own bakery, its own fountain, and its own *medersa,* or residential Koranic school. To the inhabitants of those quarters I have traversed, I am both visible and invisible, relevant and irrelevant, foreign flesh to be roughly elbowed aside, an intrinsically uninteresting object to whom objects can be sold. This is not a comfortable state of affairs. I have caught glimpses of women peering out from grills; streets hung with colored wool; a *fonduk,* or caravansary for Berbers and for animals, with two-tiered lacy wooden balconies projecting into a dirt courtyard; tattooed Berber women unveiled; girls in caftans wearing lipstick; stalls selling junky rayon next to stalls selling jewelry of eighteen-karat gold. The soapy smell of cedar from the Atlas Mountains, the sharp smell of spices, and the hot masculine smell of copper welding shroud—almost, but not quite—the sickening smell of the tanneries. Walter Harris, who as the London *Times* man in Morocco at the turn of the century enjoyed the friendship of the sultans, said Fez smelled of incense and dead cats.

At dusk, the lights of the bazaar are turned on. It is enchanting here, and it is sinister. The commonplace—heaps of boiled eggs in straw baskets, glasses of fresh orange juice, a picture of Paul Newman—seems mysterious in this candid light on these narrow, winding streets. And all human activities seem both familiar and opaque.

If I spoke Arabic (or French) I would say to Ismail, as British civil servant and writer Peter Mayne said to a guide in Tangier in the early 1950s, "I am a mad person who does not think it strange to be alone and to know nothing, and within a few minutes I shall be gone from here, and I am praying that where I am going I shall find a world where guides are born with the mark on them, so that they can be identified by their mamas and strangled." (Notwithstanding which, Mayne, who had learned to love Muslim life during a sojourn in Pakistan, lived in the back streets of Marrakech for a happy year of his life.)

Ismail is clever, and I am capable of being seduced by that which I despise. I have mentally armed myself against being badgered, wheedled, or bullied into a shop to buy a rug. I do not want to buy a rug except when I want to buy a rug. But by a series of maneuvers as tricky and twisty as the unmapped streets of the medina, Ismail has manipulated me into the shop where he will gain a commission for any purchase of mine. Along the way, in tones as sweet as almond milk and honey, he has asked, "You trust me, sweetheart madam?" to which there is no possible polite answer. We are—how exactly did this happen?—in a shop where I have no wish to be, surrounded by more rugs than are contained in all of Christendom. I buy a rug. I could have said no. How did this happen? He made me feel clever, as if I were choosing to stop here; in fact, I actually begged him to stop in this shop—he contrived to have me do so. He made me feel clever, clever man, before he made me feel like a fool.

Ismail walks ahead of me on the way back to my hotel, all pretenses of being my friend now forgotten. *El hammdul-lah*—praise

Allah!—he says to one and all. Everyone in the bazaar knows every-one else, and Ismail is sharing his delight at having snared a sucker.

What Matisse found in Morocco was a kind of mystic vacancy, the peaceful presence of the sacred. I looked out from the balcony of my hotel room over the rooftops of the medina, and I felt noth-ing of the sort. The Hotel Palais Jamai, admirably situated just within the medina's ramparts, has a fine view of Old Fez, but that was not what I hungered for after my intimate walk through the city. I wanted a refuge. I asked for another room, one in the old wing of the former palace, overlooking a garden.

A garden makes a difference. And, indeed, the nineteenth-century vizier who built the Palais Jamai, true to the religion and cul-ture of Islam—in which material things mirror the divine and have metaphysical significance—surrounded his palace with walled gar-dens precisely so that the hurly-burly, the commerce, and even the public religion of the medina would be shut out in favor of contem-plative privacy: in the garden there is *only* the garden—and Allah.

In the early morning I sit on the porch that leads from my room. Every leaf is articulated in the deceptively pale but daggerlike light. For a Muslim, the world is full of tangible, palpable metaphysical symbols, each of which incarnates feminine and masculine princi-ples. The garden is the reflection of the beauty of God. The porch is the transitional space between the temporal and the spiritual worlds, between which the soul moves; the porch waits patiently to catch the light; it symbolizes the presence of the Divine Name *Nur*—"Light." The garden is quartered; the Koran depicts paradise as four gardens, interpreted esoterically as four stages through which the mystic travels on his inward journey toward God, and traditionally known as the Garden of the Soul, the Garden of the Heart, the Garden of the Spirit, and the Garden of Essence. The

Garden of the Soul is the feminine principle. In order to enter it, one must cultivate the feminine quality of intuition.

Every garden must contain a fountain, the fruit of trees, and flowing water. Mine did. I say *mine* because no one else ever seemed to walk through the space enclosed by quartered hedges of bougainvillea and thyme to enter the world of sultry roses, with fragrance so silken as to seem illicit, joined to banks of virginal daisies, spicy marigolds, and weedy geraniums, to date palms and apricot trees. "A garden enclosed is my spouse," wrote Solomon. Traditional Muslims have taken the holy writings to mean that the veil is an extension of this cloistered space, that the woman, seeing but unseen behind it, moves through teeming life as if sequestered in her own garden.

In my hotel room, which is called El Mizna, "the garden," the furniture is a legacy of the vizier's infatuation with France, shared by many of his countrymen before that country colonized Morocco. It is quite ugly, stolid, heavy, and uncomfortable. But the amber patterned ceiling, which looks like a pitched tent translated into wood, is fabulous. What I like best is walking into my darkened room in the heat of day—the brass key is so hot it burns my hand—and feeling the marble, cool beneath my feet. White watered-silk curtains sail on the garden's breeze.

The sky is bleached white when I awake; sky and air are one. And it is breezy and cool, almost cold. By eleven it is hot. Under these sensual weather conditions one is nicely conscious of the skin being an organ . . . that is played.

Moulay, our driver, takes me to the nearby Imperial City of Meknes to visit the tomb of Sultan Moulay Ismail, the late-seventeenth- and early-eighteenth-century despot who used everything that came to hand—he immured the bodies of dead slaves in the walls of Meknes. Moulay Ismail killed for sport, "as a matter of personal and daily satisfaction, like the pleasures of the table or of the harem." He liked to wear yellow when he killed; he envisioned Meknes as an Oriental Versailles.

Through the monumental gateway of Bab el Mansour, we drive through a triple-arched doorway to the tomb of the tyrant and his mosque—the only one in Morocco that Christians are permitted to enter. The mosque and the harem garden have connecting doors. The tomb is flanked by two seventeenth-century grandfather clocks, a gift from Louis XIV, a substitute for the hand of his daughter, marriage to whom the sultan had ardently sought.

The clocks are not an anomaly. The palaces of Sultan Moulay Abd el-Aziz, who ruled from 1894 to 1908, became veritable playrooms, stuffed with gramophones, toy railways, typewriters, musical stuffed birds, barrel organs, and hansom cabs. A German sold the young sovereign—who was nineteen when he ascended to the throne—a motorboat, which was never put out to sea. An American sold him a British bulldog with false teeth for $40,000.

If these grotesque purchases had not in themselves drained the coffers of imperial Morocco, the commissions on them did: there were—and still are—so many middlemen in Morocco, it is believed that the sultan was obliged to pay 500 percent in commission to them. His vizier got loans from Europe to cover the boy's extravagances—and these debts led directly to Morocco's becoming a "protectorate" of France.

Among Moulay Ismail's lesser sins was cannibalizing the ancient Roman ruins of Volubilis to build his Imperial City. Its remains stand today on a windswept plain nineteen miles from Meknes, above a sea of grain through which the wind sighs mournfully. The colonnaded women's bath is populated now only with geraniums; the once-luxurious rooms of the bordello are home to nettles and scorpions; an olive press is left to rot, like the skeleton of a dinosaur (which it refuses to do); there is only the merest trickle of rusty water in the troughs where white and purple togas once were washed. The rocks are worn where clothes were beaten centuries ago—it is lovely in the sun to touch the smooth rocks, the palpable past. Even lovelier are the faded mosaics. The Muslim interdiction against portraying animals, birds, humans, and flowers in art, taken seriously in Morocco, produces what often appears to be a sterile sameness—calligraphy and diamond-shaped mosaics and stucco fretwork—which in turn breeds ennui. But here are dolphins sporting, a man riding a horse backward, a jolly squid, a witty prawn. On a stone block there is a representation of an enormous phallus, perhaps three feet long. Moulay points me toward it, then retreats, smirking.

From Volubilis we can see the holy city of Moulay Idriss, white and shining on a conical hill (giving the architects of Islam the last, radiant word). White birds escort our car. Moulay plays Vivaldi on the car stereo; he calls it "American music."

In Morocco, Moulay Idriss, which dates from the late eighth century, is considered in holiness second only to Mecca—Moulay Idriss, the great-grandson of the prophet Muhammad, having been the founder of the first Arab dynasty in Morocco. NON-MUSSELMAN FORBIDDEN inside the holy man's tomb, however; a low cedar gate bars the way. In this spot in the 1920s Edith Wharton saw blood dripping from the whirling caftans of dancers, "forming fresh pools among the stones . . . pools [that] were fed from great gashes which the dancers hacked in their own skulls and breasts with hatchets and sharpened stones." The dancers, howling, a brotherhood of mystics and martyrs, were baptized in their own blood.

It is pacific now, where religious frenzy on occasion still reigns. Boys with fingers interlaced lounge against rough walls, breathing their love at each other (the casualness of homoeroticism in Morocco takes one's breath away); a young boy wears a shirt stenciled with a picture of Madonna; a man with double-jointed crippled fingers brays like a donkey and collects alms; a tall, handsome, elegant old man in a blue *djellaba* smiles at me with blinding blue eyes and seems inclined to pat my head. (How I wish he would. I have never felt such an outsider as I do here.)

Outside the holy place, lollipops are sold, and beads and nougat, of course. In the town there is a multileveled market where I find the season's first apricots, white; and artichokes and lambs' heads and cows' feet and beans and peaches and plastic sunglasses and henna—powder and leaf—and the ubiquitous boiled eggs and bulls' testicles. And a pale, blue-eyed attenuated hippie, drunk, who Moulay—who is dreadfully stubborn—insists is a Berber. I am a hair away from being enraged at Moulay: he has smoothed a young girl's behind. Giving him the benefit of the doubt, and for the moment attributing nothing more to him than tenderness, I say, "Why don't you get married?" He is thirty-eight. "Because the mothers I hate," he says. The "Berber" turns out to be an American, from Philadelphia (and high on *kef*, hashish). This doesn't bother Moulay at all; in some basic way he can never, where I am concerned, be wrong: I am a woman, he is a man.

By happy accident, I chance upon a local communal bath, a *hammam*, at women's hour. In a large room, logs and sugar burn to heat and sweeten the water for the bath; they produce the smell of barbecued sausages. A crone leads me by the hand down crooked stairs to a room so dark and hot that I think I have found Hell, an inferno of flesh, pinky beige. Women, as unselfconscious as young animals, wash their bodies with hot and cold water from plastic buckets, pull at their nipples and their breasts, entirely self-bemused. They are as alien to me as the moon . . . and as familiar.

On the way back to Fez, Moulay plays Christmas carols: "And the snow lay round about . . ."

We leave Fez for Erfoud and the deep south; a nine-hour drive, a jeweled blur. (Fez—in which the past and the present, elegance and incipient violence, formality and decay, are braided—is working in me; I think of it with mingled revulsion and longing. I miss it.) P.L. and I are never quite sure where we are, assiduous consideration of maps and guidebooks and signposts notwithstanding. Moulay's command of English serves only to confound us. ("What's that, Moulay?" "King house." "Which king?" "Yes. King.") Palm trees yield to sycamore and cedar; then we are in the midst of apple trees and lilac bushes. We see storks in giant nests on pitched roofs in ski resorts. We know we must cross the Atlas Mountains—the Middle Atlas? the High Atlas?—to get to Erfoud. It would be nice if we could judge, which we cannot, when we have crossed the mountain pass. ("Moulay, is this the pass?" "Pass." "Have we passed the pass?" "No pass. This pass." "What?") Now the world is rocky; snow-covered mountains are in the near distance. On top of rock, rock is piled—fetishistic piles of rock; perhaps they are messages. Endless plains. Goldenrod. Miles of stone walls without mortar. This air is ambrosial, mountain-sweet—does that mean we haven't yet crossed the pass? There is a porcupine on the side of the road. Only his feet and his quills. His meat has been eaten by a shepherd. (Rumi: "The soul is a porcupine, made strong by stick-beating.") Fresh animal ordure, a good smell. A lake of small white flowers. Fluorescent purple ice flowers.

Now black, forbidding mountains rear, and then we are in a tunnel and exit into a land of casbahs and *ksour*—pure, simple, robust Cubist forms by the River Ziz, sand castles. (Properly speaking, a casbah is a fortified castle, while a *ksar* is a fortified town. This is almost a distinction without a difference in the desert. Both are made of mud mixed with fibers from palm trunks, a material called *pisé;* almost all have high small windows and incised geometric carvings on crenellated towers. They are designed to look inward, to courtyards and communal space, and they are defensive. They are grand, but should a heavy rainstorm come—not unknown in the desert—they melt.)

We pass groves of palm trees, oleander, almond. We drive through arcaded garrison towns, town after town, arcade after arcade. Animals' heads, hairy, unskinned, are cooked on open fires. We eat hot bread and ripe bananas that have a slightly bitter after-taste. Inky hills, a slight underglaze of green. No sound in the world at all. Houses crouch on bare hills; there is no presumption in them. A salmon-colored mosque; red canyons; Nubian faces. Triumphal arches that lead to more nondescript arcades, an absurdist's dream. Smells from municipal abattoirs. Fields of jagged upright stones no different from other stones—till one sees the design in the apparent randomness: these are Arab cemeteries, the dead are an intimate part of the landscape.

Twilight is the magic hour. We pass through white horseshoe gates with green enameled tiles and find ourselves in a market square that might have been painted by Carpaccio or Bellini. We are in another, very old world, a world of incantatory charm and volup-tuousness. The hallucinatory confusions of the drive from Fez have been preparation for this moment; weariness and irritable exhaus-tion have been wayposts on the journey toward delicious languor and untroubled acceptance. Now no question demands to be asked, no conflict resolved: we are in the sandy south, gateway to the great sand desert of the Sahara. Erfoud. Where everything and everybody is self-possessed and necessary, and every object has unquestionable integrity. The bruised and excited uncertainties of the last nine hours have led to this absolutely perfect moment at dusk; time is timeless here, endless and circular, as it is in arabesques. There is nothing one could possibly quarrel with, each thing being indisputably what it is and whole unto itself.

White-turbaned men sit along palm-lined walls, their faces turned to the storyteller in the center of their rapt group. Lanterns light the way for cartloads of black-robed women, heavily veiled, and even this seems poetically right here, even the kohl-lined eye peering out from its enveloping garment. Wharton: "All the mystery that awaits us looks out through the eye-slits in the grave-clothes muffling her. Where have they come from, where are they going, all these slow wayfarers of the unknown . . . ? Interminable distances unroll behind them, they breathe of Timbuctoo and the farthest desert. . . ." Blue men, tall handsome men wearing indigo turbans and robes that stain their skin, ride by on white camels, their beautiful dark faces veiled (black eyes flashing) to keep away the sand.

In the morning the square has lost its magic. It is just a provincial square, tawdry, sober, penitential. Outside our hotel, the Salam, we meet an Englishwoman, M., who looks like a spinster schoolmarm. She has lived here five years. She sells her indifferent watercolors at the hotel, where she sits from morning to night. One cannot imagine her life; she is plump, pleasant, a woman of few words—and, one imagines, a few compelling obsessions. "The light," she says.

We drive south from Erfoud, past irrigated fields of brilliant green, rivers in the desert, to the town of Rissani, where there is a souk in the ruins of a seventeenth-century casbah, and a *ksar,* too.

I love the market in Rissani. Shopping in Morocco has become for me a transaction almost as personal as sex. And having Moulay around is like having a third person in bed; he insists on interceding and thrusting himself into my experience. Somewhere on the long drive from Fez to Erfoud we passed stalls where crystal quartz and emerald quartz and amethyst quartz were sold; it was very beautiful. "I you no me like buy here," said Moulay, who has trouble with his pronouns, perhaps because he can think only of himself. "Wait Marrakech." Marrakech, his hometown, is where he is best able to collect commissions. At that time I was still trying to humor him—like many women, I am afraid men will exercise retribution behind the wheel of a car for slights—so I didn't buy the glittering stones. . . . Naturally, I never saw anything like them again.

In the animal souk, donkeys and sheep and goats are being sold. There is nothing for me to buy here, so Moulay deserts me, and I feel the returning happiness of being alone, unregarded, ignored, unessential to the world I move in. The tall, gaunt countrymen who come to buy here have no contract with us; their disinterested naturalness amounts to majesty. I am the only woman in this market, and it makes no difference to the men in turbans and wool caps—their business is not with me. There is nothing hostile in the din.

In another part of the market I make out the forms of babies hidden in the depths of black *haiks*—a life in the sun begun with months in a postwomb darkness. A Berber woman with bright green eyes sells jewelry—the Berbers have a special fondness for Venetian beads, which they mix and match with old coral and dull silver—twigs for cleaning teeth, dried roses, and musk, the sexy smell of which threads its way through the more pungent and less aphrodisiac smells of the market.

Dust to dust. The *ksar* of Rissani—three centuries old, built by Sultan Moulay Ali Cherif, first king of the ruling dynasty of

Morocco—is a kind of extended cave. We walk through cool underground streets, like tunnels in a womb. Pools of light from high windows illuminate great doors and hinges. Women in black glide through distant arches; in this prenatal light they are all beautiful. Four beauties lean negligently against a low doorway. This is like our first home; and what we can imagine of our last. No wonder these men think women are dangerous—they are wombs within wombs, the beginning and the end.

On the road back to Erfoud we enter another kind of cave, a Berber tent formed of waterproof sheep's wool rugs, on a windswept plateau. Outside are two circular enclosures, one of wire and one of stone, for sheep and goats and sheepdogs. I hold a baby lamb six days old in my arms, and he licks my neck and chews on my hair; and all of a sudden I miss my children. Moulay points out the lamb's sex; he is always doing this.

It is clean and fragrant inside the tent, but there are flies. An old man rests in the corner, leaning, in striped robes, on his staff. This is all, I can't help thinking, very MGM. The tent is divided (after a while the exotic becomes familiar, or you translate it into familiar terms so as not to go mad with a multiplicity of impressions) into a kitchen, where on a brazier tea is being prepared by a blue-eyed woman, and a visitors' parlor, where on many rugs we drink the sweet tea. The tattooed woman competes with me for the attention of a cat. This has very little to do with the cat, and everything to do with the men I am with. Her hennaed hands flirt with the cat—with the men.

The Land-Rover bounces south from Erfoud over miles of greenish-black scrub, trackless desert, to get to the sand dunes of Merzouga. In this altogether lonely and dry place, a solitary man faces Mecca in prayer, his red motor scooter resting at his side: if you are a Muslim you are always oriented in the world Allah has made for you.

Ahead of us, light plays on sugary sand—purple, mustard, rose, green, pink light, all of these colors and none of them. The sun is setting in the desert, and a new palette has to be invented to describe this. Saffron, ocher, violet. Camels—silly, supercilious, and remarkably dignified—stretch their necks on the ground like lazy cats. Every fold and curve and hollow of every dune is maternal and alluring. The silence is profound.

We are heading west to Ouarzazate, at the junction of the Dadès and the Drâa River valley. Once again we pass through wildernesses of rock, through canyons straight and sheer, like impending doom in the form of a vise. This is the kind of landscape that breeds fanatics. We drive over wrinkled, fat mountains that look like soft constructions in a cheap amusement park and mountains that look like an illustration for the travail of creation, the dry torment of God, the dry despair of man. Once again we are subject to weariness, ennui, the lethargy induced by a surfeit of impressions, and once again we are never quite sure where we are. We are rescued from nervous irritability by the casbahs—dense and dramatic, those defensive sand castles that look both barbaric and domestic—that line our path, and by the valley palmeries, the seas of palms that gather by the rivers. Imagine! There are hollyhocks in these palmeries, hollyhocks from *Dick and Jane,* flowers straight from an American childhood . . . and cabbages and corn and pomegranates and figs. ("This River Water is an orchard that fills your basket"— Rumi.)

A woman is picking roses. She is black. The roses grow near the high corn, which rustles like torn silk. They are pink. The intense, orgasmic sweetness of roses in the dry desert air and the sweeter, more urgent cry of the muezzin calling the faithful to prayer persuaded romantic Victorian ladies (Isabel Burton, Jane Digby el

Mezrab, Isabelle Eberhardt) that wild men would be good to them; women fall in love with a country and marry a man.

The car never smells of "car"; it never smells neutral. It smells of woodsmoke and of mint, of roses—what an extravagant country this is. And when you think you have reached an apotheosis, more is added: now, sweetness upon sweetness, it smells of moonflowers.

Men who want nothing in return stop to offer us small green apples.

These are the good things about our hotel in Ouarzazate, an unremarkable town well placed for excursions: the vanilla smell of pink oleanders (which are poisonous); jasmine, white and yellow; roses, eight feet tall, that miraculously do not droop of their own weight; the fig jam we have for breakfast. And the fun of regarding rich Arab ladies who lunch: silk caftans, Gucci bags, red toenails, modest head coverings. Their bodies are like battlefields of cultures in contention, cloistered East and brazen West.

We have dinner in the Glaoui Casbah of Tiffoultoute, seven miles west of Ouarzazate. They were wild men from the south, the Glaoui. It is said of T'hami el Glaoui, pasha of Marrakech from 1918 to 1956 and staunch supporter of the French, that he never pardoned and he never forgave. He was a falconer. He had "talent scouts" in France and everywhere in Morocco, agents positioned at railroad stations who pretended to be guides and procured for the Glaoui fine European women. He is said never to have forced his favors upon Europeans; he was barbaric, intelligent, ambitious, insatiable, and generous with jewels. Winston Churchill admired him. The casbah that bears his name is best seen in the moonlight, when its deficiencies of style yield to its magnificence of size.

There are rooms for rent in the casbah that used to house the Glaoui's wives and concubines. "Once the doors of the harem closed behind a new acquisition," wrote Gavin Maxwell in his book on the Glaoui, *Lords of the Atlas,* "she knew that she would never again leave the women's quarters of her master until she was carried out to the cemetery. From then on she was a woman of the harem, her life bounded by its jealousies and rivalries and petty squabbles and household breakages that were judged and punished by the Glaoui himself; her conversation limited to the endless sexual gossip of her fellow concubines; her sexual life limited to her necessarily infrequent turn in her master's bed and the sometimes passionate solace of her own sex. She would never again see any other man than T'hami face to face."

Nature goes on and on, and it is completely indifferent. We are driving south from Ouarzazate, through the Drâa River valley to Zagora. The countryside is dun, the *ksour* are dun. Coca-Cola signs and colored drawings of Mickey Mouse on dun-colored school walls break up the monochromatic color scheme. Immured in the car, watching everything through plate glass, I feel neurotically removed from everything I see; I want to walk in the *ksar;* what good is looking at a *ksar* if you can't walk in it? Moulay says, "There they you kill madam me not want trouble you." Of course they won't kill me; why should they?

The walls of the *ksar* are very high; you have to be at least five feet tall before you can see the mountains—the world—above the walls. Old men and women and boys and girls gather around me, candid and friendly, their rough hands curious, their manner kind. They invite me in. In a long, narrow room of Amish simplicity (clothing hooks, pillows, a Koran, a calendar, a bellows, a soccer poster, a radio, a flashlight, a brazier) I sit on a rush mat and drink tea—mud still adheres to the roots and stems of the mint—and make minimal conversation without language: incomprehension and goodwill. An old man with a sweet disposition crushes

almonds, still in their furry shells, with a rock. Almonds and bis-
cuits and sweet tea. A toddler looks on. More babies are brought in,
more children wander in, more tea is served. Palm fronds are
brought in to ward off flies, but the women and children don't trouble to use them. Fancy new glasses appear from a hidden cupboard,
and I drink fresh buttermilk, into which I dip chunks of unleavened
whole wheat bread. It is delicious. The tattooed woman of the
house tells me that I am happy; I am. She takes me to see the cow
from which the buttermilk came, in a courtyard where squash and
henna grow. How nice to be so close to the source of production. In
the nature of a gift, she takes me to another room, where there is a
baby six days old. The baby is beautiful, its eyes and brows kohled
against flies. It is wrapped in swaddling cloth tied with striped wool
yarn. It lies very still in my arms.

    The sky in Zagora is white, metallic, huge, unfriendly. The sun
is a paler shade of white, the sun of an Arctic winter. What makes
one place brutish and another kind? We are at about the same lati-
tude as Erfoud, but we might almost be on a different planet. Our
hotel, the Reda, has four swimming pools and two guests—P.L. and
me. They call me "the woman." The wind is a *jinni*, knocking
everything over—pool umbrellas, our dinner. It comes from
nowhere and leaves in its wake an intense dry heat. The air is taut.
The dining room smells of offal. Only in the pale fires of night is
this town of tired gray and timid pink bearable. We go at night—
led by a child who burns rags to light our way (there are no stars)—
to the house of one Hassan, who sells amber and coral.
    Hassan has curly ropes of hair and is handsome. He is a nomad
from the Sait Tata tribe (he says), on the road six months of the
year, traveling (he says) on his white camel along the silk route, from
Zagora to Mali and Mauretania. The rest of the time he is seden-

tary; he sleeps on his roof under the stars. He takes American Express. Neither P.L. nor I believe a word he says—except for the part about American Express—though I almost like him for using the word *sedentary,* an ambitious word. He puts a string of amber beads around my neck and grinds his body into mine, a sexual gesture devoid of sensuality. He counts too much on his good looks; his eyes are cold.

Dinner in an outdoor pavilion in a garden restores my good humor. But when we leave the lovely garden. Moulay is fighting with another guide over a commission—the commission from our meal. The violence born of desperation and extreme ill will scares me. (It is seared in my consciousness that women are considered dangerous, and paranoia reaching great heights, I am sure that the fight will have consequences affecting me, my person.) My hotel room opens into the courtyard; anyone could get in. I lock the picture windows and secure the door by means of a steel door sheath; the air-conditioning does not work—this is a tomb. Casbahs and *ksour* are defensive buildings, and communal ones; it is too much to hope that the people who build casbahs could build a hotel to suit a Western woman's mood.

"The sun's flame is a white hawk," writes Rumi. The Sufi brotherhoods court meaning in nothingness, affirmation in negation; they whirl to fulfillment in the emptiness of the desert, under a blank, white, meaningless sky. But I am unhappy on the edge of the world. My head aches and my eyes hurt, my teeth are attacked by flies and my blistered lungs by sand. I read *Murder at the Old Vicarage* and announce my intention to stay in the car until we reach the oasis of Taroudant, three hundred miles to the west.

Orange trees, their burden of fruit like Christmas decorations, screen the windows at the head of my bed. From the French doors to my terrace—where I have a breakfast of crepes with butter and honey and a steaming mug of strong white coffee—I see a wide lawn, watered in lazy arcs. A single rose leans against a palm tree; two lacy purple jacaranda trees cast their dimpled shadows on cool tiles. I light the fire in my fireplace; the logs are eucalyptus, pungent and sweet, and their fragrance mingles with the fragrance of roses resting on a small blue marble-topped table. Everything pleases me.

In the 1930s, Baron Jean Pellenc built the sophisticated hunting lodge that, with the addition of fifteen bungalows, has become the fabulous La Gazelle d'Or, perhaps the most luxurious hotel in Morocco and possibly in all of North Africa—and all of this derived from two wells outside the red-walled, dusty, somnolent, amiable town of Taroudant. The long-windowed halls of pale peach and blue, the circular rooms covered with antique silk Berber embroideries and floored in onyx marble (and stylized astrological symbols—Moroccan Art Deco) are full of fabulous stuff massed in stylish abundance: Aladdin meets Erté.

I walk from my villa to the pool on a herringboned brick path, past lipstick-red pomegranate flowers, olive trees, and oleanders and into gardens of controlled luxuriance: calla lilies and nasturtiums, hibiscus, lotus and water lilies, and banks of papyrus and elephant palms. The swimming pool is polar cold. After a while, cold feels like a different kind of warmth, hypothermal hypnosis, a fugue state, sweet.

When the sun goes down, and light leaches from the sky, the jacaranda blossoms form a haze of bluey purple and provide the color that the sunset did not. In this deceptive light, palm fronds look like velvet and caress the white-blue-gray-yellow sheltering sky. Servants prepare tea, running across the lawns in the long white silk-embroidered Moroccan-cotton *gandouras* in which they look so stately and graceful.

Outside La Gazelle d'Or beautiful boys lounge in groves of olive trees, motorbikes at the ready, to follow tourists to the souk, where they will offer their services as guides. They are prepared to offer services of another kind as well. They are singularly unthreatening; they look like a Grecian frieze.

In the market, sheer white nightgowns are fingered by women in heavy white veils. A date merchant offers me a meal of dates—dates of every grade (this is like wine-tasting, sugary), dates for sheep and dates for sultans. I love this market and the courtesy and gravity of its artisans. I learn how to mix henna with lemon juice to stain my palms. I buy stencils used to apply henna to hands and feet. (The stencils look like Matisse's 1953 *Decoration, Flowers, and Fruit,* paper cutout and gouache, which hangs in the museum at Nice.) A silversmith invites me to watch him make crude silver bracelets; he is proud of his mud mold and of his crucible. He is more interested in explaining his craft than in making a sale, which is nice.

I sit in the pink square of the town, utterly at ease and seduced by the pulse and rhythms of life, of this life in particular, which seems to me to encompass, in a little space, all that life can hold.

In a white-tiled room an applecheeked girl anoints me with hot water from a brass bowl filled at a tap. I am in La Gazelle d'Or's *hammam,* and she is bathing me. In clouds of steam she soaps me and scrubs me with an abrasive mitt. Beads and rivers of dead dirty skin form a mosaic on my body. I lose track of time. She scrubs like Mama did. I am a child again; and surrender and vulnerability are—I know with a child's lost trust—good and will be rewarded. She applies mud the color of burnt coriander to my body. Her fingers are practical, assertive, not inquiring, not lewd. This is innocent sensuality, sensuality without sex. . . . First you got dirty, then Mama washed you, usually angrily. The rosy girl reverses the order: first she makes me clean, then she applies mud—and then she washes me again. Buckets and buckets of water. She washes all my tiredness and all my anxiety away; every crevice is cleansed. Not a word is spoken between us. I can no longer tell one part of my body from another; it's all flesh, one organ. Sweat rolls into my eyes and I don't care. The girl tucks my foot in between her thighs. This is strange but not alarming. Did the harem include these pleasures? She covers me with a silken cream, rose petals and spices, musk. I am wrapped in herbal towels in an anteroom where diffuse light enters by a skylight, and I hear birds sing. I am too pleasured to sleep.

I walk home along a path of roses.

My spirit swings like a pendulum between delight and tension. Essaouira, where we go from Taroudant, is an agreeable seashore town, white and blue, of lost minor glories, its fortified walls and toylike ramparts and straight-as-an-arrow medina designed by an eighteenth-century sultan's captive French architect. At dusk, along the seawalls, women in rose caftans and black and white *haiks* take their ease in the pale light of street lamps and glide tantalizingly through the medina—twilight is Morocco's finest hour—pausing under arches theatrically stage-lit by naked bulbs. This is Morocco's Bath.

At noon gaily colored fishing boats bring great bloody white fish and serpentine fish, conger eels and jellyfish, and baby stingrays and sardines into the busy little working port that was once a pirates' haunt. They are sold under reed awnings, amid fish-kabob stalls with umbrellas of primary colors. Parallel to and behind this world of apparent simplicity is another world, a world of omens and portents and poisons and spells and sorcery, pack-aged magic. In shops like those I browse in, *tseuheur* is sold: a paste of antimony, pubic hair, and menstrual blood given by women to recalcitrant lovers. In the "herbal store" one buys a white stone, *pierre d'alun,* that stanches blood; roots and leaves to cure rheumatism, toothache, bleeding gums, gas, diarrhea, and infidelity; *kef;* opium; "secret incantations" to make one thin and to make one fat; the ground horns of animals to promote desire and ground bones to reduce enemies to impotence. One of the stated reasons men fear women—the older the woman, the more dangerous—is that women are geniuses of spells and poisons.

Sun and sea purify, scour away filth. But into the *mellah* of Essaouira the sun never comes. *Mellah* is the word for salt. To Jews, who came to Morocco from Spain to escape the Inquisition, was relegated the task of salting and preserving the severed heads of the sultans' enemies (so they could be exhibited on walls as trophies of battle); and the area to which Jews, who paid a special tax for "protection," were consigned was called the *mellah*. The *mellah* is no longer the exclusive domain of Jews; it belongs to all the poor. Its buildings, tenementlike, lean against one another. Sewage runs in the dark streets. (Moulay, who has followed me everywhere, does not follow me here.) An old lady bounces from wall to wall, stoned on *kef.* I slip on a fish head. A rat runs over my foot. Whores laugh at me. When I get back to my hotel, I throw my sneakers away, having fetishistically projected all my fear and loathing onto them; animism is making inroads in my soul.

In the Sufi school of Muslim theology, the enlightened soul is said to comprehend that, just as permanence is contained within flux, so change is contained within repetition: "The world is in intense motion, ascending . . . to meet the descent of the Absolute in manifested forms. . . . The flow occurs in such an orderly, successive manner, according to definite patterns, that we are unaware of it." I began to fear that I was spiritually infantile, for I grew weary of the patterns, the repetition: of the unchanging geometric mosaics, the stucco fretwork and endless scalloped arches, the predictable admixture of cedar/marble/tile and calligraphic arabesques of Moroccan architecture. It wasn't the pattern in the randomness that I was looking for, it was the randomness—the surprising wonder and aesthetic jolt—in the pattern. Perhaps I would find it in Marrakech, the spacious Red City, the marketplace of southern riches, the common ground and pleasure ground of all the Moroccan people, a city accessible to mountain tribes and Atlantic ports and camel routes, to sailors, farmers, tradesmen, and tourists.

Everything glorious—everything purple and red and apricot and gold, everything tunneled and tendriled and muted and blazing and mysterious and gay—that is found in Morocco is found in superabundance in Marrakech, a city on a plain surrounded by the horseshoe of the High Atlas.

I went to see The Sights.

I saw the sixteenth-century *medersa* of Ben Youssef, a somber building with a prayer hall, an interior courtyard—to which one guidebook attributes a "distinctive unhurried harmony" and "severity" (another way of saying that its virtue lies in its extravagance of space)—arches within arches, and more than a hundred student rooms that receive light from skylights.

I went to the nineteenth-century palace of the vizier of Sultan Moulay el Hassan. In what Wharton described as "the loveliest and most fantastic of Moroccan palaces," the fountains no longer play. If it were not for the niche—which orients the devout to Mecca— one couldn't, in the jumble of faded and moldy rooms, distinguish the mosque from the harem, once a "lovely prison" where wives and concubines spent day after patterned day in the company of eunuchs with names like Musk, Amber, Thyme, Essence of Roses, and Camphor.

I visited the Saadian Tombs set in a rectangular garden, into which, in their perfumed winding sheets, the Saadian dead were carried. Servants of the Saadians, who were descendants of the prophet Muhammad and who came to Morocco in the twelfth century, were buried anonymously. Members of the royal family were buried under a carpet of green and red and black diamond-shaped tiles, under pavilions with scalloped arches and honeycombed faience, and identified with calligraphic arabesques.

I didn't see the blue walls of the Atlas rising over the red walls of the city, a sight that has moved men to tears; they were shrouded in a haze of heat and dust (though I guiltily persist in believing that it was my weariness that obscured them).

I saw, from almost every place, the venerated twelfth-century Koutoubia mosque, its minaret surmounted by three golden balls and a tear, and—five times a day—by a white flag raised on a rough wooden scaffold, heralding the hours of prayer. I fancied that if I had been permitted to enter a mosque, the architecture—and so much more—might have been made clear to me. (I peered into one, feeling like a thing illicit. I saw, through a metal grille backed by a wooden grille covered with chicken wire, a cool forest of columns, a cool male world. My heart beat fast.)

Then, on my last day in Marrakech, and in Morocco, I finally saw the blue mountains in the light of a sinking orange sun. I was in the Djmaa el Fna, the great dusty square of Marrakech, a daily nighttime carnival from which the souks radiate—vanity fair, bedlam. My first impression, as I walked through circles of human onlookers surrounding circles of acrobats and witch doctors, snake charmers and letter writers, was that Hell was better organized than this. No harmonic rhythms here, no patterns or arabesques. Birds of carrion flew overhead. Dentists sat at wooden trestles with heaps of loose teeth, ready-to-wear dentures, pliers. Lice pickers sat next to haircutters. Elsewhere, a man did a lewd approximation of a belly dance. Another wore rubber flip-flops on his ears, the better to mimic a donkey. A three-piece band—flute, drums, and a kind of guitar—punctuated the storytelling of a Berber. A snake was draped around the shoulders of a protesting tourist. Cobras and monkeys competed for the attention of men who take onanistic pleasure in fishing with red plastic doughnut-shaped rings for liter bottles of Coca-Cola. Crowds collected at numbered food stalls: fish in cauldrons of fat, with yellow cumin-stained grease rising to the surface; eggs in vats; chicken tripe with chickpeas; lamb sausage; pots of *harira*, a thick soup of mutton broth and mutton chunks and chickpea mash; fried offal; foul-smelling gray meat from a deep pot of boiling liquid, grasped and pulled apart by hands. Electric lightbulbs competed with the fires of the braziers, burning pale against a pale sky.

I left the hurly-burly for the terrace of the Café de France, above the mandala of circles, the crowds. And suddenly, while I was not looking, the pale hour flared into orange and as quickly turned into night; the night lights no longer competed with day, and it became possible to believe anything: that people feasted in the anticipation and consciousness of satiety, that the stories they heard were true, even that they were happy. I was. Everything rose and converged: incense, smoke, voices, flutes. And the enduring, punctual call of the muezzin from the Koutoubia threaded its way through this tapestry of sound, which amounted to a kind of silence that encompassed singing, drums, wailing, ululating. Voices curled in the smoke, all part of the intricate pattern, a sensory flash frozen, stasis and movement: a unity. My friend Biaggio told me to see Morocco from the corners of my eyes. I didn't understand him. Perhaps he meant that everything happens when you are not looking.

Morocco Bound

The sun shines all year in Morocco, although it is very hot (and dry) in the summer months. The countryside is particularly beautiful in the spring.

No tourist visas are required for American citizens, and no vaccinations. Royal Air Maroc has frequent direct flights to Casablanca from New York, London, and Paris, as well as direct flights to Marrakesh from Paris and London.

You can arrange for a car—and a driver if you like—with a reputable tourist agency before you go. Both Flag Tours (5629 FM 1960 West, Houston, Tex. 77069; 713-580-1700 or 800-223-8889) and Le Soleil Tours (25 West 39th Street, Suite 902, New York, N.Y. 10018; 212-869-1040 or 800-225-4723) specialize in travel to Morocco. If you're planning a driving tour of the country, insist on an air-conditioned car in the summer months (the price will be higher) and, if you don't know French, on an English-speaking driver (a word of warning—levels of proficiency can vary significantly). Take along a couple of bottles of mineral water in the car, especially if you're venturing into the southern pre-Saharan regions, and a box of premoistened towelettes.

In each city, it is advisable—even if you're an experienced traveler and however much you may chafe at the idea—to hire a guide to visit the medina and the souk. As unemployment in Morocco approaches 15 percent and tourism continues to be the country's most important industry, more and more people are offering themselves as guides, but your best bet is to secure an official guide through the concierge of your hotel or the Moroccan National Tourist Office (20 East 46th Street, Suite 1201, New York, N.Y. 10017; 212-557-2520). You shouldn't have to pay more than $25 or $30 a day.

Accommodations range from youth hostels to world-class luxury hotels. The government has strict standards, and—although it's entirely possible that you'll find a hotel where the air-conditioning doesn't work, meals are arranged at odd hours, and the "heated" pool is icy—you are unlikely to find a hotel that isn't clean.

In Fez, the Hotel Palais Jamai is admirably placed just within the walls of the old city. The new wing has balconies overlooking the medina; the old wing has more personality and overlooks gardens. There are two very good restaurants in the hotel—one European, the other Moroccan (Bab Guissa, 055.63.43.31).

In the more remote, pre-Saharan south, the Hotel Salam in Erfoud (Rue de Rissani; 055.57.64.24); the Hotel Reda in Zagora (044.84.70.79); the Club Karam in Ouarzazate (Boulevard Prince Rachid; 044.88.22.25); and Des Isles in Essaouira (Boulevard Med 5; 044.78.46.20) are unremarkable but adequate resting places, complete with meals and swimming pool.

The five-star Hotel La Gazelle d'Or in Taroudant is pricey—and worth every penny. The gardens are exquisite, as are the individual villas, all of which have working air conditioners and fireplaces. The staff is exceptionally knowledgeable and friendly, and in the dining room beautiful food is graciously presented. Although you may never want to leave this peaceful paradise, a hotel car will take you into the town; the bazaar here is small and friendly and you *should* go. Have a bath—be bathed—at the hotel's *hammam* (048.85.20.39).

Another option in Taroudant is the Palais Salam, a nineteenth-century palace within the city walls that is very popular with smart British travelers (048.85.25.01).

Marrakech has many luxury hotels and one famous one: the Mamounia, which Winston Churchill was particularly fond of. The pool and gardens are lovely; but the coffee costs $5, the European food is pretentious, and the service condescending. It has been recently restored—but I found its Deco–*Arabian Nights* combo kitschy, chilly, and overwhelming (Avenue Bab Jdid; 044.44.89.81).

The trendies have moved on to the Tichka, which is somewhat inconveniently located (Route de Casablanca; 044.44.87.10).

Also comfortable and pleasant is the Es Saadi, which, like a smaller version of the Mamounia, has a roulette wheel and a pool. The food—European—is very good (Avenue El Qadissa; 044.44.88.11).

If your taste buds crave Moroccan cooking, you could have your most enchanting dining experience ever, as well as a walk on rose petals, at the Yacout (79 Sidi Ahmed Soussi) or the Stylia (34 Ksour Street). Both are in the old city, and your concierge can give you details.

Reading

In Morocco, by Edith Wharton (Hippocrene Books). Though published in 1920, this view of Morocco from a novelist's perspective still holds.

The Spider's House (Black Sparrow) and *The Sheltering Sky* (Vintage International), by Paul Bowles. Bowles currently enjoys a revival, in the wake of Bertolucci's film. The first novel is set largely in Fez's Hotel Palais Jamai.

Lords of the Atlas, by Gavin Maxwell (Century Travellers, London). A fascinating, superbly entertaining history of Morocco from 1893 to 1955.

A Year in Marrakesh, by Peter Mayne (Hippocrene). A charming, clear-sighted, funny memoir affectionately written by an English civil servant.

The Wilder Shores of Love, by Lesley Blanch (Carroll & Graf). About those strange Victorian Englishwomen who fell in love with the desert, and with the men of the desert. Their passions are at once absurd and touching.

Adventuring in North Africa, by Scott Wayne (Sierra Club). Both an intelligent guidebook and a good read, with information on the natural environment, bird-watching, and Morocco's flora and fauna.

For a greater understanding of Islam, read: *Readings in the Qur'an,* by Kenneth Cragg (Collins, London); any volume of poetry by the Sufi mystic Rumi, *Unseen Rain* (Threshold Books) or *Rumi: We Are Three* (Maypop Books), for example; *Islam,* by Frederick M. Denny (Harper & Row); or *The Sufi Path of Knowledge,* by William C. Chittick (State University of New York Press).

I found the following guidebooks useful for information on how to travel, what to buy, where to stay, what and where to eat: Fodor's; the more detailed *Morocco* from the Cadogan Guides series; the Morocco Blue Guide (essential if you're driving); and the very readable Insight Guides' *Morocco.*

Morocco en Vogue

By Peter Theroux

∾

editor's note

Here is a good piece about Morocco, from the North Atlantic coast to Ouarzazate.

Peter Theroux is the author of numerous books, including *Sandstorms: Days and Nights in Arabia* (W.W. Norton, 1991) and *Translating L.A.: A Tour of the Rainbow City* (W.W. Norton, 1994), and has translated a number of works, including *Children of the Alley* by Naguib Mahfouz (Anchor, 1996), *Dongola: A Novel of Nubia* by Idris Ali (University of Arkansas Press, 1999), and *Variations on Night and Day* by Abdelrahman Munif (Vintage, 1994).

Casablanca has a landmark at last: the soaring 656-foot Hassan II Mosque, the largest in Africa, whose creamy marble and swimming-pool aqua tiles dominate Casablanca's sapphire sky. On the seaside corniche outside its gates, I met a young Moroccan selling snapshots of the mosque at its recent nighttime dedication, bathed in yellow and purple spotlights, with blue lasers pointing the way to Mecca from its smooth battlements.

Part of the Hassan II (pronounced *deux*) Mosque's prestige is that every Moroccan, from the poorest to the richest, is supposed to have contributed something to its construction. When I asked Khaled, the photo peddler, whether he had contributed, he flexed his muscles theatrically, then hastily dug into his back pocket for a tightly folded fax whose frayed hinges barely held its six panels together. It was a to-whom-it-may-concern letter from a French contractor certifying that Khaled had worked for three months laying marble for 6.60 *dirhams* (about eighty cents) per hour.

"We worked from eight in the morning until one, then from two until midnight," he boasted. "During Ramadan, I fasted and kept working. I have no job now."

Khaled summed up a great deal of Morocco's biggest city: skill, optimism, piety, unemployment.

"We have given up hope in Casablanca," a Moroccan tour guide told me. All he meant was that, for tourist purposes, the kingdom's business capital cannot compete with the dreamy exoticism and beauty of the rest of Morocco. The city is not even marketed for its raffish charm, which is considerable. Tourists arrive at Casablanca's Mohammed V Airport and beat it: to the beaches of Essaouira or

Agadir, to the old imperial capitals of Fez or Marrakech, or north to Tangier. There are, of course, no artifacts from the Bergman and Bogart *Casablanca* (which of course was filmed almost exclusively on Warner Brothers' Burbank lot) except for the Casablanca Bar at the Hyatt Regency, which recreates Rick's Café Americain. From the lobby you can hear near-period music: Louis Armstrong singing "What a Wonderful World" to organ accompaniment. You enter the Bogartesque ambience to see that the vocalist is actually a trim young tuxedoed Moroccan at a Wurlitzer, doing a dead-on Satchmo. Casablanca is thick with lovely palm-lined boulevards and a Gaudíesque cathedral, but the Hassan II Mosque and the Hyatt's convivial specimen of nightlife imitating art are the city's main attractions. In sixteen years of living and traveling in the Arab world, I found, on this first visit to Morocco, the only Arab city I ever saw that was so nonchalantly un-Arab.

Morocco lives at a comfortable distance from the Arab world; the Moroccans, who culturally might be described as Euro-Afro-Arabs, find it easy to be Arabs sentimentally while far from the geographical heart of the Arab Middle East. They talk about *le Proche-Orient* as if it were a thousand miles away; and technically it is.

Well over half the Moroccans I met had been to Spain or France; almost none had ever visited any Arab country. Why not? "Because," the answer always ran, "I figured, since *this* is the best Arab country, why bother?" This kind of national feeling is often accompanied by a chip on the shoulder, but Moroccans always said it with an air of disarming pragmatism. (Some added that they would not mind seeing Egypt.)

Morocco's mythical aura is very different, too—of flowing robes and intrigue, the French Foreign Legion, leatherbound books, and snake-charming. There are no suggestions of the usual attic full of Arab associations: the Fertile Crescent, the Bible, the Nile, the Middle East's modern wars.

Its history is the history of its cities, and here too it is different because it has so many. Every other Arab country has a great city and an alternate: Cairo and Alexandria, Damascus and Aleppo, Baghdad and Basra, Tripoli and Benghazi. Only Morocco has a prize collection of major cities: Fez, Meknès, Marrakech, Rabat, Taroudant, Tangier, Tetouan, Agadir, Ouarzazate, Casablanca, Essaouira, and still others. The first four are imperial capitals—former capitals, that is, of successive Arab dynasties.

Morocco was the first country to recognize the newly proclaimed United States, and it's remarkable for being not only pro-American but openly so. I took only three pictures in Casablanca: the Hassan II Mosque, a classic palm-crowded boulevard, and the street sign on what surely must be the Arab world's only Rond-point Général Patton. Despite this, and the fact that Mohammed V Airport is just six and a half hours from New York, Morocco is chiefly a European destination. It is Europe's Mexico.

Almost every train in Morocco is the Marrakech Express. The lines run from the north to the south, where Marrakech is the terminus. I planned to work my way south, down to the High Atlas Mountain range. My destination, after Casablanca, was Fez, and I was armed with the usual facts about this most austere and intellectual of North African cities. The oldest part of the city is Fez el Bali, or old Fez, even though Fez el Jdid (new Fez) is seven hundred years old; and there is the Ville Nouvelle, a colonial French creation. Passing through Rabat, I had been assured by a travel agent that Fez el Bali was the loveliest place I would ever see; in 1984, UNESCO had declared it a World Heritage City, like Venice, "one of the purest jewels of Islamic civilization," and had embarked on massive restoration projects. Hearing Fez so highly praised made me ask a Moroccan friend why Morocco is reputed to have the lowest tourist return rate of all Mediterranean countries. Rather than frowning, he shrugged.

"Wait until you get off the train at Fez, or go to the medina. The guides! These young men have no job but to show tourists around and lead them into shops and take a commission. Tourists don't like being so harassed! And the beggars!"

It is true that the guides are everywhere, but I feel compelled to add here that the beggar factor is largely hype. Morocco's beggars typically are diminutive old ladies, sometimes veiled, with one palm unobtrusively out. (Although upper-class Moroccans consider the informal guide business a form of begging.)

Warned about the aggressive guides, I was relieved to meet a polite young Fassi on the train who wanted to show me around. Ali, who had just got on at Meknès, happened to be starting a three-day vacation and had nothing better to do.

"I will show you my city!" he exclaimed, as if discovering an elusive truth. "You will have lunch with us today! My mother will prepare a couscous for you!"

I could scarcely conceal my delight at this chance discovery of native hospitality.

"Yes, well, of course these boys work the trains," an experienced Moroccan traveler pointed out to me later. "They just get on and sit with the first likely-looking foreigner they see. He took you around for shopping? You got a lovely meal at his house? You met Mother and the babies, yes?"

Yes, yes, yes. It should spoil no one's pleasure that snagging foreigners off trains and springing hospitality on them is something of a cottage industry in Morocco. With more than half the population under twenty-five and nearly 75 percent of these unemployed, it is a harmless living, and imparts something of Morocco's warmth.

Ali's family lived on the hillside overlooking Fez el Bali, the medieval city of Fez, near the splendid gate called Bab Guissa. While Ali's mother was cooking a large fish couscous on one hour's notice—while I went to my hotel he had raced home from the station to tell her to expect a guest—he pointed out to me the attractions of the old medina. There below us was the ancient Kairouyine Mosque, built in 859; the tannery neighborhood; the Andalusian quarter of the old city. He proudly noted that a large community of Moors expelled from Spain in 818 had brought much of their learning and artistry to Fez. A few years later, Fez welcomed a large migration from Kairouan, Tunisia. It is a tribute to the rapid growth of Fassi culture that the Moors were evicted from Córdoba by Christian intolerance; the Tunisians were eager emigrants from one sophisticated capital to another. These two groups settled on opposite sides of the river Fez, and the districts are still called the Andalusian and Kairouyine quarters. Further influxes, especially of Jews and Muslims expelled from Spain in 1492 during the Inquisition, made Fez—though we were speaking Arabic, Ali switched to French, Morocco's lingua franca—*"la ville la plus raffinée du Maroc."* As we trekked down the hill, he changed the subject to the refined merchandise available in Fez. The payoff for most guides is not the daily rate you may or may not pay, but their rake-off on your purchases.

"I know the best places, where they don't boil their merchandise," Ali assured me earnestly over our delicious lunch. A tiny niece came shyly into the small, whitewashed dining room to pour us two glasses of Coca-Cola. I asked him to repeat what he had said, and he smiled. "Where they don't boil? Oh, we say that. Boiling means overcharging."

For as long as people have written about Morocco, from Ibn Battutah in the fourteenth century to Edith Wharton in 1920, they have compared its Imperial Cities to dreams. Edith Wharton spoke of "the dream-feeling that envelops one at every step." This is especially true of Fez, whose spaciousness and cleanliness—the Fassis spend an inordinate amount of time scrubbing the streets with buckets of water and brushes—give way, at Bab Guissa, to the labyrinth of its medina, which has been called the most complicated square mile on earth. There are no cars: Many of the streets and passages can barely accommodate two people walking side by side, and some are so steep that you are almost tempted to try going up on all fours. In the dyers' street, the cobblestones are stained a brilliant amethyst here, dandelion yellow there. The narrow lanes are like tunnels lined with caves, where leatherwork, silver, carpets, and ceramics are piled. Where the splendid entrance of the Andalous Mosque overlooks a steep stone stairway, I simultaneously marveled at the artistic genius of the Fassis and wondered whether this old medina had inspired any of Dr. Seuss's fantasy cities.

Possibly because the refinement of Fez is largely the legacy of immigrants, the sensibility that produced the tolerance and learning of the city, and its great scholars and courtiers—Ibn Battutah, Ibn Khaldun, and Leo Africanus (a native Granadan and adopted Fassi)—was ecumenical. Jews may have been second-class citizens, but they were safe in the ghettos, called *mellahs*. Every Moroccan city has one, and knowing that *milh* means salt in Arabic, I asked about the etymology and, for better or worse, got my answer: when the sultans' enemies were beheaded, the job of salting the heads for preservation (and display) fell to the Jews.

The Jewish cemetery is almost immediately adjacent to the royal palace (King Hassan II maintains palaces in all five imperial capitals), because of the royal popularity of Jewish goldsmithing "and," Ali boasted, "because the kings have loved the Jews." The *mellah* is a busy market sheltering few Jews these days, but the tradition of harmony has continued at the palace. A close adviser to King Hassan and the former tutor of his sons, André Azzoulay, is Jewish, and Morocco is the only Arab country to have a Jewish cabinet minister—Serge Berdugo, minister of tourism.

Nevertheless, it is the fervent Islam of Fez that is most famous. The beautiful Kairouyine Mosque can hold twenty thousand worshipers, and every cascade of arches—tilework, hammered gold, and bronze—is a Muslim holy place. The piety of the city was shown to me on my last day there. It was a Friday, and the intervals between the muezzins calling prayers were padded with dead silence. The lanes of the medina were empty except for men in white *djellabas* with pointed hoods and yellow or white *babouches,* sometimes leading identically clad young sons by the hand. Strong but unobtrusive religious feeling permeates Morocco. The king is a descendant of the prophet Muhammad but is on good terms with the opposition parties, which are secular. There are no major fundamentalist Muslim movements. Tolerance makes for a general lack of demonization: of former colonial powers, of the Israelis, of liquor, pork, hashish, and forbidden or foreign things in general.

"Vous êtes americain?" was the first question I was asked on the train from Fez to Marrakech; Fatima, my questioner, was a gazelle-eyed young woman going to college in Meknès. Her second question was *"Êtes-vous croyant?"* Was she asking whether I was a Muslim, or a believer in general? A believer, Fatima said—she did not expect an American to be Muslim, though that would be nice. Why had she asked—was it important? "It's important, if we want to have a truly nice conversation," she pointed out.

We did, for an hour, never discussing religion, but she wanted to know that she was sharing a compartment with a believer. She got off at Kenitra, where I got two new companions. Mohammed and Saad were professional Moroccan tour guides who had just seen off their tour groups—Mohammed's Americans and Saad's Spaniards. I wanted to pick their brains about how foreign tourists were viewed.

"The French can be good or bad," said Mohammed. "The English can be difficult. Italians are the best. Americans are extremely difficult."

I asked the obvious question.

"You cannot satisfy Americans. It is always their first exposure to an Arab country. They are so jumpy. You remember the dentist?" he asked Saad, who nodded. "A little girl was selling tissues for fifty *centimes* a packet. That's five cents. She was a little dirty, but not a beggar. He ignored her, but she was making him jumpy. Finally he screamed at her, and I mean screamed. She was terrified! She ran away crying. See, these Americans tend to be old and rich and not very cosmopolitan. An Italian wouldn't have made such a big deal—he'd have given her a few *dirhams* and got some extra Kleenex."

"Americans hardly talk to one another on the buses," Saad added. "They're wooden. You put Italians, even rich ones, on a bus ride, and what happens? In five minutes they're all singing. They play card games. They share food. The Italians!" He kissed the bunched tips of his fingers.

The train rolled through Rabat, Casablanca, and then went inland again. The flatlands and far-off cliffs looked like New Mexico. This was a second-class compartment, but cushy and spotless, and just slightly more expensive than taking the bus. Only the passing landscape and the *clickety-clack* underneath us reminded me that I was not on a plane. Saad abruptly asked whether I was planning to move to Marrakech. No . . . why?

"A lot of foreigners do. The climate is beautiful. Rent is about two hundred dollars a month for an apartment, and you can buy a fabulous place for sixty-five thousand dollars. Is this your first visit? Ah. You might decide to move after you see Marrakech."

The train began to slow as it passed the lush palm groves ringed by blue mountains. I could see the Red City beyond the palms. The graceful scalloped patterns on the square tower of the Koutoubia minaret came into focus as the train pulled into the little station.

The colorful irony of Marrakech le Rouge is that it was founded by Yusuf ibn-Tashfin, an eleventh-century conqueror and reformer who swept out of the Sahara with his Berber army to cleanse Morocco of its decadence. When he made Marrakech his capital city, it had only a mosque and a casbah; now the central attraction behind its high red walls, the Jema al-Fna, or Square of Death—it was once an execution ground—is the antithesis of the serene piety of Fez. You can hear the songs, shouts, and booming drums three blocks away. Its snake charmers, transvestite dancers, monkey tamers, acrobats, fire-eaters, and traffickers in spells and talismans would be unthinkable in any of Morocco's more northerly cities. It may not be darkest Africa, but it is a shade darker than the delicate tiles of Fez.

"I swear to you all, I was crippled with arthritis!" shouted a turbaned man sitting in the middle of a whole pharmacy of powders, roots, and dried herbs in straw baskets. I could not follow the rest of his sales pitch, but dozens of onlookers were crowding in to watch him hoist himself up and caper around the small clearing amid the baskets.

No arthritis was in evidence in a much larger clearing nearby, where two teenage acrobats in red warmup suits were locked stomach to stomach in a rigid sixty-nine position; one hugged the other around the waist, and the other one had his arms outstretched to grasp his partner's ankles. They were rolling in a wide circle, on their feet, like a huge red wheel, and when they finally collapsed, smiling proudly through streaming sweat, the crowd applauded and showered them with paper money and coins.

The fear that the whole gaudy carnival, at its most enthusiastic at night, is a tourist trap is alleviated by the mobs of Moroccans buying herbs, watching the dancing monkeys, and dropping coins on the snake charmers' blankets. I noticed that for foreign tourists, five *dirhams* (sixty cents) seemed to be the going rate for using a still or video camera, and given the consequences of stiffing a snake charmer, it seemed cheap.

"Cinq dirhams!" snapped a snake charmer's assistant as a Frenchman began to move away after tossing down a half-*dirham* coin. The man had taken a close-up picture of the flutist and his three pitch-black cobras. The tourist was quick, but the snake man was quicker; he overtook the Frenchman in three steps and in seconds had a fat black-and-white viper around the horrified man's neck.

"Prenez une photo, Madame!" the now-amiable snake man encouraged the Frenchman's wife, who took no picture, but had no trouble finding a five-*dirham* coin.

Marrakech, too, has its refined attractions. It is Morocco's pre-eminent city. *Marrakech* is the old Arabic name for Morocco itself and is the origin of the name Morocco. One of the earliest travel books about Morocco, R. B. Cunninghame Graham's *Mogreb-el-Acksa* (1898), alternately refers to the city as Marakesh and the City of Morocco. The Bahia Palace may be the world's greatest example of Moorish architecture. The medina is home to the tombs of the Saadians, the Arab dynasty that conquered Marrakech in the sixteenth century and filled it with Andalusian culture—thanks to Spanish influence (transmitted by war) and West African gold (plundered). The marble tombs are like high, narrow butter dishes and are often barely visible among the mobs of German, Italian, and French tourists.

Although their capital was Fez, the Saadians spent a fortune beautifying Marrakech, eventually adopting it as their capital. Even today the El Badi Palace may be the city's most impressive relic. It is a vast ruin with spacious plazas, sunken orange groves, thick walls, and tunnels. Saadian Sultan Ahmad al-Dhahabi ("The Golden"—he had plundered West Africa) had sheathed the palace in fifty tons of marble, none of which survived its destruction by his successors.

No one agrees on the color of the walls of Marrakech. Edith Wharton found them red, Paul Bowles "bisque-pink," Elias Canetti "ever-changing." The earth they are built from is red, and most of the time the walls are the color that paint stores call dusty rose. The best time to see them is late afternoon, when the westering sun paints them successively orange, rust, boiled lobster, scarlet, blood-red, and chocolate. The walls are interrupted only by Marrakech's big gates: Bab el Khemis, near the Thursday market (for which it is named); Bab Jdid, which conceals the seventeen acres of La Mamounia Hotel's gardens; and Bab Doukkala, which is the last sight many travelers have of Marrakech. It is the city's liveliest taxi market, spread out before the bus station.

There is a sensory overload that hits travelers in elaborately civilized places, and in Morocco it hits very hard, particularly after Marrakech. After the cobras, the marble tombs, the magic walls, the sounds, the atmosphere, it is impossible to head somewhere else and start from square one, admiring more mosques or medinas; you need a break. Fortunately, Moroccan geography almost demands a break after Marrakech. You can head to Agadir, a beach resort said to be Morocco's Miami Beach, dominated by topless

Germans, or to Ouarzazate, at the edge of the desert, to cleanse your palate, so to speak.

Anyway, after only a week in Morocco, I had begun to feel like a water drop running down a porous surface: instead of proceeding briskly south, I was being absorbed as I moved along. There was too much to take in; it was hard to travel onward, and even harder to think of leaving. Under these circumstances, I opted for the desert.

It was not frugality that sent me to Bab Doukkala to buy a bus ticket for Ouarzazate, to the southeast. You can go by air; the flight, like most internal Moroccan flights, is a bargain at about sixty dollars, but it was impressed upon me that the four-hour scenic drive was half the fun of a visit to Ouarzazate. "The shade is the most important part of the tree," according to a character in Moroccan novelist Tahar Ben Jelloun's *La Prière de l'Absent*. A private taxi costs about a hundred dollars. The bus costs $2.50, and I made a point of riding with a group of Italians to see if Mohammed and Saad were right about their being good traveling companions.

They were; the Italians even sang, at least until their children fell asleep. As we climbed the High Atlas Range, some woke up their children so they could see the Tizi n'Tichka, or Tichka Pass. It is regarded as the second most spectacular mountain pass in Morocco, after the Tizi n'Test, but at 7,415 feet it is more than 500 feet higher. After seeing the bus chug by a railless hairpin turn, with the desert floor a mile below, few went back to sleep.

We had passed through endless olive and walnut orchards and green farmland from Marrakech to the mountains; the vegetation, as we descended toward the Sahara, grew noticeably scrubbier. Unlike the ascent to the Tizi n'Tichka, the downhill road was a bone-rattling distraction from the winding passes that often revealed a village in the elbow of a switchback.

Ouarzazate finally appeared on the top of a low hill, and I was almost alarmed when the bus turned into Avenue Mohammed V.

Here were restaurants, gift shops, and even banks and airline offices—not the remote refuge I was after. This fear calmed as soon as the bus pulled into the small dirt lot that served as the central bus station. A short walk up a neighboring hill to the Berbère Palace Hotel revealed that Mohammed V was the only boulevard in town.

Something is cooking in Ouarzazate. Not only is the lovely little desert town becoming surrounded by hotels, but all the hotels, most with vast outdoor pools, look the same: a cross between *Beau Geste* forts and Yoruba palaces, or the grand mosque of Djenné near Timbuktu. All this is appropriate, since the place was founded by French forces in 1928 as a garrison and administrative center in what was still the French protectorate of Morocco. Most likely, the fact that scenes from *Lawrence of Arabia* and *The Jewel of the Nile* were shot nearby persuaded the Moroccans that tourists would flock here.

The casbah of Ouarzazate, behind the so-called *zone hôtelière,* has an outer row of shops selling local tribal carpets. Not only are they less expensive than those on offer in Fez and Marrakech, but the sellers are not as polished.

"Six hundred is my last price for this," one dealer said firmly as he displayed the lovely yellow and blue design of a tribal Ouaouzguit carpet. "Or five-fifty," he added before I could answer.

I took advantage of his candor to ask something I had been too shy to ask anyone else: What exactly was a casbah?

"A medina, you see, is a traditional closed city with several gates. A casbah is smaller, a settlement or district with one exit and one entrance," he responded promptly.

Carpets and Tuareg clothing dominated the shops along the town's main boulevard. A shopkeeper explained that the long strips of diaphanous blue and black cloth—about seven feet long—which I took for hangings were Tuareg turbans. The bright strips of carpeting, narrower but just as long, were belts. Belts? "The Tuareg are desert people," he said, pointing to a wall hung with bulky cloaks and billowing robes. "They wear layers and layers—they need long belts."

In addition to the shopping, the obvious treasures of this non-imperial city are space and quiet. This was the first big-sky country I had seen in a Moroccan city; there was almost more movement in the sky, where fat cumulus clouds scudded by on autumnal winds, than in the quiet streets, where a few wizened old men swept the gutters with palm branches.

Ouarzazate has a little airport—it even has flights to Paris—but I decided to opt again for the bus to head to the coast and home. Just fifty miles before Agadir stands the old imperial city of Taroudant; it was briefly a Saadian capital in the 1500s. Conquest has deprived it of all its glories, with the exception of its magnificent walls, the Hotel Palais Salam (located in a former pasha's palace inside the walls), and a market street selling mostly heavy silver jewelry and Judaica. It is also the ethnic cradle of the Asian-looking Shluh, or southern Berbers, who create most of the heavy jewelry. Their dancing boys are famous too. They are said to perform at the Jema al-Fna in Marrakech, but I did not see them in either city, though of course I only passed through Taroudant, barely staying long enough to have lunch, a walk, and mint tea in a café, unobtrusively trying to pronounce *Shluh* correctly. (The old spelling was Shilah, but the sound is *shu-LOO*).

Even so, I did not get out of town without a piety check, administered by a nine-year-old boy who approached me as I strolled past the Shahid Ibrahim Rouada Park on my way out of town. Beginning with a polite *"salaamu aleikum,"* he questioned me solemnly in Arabic: "Are you Libyan? Tunisian? Saudi Arabian?" I asked him his name. "Touhami." Brushing aside my nationality, he got right to the point: "Do you pray?" When I rashly said yes, he smiled for the first time and said, "The noon prayer is now. Please come pray with my family." I expressed my regrets—I had *already* prayed.

Back in Casablanca, this city felt almost familiar: it was the only Moroccan city I had arrived in twice. Crowded and full of car exhaust as I lugged my bag from Casa-Port station, it felt like home. Only a foreigner would carry his own bag in this way, and as I waddled down the Boulevard El Hansali, the hashish sellers dogged my steps, murmuring, *"Chocolat! Chocolat!"* A glass of mint tea appeared as I reached the hotel reception desk for my last Moroccan slumber. I don't usually get sentimental about travel destinations, but it did seem to me a tragic irony that my favorite movie had portrayed this place as famous only for people trying to leave it.

Beauty and Babouches

Visas are not required to enter Morocco, but bringing dollars is advisable. Because Moroccan *dirhams* may not be taken in or out of the country, cash, of any sort, is necessary to cover the 150 to 200 *dirhams* (about $20) taxi fare to the town center. Alternatively, an excellent train now connects the airport to the centrally located Casablanca Musafirin (or Casa-Port) station—the ticket is about $5.00.

The best advice on dealing with young Moroccan men who insist they should be your guide is to be diplomatic, firm, and *pleasant,* whether you want a guide or not—although they are essential in the maze of the Fez medina, and desirable in Marrakech as well. If you really do hate being pestered, hire the biggest and meanest-looking guide available and use him as a bodyguard.

Intercity taxis and trains are reliable and can be booked in advance, and Royal Air Maroc offers frequent air service between major cities. Many travelers, however, prefer to rent a car (about $400 per week for a subcompact).

Casablanca

At first glance, it could be Nice. Only after you've seen the truly fabulous cities of Morocco does it look like nothing special. But for restaurants, movies, café-hopping, and strolling along a lovely oceanside corniche, the great metropolis gets high marks. Hotels include the legendary El Mansour and the very good Safir.

Fez

If you must break down and take on a guide anywhere in Morocco, Fez is the place. The architectural treasures—palaces, mosques, tombs, and *fonduks* (caravansaries)—as well as most of Fez's shopping and all of its charm—are located in the labyrinthine old city. Fassi artisans are the best in Morocco, and this is the place to buy fine carpets; hammered silver, brass, or copper objects; glass; ceramics; and even *babouches,* the pointy-toed leather slippers that all Moroccans wear and all tourists buy.

The most desirable place to stay is still the Palais el Jamaï, a Moorish palace built in 1879 within the walls of the medina at Bab el Guisa, although the very modern and slightly more expensive Hôtel Les Mérinides, on a nearby hilltop, is at least as luxurious.

Marrakech

The crowning must-see city of all North Africa is full of hotels— to the despair of traditionalists and the delight of the Marrakchis. La Mamounia—with its location just inside the ancient city across from the Koutoubia Minaret, and with its seventeen acres of gardens and a lobby crammed with one of the world's priceless mother lodes of Art Deco furniture—is expensive and worth it. The Avenue de France is lined with other top-notch hotels, including the Atlas-Asni and Les Idrisside. The Hôtel Andalous, the Hôtel Farah Safir, and the Hôtel Siaha Safir are on the Avenue du Président Kennedy.

Marrakech's signature handicrafts are stonework and leather, and the souks fan out from the Jema al-Fna. This area of old walled Marrakech is also where the historical treasures are found: the sixteenth-century El Badi Palace, built of Italian and Indian marble, the rambling El Bahia Palace, and the Saadian Tombs.

Ouarzazate

An oasis in every sense, this quiet town—popular with travelers heading deeper into the desert, to Zagora, M'Hamid, and the Oued Drâa—offers pampering with shopping. The specialties are carpets and nomadic merchandise, especially the long turbans and brightly colored woven belts. Hotels, most with bungalows and pools, include the hilltop Berbère Palace, the Pullman Karam Palace, and the Hôtel Riad Salam.

Taroudant

As in Marrakech, the stately city walls and gates are a major attraction, although the souks are also the best in Morocco for buying silver Berber jewelry and local stone carvings—mostly human figures, which have nothing to do with Morocco's Islamic aspect and everything to do with its African side.

The beautiful old Hôtel Salam is built into the city wall, half a mile from the Place Assarag, where most of the city's hotels and taxi stands are located. The Hôtel La Gazelle d'Or, outside town, offers bungalows, tennis, and horseback riding.

Reading

Among the comprehensive guidebooks are Cadogan's *Morocco,* by Barnaby Rogerson (Globe Pequot Press), the *Blue Guide to Morocco,* by Jane Holliday (W.W. Norton), and *Lonely Planet Morocco,* by Frances Linzee Gordon, Dorinda Talbot, and Damien Simonis.

You do not need to use your imagination to enjoy the rich ambience of Morocco, but some history and literature can make the exotic even more so. You might ferret out Edith Wharton's *In Morocco, The Collected Stories of Paul Bowles,* or Bowles's non-fictional *Their Heads Are Green and Their Hands Are Blue,* a delightful Moroccan travel memoir. Tahar Ben Jelloun may live in France and write in French, but the novels *Harrouda* (Schoenhof's Foreign Books, in French only) and *La Prière de l'Absent* (French and European Publications, in French only) reveal that his roots are still in Fez.

Northern Morocco

By Doone Beal

∽

editor's note

Here are two pieces that divide up the country in the way my *next* books will: northern Morocco and southern Morocco.

DOONE BEAL, who lives in London, has contributed a great many articles on Mediterranean destinations over the years to *Gourmet,* where both of these pieces originally appeared. Her work was also featured in the *Central Italy* and *Provence* editions of *The Collected Traveler.*

Though a relatively small part of the African continent, Morocco is a country huge in scale. Its shores are washed by both the Atlantic and the Mediterranean, and its terrain is magnificently spined by the Atlas Mountains, whose peaks are snow-capped some eight months of the year. North of them the climate and culture are Mediterranean; southward, the country looks to the Sahara. Sheer geographic variety is a prime attraction, but Morocco is not quite like any other country—not even like its North African neighbors. Farthest-flung of all the Ottoman Empire territories, it was influenced much more by its Spanish associations in Córdoba, Seville, and Granada than it ever was by the sultans of Constantinople. Founded by Phoenicians in the twelfth century B.C., and subsequently under Roman rule for three centuries, it has scarcely—but for Arab rule briefly in the late seventh century—known invasion by foreign powers. Its indigenous people, the Berbers, date back to 200 B.C., when their kingdom of Mauretania occupied the northern half of present-day Morocco, and they, together with Arab tribes, remain a large percentage of the population, which partly explains the unique character of the country.

The overlay of French civilization, particularly evident along the coast and within the main tourist centers, results from a mere four decades of French protectorate status. It ended in 1956 but left its language and its education, as well as excellent roads and railways. Viticulture was improved (and continues to be so, as is especially apparent among the white and the excellent rosé wines), and the French donated as well the *bonne bouche* of their cuisine. Now, I might add, this French expertise has been deftly adapted by the Moroccans to their own very different cooking methods, which are long and slow and subtly scented with coriander, cumin, mint, lemon, cinnamon, and ginger. Including excellent seafood—especially lobster, *langouste,* and oysters—the cuisine offers visitors a tempting array of options.

Arriving in northern Morocco at Casablanca's Mohammed V International Airport late one evening, we took a cab and bowled—to the lilt of Arab pop music—north along the fast main coast road to Mohammedia and the Hotel Meridien-Miramar, doyen of the old

French resort hotels, with its luscious gardens and swimming pool, now handsomely refurbished. The front desk staff exhibited the first evidence of that remarkable Moroccan *politesse* that was to grace our entire journey. The following morning our rented car was delivered, and we headed north again, this time for Rabat, the capital.

Morocco is a country of capitals: Fès, Meknès, and Marrakech have all fulfilled that function at some time in their history. Rabat dates to the time of Ptolemy and earlier; it was the Almohad stronghold during the eleventh century and later became a trading center and corsairs' hideout. The French made it capital of the protectorate, and thus it has remained, housing the royal palace and the ministerial buildings in the new part of the city. Built of rosy copper sandstone, like so much of Morocco, and still partially walled, the Tour Hassan, Rabat's most dramatic sight, indeed its signature, has a minaret that soars to an impressive 144 feet above 200 columns of a mosque that was never completed. Some eight centuries separate it from the other massive building on this esplanade above the city—the mosque that houses the mausoleum of Mohammed V, hero of the transition to independence and father of the equally respected monarch, Hassan II.

The most beautiful panorama is the broad estuary with the whitewashed town of Salé on one side and the kasbah, or Rabat, on the other. This, the original fort, is entered through a magnificent twelfth-century gateway. Turning to the right, one strolls through graceful tropical gardens, known as the Jardins Andalouz and built along the lines of Granada's Generalife, in one of the many images of Andalusian nostalgia.

The Museum of Moroccan Arts, housed in a seventeenth-century palace and famed for its collection of Berber jewelry, musical instruments, costumes, and manuscripts, is alongside the Café

Maure, on whose terrace one can sip mint tea, gaze across that lovely estuary, and consider the ebb and flow of history that linked Spain to Morocco. The fall of Granada in 1492 marked the triumph of Ferdinand II and Isabella and the culmination of the Christian reconquest, just as it spelled defeat and exile for the Moors, whose last and most cherished stronghold it was. In fact, many of the peasants continued to live in this part of southern Spain, working on the land; but as early as the ninth century, when the caliphate of Córdoba began to disintegrate, the Moors returned as refugees to a homeland that most had never known. Called Moriscos by the Spaniards, they were known as Andalusians by the Moroccans, to whom they brought refined architectural and decorative skills; and thus it is that the Alhambra-like architecture—of which there is a great deal in Fès, for example—is still known as Andalusian.

Even the terrace portals of the Rabat Hilton, out beyond the western walls of the city, are touched by it; and though I wished that the coffee shop where we lunched had not been in a viewless corner, this is a handsome, beautifully equipped hotel with lovely gardens and a pool. Rabat is a better base for a couple of nights than Mohammedia, in spite of the charm (and the good food) of the Meridien-Miramar—but it is at least an hour's drive from the airport at Casablanca.

The road from Rabat east to Fès, which we took the next morning, runs through pretty cork and olive country, and as you climb, it begins to open out dramatically into sweeping contours. There was a moment—when I caught distant sight of the Atlas peaks—that I began to feel, for the first time, truly in Morocco. The route is strung with engaging roadside stalls (Moroccan salesmanship, an abiding passion, starts here): ceramics, bamboo furniture, rugs, piles of fruits and vegetables—even live chickens and baskets of eggs. One stall was festooned with particularly outlandish hats, their already vivid colors embellished with brilliant ribbons, feathers, and glittering sequins. Who on earth would wear them, I wondered. Much farther out into the wilds there came the answer. I saw a handsome, elderly couple riding on mules, she swathed in white, but he wearing the traditional version of the hat: natural straw, broad-brimmed, and magnificently caparisoned, jingling with bells and glinting with metal baubles. I asked their permission (an important etiquette in Morocco), and with touching dignity they posed for a photograph.

As we drove through the little towns of Tiflet and Khemisset, where the air is scented by grilling kebabs, we were struck with pangs of hunger, but Meknès was only a few more kilometers. The jade- and turquoise-tiled Bab Mansour in the formidable-looking red sandstone walls is like something out of the Arabian Nights; in fact, during the seventeenth century the tyrant ruler Moulay Ismail was harbored here in one of the darker chapters of Morocco's history. The old city was a-babble with Sunday markets and Arab music, crackling out of transistor radios. Thirst and hunger had by now become undeniable, however, and we headed straight on, some three kilometers beyond the city, to the pleasant garden restaurant, Hacienda. Welcoming service, a shady patio, delicious kebabs, and a good dry Guerrouane rosé from the local vineyards (which are among the best) made a refreshing interlude en route to Volubilis.

Following a brief but spectacularly lovely drive through the hills, we arrived at the Roman remains of Volubilis in the dry heat of midafternoon—siesta time, mercifully, for the site is easy enough to explore and piece together, and solitude is an important element of its enjoyment. Offset by slender, ink-green cypresses, the principal monuments left standing are the Forum and the Arch of Caracalla (sometimes known as the Arc de Triomphe), but further exploration reveals the mosaics of Orpheus charming the animals with his lute in the house named for him, as well as of Dionysus and Ariadne in what is known as the Knights' House. Volubilis's splendors are enhanced by limitless views over rolling plains, striped green, black, and tan in one direction and, in another, the hillside town of Moulay Idriss. This animated village, filled with kebab and sweetmeat stalls, piles of sticky dates, and gaudy necklaces, is in fact an important religious shrine. Moulay Idriss, the eighth-century ruler whose son founded the city of Fès, was a descendant of the prophet's daughter Fatima. The non-Muslim infidel, however, is permitted no more than a distant glimpse of the beautiful white mosque with its green tiled roof. There is reputedly a great view from the summit of the village, but I would advise a visit early in the day or toward sunset to make the climb bearable.

As it was, we were rewarded by a splendid, if roundabout, drive to Fès by taking a secondary road to the main Sidi Kacem/Fès highway. It was skirted at one point by rocky cliffs, which were pocked by troglodyte dwellings. A white mule walked its solitary way through the fig orchards, like a creature out of a Mogul primitive. Once on the main road we took in the hilly landscape—pale golden green and quite barren but for a few meticulous olive plantations.

On the outskirts of Fès a motorcyclist pulled up alongside. "You stay at the Palais Jamaï?" he inquired. "Follow me! Is on my way!" Such guides are part of Moroccan life. They can spot a foreigner like a laser beam, and I have to admit that our ten *dirhams* (roughly equal to one dollar) was well spent. The walled city of Fès has some half dozen different points of entry, and we were indeed swiftly and painlessly escorted to our hotel, parting with much smiling and handshaking.

Converted from a late-thirteenth-century palace, the Palais Jamaï, with its lovely swimming pool and terraced gardens, is certainly among the top hotels of North Africa and can stand comparison with many of the greats of Europe. Its charm, however, lies in being so thoroughly, so seductively Moroccan; but its cool, calm luxury makes it the perfect ivory tower. The first sight of our bedroom made me gasp, for beyond the platters of fruit and roses, beyond the broad, enclosed balcony with its comfortable chairs, there lay the very heart of the Moroccan experience: a bowl of low white buildings spiked with the towers of minarets, splashed here and there by palmy greenery, and seemingly quite silent, save for the twittering of birds. Just as the infidels poured their first drinks, though, the silence was broken by the wail of the muezzin—as it would be at five o'clock each morning with the cry, "Better to pray than sleep!"

We were poised for our first truly Moroccan meal, served in the Al Fassia, Palais Jamaï's restaurant in the oldest part of the building—all arches, low banquettes and cushions, old tiles, painted doors, candlelight, and immense brass trays. We broke with tradition by ordering *pastilla,* the famed *feuilleté* of pigeon, as a main course (for I still insist that it makes a weighty starter), preceded by *harira,* a soothing chick-pea, rice, and tomato soup scented with coriander. Also quite filling, *harira* is the traditional restorative when the day's fast is broken during Ramadan. The *pastilla* was indeed delectable, though the sugar and cinnamon topping—Fassi cooks are especially sweet-toothed—is not for all tastes.

I may have shocked our waiter by requesting a green salad. It is not traditional to Moroccan meals, and he produced instead a variety of cold cooked vegetables that were almost hors d'oeuvres: zucchini combined with sliced tomatoes, olive oil, and onions; eggplant; bell peppers with cumin and lemon; and a savory mystery that proved to be lambs' brains dressed with olives, onions, and lemon. The only dessert apart from traditional honey and almond sweetmeats, unsuitable following the *pastilla,* was slices of peeled orange, again with sugar and cinnamon.

We fared better the following evening, with tiny *feuilletés* called *briouates belkefta,* stuffed with spicy minced lamb; and then *ghalmi m'kalli,* a *tajine* of lamb with olives and lemon, which, touched with ginger and other exotic seasonings, was superb. The *tajine* comes in an earthenware dish with a volcano-shaped top; and the long, slow cooking combines melting tenderness with a heat that is amply maintained for second helpings. Apart from an excellent table d'hôte menu, one can order twelve hours ahead such delights as *méchoui à la broche* (spit-roasted lamb) or the more recherché dish of lamb steamed with potatoes, carrots, and onions called *méchoui m'bakhar,* considered a great delicacy. There are *pigeons aux amandes* and *poulet farci aux amandes et raisins secs* as well as simple *kefta* (minced lamb cooked on the skewer) and brochettes, also known as kebabs. This is a tantalizing cuisine and one whose subtle mysteries repay a sense of adventure. Lured by the prospect of a moon, as well as sitting up—rather than down—to table, we dined on the terrace of La Dienina, the hotel's international restaurant, on our third and last evening; in spite of the glamour of the setting, the European food seemed dull after the exotica of the Moroccan.

Fès is known as a three-night, two-day city, which may sound like a harsh and philistine judgment; but certainly it cannot be appreciated in less, especially if one is to make any excursions. The hotel lobby displays notices advising guests to use only the official guides (the amateurs, mainly English-speaking students, cluster in wait beyond the parking lot). We set off with a doughty, elderly Monsieur who claimed to speak French, but his heavy Arab accent did not improve communication. His chief virtue was as navigator, for any good guidebook will give you the facts, but it's not always easy to find the buildings. Walking from the Palais Jamaï, one approaches town from opposite the normal direction (via the

Boujloud Gate), which leads straight into the Grand Rue. But from any vantage, one plunges into the maelstrom of this warren of a city, its layout scarcely changed since the tenth century. The predominant cry of *Balek! Balek!*—Look out!—alerts you to do just that, as mules and donkeys laden with charcoal, vegetables, and even furniture or ridden by men with hefty boots fill the narrow alleys as they pass. The air fairly sings with a myriad of scents, both fragrant and pungent—carcasses of lamb offset by vast bunches of mint and coriander; dung, dust, and new wood shavings; jasmine oil and rose water; leather, varnish, and potato fritters, the ubiquitous snack, sizzling on wayside griddles. The whole of life, it seems, is accommodated within this tiny area. Tailors stitch gold thread onto lustrous silks and satins; and the dyers' quarter leads to the spectacular clamor of the coppersmiths' and metalworkers' area. The craftsmen wield their great hammers with breathtaking precision, and the scene—conducted on open ground shaded by trees—lacks only Verdi's Anvil Chorus from *Il Trovatore.*

There are, according to our guide, some three hundred mosques in a medina that holds 350,000 people. The Qaraouyine Mosque is the seat of a university that dates back to the tenth century, predating Oxford, Bologna, and the Sorbonne. They are all, of course, barred to non-Muslims, and, though one can imagine some of their splendors, a mere peep around the door is no substitute for being inside among that ethereal forest of pillars. The next best thing—the only opportunity to visit religious buildings of any kind—are the *medersas,* or theological colleges, with their exquisitely carved lintels, doors, and coffered ceilings and their fountains and pools for ritual ablutions in the courtyard outside the prayer hall. One of the loveliest and most Alhambra-like in the delicacy of its marble and honeycomb stucco is the Medersa Bou Anania, built in the fourteenth century. Its cedar-wood carving is especially fine and so, evidently, thought a handsome tortoiseshell cat with snowy breast, cabochon eyes, and lustrous whiskers, sitting high among the lintels as though he owned them. Dar Batha, the Museum of Moroccan Arts, is not far away—but here is where a guide is invaluable, for the museum contains all kinds of beautiful carvings and artifacts rescued from disused *medersas,* palaces, and mosques, which one can examine at leisure in detail. Other interesting incidentals include the *fondouks,* or caravansaries, used for dwelling as well as storage. Their courtyards stable mules and donkeys or are used for storing and sorting the great clouds of raw wool. The most impressive is the Fondouk-en-Nejjarine, still used as a hostel for impoverished students.

Apart from copper, brass, and leather, the best buys are undoubtedly rugs and carpets, and there is no guide—official or amateur—who will not lead you to "my friend, special prices" and get you firmly ensconced with a glass of mint tea while the wares are unrolled for your benefit—and, need I say, his own. Among several dealers, Aux Merveilles de Fès is a respected establishment at 11, Rue Bahabt, facing the En Attarine *medersa* (another beauty of its kind).

Following a morning of intensive sightseeing and souk-trailing, we plunged into the pool of the Palais Jamaï and lolled under an umbrella with a club sandwich and a long, cool drink. The day got into gear again toward five with a drive around the city ramparts, timing a sunset drink on the terrace of the Hotel Merinides, near the Merinid tombs, which has the best view of all. Part of the loop takes you past the royal palace into the *mellah* (the old Jewish quarter), which contains some jewelry souks. Nearby, on 10 Rue Bouksissat, a much more sophisticated leather shop than any I found in the medina has Fendi, Gucci, Hermès, and Cartier bags and overnight cases, selling at bargain prices.

After dark the Place Baghdadi, outside the Boujloud Gate, leaps to life like a fairground with a flea market, wrestlers, and tom-tom drummers, and you get another marvelous view of the lighted city from the southern loop of the ramparts, curving finally around the periphery to the gates of the Palais Jamaï.

The classic day excursion from Fès is to Volubilis and Moulay Idriss but, having seen them, we headed south for Ifrane and Azrou, leaving Fès via the old Jewish town of Sefrou, which lies in a picturesque clutter alongside a river. It is a route worth taking chiefly for the *circuit des lacs,* well signposted about twenty kilometers south of Sefrou and quite beautiful country. Rolling and tawny, it is punctuated by black Berber tents pitched like sleeping bats, by white ibis flocking to the waterside, and by herds of sheep and goats, in the charge of grinning Berber children. The *circuit* emerges on the main Fès/Ifrane road at Dayet Aoua and the Chalet du Lac, a recommended restaurant where we had an excellent—and very French—lunch. The great treat was the local *escargots,* sizzling in little crocks of aromatic butter. But everything was good: the feathery stuffed crêpes, the grilled lamb cutlets, and the *crème caramel.* Only half an hour on the main road from Fès, this is cool and lovely walking country, and the chalet is a great—and understandable— weekend favorite.

High among the cedars and the best excursion center for the Moyen Atlas stands Ifrane, where King Hassan maintained a summer palace. Ifrane is both a winter ski and a summer resort. With its rather spalike hotels and its *salons de thé,* plus its heavily eaved and timbered houses, it is an endearing anachronism, dating back to protectorate days, that suggests a combination of Le Touquet and Mégève—and also a way of life that the expatriate French must have abandoned with some reluctance.

The brief but spectacular road to Azrou runs through the cedar forests, with views of the Atlas like bubbles in a blue cauldron. Azrou itself, another world from Ifrane, was filled that day with a vast market that spilled over the hillside with livestock and produce. The chief attraction, other than the mere charm of this lively Berber town, is the best artisan center I saw in the whole of our Moroccan journey. Berber art tends to a naïve elegance, stylized rather than representational, as witness the wood carvings of animals, particularly monkeys (prevalent hereabout). There are attractive sequined cushions, which grace by the pile the richer Berber tents, good ceramics, wrought-iron work, and absolutely beautiful rugs. Typically they are white with spare motifs in navy blue and oxblood red, and they are loomed on the premises. What also caught my eye were a pair of sleek, handsome pewter water carriers, suspended from chains and intended to hang from a wall—or, in their traditional use, from a saddle. From Azrou a fair road runs via Khenifra to Marrakech—to which the total journey from Fès is nearly eight hours—though a plane may be preferred. But that is next month's journey. . . .

Southern Morocco

By Doone Beal

～

The very name of Marrakech carries a lure of mystery and adventure, of caravans and endless desert, as romantic as that of Russia's Samarkand, to which it is often compared. In the old quarter the streets echo the clip-clop of carriages and the jingle of harnesses. Spring blooms with jacaranda and bougainvillea and summer with roses—roses everywhere. Disparate smells mingle: blossoms, stables, burning charcoal, roasting kebabs, mint, and the earthy scent of tanning hides, which lie out to dry in the heat of day near the Bab ed-Debbagh, or Tanners' Gate. Marrakech is the last great oasis before the Sahara, and it is a city that has vied through the centuries with Fès in the north as Morocco's capital. The classic view of Marrakech is of walls and towers ranging in color from shrimp to deep terra-cotta, surrounded by palms, with the distant peaks of the High Atlas, snow-capped for much of the year, standing like some huge celestial balcony in the clouds.

From the air Marrakech must surely be a mosaic of pools, for every hotel worthy of the name—and the tally is increasing rapidly—is thus equipped. No longer dependent on its famed winter climate, which drew the latter-day Grand Tour visitors, the city has become a year-round resort that, thanks to its low humidity and proximity to the mountains, is rarely oppressive, even in high summer. It is an intriguing amalgam of the remains of French protectorate—sidewalk cafés and *pâtisseries* by the score; of ruler-straight, tree-lined avenues; and of such deluxe hotels as the Mamounia and the Es-Saadi, where doormen attired in white burnouses help guests in and out of their taxis as though they were royalty. Another attraction is the medina and the famed Place Jemaa el-Fna, which, for natives and visitors alike, is the very hub and the chief lure of Marrakech.

Surrounded by walls that look like gingerbread, as if one could break off a piece and eat it, the old city with its maze of souks extends over two square miles. Landmarked from the outside by the tower of the twelfth-century Koutoubia Mosque, the main entrance leads directly into the arena of the Jemaa el-Fna and its buzz of humanity. Snake charmers, storytellers, acrobats, scribes, performing monkeys, and medicine men with their little piles of herbs and potions—all mingle among charcoal braziers sizzling with fried eggs, fish, and kebabs and stalls dispensing mint tea and nameless sticky pastries. Each performance has its knot of customers, listeners, and spectators, and the first evening we went there, at the very height of the action, the crowd was well-nigh impenetrable. We retreated first up four flights of tiled stairs to the Café de France and then across the street to the rooftop restaurant Le Marrakchi, both of which offer the thrill of overlooking the flare-lighted *place* without the hassle of being in it. It was a moment to treasure, sinking into a comfortable low chair and rinsing my fingers in cool, scented water before discussing the food with the delightful and knowledgeable *patron,* Dr. Aziz. Le Marrakchi is among the most locally respected restaurants in the city, and I wish we had had stamina enough for the ten-course Festive Menu. As it was we began with *briouates belkefta:* little *feuilletés* stuffed with spicy minced lamb, with only the merest hint of the sugar to which Moroccans are so addicted; rather, ground cumin is used as a condiment—and very effectively, too—along with salt and pepper. I flirted with the thought of *cervelles au coriandre* (brains with coriander) but opted instead for a *tajine* of pigeon with almonds that was subtly gamy and very good. We finished with honeyed crêpes and drank Oustalet—an excellent dry, fruity wine.

The souks of Marrakech are much more open and easier to navigate than those of Fès, and one morning, intent on a shopping spree, I set off to discover them on my own. A naïve hope, indeed. Moroccans, and especially the Marrakechi, are truly helpful and kind-hearted, but visitors are rarely left alone. Amateur guides, mostly fourteen-year-old boys, pester and persuade tourists until they are employed. I found myself in the exclusive company of one Jemal, a child with the broken nose of a boxer but a gentle disposition—at least toward me. To the merchants, though, he was a fiend, prepared to throw their goods back in their faces if he perceived my genuine disinterest. Otherwise he was a good, mean bargainer. "Offer him thirty!" he would hiss in my ear, naming a quarter of the asking price. "He take it, he need the money."

Through the rope-makers' souk we walked to reach the wood-turners' souk, where the specialty is kebab spears with beautiful wooden handles. Several souks are devoted to jewelry and armory: knives, daggers, pistols with chased silver handles, and *boîtes à poudre,* circular and often handsomely enameled, which are intended for gunpowder and are still used, slung on the belts of Moroccan horsemen to fuel their muskets. (They are also the perfect ornament for the executive desk.) Among my other finds that morning, Mustafa is an excellent leather shop, with French and Italian couture bags at tempting prices; and both Bazar Ikhouan and Bazar Ddakhla offer a good general selection of rugs, old pistols, silver, pottery, and embroidery. Shopping aside, the dyers' souk is perhaps the most spectacular of them all, bannered with swags of wool and silk in indigo, saffron, emerald, crimson, and gentian violet. The water carriers, walking carillons with their hand bells and tinkling metal cups, seem to appear on cue. (Keep plenty of small change if you want to photograph.) After a few hours I came away content with two baubly necklaces and, from the pottery souk, a lovely peacock-colored vase that, stuffed and wrapped with newspaper, safely survived three flights.

For serious sight-seeing I sought the advice of Menara Tours, which is a most helpful firm to deal with whether one seeks guidance on restaurants and routes or wants to arrange day excursions. I was assigned an excellent guide, and we went first to the Saadian Necropolis, where virtually an entire dynasty—twenty sultans, along with their wives and children, who ruled during the sixteenth and part of the seventeenth centuries—is interred. Judged to be perhaps the finest example of Hispanic-Moorish architecture and the closest equivalent of the gloriously intricate Alhambra, with which it is a late contemporary, the Necropolis, with its coffered tiled pavilions, painted wood ceilings, and slender pillars of Ferrara marble, is more suggestive of a palace. For sheer beauty alone, it should be seen. We returned, then, to the less familiar residential area of the medina, where the domestic streak runs strong and the voices, particularly when raised in dispute, sound like high-speed tapes. Every tiny *quartier* has its fountain, its *hammams* (communal steam baths), its bakery, its mosque, and its Koranic school. One of the most famous—and beautiful—is the Ben Youssef Medersa, built at the end of the seventeenth century and now preserved as a historic building, so that one may roam through it at will. There was no time to see the El-Badi Palace, another magnificent Saadian building, within whose ruins the Festival of Folklore is held in June; but the Dar Si Saïd, which contains the Museum of Moroccan Arts, exudes the feel of antiquity with its splendid collection of decorative musketry, of *kelim* rugs and embroidery, and also of Berber jewelry. Some of the dangling silver earrings, strung with lumps of coral and amber, are as large as a bunch of baby carrots—but they are worn over and around, not (fortunately for the wearer) from, the earlobe. Judging by the museum displays, the women were not afraid to dazzle, and the exotic burnouses and elaborately embroidered boots made of the softest leather suggest what glorious peacocks their men, also, must have been!

Our home away from home—for that was how it felt—was the Hotel Es-Saadi, which, though no architectural beauty, was welcoming and filled with light and roses, as well as staffed with kind and efficient people. A hotel to which regular guests return year after year, it features a pool that was a tempting midday refuge from the dusty souks and a terrace with shops including Fekhita Sebti (for pretty caftans, sensibly adapted to European taste), as well as an antique jeweler's, where Berber necklaces and pendants of top quality are probably a better buy than some dubious bargains in the souks.

We lunched one day, dined another, on the pleasant poolside terrace of the hotel's restaurant. Much of the clientele is French and the food was light, fresh, and beautifully prepared: artichoke hearts with vinaigrette and segments of fresh orange; a zingy gazpacho; a brochette of *lotte* with eggplant fritters; and sea bass with an irreproachable *sauce Choron* were some of the treats, accompanied by a bottle of well-chilled Valpierre, which became a favorite from among the local whites. The Es-Saadi has a casino and a (reputedly) terrific floor show in a separate building beyond the rose gardens. At La Mamounia, a floor show accompanied dinner in the Moroccan restaurant, and the undulant gyrations of the belly dancers left me thinking that there could surely be no more effective exercise. Ideally your party should be of at least four and in the mood for a gift-wrapped folkloric evening of noise and spectacle. Indeed, orders for two will certainly feed four: our chicken with crêpes was a meal in itself, though listed as a starter; and similarly, the *tangia Marrakchia,* which is shin of lamb cooked in an earthenware jar and rather spectacularly decanted, was tender and steaming hot. We had ordered in advance—as one must for specialties—but there is a very adequate à la carte menu that actually allows more freedom of last-minute choice, such as a delectable-looking roast shoulder of baby lamb *(m'hammar)* that I coveted at a neighboring table. Though it lacks the personal warmth and friendly rapport of the Es-Saadi, La Mamounia lives up to at least some of its legends. The gardens, laid out at the end of the eighteenth century, full of pomegranates and citrus trees, are dreamy; and friends staying there remarked on the barbecue lunches and the peace and seclusion of the pool. The shops are surely the most sumptuous (and sumptuously priced) in Marrakech, and there is a pleasant French restaurant, as well as the aforementioned Moroccan restaurant, on the premises.

Another most pleasant French restaurant is the Samovar—an intimate bistro at 143 rue Chammed Elbergal. But the greatest surprise—and delight—was Italian: Villa Rosa, 64 avenue Hassan. Elegant and charmingly decorated, with flowers at every table and in huge copper urns, the restaurant has the ambiance of a private house—*"comme chez soi,"* as Madame Vasari, who is very much the hostess, put it. A Florentine who has spent much of her life in France and Morocco, she offers domestic cooking of the highest order, employing her own personal staff. Never, even in Florence, have I tasted lasagne quite so exquisite. Pasta apart, seafood, which includes the famed oysters from the lagoons of Oualidia, is a specialty of the house. Madame secures the morning catch, nothing less, as witness the flavor and texture of the huge *gambas* (shrimp) we ordered; and service was such that not only were they neatly shelled and decapitated, then reassembled, but a second relay was kept hot and served with fresh plates and cutlery. We finished with an airy froth of chocolate mousse, reveling in the pleasures of contrast—for surely, no two Marrakechi restaurants are alike in either ambiance or food.

And neither is the country itself lacking in contrast. It was a sparkling late September morning when we left Marrakech for a day trip south to Ouirgane, in the foothills of the High Atlas. The transition from the plains is abrupt, and the rosy clay of the rising valley had formed fantastic pinnacles and cones, sometimes with trees sprouting from them like outlandish hats. In one direction the view was all palms and greenery and in another, fold after fold of mountains, culminating in the spectacular peak of Jbel Toubkal. Outside Ouirgane, terraced above the valley in a grove of olives, willows, and citrus trees, there stands a little patch of paradise: the hotel and restaurant La Roseraie. At such a height the air is like warm crystal, and with the gleaming blue pool and garden full of coral roses (no others seem to have quite the intense fragrance of those in Morocco) a feeling of euphoria sets in. This would be the perfect spot to spend a weekend: there is a riding school nearby, and each of the pink adobe bungalows has an open fireplace, with logs lying ready to light at the first chill of the evening. Having swam and lolled away the rest of the morning, we settled down to a memorably good lunch on the tree-shaded terrace: fresh pasta tossed in saffron and butter, an excellent terrine, a brochette of chicken grilled over an olive-wood barbecue, and a classically perfect *blanquette de veau*. There were pitchers of delicious local rosé and traditional flatbread warm from the oven, and we finished with a fine lemon meringue tart. About an hour and a half from Marrakech, La Roseraie is another world—and one that was hard to leave.

But this is essentially wanderlust country, and it was with elation that we headed southeast for Ouarzazate, driving over the dramatic High Atlas pass of Tizi-n-Tichka, which, indeed, separates two worlds. The lush fertility of the steep, northern slopes is exchanged for the almost treeless landscape that merges into the pre-Sahara, and the pass itself marks the boundary between the provinces of Marrakech and Ouarzazate. The local youths had set out their inevitable stalls full of mineral stones—amethyst, green agate, and crystal—but it was the landscape that claimed the attention. One sees walled villages almost indiscernible from the soil, perched on the ridge of a hill and looking oddly like Egyptian temples. There are patches of velvety moss among the red rocks, and the seeming wilderness is softened, here and there, by spinneys of plumed cane, olive, and fig trees, probably watered by the melting snows. Another curiosity are the pop-art mosques with wildly decorated minarets, and some of the heavy alabaster ornaments one finds hereabout are remarkable works of art in themselves.

Standing at the head of two river valleys, the Dades and the Drâa, Ouarzazate—grown almost unrecognizably prosperous since I last saw it twenty years ago—is an undramatic though pleasing town, complete with a *Beau Geste* fort built by the French, which now houses the *gendarmerie*. In the center of town the Salam Tichka Hotel, where we stayed, is new, small, and pretty, its rooms—not much more than adequate—balconied above and around the tiny pool. The service is friendly and willing, and the food a pleasant surprise. In this country of lucky-dip gastronomy I wish more Moroccan restaurants would serve such buffets as served here. Done with imagination, ours included excellent salads, soup, cold meats, pasta, and some half dozen traditional dishes. (The *kefta,* well seasoned with cumin and parsley and grilled to order, were the best ever).

Beyond the town limits, with a lovely open view over the hills, the Hotel PLM Le Zat offers better conventional comfort and more space as well as a huge terrace pool. But whichever hotel, among the several available, you choose—and during the high winter season all accommodation is at a premium—Ouarzazate's chief claim is as a springboard from which to tour the fascinating Drâa Valley en route to Zagora, farther south.

The first part of the journey is over a pass in the Anti-Atlas, which lies to the south of the main range, before the road drops down toward Agdz, scene of a lively Thursday market—a-babble with crackling loudspeakers and a-bray with donkeys—to which the outlying villagers bring their livestock and their produce. A little farther up the road, and then from a height there was the first, fabulous view of the broad valley, a Shangri-la of palms flowing along the course of the riverbed and, on the far side, canyons and canyons of red cliffs, now haloed with the early morning light. Every oasis village seems to begin with T: Tamangouli, Timiderte, Tansikht, Tamezoute, Timsala, and Tinsouline—each of them a stage set of dwellings proclaimed by intricately decorated walls and towers. Rosy copper against the cloudless sky, sometimes they suggest a particularly elaborate child's sand castle, sometimes a Gothic turret with crenellated edges: indeed, the Berbers' natural artistry, their unwitting sophistication of shape and line, is extraordinary.

The women gather at the wells to draw water, their zinc buckets high on their heads. Some with bundles of cane, some with babies strapped to their backs, they walk the long, dusty roads, their brilliant robes clutched around the waist with ropes and ribbons, necklaces jangling, earrings swinging as they move, and often a headband slung with silver coins to which is attached a vibrantly colored kerchief. But by no means are they simple. With camera poised I approached an elderly woman, who accepted the few *dirhams* I proffered but walked on with dignity, smiling slyly and waving a negative hand.

The closer to Zagora, the more prosperous and new-looking—though, inevitably, the less picturesque. Zagora is a desert shanty town (but still some ninety kilometers from the Sahara proper), and I was amused to see in the main roundabout a placard of a camel with the caption: *Timbuktu, 52 days.* For all its remoteness, however, Zagora is a desert resort of sorts and, given its sublime winter climate and setting, is likely to become more so: the Palm Springs of Morocco is not so far-fetched a prospect come A.D. 2000. The Hotel Tinsouline, where we spent the night, looks glamorous and is adequate for lunch and a swim but, alas, is not otherwise commendable. However, PLM will open a hotel in 1985, and judging by other examples of the French chain in Morocco, that augurs well.*

Nobody had mentioned to us the beauty of the road that runs southwest from Ouarzazate to Taroudannt between the two ranges of mountains. The stretch is so bold, so empty, so infinite in perspective that the hand of Atlas himself might have drawn it. The kasbah at Taliouine is one of the most impressive of those built by the Glaoui (dynastic lords of the High Atlas) and reason enough to pause en route. But so is the Hotel Ibn Toumert, where one can spend the night in a comfortable, well-decorated room, enjoying this sensational landscape. We lunched—and very well—on eggplant fritters with spicy tomato sauce, a delicious *tajine* of veal, and a *risotto Andaluz,* whose quality suggested more than local talent in the chef. We drank a particularly good Oustalet rosé.

As the air got warmer by the minute, we approached the overture to Taroudannt: a cluster of little pincushion hills; argan trees (akin to olives), upon whose branches the goats clamber to nip the sweet, rich fruit (much prized for its oil); acres of olives and orchards; roadside eucalyptus; and rows of talipot palms. Ancient capital of the Sous, this walled city is an oasis, a miniature Marrakech and (so claim the inhabitants) even older. Certainly the Saadi ruled it before they conquered Marrakech, and for many cen-

*The author, writing this in early 1985, was rather prophetic.

turies it enjoyed a certain autonomy. The medina is small enough to be manageable; a wonderful view of it can be seen from the ramparts—women dressed in blue robes traditional to Taroudannt flit through the narrow streets.

Some of the best buys are blankets, woven from camel wool in bold stripes of black, brown, gray, and white, with touches of bright coral. Investigate the wares of Bazar Tafrout and Bazar Cleopatra, which have a good general selection of silver, brass, rugs, and caftans. Alongside, a spice shop doubles as herbalist and pharmacy; where, according to my companion, the *fakih* helps women exorcise spells—mostly those cast by others upon their men's affections—with the aid of a tame chameleon, colored powders, pickled snakes, perfumed oils, and, no doubt, pithy advice. Sunday and Thursday are the chief market days—though the souks never close. And the terrace of the Hotel Taroudannt in Asarag, the main square, is the best place to rendezvous. Over a glass of fresh orange juice, one might be serenaded on a primitive guitar by a distinguished old Berber from the Sudan.

Its local charm aside, Taroudannt is a byword for one of the most lovely and celebrated hotels in Morocco: La Gazelle D'Or, which stands at the end of a long, oleander-lined *allée* a couple of kilometers outside town. It was formerly the private residence of the late Baron Jean Pellenc, and private is how it still essentially feels. Guests stay in secluded, charmingly decorated bungalows each with an open fireplace and a garden terrace that trails with moonflowers and overlooks a cool, green stretch of long grass and poplars, the entire vista rimmed by the distant Atlas. The only perceptible sounds when I was there were those of tree frogs and twittering birds, save for the house cats who became our breakfast companions. Fellow guests had dinner served on their terrace one moonlit evening; it is that sort of hotel.

The main building, a series of elegant pavilions with inlaid marble floors and silk-tented ceilings, is casually scattered with collectors' *objets:* huge old samovars, beautiful copper lamps, and handsome silver scimitars, as well as priceless ceramics. Attended by silent, smiling staff who glide rather than walk in their white robes, one feels like a guest in a Mogul palace—an impression encouraged by the long, formal waterway, threading between an enchanted jungle of a garden and the silky blue Olympic-size pool, all set about with chaises. We were only a few guests in early October, and the poolside lunch was basic, but barbecues and buffets are set up for high season.

Tennis and riding are the chief diversions, other than Taroudannt itself, and the evenings are as convivial as the guests (an optimum of twenty-five residents) happen to make them. The food is a sophisticated mix of international and Moroccan cuisine, with all the traditional specialties such as couscous and *pastilla.* One of the best dishes we had was a deliciously aromatic *poulet au citron aux olives,* accompanied by a crisp green salad and a Cabernet, one of the prizes of an excellent cellar. One can order, on twenty-four hours' notice, lobster and *langouste* or discuss any other fancied item not listed on the menu: whims are obligingly indulged. One of the most charming ceremonies of late evening is the rolling out of the rug, when the oldest member of the staff sets out his apparatus to make mint tea and dispenses it in tiny glasses from a huge brass tray.

Capturing some of the flavors of Morocco are the following recipes.

Moroccan Chicken with Prunes

2 tablespoons olive oil
a 3½-pound chicken, cut into serving pieces
1 onion, minced
1 garlic clove, minced
½ teaspoon crumbled saffron threads dissolved in ¼ cup hot water
¾ teaspoon ground cardamom
1 teaspoon ground cinnamon
½ teaspoon ground ginger
1 cup pitted prunes
2 teaspoons fresh lemon juice
1½ teaspoons sesame seeds, toasted lightly

In a large heavy skillet, heat the oil over moderately high heat until it is hot but not smoking. In it sauté the chicken, patted dry and seasoned with salt and pepper, until it is golden, and transfer it with tongs to a platter. In the fat remaining in the skillet cook the onion and the garlic over moderately low heat, stirring, until they are softened. Add the saffron mixture, the cardamom, the cinnamon, the ginger, and 1½ cups water. Bring the liquid to a boil, and add the chicken with any juices that have accumulated on the platter, and the prunes. Simmer the mixture, covered, for 30 minutes, or until the breast meat is springy to the touch and the dark meat is tender, transfer the chicken and the prunes to the platter, and keep them warm, covered loosely with foil. Bring the cooking liquid to a boil and boil it until it is thickened. Season the sauce with the lemon juice and salt and pepper to taste. Sprinkle the chicken and prunes with the sesame seeds and serve the sauce separately. Serves 4 to 6.

Moroccan Orange Salad

4 navel oranges
¼ cup sugar
3 tablespoons fresh lemon juice
1 teaspoon orange flower water (available at specialty foods shops)
12 unsprayed orange blossoms for garnish if desired

Cut away the peel and the pith from the oranges with a serrated knife, cut the oranges crosswise into ¼-inch slices, and arrange the slices, overlapping slightly, on a platter. Sprinkle the oranges with the sugar, the lemon juice, and the orange flower water and arrange the orange blossoms over them if desired. Serves 4 to 6.

Morocco's Veiled Charm
By Nancy R. Newhouse

~~

editor's note

This piece almost reads like fantasy, but that is exactly what a visit to Morocco can be like. As the writer notes, very often in the medinas of Morocco, one is confronted with (and confounded by) completely unassuming exteriors that reveal absolutely nothing of the splendor and spaciousness of the interiors.

NANCY NEWHOUSE is editor of the travel section of *The New York Times*.

It may be the prettiest restaurant I've ever seen; certainly it's in the top five. Yacout, behind high walls in Marrakesh's ancient medina, is set in a ravishing small seventeenth- and eighteenth-century palace, its various rooms in early January glowing with crackling fires in the fireplaces, lighted by ornate filigree and colored-glass fixtures, its walls miracles of colorful tilework. Waiters in long white caftans moved silently about, and from the roof terrace one could look out over the old quarter, or back to the inner courtyard and its pool.

I can't testify to the food, because to our regret we hadn't reserved days ahead, and it was New Year's week; the city was full of visitors. But we were cordially allowed to walk through the restaurant before dinner, and we noted the quietly splashing fountain in the entry, the pool in the courtyard, and the fresh rose petals scattered on the tablecloths, muttering to ourselves about "next time."

Three of us—my husband, Michael, my brother Fen and I— were in Morocco for ten days in December and early January. It was the end of Ramadan, so the city was quiet during the day, despite holiday visitors, and came alive at night, when the renowned square, Jemaa el Fna, was transformed into a theatrical scene of food stalls where busy cooks worked at charcoal grills, Berber storytellers regaled their Moroccan audiences, and snake charmers sat on the ground surrounded by the curious.

Our trip started in Marrakesh; we then made the spectacular four-and-a-half-hour drive south in a rented car over the Atlas Mountains to Ouarzazate and the picturesque Valley of the Draa, afterward flying from Ouarzazate to Fez, our final stop.

Throughout the trip, we were struck by the perfect winter climate—60 to 65 degrees in the daytime, cool at night—and the remarkably preserved Moroccan culture, seemingly untouched by modern mores or mall blight.

And everywhere, we reveled in the beauty of Moroccan architecture, and the fact that in the old quarters of Marrakesh and Fez,
grand houses and small palaces are being converted into wonderfully beautiful restaurants, small hotels, or B&Bs. Here the *Arabian
Nights* fantasy is based in reality. Time and again, whether at a
museum, a historic monument, a restaurant, or a small hotel in the
old quarter, you would step out of a dusty, hectic street into a cool
hallway leading to a courtyard with a fountain or a small garden,
surrounded by white walls brilliant with patterned tile or pierced
with improbably delicate windows.

When Morocco was a French protectorate (from 1912 to 1956),
the colonial government maintained an active program of historic
preservation. But we were impressed that now so many individual
owners or entrepreneurs, some of them Moroccan, were restoring
and converting buildings in the old sections, rather than in the
neighborhoods established by Europeans.

Of course, the country has long had its legendary grand hostel-
ries, the Mamounia in Marrakesh, the Gazelle d'Or near
Taroudant, and the Palais Jamai in Fez. A luxury resort opened this
spring twenty minutes outside Marrakesh, the vast and stunning
Amanjena (part of the Amanresorts group); we were able to walk
through as it was close to completion. But what we found most
exciting were the renovations or reinterpretations of old Moroccan
buildings that have been carried out in or near the medinas.

One of the pleasures, and sometimes frustrations, of finding a
restaurant in the medinas of Fez or Marrakesh was making our way
on foot or being let off by a taxi in a dusty, dim street in front of an
unpromising high blank wall. But then either a large door would
quietly open, or a robed attendant would appear, to lead us through
the entrance. Invariably, we were in another magical interior.

This is the delightful game of inside-outside that plays out in the
old quarters of Morocco, where you go from the sunny, noisy hus-

tle of the souk or a dusty roadway into the shadowy coolness of hallways of tile or filigreed stucco. In the many palace museums, long sequences of rooms are punctuated by small interior gardens.

Our introduction came at our hotel, the Villa des Orangers, which opened the week we arrived. We felt as dubious as our cab driver about 6, rue Sidi Mimoun. Although it was farther down the same broad avenue as the Mamounia, inside the old city walls but outside the teeming souk, No. 6 was next to a derelict building, and we couldn't see a sign. We eventually made out a small door, walked down the narrow entrance hall, and—the Moroccan surprise.

Just behind the concierge desk, where we were warmly greeted, we peered into an enchanting courtyard with four small orange trees and a quietly dripping fountain. It was framed at ground and second floors by delicate columns supporting arcades of lacy white carved stucco and gleaming twelve-foot-high cedarwood doors.

The 1930s mansion with two courtyards was converted and restored by a French couple, Pascal and Véronique Beherec, with great attention to detail. We had some small quibbles—our split-level ground-floor rooms were not as appealing as the second-floor rooms we saw later, some with tiny terraces adjacent to the small swimming pool on the roof (although our bathroom was immense); only breakfast and beverages were available (now guests can order light lunches and a set-menu dinner). But the warm, attentive staff, the delicious Moroccan crepes and fresh orange juice for breakfast, and the delicate beauty and tranquillity of our surroundings soon had us congratulating ourselves on our good fortune.

To celebrate New Year's Eve, we went to a restaurant in the medina, Le Tobsil, opened a year and a half ago in a lovely renovated house. The *réveillon* dinner was a festive feast, starting with a delicate fish *pastilla* (layers of flaky pastry with filling), then chicken with olives, boned stuffed pigeon, or whole fish stuffed with semolina and raisins, all accompanied by pleasant Moroccan red wine. (French diners were having champagne.) Tables were artfully placed around the open candlelighted courtyard spread with bright rugs. At the stroke of the millennium midnight, Gnaouas musicians, from southern Morocco, in white robes burst in with songs and powerful drumming.

Although Le Marocain, the Moroccan restaurant in the Mamounia, was created by European architects in 1922, it has exotic mood to spare. Despite hearing almost exclusively American voices as we crossed the hotel's vast lobby, we fell under a spell in the rose-pink aura of this period piece restaurant. Here the belly dancer seemed to belong, as we watched her from our comfy divans.

While we were starting to get used to dining in exquisiteness, when our hotel proprietor told us about Al Fassia, a restaurant in Gueliz, the new section of the city that was built by the French, we jumped. Gueliz is unexciting but modern on a walkable human scale, and Al Fassia's interior, while pleasant, does not have the allure of the old city. However, here one can order à la carte.

After a few days we realized that Moroccan cuisine, superb when well prepared, is traditionally served in a set series of courses. Meaning that meals tended to be long, rich, and stately—splendid, but not every night. At Al Fassia, where we ate twice, we could limit ourselves to spicy traditional *harira* (chick-pea and lentil soup) followed by *salades marocaines,* the first course of a selection of cold salads—here there were fifteen delicious choices. And, we discovered, Al Fassia is an all-women operation. It was the only restaurant we encountered where the servers were not male, and these women, in charming regional dress, radiated graciousness and efficiency.

During the day, we would snack or find a café. And, always avid for interiors, we compulsively roamed the old city. We had heard from friends of an original spirit in the medina, Meryanne Loum-

Martin, who had converted a grand house into Ryad Tamsna. After our usual arduous search (Ryad Tamsna, too, has no sign), we had a delightful lunch and heard Ms. Loum-Martin recount how she came to Marrakesh ten years ago and fell in love with the city. Her outpost is an unusual combination boutique, bookstore, art gallery, and restaurant (for brunch, lunch, or tea; reservation only). The small boutique has a choice selection of jewelry, fabrics, and home accessories.

Another afternoon, we took a taxi to the far side of the medina to the Maison Arabe, once a legendary restaurant, now reopened as an enchanting small hotel. (Its restaurant opened after we visited.) If one were six foot four, one might hesitate to stay here because this jewel box is done to a rather Lilliputian scale. The feeling is of delicious cosseting: warm carpets, deep divans, and a small flower-edged courtyard. The two rooms we looked at were cozy and inviting, one with a minuscule terrace; each of the ten rooms and suites, we were told, is different.

On foot in the medina again, the three of us feeling exasperated after several dead ends, we eventually found the Dar al Assad and looked around this quiet B&B, with three rooms handsomely decorated with Moroccan pieces and area rugs—and the requisite charming courtyard. Its prices were also more reasonable than the upper-level ones we had encountered so far. The inn is now reportedly being sold. Several other B&Bs in a similar spirit have opened in the medina in the last few years.

The strongest evocations of the poetry of Moroccan interiors and long-ago life at the top can be had at the city's great sites: the superb sixteenth-century Saadian tombs, set in a jumbled garden full of birds; the haunting ruined El Badi Palace of the same era, with its vast empty pools and storks perched on the high exterior walls; or the nineteenth-century Bahia Palace. There, an endless sequence of empty rooms and small hidden gardens leads into a vast tiled courtyard, the whole built for a black slave who became a powerful vizier.

Although most mosques cannot be visited by non-Muslims in Morocco, there are intriguing courtyard glimpses to be had. Next to the mosque of the same name is the Ibn Youssef Medersa (which can be visited), built in the fourteenth and sixteenth centuries to house religious students; its courtyard of delicate stucco, tiles, and carved wood is a revelation of craftsmanship, work so fine it resembles old lace. Two splendid palace museums in the medina also have storybook settings: the Dar Si Said Museum and the recently opened Musée de Marrakech. The latter had one small but fine display of objects from Moroccan synagogues, now sadly almost vanished from the country.

At about the surfeit point for this kind of opulence, we left Marrakesh and drove over the slightly dizzying mountain road (good highway, no guard rails) to Ouarzazate. Long a separate culture when the mountains formed an almost impregnable barrier, this Berber region recalls the sweep of the American Southwest. Even more powerfully, it recalls scenes from the Bible. On the most remote and barren reaches, robed shepherds stood guarding their flocks of goats or sheep. Mysterious mud-walled casbahs, or fortress villages, loomed from distant hilltops.

A few days were not enough to see the picturesque countryside around Ouarzazate, a rather charmless town with several comfortable chain hotels. But driving south toward the Sahara as far as Zagora gave us a powerful sense of the Berber lands: harsh near-desert, then rich green date-palm groves stretching the length of the Draa Valley.

It was a perfect contrast to Fez, the Moroccan city whose old quarter, Fez el Bali, seems most unchanged by modern intrusions (and where the aggressive guides and hustlers are deeply trying to Western tourists). Here we stayed at the wonderful Palais Jamai, a nineteenth-century palace (its rooms are now suites) whose larger section was added in 1930 and refurbished in 1998–99.

Ornate tiles, high ceilings, and knowing decoration create a cool, gracious atmosphere. Most rooms overlook the superb garden with a pool and fountains and beyond them the medina. Our attractive sixth-floor room with a 1930s feel had a semienclosed balcony. Sitting there as night fell, looking out over the medina, watching the lights go on and hearing the muezzins' call to prayer, is a lasting memory of Fez.

Like the Mamounia, the Palais Jamai has a Moroccan restaurant with full-fledged fantasy décor, but our favorite discovery was the Maison Bleue. We went for the food, and it was the best we had in Morocco. But the décor, too, was astonishingly lovely in this small 1915 palace in the medina. The home of the el-Abbadi family, who still own it, it became a restaurant a few years ago, and more recently, guest suites were created upstairs. We were greeted in the rather bleak hallway by a *djellaba*-clad attendant who preceded us into the enclosed courtyard restaurant ringing a small bell—no doubt the closest the three of us will ever come to making a royal entrance.

Surrounded by vertiginous white walls pierced with lacy windows and enormous cedar doors, and entertained by a terrific three-man orchestra playing trance-inducing southern Moroccan music, we sat back on cushioned divans and were regaled with a superb array of first-course salads, then *tagines,* one specially prepared for the vegetarian in our group. I tried to memorize the taste and texture of the fabulous dessert, called *jouhara*—a delicate concoction of crackling superthin pastry and crème pâtissière flavored with orange water and cinnamon so ethereal it was like eating cloud.

After dinner, a manager showed us the one unoccupied suite upstairs. The charmingly eccentric space had very high ceilings, attractive Moroccan furnishings (marred somewhat by banal contemporary paintings), and a stunning tile floor.

We could picture ourselves being happy here.

Finding the Right Doors to Knock On

Marrakesh Hotels

The **Villa des Orangers,** 6, rue Sidi Mimoun: telephone 044.38.46.38; fax 044.38.51.23; www.villadesorangers.com. Sixteen rooms and suites; doubles about $230 to $276, suites $322 to $415, including breakfast and light lunch; dinner available for hotel guests. Prices are calculated at 11 *dirhams* to $1. Small swimming pool on roof. Rates include an airport shuttle and guest laundry.

Dar al Assad, 29, Derb Hajra; 044.42.70.65; a B&B with three double rooms. Rates were about $100, with breakfast, when we visited.

The **Maison Arabe,** 1, Derb Assehbe, Bab Doukkala; 044.38.70.10; fax 044.38.72.21; www.lamaisonarabe.com. Four rooms and six suites; double rooms about $190 to $230; suites about $280 to $350. The hotel has recently opened a large swimming pool in a garden. On the outskirts of town, ten minutes by hotel shuttle. Restaurant open daily for à la carte lunch and dinner (about $80 for two, with wine); hotel guests receive priority in reservations.

Amanjena, BP 2405, Marrakesh; 044.40.33.53; fax 044.40.34.77; www.amanresorts.com. Full resort facilities. Double rooms, about $600 to $750; two-bedroom *maisons,* about $1,300 to $1,600. Tax (20 percent) and meals extra.

Yacout, 79, Didi Ahmed Soussi; 044.38.29.29; fax 044.38.25.38. Dinner only, closed Monday. Fixed-price dinner, including wine and aperitif, about $60 a person.

Al Fassia, 232, avenue Mohammed V in Gueliz; 044.43.40.60; 044.44.83.49. Open daily for lunch and dinner; à la carte menu. Three-course meal with wine, about $18.40 to $23.

Le Tobsil, 22, Derb Moulay Abdallah Ben Hessaien, Rmila Bab Ksour; 044.44.40.52; fax 044.44.35.15. Dinner only, closed Tuesday. The set menu, which changes daily, is about $50.70, including aperitif and wine.

Le Marocain, Hotel Mamounia, Avenue Bab Jdid; 044.44.44.09; fax 044.44.40.44; on the Web at www.mamounia.com. Although the hotel just completed an $18 million renovation, Le Marocain has retained its original décor. Open nightly for dinner. À la carte menu, about $60 to $90 a person without wine.

Ryad Tamsna, Riad Zitoun Jdid, 23, Derb Zanka Daika; 044.38.52.72; fax 044.38.52.71. Open daily 10:00 A.M. to 7:00 P.M. There is a small art gallery, bookstore, and boutique. Brunch, tea, and lunch by reservation only; set menu three-course lunch, about $20 a person.

Fez Hotels and Restaurants

Palais Jamai, Bab Guissa; 055.63.43.31; fax 055.63.50.96; website: www.palais-jamai.co.ma; Sofitel in the United States, 800-763-4835. Double rooms start at about $193; be sure to request garden side. Suites about $461 to $1,658. Swimming pool and large garden. The hotel's Moroccan restaurant, Al Fassia, is open for dinner only, with a regular menu or à la carte; with wine, about $36 a person.

La Maison Bleue, 2, place de l'Istiqlal, Batha; 055.63.60.52; fax 055.74.06.86; www.maisonbleue.com. Restaurant open daily for dinner, about $46, with a different set menu each night. For the B&B, one junior suite, about $190; suites, $280.

Looking for Abdelati

By Tanya Shaffer

~

editor's note

This piece originally appeared in the on-line magazine *Salon.com*. Then it was included in a book entitled *Salon.com's Wanderlust: Real-Life Tales of Adventure and Romance* (Villard, 2000), which initially made me think I would not include it in this edition, as *The Collected Traveler* consists of previously published articles, not excerpts from books; but I love this tale so much, and since it began its life as an article, I decided I couldn't leave it out of this collection.

TANYA SHAFFER is a writer, actress, and solo performer who often creates pieces based on her far-flung travels. She contributed frequently to the now-defunct *Wanderlust* section of *Salon.com,* where this piece originally appeared, and her most recent theater production was *Let My Enemy Live Long!* based on her travels in West Africa. Shaffer is cofounder of the Contemporary Shakespeare Company and has worked as a writer for the Tony Award–winning San Francisco Mime Troupe. Readers may track Shaffer's adventures by viewing her website, www.TanyaShaffer.com.

Here's what I love about travel: strangers get a chance to amaze you. Sometimes a single day can bring a blooming surprise, a simple kindness that opens a chink in the brittle shell of your heart and makes you a different person when you go to sleep—more tender, less jaded—than you were when you woke up.

This particular day began when Miguel and I descended from a cramped, cold bus at seven A.M. and walked the stinking gray streets of Casablanca with our backpacks, looking for food. Six days earlier I had finished a stint on a volunteer project, creating a public park in Kenitra, an ugly industrial city on the Moroccan coast. This was my final day of travel before hopping a plane to sub-Saharan Africa and more volunteer work.

Miguel was one of five non-Moroccans on the work project, a twenty-one-year-old vision of flowing brown curls and buffed golden physique. Although having him as a traveling companion took care of any problems I might have encountered with Moroccan men, he was inordinately devoted to his girlfriend, Eva, a wonderfully brassy, wiry, chain-smoking Older Woman of twenty-five with a husky scotch-drinker's voice, whom he couldn't go more than half an hour without mentioning. Unfortunately, Eva had had to head back to Barcelona immediately after the three-week work camp ended, and Miguel wanted to explore Morocco. Since I was the only other person on the project who spoke Spanish, and Miguel spoke no French or Arabic, his tight orbit shifted onto me, and we became traveling companions. This involved posing as a married couple at hotels, which made Miguel so uncomfortable that the frequency of his references to Eva went from half-hour to fifteen-minute intervals, and then to five as we got closer to bedtime. Finally one night, as we set up in our room in Fès, I took him by the shoulders and said, "Miguel, it's okay. You're a handsome man, but I'm over twenty-one. I can handle myself, I swear."

This morning we were going to visit Abdelati, a sweet, gentle young man we'd worked with on the project in Kenitra. He'd been expecting us to arrive in Casablanca for a few days, and since he had no telephone, he'd written down his address and told us to just show up—his mother and sisters were always at home. Since my plane was leaving from Casablanca the following morning, we wanted to get an early start, so we could spend the whole day with him.

Eventually we scored some croissants and overly sugared *panache* (a mix of banana, apple, and orange juice) at a roadside café, where the friendly proprietor advised us to take a taxi rather than a bus out to Abdelati's neighborhood. He said the taxi should cost twenty or twenty-five *dirhams*—under three dollars—and the buses would take all day.

We hopped into a taxi, which took off with a screech of rubber before we'd agreed on a price.

"Forty or forty-five *dirhams*!" the driver shouted over the roar of his engine. He was already careening around corners at top speed.

"Why isn't the counter on?" I asked.

"Broken!" he said.

Miguel rolled his eyes. "Eva would hate this," he whispered.

"If I had the counter, it would cost you fifty," the driver said.

Since the man in the café had told us twenty or twenty-five, I asked the driver to pull over and let us out. At first I put it politely: "We'd like to look at other options," but he simply said okay and kept driving. After four such attempts, I said sharply, *"Nous voulons descendre."* We want to get out.

Reluctantly he pulled over, saying we owed him ten *dirhams*. "Fine," I said. "Let me just get our bags down first—the money's in there." We yanked our backpacks off the overhead rack and took off, while the taxi driver shouted after us.

Miguel shook his head. "Eva would've killed that guy," he said.

It was an hour before we caught another taxi. Finally one pulled over, and a poker-faced man quoted us an estimate of eighteen or twenty *dirhams*.

"Très bien," I said with relief, and we jumped in.

Apparently the address Abdelati had written down for us was somehow suspect, and when we got into the neighborhood, our driver started asking directions.

First he asked a cop, who scratched his head and asked our nationalities, looking at our grimy faces and scraggly attire with a kind of bemused fondness. After more small talk, he pointed vaguely to a park a few blocks away. There a group of barefoot seven- or eight-year-old boys were kicking a soccer ball. Our driver asked where Abdelati's house was, and one of the boys said Abdelati had moved, but he could take us to the new house. This seemed a bit odd to me, since Abdelati had just given me the address a week ago, but since a similar thing had happened in Fès, I chalked it up as another Moroccan mystery and didn't worry about it too much.

The little boy came with us in the cab, full of his own importance, squirming and twisting to wave at other children as we inched down the narrow winding roads. Finally the little boy pointed to a house, and our driver went to the door and inquired. He came back to the cab saying Abdelati's sister was in this house visiting friends and would come along to show us where they lived.

Soon a beautiful girl of about sixteen emerged from the house. She was dressed in a Western skirt and blouse, which surprised me, since Abdelati's strong religious beliefs and upright demeanor had made me think he came from a more traditional family. Another thing that surprised me was her skin color. Whereas Abdelati looked very African, this young woman was an olive-skinned Arab. Still, I'd seen other unusual familial combinations in Morocco's complex racial mosaic, so I didn't give it too much thought.

We waited in the yard while the sister went in and returned accompanied by her mother, sisters, and brother-in-law, all of whom greeted us with cautious warmth. Unlike the younger girl, the older sisters were wearing traditional robes, though their faces were not veiled. You see a range of orthodoxy in Moroccan cities, caught as they are between Europe and the Arab world. From the younger sister's skirt and blouse to the head-to-toe veiling of the women gliding through the streets with only their eyes in view, the women's outfits seem to cover the entire spectrum.

We paid our taxi driver, tipping and thanking him profusely, until he grew embarrassed and drove away.

We were ushered into a pristine middle-class Moroccan home, with an intricately carved doorway and swirling multicolored tiles lining the walls. The mother told us in broken French that Abdelati was out but would be home soon. We sat on low cushioned seats in the living room, drinking sweet, pungent mint tea poured at a suitable height from a tiny silver teapot and eating sugar cookies, while the family members took turns sitting with us and making shy, polite conversation that frequently lapsed into uncomfortable silence. Every time anything was said, Miguel would say, "What?" with extreme eagerness, and I would translate the mundane fragment into Spanish for him: "Nice weather today. Tomorrow perhaps rain." At this he'd sink back into fidgety frustration, undoubtedly wishing Eva were there.

An hour passed, and as the guard kept changing, more family members emerged from inner rooms. I was again struck by the fact that they were all light-skinned Arabs. How did Abdelati fit into this picture? Was he adopted? I was eager to find out.

After two hours had passed with no sign of Abdelati, the family insisted on serving us a meal of couscous and chicken.

"Soon" was the only response I got when I inquired as to what time he might arrive.

"You come to the *hamam,* the bath," the young sister said after we'd finished lunch. "When we finish, he is back."

"The bath?" I asked, looking around the apartment.

The sister laughed. "The women's bath!" she said. "Haven't you been yet?" She pointed at Miguel. "He can go to the men's; it's right next door."

"What?" said Miguel anxiously, sitting up.

"She wants to take us to the baths," I said.

A look of abject horror crossed his face. "The—the bath?" he stammered. "You and me?"

"Yes," I said, smiling widely. "Is there some problem?"

"Well . . . well . . ." I watched his agitation build for a moment, then sighed and put my hand over his.

"Separate baths, Miguel. You with the men, me with the women."

"Oh." He almost giggled with relief. "Of course."

The women's bath consisted of three large connecting rooms, each one hotter and steamier than the last, until you could barely see two feet in front of you. The floors were filled with naked women of all ages and body types, sitting directly on the slippery tiles, washing each other with mitts made of rough washcloths. Tiny girls and babies sat in plastic buckets filled with soapy water—their own pint-sized tubs. The women carried empty buckets, swinging like elephants' trunks, to and from the innermost room, where they filled them at a stone basin from a spigot of scalding-hot water, mixing in a little cold from a neighboring spigot to temper it.

In a culture where the body is usually covered, the women's absolute lack of inhibition surprised me. They sat, mostly in pairs, pouring the water over their heads with small plastic pitchers, then scrubbing each other's backs—and I mean scrubbing. Over and over they attacked the same spot, as though they were trying to get out a particularly stubborn stain, leaving reddened flesh in their wake. They sprawled across each other's laps. They washed each other's fronts, backs, arms, legs. Some women washed themselves as though they were masturbating, hypnotically circling the same spot. Two tiny girls, about four years old, scrubbed their grandmother, who lay sprawled across the floor facedown. A prepubescent girl lay in her mother's lap, belly up, eyes closed, as relaxed as a cat, while her mother applied a forceful up and down stroke across the entire length of her daughter's torso.

I was struck by one young woman in particular, who reclined alone like a beauty queen in a tanning salon, back arched, head thrown back, right at the steamy heart of the baths, where the air was almost suffocating. When she began to wash, she soaped her breasts in sensual circles, proudly, her stomach held in, long chestnut hair rippling down her back, a goddess in her domain.

Abdelati's sister, whose name was Samara, went at my back with her mitt, which felt like steel wool.

"Ow!" I cried out. "Careful!"

This sent her into gales of laughter that drew the attention of the surrounding women, who saw what was happening and joined her in appreciative giggles as she continued to sandblast my skin.

"You must wash more often," she said, pointing to the refuse of her work—little gray scrolls of dead skin that clung to my arms like lint on a sweater.

When it came time to switch roles, I tried to return the favor, but after a few moments Samara became impatient with my wimpiness and grabbed the washcloth herself, still laughing. After washing the front of her body she called over a friend to wash her back, while she giggled and sang.

"What was it like in there?" asked Miguel when we met outside. He looked pink and damp as a newborn after his visit to the men's baths, and I wondered whether his experience was anything like mine.

"I'd like to tell you all about it," I said eagerly, "but . . ." I paused for emphasis, then leaned in and whispered, "I don't think Eva would approve."

When we got back to the house, the mother, older sister, and uncle greeted us at the door.

"Please," said the mother, "Abdelati is here."

"Oh, good," I said, and for a moment, before I walked into the living room, his face danced in my mind—the warm brown eyes, the smile so shy and gentle and filled with radiant life.

We entered the lovely tiled room we'd sat in before, and a handsome young Arab man in nicely pressed Western pants and shirt came forward to shake our hands with an uncertain expression on his face.

"Bonjour, mes amis," he said cautiously.

"Bonjour." I smiled, slightly confused. *"Abdelati—est-ce qu'il est ici?"* Is Abdelati here?

"Je suis Abdelati."

"But . . . but . . ." I looked from him to the family and then began to giggle tremulously. "I—I'm sorry. I'm afraid we've made a bit of a mistake. I—I'm so embarrassed."

"What? What?" Miguel asked urgently. "I don't understand. Where is he?"

"We got the wrong Abdelati," I told him, then looked around at the assembled family who'd spent the better part of a day entertaining us. "I'm afraid we don't actually know your son."

For a split second no one said anything, and I wondered whether I might implode right then and there and blow away like a pile of ash.

Then the uncle exclaimed heartily, *"Ce n'est pas grave!"*

"Yes," the mother joined in. "It doesn't matter at all. Won't you stay for dinner, please?"

I was so overwhelmed by their kindness that tears rushed to my eyes. For all they knew we were con artists, thieves, anything.

Still, with my plane leaving the next morning, I felt the moments

I could share with the first Abdelati and his family slipping farther and farther away.

"Thank you so much," I said fervently. "It's been a beautiful, beautiful day, but please . . . Could you help me find this address?"

I took out the piece of paper Abdelati had given me back in Kenitra, and the new Abdelati, his uncle, and his brother-in-law came forward to decipher it.

"This is Baalal Abdelati!" said the second Abdelati with surprise. "We went to school together! He lives less than a kilometer from here. I will bring you to his house."

And that was how it happened, that after taking photos and exchanging addresses and hugs and promises to write, Miguel and I left our newfound family and arrived at the home of our friend Abdelati as the last orange streak of the sunset was fading into the indigo night. There I threw myself into the arms of that dear and lovely young man, exclaiming, "I thought we'd never find you!"

After greetings had been offered all around, and the two Abdelatis had shared stories and laughter, we waved good-bye to our new friend Abdelati and entered a low, narrow hallway, lit by kerosene lamps.

"This is my mother," said Abdelati.

And suddenly I found myself caught up in a crush of fabric and spice, gripped in the tight embrace of a completely veiled woman, who held me and cried over me and wouldn't let me go, just as though I were her own daughter, and not a stranger she'd never before laid eyes on in her life.

Bibliothèque

Morocco is a member of several communities: Mediterranean, African, and North African, and by extension, Andalucian and French. An understanding of them all is essential to understanding Morocco, so I have included titles that represent the full range of Morocco's history.

Africa and North Africa

Inside Africa, John Gunther, Harper & Brothers, 1953. I have long been a fan of Gunther's *Inside* books and wish someone were writing and publishing a series like this today—there really is no contemporary equivalent. This edition I find particularly interesting because all three "updated" editions were published before Moroccan independence in 1956, and the country was still divided into three parts: the French Zone, the Spanish Zone, and the International Zone (consisting almost entirely of Tangier). Though the section on Morocco is necessarily slim (the book addresses the entire continent, after all), it's quite good and still very much worth reading today, nearly fifty years later. A point Gunther stresses that we would be wise to be mindful of in the twenty-first century is that "North Africa—at least its coast—is not merely Africa, but

TANGER
Scène de Rue
Street Scenery

Europe . . . Morocco in particular is considered to be 'occidental'; General Guillaume has described it as 'an unattached fragment of the European continent.' Morocco commands Gibraltar, and its history is inextricably intertwined with Spain. The basin of the Mediterranean is indivisible; this great sea separates two worlds, but also joins them. Superfinally, North Africa is part of Asia too. Profound Asiatic influences—one need only mention Islam—have penetrated it. So, at outset, we should keep in mind that we are dealing with an area that is European, African, and Asian all at once."

A Traveller's History of North Africa, Barnaby Rogerson, Interlink Publishing Group, Northampton, Massachusetts. This edition is one in a great series for which I have much enthusiasm. Each edition gives readers a compact, historical overview of each place, highlighting the significant events and people with which every visitor should be familiar. Think of it as a mini "what you should know" guide, a minimum of milestones to help you really appreciate what you're seeing. Rogerson is also the author of the Morocco guide in the esteemed Cadogan series, and in this book he "shows a mastery of his subject," to quote from a *Library Journal* review of the guide. Each book in this series is small enough and light enough to carry around every day. *De rigueur.*

Andalucía

Alhambra, Michael Jacobs, photographs by Francisco Fernandez, Rizzoli, 2000. This is that rare coffee-table book with beautiful photographs and insightful text. With a chronology of Islamic Spain and so many detailed photos of architectural details, this is *de rigueur* for anyone visiting Morocco.

Andalucía, Michael Jacobs, Pallas Athene, London, 1998. Readers of my *Provence* book know how fond I am of Jacobs, who wrote one of the very best guides ever to that region. If it's possible, he is even more of an expert on Spain, where he spends at least four months a year. The Pallas Guides focus on landscape, people, art, and architecture, and this is the single best book on Andalucía I've ever seen. With a variety of well-explored themes, a gazetteer, a color photo insert, and an outstanding bibliography, this is probably more than the average reader wants to know, but as *Cosmopolitan* praised, "No other book can compare." *De rigueur.*

Convivencia: Jews, Muslims, and Christians in Medieval Spain, edited by Vivian Mann, Thomas Glick, and Jerrilynn Dodds, George Braziller in association with The Jewish Museum, New York; published in conjunction with an exhibition of the same name held at The Jewish Museum, 1992. *Convivencia* is the word used to describe the coexistence of Jews, Muslims, and Christians in Spain from 711 to 1492. The book covers all of Spain, but Andalucía is, of course, best represented.

France on the Brink: A Great Civilization Faces the New Century, Jonathan Fenby, Arcade Publishing, 1999. This good volume provides us with thoughtful fodder for the early twenty-first century. Journalist Fenby—who has written for *The Economist, The Christian Science Monitor,* and *The Times* of London and has been editor of the *South China Morning Post*—is married to a Frenchwoman and was named a chevalier of the French Order of Merit in 1990. He's been reporting on France for over thirty years, and in this work he presents a full array of the country's ills and contradictions, some of which are familiar (the Resistance, which was smaller than we like to think; high unemployment; immigration; government corruption) but nonetheless remain for the French to reconcile. Readers who haven't kept up with the France of today may be alarmed to discover that some classic French icons—berets, baguettes, accordions, cafés, foie gras—are fading. In his review of the book for *The New York Times,* European cultural correspondent Alan Riding wrote that "the entire book serves as a valuable introduction to contemporary France." I would add that it is also *de rigueur* reading.

Mission to Civilize: The French Way, Mort Rosenblum, Doubleday, 1988. When Rosenblum wrote this book, he was senior foreign correspondent for the Associated Press in Paris. (He is now a special correspondent to the AP and is also the author of *Olives,* North Point Press/Farrar, Straus & Giroux, 1996.) His career as a journalist took him to North and West Africa, the South Pacific, Asia, the southeastern United States, the Caribbean, the Middle East, Canada—all the former and present DOM-TOMS (*départements d'outre-mer* and *territoires d'outre-mer*) of France. Yes, this book is about France and the French, but more specifically it is about the importance of *la mission civilisatrice* (read: colonization) to the French. Rosenblum recalls Charles de Gaulle's famous remark: *"La France est la lumière du monde"* (France is the light of the world). The "North Africa: Beurs and Beaufs" chapter is particularly appropriate reading, and though the situation in Algeria has all changed and is actually *worse* now, it's extremely interesting and revealing. There is also a little more background on the Polisario.

Paris in the Fifties, Stanley Karnow, Times Books, 1997. I include this title here for the final chapter, "The Maghreb," which is an honest, disturbing report on the events Karnow witnessed in Morocco, Tunisia, and Algeria.

Mediterranean (History and Narrative)

The First Eden: The Mediterranean World and Man, Sir David Attenborough, William Collins Sons & Co. Ltd./BBC Books, London, 1987. The four parts of this book deal with natural history, archaeology, history, and ecology, and there is very good coverage of plants and animals found around the Mediterranean.

The Inner Sea: The Mediterranean and Its People, Robert Fox, Alfred A. Knopf, 1993. *De rigueur.*

Mediterranean: A Cultural Landscape, Predrag Matvejevic, translated by Michael Henry Heim, University of California Press, Berkeley, 1999; previously published as *Mediteranski brevijar,* Zagreb, 1987; *Bréviaire mediterranéen,* Paris, 1992; and *Mediterraneo: Un nuovo breviario,* Milan, 1993. A beautiful, unusual book combining personal observations with history, maps, maritime details, people, and language.

The Mediterranean, Fernand Braudel, first published in France, 1949; English translation of second revised edition, HarperCollins, 1972; abridged edition, HarperCollins, 1992. Still the definitive classic. *De rigueur.*

On the Shores of the Mediterranean, Eric Newby, first published by The Harvill Press, London, 1984; Picador, 1985. You have to travel with Eric and Wanda Newby to Italy, the former Yugoslavia, Greece, Turkey, Israel, Spain, and France before arriving in Morocco ("View From a Hill" is the chapter about Fez), but it's a pleasure every word of the way.

The Phoenicians, edited by Sabatino Moscati, Rizzoli, 1999. Any presentation of the Mediterranean without note of the Phoenicians would be a glaring omission, and though the Phoenician civilization remains mysterious, this beautiful and fascinating paperback reveals a treasure trove of information in the form of essays contributed by a number of scholars. One chapter is devoted to North Africa, and there is a good map in the front of the book showing the Mediterranean at the time of Phoenician expansion.

The Pillars of Hercules: A Grand Tour of the Mediterranean, Paul Theroux, G. P. Putnam's Sons, 1995.

The Spirit of Mediterranean Places, Michel Butor, The Marlboro Press, 1986.

Mediterranean Architecture and Style

Mediterranean Color: Italy, France, Spain, Portugal, Morocco, Greece, photographs and text by Jeffrey Becom, foreword by Paul Goldberger, Abbeville Press, 1990.

Mediterranean Living, Lisa Lovatt-Smith, Whitney Library of Design, Watson-Guptill Publications, 1998.

Mediterranean Style, Catherine Haig, Abbeville Press, 1998; first published in Great Britain in 1997 by Conran Octopus Ltd., London.

Mediterranean Vernacular, V. I. Atroshenko, Milton Grundy, Rizzoli, 1991. The chapter on Morocco features Tetouan and Chaouen.

Villages in the Sun: Mediterranean Community Architecture, Myron Goldfinger, Rizzoli, 1993. The chapter on Morocco features a village near the Tizi-n-Tichka pass; a village in the Ourika Valley; Ait-Benhaddou; *ksours* in the Dades Valley; an oasis of Tinerhir; and a village near Khenifra.

Morocco

Dreams of Trespass: Tales of a Harem Girlhood, Fatima Mernissi, photographs by Ruth Ward, Perseus Books, 1994. This wonderful, wonderful book is beautifully written and impossible to forget. Author Mernissi was born in a domestic harem in 1940 in Fez, which she describes as a ninth-century medieval city about 5,000 kilometers west of Mecca and 1,000 kilometers south of Madrid, "one of the dangerous capitals of the Christians." Her father had told her from a young age that problems with Christians—and women—always begin when the *hudud,* or sacred frontier, is not respected. The way Mernissi saw it, she was born in the middle of chaos, since neither Christians nor women readily accepted the frontiers. Her father also explained that when Allah created the earth, he not only separated men from women, but he put a sea between Muslims and Christians. Harmony could thrive only when each group respected the prescribed limits of the other, and trespassing could lead only to sorrow and unhappiness. "But women dreamed of trespassing all the time," Mernissi informs us. "The world beyond the gate was their obsession. They fantasized all day long about parading in unfamiliar streets, while the Christians kept crossing the sea, bringing death and chaos." By turns funny, moving, charming, and sad, this is a not-for-women-only read. *De rigueur.*

Imazighen: The Vanishing Traditions of Berber Women, Margaret Courtney-Clarke, essays by Geraldine Brooks, Clarkson Potter, 1996. As Geraldine Brooks (author, *Nine Parts of Desire: The Hidden World of Islamic Women,* Anchor, 1996) notes in the opening essay of this wonderful book, "The list of threats to the Berber heritage is a long and diverse one. As overgrazing denudes the hillsides, making fuel and fodder harder to come by, jobs in the cities beckon Berbers from their ancient lands. As they leave, tourists arrive—their money and their tastes creating income opportunities, but often at the price of abandoned traditions. In Algeria, radical Islamic movements and the government's uncompromising resistance have brought violence and upheaval to the remotest villages. Everywhere, the growing acceptability of intermarriage with Arab neighbors strengthens national identity and opens new opportunities, but gradually erodes the individual character of Berber culture." The changes in Morocco aren't affecting only city dwellers but the predominantly country-dwelling Berbers, too, and in just a short number of years, centuries of traditions have been altered or abandoned entirely. Many of these traditions—especially weaving and pottery—are carried out by women. Male readers, however, should not dismiss this book from their reading list. Visitors who travel around the mountainous areas of Morocco will quickly see that much of Berber daily life and activity is women's work, and certainly anyone contemplating a Berber rug purchase will find the "Weaving" and "Motif" chapters a good introductory resource. The book's scope isn't limited to Morocco but includes Algeria and Tunisia. The map that appears on a double-page spread in the early pages of the book gives a better overview than most as it indicates the spread of the Atlas Mountain chain into Algeria, which also has the Little Atlas and Saharan Atlas ranges. Courtney-Clarke notes in her preface, "Behind every photograph in this book is an adventure—and the life of a Berber woman continuing the traditions of her ancestors." These are photographs that deserve to be seen, again and again. *De rigueur.*

In Morocco, Edith Wharton, The Ecco Press, 1996; first published by Charles Scribner's Sons, 1919. It is hard not to be envious of the trip Wharton took to Morocco, in 1918, for one month. Because the First World War was still on, she had to endure shortages of petrol, the rainy season, and a treacherous crossing of the Strait of Gibraltar. Yet "these drawbacks were more than offset by the advantage of making my quick trip at a moment unique in the history of the country; the brief moment of transition between its virtually complete subjection to European authority, and the fast approaching hour when it is thrown open to all the banalities and promiscuities of modern travel." She penned her book after the war was over and so could then write, "no eye will ever again see Moulay Idriss and Fez and Marrakech as I saw them." No one could argue with that statement, but as I noted in my introduction, even now, approaching one hundred years later, the sites and cities Wharton experienced are still as exotic and interesting. This account of her travels, however, makes this book that much more valuable. She was, we can now see, a bit too complimentary of the French (though I maintain not overly so of Lyautey, to whom she dedicates the book). In addition to chapters on Rabat and Sale, Volubilis, Moulay Idriss and Meknez, Fez, and Marrakesh, there are fascinating chapters on harems and celebrations, General Lyautey's work in Morocco, and Moroccan history, as well as a note on Moroccan architecture, with two inserts of black-and-white photos. *De rigueur.*

Lords of the Atlas: The Rise and Fall of the House of Glaoua, 1893–1956, Gavin Maxwell, E. P. Dutton, 1966. A quick scan of other good bibliographies reveals that this excellent book is included in every one, without exception. And with good reason, as it is not only an extraordinary story about the brothers Madani and T'hami El Glaoui but a fairly recent history of Morocco and the Moroccans as well. The tale of the Glaoui brothers is not only unique to

Morocco but may in fact be unique in the entire world. Readers will already have noted that I have quoted from this magnificent book more than a few times; it's impossible not to, such is the significance of this epic tale. The Glaoui brothers, by the late 1800s, had a number of kasbah strongholds throughout the High Atlas and southern Morocco, but the castle at Telouet became legendary. Its interior was decorated with tiles and mosaics and elaborate wrought-iron work, and its exterior was nothing but *pisé*. Before the French Foreign Legion redirected the route over the High Atlas in 1936, the Telouet kasbah was seemingly in the middle of nowhere, but it strategically overlooked the pass known as Tizi-n-Telouet or Tizi-n-Glaoua. (Visitors today who take the road from Marrakesh to Ouarzazate will notice the turnoff for Telouet, which is no longer on the main route.) As Maxwell notes, "From this desolate group of ruins in the High Atlas, so far from the seat of government at Fez, there arose by a strange chain of coincidence a generation of kingmakers. They were two brothers, chiefs of an insignificant mountain tribe, and they rose in that one generation to depose two Sultans, to become the true rulers of Morocco, to shake the whole French political structure; and, with their downfall, to add a new and uncomfortable word to the French language. The name of the tribe was Glaoua, and *glaouise* now means, in French political jargon, betrayed. Neither France nor Morocco is over-anxious to recall the tale behind the word." Maxwell reveals many historical facts in this book, some little known or at least not very well documented elsewhere. (I think his account of the weeks and days leading up to independence is unmatched and reads like a work of fast-paced fiction.) One of the little-known facts I have not run across in any other work is that "from 1937, the French began to employ the Jewish youth of Morocco in all minor positions of Protectorate administration, as a blockade to the infiltration of newly qualified Islamic Moroccan students whose political views might be anti-French. Over all Morocco some ten or fifteen per cent of minor posts under the Protectorate were nominally held by Moroccans, but of these more than seventy-five were in fact Jews. The small handful of Islamic Moroccans whom France proudly claimed to have educated were unable to find work in their own country; these formed the hard core of malcontents around whom the independence movement grew towards a virile maturity ten years later." Little wonder that Moroccan Jews felt they had to leave after '56. The book has three black-and-white photo inserts, three maps, a table of principal events, a genealogical table of the House of Glaoua, and lovely black-and-white illustrations drawn by a Berber from Marrakesh. The lengthy appendix is just as fascinating as the main story. If told I could not have a single drop of *thé à la menthe* until I divulged the title of only one must-read book on Morocco, this is the one I would reveal. *De rigueur.*

The Magic of Morocco, Tahar Ben Jelloun, Alain D'Hooghe, Mohamed Sijelmassi, translated by Robin Buss, authorized English-language edition published by Vilo International, Paris, 2000; originally published as *Le Désir du Maroc,* Marval, Paris, 1999. Unique and beautifully produced, this oversize book features more than 150 images taken by Western photographers "who spontaneously selected strong scenes and moments which distanced themselves from their own culture." As Alain D'Hooghe notes, when photography first appeared in 1839, "Morocco had not yet been 'pacified' and had only distant connections to Europe." The country was perceived as being a bit too dangerous and unsettled, what with a seemingly endless number of internal conflicts and rebellions. Morocco was not, therefore, included in anyone's Grand Tour, which typically meant travel to Italy, Spain, Greece, Turkey, Egypt, Palestine, and Lebanon. A few intrepid travelers and photographers deviated from this route, but not many. "These two partly linked factors explain why Morocco remained for a rather long time *terra incognita* for photography. Despite its geographical proximity, Morocco did not arouse sufficient interest, either among genuine travelers, or those others who took the Grand Tour by proxy without leaving their libraries." The photographs selected here have either not been previously published or are little known to the public, and they're presented chronologically, from 1885 to 1992. The selection includes works by Henri Duveyrier, Gabriel Veyre, José Ortiz Echague, Marcelin Flandrin, Jean Besancenot, Paul Bowles, Paul Strand, Bernard Plossu, Christophe Bourguedieu, Brassai, Henri Cartier-Bresson, and Toni Catany. The only color image in the book is the final one, and though the stunning photographs are obviously the raison d'être for the project, the text is equally as memorable and inspired. (I did notice one error, however: in "With Desire as the Sole Guide" by Alain D'Hooghe, it states that Delacroix came to Morocco in 1932, when in fact he visited in 1832.) With a bibliography, a glossary, and chronology of recent Moroccan history, this is my favorite book in this vein and a very special edition. *De rigueur.*

Maroc, Albert Watson, Rizzoli, 1998. Internationally celebrated photographer Albert Watson, who grew up in Scotland, spends part of his time at his house in Morocco. He has an enormous amount of respect and affection for Morocco, amply conveyed in this handsome book. As he writes in the dedication, "The magic of Morocco is not in the snow-covered High Atlas Mountains, the magnificent endless coastline, the fertile valleys, or any mysterious souk of the ancient cities, or even the bustling modern metropolis of Casablanca. The magic is in the people to whom I dedicate this book." So, in his words, he has made a "sketch" of Morocco and its unique peoples, over a period of thirty-nine days. The images—some of which are incorporated into a collage—and their accompanying explanatory text make for an amazing, one-of-a-kind book. It has the distinction of being published under the patronage of His Royal Highness Crown Prince Sidi Mohammed.

Maroc: Aux Multiples Visages, Yves Korbendau, ACR Edition Internationale, Paris, 1999. Even though this big, beautiful, heavy, and expensive book is in French, it's really the only one of its kind that I've encountered and therefore may be of interest even to those who don't read a word of French. There are no long, beautifully written essays or even an introduction, but there is a time-line of Moroccan history, a number of maps, four pages of principal Moroccan dynasties, and page after page (more than three hundred) of color pho-tographs. The book is divided into eight distinct regions of Morocco: La Côte Atlantique, Le Rif, Plateaux et Plaines, Le Moyen Atlas, Le Haut Atlas, Le Versant Sud du Haut Atlas, L'Anti Atlas, and Les Ports du Desert. As the title suggests, this slipcased book is better than other coffee-table photography books at helping readers establish a visual image of each region of Morocco. Entirely too heavy to bring along, unless you're bringing a steamer trunk, this is a volume Morocco enthusiasts will be happy to have before and after a trip. I found my copy at Rizzoli's Fifty-seventh Street store in New York (see "Bookstores" in *Renseignements Pratiques* for contact information), but it's also available in Morocco. *De rigueur.*

Medinas: Morocco's Hidden Cities, photographs by Jean-Marc Tingaud, poems by Tahar Ben Jelloun, calligraphy by Lassaad Metoui, Assouline, Paris, 1998, distributed in the United States by St. Martin's Press. One of the most amaz-ing experiences a visitor to Morocco can have is a walk through one of the country's medinas at night, after all the shops have closed and no one is walk-ing about. (Make arrangements with your guide for a nighttime walk.) The photograph on the cover of this book so perfectly captures the nighttime view of a medina that I knew that this would be a special volume. Photographer Tingaud visited the medinas of Marrakesh, Essaouira, Rabat, Casablanca, Tangier, Tetuan, Fez, and Meknes at night and took a series of pictures, which for this book he divided into vertical and horizontal images. Morocco's medi-nas are often what visitors remember most about their journey, and since tak-ing photographs in medinas—day *or* night—can prove challenging at best, this is a good book to have. Ben Jelloun's final page of poetry is the best descrip-tion of a medina I've encountered: "The medina is more than a city / higher than walls / greater than passion / the medina is a meadow / a field of mauve poppies / a marker for the abyss / a desert swallowed up / the medina is a long night / dreamless trouble-free / an idea that revolves / round certain myths / it's a rumour that goes up in smoke / a bowl of the incense of paradise / a windfall for the memory / the medina is a tired heart / a bent body lashed by the winds / a face full of holes / a foul breath / but it's the house of our birth / a type of promised land." I have sometimes found it difficult to describe what it's like to walk through a medina, and when words fail me, I pull out this book. *De rigueur* for all medina mavens.

Mogreb-El-Acksa: A Journey in Morocco, R. B. Cunninghame Graham, introduction by Edward Garnett, The Marlboro Press/Northwestern University Press, 1997; originally published in 1898. Out of print for many years, this is a classic of Moroccan literature, and I was so pleased when Marlboro/Northwestern published the handsome paperback edition. Graham was reportedly one of the most colorful and eccentric figures of his era, and his journey to southern Morocco was first and foremost for the purpose of entering Taroudant, which was at that time (1800s) forbidden to outsiders. He wanted to be the first Christian ever to set foot there and disguised himself, twice, in the attempt (I am not really giving anything away by saying he failed in his mission). This is a wonderful book. As Barnett relates in the introduction, "The book written as a record of a journey in Morocco and treating of Moroccan affairs *vis-à-vis* with Europe, incidentally challenged many social shibboleths of the day. The author had no particular thesis, but he generally derided the Victorian practice of putting the glass to the blind eye while declaring that it could see the blessings of Western progress but not its blight. Now that the intelligent person is getting alarmed at the congestion of mechanized civilization and knows he is unable to escape from the tentacles of the octopus 'progress,' it is difficult to realize the irritation Cunninghame Graham's heterodoxy gave to the 'leaders' of opinion thirty years back, to men 'thinking imperially,' to politicians, dons and business men and to the newspaper scribes." Apparently, the book was hailed by only a few in 1898, and was too unorthodox and too witty for the Victorian British taste. *De rigueur.*

Morocco: Its People and Places, Edmondo de Amicis, translated by C. Rollin-Tilton, G. P. Putnam's Sons, 1893. This work by de Amicis (a travel writer of some renown in his day, also the author of books on Constantinople, Holland, Paris, Spain, and Italy) remains one of the classics on Morocco. It is very much of its time in terms of language and interpretation (which is to say that some passages are outdated or may rub some of us the wrong way), but it is still considered a classic because of the author's astute observations and the adventurous nature of his journey. The opening paragraph could serve as an opener in a contemporary book, the only adjustment being the length of time it takes to cross the Strait of Gibraltar: "There are no two countries in the world more entirely different from each other than the two which are separated by the Straits of Gibraltar; and this diversity is peculiarly apparent to the traveler who approaches Tangiers from Gibraltar, where he has left the hurried, noisy, splendid life of a European city. At only three hours' journey from thence the very name of our continent seems unknown; the word 'Christian' signifies enemy; our civilization is ignored, or feared, or derided; all things, from the very foundations of social life to its most insignificant particulars, are changed, and every indication of the neighborhood of Europe has disappeared. You are in an unknown country, having no bonds of interest in it, and every thing to learn. From its shore the European coast can still be seen, but the heart feels itself at an immeasurable distance, as if that narrow tract of sea were an ocean, and those blue mountains an illusion. Within three hours a wonderful trans-formation has taken place around you." The book's publication date would seem to indicate this would be nearly impossible to find, but copies do turn up surprisingly often, in various editions. The first edition includes a number of black-and-white drawings.

Morocco: Sahara to the Sea, photographs and text by Mary Cross, preface by Paul Bowles, introduction by Tahar Ben Jelloun, Abbeville Press, 1995. "I am not moved by 'photo opportunities,'" writes Cross in her author's note, adding that for the most part, "monuments do not excite me—with the exception of the soaring towers of Chartres Cathedral, Luxor's Karnak Temple, the quiet majesty of the ninth-century mosque of Ibn Tulun in Cairo, and a view of the Dome of the Rock in Jerusalem. What I cherish in Morocco, land of the far-thest West of the West, are my memories of the people and the extraordinary beauty of the land." And that is why you must get this book if you really want to see and understand the real treasure of Morocco: its people. As readers know by now, it is sometimes improper to take photographs of Moroccans, or at least it usually requires a pocketful of *dirhams* to pay to subjects who don't find cameras an intrusion. You don't need to take any pictures of people at all if you have this book to come home to, and you'll recognize the same faces: of elderly observant men in *djellabas* and skullcaps, Berber women with tattoos on their chins, merchants and craftsmen in the souks, young children running through the streets of cities and dusty villages. The book is divided into five chapters ("The Pre-Sahara," "Marrakesh and the High Atlas," "Fez and Meknes," "The Coastal Plain," "Tangier and the Western Rif"), and Cross spent time with Moroccans in all corners, including the High Atlas village of Aremd, where she was the guest of a Berber family in their home. As she notes, "There are no toys in these simple households, but there is a remarkable amount of love." *De rigueur.*

Morocco: Timeless Places, Annette Solyst, Friedman/Fairfax publishers, distrib-uted by Sterling Publishing Co., 2000. This is one volume in the Timeless Places series (others include *Provence, Paris, Tuscany, Venice,* and *The Greek Isles*), which seeks to highlight special places in the world that possess a unique ambi-ence. Each slender book features color photographs and some text. The books are not meant to be authoritative or to compete with much larger and higher-quality coffee-table books; rather, they are distinctive in their own way, with just enough text and color photos—some of which are quite unusual—to whet one's appetite for more (and for far less money than most illustrated books). This Morocco edition features short essays on Marrakesh, Fez, Tangier, the mountains, and the Atlantic coast cities as well as a number of uncommon images.

Orientalism, Edward Said, Pantheon Books, 1978. A few other books have appeared on the subject of Orientalism, but Said's is head and shoulders above the rest and is widely considered to be *the* volume to consult. It's quite interesting, and Said is quite an intellectual; in fact, at times I found I could not follow a certain thread and had to reread entire passages. Said is in a unique position to have written this. As he states, "Much of the personal investment in this study derives from my awareness of being an 'Oriental' as a child growing up in two British colonies. All of my education, in those colonies (Palestine and Egypt) and in the United States, has been Western, and yet that deep early awareness has persisted. In many ways my study of Orientalism has been an attempt to inventory the traces upon me, the Oriental subject, of the culture whose domination has been so powerful a factor in the life of all Orientals." There are a great number of passages I admire in this book, and I especially like the entire chapter entitled "The Scope of Orientalism." (I think it could stand on its own as a separate little book and should be required reading for anyone visiting any Muslim country in the world.) I also especially like the way Said qualifies the phrase "The East is a career" by Benjamin Disraeli: "When Disraeli said in his novel *Tancred* that the East was a career, he meant that to be interested in the East was something bright young Westerners would find to be an all-consuming passion; he should not be interpreted as saying that the East was *only* a career for Westerners." A brilliant, important work. *De rigueur.*

Their Heads Are Green and Their Hands Are Blue: Scenes From the Non-Christian World, Paul Bowles, The Ecco Press, 1984, paperback; originally published by Random House, 1963. This collection of travel essays features a few pieces about Ceylon, Mexico, and Istanbul but is in the main about Morocco. I *love* this entire book—it is, in fact, one of my most favorite volumes in my library. The best chapters are perhaps "The Rif, To Music" and "The Route to Tassemsit," which are logs of the trip Bowles and two companions took all around Morocco in 1959 to record all the musical genres of the country. (Bowles was awarded a Rockefeller Foundation grant to support the project, and the recordings now live in the Library of Congress.) One can't help but think how extraordinary this venture was, and reading about it is equally so. *De rigueur.*

There aren't many books at all devoted to the Moroccans, unfortunately, though thankfully the Culture Shock! series offers the very good guide discussed below. Though a work of fiction, Paul Bowles's *The Spider's House* is an excellent book to read about Moroccans. In one particularly revealing passage, Lee, an American woman new to Morocco, is having tea with Stenham, an American man who's been in Morocco for a number of years. Lee expresses puzzlement at the Moroccans, saying she wishes she knew what made them tick. "There's one thing I've found that helps," Stenham replies. "And that is that you must always remember it's a culture of 'and then' rather than one of 'because,' like ours." Frowning, she says: "I don't think I follow." "What I mean is that in their minds one thing doesn't come from another thing. Nothing is a result of anything. Everything merely *is,* and no questions asked. Even the language they speak is constructed around that. Each fact is separate, and one never depends on the other. Everything's explained by the constant intervention of Allah. And whatever happens had to happen, and was decreed at the beginning of time, and there's no way even of imagining how anything could have been different from what it is." "It's depressing," she says. He laughs. "Then I've said it wrong. I've left out something important. Because there's nothing depressing about any of it. Except what the place has become under the Christians," he adds sourly. "When I first came here it was a pure country. There was music and dancing and magic every day in the streets. Now it's finished, everything. Even the religion. In a few more years the whole country will be like all the other Moslem countries, just a huge European slum, full of poverty and hatred. What the French have made of Morocco may be depressing, yes, but what it was before, never!" "I think that's the point of view of an outsider, a tourist who puts picturesqueness above everything else. I'm sure if you had to live down there in one of those houses you wouldn't feel the same way at all. You'd welcome the hospitals and electric lights and buses the French have brought." This is certainly the remark of a tourist, and an ignorant tourist, too, he thinks, sorry that it should come from her. "At least you can say you were in on the last days of Morocco," he tells her.

Culture Shock! Morocco: A Guide to Customs and Etiquette, Orin Hargraves, Graphic Arts Publishing Company, Portland, Oregon, 1995. Each Culture Shock! edition is authored by a different writer, and each is eminently enlightening. The Morocco edition covers such topics as "The Moroccan Within," "The Moroccan You Know," communication, food and drink, work, business and trade, hospitality, and leisure time. There really is no other book quite like this one, and even though there is a lot of practical information for foreigners who are living in Morocco, even short-term visitors will find it indispensable.

Here are just a few examples: bargaining—"As a primer, familiarize yourself with what is bargained for and what is not in Morocco." The "bargain for" list includes articles of clothing; anything bought from a roving street vendor; *petit taxi* fares if the meter isn't working; any handicraft item; anything bought in a souk, except price-controlled items (see next list). The "seldom or never bargain for" list includes *grand taxi* fares on regular runs; everyday purchases such as mint, bread, parsley, and coriander; gas bottle refills; cigarettes and alcohol; meals and beverages in restaurants; bus fares between scheduled stops; price-controlled staple foods such as flour, butter, sugar, oil, tea, and milk; and bulk purchases in the souk—there are very few prepackaged goods in Morocco, so visitors who want to buy some olives or spices, for example, have to ask for them by weight. Hargraves provides a very useful chart for a variety of goods with French, Arabic, and English equivalents. And he gives us this very-much-worth-remembering quote: "Everything takes longer in Morocco than you hope, think, or expect it will, and this is as true in the work place as anywhere. Delays of every kind are endemic. It is a fact of life, so try not to let it be a source of stress. Just count on things taking longer." The "Culture Quiz" at the end of each Culture Shock! book is one of my favorite features of this series. Here are two from this Morocco book (you'll have to get the book to learn the correct answers). Situation 1: You are walking through a narrow passageway of a medina and hear someone shouting behind you, *"Balak, balak."* Immediately you (a) reply *"Allah iatik al-bal";* (b) get out of the way; (c) stop and have a look at the *balaks* on offer; (d) reply *"Balak* to you too, buddy." Situation 10: You are seated at a pleasant outdoor café where you are approached by a very ragged beggar, holding out her hand to you. The only money you have is a 50 *dirham* note. So you (a) hand it over; (b) dismiss the beggar with *"allah isehhal";* (c) ignore the beggar; (d) hold up your hands, palms forward, indicating that you are unable to help. If I haven't already convinced you that you simply must read this book, perhaps Hargraves's own words will: "If you want to become an expat armchair expert on Moroccan culture, the facts are here. If you want to make a sincere attempt to cross the bridge to Moroccan culture and be at home in the country, this book will help to get you there." *De rigueur.*

Tax Com. Rurale
Tazas C. Rurales
Province de
MEKNES
Com. Rurales

عمالة
مكناس
القروبة

Nº 226871

1,00
Uu Dirha
Uu Dirha

درهم

SYNDICAT D'INITIATIVE DE FEZ

Ponloy
1934

VENEZ
VISITER **FEZ**

ROYAUME du MAROC
المملكة المغربية
POSTES

0.50
RECONSTRUCTION d'AGADIR

comarit ferry
كوماريت
CARTE D'EMBARQUEMENT
TARJETA DE EMBARQUE
BOARDING CARD

TANGER - ALGECIRAS
2eme CLASSE

Serie P Nº 068847

17 MAYO 1997 17 09

Cachet date et heure

Des Villes Marocaines
(Some Moroccan Cities)

"The contrast of the ancient way of life in the medinas, with their bustling souks *and narrow streets, each dedicated to a particular craft or commerce, and the spacious, modern* villes nouvelles *is a fascinating one. It is a metaphor for another confrontation, that of a traditional Islamic society attempting to embrace the latest technology without losing its religious and national identity. The country has effectively leaped forward several centuries in the space of three generations."*

—Lisa Lovatt-Smith, MOROCCAN INTERIORS

The Mysteries of Fez

By Susanna Moore

~

editor's note

In Paul Bowles's masterpiece *The Spider's House,* the two American characters, John Stenham and Lee Burroughs, are sitting in a particular spot that affords them a view of the entire city of Fez. They gaze upon the city and the surrounding hills without speaking for a few moments. "What's very hard to believe," Lee says presently, "is that this can be existing at the same moment, let's say, that people are standing in line at the information booth in the Grand Central Station asking about trains to New Haven. You know what I mean? It's just unthinkable, somehow." Readers who have been to Fez understand exactly what Lee means, and readers who haven't yet will comprehend it immediately. Fez is simply astonishing.

Novelist SUSANNA MOORE is the author of *In the Cut* (Knopf, 1995, hardcover; Plume, 1999, paperback), *The Whiteness of Bones* (Knopf, 1989, hardcover; Penguin, 1990, paperback), and *My Old Sweetheart* (Knopf, 1982, hardcover; Vintage, 1997, paperback), which was nominated for a National Book Award. She contributed this piece to *Travel & Leisure.*

I wasn't looking for trouble, love-induced or any other kind. As I left Tangier I kept thinking of the old story, perhaps apocryphal, that the writer Jane Bowles had been poisoned to death there by her love-struck housekeeper. Tangier is a place for trouble. Fez, on the contrary, has always been a mysterious hillside fortress of scholarly intrigue and religious refuge. A journey of introspection, the seeking of sanctuary with the possibility of an intellectual intrigue, seemed fairly irresistible. Surely I was headed for the right place.

I drove three and a half hours south through the low, cultivated foothills of Morocco's Rif Mountains, past the remains of the encampments of Caesar's legionnaires, and the ruins of Roman villas and baths in the small town of Volubilis, where the wheat fields have been under cultivation for nearly two thousand years. In roadside markets rough herdsmen and veiled women bargained fiercely with the sellers of mint or sheep or imitations of American running shoes. The markets are not meant for foreign passersby: there are no tourist goods, and no tourists. I went into a crowded encampment, and as I picked my way past the canvas tents and dark ponies, the villagers stared at me as if I were the first foreigner they had ever seen—perhaps I was.

The fields gave way to small settlements, and then suddenly across the plain, through the dust and heat, I saw the city. Once known as "the well-guarded," Fez sits in the lap of two bare, low hills and spills beyond its ramparts onto the wide and fertile plain that stretches south to the mountains of the Middle Atlas.

It is an ancient and noble city, established in A.D. 789 by Idriss I, an Arab chieftain fleeing from the caliph of Baghdad. A descendant of the prophet Muhammad through his daughter Fatima, Idriss I founded a dynasty that became the first Arab kingdom in Morocco. Fez quickly grew into a religious and civic center that embraced the tribes of the surrounding mountains; today, Arabic is used in both formal and everyday speech, while Berber is heard among the farmers in the market.

By A.D. 859, only seventy years after the founding of the mountain refuge, the great Karaouyine Mosque was constructed, as well as the simple and lovely mosque built in the Andalous quarter, home to thousands of Islamic refugees who made the journey from Spain. Since its origin, then, Fez was a place of learning and religious study, attracting to its cloistered mosques and shaded courtyards clerical leaders, intellectuals, and artists. Now a city of some 600,000 residents, Fez still attracts the pilgrim, and I was eager to join the long line of travelers who have sojourned there to look and to study. Although I did not pray in the tradition of some of my predecessors, I fell willingly into a state of reverie, and reverence.

I passed along the broad avenues of the *nouvelle ville*—a colonial town that rose outside the walls of Fez in 1916, during the time of the French protectorate—then through the carved and ornamented city gate, the Bab Bou Jeloud, built in 1913 in a traditional style, with a pattern of terra-cotta arabesques in tiles of blue (the color of Fez) and green (the color of Islam). I circled the old city, up through large olive groves on the low brown hills that embrace the town, past the scant ruins of the Merinide tombs standing like chipped sentinels, the big Saadian fortress (now a museum of weapons), and the ancient caves of the country's nomadic first inhabitants.

The silence of the city was puzzling, until I remembered that no cars or trucks and few motor scooters can enter the covered medina of Fez el-Bali. Here and there, the green of trees escaped from enclosed and hidden gardens, and everywhere I could see the green-tiled square minarets of the mosques from which the muezzins call people to prayer.

Overexcited, nervous, I walked down the hill into the medina and, as I had hoped, was drawn immediately and without recourse (except to turn and flee, in the wild hope that I would remember the way I had come) into the Middle Ages. I was both seduced and alarmed by the exoticism, the loss of all ties to the greater and more familiar world that lay beyond the souks, the ramparts, the hills, the desert.

The mystery of Fez, the sense of exclusion and strangeness, is the result not only of custom and religion but of the very architecture. Each small neighborhood within the medina has five requisites: a communal oven, a mosque, a Koranic school, a fountain, and a *hammam,* or public bath. These neighborhoods, which were built first as forts to withstand the incessant raiding of the local tribesmen and incursive Europeans, are designed to reveal nothing of an interior life. The high stucco walls of the houses and shops are windowless, seamless; it is impossible to know where one house begins and another ends. The only indications that something lies behind the walls are the carved wooden doors studded with big iron nails and bolts, the hinges a rendering of the five fingers of Fatima, and an occasional trailing grapevine or leaf of red pomegranate making its desultory way through a rotting trellis. If one is lucky enough to be invited inside, or even to be passing as a door is pulled open (the doors have two knockers, one at a man's height and one high up for horsemen), it is as if paradise were suddenly revealed: blue-and-white-tiled courtyards with pink oleander and pale plumbago around a small fountain; rich carpets and the rare blue-and-red embroidered Fez cloth thrown over a second-floor railing to air; the sky blue and fresh, filling the secret place with light. And then the heavy cedar door is pulled to, and paradise disappears.

The maze of narrow, damp, rush-covered alleys is as dark as a tomb and is managed only by crouching, arms flung wide to feel the way. A file of patient donkeys brushed past, and I flattened myself against a stone wall to avoid their straw panniers loaded with dates and grain and empty soda bottles. The glass bottles jostled against one another, louder than the more romantic sound of the animals' hooves on worn cobblestone. Speaking in French, a stranger walking behind me remarked that many of the town's residents cannot find their way through the labyrinthine lanes, and I remembered what Colette had written about Fez: "Between the closed doors, the too-high walls, along the stifling streets where my outstretched arms touch both walls, we return in imagination to those recent times when the blameless traveler who ventured into the half-roofed alleys below the Palais Jamai risked an encounter with a well-placed blade."

Old women squatting against a wooden door pressed me to buy yellow and red powders, and tiny stems of gray-green herbs bound with raffia to cure all that troubles a lover. Young, boisterous men in the souk filled my hands with dates of all sizes and softness, and almonds and figs, whispering convincingly that their fruit, and no one else's, was truly an aphrodisiac. There was nothing intellectual or religious about these inducements—and for a moment it was tempting to abandon all logic and canon. My basket was soon full of fruits and powders and magic potions.

The plaintive song of the muezzin drew me deeper into the medina. No matter how circuitously, all roads lead to the great Karaouyine Mosque. It is said that the mosque was founded by a noblewoman fleeing persecution, or by one of two rich sisters who were jealous rivals. As with the poisoning of Jane Bowles, it is difficult to know the truth, and unimportant.

Home of one of the oldest universities in the Muslim world, the Karaouyine was a center for the *halaqat*, groups of scholars and religious men who gathered during the tenth century to study the thousands of manuscripts and scrolls and rare books in its library. It is the most magnificent of the Fez mosques, with an enormous carved and painted wood gate and canopy. Because I am not a Muslim, I was not allowed inside, but I could see a section of the white stucco walls with their wainscoting of finely woven straw panels. I watched quietly as the men splashed their bare feet and ankles in the ritual ablutions required of Muslims five times a day. The voice of the imam, invisible to those of us standing in the dark alleyway, murmured the noon prayer. I longed to see more—there are, I have read, 270 pillars of marble in the great courtyard—but stepped back, happy at least to be allowed inside the little Attarine Medersa, a Koranic school, nearby.

The four walls of the *medersa* courtyard are sheets of exact and formal stuccowork, and blue-and-white mosaic tile. Verses from the

Koran are incised in continuous friezes, but to an eye that cannot read Arabic, the pattern of cedarwood and stucco filigree and arabesques that represent the 114 *suras,* or chapters of the Koran, are dizzying in their intricacy. Although it was primarily the study of the Koran, regulating religious custom as well as law and social order, that drew the learned to Fez, lectures were also given in astronomy, medicine, mathematics, and, not least, angels and *jinn.* Young students from throughout the Islamic world lived in the small damp cells on the second-floor gallery overlooking the tiled court-yard with its fluted white marble basin. It was named the School of Spices, after the neighborhood of the spice souk where it was built in A.D. 1325. Although Fez was founded on the Oued el-Jawahir, or River of Pearls, a few small and dirty streams of which straggle through the city, and although the lanes themselves sometimes feel and always smell damp, there is little water to be seen save in small fountains in the mosques.

From the big public garden, the Bou Jeloud, I walked to the nineteenth-century Dar Batha Palace to look at the small collection of carpets and arms and pottery. An affable woman accompanied me through the cool rooms, turning the lights on and off as I trailed happily after her. The palace is most remarkable for its architecture and its slightly overgrown Andalusian garden. The arcades leading to what were once the women's quarters are oddly Japanese in feel-ing, reminding me that despite the Hispano-Moresque style, it is essentially an Oriental palace. Slavery, polygamy, and the seclusion and segregation of women were among the precepts of secular Islamic architecture, so this lovely place is not without its ghosts. I wondered if the attendant was the descendant of one of those Circassian slave women or Turkish sultanas.

Leaving the shaded cloisters of the museum, I walked to a spice shop where Mr. Khalid, the gentle and elegant owner, suggested that I take home one of the dried chameleons hanging from the ceiling like a desiccated gray mouse, in case I should someday have difficulty holding the attention of a lover. I bought several. Khalid was also happy to sell me handfuls of fragrant dried verbena for a calming infusion, and chunks of waxy attar of roses and musk to scent my fine robes. For a small fee he made designs in henna on my hands, my feet, and, as an added honor, my neck. If I was self-conscious before, I was now, on every visible surface except my face, decorated with lacelike maroon-colored designs of birds and vines and flowers.

The dark-eyed, mischievous boys selling sweets from handcarts tried to put chunks of candy into my mouth as I passed. There is no obligation to buy, you are told, if you eat the moist dates or the pink almond nougat dropped into your palm, but one is never sure. It would be possible, I thought, to buy nothing and to eat my way through the souk, drinking the small glasses of hot sugared mint tea that the carpet sellers and antiquarians offer if you happen to stick your head into one of the dark, aromatic shops which look like Aladdin's den. But since word spreads quickly, absorbently, through the souk, preceding you by only minutes, it would not be long before one's stately progress was shy of dates and candy.

In the tailors' shops and behind the high, orderly piles of olives or dried lavender or decorated candles for the mosque, the men sit cross-legged, chatting with friends, drinking tea, calling to passersby. Each trade has its own area, including the neighborhood of the potters, outside the city walls, and the tanners and dyers at the edge of the medina.

Tiny Café Laglali is where locals go to have what they consider the best tea in the country; I sat outside at one of the small, rickety tables. From the stall across the street, I bought a piece of flat coarse-grained bread and a bowl of fava beans cooked in cumin and oil and sprinkled with chilies.

I walked to the Place Nejjarine, with its small and lovely fountain behind a carved-wood proscenium arch. There was once a *fonduk* there, a lodging house and stable for travelers. Wandering through the modern market of embroidery and silk known as Kissaria, I came upon the sacred wall surrounding the tomb of Moulay Idriss II, which Muslims visit in search of good fortune. I touched the walls for luck.

There is an old *hammam* at the Palais Jamai Hotel, where one may have a traditional massage and steam bath in an enormous tiled room. I wore my bathing suit, reluctantly, and sat expectantly on the heated tile floor until an attendant came in to scrub me with loofahs and a brown gluelike soap made from cedar and olive oil. I stood under a cold shower and sat again on the hot floor while the attendant pulled and stretched me (I was happy about the bathing suit) and rubbed my shoulders. I breathed the heavy steam, convinced it had the fragrance of frankincense or myrrh, while the weariness of travel fell from me, and my head cleared, and my skin looked as pink as the nougat in the souk.

I sat in the garden of the Palais Jamai, overlooking the Old City, to wait for the evening call of the muezzin. I like best the earliest call of the day, long before first light, when I am awakened by the muezzin intoning from the top of the nearest minaret, his voice echoing and reechoing as the chant is begun, seconds later, in towers across the city, as if a round were being sung in the dark of my bedroom. To the uninitiated it seems like a mournful love song.

Beneath me the walls of the medina turned the color of lavender as the sun slipped slowly into the distant desert. I had not met with a well-placed blade, or poison, or intrigue of any kind, for that matter, but I had been studious, very mindful of angels and *jinn*, and certainly, I had found refuge.

The Facts: Fez

Because Fez still belongs partly to the nineteenth century—as well as to the tenth—there is an abundance neither of tourist places nor of tourist goods. Authenticity is its appeal.

Hotel

Palais Jamai Hotel, *Bab Guissa.* Built as a palace in 1879, this luxurious hotel is the best in Fez and one of the most charming in all Morocco. Ask for a room overlooking the medina.

Restaurants

Al-Safia, *Palais Jamai Hotel; dinner for two about $15–$35.* Traditional and refined, with belly dancers who are plump (that's how you know they're the real thing) and very good food served in beautiful rooms.

Au Palais Menebhi, *15 Souikt Ben Safi; dinner for two about $15–$35.* Housed in a lovely eighteenth-century palace that became the residence of Marshal Lyautey, who established the French protectorate in 1912.

The Sights

Dar Batha Palace, Place de l'Istiqlal. This small museum has armor, porcelain, rugs, even the ghosts of homesick slave girls and lonely queens. There is a pretty, fragrant courtyard garden.

Attarine Medersa, near the Karaouyine Mosque. Unlike at the mosque, nonbelievers are allowed inside. Built in the fourteenth century, the school is tiny and exquisite, with lacy carvings of Koranic verses in an elegant courtyard.

Andalous Mosque in the medina is a simple and graceful ninth-century building founded as a haven for Spanish refugees fleeing the Inquisition.

Shops

Antiquité Nejjarine, *3 Place Nejjarine.* This shop has the beautiful ceramic ware known as Fez blue, Berber pottery, and a collection of rare textiles.

Maison Berbère, *4 Riad Jouha Sagha.* The charming and persuasive gentleman who owns the store will ply you with mint tea and show off a treasure of antiques that includes Sephardic Judaica.

Nour Driss Khalid Spice Shop, *15 Moulay Idriss.* An alchemist's cave. Mr. Khalid will sell you herbs for lovesickness as well as bronchitis. There are dried chameleons, oils and soaps, teas, cosmetics, animal pelts, and eye of newt.

Mr. Bouchta, *23 Zenkt Hejjama.* He keeps a good selection of conventional clothing as well as pretty caftans and *djellabas* and Moroccan trousers.

In the Bazaar

Although the received wisdom is that Morocco teems with beggars and hawkers, you'll find very few in Fez; the visitor is regarded with circumspection and courtesy. It is wise, at least for the first few sorties, to have your hotel hire one of the government-licensed guides, who will help you bargain for your purchases.

There are few fine antique or clothing stores, but it is possible to find beautiful silver and coral Berber jewelry. There are big red clay pots from the Rif Mountains, as well as the more sophisticated ceramics from the towns. An occasional piece of fine clothing may be searched out, and the lovely embroidered panels of linen and cotton called *aleuj,* which are particular to Fez.

The most interesting shops are in the spice souk, with its piles of greenish henna and dried Marrakesh roses and chilies, and the carpenters' souk, scented with pine and cedarwood. In the tanners' market the skinning and pickling and dying of animal hides doesn't make a good smell, so buy a fistful of mint to hold to your nose.

Preserving a City's Soul

By Michael Kimmelman

～

editor's note

The Fez medina is home to approximately a half million people. Within the medina there are about 187 neighborhoods, 200 community ovens, 200 *hammams,* 320 mosques, 200 Koranic schools, and 200 fountains. It is little wonder, then, that Fez is a UNESCO World Heritage Site. But Fez poses no little difficulty to UNESCO's efforts to repair monuments, sustain its residents, and make the medina a safer place in which to live and work. Susan Searight, author of the Maverick Guide, has noted, "Today, most of the businessmen and traders have deserted Fez for Casa [blanca]. Their rich dwellings in the medina have become occupied by poor families from the Rif with their numerous children, many often sharing the house with several other families. The result is a degredation of the urban tissue in the medina, not designed for such an influx of population, which is today estimated at around 200,000. Its medina is on UNESCO's list of World Heritage Sites and is the object of many restoration projects, for its renovation has become a preoccupying problem. At the end of 1988, the World Bank granted Morocco a new loan of fourteen million dollars as a contribution towards this conservation and rehabilitation program. The city's present population—medina and new town—probably numbers almost 1½ million. Its many unemployed young people, poor housing, and general difficulties met

with in daily life led to violent rioting in 1990. Even if it is not the administrative or economic capital of the kingdom, Fes represents a spiritual and
political force to be reckoned with." Here is a thought-provoking piece
about architecture, good intentions, and restoration.

MICHAEL KIMMELMAN is an art and architecture critic for *The New
York Times*.

The peak of development for the old walled center, or medina,
of Fez came during the fourteenth and fifteenth centuries, and
the place looks as if it has hardly changed since then. There are
almost no cars. Mules still lug goods through the narrow,
labyrinthine streets. Metalworkers bang on pieces of copper in
storefront shops barely bigger than steamer trunks. This is a city
outside time.

It has also been a religious center for more than a thousand
years, anchored by the Karouinye Mosque and university. For first-
time visitors, one of the unforgettable experiences is to be awakened
around four A.M. by thousands of people at morning prayers. The
sound fills the medina.

Fez is an ancient place, in other words, but also a functioning
city, and one in need of repair. Several years ago UNESCO named
it a Heritage of Mankind City, like the Old City of Jerusalem. But
a major difference between the medina of Fez and almost all other
ancient city centers in this part of the world is that it remains the
hub of the local economy.

Medinas elsewhere have degenerated into slums or been superseded by civic development beyond the medina's walls. The Old
City of Jerusalem, for example, is no longer the locus of that city's
economy or civic life. Rome, which is a very different kind of
ancient city in a different part of the world, remains a capital, but
at the cost of a certain modernization, as everyone who has dodged
the traffic there knows.

People from throughout this part of Morocco, on the other hand, still shop in Fez's medina. Weavers work in it as they have for centuries.

The problem here is how to fix up the medina without fundamentally changing it, how to preserve it as a religious and economic center. And you don't have to have read Jane Jacobs to know that countless downtown areas, from Detroit to Moscow, have been turned into ghettos or theme parks or been blighted by shoddy development because of decades of misguided urban plans.

The remarkable news about Fez is that it seems to have learned from such mistakes without really having made any yet. Or at least there is an organization here that has begun to do things the right way. The Agency for the De-densification and Rehabilitation of the Medina is now working to preserve not only the great art and architecture of the place but also its most precious commodity, its historic soul.

The agency is still in its infancy, a small organization without much money but with some big ideas. The implicit question that the agency has raised seems to be no less than, What is civic culture? Is it an object like a building or a sculpture? Or can it be the life of a community, of which great architecture and art are parts? Westerners tend to see culture in terms of things. ADER-Fez (the agency is known by an acronym in French) is making a case for the other view.

It regards the medina as a neighborhood whose living links to the past are the city's truest legacy. A historical artifact like a city, it recognizes, has an economic value that goes beyond tourism. Consequently the agency is hoping to accomplish several things at once: to repair the major monuments, a project that benefits tourists, but at the same time to improve the infrastructure for residents, cleaning up a polluted water system, for example.

The agency wants to obtain loans for homeowners to fix up their houses and to ease the severe housing crunch in the medina by giving incentives for some people to leave, thereby making it more appealing to the people who stay. Also, ADER-Fez is trying to rejuvenate industries that have been part of the life of the medina for a thousand years.

For example, the agency has backed a school to train craftsmen in ancient Islamic building techniques, which include the sort of intricate stucco filigree that is one of Islam's great contributions to art. Some of the techniques were nearly forgotten here. Now they are being revived. The idea is that monuments in the medina can be restored in keeping with the original designs, but creatively: craftsmen have added their own new decorations to buildings where old decorations like painted tiles or carved stucco have been lost.

One case is the Bou Inaniya, a lovely fourteenth-century *medersa,* or religious school, which was a picturesque but complete ruin until recently. With a private grant from King Hassan II to the agency, its stucco designs have been recreated and augmented and the place generally adapted to make a dormitory.

As great examples of religious architecture, such buildings in the West might be treated as museum objects, but here they are considered practical parts of the community and adaptable. They are being returned to use in a process that provides jobs to local craftsmen doing local kinds of handiwork. In other words, no division is drawn between the past and the present, so that what's old is made new through what's old.

The agency's approach is slow and incremental, and not everyone in Morocco agrees with it. Detractors have asked, Is this the best way to preserve historical monuments? Tradition notwithstanding, wouldn't modern building techniques be more efficient and less expensive?

But ADER-Fez is devoted to a broad, long-term view of historical preservation. A private organization, it receives some help from the Moroccan government. It is run by a local man named Abdel-Latif El Hajjami, whose father was a religious adviser to the king.

People's Needs Taken into Account

He is a passionate and unshakable spokesman for his cause. Mr. Hajjami's focus was on the major monuments until people in the medina began to complain that their needs were being overlooked. Then a new plan was devised. Mr. Hajjami formulated a vision of preservation here that better took into account the whole community.

The World Bank paid for a team from the Unit for Housing and Urbanization at Harvard's Graduate School of Design to help. The Moroccan government then donated land outside Fez that the agency would be able to develop and sell to raise money for its operations.

Now the World Bank is providing the Moroccan government with a loan of more than $20 million for infrastructure improvements, emergency repairs, and short-term loans for tenants and homeowners in the medina.

The plan involves some small-scale modernizing interventions, for example to provide limited access in the medina for ambulances and fire and sanitation trucks to replace the donkeys, which happen to be heavy polluters. Some miniparks will also be created, because the medina has no places for children to play.

Already about two hundred buildings have received some sort of emergency help in the last several years from ADER-Fez. Because the medina is so overcrowded, the agency is not always able to find temporary homes for people in crumbling buildings during the repairs. One of the oddest sights in Fez is of families living in the middle of construction projects.

The Ansari family, for example, live behind a pile of rubble that, not long ago, had been the outside of a house next to theirs. Scaffolding shores up what remains of their walls. Workers on ladders busy themselves with repairs. And in a room open to their small central courtyard, now muddied by construction equipment, the Ansaris calmly sit at a low round table, sipping sweetened Moroccan tea and watching television.

Some of the agency's more conspicuous successes, besides the Bou Inaniya, include the restoration of the Foundouk Nejjarine, for example, a lodge, then a mosque that has now become a handsome woodworking museum in the carpenters' quarter. But the Ansaris' house encapsulates the crucial connection being made here between the preservation of local culture and daily life—a profound idea, once you think of the medina in Fez, its community, both physically and socially, as a living work of art.

Trying to Avoid a Theme Park

In the end the question is whether it will really be possible to make the place more amenable to tourists yet not turn it into a theme park. Can housing in the medina be improved, and the prices of houses made to rise, giving a lift to the economy, without gentrifying the community? With Fez especially burdened by building codes and fragmented ownership patterns, can the agency help eliminate the red tape to encourage more homeownership so that residents will feel it is worthwhile investing in the medina's improvement?

Mr. Hajjami sees a few trickle-down effects so far: the hiring in Spain, for instance, of craftsmen trained in Fez in the old arts of building, and voluntary improvements by some homeowners with faith in the medina's fiscal prospects. But who knows yet? It will take time merely for ADER-Fez to develop the land it received from the government to maintain its staff and offices.

What's intriguing for now is the concept alone. Americans often judge culture in terms of money, asking how much a painting is worth. Fez is a reminder that elsewhere in the world, culture is more a matter of public identity, of local or national self-worth. It is inseparable from the people who made it, and defines them. The lesson here is that the life of the medina, its residents, and their art and architecture are inextricably linked.

Lifting the Veil on Marrakech

By Alexander Lobrano

editor's note

"Marrakesh as a whole gives a totally African impression," wrote John Gunther in *Inside Africa*. "The pulse is that of Saharan Africa at its most intense beat." Marrakesh, perhaps more than other Moroccan cities, is also the epitome of opposites: familiar and mysterious, private and public, chaotic and calm, sensual and ethereal.

ALEXANDER LOBRANO is European editor for *Gourmet* and contributes frequently to a number of magazines, including *Departures, France Discovery Guide*, and *FRANCE Magazine*. His work has also been featured in two previous editions of *The Collected Traveler: Paris* and *Provence, Côte d'Azur, and Monaco*.

Marrakech is jarring, a shock. Most fabled destinations upset our habitual perception in some way, which is why we love them. The lonesome elegance of Paris brings on a nagging doubt that you've ever really known romance; the rot of history in Rome leads to musings on your own mortality. Marrakech unnerves by flooding the senses and then soothes with the freedom of instinct. Nothing is so known about this place as to prevent us from appreciating the chaos at face value. You spot something—a mosaic, a carpet, a carved wooden doorway—and love it simply because it is beautiful. For all you can tell, the flowing Arabic script on the plate you've just purchased says "EMPLOYEES MUST WASH HANDS BEFORE RETURNING TO WORK." Such an escape from educated appreciation comes as a relief.

But first you must yield to the chaos. And there is no place more disorienting than the place Djemaa el Fna, the great square where all the nerve endings of this ancient city come together. At dusk, the air is heavy with the scent of dung and diesel and the perfume of orange blossoms. Men squat in rapt attention to the incantations of storytellers; horse-drawn carriages plow through the square, already bisected by a noisy parade of taxis, motor scooters, buses, and vans. There is no empty space in which to stand still for more than a moment.

Surprised by a flash of veiled green eyes, I narrowly miss a donkey pulling a cartload of coriander. I step aside and accidentally jostle a snake charmer, who thrusts his cobra at me (at least I think it was a cobra). I cross the street and follow a neon-lit staircase to a second-story terrace café. From here, I can survey the frenetic scene from a comfortable distance.

On the horizon, the snowy peaks of the Atlas Mountains turn indigo in the tawny light spreading across the landscape of palm trees and hundreds of white satellite dishes, the latter sprouting from flat roofs like mushrooms. As the sun sets, more and more people spill into the square. Strings of white lights illuminate a hundred food stalls where meat sizzles on braziers. Dark-eyed adolescents giggle at khaki-clad tourists; would-be guides tug at their sleeves. Pairs of soldiers strut through the crowd, backpackers thumb guidebooks under streetlights, and a self-consciously elegant American couple, dressed in crisply ironed linen, stride by on their way to dinner.

Tension between tourists and international tastemakers is yet another flashpoint in this tightly wired city. The French visit Morocco the way Americans go to Florida—it's only a two-and-a-half-hour flight—and they feel a proprietary satisfaction in the fact that theirs is the country's second language. The foreign elite may dote on the delicate, honeycomb carvings of the Saadian Tombs and the sixteenth-century mausoleums that are among Marrakech's most famous sites, but thousands of others swarm in for a cheap sun holiday set against an exotic backdrop, quickly vanishing into the bunkerlike hotels outside of town. Marrakech, like Capri, has a spectacular ability to absorb all comers into the landscape. Yet I suspect that ordinary tourists love Marrakech for more or less the same reasons as the head of Hermès, Jean-Louis Dumas, who has a house in the Palmeraie; or Bernard-Henri Lévi, France's best-known philosopher, and his actress wife, Arielle Dombasle; or any of the other glamorous types who stay in the stylish small hotels that have opened in the medina. They come to Marrakech to take in the languid rhythms of a culture that is teetering on the cusp of irrevocable modernity but has yet to buy the required assumption that time means money.

Before 1912, when Morocco became a French protectorate and transportation improved, few Europeans had visited Marrakech. In 1922 the painter Jacques Majorelle, who was suffering from tuberculosis, came to Marrakech for its healthful climate. His boldly colored canvases became cult items in Paris, serving almost as tourism posters. In the same year, La Mamounia opened. The sumptuous hotel, a lavish hybrid of Art Deco and Arabic motifs, became a destination in itself, and Marrakech slowly found its way onto the itineraries of wealthy but venturesome souls with a taste for the exotic.

During the 1960s, of course, the city became a magnet for the counterculture, not least because Morocco was a major producer of hashish. In the decade that followed, Yves Saint Laurent bought Majorelle's villa and helped to restore a little of the city's glamour. But by the 1980s, the hotel boom on the edges of town had tipped the delicate equilibrium between locals and tourists: Marrakech became overbuilt; shopkeepers, aggressive.

Then, in 1994, a stern force of tourist police spread the word during the GATT trade talks that foreigners were not to be hassled. Europeans and a few Americans trickled back into town, and some started buying *riads,* the old medina houses with interior court-yards. Now people from all over the world scramble to buy *riads* in the walled city, the same ones who went to Figueres in Spain in the 1950s or Provence in the 1960s.

Today, when you arrive in Marrakech, Mohammed VI—a natty-looking fellow in a rakish white suit that could pass for formal dress in Monte Carlo—is there to greet you: his portrait is all over the air-port, adding some chic to a terminal that looks more like a high school auditorium. The Moroccans affectionately call their young king "M6," which also happens to be the name of a French TV sta-tion that's a Gallic version of MTV. His liberal policies, including an interest in the rights of women, are among the reasons why Morocco, and Marrakech in particular, has once again become popular.

But your duties as a traveler in Marrakech are still wonderfully light. You'll see the Koutoubia Mosque—tiresomely referred to as Marrakech's Eiffel Tower or Empire State Building—every day on your way into town. It's beautifully lit but closed to non-Muslims. The only other things worth braving the heat of the day for are the aforementioned Saadian Tombs, the souks, and perhaps La Bahia Palace.

And so, instead of sightseeing, you slow down and start to notice things—the powdery scent of fig leaves bruised by the desert heat, the slick green olive-oil soap sold by the scoop from big vats all over town, the vivid pyramids of loose spices in the market, the melancholy call to prayer from a neighborhood mosque, and the undertone of lust in a country where virginity is prized and half the population is currently under twenty. Like a photo slowly developing, it is the contrast and tension between the unseen and the observed that finally creates your personal picture of Marrakech.

To really savor Marrakech, you must stay somewhere that has a garden and is an easy walk into town. Behind closed doors, perhaps on a terrace of your own, you'll listen to the doves cooing in the morning and the starlings chattering at sunset. You'll spend unmeasured hours on a chaise reading and dozing. The rhythms of life follow the heat of the day, so you rise early to wander, retreat from the sun at noon, lunch, rest in the afternoon when shade and silence are the city's priorities, and then join in its explosive nocturnal life after sundown.

It's easy to find your way around and easy to get lost. The ramparts of orange-colored earth pierced by peacock-tail gates, each called a *bab*, are the skin of the medina. If this city within a city seems a random labyrinth of alleys and lanes, it is on the most basic level a maze, which is to say that the only way to learn your way around is to make the same mistake so many times you couldn't possibly make it again. Since few travelers to Marrakech are here long enough to attain this subconscious level of familiarity, the city will remain ever mystifying, a situation that is heightened by the lack of street signs.

The souks—the warren of alleys, lanes, shops, and ateliers that make up the market—lie buried in the middle of the medina. The cleanest activities—selling books and gold or making silver jewelry—are at the center of the souks, while the dirtier jobs—tanning and trading leather—are on the edges. And everywhere food is being prepared. At the end of a lane near the Bab Agnaou, an old woman grates carrots in the early morning while two others sit at a table making olive-size meatballs from a bowl of *kefta:* ground mutton mixed with rice and seasoned with cumin, cinnamon, fresh mint leaves, parsley, onion, and coriander. Suddenly aware that they have an audience, the women grin; one of them quickly flicks a curtain so their work can again be anonymous.

The Moroccan kitchen, one of the most refined in the world, has traditionally been the preserve of women, and recipes are transmitted from generation to generation as a sort of culinary dowry. Although the mass-prepared couscous and *tagines* that have become the tourist idiom are often heavy, reflecting their origins as high-caloric meals once meant to sustain laborers in the fields, the food most Moroccans eat at home is remarkably delicate. One of the glories of the Moroccan table is the wonderful array of salads and appetizers that precede the main course, sometimes spinach cooked with paprika, cumin, preserved lemons, and pepper; or *briouat,* a fragile, flaky turnover filled with meat, cheese, fish, or sausage, sweet tomato relish, and grated carrots with sultanas, those yellow raisins I kept finding stuck to my heels.

These sorts of preparations are time-consuming, which is why they are seldom found in restaurants. But things are changing. A new generation of professional cooks, including a growing number of male chefs, are codifying the country's culinary heritage at the same time that increased professional opportunities for women are freeing them from the kitchen. The assumption that most menus offer the same standard dishes is much less true these days.

What remains unchanged is Marrakech's thriving café culture, one of the best legacies of the French. A terrace with ceiling fans in the arcades of the Gueliz district, the 1920s French-designed new town, is perfect for waiting out the heat of the day with a drink and a book.

"Voulez-vous goûter le rafraîchissement local?" asks the waiter when I settle in at the Café Les Négociants. I expect mint tea. But a minute later he returns with a bright orange bottle of Fanta and a big grin. A fine joke—who could resist needling a tourist now and then?—and a telling bit of irony. Everyone else on the shaded terrace is drinking Fanta, too.

A Day in the Life of the Jemaa el Fna

BY RACHEL BILLINGTON

∽

editor's note

Readers who have seen the Grateful Dead will know what I mean when I say that the Djemaa el Fna is like the parking lot scene after a Dead show magnified times fifty. "There can be no more oriental sight this side of the Atlas and the Sahara," wrote Edith Wharton of this frenetic *place*. And John Gunther added his own two cents: "This is one of the supreme sights of Africa or anywhere else."

It's tempting to say I never tire of the Djemaa el Fna, but the truth is, I do, eventually. But that's why the Café Argana and Café de France are there, so I can sit down and continue taking it all in.

RACHEL BILLINGTON is the author of *Loving Attitudes* (William Morrow, 1988, hardcover; Penguin, 1989, paperback), *Occasion of Sin*

(Summit, 1982), and *All Things Nice* (Black Swan, 1969), among others. Her work has also been featured in the *Provence* edition of *The Collected Traveler*.

Geographically, the Jemaa el Fna is nothing, a space in the middle of the city of Marrakesh, not even a square, a circle, an oval, or any other recognizable shape. It is a negation of buildings that for seven hundred years has acted like a magnet for the various races of southern Morocco. They come from the deserts of the Sahara, crossing the High Atlas Mountains, which remain snow-capped even while the desert burns. They come from the mountains themselves, from rocky fortresses where until recently rulers defied even the fiercest sultans. They come from the towns of northern Morocco, like Casablanca and Rabat. Arabs, blacks, Berbers, and Bedouins, they all mix in this square that is not a square, which is not beautiful, and which boasts only one historic sight—the Koutoubia Mosque—and that is half a mile away.

Yet the extraordinary qualities of the Jemaa el Fna have been recognized by travelers as different as Edith Wharton, Elias Canetti, Winston Churchill (although he rather preferred the luxuries of the Mamounia Hotel), and Paul Bowles. It is a marketplace, a fun fair, a medieval fete, a lecture hall, a dance hall, a zoo, a hospital, a psychiatric clinic, a place in which magic still gives science a run for its money. Its name means "Place of the Dead"—until recently the Moroccans had a habit of displaying the heads of their enemies in public—but it is, above all, a place of the living. For it is the people who congregate there who define the character of the place and also, as anyone will discover who tries to map its outline, its actual shape.

Recreating a day in the life of the Jemaa el Fna is like trying to chart the ebb and flow of a sea filled with complicated eddies and undertows. In the few odd moments when the images are so thickly registered that there is hardly room for movement, the viewer from above can suddenly perceive a pattern, like those of the brilliant carpets that hang from rooftops or are piled in jewel-colored bundles in the narrow shops of the souk. The Jemaa el Fna has a curiously self-contained organic life; a visitor like myself, though pestered by guides and/or hustlers in the time-honored Arab fashion, senses at once that the proceedings would proceed whether I were there or not. If the drums bang louder when I pass, then that's only capitalist good sense. And if the gloriously behatted and coin-decorated water sellers now pose hopefully for photographs while the actual task of refreshing weary travelers is given to a humbler bearer of an earthenware pot, that is about the limit of the tourist influence. Even the Moroccan government was defeated in an attempt to clear the Jemaa el Fna. Soon after independence, in 1956, they deemed the area incompatible with a modern state and banished the people to a space outside the city walls. But after a few years they were back again, just as they had always been.

The day starts early, with the arrival of Berber women, bundled up in layers of clothes topped by a *djellaba* and veil. They travel in from the mountains, setting off on foot or by crowded buses at four or five in the morning. They settle themselves around the northern edge of the square, laying their handwoven baskets and intricately crocheted caps in front of them. Some bring herbs or vegetables, but these are generally sold in the souk, a tangle of dim streets leading off the northern side of the Jemaa el Fna. The southern edge of the square is defined by a row of barrows piled high with oranges, interspersed with stalls selling six kinds of nuts, artfully arranged in woven baskets. Smaller carts are piled with sweet cakes smelling of cinnamon or trays of sultanas, rows of black licorice, or thin slices of coconut.

The center fills in more haphazard fashion. Soon I find myself standing next to a dignified old man sitting cross-legged under a black umbrella. He wears a black robe and, surprisingly, bright red shoes. In front of him is a pile of paper and a pen. My student interpreter explains he is a holy man, a fakir (but not the sort who treads on nails, for which he looks far too frail), someone the good Muslim turns to for advice. He selects an appropriate quotation from the Koran and writes it on a paper for his petitioners to keep. He takes no money—for which, indeed, he has no need since the people, following the rule of Allah, feed and clothe him.

Not far away sits another fakir, although he is more of a magic man than a holy man. He also has pieces of paper in front of him and quite a large circle of interested customers. He hands over a blank piece of paper, neatly folded; the paper is then wetted. If the recipient has a problem, writing will appear, but if the paper remains blank, all is well. This fakir does accept money but refuses mine for I am, unquestionably, an infidel. A third old man is a scribe, busy as we pass, writing out a letter for an intensely huddled Berber woman.

Now the crowds are beginning to gather, and across the other side of the square, two tall younger men each entertain a large circle of listeners. One is a religious teacher, dramatically telling stories of the prophet Muhammad. Every now and again he bangs a skin drum, either to attract more listeners or to punctuate the climax of a story. The other man is a Berber, a secular teller of stories whose plots, I am assured, are both salacious and very funny.

As the morning warms up, the snake charmers begin to appear with wooden crates in which six or seven snakes are coiled. They find a clear space and take out the long flutes whose penetrating wail is as a siren song for snakes and audience alike. (Moroccans are fascinated by snakes, particularly the great black cobras with their malicious eyes and flaring hoods; there is a story that the infamous pasha of Marrakesh, Thami el Glaoui, who died in 1956, reappears in the shape of a black cobra rising out of his tomb.) One of the snake owners tells me they are fed on live birds and that it took him six years of training with the holy man Sidi ben Ase to learn how to handle them. Allah, I understand, is part of everything, most particularly with such potentially dangerous creatures as snakes.

The sun rises higher and the air blurs with the tiny particles of sand that float all around. I'm surprised to hear the voice of a woman, a majestic creature wrapped in shawls and chiffon scarves who leans against a Volkswagen camper and talks into a microphone. In front of her a multicolored rug is spread with bottles filled with a red liquid, baskets of colored powders, and large china eggs. She is offering cures "for female ailments," repeating, with perfect sense, that "good health is more important than money." Her voice, unceasingly persuasive, joins with those of the other salesmen, the drums, the flutes, and the bells on the hats of the six-year-old dancing boys, to make a rising tide of noise.

Edith Wharton, arriving in the Jemaa el Fna in 1917, and asked whether she would like to see the Chleuh boys dance, felt it would be impossible to penetrate the throng. Beating a strategic retreat, she climbed up to a rooftop where she was able to look down in solitary comfort.

When the noise and heat become too much for me, I gratefully follow her example and mount upward. There are many cafés around the Jemaa el Fna, all with roof terraces. The Café de France is the best known, with two terraces, but the Café de Glacier has the best view (although you can drink but not eat on the very top). The Café Fleur de la Place serves the best lemon chicken or kebab or couscous. All of them have cool, clean marble interiors and are patronized, particularly at ground level, by the Moroccans, who sip fresh mint tea, laden with sugar lumps.

From above, the square, which is even less square than usual now that one can see its every undulation, is backed by the tall minaret of the Koutoubia Mosque, which was built in the twelfth century and is still the most magnificent monument in the city. There are many other mosques, some with shining emerald green roofs and delicate minarets that are visible from where I stand. Elias Canetti was struck by their dissimilarity to church spires. "They are slender, but they do not taper; they are the same width top and bottom, and what matters is the platform in the sky from which the faithful are called to prayer. A minaret is more like a lighthouse, but with a voice for a light." He also mentioned the swallows, which now swirl around my head in a reflection of the crowds below.

In the afternoon, the Jemaa el Fna enters a desultory phase. Mysteriously, the eastern end has become covered with odd shoes, crossed in unmatched but friendly embrace. Shoeshine men doze under robes or umbrellas. A row of plastic sheets, filled with shorts and shirts and hats, runs at right angles to the shoes. Around the far reaches of the square, the permanent shops, decorated with studded belts and leather bags, or engraved brass kettles or knives or trays, or twigs for cleaning the teeth, or fresh henna leaves, stay open but unattended. The holy men and the Berber women have sensibly retreated. Now the big buildings around the northern side of the square are revealed, large pinkish-red edifices, some with crenellations reminiscent of Foreign Legion forts in the Sahara as seen in old French movies.

Leading off this corner is the long palm-lined street that passes by the Koutoubia. Under the shade of the palm trees, the *calèches*— horse-drawn carriages—are lined up, their Berber drivers hunched over and half asleep. Later they will come to life and move briskly about the city, filled with half a dozen local passengers, or else two self-conscious tourists on their way for a tour of the city walls.

By four or five, the square is beginning a second run of life. Young girls, still unveiled because unmarried, come out in their best clothes for a promenade. The streets roar with the sound of mopeds, bearing, sometimes, whole families, including baby on the handlebars. The cafés are at their fullest and the buzz of conversation audible streets away, although the dominant sound becomes once more the monologue of the philosopher, the salesman, the faith healer, or just in front of me, the dentist. He has a stall loaded with long yellow teeth, presumably to inspire confidence. A small and terrified boy is being held in the dentist's viselike grip as he demonstrates his understanding of the molar. Surprisingly, there seems to be a queue for his services.

Large circles of people are forming. In the middle of one I find a boxing match in progress, with champion, challenger, and promoter. The promoter, on mike, talks continuously, describing the art of the knockout punch, handing over the gloves only when he feels a sufficient level of excitement has been reached. In another circle a less ambitious promoter has young boys of about eight or ten fighting. They are fiercer than the men, sometimes ragged and barefoot, watched by their avid-eyed contemporaries.

In a quieter corner a turbaned man sits under a wide canopy spread over a multicolored rug decorated with feather arrangements. He is selling "liquid amber," a cure for rheumatic pains, but the main force of his argument centers on a foot-long live iguana. He is explaining its healing properties, sometimes stroking it or, when he needs both hands free, holding it down with the big toe of his bare foot.

As the sun's rays slant across the square, outdoor kitchens are carried out. A fire is set in the middle, burning a kind of charcoal that sends up a pungent, sweet-smelling smoke and increasing the scenic haze. Around the fire are placed benches that are soon filled by ravenous-looking men—no women, of course. During the fast of Ramadan they wait tensely for the sun to drop altogether and the siren to announce the time to eat. The poorer clients eat a thick chicken-based soup of vegetables and beans, served in painted earthenware bowls. To my amazement hungry men sit for quite half an hour with their soup in front of them, wooden spoon in hand, even bread dipped in soup, waiting for the proper moment. The power of the Muslim faith could not be illustrated more vividly.

I penetrate the southeast corner of the Jemaa el Fna, where a huge oak door in a high wall marks the entrance to the Albaraka Restaurant. The doorman bows me into a marble-lined courtyard, planted with glowing orange trees. The noise and smells of the Jemaa el Fna disappear as if by magic. This is the world of the great sultans, and it is quite appropriate to find a woman who is pointed out as one of Thami el Glaoui's widows sitting at the next table.

Filled with chicken and almonds and pigeons and prunes, I stagger back to the square for its final phase. At once I find Edith Wharton's dancing boys performing to the resounding beat of a four-piece band. The principal dancer is a plumply pretty boy of about thirteen who wears a wide band of flashing sequins around his hips. His movements are a kind of sinuous belly dance—if boys can be said to have bellies. His partner is older, a strange gaunt man with hennaed hair to his waist and a wild whirling style. I soon realize that the whole atmosphere of the place has become charged with a higher level of excitement. I am the only woman around, and for the first time, I feel a man's hand touching me.

Changing circles, I am confronted by a bare-chested man with oily ringleted hair, who takes a live snake in his mouth and begins to tear at it with his teeth. He peels the snake like a banana and then pops it, scarlet and slimy and, one hopes, dead, into a kettle of boiling water. "It's magic," I'm told, not altogether necessarily. Later he uses sections of the skin to help cure the illnesses or anxieties of his audience. They come up singly and crouch down with him. I am not tempted to join them.

Another magic man has not only snakes but also a large dignified owl and several sleepy-eyed baby owls. Before I can turn away he chops off chunks of a live snake and drops them into the open beaks of the suddenly wide-awake babies. A revenge, I suppose, for all the live birds eaten by cobras. Nobody seems able to explain the exact significance of these macabre rituals. "Magic" is the word constantly repeated, and that's how it feels—black magic turned against the powers of darkness. In yet another, noisier circle the Devil himself appears, with long flapping ears and trailing tail. He acts out a shout-and-tumble story with a man who squirts water on the crowd from a long thin tube that he manipulates suggestively.

As I make the fifteen-minute walk back to my hotel, I am passed by waves of people and *calèches,* crowding down to where the live action never stops. Having fallen asleep to the cacophony of far-away sound, I am awakened in what I assume to be the middle of the night by a climax of all the noises in the world. Then, suddenly, as if at the hand of an unseen conductor, absolute silence reigns. But only for a second, because almost at once a cock crows long and loud, and I realize that this is the end of one day but also the beginning of another, and that even now, the Berber women will be setting out on the trail that leads inexorably to the Jemaa el Fna.

Reprinted by permission of Harold Ober Associates Incorporated. First published in The Sophisticated Traveler section of *The New York Times,* October 5, 1986. Copyright © 1986 by Rachel Billington.

Marrakesh Is Alive with Sights and Sounds of Another Century

By David Aldrich

～

editor's note

Though this piece was written nine years ago, I still feel it is one of the best I've read, and it accurately portrays the fabled city. The writer wisely addresses one of the potentially annoying aspects of Marrakesh (hustlers; and by the way, if someone is truly pestering you, try the word *"imchi,"* which is not very nice—it translates as something like "get lost"—but will do the trick) and also recommends a visit to Gueliz (Marrakesh's *ville nouvelle*). I was happy to see this because most writers dismiss all *villes nouvelles* as being uninteresting and not worth visitors' time. But the truth is that the majority of Moroccans live in the *villes nouvelles,* and Gueliz especially is quite pleasant, with big avenues and quiet streets, good cafés and restaurants, modern shops, and major offices of tourist-related services.

DAVID ALDRICH, who has contributed to more than fifty newspapers in the United States and Canada, told me that "I earn my living as a technical writer but do my living as a freelance travel writer and photographer."

No one travels to Marrakesh without visiting the Jemaa el Fna, the sprawling, tumultuous market square just inside the tan ramparts of the old city. Guidebooks give the Jemaa el Fna great prominence—too much prominence, I thought. And they speak of how over the years it has become less of a bazaar and more of a tourist attraction. I soon had my doubts about the place. Too much hype.

And then I went there, and changed my mind in five minutes. It was a movie set. It was from another century. It was acrobats, Berber storytellers, snake charmers, ageless and toothless female fortune-tellers in veils and bright robes, hashish sellers, monkey trainers, and rows of food stalls with their bubbling, smoky, pungent dishes. It was like nothing I had seen before.

As for the other visitors to the "Big Square," who were they? French tourists? Germans? Some. But fewer than one in a hundred, and the rest were Moroccans. If they were Berber farmers in town for trading, they came wrapped in traditional desert robes and arrived by donkey; if they were from the city, they wore modern dress and came to bargain for leather goods and clothing and to eat and be entertained.

For centuries, the Jemaa el Fna served as a bazaar, a sideshow and public place for beheadings. As a foreigner in the square, expect to be ignored, hustled, and tolerated in turn. During your stay you'll visit most monuments once, but you'll keep returning to the Jemaa el Fna and the adjacent labyrinth of crafts shops. And you'll never quite believe that you're in the twentieth century.

A city of a half-million today, Marrakesh began in the eleventh century as a caravan town, gateway to the Sahara beyond the High Atlas Mountains forty miles to the southeast. The first permanent fortified walls were built in the twelfth century, and along with them came the first dynastic wars, pillagings, and burnings. Over the succeeding centuries, Marrakesh experienced palace-building, tribal warfare, glory, violence, decline, rebirth. During the colonial period (1912–56), the French imposed their language and culture on much of Morocco, and they built the bustling modern city (the Gueliz) outside the ten miles of walls encircling the old city (the medina). The plush hotels are in the Gueliz, the action in the medina.

No matter where you go in Marrakesh, the sights, sounds, and smells overwhelm you. Hire a horse-drawn carriage for a leisurely sunset trip around the high ramparts, and watch their color progress from tan to pink to brick-red; linger at a sidewalk café while robed women in pinks and greens and blues sweep by, their feet not seeming to touch the sidewalk; stroll under date palms and olive trees filled with squawking birds of every color; listen for the muezzins calling Muslims to prayer five times a day from a dozen minarets rising above the city.

To all this color and excitement, you can add perpetually sunny skies, good food, and low prices. So what's the down side?

Hustlers. Definition: A hustler is that young man who pops up the instant you set foot outside your hotel, who insists on being your guide, who refuses to go away. ("You want to see the medina? I show you the sights. I'm not guide. I'm just student who wants to learn better the English.") The Marrakesh hustler is persistent beyond belief. He is also charming, multilingual, subject to arrest (hustling is illegal, although spottily enforced), and on rare occasions dangerous. Promising to show you all the sights, he instead steers you to craft shops and restaurants with whose owners he has cut deals.

Politeness or firmness will not get rid of Marrakesh hustlers. Unless you've dealt with them before, you cannot imagine their tenaciousness. No matter how often or how firmly you tell one that his services aren't needed, he will nevertheless fall in beside you in the hope of wearing you down. And often will.

The tamest and least-hustled introduction to the city is by guided tour bus (four hours, approximately $12). Comfortable, air-conditioned buses pick you up and drop you off at your hotel. You'll tour palaces, museums, and gardens. Expect to end up at a rug shop, however. ("Just to look, not to buy," your guide reassures you.) There you're seated on a bench lining a wall, handed sugary mint tea, and worked over by perhaps the smoothest salesman you've ever encountered. An assistant unrolls one woolen rug after another at your feet. The carpets are gorgeous; the prices reasonable even before bargaining begins; the temptation a thing growing inside you. Warning: Enter with half a mind to buy, and you're doomed to walk out with a rug over your shoulder. And the tour guide will be pleased as punch with you (and his 30 percent cut).

A more expensive but more personal alternative to a bus tour is to hire an official guide (about $12 a day, plus transportation). Take your tour in a three-passenger *petit taxi* or—better—one of Marrakesh's wonderful horse-drawn carriages ($6–$10 an hour). Bargain hard with the drivers. You'll recognize an official guide by his red fez, long white robe, and the circular medal dangling from his neck. Although government trained and licensed, official guides nevertheless have their money-making schemes (understandable in light of their low fees). Make it clear exactly what you want to see, or you'll spend half your day dropping by car-rental offices run by a "good friend who likes to meet Americans." Expect to be led to a rug shop.

Despite yourself, at some point during your stay you'll probably end up hiring a hustler. One will simply not go away, and you'll give in. Their main usefulness lies in keeping other hustlers at bay. If you maintain your sense of humor, however, some are good company and will answer the sensitive political and social questions that official guides dodge. But many know little about the palaces, museums, and history of the city. All are victims of Marrakesh's high unemployment rate.

Regardless of how you see the city, here are my favorite sites and activities:

~The souks. It is said that six thousand craftspeople work in the medina with its hundreds and hundreds of shops (souks). It is also said that a stranger cannot navigate the medina alone. This is true. Nameless alleys go a hundred feet and turn; two-story buildings tilt against each other, cast permanent shadows, and make landmarks impossible to spot; one row of shops soon looks just like the next, and the next. You can spend hours wandering through the noisy, bustling, cramped, stimulating medina, with its great blur of activity, of bargaining, shouting, beckoning, of mystery and the tingle of physical danger, and never get your bearings. Go with a guide.

~The Jemaa el Fna after dark. The most exciting time to roam the Jemaa el Fna is at night—and the most unnerving, and perhaps not always wise (pickpockets are world-class). Instead, you may want to take a carriage ride through the square and then withdraw to the rooftop terrace of the nearby Café de France and watch the show below.

~The Dar Si Said Museum of Moroccan Art, rue Zitoun el Jdid. Go there for an hour or two of tranquillity. You'll see hanging red rugs, jewelry, pottery, and intricately tooled curved knives. But the real attraction is the former palace itself, with its cool white rooms and jasmine-scented courtyard.

~The Saadian Tombs, Bab er Rob. This sixteenth-century mausoleum contains the remains of many Saadian rulers, along with one hundred or so princes, concubines, children, and servants. In the seventeenth century, Sultan Moulay Ismail ordered the tombs sealed off in a fit of jealousy over the glory of his Saadian predecessors (of whom eight of eleven had been assassinated). The Saadian Tombs lay hidden until 1917, when the French rediscovered them from an aerial photograph of the lower medina. Today the site fills with tour groups but merits a visit for the architecture, carved columns, and flowering trees filling the courtyard.

~Gueliz cafés. For a change of pace, head for one of the French-style sidewalk cafés along Avenue Mohammed V in the new city. Here you'll mingle with office workers and businessmen, and here you'll buy your foreign newspapers. But in Marrakesh, you're never far from the old way of life. Now and again, you'll look up to see pass by a Berber woman with a tattooed chin, or watch uneasily as a brown-robed farmer and his donkey—both old, both pensive— slowly clop down the street while taxis and motor scooters whiz by on all sides.

~The tanneries. Go to a tannery to see how the world-famous Moroccan leather is prepared and for a quick glimpse into hell-on-earth. You'll enter a large, smelly courtyard of concrete tubs two yards across and filled with gray-green slime. Men and teenage boys climb in and out of this waist-deep ooze, under the hot sun, all day long, and splash sheepskins up and down in the odorous mixture. Visit a Moroccan tannery once, and you'll never utter a word of complaint about your own job for the rest of your life.

~The Ourika Valley. The most popular of day trips is through the Ourika Valley into the snow-peaked High Atlas Mountains, visible from Marrakesh as a gray-blue curtain stretching across the southeastern horizon. The usual destination is the village of Setti Fatima two hours away, a valley settlement of mud-walled cube houses and a few cafés. To get to the valley, take a tour bus, rent a car, or haggle (hard) for a *grand taxi* at the rampart gate named Bab er Rob. The trip is worth it even if you don't climb the mountain trail at Setti Fatima (which, you should be warned, starts out easy but becomes hand-over-hand in places).

Marrakesh may not be the easiest trip you'll ever take, but it could be one of the most stimulating. As for the hustlers, be patient and polite and use your wits, and they won't spoil your good time. And don't treat everyone as a hustler. While hiking in the High Atlas, I met Said, a young man who said he wanted to improve his English. (Where had I heard that before?) But this turned out to be true. As a result, in what became the high point of the trip, I spent several evenings with him and his brother as they sold *babouches* (pointy-toed leather slippers) from a blanket at the Jemaa el Fna. We lounged on wooden crates, drank mint tea, and traded Arabic lessons for American slang.

As a result, there's now a trader in the Jemaa el Fna who'll tell you that his leather slippers will (no pun) "knock your socks off."

This piece originally appeared in the travel section of *The Boston Globe* in 1992. Copyright © 1992 by David Aldrich. Reprinted with permission of the author.

Exploring the Heart of
Old Rabat

By Jeanie Puleston Fleming

～

editor's note

As many of the guidebook writers will tell you, Rabat is a good city in which to begin a visit to Morocco. I wholeheartedly agree. It's extremely pleasant, quite beautiful by the Atlantic, and not at all frenzied like some of its sister cities.

The Rabat souk is a much calmer introduction to the ways of the bazaar, and it was from this article that I learned about the wonderful "natural" olive oil soap. It's actually available in many souks in Morocco, but I didn't know what it was until I stayed at La Maison Bleue in Fez, where it was in a little ceramic container next to the bathtub. I bought a handful in Rabat, just as the author did (the merchant simply scoops it out and puts it into a plain plastic bag), but I didn't buy nearly enough. I am addicted to it, and next time I'm in Morocco I plan on buying at least a tub's worth.

JEANIE PULESTON FLEMING is a writer who lives in New Mexico.

The Kasbah des Oudaïa in Rabat stands as it has for centuries, aloof atop the cliffs overlooking the Atlantic and the Bou Regreg River, keeping watch over the mouth of the river, the inland plain, and the little boats ferrying people to Salé, Rabat's gleaming white sister city on the right bank of the river. Gauzy light, particular to the North African Atlantic coast, warms the air gently but effectively as the morning advances, and the streets of the medina— the old city wrapped around the base of the casbah—begin to empty around midday.

That was why, on our first day in the Moroccan capital, we found ourselves on a dusty terrace, high in the casbah, with the broad, sweeping view all to ourselves. After a late-night arrival, and tardy start, we were not ready to stop exploring. So we climbed the ceremonial stairway to the magnificently carved sandstone arches of the Oudaïa Gate, entered the casbah, and wandered along Rue Djmaa to the wide terrace marked on the Moroccan tourist map from our hotel.

Rabat's casbah and medina form a compact cornerstone of the city, which is bounded by the sea and river on two sides and by high walls on the others. Within these boundaries, visitors' paths inevitably lead through the lively market streets, then to the quiet walks of the Andalusian gardens and storybook casbah.

Outside the medina walls are the modern city's grid of European-style boulevards, with their sidewalk cafés and prome-nades peopled by government workers, students, and cosmopolitan residents.

But like its citizens, who move between the modern grid and the traditional byways of the medina, Rabat old and new spill over into each other in often surprising juxtapositions, particularly in the crowded, narrow streets of the old section.

Along Rue Souika in the medina, women in full-length *jalabas,* their faces veiled, cross paths with their sisters in high heels and tai-lored suits. Men, often in long *jalabas* too, may have a starched white shirt, tie, and collar of a business suit showing at the neck, or perhaps pointed yellow leather slippers right out of the Arabian Nights showing below the hem.

Antique brass bowls and modern plastic ones are on sale at adjacent stalls, where salesmen pull out pocket calculators to tally prices. Across the street, meanwhile, a grain seller is figuring his totals on an abacus. Elaborately packaged—and priced—soaps and perfumes from France are displayed behind a large dish of "natural" olive oil soap that looks like stiff molasses, smells fresh and clean, and costs about five cents for a fist-sized portion, sold by weight. Above it all looms the medieval casbah, which was once home to sultans, slaves, and pirates and has acquired a certain cachet as an address.

While a tour of the oldest part of Rabat must include the Roman ruins of the village of Chellah on the southern edge of town and the 144-foot-high Tour Hassan, ancient Rabat is the still-living medina and its casbah.

The view from the terrace is spectacular, though the terrace itself, sometimes called *le plateforme*, has the vacant-lot look of many casually tended public places the world over.

The day we were there dusty patches strewn with a few crumpled papers and clumps of weeds provided a playing field for three little boys running and shouting with their ball, as oblivious to the heat and slow-moving adults as are small boys everywhere.

In one corner of the terrace stood a low building housing a carpet-weaving factory. Since the door was open, we stepped inside to watch the weavers—all women—manipulating the woolen weft in the dimly lighted interior. When the workshop prepared to close only minutes later, we returned blinking to the brilliance outside.

The ball players were leaving, probably to retreat to cooler courtyards or shaded rooms where their families gathered for lunch. After the giggling workers filed out and down the street, we were left alone with the shimmering, wide-angle view and a sudden, heavy stillness.

Below to the northeast, where the Bou Regreg empties into the sea, Spanish galleons were lured close in pursuit of pirate ships, only to be caught fast on a barely submerged sandbar. Then the low-keeled pirate vessels breezed a few hundred yards upriver to safety while the cannons of the casbah loosed their firepower on the stranded ships.

On the pirate ships there may have been recently captured slaves who would stumble ashore in confusion and terror as they were prodded up to the slave market near the casbah gates. Such thoughts led to speculations on the fair-skinned, red-headed Moroccan merchants we had met in the market of Fez only a few days earlier. Could their ancestors have been transplanted involuntarily from some Irish village two centuries ago? Or perhaps the Fez merchants were descended from a northern European renegade known as El Inglizi, who as one of the pirate rulers of Rabat-Salé had helped remodel and fortify the casbah?

Much later that afternoon, after the customary North African pause in the day, we retraced our ten-minute taxi route from our hotel in the *ville nouvelle* to the medina. The European-style "new town," built under the French protectorate (1912–56), was coming back to life as the day moved past four o'clock. We rode along the rows of palm trees lining Boulevard Mohammed V, past sidewalk cafés (patronized almost exclusively by men), and past the elegant boutiques with $200-and-up famous-name bags and the sidewalk merchants hawking faux Cartier or Louis Vuitton wallets for two dollars. We then turned right on the boulevard Hassan II.

On the north side of this busy thoroughfare rises the medina wall, about twenty feet high and punctuated along its several-block length by five major gates, their high arches dwarfing the stream of people strolling in and out. Roughly parallel to Boulevard Hassan II but inside the wall runs Rue Souika.

This so-called Andalusian portion of the medina wall dates from the seventeenth century, when Muslim refugees fled southern Spain for North Africa. The refugees, who included not only a number of talented artisans but the nucleus of the pirate empire bent on revenge against Spain, built a settlement reminiscent of their homeland at the base of the casbah.

The western wall of the medina is much older, and longer. It runs from the north cliffs of the casbah, along the old city, and more than a mile and half farther south. Yacub el-Mansur, one of Morocco's greatest builders, was responsible for much of this Almohad wall. Just beyond the massive Bab er Rouah, Gate of the Wind, the present royal complex stretches south and west to the outer walls. Mansur also ordered construction of the Hassan Tower, a never-completed minaret that stands in a never-completed grand mosque above the river in the eastern *ville nouvelle*. The opulent mausoleum of King Mohammed V, who died in 1961, has been built beside this centuries-old landmark.

Near the river end of Boulevard Hassan II we asked the taxi driver to let us off at the gate nearest the Andalusian gardens, since they close around six in the evening.

Though created during the French protectorate, the graciously elegant walkways, the plant groupings, and the sound of water are far more reminiscent of Moorish Granada than of France's regal gardens. By day veiled women in dark blue and black *jalabas* often sit quietly while children play around them on the steps by the entrance. Inside, other women walk the flower-lined paths together.

The Museum of Moroccan Arts in the gardens proved well worth a visit, not only for the well-displayed jewelry, costumes, pottery, weapons, and carpets, but for the seventeenth-century building itself. Originally a palace with rooms typically opening onto a central courtyard, it was built for the occasional occupation of Sultan Moulay Ismail of Meknes, a ruler who united the country and reigned—with touches of remarkable cruelty—from 1672 to 1727.

Along the west wall of the gardens, the museum has expanded into another building with additional displays, including a luxurious desert tent, more costumes, and photographs of Moroccans from different areas.

Café des Oudaïs, a superbly sited terrace tearoom with a view of the river and Salé, can be reached through a gate on the east side of the Andalusian gardens.

Though coffee is readily available, the preference is a twenty-five-cent glass of sweet mint tea—Moroccans down four or five cups a day—and pastries such as coconut macaroons, *cornes de gazelle* filled with almond paste, or *cigares* dripping with honey in the shape of a finger or a triangle. With cakes costing about thirty-five cents each, we tried several, then returned fortified to the streets of the medina to join the early-evening crowds.

Rue des Consuls and Rue Souika were buzzing with the business of buying and selling. Between shops featuring brass and leather-ware, jewelry, thula-wood carvings, mosaics, clothing, spices, and plastics were several inner courtyards used as artisans' workshops.

From Rue des Consuls we saw bags being made by men and boys who formed an assembly line of cutters, toolers, and stitchers.

Just around the corner, on Rue Souika, similar bags and others were priced at $15 to $25, and a handsome saddlebag-style shoulder purse was $30—all prices, of course, subject to discussion. Farther along, Rue Souika has a roof and is lined with stalls selling slippers *(babouches)*. The yellow ones worn by men were about $10, and embroidered ones for women about $15. Food and jewelry shops take over as the street nears the grand mosque.

Between the river and Rue des Consuls runs the Sidi Malouf ramp, where ferryboats from Salé arrive and leave. Closer to the casbah along this road is a government-sponsored artisan center, laid out in cubicles of workshops and salesrooms. Across the street is a traditional arts museum built around a pretty courtyard.

Rabat carpets, often deep red with a medallion design in the center, hung in front of several shops at the top end of Rue des Consuls.

To the smells of fresh bread and sidewalk grills, we moved along with the crowd, acquiring along the way a pair of roomy Moroccan pants for about $7, several small leather evening bags for $5 each, and a few strings of exotic-looking beads that at $2 each contained plastic "amber" that nonetheless had a certain style.

The thula-wood boxes at $15 to $20 each were tempting, as was an enormous brass pot for under $40. But after a streetside vendor persuaded us to try some of his delicious fried bread as an hors d'oeuvre, appetite-whetting images of lemon chicken and hearty *tajine* stews being served in the city's many restaurants began to appear, signaling the end of the evening's stroll.

During the next days we found that Rabat's medina and casbah are easily accessible to first-time visitors, who can wander on their own for hours without fear of becoming lost. The medina, though compact, is fairly open and its streets relatively straight. The casbah itself covers an area hardly larger than a football field, and though streets curve and twist within it, sometimes to end abruptly at someone's locked gate, a few minutes' wanderings inevitably lead to an exit.

On the last day we returned to the casbah terrace and found it still an evocative setting—even though two lovers, not pirates, sat beside the old cannon, and the desperate shouts in the distance came not from a besieged ship but from a lively yet decidedly civilized game of soccer on the beach below.

From Taxi Rides to Dining Out

Getting Around

Taxis are usually plentiful and inexpensive, though they can be scarce out by the Chellah ruins, especially in the afternoon, and anywhere in the evening rush hour.

Guides

Official guides are available through most hotels and at the Syndicat d'Initiative, an official information office on Rue Patrice Lumumba in the new part of town. A full-day escorted visit, including taxi, will cost about $40 and can include a few or all of the major sights.

At the Oudaïa Gate, the main entry to the casbah, a knot of young men usually waits for foreigners arriving without a guide. For $2 or $3 one will guide you around the casbah—up to the terrace, to the Moorish café, and into the gardens. If you prefer to wander on your own, be prepared to turn them down firmly.

Shopping

The following museums and shops are in or close to the casbah:

Museum of Moroccan Arts has displays of jewelry, costumes, pottery, weapons and carpets.

Museum of Traditional Arts. Opening hours are marked on the gates as 8:30 A.M. to noon and 3 to 6:30 P.M., though it had apparently closed early on the occasions we visited.

Maroc Artisanal, 20–22 Rue des Consuls, has displays of Rabat carpets. Prices for the best quality, *extra supérieur,* begin at about $125 a square meter, with a typical size being about four square meters (about four square yards). Farther along the street another Rabat carpet merchant showed us a high-quality carpet from Fez and said it would fetch $25 less a square meter than his best from Rabat.

Some merchants will provide customs forms and insurance and will ship carpets (by air only) for about $70 to the United States.

Hotels

The city has a wide choice of hotels:

Hôtel La Tour Hassan, 26 Avenue Abderrahmane Annegal, has large reception rooms, elaborately decorated with Rabat carpets, marble, mosaic, and mirrors.

Hotel Safir, Place Sidi Makhlouf, is a favorite of French tour groups. Many of the 200 rooms overlook the Hassan Tower and the casbah.

Hotel Belere, 33 Avenue Moulay Youssef, is two blocks from the train station. It has 90 rooms that are simply furnished and rather dim.

Restaurants

A 10 percent service charge and 12 percent tax are usually added to the prices.

Hôtel La Tour Hassan has two lavish dining rooms: one Moroccan, the other international.

Oasis, 7 Rue Al Osquofiah. Customers are seated in booths with thick cushions, amid tiles and wood décor.

Koutoubia, 10 Rue Pierre Parent (601–25). The menu features typical Moroccan fare: lemon chicken *tajine,* almond chicken, or lamb brochette.

Tangier: Morocco's Mystery City

By Naomi Barry

✑

editor's note

Author Iain Finlayson opens his book *Tangier: City of the Dream* with, "They say, weathered old colonials, 'Morocco is not Africa.' A faraway look in their eyes settles irritably on the Rif Mountains which rise beyond Tangier. They say, experienced travellers, 'Tangier is not Morocco.' Their minds are on sandfast Marrakesh, perhaps, or Fez, most sinister and disorienting of the Imperial cities of the south. They say, elderly Tangerinos, 'Tangier is not what it was.'" It seems so many travelers are obsessed with the fact that Tangier is not what it used to be. But people say that about every place I've ever visited and lived. And as Paul Bowles noted, "Recalling that usually one writes best where one feels the most intensely, I tell myself that I'm justified in speaking of a Tangier which now exists only in memory but which, in spite of having been left behind by the passage of time, is in this case no less valid."

It is sometimes difficult to fit Tangier into an itinerary, as it's all the way up there at the tip of the country, but it is a most rewarding city in a gorgeous setting.

NAOMI BARRY lives in Paris and has been a frequent contributor to *Gourmet,* where this piece appeared in 1996. She is also the author of *Paris Personal* (E.P. Dutton, 1963) and *Food alla Florentine* (Doubleday, 1972).

The cloth button was small, round, and hard, with not a hint of any secret within, which made it rather like Tangier itself, the Moroccan city that has inspired a thousand fantasies. Ninety-nine of these buttons ran down the front of a striped antique caftan in shimmering pale green, lime, and gold.

"That button is a specialty of the Jews," said shopkeeper Majid. "If you were to take it apart, you would find it is made from a single thread. Nobody works like that anymore."

I was moved by the painstaking artistry and even more by Majid's caring so much. At that moment, I knew I was going to like Tangier.

From the heights of the kasbah—which simply means castle—Spain is a visible reality. To stand in Africa and look at Europe is a thrill of geography. Down the steep hill in the other direction, the houses look like a tumble of sugar cubes tossed by a careless hand. A great many artists and writers from many lands have recorded their impressions of Tangier in prose and paint, and they challenged me to unravel the button and follow the thread.

In the popular imagination, Tangier is a cocktail of sin, sex, smugglers, spies, and *kef,* a concoction of dried hemp leaves that, when smoked, produces a mild high. Such a titillating reputation must have some basis in fact, I told myself. Foreigners, tremblingly primed for the worst, are pleasantly surprised—or slightly disappointed—to find themselves in a comparatively small town where nobody hassles them and even the hustling is gentle. Should a wander through the labyrinthine medina (the old walled quarter) turn into a frustrating game of blind man's buff, someone inevitably offers to lead the way out. The mystery city suddenly seems like a friend.

Once a visitor is insinuated into the cat's cradle of local gossip, it is clear that Tangier is no average town. The tales are a thousand and one: exaggerated, improbable, and most of them at least half true. During the 1950s and 1960s, the Café Central was to Tangier what the Algonquin was to New York; its own "Round Table" was that of the expatriate Beat elite. They drank; they drugged; they talked in torrents, acted out their hallucinations, and fed the image of Tangier as a Nirvana Gomorrah where the living was cheap. People who saw them every day were astonished to learn that some of the oddballs actually had put pen to paper. Poet Allen Ginsberg, guru of the flower people, bowed to William Burroughs as his "teacher." Mary McCarthy called Burroughs, author of *The Naked Lunch*, "the greatest satirical writer since Jonathan Swift." Truman Capote also had his Tangier period.

Colorful characters have enlivened Tangier for several hundred years. The bandit-chief Raisuli pulled off a profitable pounce on May 18, 1904, by snatching American millionaire Ion Perdicaris and his British stepson from their dinner table. His demands were $70,000 in cash and the dismissal of the pasha-governor of Tangier, who was to be replaced by Raisuli. The British and American governments were informed they were to guarantee that the sultan meet the bandit's terms.

President Theodore Roosevelt was so outraged at this audacity that he ordered seven warships to Tangier Bay, and Washington debated whether to land the Marines. Secretary of State John Hay dispatched a telegram to the effect that the American government wanted "Perdicaris alive or Raisuli dead."

Fearful of foreign intervention, the poor sultan paid up. The much-headlined story turned out to be a real egg-on-the-face incident. Perdicaris was not an American citizen. He blithely explained that he had been naturalized Greek some years prior in order to protect an inheritance.

The discovery was kept fairly mum. To an enthralled American public, Perdicaris was the daring hero who had escaped the clutches of the terrifying brigand. The famous kidnapping was made into the film *The Wind and the Lion*, with Sean Connery playing the roguish, handsome bandit-chief. For romantic interest, the victim was changed to Mrs. Perdicaris, played by Candice Bergen.

Tangier's first hero was Hercules, who pushed apart the continents of Europe and Africa, allowing the Atlantic to meet the Mediterranean. On the African shore of his newly created straits, he founded a settlement and called it Tanjah, after the beauty he married as soon as he had done away with her former husband. Tanjah is still the city's local name. The inhabitants are Tanjawis— when they are not Tangerois or Tangerinos.

Because of the military and commercial advantages of Tanjah's strategic position, everybody wanted a piece of it. The contenders read like a roll call of both the ancient and the modern worlds. Little wonder that Tangier became the most cosmopolitan city on the North African coast.

The Sharifian Empire was too weak to withstand the great powers, and the city became an international zone in 1923. During one giddying phase, its judges were French, Spanish, and British. The Moroccan franc *and* the Spanish peseta were the official currencies. French, Spanish, and Arabic were the official languages.

In 1956 Mohammed V, father of Hassan II, incorporated Tangier into an independent Morocco. With the demise of the international zone, private fortunes fled, the foreign banks packed up, and the glitter dimmed. In recent years, however, soft voices have been whispering that Tangier may make a comeback as a crossroads financial center.

I wish I had been in Tangier on January 25, 1832, the day thirty-four-year-old Eugène Delacroix stepped off the corvette *La Perle* as official painter to the French diplomatic mission. Through the artist's eyes one sees Tangier afresh: the white-washed Moorish city built in an amphitheater around the spacious bay, the exuberant colors of its inhabitants' costumes.

"Every street corner could be a painting . . . ," wrote Delacroix to a friend in Paris. "I would need twenty arms and forty-eight hours a day to do justice to all this."

Feverishly the painter filled his Moroccan journals with pen-

and-ink sketches, watercolors, and copious notes for pictures to be finished later. The scribbled notes are reminders of colors and attitudes he feared might otherwise vanish like the visions of a dream. "Handsome man, green sleeves, undershirt in dimity cotton, barefoot before the pasha. The old man who presented the rose, caftan deep blue. . . . The mulatto slave who poured the tea, in yellow caftan and burnoose attached at back, turban."

Abraham ben-Chimol, interpreter for the French consulate, was Delacroix's constant companion during his Moroccan sojourn. Moorish women were shrouded in their veils, so Delacroix used the women of Abraham's Jewish family as his models. He was invited to one of their weddings, and the scene he painted of it, now in the Louvre, is one of his Moroccan masterpieces.

Another artist, Henri Matisse, was inspired by Tangier. Though he spent only three months there in 1912 and four months in 1913, sixty-odd drawings and paintings attest to the significance of those sojourns.

Matisse was less interested in the city's picturesque possibilities than in its extraordinary luminosity. Nonetheless, certain landmarks in the pictures are identifiable, such as the minaret of the kasbah, the English Church of St. Andrew, and the arched gateway of Bab el Aassa.

In Morocco, Matisse rode horseback daily across Tangier's vast wide beach. One day he followed the track eastward to Tétouan through a landscape of rolling green hills and perfumed fields that were a tapestry of daffodils, asphodels, and irises. Those fields have not changed, and country women still gather the flowers by the armload to sell in the market.

Morocco is a land of sun blessed with water in abundance. As a result, the natural products are wonderful and the cuisine lives up to the excellence of what goes into the pot. Daily fare is simple, but after leaving the country one hungers for its tantalizing tastes and aromas; ceremonial banquets, on the other hand, are sumptuous, their pinnacle being the royal *b'stilla* (pigeon mixed with spices and baked between layers of feathery pastry).

Rachel Muyal is the manager of Librairie des Colonnes, a small bookshop on the Boulevard Pasteur that is an intellectual meeting place of Europeans and Tanjawis. English, French, American, Spanish, and Arabic authors flock here. Their photos are posted on a wall: Rachel's pinups. Among the books at the Colonnes are cookbooks, and one popular with foreigners is *Moroccan Jewish Cookery* by Viviane and Nina Moryoussef. This cuisine is as different from that developed in Eastern Europe as the fig and the pomegranate are from the potato and the beet. There's orange-flower jam. Or jam made from little purple eggplants. ("Surprising, but very good," say the Moryoussefs.) To their lamb *tajine*, with onions and raisins, I added a few almonds. The dish was such a success, it immediately became part of my personal repertory.

Restaurant "San Remo" (Chez Toni, to all who knew the original manager) is a convivial Italo-Tangier restaurant, a favorite with residents. Toni had come to town as a boy in the mid-1940s to help in his uncle's butcher shop. Not surprisingly, the San Remo's meat was and is first quality, as is the fish, fresh from the sea.

The restaurant's triumph for me is a Moroccan specialty, *briouatt,* a cocktail party–size triangular turnover that is either deep-fried or oven-baked. Its thin pastry wrapper, or *ouarka*, resembles the *phyllo* pastry of the Greeks and the *yufka* of the Turks. The fillings may be either savory or sweet, but the *briouatts* that turned me into an instant addict are filled with a suave seafood mixture.

Wanting more of something similar, I asked around for the name of the best restaurant serving all-Moroccan food. "The El

Minzah Hotel does a Moroccan evening three times a week—expensive but very good," I was advised.

The hotel's dining room is attractive, redone some years back in old Tangier style, and the traditionally costumed waiters are smoothly skilled. The evening I went, a plump dancer gyrated to the strains of Andalou musicians. The food was up to the setting. It was all very "Moroccan Nights," and I had a sugary *briouatt* for dessert.

The Museum of Moroccan Arts is installed in the former governor's palace, built in the seventeenth century. It is here that Delacroix was received by the pasha, and to miss this museum would be a definite oversight, for it is one of the most rewarding places in Tangier. Its ceramic collection is among the finest in a country where pottery is one of the glories of the table. The various distinctive patterns inform the initiated as to their origins: Tétouan, Fès, Meknes, Marrakech. (Similar shapes and patterns continue to be produced, and bowls, platters, and covered jars are on sale in many shops.) Behind the museum is a walled garden, a peaceful retreat of birds, flowers, palms, and Seville orange trees.

The most impressive building in the medina is the American legation. The three-story palace was presented to the United States government in 1821 as a gift in perpetuity from sultan Moulay Slimane. When, during the early 1960s, consulates and embassies moved to Rabat, the forty-room palace became a research library, a kind of public drawing room, and a museum that is open three days a week or by appointment.

In the Marshan neighborhood, west of the kasbah, is the Forbes Museum, which houses the late Malcolm Forbes's impressive array of military miniatures in his former villa overlooking the Straits of Gibraltar. The collection contains more than 115,000 pieces, many arranged to recreate historic battle scenes. Visitors with no interest in toy soldiers often come anyway to see where the millionaire's well-publicized seventieth birthday party took place in 1989. The museum's gardens offer excellent views of the straits.

The beating heart of Tangier is its marketplace, and a good spot to start is Majid's shop, Boutique Majid, in the medina. It is spacious and uncluttered: there is no junk; everything is beautiful. Offered the hospitality of a glass of mint tea, you will be free to wander around looking at rugs, embroidered curtains, painted cornices from an old Koranic school, lanterns from disused synagogues and mosques, caftans, and fabulous necklaces, which can be reset by Majid's Danish wife to remove any excessively folkloric elements if customers wish. You always find something, and you always buy. Majid's place is more palace than store.

The Parfumerie Madini is not much deeper than a counter, behind which are shelves lined with perfume bottles. Famous past and present brands are represented, and a scent can be concocted to suit individual personalities. The family secrets of blending have been passed down from father to son.

Boutique Volubilis features nontraditional clothes that are unmistakably Moroccan. Elizabeth Taylor is pictured on the wall in a Volubilis caftan. Majid's artist-brother, Mohamed, designs the fabrics, which are handwoven in his atelier a few streets away. The fabrics can be bought by the yard and make stunning draperies. Mohamed's American wife, Carla, designs the clothes and often models them.

A small kiosk located near the medina's jewelers' shops sells irresistible nougat. The affable vendor usually adds a few extra chunks for eating on the spot. You may rue the day you ever got into this habit.

The medina is dense, but the countryside begins abruptly at the edge of town. Certain excursions take visitors to places as essential to Tangier as a setting is to a gemstone. Fourteen miles to the west, the lighthouse of Cape Spartel is the dramatic exclamation point that marks the land's end of Africa. About six miles from Tangier are the Grottoes of Hercules. Nature's grandiose suite of vaulted limestone ballrooms in the cliff was, some years ago, a fitting site for a ballet performance. Through the windowed apertures is the vision of a powerful Atlantic pounding at the rocks.

The most interesting person ever born in Tangier probably was the geographer Ibn Batouta. He wanted to see the world so he got up and walked. He didn't meet Marco Polo, but the Venetian and the Tanjawi were likely in Cathay at the same time. Batouta then walked his way back home again, arriving in Tangier some twenty-eight years after leaving.

The thread of the button had led me in many directions. At first nothing seemed to fit, but then Tangier all came together like a tapestry.

Tangier en Vogue

BY CHRISTOPHER PETKANAS

～～

editor's note

Tangier has been referred to as a supremely secretive city, but no one reveals all its best better than Hamish Bowles (no relation to Paul), *Vogue*'s European editor at large, all-around style maker, and Tangier habitué.

CHRISTOPHER PETKANAS, who is passionate about Morocco, is a special correspondent for *Travel & Leisure,* where this piece originally appeared. He is also the author of *At Home in France: Eating and Entertaining with the French* (Phoenix, London, 1990; distributed in the United States by Sterling Publishing Company). (As an aside, Christopher and I believe that the Imperial City of Meknes is too often overlooked or dismissed entirely by travelers, and is worthy of more than a few hours' visit from Fez.)

A blurred vision in lime linen and a straw planter's hat, Hamish Bowles is darting across Rue de la Liberté, the teeming artery that snakes down to Tangier's medieval medina. After a week's worth of tea parties and cocktail parties and dinner parties (so many that Bowles is often double-booked), he is about to leave Morocco for his home in Paris. In his slender British hand is a checklist as arduous as any he has worked through as *Vogue*'s European editor at large: Pick up monogrammed leather portfolio at Art de la Reliure. Pay for eighteenth-century Mughal miniature at Galerie Tindouf. Try again (maddeningly) to find souk selling straw slippers.

"There's nothing obvious about Tangier. Its charms and beauty are real but elusive, not overt the way Marrakesh's are," says Bowles, dodging a baby carriage rigged to carry bales of the fresh mint used for making tea. Gently swiped by another cart, this one selling water in white plastic bleach bottles, Bowles doesn't miss a beat. His brow isn't even damp.

"Tangier appeals to the sophisticated," he continues, picking up the pace (shops close in ten minutes!) as the muezzin calls the faithful to prayer. "For Westerners, it's delightfully familiar on some levels and disturbingly alien on others. You're always making discoveries by taking wrong turns, pushing open closed doors. Tangier has an edgy, louche, flyblown character that I'm strangely drawn to. I visit

Naples and Marseilles for those same Mediterranean port-town qualities."

Pinned to the tip of North Africa, Tangier is within winking distance of Spain, across the Strait of Gibraltar. In 1923, eleven years after Morocco became a French protectorate, France agreed to share Tangier with its World War I allies—Spain, Portugal, Italy, Belgium, the Netherlands, Sweden, and Britain. Thus began the city's gilded age as a free port and proudly sinful International Zone governed by European delegations. Anything went: drugs, smuggling, espionage. Sex—any way you liked it—was cheap and plentiful.

Whose interest wouldn't be piqued? The Beats came: William S. Burroughs, Allen Ginsberg, Jack Kerouac. Woolworth heiress Barbara Hutton showed the beau monde that Africa—Africa!—was safe for its kind. Cecil Beaton and Tennessee Williams got their feet wet. When Truman Capote called Tangier "that ragamuffin city," he meant it as a valentine. Paul Bowles visited and never left. He and Tangier are a perfect fit, the place supplying the writer with the mind-bending disorientation that powers his work. He has celebrated his adopted home as "a dream city . . . [with] the classical dream equipment of tunnels, ramparts, ruins, dungeons, and cliffs . . . a doll's metropolis."

The party has been a lot less festive since 1956, when France and Spain handed Morocco back to the Moroccans. Nasty hotels offering holiday packages have gone up on the beach, and everyone from the Rolling Stones to Malcolm Forbes has stepped in when Tangier needed a jump start. One of the figures steering the current renaissance is the city's other Mr. Bowles, Hamish.

"With its layers and remnants of many periods, Tangier is just so achingly nostalgic," says Bowles, whom *Vogue* relies on to tell its readers how to get into the late decorator David Hicks's landmark Oxfordshire garden (by faxing Hicks's son, Ashley), and about the unknown Paris artisan who makes by hand the signature braid on Chanel couture suits (Raymonde Pouzieux). "And the contrasts in Tangier are thrilling. The mountain ladies who ride down on donkeys to sell their bouquets look like Chaucer's Wife of Bath; it could be 1399. Middle-class Tangerine teenagers walk side by side with their mothers, the young women with Spice Girl midriffs and platform sneakers, the mothers in all-enveloping robes, heads covered, faces veiled, eyes flashing. The young Arab men wear royal-blue nylon soccer shorts under their *djellabas*. And there's a whole subcommunity of campy English seaside landladies and old French diplomats' wives who have stayed on."

Did Hamish mention the burgeoning colony of international designers and decorators, painters and photographers? "It all makes for a very mad, stimulating vibe," he promises. And on questions of vibe, no one argues with a *Vogue* editor.

Where to Stay

Before Bowles traded up to deeply glamorous rental houses that allow him to bring friends, entertain, and settle in for longer periods, his address in Tangier was always El Minzah Hotel (85 Rue de la Liberté; 099.935.885, fax 099.934.546; doubles from about $130). Built in 1930 in a pleasing Hispano-Moresque idiom by an English lord, it is as close to a full-service luxury hotel as the city has to offer, with a pool, health club, and sauna. El Minzah's sterling location in the heart of town puts the medina, souks, boutiques, casbah (the ancient military and political center), and beach—and the most interesting cafés and restaurants—all within strolling distance. The hotel also presents the delicious contrast between the rough-and-tumble of Tangier street life, one step outside the front door, and the serenity of vivid gardens, grassy terraces, and a fountain-cooled, blue-and-white-tiled courtyard. Birdsong is another lovely de-stresser.

The best (and only a handful) of El Minzah's 123 rooms and 17 suites have balconies facing the Strait of Gibraltar, serving up wrap-around palm-fringed views some say are alone worth the trip—even if the balconies themselves could use a good sweep. While rooms are a little on the *fatigué* side, they and the public spaces are appointed with a catalog of Moroccan style elements, including pierced metal lanterns with colored glass panels, furniture inlaid with mother-of-pearl, the straw wallcoverings known as *hsirah,* and bedspreads shot with metallic thread. Wonderfully knowledgeable about Tangier, the front desk staff turn on a dime, never stopping to relax their imploring how-can-I-help? smiles. "I love that typically Moroccan thing of always wanting to please," says Bowles. "At the Minzah, if you express the least concern about the weather, somebody will always assure you it's going to clear up."

Shopping for a romantic, potently nostalgic venue for the fortieth birthday party of his boyfriend, British designer-architect Peter Kent, Bowles settled on the hulking, labyrinthine, 70-room Hotel Continental (36 Rue Dar El Baroud; 099.931.024, fax 099.931.143; doubles $28, including breakfast). "It's a fabulous period piece," says Bowles, "with a traditional Moroccan smoking room lined with low banquettes just off the lobby. The Continental is for the more adventurous—and for those seriously into Bowlesiana," he adds, noting the hotel's reputation for evoking the Tangier of Paul Bowles's books. Parts of *The Sheltering Sky,* Bernardo Bertolucci's movie version of one of those works, were shot here, and the director made the Continental his home during filming. Painter James Brown is also sensitive to the hotel's poetry and always books room 108.

Built on the edges of the medina, the Continental opened in 1872, with Queen Victoria's eldest son, Edward VII, among the first to check in. His endorsement ensured that it would become *the* place to spend the night in Tangier. The next year, according to the original guest book, which patrons are invited to thumb, Degas and society portrait painter Giovanni Boldini visited. Today, to be fair, the Continental strikes some as underfunded and gloomy. Still, an ambitious renovation program is under way, netting stylishly off-beat rooms with sculpted plaster ceilings, brass four-poster beds, wacky upholstery, and wrought-iron tables topped with *zelliges* (geometric mosaic tilework). Rooms at the back of the hotel over-look the exhilarating whitewashed chaos of the medina. If you're predisposed to like the Continental, the derricks visible from the front rooms will seem an ineluctable part of the Tangier har-borscape.

If El Minzah is full and you aren't up to the moody atmosphere of the Continental, consider the Rembrandt, a hotel whose rather anonymous feel is partly balanced by a pool and a central location (Boulevard Mohammed V; 099.937.870, fax 099.930.443; doubles from about $41).

Le Mirage (Grottes d'Hercule; 099.333.332, fax 099.333.492; doubles about $195), a resort of 22 newly minted, blindingly white attached bungalows crowning a rocky Atlantic promontory nine miles from Tangier, is "overlandscaped but a good option in blis-tering summer," says Bowles. The bright and fresh accommoda-tions have kitchenettes, private terraces, wicker furniture, and ceramic globe lamps.

If you want to follow Bowles's lead, consider renting a house. Dar Sinclair, his five-bedroom villa, with a large garden, a pool, and sweeping views of the city, goes for about $1,680 a week. It is avail-able through CLM Morocco (69 Knightsbridge, London; 011.44.171.235.0123, fax 011.44.171.235.3851), an agency with a good range of listings, including Dar Kharroubia, or La Maison Rose ($1,600 a week), the deep-pink four-bedroom villa that once belonged to the late Honorable David Herbert. The younger son of the sixteenth earl of Pembroke, and one of the expatriate personalities who got Hamish Bowles interested in Tangier, Herbert ruled English society in the city like a despot from the late 1930s until his death in 1995. His house, ten minutes from town, is a kind of Moroccan Grey Gardens, strangled with oleander and hibiscus and filled with the exquisite furniture, paintings, and objects he collected. A picture of the queen is inscribed "For David from Elizabeth R. 1984." Herbert was known acidly as "the Queen of Tangier." His wizened ghost fills Dar Kharroubia.

Where to Eat

There aren't even a half-dozen places serving authentic, high-quality Moroccan food in Tangier, so don't waste your time looking for them. The finest is El Korsan in El Minzah Hotel (dinner for two about $30). On almost every trip, Bowles indulges in the restaurant's ceremonial *méchoui,* typically a hindquarter of lamb patiently baked in a slow oven. When properly cooked, the meat should be falling apart and have the marvelously fibrous texture of confit. "*Méchoui* is one of those traditional North African fête dishes that works best when there are a lot of people," Bowles says. El Korsan is also noted for three other Moroccan grand classics: *m'qualli tagine,* a luscious chicken stew with preserved lemons and pungent olives; *pastilla,* a flaky pastry pie filled with squab or chicken and almonds, and finished with a lattice of confectioners' sugar and cinnamon; and couscous, accompanied by lamb and seven vegetables, or by meltingly soft onions and plump raisins.

Saveur de Poisson (2 Escalier Waller; 099.336.326; lunch for two about $30), a quirky little hole-in-the-wall, "is another spot people swear by," Bowles says. "The owner, Belhadj Mohamed, brings in all these strange herbs, grains, and spices from the Rif Mountains, where he's from. Not only is his cooking healthful, he claims it will improve your sex life."

What is known for sure is that Mohamed's food is earthily delicious: barley-and-seafood soup simmered in an enormous teardrop-
shaped terra-cotta vessel over a charcoal fire on the steps in front of
the restaurant; grilled bass stuffed with succulent baby shrimp.
Burst figs slathered with a rustic honey taste like a bite of the
Moroccan countryside.

The restaurant is hung with naïve fish paintings and basketwork
ceiling lights. Following Arab custom, diners wash their hands
before eating—at a sink in the middle of the room. A meal at Saveur
ends with a musky, viscous, plum-colored drink made by boiling
down peaches, bananas, and a handful of other fruits for a full day.
Mohamed is such an eccentric personality that, while discussing a
dish with you, he may suddenly begin eating off your plate. With
the check comes a surprise gift of wooden cooking utensils.

The real draw at the Nautilus (9 Rue Velázquez; 099.931.159;
dinner for two about $27), down on the beach, isn't the food—
though the grilled fish is good enough—but the surreal show of
camels prancing across the sand in a mixture of floodlight and
moonlight. "It's one of Tangier's great spectacles," Bowles says.
"And the view of the glittering town rising behind you is wonderful." The Nautilus's cool, restrained (for Tangier) design is the work
of Stuart Church, the city's well-regarded American architect-in-
residence. One nod to local building traditions is the *tataouni,* or
oleander-reed, ceiling. Hostess Sally Wool-Lewis's playful bossiness
and deadpan Englishness ("Anyone into pud?") definitely plays a
part in the restaurant's popularity with the Bowles camp.

The comfort level is low, and the place even looks a little grubby,
but the Valencia (6 Avenue Youssef Ben Tachfine; 099.945.146; dinner for two about $22) is probably the most serious seafood restau-
rant in Tangier. Check any hesitations at the refrigerated case of
clear-eyed, red-gilled fish by the entrance. The crowd, too, tells you
you're in the right place: old-guard French rug designer Jacques

Demignot; bourgeois Tangerine families; bands of the city's sexy *jeunesse dorée*. Order the giant platter of deep-fried fish and shell-fish and an iced bottle of Guerrouane Moroccan rosé.

Exuberantly designed for an earlier generation of Tangier tourists, Hamadi (2 Rue Kasbah; 099.934.514; dinner for two about $40) is another of Bowles's favorite period pieces. Mile-long banquettes nuzzle the walls, cushions and curtains are of red-and-green-flocked fabric, and vintage Morocco tourism posters dot the room. The intent isn't kitsch, but that is the overwhelming effect. Hamadi is especially pleasant in late afternoon, when mint tea and an assortment of Arab pastries are a mere $2. The restaurant also serves respectable *pastilla,* couscous, and *kefta* (small skewered lamb patties).

What to Buy

All the best shopping in Tangier can be done on foot. Set aside at least two full days, one in the *ville nouvelle,* or modern city, and one in the adjacent medina. Never agree to the first price announced by a merchant—bargaining here isn't a sport, it's a way of life. Many shops close from early to mid-afternoon.

In the Ville Nouvelle

"The genial Temli brothers have the monopoly on boutiques in Tangier," Bowles says half-jokingly of Boubker Temli, who runs Galerie Tindouf (72 Rue de la Liberté; 099.938.600), a high-end antiques shop, and Mohámed and Ibrahim Temli, who operate Bazar Tindouf (64 Rue de la Liberté; 099.931.525), a more accessible crafts shop.

"The Galerie offers a perfect, concentrated look at the eclectic taste of high-style Tangerine interiors," adds Bowles. Boubker Temli explains the eclecticism: "The Tangier look was never purely Moroccan, because of all the Europeans and the diverse possessions they brought with them." Typically, his boutique might be stocked with towering Imari vases, Bohemian crystal made for the Turkish market, and Orientalist paintings. A caftan in ice-blue Lyonnaise silk, embroidered locally with metallic flowers, once belonged to Barbara Hutton. Old sepia postcards of Tangier make nice keepsakes. Designer Jacques Grange became a Galerie customer while decorating the Tangier villa that Yves Saint Laurent recently bought.

Ibrahim Temli worked on the decoration of Chez Es Saada, New York's fashionable North African restaurant. His Bazar Tindouf offers the closest thing to one-stop shopping for Moroccan crafts that can be found in Tangier. This is the proverbial cavern made famous by Ali Baba, a deliciously shadowy place with, indeed, a piled-high basement, back room after back room, and merchandise coming at you from every direction. Keep your elbows in as you squeeze through the aisles, examining amber-and-resin snuffboxes, *kef* pipes, silver-and-glass bottles for dispensing rose and orange-flower water, and brass star lanterns. For their "almost Jacobean simplicity," Bowles admires the geometric motifs embroidered in cranberry wool on straw rugs. Silver tea services come with everything needed to follow the highly codified Moroccan tea-making ritual: a squat, potbellied teapot ("They've been using the same mold since 1845," Bowles says), plus containers for tea, sugar, and mint.

Bowles is as seduced by the quality of the traditional clothing at Bambi (6 Rue de la Liberté; no phone) as he is by the courtly manners of the gentlemanly owner, Mohamed Larbi Homrani. Vintage fezzes are sold in their original boxes, whose fadedness adds to the charm. With its terrazzo floor, old-fashioned fittings, and whispering echoes of Tangier's International Zone era, Bambi is one of the few places where you find *djellabas* and caftans that are not only of the best handloomed fabric but also entirely hand-sewn.

Hand-tooled and -stamped leather goods are sold directly out of the minuscule atelier Art de la Reliure (Rue de Belgique; 099.932.580). Everything made by this friendly team can be quickly personalized: address books, frames, pencil cups. Bowles relies on Reliure for last-minute gifts, usually in the "rather over-the-top Moroccan" combination of lipstick-red leather with gold tooling.

De-Velasco (26 Boulevard Mohammed V; 099.322.495) is "less about antiques than what I call 'haute decoration'—overscaled pieces that make a big impression and are not too bothered about pedigree," Bowles says. Ormolu-tipped rosewood furniture represents delirious feats of cabinetmaking. Porcelain cachepots stuck with realistic fruit are sized for mature palm trees. The boutique itself has a tented ceiling, a staircase with mirrored risers, and wooden tassels dangling from fabric swags. According to Bowles, De-Velasco's capes with padded shoulders—made on the premises as a sideline—were endorsed by fabled *Vogue* editor Diana Vreeland and are now a favorite of Carine Rotfeld, muse of Gucci designer Tom Ford.

At Z'Rabl (122 Avenue Sidi Mohammed Ben Abdellah; 099.943.214), the made-to-order hand-knotted wool rugs with a repeat pattern of interlocking initials are "a page out of British decorator David Hicks's book," Bowles says. Jacques Demignot is the owner of this small factory and showroom in a dusty modern suburb five minutes from town. He started his career in the 1950s, as an assistant to Hubert de Givenchy in Paris, then set himself up as a decorator in New York City. Demignot's own innovation is hemp-and-cotton rugs, cool and crunchy underfoot, that are especially suited to beach houses.

In the Medina

As a kid in the late 1960s, Abdelmajid Rais El Fenni earned five *dirhams* a night emptying ashtrays at Barbara Hutton's parties.

Today his Boutique Majid (66 Rue Zankat El Mouahidini; 099.938.892) is one of the top antiques shops not just in Tangier but in all of Morocco. When El Fenni crows, "I've got the finest, most extensive collection of antique textiles in the country," no one challenges him. Mountains of beautifully rehabilitated brocades, lush velvets, humble checks and ticking stripes, muslin wedding sheets, and elaborate floral crochetwork fill his well-tended, atmospheric shop. Bowles goes jelly-kneed over a nineteenth-century felted cashmere caftan in raspberry with plum trim—"So Schiaparelli, don't you think?" Berber jewelry of coral, silver, and fragrant hand-polished amber is another Majid specialty.

You can practically reach across the alley from Majid to Coin de l'Arts Berbers (53 Rue Zankat El Mouahidini; 099.938.094), which Bowles says has the best rugs in town, "including the kind of grid designs in ivory-and-black shag that the legendary decorator Billy Baldwin used in so many houses." The rug inventory encompasses styles from forty-two Berber tribes. The shop is also known for architectural salvage, such as carved cedar keyhole doors from the Sahara.

Part of the fun of shopping the medina is not having a plan. But if an improvised expedition doesn't lead you to the following souks, make a point of seeking them out. Bakkali Jaafar (1–3 Rue de la Fontaine Nouvelle; 099.933.321) sells cotton velveteen cushions and tissue-box covers in juicy colors. Alaoui Lamrani (9 Rue de la Fontaine Nouvelle; 099.938.646) has the wide gold passementerie-and-rhinestone belts worn by Muslim brides, and bright yellow leather babouches, or slippers. "Our décor hasn't changed in seventy years!" proclaims the owner of Madini (14 Rue Sebou; 099.934.388), an adorable closet-size shop that sells twenty-seven essential oils from crystal decanters, as well as copies of ninety-seven brand-name perfumes. Bazar Najah (10 Rue de la Tennerie; no phone) stocks a wide selection of verre eglomisé (reverse paintings on glass) of folk scenes and peasant portraits. The staff at Secret des Plantes (50–52 Rue des Almohaden; 099.939.585) is precise and unhurried when explaining the uses of exotic medicinal herbs. The shop also sells chunks of amber for scenting linen cupboards, and sandalwood bark for cleaning teeth.

What to See

Depending on which concierge you talk to, the Grand Hôtel Villa de France (Rue de Hollande) is on the brink of being either razed or renovated. "It's utterly derelict, but the hotel's place in Tangier history makes it worth a look from the outside," Bowles says. "If you were to open the shutters of room thirty-five, you'd see exactly the view Matisse painted of the Grand Socco, the city's main square."

Even cultural institutions are steeped in funky charm. Built in the seventeenth century as a sultan's palace, the Dar el Makhzen Museum (Place de la Kasbah; 099.932.097) houses ravishing mosaics from the Roman city of Volubilis, as well as Moroccan costumes and household implements. Any of the gamins playing outside the museum will eagerly lead you to Sidi Hosni, Barbara Hutton's former villa.

Bowles's second trip to Tangier, in 1989, was to cover the $2.5 million seventieth birthday party Malcolm Forbes threw for himself at his Palais Mendoub. "This was during Malcolm's Elizabeth Taylor period. Guests thought they were coming to Monaco, not Morocco. You never saw so many hairpieces and Scaasi ball gowns." Following the publishing magnate's death in 1990, his bougainvillea-swaddled mansion became the Forbes Museum of Military Miniatures (2 Rue Shakespeare; 099.933.606). Stirred in with toy soldiers and war memorabilia are snapshots of Forbes's famous balloons and his infamous *Vanity Fair* portrait as a biker. Weird.

"Morocco in its infinite wisdom was the first country to recognize American sovereignty after the Revolutionary War," says Bowles. Sultan Moulay Suleyman even made a gift to the United States of the eighteenth-century building that served as the country's consulate and is now the American Legation Museum (8 Zankat America; 099.935.317). Straddling a passage in the medina's old Jewish quarter, the museum has an enchanting collection of works with Moroccan themes by Claudio Bravo, Oskar Kokoschka, Cecil Beaton, Yves Saint Laurent, and others. Pretty reception rooms are adorned with nine gilded Louis XV mirrors made for the African market. Another exhibit is devoted to correspondence between the sultan Moulay Abdullah and George Washington, and an entire room is given over to Paul Bowles—his first editions, photographs, original manuscripts, a study for Lawrence Mynott's noted oil portrait, and even the writer's old luggage.

The Perfect Day Trip

Exploring Tangier's environs in a taxi cannot be considered an indulgence, not when $100 buys up to twelve hours in a roomy, gently worn, if slightly antique, Mercedes-Benz. Asilah, 28 miles south of the city, is close enough that you're not exhausted once you get there, and different enough to make you feel that you've been somewhere. "The drive hugs the Atlantic almost the entire way," Bowles says. "And once you arrive, there's this big surprise—a jewel of a port that looks as if it was lifted straight out of the Aegean."

Asilah's medina is cleaner, more orderly, and easier to navigate than Tangier's, and strolling the waterfront is more pleasant. The other secret is that its restaurants are better. Every season, lines are drawn over whether Oceano Casa Pepe (22 Plaza Zalaka; 099.417.395; lunch for two about $15) or Casa Garcia (51 Rue Moulay Hassan Ben El Mehdi; 099.417.465; lunch for two about $20) does a superior version of the Spanish specialty, threadlike baby eels sautéed in olive oil, chili peppers, and garlic. Le Pont (24

Avenue Amir Hassan Ben Mehdi; 099.917.461; lunch for two about $15) is a humble, pristine new restaurant right on the beach that specializes in Moroccan fish dishes.

Asilah's shopping is as good as its food. Lining the main road into town are makeshift wind-raked stands displaying *tagines* and other terra-cotta cookware for next to nothing. The kilims and crafts at Bazar Atlas (25 Rue Tijara; 099.417.864) are several notches above what you see almost everywhere else. And Tangier has nothing to match Jasmin et Corallo (8 Rue Sidi Libenhamdouch; no phone), which sells sophisticated contemporary jewelry (cord chokers strung with coral and silver beads) and home accessories (mirror frames covered with beach glass and coral). It's the kind of smart boutique you expect to find in St.-Tropez or Positano, not on the far-flung North African coast.

Hamish's Essential Tangier Checklist

~At the daily **Marché de Fès** (Rue Moussa Ben Noussair at Rue de Fès), buy dozens of electric-colored flowers—gladiolus and zinnias—for your hotel room.

~Eat an almond-filled *corne de gazelle* from **Traiteur Al Mouatamid Ibn Abbad** (16 Rue Al Mouatamid Ibn Abbad; 099.943.072), a pâtisserie with more than seventy different Arab pastries.

~Visit the lighthouse at **Cap Spartel,** nine miles west of Tangier, and then lunch on fried calamari at the **Mirador** (Cap Spartel; 099.933.722; lunch for two $20), "a crazy fifties restaurant."

~Swim in one of the **Atlantic coves** between Cap Spartel and the Grottes d'Hercule.

~After a trip to the beach, sip mint tea at the clifftop **Café Hafa** (Marchane Quarter, near the Forbes Museum; no phone), the best place to experience Tangier's famous lassitude. That's *kef* (or hashish) you smell wafting from the next table. On a clear day, look for Spain.

~Walk through the daily **main food market,** with its hillocks of olives. (To find your way, enter the medina via the Grand Socco's big gate, then walk through the first archway on the right.)

~Take a front-row seat at the **Gran Café de Paris** (Place de France) at 7 P.M., when the evening *paseo,* or promenade, is in full swing. Same time another day, nurse an espresso on the Petit Socco, "a square that looks like a magical stage set—all false perspectives and foreshortened buildings."

~Have cocktails at **Guitta's** (110 Sidi Bou Abib; 099.937.333), a seen-much-much-better-days bar, restaurant, and guesthouse. Try to get owner Mercedes Guitta talking; she happens to be one of the last conduits to Tangier's heyday as an International Zone.

~End the day in **El Minzah's Mirador bar** (85 Rue de la Liberté; 099.935.885) with a Barbara (vodka, crème de cacao, and crème fraîche), a cocktail named for Barbara Hutton.

Originally published in *Travel & Leisure,* February 1999 © 1999 American Express Publishing Corporation. All rights reserved.

A Cache of Roman Mosaics

BY NICHOLAS FOX WEBER

〜

editor's note

I realize that it isn't quite correct to identify Volubilis as a *city,* though it once was quite a thriving one, if far-flung from Rome. It's not only the site itself that is amazing but the countryside around it, with a view over to Moulay Idriss, which is what stays in my mind even more than the ruins. If you visit in the springtime, the hills all around will be a shade of green like you've never seen before. As some guidebook writers suggest, try to arrange a visit in the late afternoon, so that you can be there for the sunset. It is truly unforgettable, and at that time of day you may see, as I did, donkeys munching on sweet clover along the main "avenue" and local women filling big baskets with the herbs and wildflowers that grow among the stones.

NICHOLAS FOX WEBER is a cultural historian who writes about art and architecture.

Coming from any direction, travelers have a memorable first glimpse of Volubilis. Whether you approach this Roman city in Morocco from the exotic labyrinth of Fez, about an hour and a half away by car, or the bustling city of Meknès, a drive of half an hour, you spot the spectacular ruin first from a hilltop. Suddenly you see in the distance an agglomeration of columns and arches. This concentration of intensely civilized forms is on a high plateau surrounded on all four sides by land that drops down to a fertile river valley.

In her guidebook to Morocco written in 1925, Edith Wharton described this site: "After a time we left oueds and villages behind us and were in the mountains of the Rarb, toiling across a high sandy plateau. Far off a fringe of vegetation showed promise of shade and water, and at last, against a pale mass of olive-trees, we saw the sight which, at whatever end of the world one comes upon it, wakes the same sense of awe: the ruin of a Roman city."

Although the heyday of Volubilis was during the Roman Empire, its name is actually Arabic for "Castle of the Pharaohs." There had been a settlement on the spot ever since the Neolithic period, and the Berbers had built it into a significant town at the point when the Romans arrived in the last century B.C. The Emperor Augustus granted the Berber kingdom of Mauritania to King Juba II in 25 B.C., and by the year A.D. 1 Volubilis was the kingdom's western capital.

In 19 B.C. Juba married Cleopatra Silene, the daughter of Mark

Antony and Cleopatra, and under them and subsequent Roman leaders Volubilis prospered. It thrived as a granary and producer of olive oil for the empire, and as a base from which to control the rebellions of Berber tribes nearby. For centuries it remained a center of Roman culture and the largest city in Morocco, abandoned only after 787 when Moulay Idriss, a refugee from Arabia and the great-grandson of the prophet Muhammad, was acclaimed sultan there but decided to live elsewhere. With the rise of Islam, Volubilis was deserted and fell into decay.

For Edith Wharton this ancient place represented "a system, an order, a social conception that still run through our modern ways." But it had been recognizable as such for less than a decade; if she had arrived there ten years earlier, she would have found a pile of rubble.

When restoration by the French began in 1915, the city had been in ruins since the eighteenth century. Destruction had begun even before then; in the late 1600s, the Sultan Moulay Ishmael, known for the frequent arbitrary executions that marked his fifty-four-year reign of terror, needed its hard-core stone for foundations in the imperial city of Meknès. The Lisbon earthquake of 1755 pretty much finished Volubilis off. But an English antiquarian had made sketches there in 1722, which constituted a partial record. Moreover, the rubble contained some recognizable building remains, and a number of mosaics remained underneath them, facilitating restoration and reconstruction. French archaeologists discovered the site and started excavation and rebuilding in World War I, working on the project with the aid of German prisoners. The Moroccan government has been continuing excavations and restorations there ever since.

Never extensively publicized, not yet obscured by chain-link fence or an excess of souvenir stands, the sites of Volubilis are remarkable. There, on the floors of the houses of prestigious citizens, are mosaics of an earlier era. Austere, graceful, and articulate, these are sure reminders of why artists like Picasso turned to Classical art for a power and clarity they wished to inject into their own work. These Roman floors are surrounded by a city plan and the remains of buildings of equal intelligence and force.

Touring Volubilis today, you start at the original southeast gate. Whether you are with a tour group or on your own, you should have a guide; a number of available guides—both official and independent, and many who speak English—will invariably be waiting near the ticket office. He (the guides are all male) will lead you along a prescribed route: through an unexcavated quarter of the ruined city, past ancient stone olive presses, to the waist-high walls of the mansion called the House of Orpheus. Here you will see the first of the city's extraordinary mosaics, some of which date back close to the inception of this art form. Their multicolored tiles form into flowers under foot; they gyrate around one another as animated Arabic script and vibrant ornament on building walls. The precise geometry and rhythmic repetitions of those small pulsing squares are meant to invoke the order of the universe, to provide an antidote to the confusion of everyday living.

On one floor of the House of Orpheus, perfectly intact although surrounded by nothing but the remains of rough foundation walls, are nine mosaic dolphins. Their rendition is highly abstract, but their lithe, undulating forms make them seem alive in the water, which is suggested by jagged, wavy lines. The square sea is surrounded by a geometric design of interlocking circles and a diamond grid that recall the patterns of Berber carpets. On the floor of the atrium is a scene of Amphitrite, the sea goddess, pulled by a sea horse and accompanied by sea leopards. In the large dining room is the mosaic of Orpheus for which the house is now named. The central panel, framed by an eight-sided form made by gently curving tree branches, portrays the god playing his harp. The lovely foliage that surrounds him is filled with animals seduced by his music.

This is an artwork that warrants ample viewing time. The small, brightly colored mosaic tiles give each bird in Orpheus's audience its own distinct plumage. One has a sapphire breast and pale blue wings. Another is a mix of brilliant orange, brick red, and the blue of the desert sky. The profile of a dog enraptured by Orpheus's playing is, perhaps because of the limitations inherent in the medium, rendered rather crudely, almost in the style of children's art; but with its open mouth, wide eye, and eager stance, the animal makes its enchantment palpable. A monkey, seated with its elbows on its knees, looks out at us and points toward the toga-clad harpist, as if to say that music is a religion that we should all join.

A fascinating feature of the Orpheus house is the remnants of a kitchen with empty niches in which there were once statues representing the gods who kept food and drink from going bad. The various cooking and storage areas, the ice box, and the boiler room are difficult to discern without the guide indicating them, but fascinating to contemplate in this civilization that preceded ours by practically two millenniums. Next door are the ruins of public baths—enlarged and redecorated in 160–68 under orders from the Emperor Gallienus—that give yet another indication of everyday life here. This is in fact a *hammam*—a steam bath in which people lie on hot stones on the floor and are washed from buckets. If you are lucky, by the time you see the faded mosaics on the wall of this one, you will have discovered that the tradition of these *hammams* is still alive in modern Morocco. Like the mosaics, the *hammam* at Volubilis is the ancestor of more recent glories.

You walk through the main public spaces of the city and past its monumental buildings. They surround the forum, where public meetings were held and political speeches given. The statues that once lined this space are now elsewhere in Morocco, but one can envision the forum in use. Remains of the basilica—the courthouse—are nearby. So are the ruins of the capitol, a rectangular court marked by Corinthian columns, with a temple inside it. The temple, with its delicate pillars, was dedicated to Jupiter, Juno, and Minerva, the chief divinities of the state. The local officials would appeal to them here, at the sacrificial altar at the base of the temple steps, before declaring war or going into battle, or after returning from victory, when they would offer gold or other booty at the altar.

Next comes the triumphal arch, which in one direction faces the remnants of the broad Decumanus Maximus Avenue, the main byway of Volubilis, and on the other side opens to olive groves and rolling fields. Having survived the Lisbon earthquake with relatively little damage, the arch was the remainder of the original Roman city that inspired its excavation in 1915. Erected in 217 in honor of the Emperor Caracalla and his mother, Julia Domna, it is missing its top section but remains an impressive monument of large blocks of local stone. Simple and mathematically precise in its overall form, the arch has a wide opening capped with a perfect semicircle. Medallions, statues, and the remains of columns cover its walls.

A few minutes' walk from the triumphal arch, on the other side of town, stand the remains of the governor's palace, built in the third century with numerous courtyards and seventy-four rooms. And there are more fine mosaics in the ruins of other large neighboring houses. On the floor of the Knight's House is a vivid image of Bacchus—strong and lusty, his face and muscular body indicated crudely but vividly—discovering the sleeping Ariadne. Bacchus is aided by a winged Eros who has been largely destroyed, as has part of Ariadne's body. But in this image the shore at Naxos, where Ariadne is stretched out, is in excellent condition, and it remains a fine example of the eloquence of mosaics.

Nearby is the House of the Athlete, with another floor mosaic that is one of the glories of Volubilis. Guidebooks describe it in different ways. One calls it a depiction "of a sportsman who has won a cup for vaulting over a grey horse." Another characterizes it as an image of an "acrobat . . . who rides backwards on a horse." In any event, it depicts a horse strolling with its head down, mounted by a jubilant figure seated backward and looking toward us. The rider's face resembles, to an astounding degree, heads drawn by Picasso. Surrounded by a jubilant framework of intertwined lines and billowing curves, he conveys a spirit of sheer triumph.

The pleasures and skills that give luster to life in ancient Volubilis are remarkably like the prizes of our own era.

Visitor's Guide to Volubilis

There is no place to stay at Volubilis, but there is a café where lunch and snacks are served at low cost. There are also some souvenir stands selling fossils, locally made pottery for serving couscous, and other bits of handcraft.

The nearby town of Moulay Idriss, an ancient village and pilgrimage site, has a lively marketplace where a pot of mint tea and a lamb kebab grilled over an open charcoal fire cost about $2. (These might be especially welcome if you have visited Volubilis when it is windy and cold, as it was when we went in April.)

Most visitors will have come by taxi or bus from Meknès (half an hour) or Fez (hour and a half). A taxi from Fez costs about $75. Tour organizations run trips from hotels in Meknès and Fez for about $25.

Bibliothèque

Literary Trips: Following in the Footsteps of Fame, Victoria Brooks, editor, foreword by Paul Bowles, introduction by Bob Shacochis, GreatestEscapes.com Publishing, Vancouver, BC, 2000. Like my own *Collected Traveler* series, this unique book points readers in a number of directions, especially back to the works of fiction and nonfiction celebrated here. Also like my series, this book is not easy to categorize. Editor Brooks invited other writers to submit pieces on literary personalities who were or are inseparable from a particular locale in the world. Though those locales are on every continent, Brooks herself wrote the opening piece, appropriately enough on Paul Bowles and Tangier, which is why I've included the title in this section (other matches include Rohinton Mistry and Bombay, Tennessee Williams and New Orleans, Ernest Hemingway and Cuba, W. B. Yeats and Ireland, D. H. Lawrence and New Mexico, and American expatriates and Paris). At the end of each piece is "The Writer's Trail," a compendium of the locale's related literary landmarks, practical information, and a bibliography of books, films, and music.

Marrakesh: The Secret of Its Courtyard Houses, ACR Edition Internationale, Paris, 1999. If you will not be staying in a refurbished *riad* or *dar* in Marrakesh, and don't have an invitation to visit someone who is fortunate enough to live in one, you should at least turn the pages of this luscious book to see what you're missing. *Roud* (plural of *riad*) are rather plentiful in Marrakesh because plots of land are generally larger there than in other Moroccan cities and are therefore better suited to the occasionally immense size of *roud*. The photographs—which feature both public and private places—are gorgeous, and the text is remarkably informative for a coffee-table book. It's in English, by the way, in a slipcase cover.

Tangier and All That, Hugh Harter, Passegiata Press, 1993. This book is a little hard to find—I actually have only seen it in Morocco—but it's a good, quick read, much more chatty than Finlayson's book below. Bowles biographer Michelle Green once described Tangier as a place "where eccentricity was an asset," and all the eccentrics who ever set foot in Tangier are featured in these pages. It was in this book that I read one of my most favorite quotes, by author Angus Stewart (*Tangier: A Writer's Notebook,* a book I've heard about but have never read): "Whenever I could raise an air fare plus I left for Morocco."

Tangier: City of the Dream, Iain Finlayson, Flamingo, an imprint of HarperCollins U.K., London, 1992. Though this engrossing book has been referred to as "a masterpiece . . . of literary gossip" (it is), it's also an excellent account of the most famous city in Morocco. The initial chapter, "The International City," is not only a great overview of Tangier but mirrors the history of the country. Finlayson presents Tangier by tracing the lives of seven personalities of the city: Paul and Jane Bowles, William Burroughs, David Herbert, Joe Orton, Mohammed Choukri, and Mohammed Mrabet. I would venture to say that most readers, even if they think otherwise, dismiss Tangier too readily and do not really know its fascinating layers. To quote Finlayson, "Since Tangier has always been perceived as a territory at least on the edge of, if not beyond, the mundane world, it has been the victim of the myths, the fantasies, the dreams and ardent desires imposed upon it by its colonists. The result, of course, has been an irreparable fragmentation of the city's character. Required to satisfy—satiate—the infantile, polymorphous perversities of so many, Tangier has remained formless, eternally embryonic, never fully able to mature. Like a brain perplexed by too many conflicting demands, or like a computer fed with a mass of conflicting data, it has often been rendered inert, passive at best, at worst seized by intermittent fevers in its struggles to distinguish priorities. For the likes of Mrabet, Choukri, and many other natives of the city, the world comes inevitably to Tangier: what need is there to travel elsewhere? For most, like the Tangier-born but now Paris-based novelist Tahar ben Jelloun, the end result of travel is simply a comparison of the mother city with cities elsewhere, rarely to the detriment of Tangier." If you're going to read only one book on Tangier, make it this one.

A Year in Marrakesh, Peter Mayne, drawings by Ronald, Baillie, Eland Books, London, and Hippocrene Books, New York, 1982; first published by John Murray as *The Alleys of Marrakesh,* 1953. I love this book so much that I wanted to write something about it that would *ensure* readers would want to track it down immediately. But what I just wrote was pure over-the-top gushing, so much so that I decided you wouldn't believe me, so I am merely sharing one of the endorsements from the back cover, which is really much better than I can express myself: "A notable book, for the author is exceptional both in his literary talent and his outlook. His easy economical style seizes, with no sense of effort, the essence of people, situations and places. . . . Mr. Mayne is that rare thing, a natural writer . . . no less exceptional is his humour. Few Westerners have written about Islam with so little nonsense and such understanding." That's from *The Times Literary Supplement* in London, and I think you'll agree.

TANGER · ALGECIRAS

CARTE D'EMBARQUEMENT
TARJETA DE EMBARQUE
BOARDING CARD

2eme CLASSE

Serie V

1946

CACHET DATE ET HEURE

Au Delà des Villes
(Beyond the Cities)

"Beyond the cities is the other Morocco. It lives in the red stone, in the sky swept by scudding clouds, in the eyes of men whose memories run deep. The other Morocco turns its back on the cities, though its men and women, made desperate by drought and want, may leave the mountain to lose some of the dignity in the wide streets of the asphalt towns. The Moroccan population is largely rural, but many of today's city folk are yesterday's peasants and mountain dwellers. There is no frontier between town and country, not even a symbolic one. The lure of the city is strong, but despite everything, the mountain man, whether from the Rif or the Atlas, has not forsaken his roots. Even when he descends into the city, he retains his habits, his customs, and his language."

—Tahar Ben Jelloun, from the Introduction to
MOROCCO: SAHARA TO THE SEA

On Track in Morocco

BY MALCOLM W. BROWNE

∽

editor's note

Though this article appeared in 1987, there is much practical information about the southeastern portion of Morocco—the predesert as it's often called—that is still useful and àpropos. An added note about provisions: think ahead about your culinary desires. It has been my experience that, while you may pass several small restaurants and cafés when you enter a village, you may not want to eat at any of them, and if you then decide to buy some snacks to hold you over until the next village, all you may find is candy, bottled water, fresh bread (the only item I ever chose), yogurt (but you need a spoon to eat it), and some junk food. It's a good idea to ask the inn where you've been staying to pack you a little lunch before setting off, or allow for time to do some shopping at the *marché* or souk.

MALCOLM W. BROWNE is a science writer for *The New York Times* and a former foreign correspondent.

There's a delicious scariness about skirting the fringes of a great desert. The feeling has something in common with riding a roller coaster or making faces at a caged tiger: one can savor the proximity of danger without actually having to confront it. When an unwary visitor or downed aviator is truly snared in the death grip of a major desert, of course, survival is no joke. The Atacama of Chile and Peru, the Gobi of Inner Mongolia, and Antarctica's Polar Plateau, for instance, are among Mother's Earth's celebrated killers. Even in an age of spotter satellites and rescue helicopters, the wise traveler treats any desert with the utmost respect.

But by driving along the Moroccan perimeter of the Sahara, a moderately venturesome tourist can enjoy the stark beauty of a sea of pink sand in safety and considerable luxury. Nothing can quite compare with the setting; Lawrence of Arabia and many another desert campaigner have waxed poetic over the subtle tints and shadows, the bloodred sunrises and sunsets, the alternation of roaring winds with utter stillness.

Most of Morocco's visitors, intimidated by tales about the language barrier, highway banditry, and other real or imaginary problems seem attracted to the supposed security afforded by organized tours. Whatever their merits, such tours are not for people who like to explore on their own. Luckily, the traveler seeking communion with the desert can get along without joining a group and even without the ministrations of a private guide.

The most interesting way to get around Morocco is by driving, as my wife and I did on a recent sixteen-day visit, and a road tour is likely to begin in Casablanca. The only nonstop air route to Morocco from the United States is via Royal Air Maroc, which makes two flights a week from New York to Casablanca. The round trip can cost less than $600, which makes flights in both directions so popular they are usually fully booked weeks in advance. No visa is required for stays of less than three months.

I have found it almost impossible to get a confirmed hotel reservation anywhere in Morocco, but this hardly seems to matter. Even when there is no room at the inn, desk clerks are generally willing to help find accommodations elsewhere, especially if they perceive a tip in the offing.

The first move after stepping off the trans-Atlantic flight is to rent a car, and plenty are available at Moroccan and American agencies in the larger towns. Four-wheel-drive vehicles are recommended (at steep rates) for cruising the unpaved *pistes,* or tracks, that crisscross the desert, but for the somewhat better surfaced roads that lead to most of the interesting places, the Renault 4 is fine. This ubiquitous little vehicle is the cheapest rental car in

Morocco, and in my experience it is less likely to get stuck in sand or mud than heavier cars. A driver quickly becomes accustomed to its bouncy ride and the awkward four-speed gearshift protruding from its dashboard. (The cost of our Renault for two weeks was $793, including mileage charge—we drove 2,200 miles—insurance of $8 a day, and 19 percent tax.)

The purchase of modest provisions for a desert sojourn makes sense, just in case. The main item on the shopping list should be a six-pack of liter bottles of mineral water. The traveler will probably never need them for survival, but long drives in a dry desert are thirsty work. Bottled water is available at shops and souks in almost all villages, or, more expensively, from hotel dining rooms. Canned snacks are nice for hunger pangs, although any largish town is likely to have at least one European-style restaurant.

A good road map bought before starting out is indispensable, although even the best maps tend to be out of date and flawed. When in doubt about a direction, it is best to ask someone. Most innkeepers and filling-station operators speak some English or French, as do policemen in large towns. The people I encountered along rural roads, however, spoke only Arabic or one of the Berber dialects.

One situation to avoid is getting stuck in sand. Many roads close to the desert abut on dunes, and sand often drifts across sections of pavement or gravel. The sand flows like water and is as slippery as ice. If a driver spots a tongue of sand covering a piece of road ahead, the best course is to maintain speed and coast over it. Once a car's driving wheels are resting on Sahara sand, getting started again will depend upon the availability of willing hands and a robust pusher.

Mechanical problems can often be mended at village garages with only minor delays. The exhaust pipe of my car blew out during our trip, resulting in an ear-splitting racket for the next sixty miles. But at a workshop near the night's resting place, an expert mechanic put things right with a brazing torch in just over an hour, and charged $15.

Between Casablanca and Morocco's desert frontier with Algeria lie the Atlas Mountains and some of the most spectacular canyons, bluffs, and badlands east of Arizona. Sedimentary formations in the Atlas range date from the Cretaceous period, and roadside entrepreneurs entice drivers to buy rocks, geodes, and fossils, particularly those of the extinct spiraled shellfish called the ammonite. Unfortunately, the rock dealers usually grind down and shine their ammonites to a high polish, and this process destroys most of the fossils' scientific value.

Generally, the easiest routes to the desert run eastward from Ouarzazate through the Draa Valley to Zagora, or southward from Ar-Rachidia through the Ziz Valley to Erfoud. Between Zagora and Erfoud, a distance of about 130 miles, the roads or tracks are steeped in sandy solitude. One minor irritant stems from the fact that the border between Morocco and Algeria is ill-defined and disputed. For more than a decade, Algerian-backed Polisario guerrillas have occasionally clashed with Moroccan troops in the Western Sahara south of Morocco, although no blood has been spilled in recent years. Military checkpoints have been established along some roads.

Zagora is billed as the gateway to the desert, but the driver who heads south of Zagora toward an oasis called M'hamid soon finds himself up against a roadblock. The none-too-friendly sentinel who mans this checkpoint will demand to see a *laissez-passer* issued by regional authorities in Zagora. If the traveler doesn't happen to have one, he can always drive back along thirty-odd miles of bad road to Zagora, but if it is a weekend or holiday or lunch break, all official offices will be closed. In practice, the only expeditious way to get past the checkpoint is to hire a guide in Zagora, who is likely to be one of the desert tribesmen called Blue Men (so called because they wear bright blue caftans). Miraculously, my guide obtained the necessary travel document in next to no time, and when a Blue Man is riding in the back seat, no car will be held up for long by any sentinel.

The guide charged about $10 for the few hours he accompanied the car, but, as often happens, it was not easy to end the association. The guide had a brother or cousin who wanted to invite us for refreshments, and the invitation was couched in such terms as to be difficult to resist. The relative turned out to be an aggressive rug merchant. Disentanglement from one of these hard-sell situations can sometimes lead to sharp words.

The hotels in Zagora, while offering somewhat unpolished service, are comfortable and modern. The Reda, for example, is new and has gigantic swimming pools bounded by lush gardens, floodlit palm trees, tiled fountains, old-style Arabic gazebos, flocks of songbirds, and attentive waiters. A room here costs about $50 a day. In Erfoud, another hub of desert tourism, the Hotel Sijilmassa (telephone, 80; room rates, about $70 a day) overlooks a hamlet whose vegetable plots, pathways, yards, and cemetery are gradually being inundated by drifting sand. As the recorded prayer of a muezzin booms from the loudspeakers of a minaret, the traveler can watch a glorious sunset from the hotel's splendid pool.

Life in the wretched, sand-blasted hamlet is hard and getting harder. A foreigner watching from the hotel ramparts may be struck by the disquieting gulf between luxury and poverty in this part of the world. Then again, the Sahara has always been a land of extremes, and its beauty, at least, is there for all.

Into Berber Country

By Steven A. Holmes

∽

editor's note

....

This is a very good piece about exploring the south of Morocco, and I would remind readers that, as the author notes, "the drives to Morocco's south are long." Plan accordingly.

Steven A. Holmes is a reporter in the Washington, D.C., bureau of *The New York Times*.

A broiling sun cooked the mélange of cars, buses, trucks, donkey carts, mopeds, and taxis as our minivan maneuvered its way out of Fez. We were headed south on Highway P-24 toward the Middle Atlas Mountains and the desert beyond. Having pampered ourselves in Fez at the luxurious Palais Jamai and tasted the exotic centuries-old flavor of the labyrinthine medina, we were off to the countryside in search of new adventures.

In a country as varied as Morocco, there is plenty to see beyond the well-trod sidewalks and narrow alleyways of the imperial cities Tangier, Fez, and Marrakesh. So during a family vacation to Morocco in August, we took three days to explore the south, an arid and rugged land with sandstone hills and steep-walled valleys, and whose Berber populations have at times been quite separate from the rest of the country.

The drives to Morocco's south are long—eight hours from Fez to Erfoud. And with the exception of Ouarzazate, the south's major urban center, accommodations tend to be spare, especially as you get closer to the desert. But if you're game, a trip to the south will yield spectacular vistas of ruggedly beautiful countryside and the serenity of Saharan landscapes.

Getting around Morocco is relatively easy. The country has a good road network that includes superhighways, mainly in the north, and two-lane roads in the southern reaches. My wife, Marian, my fourteen-year-old daughter, Jenny, and I traveled with friends, a family of four from Washington. Given the size of our party and the distances involved, we hired a minivan with a driver and a guide, all for $200 a day. Split between two families that was only slightly more than renting two cars and paying roughly $3 a gallon for gasoline.

About an hour outside Fez, the road lurched sharply upward, the air cooled considerably, and the landscape became more lush as we entered the Middle Atlas Mountains. We drove through serene apple orchards, terraced farms, and dense forests of red and green cedars, evergreen boughs etched across a blue skyline. Nestled on hillsides were mud-walled Berber houses recognizable by their low doors. According to our guide, thirty-six-year-old Jawad Lahani, this was a vestige of ancient times, when you wanted anyone venturing inside to stoop low and be defenseless, in case it was an enemy.

Mr. Lahani is a slender, internationally trained economist from Fez who has been leading tours, large and small, for five years. He often remarked that Morocco was a country of sharp contrasts. If Fez resembles Morocco of the twelfth century, Ifrane, with its sharply peaked red-tile roofs suggests Switzerland at the beginning of the twenty-first. This city, about an hour and a half south of Fez, is the center of Morocco's skiing industry and has a cosmopolitan air.

When we stopped in Ifrane for a break, we wandered into a small restaurant that served sweet chocolate pastries and strong Moroccan coffee. The staff took orders in French and Arabic while the sounds of Natalie Cole crooning American ballads drifted from speakers.

Back on the road, we kept a sharp eye on the forests, hoping to catch a glimpse of a troop of Barbary apes. These rare tailless macaques, about the size of small chimpanzees, and found in Morocco, Algeria, and Gibraltar, are reportedly highly sociable and do not shy away from human contact.

Our search of the cedar boughs turned up no sign of the creatures, but as we stopped at a scenic overlook to take pictures, a brown Barbary ape leaped through the van's open door, startling everyone. She was the domesticated pet of a roadside vendor, and her name was Linda. She was quite tame and jumped into the laps of several of my traveling companions, contentedly picking at them, probably looking for a succulent insect or two.

We rummaged around in the cooler we kept in the back and found a banana for Linda. This turned out to be a big mistake. Happy to have found a steady source of food, she settled in and showed no inclination of wanting to leave the van. Finally, her master persuaded her by brandishing a stick in her direction. Linda beat a huffy retreat, showing her disdain by displaying her rump in our direction as she ambled away.

Coming out of the Middle Atlas Mountains, we sped along a high rocky plateau in a countryside resembling southern Utah. Rocky sandstone hills loomed in the distance, and after a few hours the Ziz River cut dramatic gorges in the high desert landscape. At the bottom of the gorges, an oasis that stretched for miles provided a welcome streak of green.

We pulled into a parking lot in the dusty city of Erfoud, and out of the Café des Dunes bounded Seddik Ettaiek, who was to be our guide for the next two days in the Sahara. Smiling broadly, he displayed stained teeth and what we soon learned was his normal sunny disposition.

We left our van and piled into two rented Land Rovers. Seddik wrapped his head in a blue silk scarf and climbed behind the wheel of one Land Rover with the three children and one adult; the rest of us rode in the other with another guide, Ahmed, who wore the flowing blue robes of the Tuareg people.

We headed toward Merzouga, a tiny village in the southeastern corner of Morocco that abuts Erg Chebbi, Morocco's only genuine Saharan *erg,* or dunes. The undulating hills of sugar-fine sand rise to four hundred feet and go on for miles in frozen brown waves, looking just as one would imagine when conjuring up images of the Sahara.

Some guidebooks, notably Lonely Planet, suggest that you can drive yourself to Merzouga. I recommend against it. The paved road peters out about six miles outside Erfoud. The rest of the way has to be negotiated over a moonscape of black shale that covers dangerously soft sand, best left to four-wheel-drive vehicles and expert drivers. The Land Rovers cost only $50 each for two days, and that included the driver. They were worth every penny.

About forty-five minutes into the desert we came upon a minivan stuck up to its axles. Our drivers stopped and, with the van's driver, tried to push it and its occupants—an elderly woman holding an infant—out of its trap. But the van only sank deeper into the sand. Meanwhile, several other Land Rovers, each full of tourists, sped by, not even slowing down to see if they could help.

Finally, someone produced a coil of rope, hardly more than twine. It seemed too fragile to be of much use. But Seddik and Ahmed fastened one end to the rear of the van and the other to the front of one of the Land Rovers. This time, Michael, the father of the other family we were with, and I put our shoulders into it. With all of us straining, the Land Rover pulling hard, and the van driver gunning his engine in reverse, the vehicle suddenly lurched free.

"Ahmed," I said in my rusty French after we resumed our trip, "why didn't the other Land Rovers stop to help?" They were guides from other places, said Ahmed, who was raised in the desert, and they did not appreciate the rigors of the Sahara. "They are not desert people," he said.

In Merzouga, we hopped aboard camels and, led by guides, rode out into the dunes. The sun was setting and the temperature had dropped considerably. Except for our own voices, not a sound could be heard. We spotted a few other tourists off in the distance walking among the rolling sand hills, but for the most part, there were no other signs of life. We were enveloped by a sense of timelessness, aware that the vistas we looked at had not changed from the time when they were crossed by caravans loaded with spices, gold, and indigo.

We stayed that night at the Auberge Kasbah Tombouctou Hotel, a collection of adobe buildings at the edge of the dunes. The rooms were clean but basic and, without air conditioning, sweltering. But at $15 a person, including breakfast and dinner, the price was hard to beat.

The place was also lively. Seddik, in addition to arranging and driving the Land Rovers, ran the hotel. His staff cooked a savory lamb *tagine*—the classic Moroccan stew—and he and others on the staff entertained the guests, playing drums and a banjo and singing Berber songs. Unable to resist the intoxicating rhythms, patrons, including a group of French students and Marian, were soon on their feet dancing.

Exhausted, I left the party and went to bed. But sleep was impossible in the stifling rooms. So the hotel staff set up beds on the roof, where we were cooled by desert breezes and slept under a canopy of stars and an incandescent full moon.

Southern Morocco is also known for its *ksors* (walled towns) and its casbahs (fortified dwellings that had been the homes of the gentry or local chieftains). Most that we passed as we drove northwest from Erfoud toward Ouarzazate (pronounced *WAHR-zah-zaht*) were modest one- or two-story affairs. Then there was Tifoultoute.

This casbah, three miles north of Ouarzazate, epitomizes Morocco's turbulent history. It was once owned by the Glaoui family, a colorful dynasty that ruled large stretches of southern Morocco and whose power sometimes rivaled the king's. In the 1950s, Pasha Thami al-Glaoui, the last of the line, conspired with the French to deport King Muhammad V, who had been agitating for independence. After independence, the Glaouis tumbled from power, and the casbah at Tifoultoute fell in disrepair.

Poised on a small hill, with a commanding view of the Ouarzazate Valley, the casbah presented two faces. One was of pitted mud walls that were crumbling from years of neglect. The other was a restored portion of the fortress whose pink walls were rising from decay. We climbed to the battlements and gazed out on the broad valley below, marveling at the huge nests that storks had built atop the towers.

Inside was the large central room where the pasha received visitors and supplicants. We lingered amid the plush pillows and white-washed walls hung with Berber muskets in the rooms off the large chamber, where his four wives entertained guests. Close your eyes, and you could imagine the power and intrigues of this court.

If the intrigues of the Glaouis seem made for a Hollywood script, Ait Benhaddou, just west of Ouarzazate, offers a perfect setting—so much so that the dramatic mud-walled town has been used in location shots for a number of movies, including *Gladiator*. Considered one of the finest examples of a Moroccan *ksor*, this ancient village has been declared a World Heritage Site by UNESCO.

To reach it on its steep hill, visitors cross a river bed, dry when we were there. Once inside its walls, we wandered the narrow streets and, along with our guide, were invited inside a Berber home.

The occupants—one of the few families actually living there—were shy about allowing us to take their pictures but permitted us to explore their dwelling and offered us almonds. Their hospitality was typical of what we found in southern Morocco, and it beckoned us to return.

Driving South to Casbahs and Saharan Dunes

In southern Morocco, with the exception of Ouarzazate, accommodations can be somewhat spare. It is best to make sure you have places reserved, rather than just taking a chance on what you might find.

Travel agents in the United States specializing in Morocco can be very useful. You can get a list of agents by contacting the Moroccan National Tourist Office, 20 East 46th Street, Suite 1201, New York, NY 10017; 212-557-2520; fax 212-949-8148.

We used one of those agents, Sarah Tours, 1803 Belleview Boulevard, Suite A1, Alexandria, VA 22307; 800-267-0036; fax 703-765-7809; www.sarahtours.com. They provided ground transportation, including a driver and a guide, and can also handle accommodations. Sarah Tours also offered to provide Land Rovers into the desert and a hotel there, though we found both on our own.

One thing to keep in mind. Telephone calls to Morocco from the United States (the country code is 212) are expensive, so it might be more economical to arrange your trip through stateside agents.

Our desert hotel and car were provided by the Ettaiek brothers, who operate the Auberge Kasbah Tombouctou in Merzouga. They can be contracted through the Café des Dunes in Erfoud, 055.57.67.93; fax 055.77.765.

The hotel is cheap—$15 a person a night, at 11 *dirhams* to the dollar, including breakfast and dinner—but also clean and with a friendly staff. The employees' English is pretty basic, so it helps to know a few French phrases.

There are only a few hotels in Ait Benhaddou. We stayed at the Hotel Restaurant La Kasbah, 044.89.03.02, which charges $23 a night for a double room. Like the Tombouctou, La Kasbah is not air-conditioned, and for good measure, the electricity is turned off at 10 P.M., though candles are provided. Perhaps its best feature is its chilly swimming pool, which provides a refreshing dip after a day in the heat.

Admission to the Tifoultoute casbah, near Ouarzazate, is roughly $1. For information, contact the tourist office in Ouarzazate, 044.88.24.85.

Glory in a Camel's Eye

BY JEFFREY TAYLER

~

editor's note

Just as I discovered an article by writer Jeffrey Tayler at the eleventh hour into my Provence manuscript, I discovered this one, too, at the last minute. (It was, I'm sorry to admit, buried within a tower of "to be filed" papers that fortunately fell over or I never would have found it in time.)

JEFFREY TAYLER lives in Russia and contributes frequently to *Harper's* magazine. He is also the author of *Facing the Congo* (Ruminator Books, 2000, hardcover; Three Rivers Press, 2001, paperback) and *Siberian Dawn: A Journey Across the New Russia* (Ruminator Books, 1999).

The two camels tread ahead of me, their soft, splayed hooves padding into the ocher-colored earth. A perfume of wild mint and orange blossoms sweetens the air. Dates hang from the palms in bushels of gold and tarnished bronze. Pomegranates, ripening, drop to the ground and split, spilling their rubied innards onto the oasis floor, and fresh water burbles through the irrigation channels. With the rhythmic gait of the camels, I'm growing pleasantly intoxicated, and my thoughts meander. Remembered fragments from a chapter of the Koran echo in my mind: "O which of your Lord's bounties will both of you deny? . . . Green, green Pastures . . . therein two fountains of gushing water . . . therein fruits and palm trees and pomeg ᴐnates . . . O which of your Lord's bounties will both of you deny?" The words describe the gardens of Paradise that God promises to the faithful in the afterlife, but I feel as though I'm walking through them now.

The lead camel bellows and my reverie ends. Omar, an 'Areeb cameleer in his late forties, yanks on the reins as the beast digs in its hooves, fearful of attempting, with its broad load, the narrow break in the straw fence. Ali, my guide, dressed in an indigo robe, his head wrapped in a black *chêche,* or cotton turban, sets about widening the opening; the camel negotiates a passage. Omar and I follow on foot, leaving the shade of the oasis, and emerge onto the desert tableland by the Drâa River. Mount Zagora rises ahead of us, a black anvil against a sky of white-hot glare.

I've come to southern Morocco to fulfill a dream I've nursed since living in Marrakech as a Peace Corps volunteer a decade ago: to travel by camel through the oases of the Drâa Valley and out into the Sahara. I'd felt my experience of the country had been too urban, too full of souks and merchants, when what had originally drawn me to life in North Africa and the study of Arabic was the desert. By traveling down the Drâa Valley, I would, finally, meet Arabs in terrain they had mastered, terrain that, I had read, brought out the best in people by forcing them to work together to survive. In a land of such scarcity, there is no other way to get by.

The valley begins, steep and narrow, near the town of Ouarzazate. Some forty miles to the south, on the way to Zagora, it widens into a green sea of date palms under which Arabs and Berbers till the oasis loam. The Sarhro and Bani mountain ranges— Saharan massifs of stark rock and no shade—spread to the east and west, alternating with dunes and stretches of hammada, desert tableland. For the next two weeks I will traverse this terrain as a *rahhaal* (plural, *ruhhaal*), as Bedouins are known in North Africa, with Ali, an Arab from the *rahhaal* 'Areeb tribe (the 'Areeb are among the most renowned of the caravaneers). I've chosen a route that will take us from Zagora south, through the oasis Casbahs of Ignaouen and Aït Isfoul, over the pass of Mount Beni Selmane, and east to the great dunes of Chagaga. Beyond Chagaga the Drâa goes on to meet the Atlantic, but we plan to loop back around and conclude our 190-mile peregrination where Morocco ends—at the settlement of M'hamid.

I recall the day I met Ali in the Drâa two years ago, a day of burning winds, roiling sands, and 125-degree heat. With a *rahhaal* youth as a guide, I had set out on a short drive along a *piste,* or desert track, when one of the worst *sharqis* (sand-laden winds from the east) in years struck and disoriented him. We got lost searching for the road to M'hamid and for five hours trundled this way and that over the hammada in a brownout of choking dust. Finally, when we were low on fuel, with our radiator punctured by a rock and no drinking water left, we came upon Ali's tent and were saved; he gave us shelter and later guided us safely back to M'hamid. For his knowledge of the land, I've asked him to accompany me now. No matter how idyllic its oases, the Sahara is a domain where the fury of the elements may gather without warning, where one survives by expertise, stamina, and, at times, God's will alone.

Late in the afternoon, we camp on the hammada by a lone acacia tree, a gnarled skeleton of bark, thorns, and leafless branches.

The sun slips behind the horizon, loosing a fan of gold and red beams into the cirrus clouds, and shadows fall over the ruined Casbah of Aït Isa Brahim, to our north. Omar produces a satchel of dates—"God's gift," he calls them. "They have salt, water, sugar, and vitamins. In the Sahara you need nothing more." They are *boufeggou* dates—the sweetmeat of the desert—and they taste as rich as baklava.

For hundreds of years, trade caravans bearing salt set out from the Drâa for sub-Saharan Africa; they returned laden with spices, gold, ivory, and slaves, and the Casbahs of the valley thrived. Indeed, these elaborate fortified clay villages that stand above the palms look the same now as they would have centuries ago—like palaces out of *The Thousand and One Nights*. Intertribal warfare was common, however, and in the eighteenth century Aït Isa Brahim was destroyed in a raid. Today, only broken columns and a jumbled cemetery remain here.

The west is now flushed with the violet of dusk. We're stretched out on blankets, our faces lit a trembling pale yellow by the flame of the portable gas stove. The kettle hisses. Ali opens it and drops in a chunk of sugar, pours tea into his glass, then pours it back into the kettle—the timeless ritual of the Moroccan tea service. But this isn't the mint tea drunk in the rest of the country; rather, it's a bitter khaki green potion that, to my palate at least, has little appeal.

"We used to lead the caravans across the sands to Timbuktu," Ali says. "There are places on the way where no man can go, where the wells are salty and vipers and scorpions cover the ground." He sips the tea, finding it sugared to his taste, then commences pouring, holding the kettle a foot above our glasses to give the brew the required head. "But the caravans stopped in the 1950s, with borders being established. Now only the old men remember the route, and they are fewer and fewer."

We dine on meat and vegetable stew and retire to the blankets and sleeping bags we have spread on the hammada. There is no moon. The sky is an indigo *chêche* studded with diamond stars.

At dawn we awaken to a woolly gray sky betokening a hot day. With shouts of *"Utsh! Utsh!"* Omar coaxes the camels to their knees. He and Ali hoist saddlebags onto the animals' backs and begin loading them with sacks of rice, canned goods, bottles of cooking oil and bleach, bags of tomatoes, lanterns, and jerry cans of water we have brought with us from Zagora—everything, in short, that the *ruhhaal* carry with them on their wanderings around the Sahara.

One of the camels roars and moans with every added item. Omar pats his side. "His name is Sahl [Easy], though he's anything but." With his torn left nostril, his hollering, and his habit of vomiting when angry, Sahl is tough to envision as one of the loyal ships of the desert on which the *ruhhaal* have always depended. Fed up with the tightening ropes, Sahl lunges for Omar, who laughs and lets the beast's ivory teeth graze his arm.

"Oh, Sahl, *miskeen* [poor thing]! Always complaining. Someone must have beaten you when you were little."

"Aren't you afraid he'll bite you?" I ask.

"Afraid?" He wrestles Sahl's spittle-encrusted maw toward his face and plants a kiss on his blubbery lips. *"Miskeen!"*

I climb into the saddle. Omar instructs me to hold tight to the wooden bar that serves as a pommel.

"Gum, aa Sahl, gum!"

Sahl straightens his hind legs. I lurch forward so violently that I nearly fly over his neck.

"Gum! Gum!"

Sahl then straightens his front legs, and I jerk backward. A further shake or two and he's up, bellowing and baring his teeth. Omar grabs the reins and leads the way, and with Ali we're off across the hammada.

Evening finds us camped in the wadi, or seasonal riverbed, at Anagam Pass, between walls of granite. During the night, there are scuffling sounds all around us—I take my flashlight and have a look. I find nothing, but in the morning the sands are embroidered with scarab tracks, with the slithering trails of snakes, the scratchy indentations of scorpions, the hip-hop paw prints of hares and rabbits, and the stealthy marks of desert foxes.

The next day, late in the afternoon, we catch sight of the saffron-hued battlements and crooked towers of Ignaouen, a wealthy Casbah that dominates the heart of the Drâa oasis. Children pour forth from the alleys, pounding tambourines, chanting *"'Aash al-jamalayn! 'Aash al-jamalayn!"* ("Long live the two camels!")—a refrain once sung to caravans arriving from the Sahara. Women stream past us in black shawls brocaded around the edges with the floral patterns of their tribes. Men in white turbans and blue robes hail us with *"As-salam alaykum!"* ("May peace be upon you!") We're on our way to the house of Ali's friend Driss, who lives in the Casbah of Aït Isfoul. Here, the Casbahs flow into one another, following the river.

The sun sets and the wind picks up. We emerge from the narrow lanes of Ignaouen and find more Casbahs, each a maze of lanes ending in gates and more lanes. This isn't a road Ali and Omar travel often, so we have to ask the way. Women turn their faces to the wall or scurry away as our caravan lumbers near, but men stop and shout directions over the wind.

We enter the oasis again. Now, above Mount Bani, leviathans of brown haze are churning and tumbling, splitting apart and mating like giant amoebas in the sky. Ali points to them. "A sandstorm!

Yallah, let's go!" A few minutes later a hot wind whooshes upon us, and I close my eyes against the assault of stinging sand. In the brownout I begin coughing; Ali and Omar breathe easily, their mouths and noses protected by *chêches.* My *chêche,* thin as it is, suffocates me, and I can't wear it. We slip downward into a milky haze, and I fall forward in my saddle. We've blundered upon dunes, and their undulations are invisible in the dark. With the assault of the sand and the rigors of the day's travel, I feel suddenly, painfully, fatigued. Then the wind dies, the sands settle, and we find ourselves, finally, beneath the high ramparts of Aït Isfoul.

Driss, a lanky Berber in his twenties, lives in a typical Drâa house consisting of a broad courtyard floored with packed earth and here and there strewn with cushions. It's open to the skies; on the sides are high-ceilinged chambers into which personal effects are moved during bad weather. The roof belongs to the women—there they socialize and do laundry. During the summer, the family sleeps under the stars to catch the breeze. Casbah life is lived alfresco for all but a few inclement days of the year.

Observing the Islamic customs of segregating the sexes, the women of Driss's family have sequestered themselves in a relative's house while we men prepare a meal. In the courtyard we gather around the *tagine* bowl, using shards of pita bread to scoop up chunks of chicken and rice. Afterward, Omar makes countless kettles of tea, and Driss's friends, all unemployed Berber youths, drop in to visit, greeting each of us with a soft handshake followed by a customary tap on the heart. Except for the oasis farmers, not many in Aït Isfoul have jobs. Many survive on income sent from relatives working in Marrakech or Casablanca. A few hours later, the guests depart, and we spread our blankets and turn in to the sound of palms soughing in the oasis.

～

"Haaw! Haaw!"

It is morning, and Driss is shouting. He flings open the doors to one of the side rooms and thumps the walls with a piece of wood. A rumble of hooves follows, and goats and sheep spill out, stampeding for the courtyard gate; they will spend the day foraging in the oasis. In the Drâa, people share their homes with their animals, if they're lucky enough to have any.

After a breakfast of bread, fresh honey, and bitter tea, we load the camels and Driss guides us to the path south. There we take our leave of him and make our way into the oasis, ambling through pools of shadow and puddles of sun, the scent of melons and dates on the air, the mists of dawn soothing our dry skin.

The slopes of Mount Bani are evenly grooved, as if they'd been plowed into rows for cultivation. *"Masalik,"* says Ali, as we ascend. Pathways. "For a thousand years our caravans passed along these *masalik,* wearing down the earth, making these grooves." They run clear up to Beni Selmane Pass. Omar stoops now and again to toss aside a stone, doing his share of the millennial labor.

We reach the pass. Ahead of us, the lowering sun floods the *masalik* with red and gold. Volcanic mountains rise above a sea of hammada pale with washes of sand in some places, dark with basalt rubble in others, and girded on the west by more oases. Ali gestures with his staff.

"There are the tents."

"Where?"

In the murk subsuming the hammada I can discern nothing but the contours of dunes.

We are all on foot now. We start down the mountainside, each of us guided by his own groove, each of us lost in thought and soaking up the cool of twilight. The firmament melts from azure to purple to cobalt; the earth seems to fall from under our feet as we descend; we're floating down through the dusk. The world empties and in the void anything becomes possible. Ali is loping ahead, his *chêche* trailing behind him, a hooded silhouette under the Milky Way. Omar lags somewhere behind.

Finally, pinpoints of light twinkle in the murk—the tents. A couple of hours later we reach them; they are three roped-together patchwork affairs of coarse sheeting, animal hide, and wooden beams. Four young men who look after the tents, tend the camels, and cook for the tourists Ali occasionally brings on desert treks throw out carpets for us at the edge of the dunes. They putter around, bringing us water and making us tea, but there is only one lantern lit, and to me they seem like roving shadows on the sand. This area is called Erg Lihoudi (Dune of the Jew)—legend has it that a Jewish man died here. The *ruhhaal* often name places after the dead, honoring them, investing otherwise lifeless corners of rock and sand with a comforting semblance of human spirit.

I remember coming upon Erg Lihoudi in the sandstorm and feeling saved. Now the skies are quiet, and the camp promises respite from the rigors of walking and riding; again I greet it with relief.

At sunrise the wind drives sand through the porous walls of my tent, which sieve the grains onto my face, into my mouth, and over my eyelids until I cough myself awake and crawl out of my sleeping bag. Again Erg Lihoudi is being hit by a gale from the east, a *sharqi* purveying the torrid wastes of Algeria, Mali, and Niger, very much like the one when I first met Ali. Outside, the camels sit like dark ships on an ocean of white, whirling sand.

I get up and run outside, head down, shielding my eyes with my hands, to the kitchen tent. There, Ali and I breakfast on tea and *shihma* (sheaths of pita filled with saffron, egg, and onions). Ali tells me he received a degree from the University of Marrakech, but he found nothing good in city life, so he returned to the Drâa to tend his herds. Droughts made animal husbandry unprofitable, however, and he became an official *guide du tourisme*. His 'Areeb workers recline around us, listening. Out of respect they say nothing, their faces covered in *chêches*, oblivious to the sand penetrating the tent, to the flies crawling over every patch of exposed skin.

When the wind dies down, the cook digs a hole in the sand, fills it with embers, and bakes *m'lla*, "bread of the sands," for our trip the next morning.

During the night, Ali develops a fever and chills. A cut on his foot has become severely infected, and he will have to visit a doctor in the settlement of Tagounite some ten miles away. He appoints Mustafa, a Berber *rahhaal* from Morocco's eastern deserts, to take his place. Mustafa, Omar, and I depart shortly after dawn. Beni Selmane and Bani jut up to the north, their razor ridges cutting into the steel sheet of the sky. Mustafa is more talkative than Ali. He tells me about his home and family in the eastern desert region of Merzouga, which he left five years ago in search of work. He is curious to hear about me, so I begin to tell him about my life in Russia (where I have spent the past seven years), but no country could be more unlike his world of sand and palms. Everything I say requires a verbal footnote of explanation. Eventually our conversation dwindles as the heat intensifies, and we return to our customary silence. Mustafa conducts our caravan toward the southwest, in the direction of Chagaga.

The hammada is shimmering with lakes of silver, flats of mercury—the famed *sarab*, or mirages, of the Sahara. Noon. The air is dead still, wicked hot. We march toward them, drowsy and quiet, our thoughts nullified by the knowledge that the heat won't abate until the sun has completed its arc and baked us from every angle. Flies harrow the camels, landing on their necks, upending themselves and sinking their proboscises into the cordlike jugulars, their green bellies swelling with blood. Gorged and sluggish, they buzz slowly away, to be replaced by others.

We reach the wadi of Mouzmou and halt for lunch under a clump of tamarisks. Omar and Mustafa hail the two *ruhhaal* resting there, and the salutations commence: "Peace be upon you! No harm to you! How are you? How are the family? How are the sons? How are the flocks doing? How are you getting along with the weather? Is everything all right with you?" All four spill out their greetings simultaneously, never waiting for answers. Despite the verbiage, no information is imparted; this is ritual, pure and simple.

Their talk with Omar and Mustafa is all about camels. There are ten words in Arabic describing camels of various ages and states, from the infant *hawar* to the toddler *'ashar* to the adolescent *ba'eer,* on and on up to the fully grown *jamal.* A pregnant female is known as a *shayla.* Camels are gifted with prodigious memories, *ruhhaal* assert; they must be persuaded to obey and never beaten; they must be allowed to end their lives in dignified retirement.

After lunch, the sun bears down on the wadi and the conversation dies. The feathery, needled boughs of the tamarisks flute the rising wind; they sing, they chime, they chant, Sirenlike, a dirge that puts the *ruhhaal* to sleep but unsettles me, conjuring up a time long ago when people were few on earth, hunting in scattered tribes under a red sky.

At three in the afternoon we arise groggy, torpid with the heat, our shirts damp and sticking to our backs. We set off into the sun, breasting the wind. The hammada ahead is the abstracted landscape of nightmares—charred earth, blinding white sky, gales. Low dunes rumple the desert to the south, trailing tongues of wind-blown sand across the hammada, tawny lizard tongues unraveling in our path. This is Oued l'Meyyit, Mustafa says. The Valley of the Dead.

We camp for the night at the well of Oued Naâme, by a solitary tamarisk. Exhausted, we say nothing as we unpack. A breeze stirs the tamarisk to song, but this time, in the cool, it sounds like a paean to salvation. Nothing in the Sahara is what it is for long; the desert has few features save what the sun and the winds lend it.

A spring waters the oasis of Oum Laâlague, bubbling up from under a cluster of date palms and trickling off through verdant swards. By it we meet Brahim, a youth from the Berber Aït Habbash tribe, and he invites us to his family's tent for tea.

Brahim brandishes a dagger set in a tamarisk handle. But if the Aït Habbash once excelled as warriors, Brahim's greased-back hair, fraying windbreaker, and threadbare trousers call to mind the *bidonvilles* of Casablanca, the poverty that drives Moroccans to cross the Strait of Gibraltar to seek work in Europe.

Brahim's family used to wander from the dunes of Merzouga in the east to Tan-Tan in the west, grazing their sheep and camels, moving where the grass was. Seven years ago the drought forced them to settle here. Their tent is a jumble of plastic sheets tossed up around a stunted tamarisk. Women putter about the wadi doing chores, their faces averted from mine. Radio Algeria blares the news from a sand-caked wireless. I wonder if Brahim can understand it— the media broadcasts in classical Arabic, unintelligible to the illiterate.

"Do you understand the radio?"

He lowers his head. *"Shwiyya."* ("A little.") *"Shwiyya.* But I don't need to. It's my job to stay here at camp with the women. Our tradition is that a male stays by the tents in case guests come."

The family numbers fourteen, and a newborn wails in the tent out of sight. They're all illiterate; the nearest school is in M'hamid, two days' walk away.

The name *Chagaga* derives from the Arabic verb *shaqqa,* to split. To my eyes the dunes of Chagaga, our westernmost destination, only separate barrens from more barrens, but the *ruhhaal* noticed that the wadis run around the sand and not through them, dividing the hammada of the eastern Drâa from the hammada of the west.

We reach Chagaga as the sun sets. I leave the camels and clamber up the highest ridge, slipping in the cool sand, drawn by the vista of golden dunes rippling away to the horizon. Omar soon arrives at my side and savors the view in silence. "Desert life has no equal," he says, finally. "What a pleasure it is to lie down at camp at the end of the day, your camels watered and fed next to you. They rest and you rest. You sip your tea, you eat your dates, you look at the sky. This is pure. And the children of the desert are brought up pure, with no narcotics or alcohol or brothels. In the cities, children are born sick. Here you're healthy from birth, and your mind is clear." He pauses. "This land was once filled with us *ruhhaal*. But you saw how empty the valley was on the way here. The *ruhhaal* are leaving the desert. Now, maybe three out of a hundred remain. It's because of the drought."

In his tattered cameleer's *fouqiya* and tire-rubber sandals, with his *chêche,* dagger, and Sinbad beard, Omar looks like a figure from a nineteenth-century Arabian daguerreotype—the very image of a *rahhaal.* As colorful as he is, Omar is, after all, an anachronism. With the droughts, the closure of borders, and the pull of urban life, the Drâa *ruhhaal* seem fated to dwindle. One or two generations off the sands, and the skills necessary to survive there will be lost.

A hodgepodge of low earthen ramparts and tumbledown towers, M'hamid, our final destination, hunkers on the horizon as if flattened by the ferocity of the Saharan sun. We march toward it without stopping for a drink—soon we'll have all the water we could want, and that thought quickens our steps. Just outside the walls, Ali appears and embraces us; he's recovered from his infection. Twelve days after leaving the oasis of Zagora, we penetrate the beehive lanes of M'hamid, the wind stirring tiny twisters along our path.

But our eyes are drawn to a careening segmented beast of steel and flying dust. A convoy of Land Rovers, black and sleek and bearing tourists, is rifling across the hammada into town, and the camels that have been so indispensable to us suddenly seem quaint. The vehicles look like invaders here, and the smell of exhaust burns our nostrils. But Ali doesn't object. The influx of tourists is probably as unstoppable as the *sharqi*. A survival trait of the *ruhhaal* is adaptability, and Ali is changing with the times, doing well with his guide business. It might even be that he and his *ruhhaal* will teach visitors to the Drâa the humbling and salutary lesson of the Sahara—that there's still a very big place in the world where people, without their gadgets and armor, are fragile animals indeed.

He leads us to his brother's house, where we find the family, all welcoming smiles, awaiting us. One of his cousins tosses a plastic tub onto the sand and turns on a hose full blast. The camels, dry from three days of walking without well or spring, drop their snouts to it and begin slurping the water faster than the hose can pour.

Luxuriating in a sense of deliverance, in the near bliss of arrival, I follow Ali inside the high-ceilinged Casbah house. Tea has been set up for us in the main room, an expansive stone chamber made up of cool and shade, supported, it almost seems, by shafts of liquid gold—pillars of light pouring in through the glassless windows of the roof. Only here—and in the palm-canopied oases—does the sun of the Drâa feel so soft.

Down in the Drâa

A beautiful Berber Casbah often used in desert films, Aït Benhaddou is an easy introduction to the Drâa Valley—only about a half hour from Ouarzazate (a taxi hired at the Gare Routière, the main station, will cost about $8 to $10 per hour, if you bargain). Several families still inhabit the Casbah, and their sons are happy to show you around.

A tour of the valley itself might include five or six days of visiting the Casbahs (all inhabited) and oases along the 140-mile Ouarzazate-Zagora-M'hamid road—particularly Tleta Tighoummar, Igharghar, and Ouled Atmane, which has the palace of Dar Qa'id al-Araby—as well as equal time spent trekking or camel-riding in the outer reaches. Taxis will take you from Ouarzazate, or you can rent a car (Avis, Europcar, Budget).

The most environmentally friendly way to explore the desert beyond the valley road is by camel: four-wheel-drive vehicles scar the hammada. Zagora-based itineraries of up to 6 days usually stretch southwest, toward M'hamid. From M'hamid excursions run west to the dunes of Chagaga, 2 or 3 days each way, or all the way west to Foum Zguid, about 12 days there and back.

(The area code for the Drâa Valley is 04.)

A guide is strongly recommended for *any* trip into the Sahara, even for a day. There are no accurate maps, and even well-marked pistes may disappear under sand dunes in places. In Zagora, Ali Daimin's licensed agency, Caravane Erg, arranges safe, customized treks for about $40 per person per day, and camel expeditions for about $67 (044.84.75.76). If you don't reserve in advance, look for him at the Bazar Tombouktou, across from the Hôtel Tinsouline (ask proprietor Youssef Barane). Note: No matter how cheap the rates, steer clear of youths hawking trips to meet "blue men of the desert" (in reality, urban shysters dressed as nomadic Tuaregs) or other desert escapades, some of which may include offers of hashish (illegal in Morocco, regardless of what you hear).

Weather in the Drâa Valley demands respect. Summer temperatures hit infernal highs; winter has nights of bone-dry, skin-splitting cold. October and November, and March, April, and May are best, with warm days and cool nights. Dress appropriately, as the locals do: cover up. Loose cotton works best, acknowledging Islamic modesty and the powerful sun, dust, and persistent flies. For about $30 you can buy the traditional *fouqiya* (robe), *sirwal* (undergarment), and *chêche* (turban). Sturdy-soled walking shoes are ideal; a broad-brimmed straw hat, polarized sunglasses, sunblock, and moisturizer are indispensable.

Use plastic bags to seal your baggage, documents, film, and cameras. Speaking of which, ask permission before photographing *anyone*. Not to do so is offensive, and children have been known to throw stones at shutterbugs. If you approach the Algerian border or a military post, stash the camera or risk losing your film.

I've never spent time in southern Morocco without encountering scorpions. They pop up in even the best hotels and prefer dark, cool places. Don't walk barefoot in the dark, shake out your shoes before putting them on, and be careful when collecting firewood or upending rocks. Stings from the fat, black *Androctonus* can be fatal—make sure your guide carries the antivenins, available in local pharmacies.

Lodging and Dining

Ouarzazate, at the valley's head, is the major town, and the Berber Palace the premier hotel. Built to resemble a Casbah, it has a pool and a restaurant with a decent buffet dinner. Service can be erratic; confirm your reservation (044.88.30.77, fax .71; doubles, about $103). The Hôtel Bélère is slightly downscale and slightly cheaper (044.88.28.03, fax .31.45; doubles, about $70).

From Zagora you can set out into the desert, very likely from the garden of the endearingly ramshackle Hôtel Tinsouline (044.84.72.52, fax .70.42; doubles, about $60). To get a feel for Zagoran commercial life, visit the rough-and-tumble Sunday souk (next to the station), if only to watch men in *djellabas* and turbans haggle furiously over everything from toasters to spices to goats.

Should you need to spend the night in M'hamid, the Hôtel Sahara is virtually the only option, for rooms as well as (relatively safe) food. The sociable staff somewhat redeem the spartan, dusty establishment (phone and fax, 044.84.80.09; doubles, about $7).

Reading

For essential information on how to prepare for the climate, the conditions, and the culture, pick up Cadogan's *Morocco,* which has a good section on the southern oases of Morocco, updated in 1997. With Moroccan schools Arabicizing their curricula, less and less French is now spoken, and a Moroccan Arabic phrase book, such as the one offered by Lonfely Planet, is well-nigh essential outside the towns.

A Mosque a Minute

BY ANDREW MARTON

〜〜

editor's note

This article proved to be very helpful to my husband and me when we were planning a driving route south from Marrakesh. We had a multitude of maps, a kilometer chart from the Moroccan National Tourist Office, and lots of patience, which was good because we really could not accurately ascertain how long it was going to take to get from point A to points B and C. (How much time does one calculate for windy, mountain roads? a possible breakdown? the condition of the roads on the other side of the Atlas?) In this piece—which is, after all, about driving—the writer provides estimates for the total driving time for three itineraries, two of which are Marrakesh to Ouarzazate and Ourzazate to Tamgrout to Marrakesh. It was not until we read this piece that we were able to confirm this portion of our itinerary.

ANDREW MARTON writes frequently for *Travel & Leisure*, where this piece originally appeared. He is also coauthor, with Linda Fisher, of *The Muffin Lady: Muffins, Cupcakes and Quick Breads for the Happy Soul* (HarperCollins, 1997) and is the book review editor at the *Fort Worth Star-Telegram* in Texas.

No sooner have my Timberlands hit the tarmac of Casablanca's airport than a blast of desert air blindsides me. This flying carpet of Moroccan history, with its billions of granular artifacts, is the country's signature greeting. And so the trip—part nostalgia tour, part meandering history lesson—aptly starts with a confetti shower of Morocco's past.

Several decades ago, my brother-in-law, then a Peace Corps director, called Morocco home. Now my sister, her two children, and I have accompanied him back. Friends are there to meet us, and an hour later we're in the capital, Rabat. The city's bustling souk is our first sign that the 450-mile spice trade route, a paved arrow into the heart of Berber country, is close at hand. This ancient road, skirting gorges, emerald fields, and the Sahara, is cryogenically preserved in time, an asphalt descendant of the original spice trail running from Timbuktu through the Western Sahara.

From the outskirts of Rabat, southwest to Casablanca and due south to Marrakesh, the route choreographs scenes straight out of a Cecil B. De Mille biblical epic. Camels lounge under orange trees heavy with fruit. Apostlelike elders finger worry beads; shepherds prod goats. Young and old shuffle by in long robes called *djellabas*. Concealing torso and legs, these cloaks create an amazing mirage of levitation. The hood, when raised, engulfs the face in grim-reaper shadow.

The interior of Morocco is almost entirely free of eyesores—no knockoffs of Calvin Klein T-shirts; no McDonald's signs. Any anachronisms—such as a Bryan Adams tune playing on a fellow traveler's tape deck—are drowned out by the muezzin's call to prayer. Our rented Hyundai is the only modern intrusion on a trail where traffic jams mean donkeys braying at oxen.

From Rabat, our first day's drive of just over 200 miles takes us to Marrakesh, where we spend the night at La Mamounia, the most sumptuous hotel I've ever encountered. In the morning we're on our way to the terraced fields of Taddert, the first caravan staging post in the 127 miles between Marrakesh and Ouarzazate. Today, traders still hawk semiprecious stones and fossils. A 1939 plaque from the *Guide Gastronomique de la France* honors Taddert's musty village inn, no longer a source of Escoffier-level cuisine.

On roadside bluffs outside Taddert we spot the first of hundreds of fortresslike *pisé* (clay or mud brick) manor houses, or casbahs, many surrounded by fortified palaces called *ksour* (a single one is a *ksar*). As my brother-in-law fearlessly navigates around sheer rock on one side, oblivion on the other, we chug up the 7,413-foot Tizi n' Tichka pass. Along the way we see egg-shaped Islamic shrines, women swatting indigo rugs, and rivers bleeding clay.

Suddenly, salesmen appear beside our car, hawking today's inventory of asparagus, lizards, and chunks of quartz-amethyst with a fool's gold interior of shocking orange. In this, one of the world's oldest shopping malls, I have entered the minor leagues of haggling. While rock bargaining, I learn the back-of-the-hand snub, that cookies are tradable, and that a Flair pen thrown into the deal means 30 percent off. But be warned: any rental car attracts a mob of faces and clawing hands. And in this market, all sales are final.

Such cutthroat commerce isn't the only heritage from the spice road. The casbahs all along the trail are lacerated by wind and rain. Nowhere is this primal battle more eloquently waged than in nearby Telouet. We drive to the cusp of the Tizi n' Tichka pass before downshifting toward the town and its casbah. Once the seat of the powerful Glaoui family, which aligned with the French during the fight for independence, the casbah has been punished with the slow torture of raindrops melting its wood-and-mud-brick towers—yet somehow its Moorish reception and harem rooms have retained their extraordinary stucco filigrees and mosaic tiling. On our way out, we spot a double rainbow.

From Telouet, the spice trail enters oases wild with date palms and spiky ferns. Bordering the Asif Imini stream, the town of Anguim has a craft cooperative devoted to carpet-making and embroidery. Tuesday is market day, and the local women tote heavy reeds while the men recline, admiring all the work they don't do.

Only thirty minutes northwest of Ouarzazate, across the Mellah River valley, looms Aït Ben Haddou, an imposing coral-tinted *ksar* of tapered clay towers, familiar from the nearly two dozen Hollywood films shot there. Our guide, Ahmet, was an extra in *Lawrence of Arabia*.

If Aït Ben Haddou is an architectural wedding cake, then

Ouarzazate shows more restraint. The town's greatest asset, besides the Krupp cannon, the Scud missile of its day, seems to be the Hotel Riad Salam. With glazed mosaic tiles, copper wall hangings, and an interior courtyard filled with orange trees, the Riad Salam bestows the mythic comforts of a trade-route oasis stop—plus indoor plumbing.

The hotel's breakfast of honey crêpes, ham and cheese, and frothy apple juice provides fuel for our third-day road plan: a 120-mile trek to the windy border of the Sahara. The Drâa River valley, land of palm groves and alfalfa fields, is scented with oleander. In Zagora, at the southern end of Boulevard Mohammed V, we pass arcade stalls displaying lamb and honey-sweet dates to find one of the world's great photo ops: a sign reading TOMBOUCTOU 52 JOURS (52 Days to Timbuktu). That's camel days.

Speaking of camels, there are six of them awaiting riders on Zagora's sandy outskirts, and more camels a dozen miles down the road past Tamgrout, where the smooth spice road disintegrates into a rutted trail. At the Tinfou Dunes we finally decide to take a ride, led by a guide named Mohammed—a Reguibate nomad, or Blue Man of the desert, wearing a sheath of blue muslin whose dye has tinted his tobacco skin pale indigo.

A single-humped camel obeys Mohammed's every command as a rope depresses its tongue. This leash brings the eight-foot animal to its knees. I climb aboard, keeping a firm grip as the camel's feet sink into the fifty-foot dune. From this perch, with my bath-towel *kaffiyeh* and local medal of valor, a rabbit made from a folded palm leaf, I am transformed into T. E. Lawrence.

Our car's bucket seats are a humbling return to reality. As we leave Tamgrout's moonscape and head back to Marrakesh, 250 miles northwest, we stop at the ramshackle town of Tadoula, where kids offer us a tour in exchange for a bushel of oranges. Farther on, in Tizirine, the entire village has gathered for a hillside funeral. It's a privilege to witness this ritual: three hundred townspeople, burial rocks in hand, stand on a bluff overlooking a swaddled body. The silence is broken by a bloodcurdling ululation from the women, signaling that mourning has begun.

For us there's one more essential stop on the spice trail: Marrakesh's medina, home to perhaps the world's most electric souks, sequestered behind a six-mile ring of salmon-colored ramparts. My family and I enter Djemaa el Fna square, "the Place of the Dead," a plaza at the edge of the souks, and immediately recognize the backdrop for the opening murder in Hitchcock's *The Man Who Knew Too Much*. We are surrounded by "Allah"-crying beggars, acrobats, soothsayers, men twirling tasseled fezzes, food carts offering goat's head soup, and scooters. (One carries recently beheaded chickens hanging from the handlebars.) I lose my nephew to two snake charmers who have him smilingly draped in deadly cobras. What salesmanship.

The souks sell everything: flutes, *tagines* (earthenware casseroles), embroidered saddles, copper, wood, textiles. Rusted palace locks lie in a basket beside writhing turtles. The merchants' persistent come-ons provide a constant din. When we enter one store, its salesman flatters us with nicknames: my nineteen-year-old niece becomes La Gazelle, and I, with pad and pen, am promoted to Ministre de la Culture.

But I'm ready for ploys like this. The spice road's onslaught of drive-by commerce has apprenticed me for the ultimate transaction: the carpet purchase. Mine begins with rounds of mint tea, aka Berber whiskey, amid twenty-foot fabric towers. Soon a procession of twenty-by-fifteen-foot rugs splashed in shades of saffron and evergreen lines the room, and I'm listening to details and more details about kilim weaving techniques, the peculiar hue of Berber rugs, and on and on.

Then dueling calculators emerge, and my brother-in-law whispers advice. Teeth clench. More rounds of tea. *"C'est impossible!"* is blurted out. Leaving the store chops the price by 20 percent. As the proprietor implores us to return, a handshake and a touch to the heart seal the deal.

At the spice trail's last stop, with my mercantile prize, I can't help but hear Paul Bowles's words: "Business is business, and prayers are prayers, and both are a part of the day's work."

The Itinerary

DAY 1: Rabat or Casablanca to Marrakesh

We landed in Casablanca (where Hertz, Avis, and Europcar all have rental desks) and spent our first night with friends in the capital, Rabat, 56 miles to the northeast; its souk is an ideal first stop on the spice route. From Rabat we backtracked to Casablanca via the palm-lined P36 or P1 motorways, passing towns such as Skhirat, Bouznika, and Mohammedian. Follow the P7 for 146 miles to Marrakesh. Stop to eat cumin-laced lamb *(imechouii)* or meatball sandwiches *(ikeftai)* at a roadside café. Total driving time: approximately four hours.

DAY 2: Marrakesh to Ouarzazate

Follow P31 southeast toward Aït Ourir and Taddert, a good place to buy blood oranges and cookies, which are useful for bartering with roadside vendors. From Taddert up to the Tizi n' Tichka pass, the road winds through valleys of birch. Take Route 6802 to Telouet and its casbah. Then return on Route 6802 to the P31 and the craft centers of Anguim and Amerzgane. Turn left onto Route 6806 and then right onto 6803 to Aït Ben Haddou and its castle. Return to the P31 for just under an hour, to Ouarzazate. Stay at the Hotel Riad Salam. Total driving time: five hours.

Most of the P31, from Ouarzazate southeast through Agdz into the Drâa Valley, is extraordinary. Stop at Zagora's arcaded market, then follow Route 6958, a rutted path, toward Tamgrout. At Tinfou, four miles south of Tamgrout, you can ride camels and scale fifty-foot Saharan dunes. Return to the Hotel Riad Salam, or head back 250 miles to Marrakesh via Ouarzazate and Routes 6958 and P31, making sure to traverse the tricky mountain passes in daylight. On the way, tour the *ksar* of Tadoula. Then do your final bargaining in Marrakesh. Total driving time: six hours.

The Facts

Marrakesh

La Mamounia, *Avenue Bab Jdid* (see *Des Belles Choses* for contact info). A luxurious hotel steeped in history, thanks to such famous patrons as Winston Churchill, Franklin D. Roosevelt, and Rita Hayworth. In recent years it's undergone a complete Art Deco facelift while managing to retain its classical Moroccan style.

Les Deux Tours, *Circuit de la Palmeraie de Marrakesh; 044.312.071; fax 044.312.057; doubles from about $115.* Six interconnected villas—each with a fireplace and plunge pool—plus 25 rooms and suites, set in a quiet palm grove just outside town. Wonderful room-service breakfasts and dinners.

Dar El Baroud, *275 Avenue Mohammed V; 044.426.009; dinner for two about $90.* A perfect respite from the medina, with vaulted ceilings and plush banquettes. Our *prix fixe* meal included lamb-stuffed pastries, seven-vegetable couscous, and a heaping fruit platter.

Yacout, *79 Sidi Ahmed Souss; 044.382.929; dinner for two about $120.* Located in a former villa, Yacout has extraordinary tilework and mother-of-pearl–accented furniture. Some specialties: lemon chicken with olives, glazed shoulder of lamb, cinnamon carrots, oil-and-vinegar peppers, and a napoleon of orange and almonds.

Ouarzazate

Hotel Riad Salam, *Avenue Mohammed V; 044.883.335; fax 044.882.766; doubles from about $90.* A 62-room spice road oasis with two restaurants, tennis courts, a pool, and sauna.

Zagora

Kasbah Asmaa, *Route Tamgrout; 044.847.241; fax 044.847.527; doubles about $55 (includes breakfast and dinner); lunch for two about $23.* A 35-room hotel with a poolside restaurant that you reach via a path of Berber carpets. To the guttural mood music of camels, feast on Moroccan salads, *tagine* of lamb with prunes, or lamb couscous.

The Jewel of Morocco

By Larisa Dryansky

editor's note

It's difficult to say whether a visit to Essaouira (known among Moroccans simply as 'Saouira) should be at the beginning or the end of a trip to Morocco. It's cool, breezy, beautiful, slow-paced, manageable, and wonderful. And perhaps thankfully, Essaouira does not appear on the itineraries of many tour operators. It's a little out of the way in that it's not on a direct route to anywhere, but it's worth whatever effort you may make to get there.

Larisa Dryansky lives in Paris and writes often for *Condé Nast Traveler,* where this piece originally appeared.

There was a rich maharaja from Mogador./He had hundreds of camels and maybe more./He had rubies and pearls, and such beautiful girls,/But he never learned to do-oo the rumba."

My father taught me this song, a jewel of prerock nonsense, at about the time I started to read fairy tales. Did he have the words right, or did he deliberately make the song wackier than it was? Mogador happens to be a maharajaless port on Morocco's Atlantic coast. But to my childish ears, all of it seemed perfectly compatible: the exotic name, with its rich sound evoking fantastic treasures— and binding the splendors of India to the sexy rhythms of the Indies.

Mogador is now called Essaouira *(es-sa-WEE-rah).* It has become harder to pronounce, but you'll be hearing it pronounced more and more often in fashionable circles. In real life, in different ways, it's as much a delicious and rich paradox as the nutty song made it out to be. Right now it is at that stage among destinations where an old eddy becomes a new wave. Already, for example, Philippe Starck, international star of contemporary design, French author of New York's Royalton, has been sniffing around the eighteenth-century town, looking for a site to create a hotel with Attitude.

Essaouira, long forgotten and smothered in its historic past, its whitewashed houses splashed with the crisp blue of indigo window frames, has, for now, no world-class hotel, no discothèque, no sizzling nightlife. The town's most hectic activity is the coming and going of the fishing boats, overladen with sardines.

Tangier used to be the fabled enclave of edgy expatriates; now it's a mélange of squalor and showiness. Marrakech? A great place for rich Europeans to hide their luxurious lives behind pink walls. What makes Essaouira different from both is its authentically Moroccan tempo and allure—and this in a place that was once designed to look like Europe, to impress European traders.

I saw old Mogador for the first time at night. Passing under crenellated ramparts, I made my way to the port. The scene was from a Hollywood pirate movie, with the moonlight softly turning the old frames of wooden trawlers into the ghosts of caravels. Where was Douglas Fairbanks? The old Portuguese fort of Castelo Real is long ruined, but I thought about another bit of drama as well—Paul Claudel's *Satin Slipper,* which uses the imagined fort as a backdrop for a tortured story about love and religion. "There is only one certain castle I know of where it is good to be locked in," Claudel wrote. "Better to die than to give back the key. It is Mogador in Africa." It is unclear whether Claudel actually traveled to Mogador, except in his imagination—which is not to say he never got there.

In the daytime I discovered more elements of paradox: a town with the look of a Breton sea village, whipped through by briny winds, but penetrated with the scent of *kamoun,* the Moroccan name for cumin, which flavors every local dish and is as essential as salt and pepper.

The port was crowded with weather-beaten fishermen in frayed sweaters—a sight not unfamiliar, yet all but vanished from the old shores of Europe, not to mention America. The fishermen were enjoying their version of a miracle: for the first time in years, this summer's catch of sardines was so bountiful that they were throwing them away. Bronzed kids armed with plastic bags kept diving into the port waters to gather up the floating fish. The quay ground was speckled with a motley haul of other fish: long, glistening eels that, combined with raisins, go into a local sweet-and-sour *tagine,* or stew; silvery pageots; delicate sole and turbot; succulent crayfish; and lobsters, which are particularly delicious in Essaouira, whose waters, blessed with a cold current, are cooler than those of neighboring ports.

Bargaining shoppers were making a ruckus on the decks of the boats, while on the pier old men were hawking sardine-and-pimento sandwiches and mint tea. Wooden skeletons on the quays resembled prehistoric carcasses: boats were being constructed. The style of building boats is peculiar to the town and, according to local tradition, can be found in only one other place, a small Breton port whose name nobody can remember.

I paint this scene in detail because soon we'll be looking at a yacht harbor here, or so Mr. Taoufik Ben Jelloun, governor of the Essaouira province, told me in his 1960s-modern office. "Yachting," he said, "is the kind of tourism we want to encourage."

Let's hope that the ship chandlers don't edge out the stalls near the custom house where a vendor will grill a fish for your lunch, to be eaten on a bench under his tent while watching the port's animation. Aficionados of freshness prefer to buy the fish straight off a boat and have it grilled in the souk.

The souk spreads through a whole neighborhood in the center of town. Bright blue carts stumble through its narrow alleys with colorful freight: heaped black-fleeced bloody goat's heads and brown shiny cow's heads whose long eyelashes seem still to be quivering; mounds of pink-and-green prickly pears; piles of mint; loads of bright vegetables and plastic bottles filled with argan oil. The argan tree grows naturally only in the region around Essaouira, and its fruit is a favorite of goats, which climb into the trees to get at it. The fruit yields a nutty kind of oil that is a staple of Moroccan cuisine. The tree, which looks like a stumpy olive tree, is actually a survivor from prehistoric times.

On the Avenue de l'Istiqlal, the souk's main thoroughfare, a wide porch beckons, leading to a patio with tables spread out in the shade of some trees. This is not a restaurant but an informal grill house, where you bring your own meat or fish to be cooked. Buy bread next door in one of the stalls, and sit down for a rustic snack. They serve nothing of their own but mint tea. Street-food lovers have a perennial picnic in Essaouira, but there are other things to do than wander around eating amid the exotica.

In fact, you don't go to Essaouira deliberately to entertain yourself—except maybe if you are a windsurfer. Writers go to finish novels, musicians bring their sound trucks and cut records, theater and cinema people come to drain their minds of old roles and plots. There's the beach, where the swimming can be dangerous because of the currents. But this is also a town in which going out for a newspaper is a moment to savor, as you let the cityscape speak to you.

The endemic wind is the true soul of the town. Orson Welles was deeply perturbed by it when he shot his Kafkaesque version of *Othello,* which earned him the 1952 Grand Prix in Cannes, on the sea-battered walls. But the Souiri, the inhabitants of Essaouira, are fond of the wind's intoxicating power. It blows a spirit of mystery through the town, turning the locals into ghostlike figures wrapped from head to toe: men in striped burnooses, their faces lost in the baroque pleats of their oversize hoods; women delicately enveloped in the white folds of their *haiks,* the age-old local costume made of a single piece of cloth, not sewn but folded several times, with an instinctive sophistication that would have intrigued Balenciaga.

Contrary to legend, Jimi Hendrix did not stay here for months. He made just a lightning visit during his one-week trip to Morocco in the summer of 1969. But since then, Essaouira has become a favorite among rock musicians. Les Rita Mitsouko, the leading French alternative rock group, cut a best-selling album here, followed by Imhotep, the leader of the controversial Marseille rap group IAM, who dedicated a recording to Essaouira.

And just as in the days when it was a consular town, Essaouira is now attracting people from world politics and finance. Two weeks before I came, the head of the World Bank, James D. Wolfensohn, had been visiting. During my stay, the British ambassador to Morocco was quietly vacationing at the Villa Maroc, a discreet, fashionable hotel set in a private home. Its understudied elegance is another expression of the town's allure.

Mogador was founded in the late eighteenth century, at about the time *A Thousand and One Nights* was being introduced to the West. It is an architectural and cultural fantasy: a Moroccan town designed by a Frenchman in the classical taste, with a grid-pattern casbah and fortifications modeled on the work of Vauban, the military architect of Louis XIV.

The Portuguese had called the site Mogador in the early sixteenth century. The name is said to be a distant cousin of the ancient Phoenician word for "watchtower." That was the heyday of Portugal's imperialist expansion into the New World and along the coasts of Africa.

The fame of the place is even more ancient. Both the Phoenicians and the Carthaginians traded here, exchanging silk, perfumes, and spices for ostrich feathers and African gold. The so-called Portuguese fort, a ruined watchtower, is the most visible Carthaginian remnant. It stands guard at the far end of the beach, an eerie pile of stones beaten by the waves—which is said to have inspired Hendrix's "Castles Made of Sand."

In Roman times, the site of Mogador—including the peninsula on which the present town is built and Ile de Mogador, the island across the bay—was known as the Purple Islands. This was where the finest purple dye was extracted from snails to color the emperors' togas. The island, where most of the Roman relics have been excavated, is now a reserve for a dying species of bird, Eleonora's falcon. Pre-ecology gourmets speak greedily of mouthwatering omelettes made from the falcon's eggs. (Each egg alone is now worth as much as $100,000 on the black market.) The island's first guard would delinquently treat himself to one of these omelettes every morning for breakfast. The scattered eggshells finally gave him away. He was chucked into the sea and, after he was fished out, replaced. The island was closed for some time but can now be visited with a special permit.

The true history of Essaouira begins in the 1760s, with an imperial decree to build a port that was to be Morocco's only contact with the West for almost a century. This Moroccan St. Petersburg, erected overnight in the middle of nowhere, became the apple of Sultan Sīdī Muhammad ibn Abdullāh's eye. He brought the town prosperity by drawing an elite of merchants from all over the country.

The sultan also ordered that all foreign representatives be consigned to the town. The Danes were the most significant. The former Danish consulate is still one of the largest houses in the medina, the town's center. Sixteen families now squat in its ruined apartments, under the vestiges of the painted ceilings. There is a plan to rehabilitate the consulate and make it a cultural complex.

With the opening in 1988 of the Frédéric Damgaard Gallery, the Danish presence was reasserted. The gallery is part of the general drive to develop Essaouira as a place for travelers interested in the arts and architecture. Run by a former Danish antiques dealer, it was founded to promote local artists, most of whom are self-taught. I wasn't much convinced by "Souiri art," which is generally of the minor outsider-art sort.

According to legend, the Arabic name of the town is derived from the word *picture:* "Show me that precious picture [*tssouira*]," the sultan is supposed to have said while examining the plans for the new town. Although today Essaouira still hardly stretches beyond its eighteenth-century walls, Souiri continue to dominate Moroccan public life. Among them is André Azoulay, King Hassan II's privy councilor, a Sephardi who is the main architect of the town's current revival.

Essaouira can be called a microimage of world culture. Here the civilizations of Morocco, Europe, and Africa meet, caught up in the trance music of the Gnaoua, the mystical descendants of slaves. Gnaoua music is part of magic healing ceremonies akin to voodoo. Its hypnotic rhythms and chants seduced jazz musician Randy Weston, who made a record here with Gnaoua musicians.

"Essaouira is a melting pot," says Kamal Ottmani, the debonair owner of El Minzah, a restaurant serving Escoffier-inspired Moroccan-international cuisine and one of the few places where you can have a late night drink. Half Jewish and half Muslim, Mr. Ottmani embodies the melting pot. In the time of Essaouira's glory,

Jews made up almost half the population. The Jewish community was so vital that the whole town would shut down on the Sabbath, and there were more synagogues than mosques. The main synagogue, on the Rue Lallouj, was entirely fitted with expensive furniture and accessories imported from Manchester by the strongly Anglophile community. Today, with most of the Jews gone to Israel, Europe, or the United States, the synagogue is in ruins, and when I passed it, a fat rat ran out through a chink in the door. But with the town again in the limelight, there is talk of restoration.

The original Jewish population was divided into two communities. The wealthy Westernized merchants lived in the casbah. Stars of David carved over doors still mark their homes. The poor Jews, on the other hand, crowded into the ghettolike *mellah,* which remains the poorest district and is the main target of a United Nations Habitat–sponsored revitalization plan. The Souiri are wary, though, of the rehabilitation of the *mellah* turning into a hasty gentrification.

With its crooked, narrow streets, the *mellah* is worlds away from the town's main square, the Place Moulay-Hassan. The square is nestled at the narrow end of a wide, empty square giving onto the port. At sundown, children gyrate on their bicycles amid the cries of seagulls and under the watchful eyes of veiled women. The fathers take over the café terraces that line the Place Moulay-Hassan proper. Attracted by the animated horse betting, I chose the terrace of the blue and white moresque Café de France. In the days of the French protectorate, this was where Mogador's high society would meet. Upper-class Jews would order their tea here in English. (The tea-drinking habit so typical of Moroccan life actually stems from the Anglomania of Jewish merchants from Mogador, who were the exclusive importers of the precious leaves.)

Later, sipping a freshly squeezed orange juice, I observed the evening get-together of Western expats at Jack's Kiosk. A newsstand run by a Swiss, it is a place where foreigners can meet and catch up on world news while making a phone call or sending a fax.

Last spring, a new meeting place opened on a corner of the Place Moulay-Hassan. Taros—café, library, and restaurant—is the prize jewel of Alain-Claude Kerrien, decorator of Le Palace, Paris's legendary nightclub. A Breton by birth, Kerrien has long felt a strong connection with Essaouira. For him, the ramparts and salt-laden air teasingly evoke the atmosphere of St-Malo.

Like all the members of Essaouira's foreign community, he tells a story of being spellbound by the town. It was not he who chose the eighteenth-century merchant's house that is home to his café, he claims, but he who was chosen. The house, with priceless nineteenth-century Spanish tiles decorating the walls, was for sale for fifteen years, but the family refused all offers—until one day Kerrien, on vacation in Essaouira, stopped by out of curiosity, and the heir said that he could have it.

There's been a kind of real estate fever recently in Essaouira. A French television piece publicized the town last summer as ideal for investment, a place where you can buy a huge historic house for nothing. In fact, good real estate opportunities are rare in town; most of the valuable houses are gone, not to mention those with sea views.

In the 1960s and 1970s, Essaouira's spirit of tolerance made it a hippie destination. The Living Theater set itself up here for a while. Judith Malina and Julian Beck soaked up the town's mystical and popular culture and entertained Anaïs Nin. The motley theater group was eventually evicted by the police, but it drew in its wake bands of "pimply, barefoot European youths begging for *dirhams,*" as the Souiri sculptor Mohammed Bouada recalled for me. Bouada allowed that his own vocation as an artist was in fact sparked by his youthful encounters with these Western originals.

Remnants of the hippie community now live outside town, in the hamlets of Diabat and Razoua. Diabat stands at the end of a dirt road. Beyond, there is nothing but dunes spotted with the half-buried ruins of an eighteenth-century palace and leading to an endless, deserted beach. Just outside the village is the entrance to the Auberge de Tangaro, an elegantly rustic hotel-restaurant in the middle of nowhere, with no electricity. The Auberge is one of Essaouira's most romantic locations. At night, the candlelit dining room becomes a club for the arty crowd of Razoua, which doesn't appear on the map.

A mystical peace still hangs over Essaouira. There is an overwhelming feeling of "lightness," as Françoise Quéré explained to me. Quéré, whose chiseled good looks epitomize the French notion of *racé*, came to Essaouira last spring for a weekend and stayed on. On an impulse, she bought the third house she visited, a ruined *riad* (a typical Moroccan home) built around a courtyard that is open to the sky. She fixed it up in no time and renamed it Dar Tissir. *Tissir* is an untranslatable Arabic word for a state of bliss and luck. For Quéré, to be in Essaouira is to be *tissir*. As she confided this, little *tibibt*—blue-headed sparrows that the Souiri say bring good luck— kept flying into her courtyard.

That evening, hundreds of *tibibt* were gathered in the rubber tree in the Place de l'Horloge, and their frenzied chirping filled the otherwise peaceful square with something like surreal music. The *place* is named after the clock tower on one of its corners, a rather whimsical legacy of French colonialism. The pride of Essaouira when it was installed in the 1920s, the clock seems now to be running on its own time—always five minutes ahead—or behind; less a timekeeper than a reminder of the town's intrinsic timelessness.

The cry of the muezzin, coming at regular intervals from the nearby mosque, is more reliable.

Souiri are known throughout Morocco for their natural elegance and their gentleness. In nearby Marrakech, someone is always trying to take you for a tourist ride. In Essaouira, horse-drawn coaches gather in the poor neighborhood near the souk at the Doukkala Gate. So far, it is housewives in *haiks* who hire them to carry their groceries home to the town's outskirts. I never saw anyone with a video camera being ridden around. Not yet.

In Old Mogador

With few hotels and fewer souvenir stands, Essaouira still counts as a discovery. The climate is mild enough for swimming year round, but in September and October the light is particularly beautiful, and the trade winds have abated, as have the summer crowds of surfers and windsurfers. The port is about a three-hour drive west from Marrakech, but regular flights now link Essaouira to both Agadir and Casablanca. The Rough Guide *Morocco* captures the atmosphere of Essaouira; the Cadogan *Morocco* is a bit more detailed, but has some inaccuracies.

Lodging

Originally a courtesan's *riad,* the Villa Maroc must be booked well in advance. Rooms have no phone or TV, and bathrooms are plain, but you get a fireplace, and terrace suites have sea views. The cuisine is unusual and authentic, the kind you get only in somebody's home (044.47.61.47 or .67.58; fax .58.06; doubles, about $62–$79). The Hôtel Riad Al Madina is in a nineteenth-century *riad* with a large patio, but the decor is Pier 1 Imports (044.47.59.07; fax .57.27; doubles, about $55). Orson Welles would hardly recognize the Hôtel des Iles anymore, except for its main, and unrivaled, asset—the pool (044.78.46.20; fax .55.90; doubles, about $64). At Jack's Place

Moulay-Hassan, Essaouira Apartments rents flats in historic buildings (044.47.55.38; fax .69.01; about $40–$60 per night).

For a true getaway, the Auberge de Tangaro, near the hamlet of
Diabat, is practically lost in the woods, a rustic compound of whitewashed one-story buildings. Elegantly sparse rooms have fireplaces
but *no electricity*. The cuisine has a very light French touch
(044.78.47.84 or .57.35; doubles, about $65, including breakfast and
dinner).

Dining

Street food, which generally costs under $10, is best for lunch. There
are fish stalls on the port, but I preferred to eat in the souk, in the
grill house in the middle of the Avenue de L'Istiqlal. Behind the jewelers' souk, ask for directions to Saïd's Café, a hole-in-the-wall
workers' canteen serving aromatic meat *tagines* and deliciously
hearty *loubieh,* a bean stew. For fresh seafood in an old-world
atmosphere, try El Minzah, at 3 Avenue Oqba-ibn-Nafia (*prix fixe,*
about $9–$20).

For a breakfast of French pastry and fresh orange juice, Driss is
a direct legacy of the French protectorate, at 10 Rue Hajjali.

Taros, at 2 Rue Sqala, is a café, bookstore, late-night bar, and
restaurant—an informal club in an elegant historic setting (*prix
fixe,* about $11).

First, the Souk, but Then . . .

Traces of Essaouira's rich past can be found, and purchased, at
Galerie Aïda, Joseph Sebag's antiques store at 2 Rue de la Skala. A
member of an influential Jewish family, Sebag is a living archive of
the history of the town and is now a part of its renaissance. His
selection includes Benchaya pottery, plates, and bowls that were
designed in the 1940s by a Casablanca potter and manufactured in
France, to comply with local snobbishness.

Omar Samat has a fine shop of crafted jewelry at 45 Rue Laattarine (044.47.49.20). Essaouira is also renowned for *thuya* woodworking, but this craft is a late introduction, and most of the artisans are from Agadir. More interesting, and part of the town's renaissance, is the raffia craft, revived by Miro. A shoe designer who often works for Agnès B., Miro produces raffia shoes and accessories. Having worked in Paris and Casablanca, he opened Rafia Craft at 82 Rue d'Agadir in 1998 because he felt that Essaouira was the right place to be. His only rival is Hajoub, a shriveled old cobbler who can be seen tressing raffia pumps in a tiny, dusty shop at 4 Rue El Hajjali, off the Place de l'Horloge.

Bibliothèque

Strangely, I do not own any books devoted to specific regions of Morocco outside of its cities, and I haven't been able to find any, either. There are plenty of books on Morocco, in English and in French, that cover the entire country, with *sections* devoted to the Rif or the Atlas or the predesert areas (see the *Points de Vue—Maroc bibliothèque*). I would be grateful to learn of any titles you may discover, so please don't hesitate to let me know!

Saveurs et Tables Marocaines
(Moroccan Flavors and Tables)

"To my mind four things are necessary before a nation can develop a great cuisine. The first is an abundance of fine ingredients—a rich land. The second is a variety of cultural influences: the history of the nation, including its domination by foreign powers, and the culinary secrets it has brought back from its own imperialist adventures. Third, a great civilization—if a country has not had its day in the sun, its cuisine will probably not be great; great food and a great civilization go together. Last, the existence of a refined palace life—without royal kitchens, without a Versailles or a Forbidden City in Peking, without, in short, the demands of a cultivated court— the imaginations of a nation's cooks will not be challenged. Morocco, fortunately, is blessed with all four."

—Paula Wolfert, COUSCOUS AND OTHER
GOOD FOOD FROM MOROCCO

God Is in the Diet

By Patricia Storace

editor's note

This piece represents the kind of article I love most: one that examines several Mediterranean countries (in this case, Spain, Morocco, Italy, and Turkey) and reveals the threads they all have in common. This is a wonderful article, a veritable cross-cultural odyssey, that I hope you enjoy reading, too. (Note: I did not include the "places and prices" information for Spain, Italy, or Turkey as I felt those details were probably outside the scope of this book; however, readers who would like that additional information may contact The Condé Nast Publications at 800-753-7276.)

PATRICIA STORACE writes often about Mediterranean travel and is the author of *Dinner with Persephone: Travels in Greece* (Pantheon, 1996, hardcover; Vintage, 1997, paperback), and *Heredity* (Beacon Press, 1987).

A n enormous rib of raw beef has been brought to the table on a platter to be displayed before carving, like a king lying in state on a catafalque. I am sitting on the patio of Córdoba's El Churrasco restaurant, its walls lined with earthenware jugs and ceramic plates and its clientele lined with cell phones. Magnificent Spanish knives detailed in wood and brass are ceremoniously laid at each place. A cutting board and a bowl of glittering coarse salt crystals are set down.

The waiter expertly carves the meat into fillets with the most perfect knife work I have ever seen, exactly as I imagine the art of the ancient Greek *mágeiros,* the cook-sacrificer. The strips of meat are lined up like soldiers, flanking the bone they were carved from, and are cooked on a heated terra-cotta plate while the smoky per-

426   M o r o c c o

fume of the meat rises, the fragrance that was once the reverential gift to the gods.

I have never eaten a more Homeric meal. The beef is accompanied only by salt and twigs of crisply fried potatoes, those treasures brought here from the Americas. Dinner has the austere splendor of a liturgy, the nourishment of death contradicted by the proof—the living, underground potato—that all that is buried in the earth is not dead. It is an ancient religious meal, deeper than any doctrine, and a fitting overture for my monthlong exploration of Mediterranean food.

Cuisines, like empires, rise and fall. At the turn of the last century, the flamboyant American gourmand Diamond Jim Brady sent a mole into the kitchens of Paris's Café Marguery to obtain, over two months of fifteen-hour workdays, its guarded recipe for *sole de Marguery*. When his spy returned to New York, Brady gave a dinner at which the guests included the composer Victor Herbert and the department store magnate Marshall Field, and declared that the sauce would render a Turkish towel edible. If Brady were alive today, however, he might send an infiltrator on a mission to Fez, famous for refined and unattainable home-cooking, to obtain the secret of a household's private recipe for *ras-el-hanout*, a mixture of up to forty-five spices whose nuance changes from blend to blend. At the turn of our century, Mediterranean cooking—virtually a new category of food, with its own listing in the Zagat guide—has the prestige that French haute cuisine did in Brady's time.

And small wonder. We have entered an era in which every part of the world matters to every other part, economically and politically, and it seems natural to hunger for the food of a region where worlds converge. A table set for a Mediterranean meal is no still life, but a setting for political and religious drama. Tracing its elements takes us as far afield as China, America, and, in fact, Heaven and

Hell, where the gods themselves have created, offered, and transported Mediterranean staples.

Along these shores, food has always been the most powerful metaphor for God. It was in the Mediterranean that gods were honored by being invited to partake of human feasts, given portions of sacrificial meat, grain, and wine. In classical Greece, cooking itself was a religious activity. And it was in the Mediterranean that the startling revelation of a new kind of meal occurred, one in which creatures could not only feast *with* a divinity but *on* one, a new kind of god that literally was food, present in bread and wine. The much analyzed health benefits of the Mediterranean diet—olive oil instead of butter, the emphasis on grains and vegetables, the fruit desserts—seem a reflection of our ancient wish for physical immortality, enacted here in religious rituals of different gods for centuries.

For me, one of the essential Mediterranean foods is the quince, which I began to cook and eat when I lived in Greece. Foods have heritages and biographies as humans do, and the quince, like the most significant foods we associate with this region—the olive, wheat, grapes, lamb—is linked with a divinity. It was the golden apple of Aphrodite and her eastern goddess predecessors. No one knows the exact route by which the fruit, native to Persia and Anatolia, spread through the Mediterranean, but one possibility is that it arrived with the Phoenicians via Crete, whose port of Chania was once named for it. And as Mediterranean history shows, when food travels, so do gods—stowaways delivered to new shores, hidden in the pith and juices and spheres and bones of the foods that symbolize them.

The quince, doing the work of its patron goddess, made me, in fact, fall in love with a gentleman named Ja'far ibn 'Uthman al-Mushafi, a love that was somewhat unrequited, since he had died in Moorish Andalusia in the tenth century. He had, though, left one of the world's great erotic poems, a description of desire as seen and felt through the medium of a quince. "A perfume / Penetrating as musk / . . . Its golden body / Naked in my hand . . . made me think of her / I cannot name / I was breathing so hard / My fingers crushed it." Miraculously, I could taste that tenth-century quince and imagine it in Ja'far's living hand. I understood the same thing he did about the undying flavor of love, and I knew him, frankly, as well as if I had kissed him. It seemed right to start a gastronomic odyssey in his own city of Córdoba.

Meandering through the city in the afternoon, I notice advertisements for *fontanerías,* fountain manufacturers, with painted images of the elaborate fountains that are the crucial foci of Andalusian patios, those domestic oases. *"¡Agua!"* flamenco audiences shout during a great passage of dancing, a praise invoking the most treasured element in this hot country. A woman in lemon yellow shorts stares into a jeweler's window, fanning herself with a matching lemon-colored fan, still an essential article of Spanish costume. I catch a glimpse of a noble Roman bridge, a form that never fails to move me—I love the architecture that unites one side with another—under which the Guadalquivir River sparkles. A *carnicería,* a butcher shop, announces itself with a round medallion enclosing a picture of a forthright pig, while hams hang like slabs of pink marble in this and many other windows. The almost aggressive presence of pork in Spanish cooking is one of the clearest emblems of Christian Spain's reclaiming of its nation from the Islamic Moors, of a religious and political divorce. A number of dishes of Moorish origin are laced defiantly with pork, a culinary *reconquista;* in fact, I will have no meal here that does not contain some trace of pork, whether as garnish, appetizer, or flavoring. Nothing, it seems, is more political than a pig.

I pause in the old town before a statue of a turbaned medieval

Muslim, one Muhammad El-Gafeoui, who was a celebrated oculist of Córdoba—a stony example of how haunted this part of Spain is by its Islamic past, veering back and forth between the world of the caliphs and the world of Rome. Here that past is simultaneously commemorated and rejected, because this image is a sculpture, a representational art that became profoundly Christian and is forbidden to Muslims.

In the old Jewish quarter, I stop at an exhibition of coins from Roman to Christian Spain—the coins of Moorish Andalusia are momentarily startling, since they are faceless, bearing only inscriptions. In the forecourt of the University of Andalusia, the matriculation lists are posted. Alongside the Angels, Isabels, and Jesúses, I find a scattering of names such as Fatima, Nadir, Sara, and Soraya, names with a fragrance of Spain's Semitic past.

I am in Moorish Spain again for dinner, at El Caballo Rojo, whose owner, Don José García Marín, has truly altered the repertoire of Spanish cooking at this restaurant named, he tells me, in honor of the local tradition of horsemanship and saddle-making. Don José, a courtly, witty man with a passion for cooking and Spanish history, has revived and reinterpreted Moorish and Jewish dishes missing from Spanish menus since the Middle Ages. My dinner is drawn from these, and as I eat his famous *cordero de miel,* lamb made with honey, a new standard in contemporary Spanish cookbooks, he shows me a well-worn volume. "This," he says, "is the most valued cookbook in my collection." It is a facsimile of a thirteenth-century collection of Hispano-Maghreb dishes, which inspired Don José to recreate these flavors. In a moment of minor culinary destiny, the book falls open to a recipe for partridge cooked with *membrillo,* candied quince conserve, a dish that my poet, Ja'far, might very well have eaten. "Look how each recipe ends," Don José points out, "always with the phrase *Si Dios quiere."* *"Inshallah,"* I say delightedly, and he nods. "If God wills." A few days later, on the Moroccan side (one instinctively thinks of Andalusia and Morocco as two halves of a whole), I am told that television weather forecasts conclude with the same *Inshallah,* since among the five things that only Allah knows is what tomorrow will bring.

From Córdoba I go to the *pueblos blancos,* the whitewashed villages in the southern mountains not far from the coast facing Morocco, some of which were the last Moorish strongholds in Spain. I want to experience the architectural continuity of these white villages throughout the Mediterranean and to taste country cooking. On the way, I stop to visit Janet Mendel, an expert on traditional Spanish food, who serves me *tapas* of velvety quail eggs dipped in cumin and salt as well as perfect fresh anchovies, along with a rosé that drinks like a scented breeze. Talking to her reminds me that cooking is a matter not only of craftsmanship in the kitchen but of knowledge of the environment, economy, and history outside it. When I ask her about the beauty and quality of the Spanish knives I have encountered even in the simplest restaurants, she speaks of the steel industry in the Albacete province and the great tradition of sword-making in Toledo. And she reminds me, with patriotic warmth, that Spain was not only a conduit for Middle Eastern influence on Mediterranean food but also had a corresponding influence of its own: "It introduced tomatoes, potatoes, and chocolate from the Americas to Europe. And American corn was translated into polenta, a new version of Roman porridge that is still eaten in Spain."

The quince trees along the road to the village of Grazalema are beginning to bear fruit, and I see a large handwritten sign, HAY CHURRO, with an arrow pointing to a man in a white booth who has some fresh fried pastries waiting on a hot tray, oil at the ready in his pans to cook more. As Janet predicted, I see fathers stopping at the booth to pick up this weekend breakfast treat. It is the birthday of the Virgin, and the little girls of Grazalema are wearing elaborately ruffled and polka-dotted fiesta dresses. I find a restaurant on a narrow street where families are having long Saturday lunches, wives studying the menus with the pleasant intensity of women having a holiday from cooking. I order a *tortilla de espárragos trigueros,* a marvelous country dish of the freshest eggs cooked with a kind of wild asparagus that grows on the verge of wheat fields, and to my delight, I find *carne de membrillo,* that confection of sugared quince that is like sherbet without the ice.

A tent is being set up for the evening celebration in the town square, overlooking surrealistic mountain peaks and a dramatic sheer drop. The view provides the unfailing exaltation of looking at something dangerous from a point of safety, a kind of visual equivalent of the rapture evangelists feel when they speak about sin. I turn into the warren of streets to find my car, and peering into the kitchen window of a house with cages of canaries flanking its front door, I see a row of labeled jars of Spanish staples. *Arroz, carne, aceite, azúcar, sal,* the words, like the foodstuffs, mixing empires, Roman and Islamic.

The ferry ride from Algeciras to Tangiers must be placed in the category of experiences that Voltaire classified as "once an experiment, twice a perversion." There are sweltering delays, and a brutal trampling chaos at disembarkation is enhanced by women wearing black bandannas bandit-style over their mouths, carrying full-size suitcases on their heads and babies tied in blankets to their backs (both of which function as battering rams), and by the game, but not entirely competent, attempt of a gentleman to steal my passport.

The fantasy splendors of the hotel La Mamounia in Marrakech, my first Moroccan destination, make a powerful contrast to the ferry. Spain itself vanishes at the sight of the Hieronymus Bosch–like spectacle of the city's Jemaa el Fna square, with its cobra charmers, startling clusters of staring-eyed calves' heads (which diners sit at makeshift counters to eat), fortune-tellers, watchful pickpockets, and storytellers delivering tales from the Koran in a haranguing style that reminds me of the theater of evangelical revivals in America. At the book stalls, French and Arabic volumes are displayed side by side, along with pictures of Muslim saints and a rich selection of portraits of King Hassan, ubiquitous in Morocco. There are drawings of trees and animals that cleverly circumvent the Islamic prohibition against representation of forms by being made entirely out of elements of calligraphy—in a sense, these are not images at all, but words. A brightly colored poster of an Arabic alphabet for children hangs in a corner, the letters illustrated by olives, lemons, a fortresslike entrance to a house (familiar here, where doors are strongholds), and a minaret—the whole stunningly different from the world of images in a Western child's alphabet. At a music stall nearby, I find a CD of Arab-Andalusian music, song after song lamenting the loss of the Alhambra, of Spain, "grieving about Andalusia . . . in this world and in Paradise may Allah be sorry for us."

Christine Rio, who has created the Marrakech restaurant Tobsil (a Moroccan word for a cooking pot), known for its elegant and innovative interpretations of Moroccan dishes, joins me for dinner at the intensely decorated Yacout, Marrakech's best-known traditional restaurant, to talk about the character of Moroccan cooking. The meal proceeds from drinks on the roof of Yacout, with its splendid view over the medina, and finishes on a patio where the moon's reflection floats in a pool and musicians play traditional songs.

We peer into the kitchen, with its tiled wall fountain, a more elegant version of the corners of the medina, where wives and daughters jostle for household water with their jugs, plastic buckets, and glass pitchers. A cook on a low stool is occupied with frying the triangular pastries called *briouats,* transferring them to a growing pyramid on a plate. Moroccan cooking, I reflect, seems to be created from low on the ground: kneeling, squatting, shaping the dishes almost as if from the earth itself. Mademoiselle Rio, knowing of my taste for quince, has arranged for a special *tagine,* or slow-cooked stew, of chicken braised with quince, the quince adding a fragrant depth, almost like a liqueur—here the fruit surpasses its use as a dessert and seems to play the role of the forbidden wine in meat dishes.

Rio describes an intricate cooking, one that seems a harem cuisine, an art grown elaborate within the walls of its enclosure, a substitute for the physical world of nature women hardly experienced. She mentions traditional dishes like lamb seasoned with cumin, placed in a great pot, which is then wrapped in cloth, and cooked for four hours at the *hammam.* "It's a dish for a party of men, making a social occasion of their baths," she says. I must try the subtle *trid,* pigeons cooked in bouillon, then wrapped in a kind of crêpe and sauced with their own broth, a dish said to be the favorite of the Prophet Muhammad. "For me," Rio says, "the nature of Moroccan cooking is in the balance of the *salé* and the *sucré,* the salty and the sweet." From the preparations she describes, I would add a third element to the salt and the sweet: time.

As we retreat to the courtyard for dessert—the little pastries called gazelle's horns that she says she recognizes as coming from the same patisserie the Moroccan royal family patronizes—she teaches me an amusing trick to decipher the gravity of a Moroccan banquet. "Count the number of courses by observing how many layers of cloth are laid on the table," she advises, "layers that will be removed course by course." Moroccan cooking has its own codes and symbols, like the different styles of calligraphy that decorate Moorish buildings. As with Moroccan houses, one has to find one's way into its innermost recesses to grasp it. It is a cuisine of defense against intrusion. It is dramatically apparent how New World foods such as potatoes and chocolate (which never appears in the desserts I encounter) have been little embraced here.

The road to the imperial city of Fez, where Boabdil, the last Moorish king of Spain, lived out his life in exile, is a liberation from the desert landscapes of Marrakech, swatches of hillside studded with melons the color of harvest moons. Breakfast in the Palais Jamaï's Andalusian garden, while water splashes in fountains and descends in channels through tiled conduits, is an even greater relief. I have chilled almond milk flavored with rose water, which I decide I would like every day for the rest of my life, and *beghrir,* the famous semolina pancakes cooked on one side only, so that honey pours through their English muffin–like perforations, in a marvelous culinary duet. From breakfast, I go straight into the medina with a hotel-procured guide, who leads me past clusters of Fassi men eating their own breakfasts, soups in which float peas, cumin, and splashes of olive oil; some are snacking on *khelea,* a preserved dried meat that is considered a useful provision for expeditions into the desert; others are eating eggs fried in *smen,* salted butter, which stands in a great tub at the cook's side.

We follow in the wake of two women, one wearing what looks like a lace-edged table napkin tied over her nose and mouth, the other voluminously draped head-to-foot in a chic leopard-skin-print robe. Down one alley, a boy sits on a sandbag in a dark corner chamber, where a level below him, like Hell itself, is the fire to which he feeds wood to keep the water for the *hammam* baths hot. Some young girls in long shapeless dresses are carrying trays of fresh breads home from the communal bakery, which, I am later told, is frequently positioned near the *hammam,* to make economical use of the same heat source. My guide seizes one girl by the shoulder and, to her dismay, peremptorily tears off a sizable wedge of her family's loaf, putting some in his mouth and handing me the rest. The girl's face works with suppressed anger and apprehension—she looks as if she is afraid of a scolding at home and is disgusted by this enforced hospitality.

I am soon, and gladly, rid of the guide and on my way to the site of Volubilis, one of the great cities of Roman Africa. It was the seat of King Juba II, who was married to the daughter of Mark Antony and Cleopatra and was the author of botanical treatises in Greek, one of which discusses the medical uses of opium. (Perhaps King Juba anticipates the famous Moroccan *majoun,* a narcotic confection made with nuts, dried fruits, and cannabis, a version of which scandalized Alice B. Toklas's readers when she published a Moroccan-inspired recipe for hashish fudge, "which anyone could whip up on a rainy day.")

On the road, we pass through tiny villages with whitewashed mosques, and crème caramel–colored fields of wheat. A woman in brilliant canary-colored drapery carries on her back a sack of olive cuttings, half as tall as her and much broader. The countryside is scattered with oleander trees, appropriately, since Volubilis was also called Oulili, or oleander, a plant whose bitterness is explained by its having sprung from the tears of Fatima, the Prophet Muhammad's daughter, when she learned that she would have to share her husband, Ali, with a second wife. I remember a parallel Christian story—in Greek folklore, the oleander is bitter because the Virgin Mary cursed it for helping to fashion the cross.

Even in ruins, Volubilis seems prosperous, with its brilliant siting amid fertile farmland that has access to three rivers and its elegant villas with their festive mosaics, whose images are bordered with serpentine twists, diamond-shaped lozenges, and other figures that recall Moroccan and Berber carpets. In one villa is a mosaic anthology of African animals, in another villa's bedroom a discreetly erotic Dionysus and a lounging Ariadne, one pretty leg left promisingly bare under her drapery. A stork nests on a column of the town's basilica, which looks incongruously like a church, reminding me that it was the Roman architecture of law that was translated first into the Christian architecture of faith.

I lunch in a nearby country restaurant, the Baraka de Zerhoun, the "blessing" of the Zerhoun, whose food is the nearest to home cooking I will eat in Morocco, unlike the impressive banquet cooking most visitors will remember. A portrait of the king and an enormous hand of Fatima, a charm against the evil eye, decorate the room, and banquettes line its walls, as reminiscent of the Greco-Roman style of banqueting while reclined as the *hammam* is of its precursor, the Roman baths. A son or relative of the family moves toward the floor fan and tenderly repositions it so that the breeze travels to our table at a perfect angle. The care with which our meal is served is almost protective, and here, as nowhere else I dine, I am reminded of the religious dimension of hospitality, of succor for strangers.

Through the arched doorway of the kitchen emerges a tray of mixed Moroccan salads, fava beans, green beans, tomatoes, and grated carrots, both noticeably sugared, as is the local practice, along with the uniformly superb breads of Morocco. We are then given a *briouat,* a triangular pastry filled with chicken, almonds, rice, and raisins, followed by brochettes of smoky lamb so fresh that I fear I know its relatives, bedded on startlingly fresh coriander. Then comes couscous with chicken, onion, and raisins, and a dessert of sweet *briouats* filled with nuts and drenched in honey. The lavish pattern of the meal was unnerving until it was explained to me that Moroccans prefer to cook and serve in large quantities, not only as a display of largesse but with the expectation of feeding an entire second tier of people—once as a consequence of large, polygamous families, now more usually employees and relatives— from the labor of making one meal.

At dawn I wake up, as I will every morning in Fez, to sit on the balcony and listen to the passionate cascade of chanting calls to prayer that leap from mosque to mosque, music that moves like the myriad waters of courtyard fountains. As the prayers, in tones of inexpressible yearning, exhort those who hearken that it is better to pray than to sleep, roosters begin to crow. The chanting seems to magically create the new day.

Later my new guide, Aziz, who is as knowledgeable and thoughtful as yesterday's guide was inadequate, takes me on a walk through the medina's narrow passageways. Again and again I am struck by a sense of the physical commitment Fassi craftsmanship involves, of the way the laboring bodies of craftsmen transform the materials they work with—the young boy on the roof within the tanner's market who cleans cowhide of hair and kneads it like pizza dough, the man hammering a copper pot in a rhythm a jazz drummer would envy. These silks, leathers, shoes, trays, filigreed vessels are made with hands, tongues, feet, shoulders, eyes—the works of *adam,* the Arabic word for human, who was created by the divine craftsman, Allah, "of fermented clay dried tinkling hard like earthenware."

Aziz leads me on through a quarter with enormous vessels for *tagine* and other mammoth cooking utensils that can be rented for banquets. I ask him about a tray the size of a wading pool—"We carry the bride in it on her wedding day." He later points out a golden belt in a jeweler's window, part of a bride's costume on the day when her elaborate caftans are ritually changed four or five times, rather like the covers of the banquet tables Christine Rio described in Marrakech. The bride herself seems to be a kind of banquet here.

Just ahead I see a man in a saffron yellow robe and *babouches* sitting on a crate, gently holding a squab pigeon. He scoops a portion of seed into his mouth, lifts the pigeon to his face, puffs out his cheeks as if he were about to play a wind instrument, then brings the pigeon's head to his and softly blows into its beak. "These are baby pigeons," Aziz explains. "They are too young to feed themselves. Only these pigeons are young enough to use for making *b'stilla,"* the elegant pie that is the masterpiece of Moroccan cooking. This intimate transfer of food to the helpless young is one of the biological origins of kissing, some anthropologists believe. And yet this extraordinary image of nurturing tenderness between man and animal is a prelude to death—the one being fed will be the other's meat. Here is the nakedly revealed truth that in cooking and eating we are brought, however unaware, to a crossroads, an intersection of sensuality, of life, and of death. It is at this crossroads that the foundations of religious experience are laid—doctrines vary, but eating will always be an encounter with the sacred, taking us to the permeable borders between life and death.

Over a crisp, thin, and gilded *b'stilla* and traditional wedding *tagine* of chicken, lemon, and olive at the Palais M'nebbhi, Aziz describes the great religious Feast of the Sacrifice following Ramadan. There is an open-air prayer, and the slaughter of the first sheep in the presence of the king is televised nationally, after which the fathers of families slaughter the sheep they themselves have specially purchased for the holiday. Although we eat with forks, Aziz tells me the old people say that eating with the hands brings *baraka,* blessing: if you are very hungry, even a small portion, if eaten with the hand after reciting the phrase "In the name of Allah," will satisfy you.

We eat in the courtyard, facing a marble fountain filled with roses, which gives Aziz a chance to make an old joke about the Moroccan sugar trade—"They ate our sugar, and we kept their marble," he says. Yes, I think to myself, but the effect of food on human destiny is more profound than we often consider, both in history and imagination. We owe Marco Polo's voyages in part to cinnamon, Athenian civilization to Athena's gift of the olive. And the sugar that seems so ephemeral to Aziz gave us the poetry of Othello, the Moor of Venice, since the Elizabethan Barbary Company, which exchanged English cloth for Moroccan sugar, was one of Shakespeare's patrons.

A Mediterranean culinary pilgrimage requires a visit to Sicily, that eternal colony invaded, as the Sicilians will tell you encyclopedically, by "everyone." Its cooking is a magma of Greek, Roman, Arab, French, Spanish, and American influences, a cuisine with an elastic character rather like that of its San Guiseppe festival soup, made of the remnant legumes from the year's harvest, a soup that changes according to what the pantry offers. Sicily is celebrated as the birthplace of the first known cookbook, *The Life of Luxury,* produced in the fourth century B.C., during the island's days as a Greek colony, so there is a pleasing symmetry in the thought that I will be visiting the current three graces of Sicilian cooking: Mary Taylor Simeti, Anna Tasca Lanza, and Giovanna Tornabene.

By accident, I arrive in Palermo at 2:30 in the morning, having gotten thoroughly lost on roads seemingly laid out by Lewis Carroll, with signs indicating that each destination in Sicily must be reached by traveling simultaneously in all four directions. Perhaps this too is a defensive legacy, designed to stymie invaders. The street that is my destination is under construction, and I collect a Pied Piper's worth of helpers as I search on foot for the hotel. Trailing construction workers and policemen, I emerge dazzled onto the Piazza Pretoria, stunned, after the imageless conventions of Islamic decoration, by a teeming senate of illuminated life-size male and female nudes, permanent residents of a monumental fountain. A bride rustles majestically toward me, wearing a bouffant wedding dress and train on the scale of the fountain. It turns out that she is not a hallucination, but a model dressed for a photography shoot that is using the sixteenth-century *fontana* as backdrop, and she knows my hotel.

She is a portent, since tomorrow, as I discover, everyone in Sicily is getting married. At every church I want to visit, a wedding is, or is about to be, in progress. It seems only fitting, after all this matrimony, to be visiting a site associated with the goddess responsible for it, Venus, who was celebrated in a famous temple of antiquity in the mountain town now known as Erice, on Sicily's southern coast, facing a corresponding shrine to the goddess across the water in Tunisia. A popular Sunday outing among Sicilians, Erice is now the center of another cult, that of Maria Grammatico, trained at the now-empty convent of San Carlo and one of the remaining experts in the making of the famous Sicilian convent sweets.

I climb up the streets of the medieval village, with its stone houses often, I am told, wrapped in mist; even today, with a sky the color of blue silk, it's chilly enough for a sweater. Trattorias promise Sunday lunches of fish couscous, an Arab dish that clung to Sicily; a shop window displays bottles of a local liqueur called the Milk of Venus and whimsical dolls that look like Polyphemus, the cheese-making cyclops of Homer's *Odyssey*, conventionally imagined to be Sicilian.

In Maria Grammatico's shop, a picture of the Virgin and Child hangs on the wall, along with engravings of pastrymakers and bot-tles of marsala and *limoncello*. Here is an array of the devastatingly sweet Sicilian pastries, explosive with the sugar that is every Westerner's culinary legacy from the Arabs. The pastries, filled with almonds, lemon, orange peel, and quince and citron conserves, are often named as if they were miniature operas: Belli e Brutti, Bolle di Neve, Minni di Virgini (virgins' breasts). Here too is the sculp-tural marzipan, which reminds me of the great nineteenth-century chef Carême's remark that pastry-making is a branch of architec-ture; it also attests to a striking quality of the Sicilian aesthetic: Sicilians insist on the image as the Spanish insist on pork, in con-tradiction to their Muslim legacy, and perhaps also because they are searching for an image they can recognize as their own amid the unstable procession of their occupiers—my quince conserve here, *cotognata,* is shaped in molds stamped with designs. And tasting Maria Grammatico's almond tart, work calibrated like a wine-maker's to bring each element of the pastry to its vintage moment, I reflect that human passion will find its way into the world through food, even if forbidden other routes, and thank God for our unchastity.

I take the train to Vallelunga, to visit Marchesa Anna Tasca Lanza at Regaleali, her family's estate and vineyard. The driver who picks me up at the station stops the car at the sight of a baby lamb, whose mother is nudging it up a hill. *"Agnellino,"* he sighs.

When I visited Giovanna Tornabene in her country house hotel in the Madoni Mountains, she designed a meal for me that demonstrated how traditional Sicilian food was evolving; Mary Taylor Simeti, whom I met at her farm near the cathedral town of Monreale, talked to me about the ingenuity of Sicilian peasant cooking, describing a fishless version of *pasta con le sarde* with the poignant name *pasta con le sarde a mare,* "pasta with the sardines still at sea."

Anna Tasca Lanza's work is the documentation of a culture, including dishes still unknown to the world because they are rarely presented outside private households, and dishes drawn from the baronial cooking she was reared on, with a *"monzù,"* a French chef, in the kitchen. In her courtyard today, tomatoes dry on tables covered with wire screens, and in the kitchen Anna Lanza, in pearl earrings and careful coiffure, supervises a cook who is filling glass jars with *'strattu,* a dense tomato conserve that is a staple of Sicilian households and is made in a painstaking series of dryings, pureeings, and evaporations. The woman filling the jars with what looks like rust-colored clay reminds me of the potters of Fez. A marble table displays traditional molds for the Easter marzipan lambs, and on the counter stand an endearing herd of horses made of caciocavallo cheese, further evidence of the Sicilian penchant for the image. We have cheese-filled *paninni* for lunch, along with a red wine from the family vineyards.

"It is in the Sicilian tradition not to give recipes," Lanza tells me, talking of her struggles to obtain closely guarded recipes before they disappear. She has, she says, been trying to persuade the prioress of a convent famous for its sweet couscous made with almonds and pistachios to divulge the secret. "Have you heard of the *pentiti?*" she asks. I haven't, but she explains that they are mafiosi who, when they "repent" and confess to the police, are given certain prison privileges in exchange. Anna Lanza, it seems, had occasion to invoke them when she was most recently stubbornly refused the couscous recipe. "Here," said the *marchesa* to the prioress, "is my card. I hope you will repent and call me with the recipe."

There is a Turkish saying, *"Allah bir peygamber hak, pekmez kara, yogurt ak,"* "God is one and the prophet real, as grape molasses is black and yogurt white." In Turkey, my final destination, God also communicates through food, and food continues to be an emblem of politics. Turkish food is the nourishment of invader and empire, a fusion of the food of expedition and the food of privilege, an amoebalike amalgam of methods and influences from conquered regions and imperial invention. Today, Turks still demonstrate an extraordinary capacity to set up camp and start cooking. I pass a scraggly corner of Istanbul's Gülhane Park, once part of the gardens of Topkapi Palace, and notice that an impromptu fast-food stand has been created with a tiny portable grill and two crates of bread hauled onto the grass. Two scarved ladies with trailing skirts are grilling kabobs and peppers for passersby. One cooks the meat, while the second splits a small loaf, scoops in some greens from a pyramid of chopped salad on a newspaper, and assembles the meal—absolute nomadic mastery of *cuisine à la minute,* which I will observe again and again.

In this country composed of disparate ethnicities and religions, food was deliberately used to forge a communal life. The emblem of the Janissaries, the troops made up of European subjects who were converted to Islam, was a soup kettle. Even the titles of the officers—soup cooks (who were commanders), chief cooks, pancakemakers, scullions—were drawn from culinary usage, emphasizing how identity is created through the sharing of food. The Ottoman rulers well understood the political uses of food, and according to the historian Philip Mansel, "the task of satisfying the hunger and quenching the thirst of Constantinople preoccupied sultans and grand viziers even more than protection of the pilgrim route to Mecca." It is apt that the showiest jewel in the Imperial Treasury at Topkapi, bought by Mehmed IV in the seventeenth century, is known as the "spoonmaker's diamond," spoons being important pieces of Ottoman private property, measures of etiquette, and actors in the multitude of Turkish proverbs concerning food.

In Hagia Sofia, the great Byzantine church with its dome like a goddess's navel, whose capture by Mehmed the Conqueror in 1453 in a sense created the Ottoman Empire, I grasp that the architecture of belief must be an architecture of miracle, using material so that it seems to metamorphose into some new element. Here the hard marbles of the walls—porphyry, pink, green, gray—look like silken cloth, and stones glitter in geometric shapes in the walls and mosaics, like handfuls of jewels thrown into the air that miraculously stay suspended. The building's gradual ascent to its central dome makes the whole a metaphor for not falling, a monumental expression of Christian theology. The Turks seem to have fallen in love with the dome, present both in many of their greatest mosques and at formal Turkish meals, where the great ragouts and pilafs— imperial, not nomadic, cooking—are brought to the table covered with elaborately worked copper and silver domes.

I myself ascend, for lunch several flights up, on a terrace overlooking the Sea of Marmara, at a deceptively simple restaurant called Develi. Tucked in among a warren of houses and a lively fish bazaar, the restaurant is known for its magisterial kabobs. I drink white wine and order *muhammara,* an elegant chickpea and red pepper puree, from the meze tray; it is served with a puffed bread studded with nigella seeds that make little pockets of intense flavor, rendering each mouthful unpredictable, one of the baker's great challenges. In fact, each dish is served with a different bread. Bread seems to play a role in Turkish cooking similar to that of sauces in French cuisine: each is perceived to enhance a certain range of flavors. I next order *fistikli kebab,* meat crusty with brown, crackling onions and jeweled with pistachios, which makes me think of the Turkish love of inlay, evident in buildings like the Blue Mosque, with its wood doors inlaid with ivory, mother-of-pearl, and tortoiseshell. The kabob comes with bread called finger *pide,* a Ramadan specialty obtainable all year; baked in a wood-burning oven, it is indented with the fingers and brushed with yogurt. I finish the meal with quince simmered in syrup and served with *kaymak,* a thick sheep or buffalo cream, so thick it is almost cheese— this must be the meat of angels, who do not kill to eat.

A train rolls by with seven or so army tanks on the open beds of its cars, and I watch the genre paintings my vantage point over the neighborhood provides. A man gently feeds pet pigeons on his roof. He climbs a little way down the sheer face of the rock that forms one wall of his house and extends a shovel for a pigeon who cannot make his own way to the roof. The pigeon and the man are so familiar with each other that the pigeon climbs on and rides as comfortably as if the shovel were an elevator.

Wandering through the fish market, I see an unpredictable range of women's dress; a shrouded woman bargains next to one with high-heeled sandals, hennaed hair, and tight black jeans. I count five different kinds of rice at one stall, including a variety especially for dolmas, stuffed leaves. I stop in at a bookstore, whose proprietor is peering out the window with a somewhat crestfallen air. "What time do you have?" he asks me, and comments anxiously that it is getting late. "Do you think there is still time for them to come?" "Who?" I ask. "The Rolling Stones. They are here for a concert, and

I was told they would surely come in to buy some books." Trained in the Deep South to soothe, I mutter involuntarily reassuring phrases to convey that there is ample time for the Rolling Stones, a rock group celebrated everywhere for its love of literature, to enhance their libraries with a visit to his shop.

A pharmacist in a shop full of sacks of dried flowers and herbs notices my pause before a jar of reddish-brown paste with a picture of a confident-looking turbaned and bearded man in Ottoman costume, his hand on what appears to be his sword. *"Macunu,"* the pharmacist grins at me, "Turkish Viagra." A small, earnest boy of five or so, carrying a silver scepter and wearing a plumed turban and sequined cape, crosses the street surrounded by family. He is wearing his circumcision costume; stretched across his chest is a banner that reads MASHALLAH, "May God protect."

On a Sunday I join Engin Akin, whose radio program discussing Turkish and international cooking is an institution in Turkey. Engin and I have already met (her name means something like "the infinite"; the Ottoman tradition of giving lyrical names to women continues, and I have been introduced, along with "Infinite," to "Daylight" and "Sea"). Our first meeting was at Istanbul's Divan Hotel, whose restaurant specializing in traditional Turkish cooking is an education as well as a delight. There we sampled such courtly dishes as *su boregi,* made of layers of rolled pastry that are boiled one by one, spread with a filling prepared from cheese, herbs, and butter, then baked; and the famous Circassian chicken, made with pulverized walnuts and paprika, supposedly the creation of the most prized fair-haired harem slaves from the Caucasus, who at the turn of the century commanded prices of up to thirty thousand dollars. I wonder how the excellent Divan version compares with the one described by the historian Godfrey Godwin and made in an earthenware flowerpot with successive layers of black walnut oil and chicken breast shredded as fine as silk threads and weighted overnight with a brick until the mixture metamorphoses into an almost mystical amalgam of flavors.

Today, Engin and I stroll up the Bosphorus, past Mehmed the Conqueror's fifteenth-century fortress, the Rumeli Hisar. The shore is lined with amateur fishermen, strollers, bread sellers calling *"simit simit simit"* and setting their wooden trays of golden bangle-shaped bread rings on tripods for sale as if they were pitching tents. We pass dessert shops that are evidence of the nomadic expertise with dairy foods and which sell bowls of dishes such as rice pudding *brûlée* and a Roman-Byzantine pudding made of chicken breast, milk, rice flour, and sugar, adapted in medieval Europe as blancmange. The milk-pudding shops, sherbet-sellers offering flavors like black grape, pâtisserie windows full of the Bursa specialty of glacé chestnuts, and sweets such as *locum* and *helva* remind me of the almost religious obligation of Muslims to relish sugar—"To enjoy sweets," says the Koran, "is a sign of faith."

On the road to Antioch, the fabled pleasure-loving city of Roman Syria (which formally joined the Turkish Republic in 1939), I stop at Toprakale castle to look out over the plain of Issus, where Alexander the Great's victory over the Persian Darius helped create the future of our own world. Looking out from the battlements of this wilderness-eaten twelfth-century castle, so ruined that it is now a geological feature rather than a building, as the *Titanic* is a marine feature rather than a ship, it occurs to me that the site of this battle is also a culinary landmark—Alexander's eastern expeditions were accompanied by botanists, who among other things introduced rice to the Greeks. Eastern and Western gods as well as armies met on this plain; as always, the political, the gastronomic, and the religious are conjunct.

Antioch itself is now pocked with ugly high-rises, and its

Orontes River is a sinister polluted yellow. But in the city's old hill-top Roman suburb, Daphne (now called Harbiye), where the nymph metamorphosed into a laurel tree before Apollo's eyes, I have a meal that is likely to be unequaled in my life. In the Bogazici (Bosphorus) restaurant, divided in halves by a fish-filled canal fed by a mountain river, under clusters of grapes the color of green tourmalines, I expect to find, and do, Turkish food at its most Eastern: we are near the Syrian border here, the first language is often Arabic, and the hotel lobby displays a clock set to Riyadh time.

The waiter, who is a combination of educator and host and manages the meal with a justified ecstatic pride, takes me back to the kitchen, where ranks of cooks preside over *meze*, meat dishes, fish dishes, and baking. Flat sesame-studded bread is baked on wooden planks, and fresh loaves are extravagantly hurried to tables as soon as the previous portion is judged to have cooled. The waiter signals to a man who is making *cig kofte,* raw meatballs made of lamb, bulgur, and a panoply of Eastern spices—cloves, ginger, cin-namon, cumin. The waiter puts one on a plate and feeds me fork-ful by forkful, waiting triumphantly for my verdict.

At the table, there is a dish of chopped herbs, in which mint is prominent, a salad of mountain oregano with pomegranate molasses, and homemade string cheese. The main course is a spicy kabob with green peppers, onions, and coriander—the waiter also hurries anxiously to the table with a supplementary plate of french fried potatoes, anxious for me to have something familiar. They are the best I have ever eaten—if the Belgians only knew.

After dinner, I am urged on to an evening of music at an open-air nightclub down the road. A singer moves from table to table, taking requests, being sprayed with shaken-up club soda in moments of passionate appreciation. A tiny enclave of mixed cou-ples dance together near the stage, but for the most part, the diners and dancers are male, shimmying and mirroring each other's movements in groups and in couples, around tables laden with water-melon. A proverb a Turkish friend once told me comes to mind: "A woman for work, a boy for love, and a melon for ecstasy."

The next morning, I wake up to the sounds of hoofbeats, as donkeys descend from the mountain laden with panniers full of fresh mountain herbs for making tonight's salads and kabobs. Antioch is home to a museum with mosaics from the luxurious Roman villas that were once the pride of Harbiye. I spend a long time in front of one nicknamed "The Buffet Supper." In the central panel, Ganymede gives drink to Zeus, who has taken the form of an eagle; the pair is bordered by a still life that shows representative courses of a Roman banquet made up of foods I have encountered in every country I have visited on this trip, an entire spectrum of Mediterranean cooking. Here, in stone, are appetizers of boiled eggs in cups, shown with the special spoons designed for breaking eggshells. Here too are roasted artichokes, a springtime delicacy in modern-day Sicily, and in the ancient world a specialty of Antioch. A silver sauce dish holds some kind of reddish condiment that makes me think of pomegranate molasses, though it is probably wine, vinegar, or even honey, and which recalls Morocco. There is a fish on a grand rectangular platter, as I have seen served on the Bosphorus, three disks of bread that resemble Turkish *pide* and Moroccan *khobz,* and a ham, the love of which the Romans bequeathed to their Christian descendants, as is apparent in Spain. And there are, of course, Zeus and Ganymede, here where food and divinity are one essence, and old gods and new meet at table. D. H. Lawrence once said, "Eat and carouse with Bacchus or munch dry bread with Jesus, but don't sit down without one of the gods." At Mediterranean tables, no one ever does.

Costumed attendants at the entrance of Marrakech's legendary hotel La Mamounia create an irresistible Orientalist fantasy, providing even the psyche with a vacation. A lunch of chicken sandwiches and champagne at the bar will make you feel like Cole Porter.

Despite less than perfect service, the Palais Jamaï at Bab Guissa is still the best hotel in Fez. Or stay in one of the four wonderfully atmospheric suites at La Maison Bleu, also in the old city (see *Des Belles Choses* for contact info). In Marrakech, don't miss Christine Rio's restaurant, Le Tobsil (04.44.4052; fax .3515; *prix fixe,* about $53), or Yacout. (See *Des Belles Choses* for contact info.) Rio also suggests that if you wish to sample a particular Moroccan dish, you or your hotel could arrange in advance with a restaurant to cook it for you. In Fez, the beauty and sumptuous hospitality of the Palais Mnebhi makes for an unforgettable experience (055.63.38.93; fax .44.05; entrées, about $18–$35). El Baraka de Zerhoun, 37 miles east of Fez, in Moulay Idriss, is the closest many visitors will come to eating in a Moroccan home (055.54.41.84; entrées, about $7–$8).

Reading

For richly detailed historical and practical information, pick up the Cadogan Guide *Morocco*. Edith Wharton's *In Morocco* is a fascinating social history and a work of great beauty. Fez cookery and household customs are described in *Traditional Moroccan Cooking*, by Madame Guinaudeau. Paula Wolfert's *Couscous and Other Good Food from Morocco* is a classic, as is the rest of her oeuvre, down to the latest, *Mediterranean Grains and Greens,* which made me suspect that she is in fact Demeter, the ancient goddess of the harvest, up to her old trick of pretending to be mortal.

Where to Buy in Morocco

Haggling is expected in the marketplace, although Moroccan merchants seem to view it as drama. In Marrakech, the Khalid Art Gallery is a good source for decorative items and jewelry (044.442.410). Galerie Tinmel has beautiful Moroccan antiques and rugs and doesn't require the bargaining practiced in the souks (044.443.2271). The entire medina in Fez is filled with lovely work—which your guide will lead you to, since part of his job is to gauge your tastes, as well as your pocketbook. You won't want to miss the five hundred varieties of perfumes, spices, and cosmetics at Nour Driss (055.63.39.48), or Poterie Fakhkhari in the Potter's Quarter, with its exquisite tiles, plates, bowls, and ornate Moroccan bread boxes (055.64.93.22).

I was extremely lucky in my guide, Abdelaziz Zgani, who is intelligent, humorous, knowledgeable, and willing to shape a route to fit the client's interests. As an *accompagnateur de tourisme,* he is a true Fassi craftsman. Reserve his services in advance in writing or by phone—but call at night, since he guides during the day (4 rue 2 Arset Bennis Douh, Fez, Morocco; 055.74.00.92).

Café in Morocco

BY PAUL BOWLES

༄

editor's note

....

I admit that this is an article I did not originally have in my files. I read
of it in Paula Wolfert's *Couscous and Other Good Food from Morocco,* in
which she spoke highly of it, in particular in the way Bowles described the
many functions a Moroccan café serves its habitués.

PAUL BOWLES lived for more than fifty years in Morocco; he was prob-
ably equally famous for being an expatriate in Tangier and the author of
*The Sheltering Sky, The Spider's House, Their Heads Are Green and Their
Hands Are Blue,* and *100 Camels in the Courtyard,* among many others. But
Bowles was also an accomplished composer in New York before he moved
to Morocco.

The beach, very wide along this coast, is protected by a crumbling breakwater a few hundred feet offshore, so that from here
in the garden the waves make only a distant murmur, a somnolent
backdrop for the nearer sounds of bees buzzing and the occasional
low voices of the men inside the café. I came into the garden a few
minutes ago and sat down on a large woven-grass mat near the well.
The mat has been provided with piles of bottle tops to be used as
counters in whatever game I may be going to play.

The garden spreads out along the foot of the town's ramparts,
hidden behind a jungle of fig trees and cactus, buried in total shade
beneath a ceiling of grape leaves. At this season the heavy bunches
of grapes hang down between the meshes of cane trellis above, and
bump against my forehead as I come through on my way to the well.
Facing me, in a corner, like a Chinese lantern big enough to hold a
man, is a wicker fish trap left to dry: this is a fishermen's café. At

night, after it is shut and the beach is deserted, the customers often return with their own teapots and invade the garden, lying on the mats talking and smoking, and when the grapes and figs are ripe, eating the fruit. Mrhait, who runs the establishment, finds this as it should be. "The fruit is here for our friends to eat," he declares. There are a few tables and chairs around for those who want them, and even these are left out all night for the customers' convenience. They represent the major part of his capital, and they could easily be carried away. But this is a small town; no one has ever stolen anything from him.

The traditional café in this part of the world is conceived of as a club where, in addition to enjoying the usual amenities of a café, a man may, if he wishes, eat, sleep, bathe, and store his personal effects. The fact that the nearest café may be five or ten minutes' walk from where he lives (it is seldom farther, for the establishments are numerous) does not prevent him from considering it an extension of his home. Each café has its regular clientele whose members know one another; the habitués form a limited little community in which the appearance of an unfamiliar local face is as much an intrusion as that of a complete foreigner. It is difficult to induce a Muslim to go into a café where he is not known: he does not enjoy being stared at.

Upper-class Muslims generally refuse to be seen in cafés at all, their contention being that one sits and drinks tea in a crowded public place only if one cannot do so in one's own house. But for these good bourgeois, as for us Europeans, the taking of tea is thought of as a relaxing pause, a respite from the affairs of the day. The hour or two spent on the terrace of a café counts as time off from the involvements of daily routine; one sits and watches life go past. The average Muslim here, on the contrary, goes into a café in order to participate as intensely as possible in the collective existence of his friends and neighbors. In a land whose social life is predicated on the separation of the sexes, the home is indisputably the woman's precinct; the man must seek his life outside. And the generally prevalent uproar in even the middle-class Muslim household makes the all-male café a necessity. Only there does the man feel free to talk, smoke his kif pipe, play or listen to music, and even, if the spirit moves him, to dance a little in front of his friends.

And it is in the café that the foreign visitor, too, can feel the pulse of the country. Nowhere else can he manage to observe a group of individuals repeatedly and at length in their daily contacts with one another, or succeed in existing at their tempo, achieving in occasional unguarded moments a state of empathy with their very different sense of the passage of time. And to experience time from the vantage point of these people is essential to understanding their attitudes and behavior. Today, when even in the farthest reaches of the bush there is beginning to be established a relationship between the number of hours a man works and the amount of wages he collects, any human institution where the awareness of time has not yet penetrated is a phenomenon to be cherished.

With its luxury of unmeasured time the Moroccan café is out of harmony with present-day concepts, and thus it is doomed to extinction. Ask any café owner. It takes approximately three minutes to prepare each glass of tea. The customer may then sit for as many hours as he wishes over the one glass. Since the maximum profit per order is equivalent to about one cent, it seems clear that economically there is no future in the café business. There are other factors, too, that militate against the continued life of the traditional "Moorish" café. It is claimed by the authorities that cafés cause men to waste time that might be used to better advantage. Whatever places are shut down in periods of civic reform (and latter-day puritanism has made these campaigns fairly frequent) are thereby permanently destroyed, since if and when they are reopened, it is invariably as European-style establishments. The change-over in clothing also has its effect. As long as the clientele was composed exclusively of men wearing the customary garments, it was sufficient to cover the floor with grass matting. The increasing number of those who sport European apparel, however, induces the owners to provide chairs, since the Moroccans like their trousers to be so tight-fitting that to sit in their normal position on the floor while wearing them would be an impossibility.

The traditional floor-café is a result of natural processes; one might say it is strictly functional, in that the intent is merely to make as comfortable and pleasant a place as possible for the greatest number of people, and at minimum cost. The cheapest materials—cane, bamboo, palm thatch, woven reeds and grass—are not only the most attractive visually, but also provide the most satisfactory acoustics for the music. The modern table-and-chair café, on the other hand, is an abstraction: its primary aim has come to be the showing off of the expensive foreign objects that have been acquired (including, in the cities, electric refrigerator and television) and that distinguish the place from its humbler rivals. Practical considerations fade before the determination to make this all-important display. Thus it is that the new-style cafés achieve only a sordid uniformity in their discomfort and metallic noisiness, while the old-fashioned places are as diverse as the individuals who created them.

This garden here by the sea with its ceiling of grapes; the flat roofs of the Marrakesh cafés where men sit at midnight waiting for a breath of cool air; the cavelike rooms in the mountain markets of the High Atlas, to which the customers must bring their own tea, sugar, and mint, the establishment furnishing only the fire, water, and teapot; in Fez the baroque wooden palaces among the weeping willows of the Djenane es Sebir, whose deck chairs line the river's wandering channels; the cafés where the tea drinkers bring their prayer mats and retire into a small carpeted room to perform their sundown prostrations; the countless little niches in the alleys of every town, where a plank along the wall and bottle crates turned on end are the only furnishings; and then the cafés with dancing boys, like the Stah in Tangier; the sanctuary cafés, whose shadiest customers remain unmolested by the authorities, like the one opposite the gardens of the Koutoubia in Marrakesh; the superb improvised tent cafés at the great religious pilgrimages in the wilderness; the range is vast. Few countries can supply such a variety of décor and atmosphere.

And what goes on in these places? The men converse, tell interminable stories, eat, smoke kif, sleep, and play games: cards, checkers, dominoes, parchisi and, during Ramadan, bingo, whose prize used to be a glass of tea for each winner, but which nowadays often mysteriously turns out to be a bottle of cooking oil. In cold weather they sit as near as they can to the bed of burning charcoal under the water boiler. At night latecomers anxiously ask as they enter: "Is there still fire?" Once the embers have been allowed to die there is no more tea until the next day. The water boiler is an improvised samovar made of copper with a tap on the side; once in a while it proves to be the real article, with Cyrillic characters incised on its flank. Being the most important item in the place, it is put in the spot where there is the most light.

The elaboration of niches and shelves around the fire and water is the living heart of the café—rather like the altar of a church. In the cities it is a complicated tile-covered construction that serves as sink, stove, and cabinet. One compartment contains the fire and the samovar, another the water tap or pail; smaller cubicles are for storing sugar, tea, and mint. In the lesser cafés the single table is put beside this unlikely looking installation. Close friends of the proprietor and the kif concessionaire generally sit here. Nowadays, what with official frowns being directed at the smoking of the herb, the kif seller is not likely to be in evidence; nevertheless, he is a very important factor in the functioning of the café. He not only brings his own raw material, which traditionally he cleans and cuts in full view of the clients before selling it to them, thus forestalling doubts about its purity, but also processes (for a price) the kif that others have brought with them, blending the tobacco with it to suit each man's individual taste. How much of this must go on clandestinely depends on local circumstances; the ban on kif is being enforced with increasing firmness.

Unless he has been at the pipe for many hours, it is impossible to tell from a North African's behavior whether or not he has smoked kif. The same observation cannot be made, I am afraid, if alcohol has been taken instead. In the bars, loosened inhibitions send tempers up in flames, but I have never seen anything more serious than an argument in a café full of men smoking kif; the prevailing atmosphere is calm and jovial.

When the tea maker gets an order, he takes a long-handled tin canister and puts in a heaping teaspoonful of green China tea (usually Formosan chun mee). Next he adds four or five teaspoonfuls of sugar. Another little canister filled with hot water from the samovar is already embedded in the coals. As soon as it is boiling, he pours the water over the mixed tea and sugar. While it is steeping he crushes as many stalks of fresh spearmint as he can into a glass. Then he strains the tea into the glass, often garnishing it with a sprig of verbena, two or three unopened orange blossoms, or a few leaves of rosemary, *chiba,* or some other locally available herb. The result, hot, sweet and strongly aromatic, bears very little resemblance to tea as it is drunk anywhere else in the world; it is *até,* a refresher in its own right, not unlike maté in Argentina but a good deal more tasty. Usually when newcomers try their first glass, they are appalled by the concentrated sweetness, and get into the habit of ordering it with less sugar. The results are catastrophic. Indeed, the cafés that cater to the tourist trade now serve an unpalatable hybrid concoction, neither *até* nor tea. The Moroccans were quick to heed the foreigners' preferences: what with the constantly rising cost of sugar, the new preparation saves them money.

All cafés provide neighborhood delivery service. A boy carries racks holding six glasses, back and forth, full and empty, all day long between the samovar and the nearby offices, banks, and shops. Boiling-hot mint tea is still the favorite drink in the land, notwithstanding the increasing sales of colas and other bottled gaseous beverages. Even the customs officials in the port may be sipping tea offhandedly while they go through the luggage; the traveler who is automatically unnerved by the prospect of customs inspection often finds this reassuring.

A part of each café is occupied by the *soudda,* a wooden platform raised a foot or so above the floor, usually with a low railing around it, and always with a covering of woven grass or reed matting. If there are any musicians they sit here, as do the establishment's most regular and esteemed habitués. After hours at night, this space may be used as a dormitory for transients. Ten or twelve years ago in the Calle Ben Charki of Tangier there was a large café with an unusual clientele. It made no difference whether you went at midnight or at three in the morning; scores of boys between the ages of eight and fourteen sat at the tables in the center of the sparsely lighted room, fiercely playing cards. A wide platform extended along three of the walls, where there was even less light. The boys lying here tossed and scratched in their sleep; even so, they were the lucky ones, for when the card players began to yawn and look around for a place to stretch out, the platform was often full, and they had to be content to move to a table where others were already asleep, leaning forward from the little straight-backed chairs, their heads and arms lying flat on the boards. Month in, month out, the ragged horde filled the café. They were the *boleros* of Tangier, children who had strayed into the city from the hills beyond, and having managed to acquire a wooden box, a tin or two of polish, an old toothbrush, and a rag, had set themselves up in business as shoeshine boys. As an old resident, I found the place a natural concomitant of North

African life; however, the foreign visitors I took there thought it offensive. Children ought not to live that way. Apparently the authorities shared these prejudices, for the establishment has long since ceased to function, nor are there any others similar to it.

Like all the African countries, Morocco has been thrown open to the forces of rapid modernization. The fact that its indigenous culture is so much more highly evolved than that of most other places on the continent tends, however, to retard the process. In a primitive land where the disparity between the old and the new worlds is total, the conversion conceivably can be effected in one generation, but where there is a perfectly viable, if archaic, tradition of civilization already in existence, as there is in Morocco, it will naturally take more time. This spirit of resistance to arbitrary, senseless change is a stock subject of the humorous anecdotes exchanged among café sitters, particularly in small towns.

A story I heard here in Mrhait's café the other day delighted me. This was a factual account of something that happened in a little country market up in the hills behind Larache. It was the day of the week when all the peasants of the region come on foot and on donkeyback to the village and sit in the market selling the things they have brought in with them. Swaggering through the throng of rustics came a young man who, if he was not really from the city, at least was doing everything he could to create that impression, his most blatant claim to urban refinement being a brand-new pair of locally made Levis, so skin-tight that he had a little difficulty in walking. He came up to an old woman, one among many others like her, who sat in the dust with a few figs, a half dozen green peppers, and some tomatoes, each being arranged according to custom in a neat little pyramid in front of her. Indicating the figs with the toe of his shoe, and thus upsetting the pile, the youth asked their price in an offhand manner calculated to widen the social difference he felt existed between him and the old woman.

"Don't kick the fruit, my son," she said evenly. She had taken his measure as he came, but now she did not even look up at him. Then she added: "If you'll sit down here beside me, I'll give you a good price."

The prospect of a bargain proved too much for the young man. He squatted down, and that was the end of him. With an explosive sound the seams of his trousers split wide open. ("His face was red, red!" the raconteur recalled with relish.) To the accompaniment of loud peasant laughter the young man made his way back through the crowd and out of the market.

One night I went to Mrhait's café with the idea of telling him that what I had been writing there at the end of his garden was a piece about cafés, to see if he had anything to say on the subject. But I intended to wait until everyone had gone, in order to avoid interruptions. It was fairly late, and there was a hot east wind roaring overhead. Even there behind the ramparts I recognized the dry spicy smell of parched hillsides that is borne on the *cherqi* at this time of year. The waves rolled in across the dark beach with mechanical regularity. I sat until there was no one in the garden, and I could hear no voices inside the café. Eventually Mrhait came out of the doorway and peered through the tangle of vines toward my dim corner. He finally saw me and came over.

After he had sat down opposite me and lighted a cigarette, I began. "You know, I've been writing about cafés here in Morocco so that Americans will know what they're like. I thought maybe you might have something to say about your own café, something you'd like them to know."

The cigarette end flared; his voice betrayed a surprising degree of feeling. "For sixteen years, ever since I was twelve and my father put me in this café, I've worked here and lived here and slept here. I made all this with my own hands. Why are those roses growing there? Because I planted the bushes. Why do we have these figs and grapes? Because I take care of the trees and vines. Why is there good sweet water in the well? Because I keep it clean. This morning, this very day, I went down inside and scooped out eight wheelbarrows full of sand and mud. That's what it means to run a café—not making one glass or a thousand glasses of tea."

Failing to see just where his rhetoric was leading him, I interrupted cautiously: "But you do like your work, don't you?"

"My work is in the garden, and that's only in summer. In the winter I stay inside the café, and the wind blows, and some days nobody comes at all. Just the empty café, and outside the rain and the waves. That's not work. That's prison. There's nobody left in this town. Everybody's gone. And that's why I'm going to go to the city myself and get a job in a café where they pay you every week."

He rose to his feet. I was silent, considering again the transitoriness of everything in this land. In my imagination the café had long ago assumed the character of a landmark; it seemed impossible that Mrhait should be willing to walk out and leave it. I got up, too, and followed him slowly across the garden.

"But it's your café!" I was saying. "It belongs to you! After all these years you want to begin working for wages? At your age?"

In front of the doorway onto the beach he stopped and turned to face me. "Look. If you can't make a living by working for yourself, then you go to work for somebody else, don't you?"

"I suppose so."

"It's better to carry glasses in a busy café than own an empty one. Better to eat than starve, no?"

As we shook hands, he added reassuringly: "I'll be back. I'm sure to come back, later on. Just as soon as I get a little money together."

Fortunately it was dark and he did not see my smile, which he would have recognized as cynical. The familiar refrain: *There is money in the city! I'm going to get it.* Whether or not Mrhait gets it, once he has lived in the city he will not return here.

Of Pigeons, *Bisteeya*, Couscous, and Rose Petals

BY NANCY HARMON JENKINS

~

editor's note

The following four articles detail a variety of dining and cooking experiences throughout Morocco. If it seems that one hears of the same names repeatedly in the restaurant world, it's because it's true. Morocco is not a nation of people who dine out (Moroccans believe that a person who has to dine out should be pitied, because everyone knows the best food is served in the home), and therefore restaurants are not in great supply.

NANCY HARMON JENKINS is a contributing editor of *Food & Wine* and is the author of *Flavors of Tuscany: Traditional Recipes from the Tuscan Countryside* (Broadway Books, 1998), *Flavors of Puglia: Traditional Recipes From the Heel of Italy's Boot* (Broadway Books, 1997), and *The Mediterranean Diet Cookbook* (Bantam Books, 1994).

I will try to be as honest about this as I can. It is not easy to dine out in Morocco. Or at least, it is not easy to dine out *well* in Morocco.

True, it's easier than in Egypt or Iraq, for example, but Egypt and Iraq do not boast of celebrated cuisines that have been verbally massaged in high romantic style by American (and other) writers to the point where the food is considered an apotheosis of gastronomy. Morocco, on the other hand, does.

Ever since Paula Wolfert wrote about it in the early 1970s, Moroccan cooking has been vaunted for its synthesis of what she called the essentials of a great cuisine—a fertile mix of cultures, a rich and well-developed agriculture, and a palace tradition with an established code of elegance and refinement in the kitchen and at the table.

Morocco has it all: an Arab-Berber-Jewish, African–Middle Eastern–Andalusian inheritance (not to mention the French, a recent but nonetheless persuasive influence); an extensive agriculture incorporating Mediterranean olives, olive oil, and citrus, African dates and peppery spices, and Levantine sheep and dairy products; and an honored tradition of aristocratic palace dishes, such as *bisteeya,* the rich fantasia of minced pigeon and almonds, butter, sugar, and eggs, all layered between crisp, transparent leaves of *warka* pastry and flavored with a complex of pepper and cinnamon, ginger, cilantro, saffron, and orange-flower water.

But just try to find this food outside private homes and fewer than half a dozen restaurants.

Before setting out on my gastronomic pilgrimage, I asked Moroccans—I even asked Paula Wolfert—for restaurant recommendations. What I received in response was genuine bewilderment. "Why would we eat in restaurants," they said, "when we have such good food at home?" As in other societies that are obsessed with family and caste distinctions (one thinks immediately of India), restaurants are still considered déclassé places to take a meal, best suited to the needs of poor people and travelers.

Travelers, alas, is what we were, and hungry travelers at that. Through my guide, an American friend who has lived in Morocco and spent the better part of the last fifteen years combing the country for the intricately woven Berber rugs she imports, I was a guest in a few private houses, and there we ate very well indeed, sampling the great and still-vigorous traditional cuisine. We dined around low tables, eating with the fingers of our right hands, dipping bread into thick savory sauces, sampling salads of oranges and carrots, thick, jammy mixtures of tomatoes and hot and sweet roasted peppers, stews flavored with the curious musty tang of preserved lemons, and lush *tagines* of meat braised with quinces, prunes, or humble, sweet turnips.

Outside of private homes, there are three kinds of places to eat in Morocco, all very different from one another: a handful of palace restaurants, of varying quality, in the old royal cities of Marrakech, Fez, and Meknes; an abundance of food stalls in the old medinas or the souks in country market towns, where the food, though irresistible, should be consumed with caution; and the remarkable seafood restaurants in little fishing ports as well as great cities along Morocco's long Atlantic coast.

Among traditional palace restaurants, the finest by far is Yacout in Marrakech—an experience that should not be missed by anyone, interested in food or not. Under the inspired direction of Mohammed Zghirri, the restaurant summons up all the exotic mystery of Moroccan culture while remaining deeply true to what that culture means—a fine line, but Yacout treads it confidently. There's no tourist hokeyness here, no belly dancing (a baffling Egyptian import that is utterly at odds with traditional Moroccan music and dance). By Moroccan standards, Yacout is very expensive (about $50 a person, with wine), but it's worth every penny, even for budget-minded travelers. Work it into your budget somehow.

Housed in a palatial town house in the heart of the medina, that warren of narrow streets and alleys that makes up the old city of Marrakech, the restaurant takes some persistence to find. Once beyond the massive door, we mounted a flight of stairs, past rooms ornate with multifaceted mosaics, carved stucco, and colored marquetry paneling, to the rooftop terrace. Here we settled onto comfortable low banquettes to sip wine and gaze out at the star-sprinkled dusk over the roofs and minarets of Marrakech while a traditional Gnaoua musician played untraditional music, a soothing blend of modern West African jazz motifs.

Dinner was back in the ground floor garden atrium, where candle flames, shivering in the light breeze, were reflected in a green-tiled pool, and tabletops were strewn with pink rose petals. A meal at Yacout begins according to tradition, with an array of little dishes called salads—somewhat misleading, since they are composed of vegetables, such as carrots, zucchini, peppers, eggplant, and tomatoes, as well as cubes of lamb's liver or delicate brains, all simmered in sauces spiced with cumin and ginger, cinnamon, fresh green coriander or cool mint, and perhaps a little chili (but not a lot; most Moroccan food is not fiery hot). With these were served *braewats,* little envelopes of paper-thin *warka* pastry that were wrapped around savory ground meat, or rice and almonds, or chopped brains, and then deep-fried. It takes a fine hand in the kitchen to ensure that *braewats* are crisp and frangible and never greasy, and Yacout has several pairs of fine hands—all of them, I found out later, women who had been trained from childhood in these traditions.

Anxious to try something new, we passed on the *bisteeya*, which we had had the night before, and opted for two main courses—plump little pigeons stuffed with couscous and served with a rich brown sauce, slightly sweetened with cinnamon and garnished with raisins and toasted almonds; and a lush and hearty couscous, a pyramid of fluffy pasta grains piled with morsels of lamb and chunks of zucchini, carrots, firm yellow squash, and crisp cabbage and served with bowls of fragrant hot sauce and the deep-flavored broth on which the dish was based. Finally, the sweet, simple but no less elegant: layers and layers of crisp *warka*, heaped with sugar and toasted almonds and napped with a voluptuous sweet cream thickened with rice flour and flavored with orange-flower water.

I dwell perhaps in unseemly fashion on Yacout simply because the rest of the palace restaurants we visited, though frequently mentioned by travel writers, were so disappointing. Stylia, also in Marrakech, was appealing at first glance, but the food was overly sweetened and the powerful fragrance of roses made it difficult to appreciate. On the other hand, lamb shanks cooked with a lemon and cumin sauce were delightful, the aromatics of the sauce penetrating the gelatinous meat right down to the bone. In retrospect, I might have liked Stylia more had I not gone to Yacout shortly after.

As for the vaunted Hotel Mamounia, a word to the wise: I went for lunch by the pool, but I was not permitted even to enter the hotel dressed as I was for a morning of exploring in the souk in a pair of clean jeans and tennis shoes with a good-looking (at least *I* thought so) sweater and blazer. Unacceptable, said the imperious and extremely disagreeable man at the front door who called himself *directeur de restauration.* If Mamounia is on your list, check the dress code first.

And in Fez, the restaurant in the Palais Jamai, the fanciest hotel in town and also much touted by travel writers, boasts *"les plaisirs de la cuisine fassie,"* which was, to put it gently, a farce. The six specialties of Fassi cuisine were available only *sur commande,* meaning at least twenty-four hours in advance, the waiter said. "Could not the person who took my reservation perhaps have informed me of that?" I inquired. The poor waiter—it wasn't, after all, his fault— struggled to explain. We could have couscous, *tagines,* and kabobs, he said. But I could get couscous, *tagines,* and kabobs in any street market in the country.

And I did—in the rollicking Djemaa el Fna, the amazing vast and crowded square just outside the Marrakech souks, where at sundown billows of blue smoke signal the start-up of the grill stations; at open-air restaurants lining both sides of the road for a mile or so through the town of Khemesset, where travelers pause midway between Rabat and Meknes to select their meat from local butchers, closely supervise its spicing and grilling over charcoal fires along the sidewalk, and consume it at tables set up nearby; in the two- and three-person stalls in the medina of Fès-el-Bali ("Old Fez," to distinguish it from the seven-hundred-year-old new Fez), where you pause just long enough to down a bowl of pureed fava beans drizzled with olive oil and cumin before being jostled along by the crowd; and in tented enclosures, hazy with the smoke of cooking fires, that surround bustling weekly country souks, like those near Rommani, east of Casablanca, and in Zeida, on the road between Midelt and Fez.

The food in these markets is amazing, seductive, tantalizing, full of alluring and provocative aromas, roasting meat, bubbling *tagines* spiced with cumin and cloves, fresh, fragrant bunches of mint and coriander. And it can be the most startling food imaginable—sheep's heads, thoroughly roasted, with ears akimbo and nasty little teeth protruding, decorated butchers' stalls in the medieval souk of Fez.

The array can seem endless—*tagines,* kabobs, and ground-meat *keftas,* deep-fried fish and chips and chunks of eggplant, *mechoui* (the pit-roasted lamb that's a deliciously festive treat all over the country), porcelain-colored snails cooked in a rich dark sauce, glasses of freshly squeezed orange juice, little *merguez* sausages made of ground lamb spiced with cumin and coriander and served with hot *harissa* sauce, chopped raw onion, and a chunk of bread. Try a potato sandwich—mashed potatoes stuffed into a wedge of bread with a hard-boiled egg if you wish, and far more delicious than it sounds. Or a fried potato croquette, redolent of cumin and colored bright yellow with imitation saffron. Or a bowl of chickpeas drizzled with oil, or the thick and meaty soup called *harira,* best for Ramadan but eaten all year round. Or plain bread—good, hard-wheat semolina rounds sold by black-veiled women who sit cross-legged atop their booths and glare balefully at the throng.

Try it all, but be careful: fried food is fairly safe, if you can actually see the cooking process, for few germs will survive a boiling oil bath; on the other hand, I would not recommend any meat that is less than thoroughly cooked. Our party of four suffered from various seizures, none of them serious and none of them *necessarily* attributable to the food we were eating. Use good judgment, but do experiment, because these country souks and city medinas are where you can see and smell and taste Morocco at its most appealing.

Beyond tradition, however, the best food in Morocco is the simplest—the impeccably fresh fish that is available up and down the Atlantic coast from Rabat and Casablanca, south through Oualidia and Safi, and on to Essaouira, a charming fishing port due west of Marrakech.

In Casablanca, we had a splendid series of skillfully prepared fish at Au Petit Rocher, out on the shore near the lighthouse—quite the best and freshest fish I have had outside of Spain—grilled *loup de mer,* or sea bass, flavored with fennel and served with a spicy remoulade; *daurade* (a type of bream) *au gros sel,* the fish encased in a thick salt crust that is broken at the table before serving; grilled swordfish with a light and savory anchovy butter; and a *brochette de lotte,* or monkfish, the chunks agreeably smoky with a nice touch of fresh tarragon and chervil. Like most restaurants in Morocco, Au Petit Rocher is astonishingly cheap—$15 to $20 a person with wine.

Farther down the coast, we stopped at Oualidia to sample the oysters from beds established in the 1950s, one of many fine touches left from the French occupation—another is good baguettes and croissants far better than most of what's available in France these days. At L'Hippocampe, a beguiling hotel perched above a winding sandy beach, salt air off the Atlantic rattled the palm leaves in the bright, sunny garden, but the restaurant was dark and cool, with windows facing the sea and distant surf. Dewy Portugaises, just opened, their shells as thick as old coral, were about $5 a dozen and so fresh that they flinched at a drop of lemon. The thick green *soupe de poisson,* flavored with saffron and hot pepper, came with a spicy rouille, and we followed it with irresistibly tiny inch-long whitebait, battered, crisply fried, and sprinkled with the juice of a green lemon. Again, astonishingly cheap—no more than $15 a person with wine.

Finally, Essaouira, romantic, pink-walled Essaouira, a town with a past. Once called Mogador, Essaouira was both home to one of the largest Jewish communities in Morocco and one of the most important ports on the West African coast. There was a Jewish festival going on when we arrived—the *moussem* of Rabbi Zal. Pilgrims had come from as far as Israel, and even Washington, D.C., for the opening of the miracle-working rabbi's tomb. The town was crowded, it was hard to find hotel rooms, and the restaurants were packed.

Down on the port, where fishing vessels dripped nets and buoys, the scene was tumultuous as holidaymakers crowded the docks. "The Jews have taken all the tables," said the proprietor of one of a dozen or so open-air fish restaurants that operate side by side along the dock. *Restaurant* is hardly the word for these slapdash operations made up of a display of the day's offerings (often alive and squirming), a couple of charcoal braziers, gas-fired deep-fat fryers, and long boardinghouse tables cheerfully decorated with bottles of the several kinds of soda pop available *sur commande*. We had selected this particular place because the colors were dazzling— pink-sequined *daurade,* alabaster sole, silvery blue sardines, and dark red *crevettes royales,* the giant shrimp from the Atlantic. Along with this the proprietor offered minuscule baby octopus, which he promised to deep-fry to perfect crispness for our pleasure—and he did.

There are other fish restaurants in Essaouira, at one of which, Chez Sam's, out at the end of the dock, we had dined amply the night before on a variety of fish, including some splendid little sardines grilled, as is the local manner, with their guts intact. But this dockside restaurant souk, with its humming holiday spirit, its gorgeously fresh fish, its smells of charcoal and burning fish, its funny, teasing proprietors, each one enticing customers

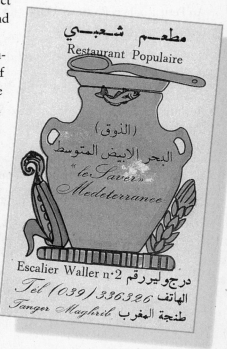

with the freshness, the skill, the perfection of his offerings, was clearly the heart of what was happening in Essaouira.

We tucked into it all as soon as the black-caftaned women, Jewish and not, made room at the table. We ate fish until we could eat no more, along with plenty of Moroccan chopped tomato-and-onion salad, good semolina bread, bowls of olives, and bottles of Coca-Cola and Orange Crush to wash it down. The day was brilliant, an African sky so blue you could see deep into it, sunlight dancing off the Atlantic, and a crisp onshore breeze keeping temperatures well within the tolerable. We had come to Morocco looking for good food, and here it was, finally, all around us.

Sound Bites

Au Petit Rocher, Phare-el-Hank, La Corniche, Aïn Diab, Casablanca; 022.39.57.48.

Restaurant L'Hippocampe, Oualidia; 033.36.61.08.

Restaurant Stylia, 34 Rue Ksour, Marrakech; 044.44.35.87.

Restaurant Yacout, 79 Sidi Ahmed Soussi, Marrakech; 044.38.29.29.

The Fragrant Food of Morocco

By Florence Fabricant

⌇⌇

FLORENCE FABRICANT writes about food for a variety of periodicals
and is the editor of the "Food Notes" column for *The New York Times*.

M orocco is a country that takes its food seriously. A stroll
through the market stalls of any souk reveals vibrant spice
stands, glistening pyramids of black and green olives, mounds of
preserved lemons, sacks of golden grains, freshly quarried blocks of
almond-studded nougat, enticing arrays of mahogany dates, and
huge aromatic bouquets of deep green mint.

It's not just this wondrously decorative array of ingredients that
is so mouth-watering. Children rush past on their way home with
palletes of fragrant bread fresh from communal ovens. Pastry mak-
ers hawk sticky, honey-dipped fritters and morsels of nut brittle.
Pause briefly to look at a rug, and the merchant will pour endless
glasses of sweetly soothing mint tea all around.

The accessories for cooking and serving, like jaunty conical
tagines (Morocco's lidded serving containers) in every size, couscous pots made of metal and clay, etched crystal glasses for mint
tea, and fine hand-embroidered table linens are also on display
everywhere in the market.

We found it easy enough to purchase a bag of dates or olives for
snacking and a terra-cotta *tagine* to bring home, but inevitably the
concentration of foodstuffs and tableware whetted our appetites.
Our foursome—myself, my husband, and another couple—had
been looking forward to visiting Morocco as much for its food as
for its historic sites and breathtaking scenery. In the major cities and

even in the country, we discovered many restaurants that produce commendable Moroccan fare, often in exotic settings.

A typical Moroccan meal usually begins with an array of up to a dozen colorful salads, many composed of cooked vegetables like carrots, zucchini, and cauliflower in various mild or peppery marinades. Cubes of cooked liver and airy morsels of deliciously spicy lamb brains are often included. Olives, the equivalent of butter at a Moroccan meal, are served with flat, round, focaccialike Arab bread. (When real butter is served, at breakfast in a hotel for example, the French influence is evident in its excellent quality.)

Diners share the salads, passing them around the table. Soups fortified with beans are another first course option, as are flaky meat or rice-filled pastries. A *tagine,* or stewlike dish, usually lamb or chicken, frequently cooked with olives, tangy preserved lemon, almonds, or prunes, could follow, served in a conical dish of the same name.

Tagines might be ordered by each diner or be presented in the center of the table, to share. Occasionally, especially in coastal towns, herbaceous fish *tagines* are available. Vegetables and starches are rarely served with *tagines.*

Dining Moroccan style inevitably involves sharing, adding a note of conviviality to the dinner hour and enhancing the already inviting food. Huge, beautifully arranged platters are placed in the center of knee-high round tables in restaurants with traditional décor. Portions in Morocco are usually generous to a fault.

And because Moroccans share food and eat it with their fingers, it's usually well cooked, making it tender enough for bite-sized portions of meat to be pulled off the bone from the central platter. For couscous, the light semolina grain garnished with vegetables and sometimes meat, spoons are provided. It may be one of the main dish options, but in a lavish multicourse meal it comes last, just before a simple dessert of fresh fruit and little pastries.

On a few occasions when we were invited to dine in Moroccan homes, we ate with our fingers, but most of the time in restaurants we used silverware. The only Moroccan restaurant that insisted that everyone use their fingers was the famous Maison Arabe in Marrakesh, which closed in 1988.

Many, but not all, Moroccan restaurants serve Moroccan wines and both domestic and imported beers. Vin gris, a type of dry rosé wine produced in the region around Meknes, is the best of the native wines. Soft drinks, juices, and still or sparkling mineral water are always available. Mint tea, made by infusing sweetened green tea with fresh mint leaves, is offered at meal's end.

Moroccan meals are frequently fixed-price, with a couple of choices for each course. À la carte menus are available in some places. Restaurants that serve elaborate banquet dishes, like whole roasted or steamed lamb *mechoui* or the flaky *bistilla* pastry enclosing pieces of pigeon, sometimes require that these dishes, intended to serve two or more, be ordered a day in advance. While many restaurants display the symbols of major credit cards in their windows, it is not uncommon for the management to say that regrettably the credit card machine has just broken or the restaurant is out of charge slips, necessitating cash.

Most of the time a diner who insists on using a credit card, and is willing to spend the time in what might prove to be a twenty-minute standoff, will discover that the restaurant's charge equipment has miraculously started to function again. Finally, always check the bill carefully, especially in restaurants that seem to cater exclusively to tourists.

Finding restaurants in the labyrinthine medinas, or old quarters, of Moroccan cities, especially after dark, can be daunting. The advice of a hotel concierge or the services of a taxi driver or a guide are advised.

Among those that are not easy to locate but worth the effort is

Yacout in Marrakesh, one of the most enchanting restaurants in Morocco. Like many other restaurants in the medinas, this was once an eighteenth-century private palace, or *riad,* with an interior courtyard and lavish Moorish tile and stucco decorations. Typically, its anonymous doorway offers no hint of the richness within.

The main dining room of Yacout, at the end of a tiled and carpeted passageway punctuated with marble fountains filled with roses, is in a large central courtyard. Some tables are outside on the terrace around the aquamarine pool; others, strewn with rose petals, are in alcoves shielded from the elements by glass doors.

Staircases lead to upper floors where there are other bars and dining rooms including the former harem room, furnished with armchairs, floor cushions, and pillow-strewn banquettes, some invitingly cozy for chilly winter evenings. A rooftop terrace paved with Berber carpets and lighted by lanterns, where cocktails may be served, has a view of the minarets and the mountains beyond.

Everywhere there is the flicker of candlelight, the splash of fountains, soft music, and the perfume of roses and jasmine.

The host, Mohammed Zkhiri, a graduate of New York University, engaged an American decorator, Bill Willis, to restore the palace, a task that consumed twelve years. The kitchen, a large, simple white tile room open to the sky, is run by women, as are most Moroccan kitchens. Men may learn European cooking and service in the country's hotel schools, but the techniques and traditions of authentic Moroccan cooking are taught to women by their mothers at home.

Dinner at Yacout consists of a succession of superb courses, usually six. Three main dishes can be selected from a list of about six, and all the dishes depend on market availability. There is no printed menu. Our dinner started with various salads, followed by a giant flaky *bistilla* of parchment pastry layered with morsels of pigeon and seasoned with cinnamon.

Delectable lamb braised with almonds, then classic couscous with vegetables and lamb follow. Fresh fruit and a four-tier stand of tiny cookies were served for dessert. All beverages, including wines and cocktails, are included in the fixed price of 500 *dhiram,* about $55, calculated at a rate of one *dhiram* to 11 cents.

Another former palace-turned-restaurant in the medina of Marrakesh is Stilya, with excellent Moroccan food served in a luxurious if somewhat less singular setting than Yacout. The restaurant has one large room furnished with banquettes, tables, and chairs and serves a fixed-price multicourse dinner, charging about $42. Beverages are extra.

After a delicious assortment of salads and some rice- and meat-filled pastries called *briouates,* we had a whole fish roasted over charcoal, seasoned and stuffed with onions, herbs, and spices. The fish was pageot, with thick succulent flesh, a variety the French call *daurade royale,* native to the Mediterranean and the Atlantic around the Canary Islands.

Lamb *tagine,* couscous with vegetables, and a dessert *bistilla* drizzled with honey, fruit, and tea rounded out another sumptuous dinner. At several intervals during the meal, a waiter with a silver basin and a pitcher of orange-flower water came by so the diners could wash their hands. Clean napkins were provided at each turn.

For fine Moroccan cooking without venturing into the medinas at night, there are Moroccan dining rooms in some of the hotels. Here the cliché about hotel food does not apply.

The Moroccan Restaurant in La Mamounia Hotel in Marrakesh is a fantasy in pink mosaic lighted with pierced metal lanterns. Plush banquettes bolstered with cushions surround the low tables.

There is an impeccably served collection of à la carte dishes, including a parade of salads, delicate lamb brains, and a *bistilla* stuffed with pieces of pigeon on the bone.

A *mechoui*, the delectable Berber-style whole roasted baby lamb, is worth ordering in advance. *Chaariya medfouna,* consisting of pieces of seasoned pigeon, is an uncommon but slightly bland dish that must also be ordered a day before. Most of the main dishes are $20.

Dessert was a platter of refreshing orange slices dusted with cinnamon. Huge bowls of fruit and trays of cookies were also placed on the table.

Waiters are in traditional Moroccan dress, from fez-capped heads to feet slipped into the heelless leather slippers called *babouches*. A belly dancer with an entourage of gaily costumed musicians weaves through the dining room.

Similar, if somewhat more intimate, is Al Fassia in the Palais Jamaï Hotel just inside the walls of Fez. It is probably the best restaurant in Fez, but unlike Yacout or the Moroccan restaurant in the Mamounia, it attracts mostly tourists. The soaring room that was once part of the original palace glitters with blue mosaic tile. Low tables are set into comfortable alcoves. There is music and a belly dancer who encourages male diners to gyrate with her.

The food is attractively presented and carefully prepared. Among the appetizers, *harira,* the hearty bean soup, was correctly served with dates and lemon on the side. Pigeon stuffed with couscous and almonds, a superbly succulent roasted baby lamb shoulder for two *(dalaa m'hammara),* and couscous with chicken, raisins, and onions were outstanding. The main dishes are $12 to $15. Specialties for two that must be ordered in advance are $20.

Al Fassia also makes a delicious dessert couscous, a mound of the feathery grain mixed with raisins and nuts, sweetened and dusted with cinnamon. Warm milk is served on the side to moisten it.

One afternoon while in Fez we ventured for lunch at Dar Saada, a converted palace in the vast medina. Our group of four plus a guide was the only party that did not belong to one of two huge bus tours that had taken over the restaurant. And while the lunch included artfully seasoned salads, spicy *merguez* sausages, and perfectly cooked lemon chicken, the service was perfunctory at best.

Unfortunately, at lunchtime, most of the elegant *riad* restaurants in the old quarters of cities like Fez, Meknes, and Marrakesh are jammed with group tours. Two or three fixed menus at prices from $10 to $20 are usually offered. At dinner the groups tend to eat in their hotels.

In Meknes, near Fez, the smallest of the imperial cities, we took a break from mosaic tile and costumed waiters and had dinner at La Coupole, a simple restaurant in the new part of the city that serves both Continental and Moroccan dishes. Beyond the inevitable portrait of the king, there is little in the decoration that suggests Morocco. But it had been recommended to us for the quality of its Moroccan food, and we were not disappointed.

An array of fine salads of carrot, cauliflower, zucchini, eggplant, lamb brains and liver, plus olives, made up one appetizer. Steaming bowls of particularly well-seasoned *harira* soup, thick with beans, was another.

A rich *tagine* of lamb and prunes with sesame seeds and chicken with preserved lemons and olives were two other felicitous choices from an à la carte menu listing a dozen *tagines*. There was also an assortment of European dishes, from omelets and shrimp cocktail to spaghetti. Most of the main dishes were around $6. Service at La Coupole was extremely accommodating.

In Rabat, we came upon one of the most alluring stops imaginable for a midafternoon break. Within the walls of the Almohade Kasbah of the Oudaias, an open-air cafe is tucked into a whitewashed Andalusian-style village surrounded by gardens.

At Café Maure, with bright blue chairs and tables, tile work, a shady trellis, and a view of the sea, waiters served mint tea, soft drinks, and pastry. Tea is 25 *dhirams,* about 30 cents, and good pastries like big, soft macaroons and crescent-shaped *corne de gazelle* cookies filled with almond paste are also 25 *dhirams* each.

Morocco abounds in exotic décor and, sometimes, splendid settings. We encountered two such restaurants deep in the Todra Gorge. About nine miles along a reasonably good but narrow road from Tinerhir in the south of the country and about as far as a vehicle without four-wheel drive can safely venture even in dry season, there are a pair of restaurants set into the base of the narrow canyon walls.

The choices are Yasmina and Hôtel des Roches. Because the latter was filling up with a bus tour and seemed to have fewer tables with a good view, we selected Yasmina, opting to have lunch outside in a tented and carpeted Berber pavilion.

A fresh if simple salad of excellent tomatoes plus olives, onions, and cucumbers in a well-made vinaigrette was followed by a choice of beef brochettes or lemon chicken with fresh fruit for dessert, 60 *dhirams,* or about $7.50, complete per person.

In general, we learned that brochettes are worth ordering only in quality places that have good meat, or when they are made of sausage or seasoned ground lamb *kefta.* And at Yasmina we sampled some of the most delicious dates we tasted in Morocco. When we commented on them the manager presented us with a bag full for the road, one of the many expressions of Morocco's warm, genuine, and often spontaneous hospitality we encountered.

Dining in Medina and Casbah

Al Fassia, Palais Jamaï Hotel, Bab el Guissa, Fez; 055.63.43.31. À la carte dinner menu. Alcoholic beverages, including a good list of

Moroccan wines, are served. Credit cards accepted. There is entertainment.

Dar Saada, 21 Rue Attarine (in the medina), Fez; 055.63.33.43.
Lunch only, with *prix-fixe* menus from about $12 to $35. No alcoholic beverages served. Credit cards are accepted with reluctance.

Café Maure, Casbah of the Oudaias, Rabat; no telephone. Tea,
soft drinks, and pastries are served, about 30 cents a portion.

La Coupole, Rue Ghana at Avenue Hassan II, Meknes;
055.52.24.83. À la carte lunch and dinner menu. Alcoholic beverages, including a good list of Moroccan wines, are served. Credit
cards may be accepted.

Le Restaurant Marocain, La Mamounia Hotel, Avenue Bab Jdid,
Marrakesh; 044.44.89.81. Serves dinner only. À la carte menu with
main dishes around $20. Alcoholic beverages, including a lengthy
list of Moroccan and European wines, are served. Credit cards are
accepted. There is entertainment.

Stilya, 34 Rue Ksour (in the medina), Marrakesh; 044.44.35.87.
Prix-fixe dinner menu. Alcoholic beverages are served. Credit
cards are accepted.

Yacout, 79 Sidi Ahmed Soussi (in the medina), Marrakesh;
044.38.29.29. Dinner only, *prix fixe* around $55 including alco-
holic beverages. Moroccan and European wines are served. Credit
cards accepted.

Yasmina, Todra Gorge near Tinerhir; no telephone. *Prix-fixe*
menu around $6. No alcoholic beverages. No credit cards.

The Kitchen of Earthly Delights

BY LAUREL DELP

~~

LAUREL DELP is a contributing editor at *Travel Holiday* and a features
writer whose work has appeared in a wide variety of newspapers and magazines. Her work has also appeared in the *Paris* edition of *The Collected
Traveler*. She is currently at work on a novel, which is set in Laos at the end
of the 1950s.

The round-faced woman nudges me, laughing, and holds up
three delicate maroon threads of saffron. Once she has my
attention, she drops them theatrically into the pot along with the
garlic, onions, and chickens. Wordlessly, she holds out a handful of
cumin for my inspection, then a bouquet of cilantro. She adds
water, and in moments the aroma envelops us like a cloud. We all
grin. The five Moroccan women, their hair tightly bound in scarves,
white aprons still immaculate at the start of day, are chefs at the
Palais de Fez restaurant, and they speak only Arabic. The waitress
who has been translating has left the kitchen, reducing us to pan-
tomime.

I am here this morning learning to cook a few traditional
Moroccan dishes in much the same way these women doubtless
learned, by watching other women. Moroccan cuisine, in all its
myriad regional variations, has been passed down orally, mother to
daughter, woman to woman, for centuries. It is, more than any
other, a cuisine of women.

Moroccan food is like the country's Moorish architecture,
deceptively plain on the exterior, elegant and sensually detailed in
the interior. Of the countries of North Africa's Maghreb—"far
west" in Arabic—it has the most refined cuisine. Tunisians rely on

fiery peppers, and Algerians use only a fraction of the spices the Moroccans use.

Most of us think of Morocco as forbidding desert, but in fact its closest geographical cousin is probably California. The two share long coastlines, high mountain ranges, and stubbly, rocky desert but sweeping fertile valleys as well. The heart of Moroccan cuisine is its rich, fresh produce; fruits and vegetables, fresh herbs and dozens of home-ground spices, lemons preserved in salt, dates and olives, along with farm-raised chickens and lamb and fresh Mediterranean fish. In Morocco a tomato tastes like a tomato.

In the end, the ingredients of Moroccan cuisine are like a taste-map of all the great empires that tried in vain to absorb this most western end of North Africa, both before and after the Arabs swept across the Maghreb in the eighth century, claiming it and Spain for Islam. The Phoenicians probably brought the first olive trees and saffron, but it was the Romans who established the olive groves and vineyards. The Arabs brought lemons from Persia, oranges from China, Asian spices and sugar. There's no doubt the Moroccan sweet tooth came from the Arabs, but the Chinese green tea that is like mother's milk to them (steeped with fresh mint and so heavily sugared it tastes like syrup) first came with the Portuguese, who, along with the Spanish, also introduced the bounty of the New World, including potatoes and tomatoes. Through it all, Morocco's indigenous Berber tribes shrugged off all the invaders, absorbing what they liked and making it their own.

"Along with French and Chinese, Moroccan is one of the most complex cuisines in the world," says Mohammed Sbai, owner of Restaurant Ryad Zitoun in Casablanca. He gestures expansively. "It takes three or four people just to prepare a *b'stilla.*"

Today Moroccan cuisine remains rigidly traditional. Years of French colonization—ending in 1956—resulted in a wealth of cafés, most of which serve Moroccan dishes as well as French, but so far there's been no fusion. No one has reinterpreted Moroccan tradition through the techniques of haute cuisine. It remains cooking of the home.

"To eat Moroccan cuisine in restaurants is fairly new," says Sbai. "And it's very conservative. You must make couscous the same way your parents did—no nouvelle cuisine. You won't find couscous with endive, for instance."

In fact, twenty years ago, to preserve the cuisine's authenticity, the late King Hassan founded a cooking school, the Centre de Qualification Hôtelière et Touristique de Touarga, located on the grounds of the royal palace in Rabat. "Our role is to keep the tradition alive," says Noureddine Boutahra, the school's director of studies. "The king was afraid it would be lost."

It's a difficult cuisine to master. The students, all women, "must learn all the regional dishes by heart," he says. "The spices are very complicated, and each city has its own variation on *tagine*"—a stew cooked in a clay pot with a distinctive conical lid—"such as lemon or prune. You can find twenty *tagines* with prunes, each with a different sauce." The young women who come here study for two years, then go on to cook for Moroccan embassies overseas or in government ministers' homes. The school provides them with a reliable profession that's considered honorable in this male-dominated society, and for many women, it's a ticket out of the grinding poverty of village life.

The crenellated earthen ramparts of Marrakesh's medina rise shimmering out of the afternoon-sun-drenched plain like a garnet apparition, the minaret of La Koutoubia Mosque dwarfed by the snow-capped High Atlas Mountains. As dusk settles under a gold gibbous moon, the vast open square of Djemaa el-Fna is a jostling mass of Marrakshis and tourists, snake charmers and acrobats, street musicians and ghetto blasters, all wrapped in a hallucinatory cloud of smoke from the dozens of charcoal braziers at food stands. There are Berbers, Arabs, black Africans—and women; women in traditional *djellabas* walking with younger women in tight jeans, women with their heads covered and women with hair streaming defiantly across their shoulders.

In Morocco women are on the cusp of a revolution, and nowhere is this better illustrated than in Marrakesh, where the tribal south meets the sophisticated north, and international celebrities like Yves Saint Laurent and Alain Delon have mansions. Most Moroccan women still lead lives devoted to the home, but a growing number are joining the professional work force, where they are more often than not faced with open hostility. Even I, several times during my travels, received lectures on the home being my proper place.

Further inside the medina, on the roof of Dar Yacout restaurant, three Gnaoui musicians are softly playing the opening strains of a trance melody. A warm autumn breeze sets shawls and dresses fluttering, and faces are eerily beautiful in the flickering light of cut-metal lamps. As people finish their cocktails, waiters summon them down the winding staircase to the dining area, a courtyard where one wall resembles a Berber kasbah and the adjoining interior rooms are elaborately tiled in traditional Moorish style. Crisp white tablecloths are strewn with rose petals, and candlelight sets the central pool glittering.

The meal mimics a Moroccan wedding feast, starting with a sea of small dishes holding cooked salads meant to be scooped up with flat bread. Next comes a chicken *tagine* cooked with preserved lemons and cracked green olives, then a couscous, and finally a crisp, airy *kteffa,* a kind of Moroccan *mille-feuille* made of layers of *ouarka* (a paper-thin dough, slightly thicker than *phyllo,* that's also used for *b'stilla*) alternated with crushed almonds and an orange-flower-flavored custard.

"Pretty soon women will have all the jobs," my dinner companion Hassan is muttering, taking a mournful sip of syrupy mint tea. Earlier in the day we passed some of Marrakesh's brand-new female traffic cops, soon to be joined by female postal carriers, and the indignity is still weighing heavily on Hassan's mind. I can't help thinking of the women who must have prepared the banquet we've just consumed. "Pretty soon," he sighs, "men will have to become belly dancers."

I've had enough of his gloom, and I'm pleasantly surprised in Fez to have a female guide, an animated, dark-haired young beauty named Amina. *"Suivez votre guide!"* she admonishes a portly French tourist who's lagging behind his group. The narrow cobblestoned streets of the thousand-year-old medina are an impenetrable maze for the first-time visitor. The souks have not changed significantly since the Middle Ages, and the constantly flowing throngs of people and the heady mix of aromas quickly become surreal. *"Balek, balek!"* someone cries, and Amina grabs me, flattening me against a stained, peeling wall, as an overladen donkey labors through, filling the entire passageway.

As we weave on through the jammed passageways, Amina deftly fends off joking from male shopkeepers that just verges on the insulting. She begins to talk about her life. Her boyfriend's family will never allow him to marry a woman working as a guide, she says, but she must work to help support her family. "Even his boss told him not to marry me," she says. "Can you believe this?"

It seems impossible this beautiful young woman will have trouble marrying. Even worse, she admits with a laugh, she can't cook at all. "In Morocco, you must prepare a special meal for your mother-in-law to show her you can cook," she explains.

"Oh! You must try this!" she cries, pointing at an unappetizing mound of dried salted beef coated in lard. I sigh and hold out my hand, and Amina finds me a piece that's nearly lard-free. As we walk along, I take a bite and laugh in surprise. It's delicious. "It's *halia*," she says. "We have it for breakfast."

Fez is Morocco's culinary capital, the city with, as everyone agrees, the most refined cuisine. We pass a small square where live free-range chickens and turkeys are being given a businesslike once-over by women shoppers. "We call these country chickens," Amina says. "The others we call industrial chickens," she adds with a sniff. "You don't serve those to guests. It would be rude."

On another street mounds of green olives mixed with chopped parsley and ground red pepper rise in pyramids next to sculptures of lemons. There are green olives, purple olives, and black olives, each with a specific use—you would use green olives, for instance, only with chicken. Across the way a man is selling dates and dried figs. Nearby in the spice souk a salesman shows me his *ras el hanout,* a mix of forty-five spices meant for "lazy" cooks. It's good, he says, for *harissa,* the mutton soup used to break the fast at the end of the day during Ramadan. When I emerge from the medina, I am dizzy from all the sensations.

We collapse at a *zellige*-tiled table on the roof terrace of the Palais de Fez, where I have my first *b'stilla,* a mix of pigeon, onion, egg, almonds, parsley, cilantro, and spices wrapped in the parchmentlike dough called *ouarka,* baked, then dusted with cinnamon and powdered sugar. Azzedine Tazi, the owner, is planning a small cooking school and is just finishing attractive guest rooms and a separate kitchen for students on the lower floors of his *dar,* a former merchant's palace at the edge of the medina. "Come back," he insists. "I will put an apron on you, and you will learn to cook!" And I do.

That night the moon is full over the valley of cream-colored buildings that is Fez. A breeze rustles the palm trees. Near the king's palace I enter Maison Bleue through a long hallway dancing in the shadows cast by candles in Moroccan lamps. Inside the tiled court-yard a man strums a guitar, singing songs that even without know-ing a word of Arabic I know to be love songs.

Mehdi El Abbadi has turned the mansion his grandfather built in 1915 into an antique-filled six-suite *maison d'hôte,* and his restaurant is Fez's best. "Most of the restaurants do the basics," he says. "Here we try to do something different, like a special couscous from the thirteenth century, or a chicken dish made with parsley, cilantro, garlic, and saffron." La Maison Bleue's female chef cooks no more than twenty-five dinners nightly, using only the best ingre-dients—starting with "country" chickens—and it shows.

The meal is far and away the best I've had in Morocco. And the Gnaoui duo that goes from table to table in the blue-tiled alcoves off the courtyard has everyone clapping as the music mounts in tempo and volume, and the castanet player stamps and bobs his head so that the tassle on his red fez spins deliriously.

The road from Fez to the seaside capital of Rabat is surrounded by eucalyptus-bordered farm fields. Just outside the stately old imperial city of Meknes lie the vast Roman ruins of Volubilis, where mosaic floors are all that's left of merchants' palaces and only bro-ken stones mark what once were olive mills. This is a rolling land full of olive and fruit groves, vineyards and valleys rich with pro-duce, where the roads are lined with farm stands selling apples, pomegranates, and garlands of brown-skinned onions. Live ducks and turkeys for sale wander perilously close to the traffic.

I spend my last night at Dinarjat, a restaurant inside Rabat's walled medina. In spite of the establishment's large sign by the me-dina's entrance, Dinarjat is not easy to find, and I gratefully accept the help of a small boy who leads me to a big wooden door, then darts away, happy with the handful of coins I've given him.

My dinner is a sampling of three *tagines:* lamb with eggplant, lamb with pear, and chicken with lemon and olives. Traditionally, *tagines* are prepared with all the ingredients assembled before baking over a charcoal brazier, but most restaurants today take a shortcut, cooking the meat first, then adding the prunes or lemons and olives and spices to order for a short blast in the oven. None of the student chefs from the Centre de Qualification Hôtelière would consider such heresy, but to a beginner like me, these faux *tagines* are still delicious.

As I eat, the kitchen door occasionally swings open, and I can see the women chefs sitting on stools, laughing as they relax at the end of a busy evening, popping bits of food into their mouths. One glances out and smiles at me. And here I am sitting in the tiled courtyard of an elegant Moorish mansion. The waiters have washed my hands over a tray of roses and sprinkled me with rosewater. A tenor is singing Moroccan love songs. What more do I need?

Essentials

Several tour operators offer culinary tours of Morocco, but to create your own, start in Marrakech, then work your way into the countryside. Start by rounding up information from the **Moroccan Tourist Office** (212-557-2520). Most flights from the United States go to Casablanca; the easiest is **Royal Air Maroc**'s six-and-a-half-hour nonstop from New York. From there, you can change to a forty-minute flight to Marrakech on RAM (800-344-6726). Driving around the country is fairly easy and safe; you can even rent from AutoEurope (800-223-5555; about $350–$550 a week).

The hands-down best place to stay in Marrakech is **La Maison Arabe,** in the medina. Each of the 10 rooms is different; some have fireplaces and terraces, and all are impeccably decorated with the best Moroccan furniture and rugs (1 Derb Asschbe; 044.39.12.83; about $190–$400).

For something more Western, try the 314-room **Palmeraie Golf Palace** (044.30.10.10; rooms start at about $220), a sprawling hotel with a golf course and six restaurants set in the chic suburb of Les Jardins de la Palmeraie. And, of course, there's the famed **La Mamounia,** with its combination of Deco and Moroccan decor and beautiful grounds set inside the medina (in the United States, call 800-888-4747; about $250).

And for dinner? While **Yacout** has good food, it's much like you'll get at any Moroccan restaurant: a *prix fixe* of about $55 per person that includes wine and then the set menu of salad, *tagine,* couscous, and *kteffa* pastry. Yacout, though, is one of the most beautiful restaurants in the entire country, and patrons (lots of locals, which is rare) dress the part (79 Sidi Ahmed Soussi; 044.38.29.29; about $110 for two; reservations are a must).

Fez is an eight-hour drive away, but it's the centerpiece of any food tour. I stayed at **Jnan Palace** (Avenue Ahmed Chaouki; 055.65.39.65; about $185), a big, modern hotel. For the most luxury, try the **Palais Jamai,** Fez's legendary hotel. A late-eighteenth-century palace set in Andalusian gardens, it has been enlarged by the French Sofitel chain to include modern rooms. Its Moroccan restaurant, Al Fassia, is worth trying, as is a night in the hotel (rooms start at about $210; dinner for two is about $80; in the United States call 800-221-4542). Don't leave town, though, without trying **La Maison Bleue,** one of Morocco's best restaurants, and my favorite. It's also an utterly charming six-room hotel (2 Place de l'Istiqlal Batha; 055.63.60.52; dinner for two about $100; doubles start at about $250).

If you have an extra few days, go to Rabat, about two hours from Fez. Rabat's version of La Mamounia and Palais Jamai is **La Tour Hassan,** which opened in 1914 and has been enlarged by the Meridien chain (in the United States, call 800-543-4300; 26 Rue Chellah; doubles start at about $180). And for a good dinner, go to

Dinarjat restaurant, one of the few places I ate at in Morocco where you actually get to choose your dinner from a menu (6 Rue Belganoui; 055.74.239; about $100 for two).

Inside Marrakesh

BY DOROTHY KALINS

❦

editor's note

Here is an outstanding piece on the splendid cuisine and legendary hospitality of this venerable Moroccan city.

At the time she wrote this piece, DOROTHY KALINS was editor of *Saveur*.

Think of Marrakesh as an oasis in the pre-Saharan desert. Warring nomadic tribes, armies of traders and invaders— every culture has left its mark. The Arabs brought our religion across North Africa around A.D. 700. The Almoravid princes who built the walled city came north from the Senegal River in 1062. The Spanish were ever present. The French protectorate lasted from 1912 until 1956. And each wave of conquerors had to contend with the local Berbers, the tribal people from the mountains who were here first. My father was a Berber from a remote village in the High Atlas Mountains. He had two wives and twenty-four children and lived to be 103."

Ahmed Zaidane Lasry is talking. He has been talking since he met us at the airport with a lipstick-red silk foulard poking from the pocket of his immaculately tailored Italian suit; his whispered Arabic chirps are all it takes to slip us through customs. He is driving us to his home in the medina (the old city) of Marrakesh, his well-used BMW negotiating the narrow alleys and almost brushing the burros they were built for—and it has become clear to us already that Lasry is a wall of words, a river of them. He went to school on life and came out a well-connected guide. "Besides Arabic and Berber, I picked up English, Italian, Dutch, and German. But *mon français est* correct. *Très* correct." To begin to understand Marrakesh—its traditions, its food—people rent houses, spend years. But we don't have houses or years: we have Lasry.

We have Wolfert, too. For an American cook, there's almost nowhere you go with Moroccan food that Paula Wolfert—who published *Couscous and Other Good Food from Morocco* in 1973 and has defined Morocco's immensely sophisticated cuisine for us ever since—hasn't been. Much from that seminal book remains with me, especially her description of the country's legendary hospitality: "an embarrassment of riches, total satisfaction, abundance as an end in itself and as a point of pride for the host." That, and the memory of some convincing meals at a Moroccan restaurant in San Francisco (where I recall the cozy community of shared eating as much as the sweet and savory food), had left me longing to visit Morocco. Last spring, I hook *Saveur* executive editor (and star photographer) Christopher Hirsheimer on the adventure, and she immediately lures to our office a group of knowledgeable Moroccans, whom we pepper with questions: "Should we go to Fez or Marrakesh?" we wonder. "Fez is more refined and sophisticated," our guests reply, "but less has changed in Marrakesh." Done. "Is our idea of Moroccan hospitality just a romantic sentimentality?" I blurt. "Does it still exist?" "Yes," they reassure us, eyes twinkling. "It still exists."

Lasry's house is full of women. Through what looks like just another door off just another noisy and crowded street, you enter a courtyard—the heart of the Moroccan house, the real living room, where polished rituals and messy intimacies alike take place. Written in Arabic over the double-height Moorish arch are the words "Whatever God wants. There is nothing stronger than God." Lasry breathes in slowly: "Now I am calm." On a banquette in the spring sun, Lasry's mother, Lalla Aicha Bouziane, almost ninety, smooths her beautiful traditional skirts. Through a bedroom door off the courtyard bursts Lasry's daughter (from his first marriage) Myriam, twenty-four, in jeans, just back from a business trip to Geneva. Lasry's wife, Asma Zaidane, about Myriam's age and pregnant with his son, fusses, along with Saâdiya, the cook, over the salads we are about to eat. We have been promised the preparation as well as the meal. Lasry turns to us. "You are not guests; you are at home here. You do what you want." Proverbs flow like honey: "My father would say: 'He who comes into my house is a friend; he who does not is a villain.' And 'A piece of bread with a glass of tea and a smiling face is better than a whole lamb on the table and a frown.' My father was a pious man. When we moved to Marrakesh, he opened his house to students of the Qur'an who came from the mountains to study but had no food. Now, every Friday, twenty poor people from the mosque come here and eat dishes like seven-vegetable couscous. They know my door is open."

Lasry's whole house is open—to the sky! Only a peaked roof three stories up shelters the courtyard from rain. Birds fly in and nest in star-shaped holes in the walls. His house is open to the world as well, we learn. "People come, and someone must be here, because if people visit and no one is here, they'll stop coming. If they come, that means they like you. And everybody has a story. It's how we get the news."

Asma carries into the room a low round table laden with ingredients for the cooked and raw salads she is about to assemble. We review the recipes in French, and I try the few Moroccan ingredient words I've learned. As Saâdiya chops parsley for the salad of cubed cooked potatoes, I venture: *"M'ednus?"* *"M'ednus,"* echoes Lasry's mother with a radiant smile. Asma sprinkles minced garlic, then cinnamon, on rounds of boiled carrots. *"Tuma,"* I chant, and *"Qerfa."* *"Tuma!"* repeats the mother, like an incantation, *"Qerfa!"* Baby zucchini are always dressed with *kamun* (cumin), and grated-carrot soup is invariably made with orange juice and orange-flower water. These are the defining flavors of iconic recipes. No free-wheeling "creativity" can screw this up.

Lasry has quietly slipped into a long white *djellaba,* a ruby fez, and those funny flat leather slippers—and in so doing, has slipped back a couple of hundred years. Except, that is, for the Ray-Bans he puts on to announce that, until lunch is ready, we're going out into the market streets.

"Dark, fierce and fanatical are these narrow *souks* of Marrakech," Edith Wharton wrote in 1919. "Marrakech is the great market of the south . . . not only the Atlas [Mountains] with its feudal chiefs and their wild clansmen, but all that lies beyond of heat and savagery: the Sahara of the veiled Touaregs, Dakka, Timbuctoo, Senegal and the Soudan." Maybe. But Lasry walks the packed, dusty alleys of his neighborhood like the local mayor. We run to catch up as a shopkeeper selling wild artichokes actually kisses his robe. In a butcher shop raised from the street like a stage, a whole cow's head hangs, its tongue lolling. A holy man from the mosque where Lasry prays five times a day carries a great bunch of mint, and its scent lingers on the air as he embraces Lasry. We ogle olives piled mountain high and bowls of the preserved lemons indispensable to Moroccan cooking.

"Look, please!" Lasry cries, as the streets act out their dramas.

"It is like in a movie." Men sit curbside beating out the soundtrack on hand drums—*pam, pam, pam-pam-pam*. We pass leather workers tooling their famous skins, and suddenly Hope and Crosby ride into my brain on a camel, singing: "Like Webster's dic-tion-a-ry, we're Morocco bound." Women in *djellabas* and veils chatter with girls in tank tops and leggings. "Look how relaxed the dress code has become," Lasry enthuses. Still, it seems women like *djellabas* for the same reason their men do: they hide everything.

Back inside the house, Asma has thrown a cloth over a large round table pulled into a corner. I count five different mosaic tile patterns on floors and walls, highly colored like their design antecedents, the patterned rugs that hang at the sides of Berber tents to keep out the desert winds. Through the open roof come the sounds of the city. At 12:30 P.M., the muezzin calls the neighborhood men to prayer from a loudspeaker on the mosque next door: "God is most great. I witness that there is only one God and that Muhammad is the prophet."

Lasry sits between his mother and his daughter. "You see?" he says, grinning (and showing off a bit). "This is how we eat lunch every day." We begin with the salads, a mosaic themselves on the tabletop, each with its distinct, bright flavor. We eat as our hosts do, with the first three fingers of the right hand, sometimes dipping with good, grainy wheat bread. Lasry cautions not to mix the flavors, to keep the salads separate on the plate. We drink as they do— Coke from big glass bottles set on the table. Asma goes to the kitchen—just a hallway with sink, burners, and more little low tables—to get the pressure cooker in which her lamb and green olive *tagine* (named for the pot it's traditionally cooked in) has been simmering. For form, she transfers the stew to a terra-cotta *tagine* for serving. Lasry's fingers find just the piece of gristly lamb his mother likes, and he offers it to her. The sauce is famously rich; its complex, spicy aromatics stretch a little meat a long, long way.

The next day, back in Western attire, Lasry meets us at our hotel, the Palmeraie Golf Palace, set in a twelfth-century grove of soaring date palms. (The Almoravid rulers once hunted here; captains of industry now play golf here.) Captive in the BMW, we speed past jacaranda trees, all bright purple blossom and no leaves. We're heading, it seems, to have tea with a woman Lasry just remet after thirty-three years. "I once had a bike. They rented it from me. I never saw them again until last week at the airport." At some point we just give up trying to picture this happening at home.

Lalla Koute greets us in an open courtyard many times larger than Lasry's. It is a garden, really—its quadrants thick with orange and lemon trees, a fountain in the center, and long salons at each end. In the kitchen, surprisingly unadorned for a house this grand, Koute, in a fawn-colored *djellaba,* welcomes us in good English: "Any time is teatime in Morocco." (It turns out she's been to UC Berkeley.) We follow her through the garden to a salon and, removing our shoes as she does, join her husband, Said, a policeman, and a young student named Mohammed Sebti. Koute brings us plates of homemade pastries—crescent-shaped *hlal,* or moon cakes; *smid,* topped with sesame seeds; *feqqaṣ,* which look like biscotti—and bowls of mixed dates, figs, walnuts, golden raisins, and peanuts. Then she twice pours the tea into a glass and back into the pot and finally, from a height of two feet, into our decorated tumblers. We sip the minty warmth of its welcome. "We did not do this especially for you," she explains. Lasry elaborates: "You prepare these things every day for guests, and every day someone comes. In Morocco, you never ask why. We are here for reasons we cannot explain. God will never let me meet bad people. I met these people last week because I wanted to show you something." After an hour, Koute sprinkles our hands with orange-flower water from a silver ewer and bids us good-bye. Inexplicably, Mohammed joins us.

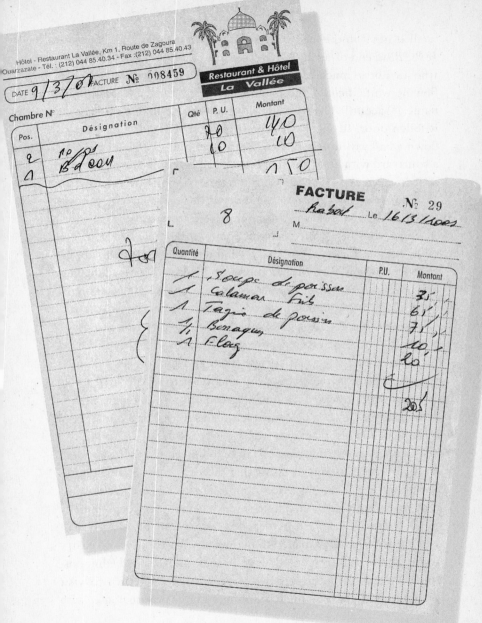

It is night in the medina. Magic and mystery. Lasry's car stops at the dead end of an alley. We descend to a scattering of little boys who are not so much begging as curious. A tall man in an elegantly flowing white *djellaba* meets us. Lasry utters only the restaurant's name: "Yacout." The man nods, we follow. He knocks at a heavy wooden door. It opens. Another beautifully robed man leads us down a hallway lit only by candles in silver-and-glass lanterns, past a courtyard with an exotic tree-lined pool, and up a narrow curving staircase. No one speaks as we climb three stories onto the roof for a drink. As we look out over the roofs of the low-lying city, we hear the drumming, always the drumming, from the streets.

Soon, another white *djellaba* comes to lead us down to our table. It is set for four, but Lasry, all graciousness, suddenly disappears, leaving us with Mohammed—and something of a language barrier. From our low banquettes, we are only vaguely aware of other guests as our dinner proceeds. We never order; we float, wanting for nothing. Salads arrive, nine in all, riffs on those at Lasry's house: silky roasted green pepper with cumin; artichokes and baby zucchini; cubed fried calf's liver; lamb and quince. Two waiters carry in a giant leather *tagine* and uncover it to reveal three whole chickens with preserved lemon and green olives. The tender flesh is deftly loosened by a waiter, then left for us to eat with our fingers. It is one of the lushest things we have ever tasted.

Another *tagine,* this time of lamb and green beans in succulent sauce, follows. I'm vaguely aware that the idea of pacing oneself has fled altogether. Then, like rice at an Asian banquet, there is couscous to end this one—a classic seven-vegetable couscous. Finally comes a dessert *beṣṭila* (often spelled *besteeya* or *pastilla*), a delicate pie as big as the table, with many flaky-leaved layers of pastry and a cream filling scented with orange and roasted almonds. Somehow I am not surprised to learn, when we return to visit Yacout in daylight, that the restaurant is a large private house, with only a house-size kitchen, where each painstaking step of preparation is a deliberate celebration of the cuisine's glorious traditions.

Another night, we slip away *sans* Lasry to check out the stuff of legend at La Mamounia, the 1920s hotel set just inside the medina's walls. Wandering its splendid gardens in the moonlight, admiring its Art Deco interiors, it's easy to imagine when this was the only luxurious doorway to the Sahara. In the elegant traditional Moroccan restaurant, with its ornate pierced plasterwork, we revel in the earthy authenticity of *mḥammar*—braised lamb.

"*Bismillah* [On God's name]," murmurs Lasry as he starts the huge Ford Explorer we've rented to drive the Ouarzazate road into the snow-capped High Atlas Mountains near the Berber village where he was born. "*Mahi mushkila?* [No problem?]" I ask. "Getting this car we had plenty *mushkilas,*" he laughs. In the back is—Mohammed. We sense he's been adopted, somehow, and don't ask. Leaving town through perfect groves of olive trees and vast fields of poppies, we try explaining to Lasry why it's funny that we're bringing Mohammed to the mountain.

"Here is every climate in the world in one wonderful country," says Lasry, becoming all guide. Quickly the red villages appear, nestled into hillsides waving with wheat. Women cut sheaves and load them into baskets on donkeys' backs. This is where the couscous begins, I think to myself.

Villages become tightly packed and isolated as the grade increases. "Look, please!" and we stop for a bunch of kids by the roadside; a six-year-old leads a cow. Lasry speaks tenderly to them in Berber. Long, deep valleys luxuriate between red hills and the ancient high towers of casbahs (medieval fortresses). Patterns repeat: square brown houses with flat red roofs, courtyards noisy with roosters and children. We're now on roads the Explorer has no business exploring—with drops so terrifying that with each "Look, please!" from Lasry, Christopher and I giggle harder.

After two hours, in the tiny town of Taddert we marvel at the Berber *tagines*—smooth mounds of saffron yellow potatoes, punctuated with strips of pepper, topped with tomatoes—cooking over coals at roadside stands. "Berbers are healthy," Lasry informs us. "They eat a lot of fresh vegetables, couscous, and only a little meat." An hour later, we arrive at a high flat place where the road seems to end. "Down there is my town, Anmeter, where twenty-four families still live." We look at the village in the valley, trying to place Lasry in his Adidas running suit in this sixteenth-century setting, still a two-hour donkey ride away. Lasry spares us the donkeys, and we turn back to have lunch at an informal restaurant in a heavy woven-wool Berber tent at the mountain outpost of Telouet. We're offered tea, a tomato salad, and a jewel-like Berber *tagine,* just like the road-side version. As we eat, I think that if, as has been said, Morocco (like Provence) is a cold country with a hot sun, it is true, too, that Morocco is a poor country with a rich cuisine.

For days, Lasry has promised us a woman who makes *warqa,* the pastry leaves, thinner and more delicate than Greek *phyllo,* used in *beṣṭila* and other Moroccan pastries, and for days, no one appears. Embarrassed, he explains that people don't make *warqa* anymore; they buy it. But on our last night, in the kitchen of our hotel's excellent Moroccan restaurant, Lasry produces three home cooks who enthusiastically take us through the complex steps of making *beṣṭila*—this symphony of Moroccan cuisine. Then Lasry, the man who unfailingly makes his monthlong pilgrimage to Mecca every year, steers us to (go figure) a karaoke bar. He turns suddenly serious. "I feel that God knows me. He gives me what I ask for and what I don't ask for. I am fifty-seven. All I can ask at the end of my days is to be in a small village and call people to prayer." Then, just as suddenly, he grabs the mike as the Blues Brothers appear on screen and belts out loud with them: "I'm a soul ma-a-an."

Where to Stay and/or Eat

Dar Marjana, *15 Derb Sidi Ali Tair (044.44.11.10; fax 044.42.91.52). Dinner: Expensive.* Drinks are served by the pool amid the Moorish arches of a classic old house, while dinner is served at heavily padded banquettes in small, lantern-lit rooms. Along with Yacout, this is one of the city's top restaurants.

La Mamounia, *Avenue Bab Jdid (044.44.89.81; fax 044.44.46.60; reservations 800-223-6800). Dinner: Expensive.* Perfectly located just inside the walls of the medina, this legendary Art-Deco-meets-Moorish palace from the 1920s is famous for its Moorish-style gardens and its hospitality. French and Moroccan dining rooms.

Palmeraie Golf Palace, *Les Jardins de la Palmeraie (044.30.10.10; fax 044.30.50.50). Rates: about $192 double. Dinner: Moderate.* A luxury hotel with five shimmering swimming pools and an eighteen-hole golf course amid groves of palms, all in a parklike setting on the edge of town. Its restaurant, Narjis, serves authentic home cooking—*beṣṭila, tagines,* and couscous—prepared by superb local cooks. It's worth a visit even if you're not staying here.

Yacout, 79 *Sidi Ahmed Soussi (044.38.29.29). Dinner: Expensive.* In the heart of the medina—and an experience like no other. Guests are met at the door and escorted inside for cocktails on the roof terrace. Exquisite multicourse dinners are served downstairs in a number of glamorous dining rooms—some surrounding a candlelit pool.

Excursion to Ouarzazate

Rent a four-wheel-drive vehicle, through your hotel, for a fascinating—if often hair-raising—drive through the High Atlas Mountains to the historic town of Ouarzazate (where scenes from many movies, including *The Sheltering Sky,* have been filmed). During the four-hour drive (though it's only 120 miles from Marrakesh to Ouarzazate), you'll traverse a riveting landscape of fertile valleys, deserts, and snow-capped peaks. Villages have an ancient feel. But don't even think about setting off unless you're up for an all-day excursion on unpaved, extremely narrow roads (literally cliff-hangers in some spots) where speeding trucks vie for right of way. It is best to spend the night in Ouarzazate.

Auberge Telouet (Chez Ahmed), *Telouet (044.89.07.17). Dinner: Inexpensive.* Step into the tent here, opposite the casbah in Telouet, on the way to Ouarzazate, for delicious Berber *tagines* and other local specialties.

Hotel Riad Salam Ouarzazate, *Avenue Mohammed V, Ouarzazate (044.88.33.35; fax 044.88.27.66). Rates: about $80 double.* A fine, first-class hotel with a swimming pool.

Leaving Home, Taking the Hearth

BY LAUREN SHAKELY

editor's note

Like the writer, I too rank visiting local food stalls and shops as a high-light of any journey, and it is especially enticing in Morocco. Unlike the writer, however, I am not overcome with the desire to find a stove while I'm away, but I usually cannot wait to return home to my own kitchen to capture some of the smells and re-create the dishes I so enjoyed abroad.

LAUREN SHAKELY is editorial director of Clarkson Potter/Publishers, an imprint of illustrated books specializing in lifestyle, gardening, decorating, and cooking, including the complete works of Martha Stewart. She contributed this essay to the travel section of *The New York Times* on July 1, 2001.

Years ago, when I was a novice traveler, I made a grave error packing for a trip to Tuscany—I forgot the pepper grinder. Others may travel to get away from the kitchen, but for me, part of the pleasure of another place is experiencing it through the market and the stove. I want to visit street vendors and tiny shops, spice markets and roadside stands.

Once I'm there I want to buy, not just sightsee. Covent Garden in London isn't about the theater; it's about raw-milk cheeses at Neal's Yard Dairy.

The snorkeling is wonderful in Belize (they tell me), but not nearly as thrilling as seeing the catch of the day at the dock. And caressing the tomatoes at the Rue Mouffetard market in Paris is worth it, even when the response to my affection is a slap on the hand.

After I have bought it, I must cook it, so no matter where we go in the world, my husband, son, and I almost always rent a villa, house, or apartment. It's my job to pack the supplies, and I have learned the hard way that you must take along anything you cannot live without, even pepper to Italy.

Fortunately, on the Tuscany trip, we discovered a delightful invention, the disposable pepper grinder, which actually served on many picnics after we returned home. But I have not always been so lucky. In a leaky Adirondack cabin, all the pots were already in use, and we had to choose whether to stay dry or boil spaghetti. Besides the pots, the rental's "fully stocked kitchen" had no spatula or mixing bowl, which made simple kitchen tasks from flipping a pancake to tossing a salad more difficult than they needed to be.

Because I don't want to spend my vacations outfitting other people's kitchens, I now plan carefully. If the owners of the house we are renting can communicate in English, I often write my wish list or send it by e-mail: salt and pepper (it's a pain to have to buy the basics in bulk), can opener, coffee maker, basic pots and pans. Some of my needs are specific to a region or time of year: pie plates and muffin tins when the blueberries and peaches are in season on Long Island, a barbecue grill in August. If I don't get an answer from the landlord, then the pepper grinder, the can opener, a sharp knife, and the plastic coffee-filter holder go into the luggage (in airports the knife is checked through, of course, to avoid problems at security). I was tempted to take a collapsible barbecue onto the plane, but my husband, Gerrit, drew the line.

Even more important than the availability of equipment is what food you can put into it.

Most of the time it is the local food I am longing to cook, but there are places, particularly in resort towns, where meat is as precious as bullion and there is no cheese or breakfast cereal. The nonperishables are easy to stow, although I sometimes resent that my son's affection for Cheerios has squeezed my extra nightgown out of the suitcase. The perishables, however, are challenging. First, of course, they perish, and not even a cooler can keep groceries perfectly fresh on a trans-Atlantic flight. (I know because I have tried it.) Second, most other countries have regulations limiting what foods can cross their borders. I'm sure it's not as bad as gunrunning, but I do feel guilty about having imported dried spices on occasion, and once, a lemon.

Our nomadic culinary experiences have had their highs and lows. Perhaps the least satisfying cooking was in an out-of-the-way haven in the Bahamas where the local market sold the most freezer-burned poultry I have ever seen. (But a woman down the road baked delectable coconut bread, which made up for it.) My proudest achievement: taking a week's worth of meat on a Christmas trip to St. Bart's. I froze it, packed it in several plastic bags, and surrounded it in bubble wrap for insulation. We ate very well, and cheaply, on an island where doing both simultaneously is usually a challenge. The plum pudding wasn't bad, either.

Vacations are about memories, and many of our family's revolve around meals we have eaten in our own borrowed "home," with or without guests. Because we are visiting the supermarkets (food museums), liquor stores, and laundries of our travel destination, we can imagine that we are local residents without having to pay the dues, or the taxes. Vacations become a seamless part of our lives, and our routines continue without the intrusion of room service.

When we think of Bermuda, for example, we think of how I nearly set the cottage ablaze by using one candle per year on my husband's miniature birthday cake. (For safety's sake, we now use one birthday candle to represent a decade.) Gerrit's surprised and slightly concerned face is captured in the photograph taken by our son, Alexander, then nine years old, but the taste of the chocolate cake on the patio at sunset is a memory that only the three of us can share.

Or there was the camping trip in Colorado when I finally succeeded, without a recipe and in a folding frying pan over Sterno, in
reinventing Tex-Mex flautas, flute-shaped fried tortillas stuffed
with chicken. They made up for the night before, when we had tried
to sauté the chicken over the campfire in an epic rainstorm. The fire
sputtered, and the pan filled with water faster than it could be emp-
tied. As the situation deteriorated, we agreed with the two friends
who were camping with us that we would simply poach the chicken,
then gave up altogether and nourished ourselves with beer.

Camping in South Africa was probably our most adventurous
journey, from both traveling and cooking perspectives. We cooked
nearly every night of a six-week tour from the northern Transvaal
to Cape Town. Using recipes from Gerrit's South African relatives,
we enjoyed sosaties (curried kebabs) and sausages on the braai (barbecue). Then, when relatives gave us a respite from camping with
the offer of a spare room, we cooked for them, using recipes we had
typed from our cookbooks onto index cards. As we drove from
South Africa into the mountain kingdom of Swaziland, we were
told that there were cholera and bandits on the road up ahead, but
a more immediate concern was that the border guards raided the
gas-powered refrigerator, leaving us with nothing for dinner.

As with any passion, the cook's tour can go to extremes. Picking
too many mussels off the rocks just means trying to make new
friends before dinnertime. But one summer on the Maine coast I
probably truly overdid it, putting up dozens of jars of strawberry
jam while others were happily swimming, sailing, and kayaking.
(The truth is, though, I like preserving jam better than I like any of
those activities.)

In March we visited Morocco, our first trip in years without
the pepper grinder. We stayed in romantic hotel rooms with luxurious whirlpool baths and colorful tile floors, but there was never
so much as a hot plate in any of them. The guides led us through

the souks of Marra-
kesh and Fez, where
shopping is still an
adventure. The sym-
phony of edibles
included heaps of
mint, coriander,
parsley, and cha-
momile in bloom;
joints of meat
hanging in the
butchers' open
windows; pre-
served meats
packed with
salt and fat in

crocks; forty kinds of olives;
snails in a plastic bucket—and many delights never
offered to us in restaurants. It was a cook's paradise, and I had no
kitchen. Needless to say, it will never happen again.

Bibliothèque

Cookbooks

Like so many other cuisines, it seems to me that one cannot separate Moroccan food from Moroccan history. Really good cookbooks—ones that offer tried and true, authentic recipes, as well as detailed commentary on the food traditions of the country or region and the history behind the recipes and the ingredients unique to the cuisine—are just as essential to travel as guidebooks. I read these cookbooks the way other people read novels; therefore, the authors have to be more than just good cooks, and the books have to be more than cookbooks. All of the authors and books listed below fit the bill, and because they are *all* my favorites, I feature them alphabetically. I use each of them at different times throughout the year and couldn't envision my kitchen without a single one. The Mediterranean cookbooks are in some ways the most interesting, because, as Claudia Roden notes in her book *Mediterranean Cookery*, "Looking for the imprint of the past in the Mediterranean can be fascinating and helps to explain why a dish on one side of the sea is like another on the other side. But it is even more exciting to discover the extraordinary regional diversity of the area. For here unity does not mean uniformity. Obviously a Berber village clinging to a rock has a different way of interpreting a stew from a city like Granada. The Mediterranean has many faces: eastern and western, Christian and Muslim, one intimate with the sea, one with the desert, one which knows the mountains and one which looks beyond the olive trees at northern Europe, one which is rooted to the land, another which glitters with ancient grandeur. And regional cooking reflects them all." I do not provide lengthy descriptions of these titles as I think it is sufficient to state that they are definitive and stand quite apart from the multitude of Mediterranean and Moroccan cookbooks crowding bookstore shelves. I have also included a few articles and titles that aren't strictly cookbooks but are equally as interesting and relevant nonetheless.

Mediterranean

A Book of Mediterranean Food, Elizabeth David, Penguin, 1988
Cod: A Biography of the Fish That Changed the World, Mark Kurlansky, Walker and Company, 1999. I include this wonderful book here because, as Kurlansky notes in one of the chapters, "from the Middle Ages to the present, the most demanding cod market has always been the Mediterranean." Fresh or dried salt cod is a ubiquitous Mediterranean staple (except in the Muslim countries), making an appearance in such dishes as *sonhos de bacalhau* in Portugal, *brandade de morue* in France, *baccala in umido* in Tuscany, and *filetti di baccala all'arancia* in Sicily. The fascinating story of cod criss-crosses the globe from

Newfoundland, New England, the Basque coast of Spain, Brazil, West Africa, and Scandinavia, but the Mediterranean is never very far from the thread.

The Feast of the Olive, Maggie Blyth Klein, Aris Books (Addison-Wesley), 1983; revised and updated edition, Chronicle Books, 1994.

From Tapas to Meze, Joanne Weir, Crown, 1994

Mediterranean: The Beautiful Cookbook, Joyce Goldstein, produced by Welden Owen, Collins, 1994. In addition to the Moroccan recipes peppered throughout, there is a four-page summary of North African cuisine.

Mediterranean Cookery, Claudia Roden, Alfred A. Knopf, 1987. I have lost count of the number of recipes I love from this book. It was when making a Moroccan dish that I learned of Roden's method for roasting peppers in the oven instead of over a flame, which is easier and equally delicious.

Mediterranean Cooking, Paula Wolfert, HarperCollins, 1994. No Moroccan recipes are featured in this book, but then that's why there is Wolfert's *Couscous and Other Good Food From Morocco* (see below).

The Mediterranean Diet Cookbook, Nancy Harmon Jenkins, Bantam, 1994.

A Mediterranean Feast: The Story of the Birth of the Celebrated Cuisines of the Mediterranean, Clifford A. Wright, William Morrow, 1999. Only seven Moroccan recipes, but an outstanding, engrossing achievement.

Mediterranean Grains and Greens, Paula Wolfert, HarperCollins, 1998. Only five specifically Moroccan recipes but still an excellent and interesting resource.

Mediterranean Light, Martha Rose Shulman, Bantam, 1989.

The Mediterranean Kitchen, Joyce Goldstein, William Morrow, 1989. A number of Moroccan recipes, both traditional and inspired, are included in this wonderful cookbook. Uniquely, Goldstein indicates how, by changing only an ingredient or two, recipes can go from being French, say, to Moroccan or Italian or Portuguese, which illustrates the core ingredients each country in the region shares and also allows for more mileage out of nearly every recipe.

The Mediterranean Pantry: Creating and Using Condiments and Seasonings, Aglaia Kremezi, photographs by Martin Brigdale, Artisan, 1994. Among the multitude of Mediterranean staples are recipes for preserved lemons and *harissa,* both fairly ubiquitous in Moroccan cuisine.

Mostly Mediterranean: More Than 200 Recipes from France, Spain, Greece, Morocco, and Sicily, Paula Wolfert, Penguin, 1988.

Olives: The Life and Love of a Noble Fruit, Mort Rosenblum, North Point Press, 1996. One of my most favorite books, with one chapter entitled "Marrakesh," which is also about the entire olive industry in Morocco. However, it is indeed Marrakesh where Rosenblum had his Moroccan olive epiphany: "For olive lovers, there is no place on earth like the little corner of the Marrakesh souks, just past the cobra charmers and pickpockets of Jemaa el Fna square. Much of Morocco is olive country, from the coastal fringe, up the slopes of the Atlas and Rif ranges, and on toward the Sahara. Trees grow most densely near Fez, a thrilling thousand-year-old imperial city of high walls and winding lanes. But Marrakesh is a holy site in olivedom." My husband and I have spent some time in this little olive corner too, buying about a hundred grams (about a quarter pound) of various olives—for about thirty cents—each time we walked by. Rosenblum packs a lot of olive facts and figures into this chapter, such as that every Moroccan village has its secret preparation and every city its specialty (in Fez, coriander is added; in Agadir, mountain herbs); in a good year, Morocco exports about 60,000 tons of olives, second only to Spain; Morocco supplies three-quarters of France's olives, many of which are sold abroad as French; and more olive production might bring down the price of oil, which would be a blessing for Moroccan families, who can rarely afford it and use seed oil instead; Moroccan olive oil is dark and strong and can therefore stand up to ingredients like honey and candied citrus. *De rigueur,* if only because, as Rosenblum states, "when it comes to olives for eating, they [Moroccans] are the world champions."

Middle Eastern

The New Book of Middle Eastern Food, Claudia Roden, Knopf, 2000; an expanded and updated version of the original edition, first published in 1968. When someone speaks of the Middle East, usually the countries referred to do not include Morocco, and rightly so. Roden has expanded her vision of the Middle East to include Morocco, which I think makes more culinary sense than political or cultural. As Roden notes, "The fourth distinctive cooking style is that of North Africa, where Moroccan cuisine is especially magnificent. It is based on the couscous of the original Berber inhabitants with centuries-old echoes from Spain, Portugal, and Sicily and the more recent influence of France. Remarkably, it bears the strongest legacies from ancient Persia and Baghdad in the art of combining ingredients and mixing aromatics." In my opinion, this is the leading book in this culinary category, and while not exclusively devoted to Morocco, is very much worth reading (and cooking from).

The Vegetarian Table: North Africa, Kitty Morse, photographs by Deborah Jones, Chronicle Books, 1996. As Morse notes in the introduction, "When a North African woman shops for her family at the city *marché* or at the open-air souk in the countryside, her basket overflows with the fruits and vegetables of the season, bunches of fresh herbs, fresh or dried fava beans, lentils, and of course, the pellets of cracked durum wheat, or semolina, called couscous. She will purchase meat, poultry, or fish mainly on special occasions, or when her finances allow." As John Buffa, an early nineteenth-century doctor, recounts in *Travels Through the Empire of Morocco:* "The Moors (as Moroccans used to be known) in general, are extremely fond of vegetables, which contribute very much to their contentment. The peasants eat meat only on certain great days . . . and their favourite dish is cous-ca-sou [sic]." I often feel that when cooks try to convert dishes with meat to dishes without meat they don't always work; but these recipes really do, which is partly due to Morse's creativity and deep understanding of these cuisines (she grew up in Morocco, teaches Moroccan cooking, and writes about Moroccan cuisine; she also organizes an annual culinary tour to Morocco—see the entry for "Cooking Schools" in *Renseignements Pratiques* for more details) and partly due to the fact that North African dishes have remarkable depth and taste rich with the use of so many spices. Besides spices, preserved lemons add a lot of flavor to North African cuisine, and Morse shares three different recipes for them here. The "quick preserved lemons," which she learned from a friend who owns a cooking school, is particularly helpful for busy cooks as all you do is prepare the lemons as usual and then freeze them overnight. The lemons aren't, obviously, as soft, but they do impart some of that wonderful scent and flavor. If you are using this book to cook for carnivore friends, they'll never miss the meat.

Moroccan

The Casablanca Cookbook: Wining and Dining at Rick's, Sarah Key, Jennifer Newman Brazil, Vicki Wells, Abbeville Press, 1992. This little hardcover volume is one edition in the Hollywood Hotplates series, and it's like a ready-made party in a book. Recipes for a complete meal (from cocktails and fruit drinks to hors d'oeuvres, salads, and desserts) and entertainment (trivia time out, Casablanca charades, Oscar interlude, and trivia finale) make for a truly fun evening. This is not, obviously, the sort of serious, authoritative cookbook I prefer; but I can't resist including it here because it is exactly the thing I love about immersing oneself in one's destination before a trip. (Plus, I really do love the martinis made with preserved lemons.) Invite some friends over, rent the movie, and have a blast.

Casablanca Cuisine: French North African Cooking, Aline Benayoun, Serif, London, 1998. *Pied noir* cooking (see "Cooking à la Pied-Noir" by Jeffrey Robinson in my *Paris* book) is rather overlooked and unknown, and this book is one of the few, in English, to focus exclusively on a varied, delicious, and healthful cuisine. As Benayoun relates, after independence her family felt they had no choice but to "return" to France, which to her was hardly more than a place to visit on school holidays. "I was just twelve when we left, and although I was raised in Antibes and now think of the Côte d'Azur as home, because we *pieds noirs* were bathed in an exotic tradition we remain very different from the rest of the French." *Pied noir* cuisine is, like Mediterranean cuisine in general, a perfect example of food as the meeting place of cultures: it's French, Spanish, Moroccan, Algerian, Tunisian, and Sephardic, with a touch of Italian. The Sephardic influence naturally tended to adhere to Jewish dietary laws, which in turn were simply adopted by non-Jewish *pieds noirs*. Some of the defining characteristics of *pied noir* cuisine are that every meal starts in the market, and in Morocco that means a morning visit to the souk; the cooking is simple, requiring little more than basic kitchen skills; though sweets were and still are brought out for tea and at weddings, family festivals, and religious holidays, desserts are not elaborate; at the end of an ordinary meal, fresh fruit follows, as it refreshes the palate and aids digestion; cheese was and is served only occasionally, as it isn't really suited to a hot climate; finally, in a less definable element borrowed from Arab neighbors, the sense of hospitality is strong. "We believe that a great meal means more than just good food; it also means a table crowded with family and friends. If there is enough for eight, we reckon there is enough for nine, so we insist that friends of friends join us. And their friends are welcome too, because if there is enough for nine, then there is enough for ten." With a number of easy-to-prepare recipes, this book stands as a valuable historical document as well. *De rigueur.*

Cooking at the Kasbah: Recipes From My Moroccan Kitchen, Kitty Morse, photographs by Laurie Smith, Chronicle Books, 1998. Though not as authoritative as either Paula Wolfert's or Robert Carrier's books (below), this is definitely the next best volume. Morse provides a good introduction to Moroccan cuisine as well as notes about Moroccan hospitality, dining etiquette, and basic ingredients and techniques in the Moroccan kitchen. Suggested menus are given for a family-style dinner, a Moroccan picnic, a Friday lunch, a Sephardic dinner, and a Moroccan tea, for example, and there is a page of mail-order sources for spices, *tagines,* Moroccan wines, dates, and more.

Couscous and Other Good Food From Morocco, Paula Wolfert, introduction by Gael Greene, Perennial, 1987, paperback; Harper & Row, 1973, hardcover. I once was introduced to a graduate student from India who was pursuing his degree here in the States, and I asked him for a recommendation of a good Indian restaurant in the San Francisco Bay Area, where I was living at the time. He replied that if I wanted to taste really good Indian food, I should buy Madhur Jaffrey's *Invitation to Indian Cooking* and cook it myself. The same seems to be true of Moroccan cooking, and this is hands-down the single best Moroccan cookbook in existence, in English (and I doubt there is a better one in French or any other language). Though the hardcover is out of print, the paperback can still be found, and you should make every effort to find it if you are even remotely interested in reading about Moroccan cuisine and/or cooking some authentic dishes at home before and after your trip. Every single recipe I've tried turns out just as Wolfert says it will, which is to say delicious.

(My husband still maintains that "Chicken With Lemons and Olives Emshmel" is the best chicken dish he's ever had, and the "Eggplant Salad, Rabat Style" is uncommonly good.) In addition to being an outstanding cookbook (there is even a recipe for *kif* candy—*majoun*—although Wolfert denies, "absolutely, that I have ever tested this recipe"; the one she gives is apparently one that her friend Mohammed made. Her advice, should you decide to try it, is "eat with care—never more than one tablespoon at a time"), this is a very good overview of the foodstuffs you'll see for sale in the souks and the dishes you'll find on restaurant menus. *Absolument de rigueur.*

Marrakech la Rouge: Les Juifs de la Medina, Helene Gans Perez, Les éditions Metropolis, Geneva, 1996. This slender volume is one in a series called La Cuisine de mes Souvenirs, and is of great interest not only for its recipes but for the author's recollections of Jewish life in the medina of Marrakesh. In French, but not difficult to read.

Moroccan Cooking: The Best Recipes, Fettouma Benkirane, Sochepress, Casablanca, 1999. This little paperback volume is part of a series called Collection Vie Pratique and is apparently the second cookbook by author Benkirane. (Her first, *Moroccan Cookery*—published in French, Arabic, German, and English—I have not seen, either in the United States or Morocco.) With this book, Benkirane presents lighter and less time-consuming versions of traditional Moroccan recipes. She especially addresses young women, "who have not learned to cook, and who therefore feel that they haven't the time to do so." She emphasizes that "the Moroccan culinary repertory is much vaster than might be supposed from the incessant repetition of the same well-known dishes" [*pastilla, mechoui,* couscous] and that, contrary to what one might think, Moroccan cooking, "based as it is on spices, the savour of herbs, and the variety of vegetables, is actually easier to prepare than French cuisine, which is based on thickened sauces."

A Quintet of Cuisines, Michael and Frances Field and the editors of Time-Life Books, photographed by Sheldon Cotler and Richard Jeffrey, photography in Poland by Eliot Elisofon, Time-Life Books, 1970. The Foods of the World series was an extraordinary publishing feat. Each edition was an amazing collaborative effort, the likes of which we'll probably never see again (a separate spiral-bound recipe booklet accompanied each hardbound edition). This edition is, admittedly, a seemingly odd quintet as it features Switzerland, the Low Countries (Belgium, Luxembourg, Netherlands), Poland, Bulgaria and Romania, and North Africa (Tunisia, Algeria, Morocco). It's true that these five regions have little in common, but as the editors explain in the introduction, "They all have fascinating foods—and for purposes of exploring their styles of cooking they are all gathered in one kitchen, as it were, in this book." This odd assemblage aside, the pages devoted to Morocco are among the best written on Moroccan cuisine. In defense of the Arab tradition of eating with your (right) hand, Field relates, "At the second or third helping of fish, I found that for the sheer sensual joy of tasting food in its pristine state, fingers are best, because a fork, even of the finest silver, intrudes with its own alien flavor and texture. This discovery prompted a stream of associations in my mind: ripe, sun-warmed tomatoes plucked from the vine and eaten on the spot; freshly baked bread eaten with the hands; a ripe banana; or even the lowly but delicious hamburger on a bun. For the first time I really understood why the Chinese and Japanese use chopsticks—as aids to direct the food *to* the mouth, but not to accompany it *into* the mouth." The recipes are not as detailed as those given in Paula Wolfert's book but are equally as authentic. Field concludes that "while not so sophisticated and complex as the French cuisine nor so varied and subtle as the Chinese, the cooking of the Maghreb combines all those attributes in a way that makes it utterly distinctive. I found myself thinking about it in musical terms, as I often do when deeply moved, and I still think of it that way: as a three-movement symphony held together by interlocking themes—Tunisia, a lively, fiery first movement, *allegro con brio;* pastoral Algeria, a slow *andante;* and Morocco, richest of all, a grand *finale maestro.* Altogether a magnificent whole, not yet fully known or appreciated by the rest of the world." Long out of print, but copies do turn up in used bookstores and specialty cookbook shops.

Scent of Orange Blossoms: Sephardic Cuisine of Morocco, Kitty Morse and Danielle Mamane, Ten Speed Press, Berkeley, California, 2001. This book will be landing in bookstores at about the same time as this Morocco edition, so as I write I have not seen the finished work. But I bring it to your attention because I think it will be very good, and I am awaiting it with anticipation.

A Taste of Morocco: A Culinary Journey, Robert Carrier, Clarkson Potter, 1987. A classic you'll find included in nearly every bibliography on Moroccan cuisine, especially since it was published both in the United States and the U.K. (Century Hutchinson, London, 1987). As an illustrated hardcover, it's a little different from Paula Wolfert's cookbook but is equally as authoritative. Actually, I think each book is indispensable, and having them both is like having the best of Moroccan cuisine at your fingertips. This title, however, is considerably more difficult to find than Wolfert's—when I phoned Kitchen Arts & Letters here in New York, the staff had a waiting list of fifteen people; persevere, though. You'll be glad you did. *De rigueur.*

Traditional Moroccan Cooking: Recipes From Fez, Madame Guinaudeau, foreword by Claudia Roden, Serif, London, 1994; originally published in Rabat by J. E. Laurent as *Fes vu par sa cuisine* in 1958 and *Fez: Traditional Moroccan Cooking,* translated by J. E. Harris in 1964; distributed in the United States by Interlink Publishing, Northampton, Massachusetts. I admit I have not made a single recipe from this book, but without hesitation I deem it *de rigueur* because it is "a contribution to the history of this country and a document of great human interest," to quote from the preface by Ahmed Sefrioui. More than an in-depth look at the refined cuisine of Fez, this is a book to approach like a history or sociology book, for, as Claudia Roden notes in the foreword, Guinaudeau describes "the way people lived and entertained, the protocol of their banquets, the activities of the kitchen and the public bakehouse." Besides the recipes (Guinaudeau shares one for *"El Majoun"*—hashish and honey— with a tip that certain grocers in the Attarine quarter are renowned for their way of preparing *majoun*, which I believe is still true), Madame covers the distillation of orange blossom and rose petals, *nezaha*, restaurants, cafés, the markets and food shops of Fez, *mechoui*, and the corporation of cooks.

World Food: Morocco, Catherine Hanger, Lonely Planet, 2000. When I first learned of Lonely Planet's World Food series (other editions include Spain, France, and Italy), I imagined that each book would be authored by the food authorities relevant to each country's cuisine. They're not, but it turns out the authors are knowledgeable culinary enthusiasts. (Publishers, however, take note: there is room on the shelves for those books I imagined!) Each title in this series is small enough to fit in a large pocket or handbag and therefore is a good companion at restaurants, as you can discreetly consult its contents without looking like a dork. In addition to a thorough Moroccan culinary dictionary and a Moroccan-English food glossary, this little book packs in information about the culture of Moroccan cuisine; staples and specialties; drinks; home cooking and traditions; celebrations; regional variations; shopping and markets; and a summary of places to eat and drink. Short, themed essays appear throughout the book, and of these I particularly like "A Tale of Two Souqs (Urban/Rural)" and "Eating en Famille." Also, I found the advice given for health concerns (like traveler's diarrhea) better than in general guidebooks, and I appreciate the author's honest assessment of street food, which is to say that it should by all means be experienced, not avoided as some other writers will advise. *De rigueur.*

Articles

"My Old Moroccan Home" by Paula Wolfert, *Saveur*, No. 7, July/August, 1995. Unfortunately, I was unable to include this wonderful article here, but it is very much worth tracking down at the library or through *Saveur* (800-429-0106). Tangier, as Wolfert notes, "was the city where I lived unhappily with one husband and very happily with another, set up households, raised children, forged friendships, learned what the Mediterranean lifestyle was and how to live it. It was also the place where I found my vocation as food writer—where I discovered who I really was."

Les Personalités
(Natives and Passionate Visitors)

"Many Moroccans think of themselves as residents of Fez, or Oujda, or Agadir, rather than as 'Moroccans.' A Tunisian is a Tunisian, but a Moroccan can be a lot of things."
—John Gunther, *INSIDE AFRICA*

"The foreigner who elects residence in Morocco is to some extent a cultural voyeur. American writer Edith Wharton in 1920 has remarked on 'the dream-like feeling that envelops with every step.' There is still a strong sense of being part of the civilisation of the ancient world. The rites and rituals of everyday life are still unchanged in many areas. The eternal aspects of mankind are always present. There is a purity that belongs to an older age, and everywhere there is a direct communication with the past: in family relationships, in local dress, in the prevalent code of manners. Morocco is and has always been a deeply mystical land."
—Lisa Lovatt-Smith, *MOROCCAN INTERIORS*

Delacroix in Africa

By Roy McMullen

◦∾◦

editor's note

Alain D'Hooghe has noted in *The Magic of Morocco* that "it could be said that, to some extent, everything began with Eugène Delacroix, who, in 1832, came here with the Comte de Mornay, on a mission from the French government to conclude a treaty of good-neighborly relations with the Sultan, Moulay Abderrahman." As students of art history know, Delacroix stayed only six months, but he filled eight notebooks with sketches, drawings, and watercolors, and his Morocco journey had nothing less than a profound effect on his life and work. Other painters, of course, crossed the Strait of Gibraltar and followed in Delacroix's footsteps. They, too, as D'Hooghe notes, wanted to discover Morocco, "to bathe their eyes in it and to gather the raw materials that would later serve for paintings of fantasias, interiors of harems, beautiful Mooresses, Jewish brides and so on, all subjects snapped up by their European customers. In the second half of the nineteenth century, the heydey of the *Thousand and One Nights* arrived." As this piece from *Horizon* reveals, Delacroix's visit resulted in much gunfire, a minor treaty, and a turning point in nineteenth-century art.

ROY MCMULLEN has been a frequent contributor to *Horizon*.

They had to get along without modern hallucinogenic drugs and without the lupine eloquence of words like "freak-out." Nevertheless, many imaginations in nineteenth-century France seem to have been addicted to trips. Baudelaire embarked for "languorous Asia and burning Africa" simply by nuzzling his beloved's hair. Mallarmé, after a night of writer's block, had Mitty-like visions of chucking everything: "I'll leave! Steamer with swaying masts, weigh anchor!" Rimbaud took off in his drunken boat for "unbelievable Floridas," among other places.

The habit raises a question that may interest students of the romantic creative process. What happened when a trip came true? When the escape metaphor materialized? Here the poets are not very helpful, since in real life Baudelaire turned back from a voyage to Asia, Mallarmé scarcely budged, and Rimbaud quit Europe and literature simultaneously. An answer, however, has come down to us from Baudelaire's friend Delacroix, who actually took a six-month journey to a reality that resembled his reveries—specifically, to Morocco, with detours in Andalusia and Algeria.

Imperialism and useful acquaintances provided the occasion. In 1827 the Turkish dey of Algiers had flicked a French consul with a fly whisk, and in 1830 French troops avenged the insult by occupying the territory. The government of Louis Philippe worried about the intentions of Abd-er-Rahman II, sultan of neighboring Morocco. In 1831 it decided to send Count Charles de Mornay, a pleasant young man about town, to the imperial city of Meknes to negotiate a treaty; he insisted on having a history painter attached to his mission. Delacroix got the appointment through the influence of several important Parisians: the director of the Opéra, the Bertin newspaper family (immortalized a few months later by Ingres's portrait of Bertin the elder), and the actress Mlle. Mars, who was Mornay's mistress. The ambassador and the artist left Paris for Toulon on December 30, after a party given by Mlle. Mars.

As these worldly circumstances suggest, Eugène Delacroix at thirty-three was not yet the monkish, compulsive worker he became in later years. Nor was he the messy bohemian sort of romantic. He was an appeaser of the establishment, with well-cut clothes, aristocratic manners, and a classical education. In a letter written shortly after her party, Mlle. Mars summed him up as "a young painter who has talent, wit, social graces and, they say, an excellent disposition."

His urbanity, however, did not keep him from projecting an unconventional image. The nervous, olive-tinted face under a mass of jet-black hair might have been that of a Napoleonic carabineer if it had not been set on such an obviously frail body. He had a peculiar way of squinting with both eyes, as if he were looking into a bright light or perhaps taking the measure of an unknown adversary. He reminded Théophile Gautier of "some Indian maharajah who, after being perfectly educated at Calcutta as a gentleman, has come, dressed in European clothes, to inspect the civilization of Paris."

Does all this imply an ordinary salon poseur? I am afraid it does a bit; and Delacroix was certainly not ordinary. He was one of the most articulate and generally intelligent painters on record. Still, it is true that up to this point he had shown a distaste for ordinary reality and for what many people would call sincerity. The fierce sexuality in his paintings, for example, had not corresponded to the reality of his bachelor life, which had been mostly celibacy interrupted by brief affairs with models. One of his finest pictures, *Liberty Leading the People* (1830), had been political make-believe, for in fact street insurrections filled him with bourgeois alarm. His interest in Eastern exoticism, which had led to such splendidly rhetorical works as *The Massacre at Chios* (1824) and *The Death of Sardanapalus* (1827), had been nourished on Byron and Turkish bric-a-brac. In sum, he had been living and creating largely on the basis of secondary sources and feigned feelings. Now he was confronted with the prospect of sunlit primary sources and violent physical sensations.

Part of that prospect was slow to become immediate. The members of the Mornay expedition reached Toulon after a rough journey by coach and horse through snow in the Rhône valley and wet gales on the littoral; on January 11, 1832, they set sail aboard *La Perle*, a small warship carrying eighteen cannons. Delacroix, who had already begun to write reports for his friends at home, found life on this "floating prison" a mixture of the boring and the very disagreeable. He was seasick for several days. The ship ran into "disheartening calms" and then into "squalls that were quite alarming, to judge by the face of the captain." As compensation he had distant views of the Balearic Islands and "the coasts of the kingdom of Granada," and he managed to do some pastels.

When they put in at Algeciras, he was disappointed to discover that they were in strict quarantine because of a cholera epidemic in France, but he "touched Andalusian soil" anyway with the men sent ashore for provisions. He moved swiftly from direct observation to memories of art: "I saw grave Spaniards in Figaro costumes keep us at pistol point for fear of infection, toss us turnips, lettuce, chickens, etc., and nevertheless pick up, without dipping it in vinegar, the money we left on the sandy beach. With the liveliest sense of pleasure I found myself outside France, transported directly into this picturesque country, seeing their houses, their cloaks. . . . All of Goya was palpitating around me."

At sea the next day *La Perle* had more trouble with unreliable winds. (One wonders how naval battles ever got fought in the days of sail.) She was half-becalmed for several hours and then, toward evening, blown out through the Strait of Gibraltar into the Atlantic. Delacroix longed for his "peaceful nest" in Paris. But at last, at nine o'clock on the bright morning of January 24, 1832, thirteen days after leaving Toulon, the ship anchored off Tangier, and the dream-trip proper got under way.

It was actually several trips. The members of the French mission remained in Tangier until March 6, waiting for the sultan's travel permit and for the end of the Ramadan fasting. They then set out on horseback, with camping equipment and a Moroccan escort, for Meknes, about 175 miles south. They reached the imperial city on March 15, had an audience with Abd-er-Rahman on March 22, and departed on April 5. Back in Tangier on April 12, they settled down to wait for Mornay's treaty. Eventually Delacroix crossed over to

Spain, endured the quarantine, and spent the last two weeks of May in Cádiz and Seville. He returned to Toulon in a roundabout way, stopping in Tangier (June 3–10) and visiting Algiers for three days (June 25–28). He did not see Paris again until July 20.

His letters and the notes he scribbled on his sketches make it clear that the going was frequently far from good. He describes the region between Tangier and Meknes as "a land in which there are neither roads, nor bridges, nor boats on the rivers." Although he was apparently an excellent horseman, he felt the strain of riding all day "at a walking pace without shade and on a bad saddle." He had spells of exasperation with "the picturesque that knocks your eyes out at every step."

As the weeks wore on, he began to have bouts of shameless homesickness: "My companions all around me have received letters. I alone am deprived. . . . The smallest event is precious to an exile. When I say news I don't mean political or literary matters, but your news, the most simple things. . . . Pray Heaven not to prolong my exile, and keep on writing. . . . I beg you, write, write." From Meknes on a particularly depressing day he asks Armand Bertin, editor of the powerful Paris *Journal des Débats,* to persuade the foreign ministry "not to leave us here to rot."

His pages echo with the roar of massed explosions and the whistle of bullets, for the Moroccans were inclined to fire their long guns on almost any pretext: as a sign of welcome, as a way of impressing infidels, as an addition to the excitement of a horse race or a mock cavalry charge, or simply as an expression of high spirits. The mission's progress south from Tangier had the form of a crescendo: "At each instant we met with new armed tribes that expended gunpowder at a frightful rate to celebrate our arrival. Each provincial governor turned us over to the next, and our already very important escort kept growing. From time to time we could hear a stray bullet hissing in the midst of the rejoicing."

On March 8 only the intervention of Ben-Abou, the commander of the Moroccan military escort, prevented the rejoicing from turning into tragedy. The French party had stopped to camp at Alcazarquivir, a locality that gratified Delacroix's romantic sense of history by being the site of the sixteenth-century Battle of the Three Kings, in which Dom Sebastian of Portugal and two Moorish rulers perished. Suddenly, according to the rather frantic sketchbook notes for that day, the usual welcome became ugly: "Population, music, gunpowder games without end. The pasha's brother hitting about him with a stick and a saber. A man breaks through the crowd of soldiers and fires his gun in our face. He is grabbed by Abou. His fury. He is dragged away by his undone turban, he is knocked down. My panic. We run. The saber was already drawn."

The crescendo reached its climax when the Mornay mission, flags flying, arrived at Meknes. The next day, March 16, Delacroix described the glorious event in a letter to his boyhood friend J. B. Pierret:

The Sultan had ordered everybody, under threat of the severest punishment, to have fun and to turn out to give us a celebration. The crowding and the disorder were terrible. We knew that during the reception for some Austrians here six months ago a dozen men and fourteen horses had been accidentally killed. Our little troop had a lot of trouble keeping itself together and knowing where it was in the middle of the thousands of guns that were going off right in front of us. We had our music at the head of our formation and more than twenty flags carried by horsemen. Our music was also mounted; it consisted of something like bagpipes and of drums hung from the necks of the horsemen, who beat them alternately on each side with big and little drumsticks. The deafening racket they made blended with volleys from the cavalry, from the infantry, and from the more rabid individuals who kept breaking in all around us to fire in our faces. . . . This triumph, which resembled the torture of some wretches on their way to the gallows, lasted from morning until four in the afternoon. *Nota bene* that we had had only a light breakfast at seven o'clock in our tent.

In addition to the heat, the fatigue, the noise, and the danger, there were restrictions that were irritating for all the French and maddening for a painter. At Meknes the whole party was confined in an old palace during the week of waiting for the audience with the sultan. When they were finally given permission to go out on the street, accompanied by a military guard for which they had to pay, Delacroix was the only Frenchman willing to face the anti-Christian populace; and even he seems to have sometimes regretted what he calls his "impulse to look": "I am followed, every time I emerge, by an enormous band of the curious, who do not spare me such insults as dog, infidel . . . and who jostle each other to get near and make a scornful face under my nose. You can't imagine how I itch to lose my temper." It was nearly impossible, at least in Meknes, to draw "merely a tumble-down house" openly. When Delacroix tried going up on the roof terrace to work, he was greeted by rocks and gunshots, for it was there that the Moroccan women sometimes went to enjoy a cool breeze.

Was the journey a disappointment? Clearly it was not. In spite of the difficulties he mentions, Delacroix succeeded in getting on paper an astonishing amount of what he saw. And each of the complaints in his letters and notes can be more than matched by evidence of a romantic tourist enjoying himself immensely.

A midsummer-night refrain, half-Berlioz and half-schmaltz, runs through his narrative. On February 12, at Tangier, he writes in his sketchbook-diary: "Indisposed, remained alone this evening.

Delicious reverie by moonlight in the garden." On March 12, during the noisy progress south: "This evening, after a gay dinner, went down, solitary, to the banks of the Sebou River. Lovely moonlight." On April 7, during the ride back from Meknes: "Distant mountains. Went out this evening after sunset. Melancholy view of this immense and uninhabited plain. Sound of frogs and other animals. The Moslems were saying their prayers at the same time." On May 18, at Cádiz: "Midnight is sounded at the Franciscans. Singular emotion in this strange land. This moonlight. These white towers in the rays of the moon." On May 23, at Alcalá de Guadaira, near Seville: "Night. The moon on melancholy water. Croaking of frogs. Moorish Gothic chapel."

From Tangier he writes of a "sentimental little love affair I am carrying on here with a very pretty and decent little English girl." (She was the daughter of the British consul.) His notes at Seville refer mysteriously to a second adventure, also with an English inspiration: "Mrs. Ford corrected the music for me, and I was near her. . . . Mrs. Ford: adieu to the Englishwoman. Flirt. I had been there during the day without finding her; I had wandered the streets like a Spanish lover."

Although at home he had never shown much interest in landscapes without personages, he was fascinated by the Moroccan scenery. Some notes apparently written on horseback near Alcazarquivir read like a forecast of Cézanne—a Cézanne equipped with a panning movie camera: "Beautiful country, very blue mountains, violet on the right; violet mountains morning and evening, blue during the day. Carpets of yellow flowers, violet before reaching the river. . . . Entered the plain where Dom Sebastian was defeated. On the right, lovely blue mountains; on the left, plain as far as you can see, carpets of white, light yellow, deep yellow, violet flowers."

He was equally fascinated, however, by the color of the costumes he saw around him. At Tangier *La Perle* was visited by "a score of black, yellow, and green marabous." In the towns there were Jewish women, beautiful as "pearls of Eden," clustered in groups like "pots of flowers," wearing vests in "gold and amaranth" and "a red skullcap, white drapery, black dress." There were mulatto slaves in yellow caftans, elderly Moors in transparent burnooses and green sleeves, and a Spanish woman with "brown arm against black mantilla and brown dress."

His eye for architecture was less professional and more sentimental, but alert. At Tangier his notes record dozens of unexpected details: the decaying columns of a Moorish palace, the ceramic wall behind a pasha, a sculptured ceiling, a stone bench, a "little white house in the shade in the midst of dark orange-trees." At Meknes he relished the sharply shadowed archways and the massive town walls, which had been built in the seventeenth century by the sultan Moulay Ismail, Morocco's equivalent of both Louis XIV and Cheops.

The surviving documents constantly remind us of Delacroix's dedication to the craft of painting. Sketches done on the way back from Meknes are accompanied by such comments as these: "Mass the personages in brown, on the assumption of lightening later to make them stand out. . . . Men in half tint . . . Michelangelo head . . . Men lit from behind . . . Red soil." A random note at Meknes reads: "Jews on the terrace silhouetted against a sky slightly cloudy and blue-tinted in the style of Paolo Veronese."

The simplicity and the immutability of Moroccan life turned him, for the time being at least, into a disciple of Rousseau. "We notice," he tells his sketchbook, "a thousand things that these people lack. Their ignorance makes them calm and happy. Are we ourselves at the end of what a more advanced civilization can produce? They are closer to nature in a thousand ways: in their clothes, in the form of their shoes. Hence beauty is linked to everything they do.

In our corsets, our tight shoes, our ridiculous sheaths, we inspire pity." In a letter to Pierret he wonders ironically about the wisdom of ever returning to France: "What new revolutions are you preparing for us with your ragpickers and your Carlists and your crossroads Robespierres? *Tempora!* Is this the price one pays for civilization and the bliss of having a round hat instead of a burnoose?"

The costumes and the dignity of the Moroccans furnished him occasions for continuing at long distance his war with the neoclassical and academic followers of Jacques-Louis David. In one letter he remarks: "The heroes of David and company with their rose-colored members would cut a sorry figure alongside these sons of the sun." In another: "Imagine, my friend, what it is to see—lying in the sun, walking the streets, mending slippers—consular personages, Catos, Brutuses, who do not lack even the disdainful air the masters of the world must have had. . . . All in white, like Roman senators and participants in the Panathenaea at Athens." Referring to the Paris custom of sending young painters to study at the French Academy in Rome, he says it would be better for them "to be sent as cabin boys on the first ship for Barbary."

The ultimate results of the trip? Among the more evident are two famous canvases painted after Delacroix's return to Paris: *Women of Algiers,* in the version of 1834, and *The Sultan of Morocco Surrounded by His Court,* in the version of 1845—variants of both pictures exist.

The origins of *Women of Algiers* are known only indirectly. During his brief visit to the Algerian capital the painter is said to have been admitted secretly to the small harem of an acquaintance of a French port official. According to the official, quoted by a friend, this is what happened: "Delacroix appeared drunk from the spectacle before his eyes. After the bedazzlement came work, and then conversation. . . . From time to time Delacroix exclaimed: 'It's beautiful! It's like Homeric times! The woman in the gynaeceum, busy with her children, spinning wool or embroidering marvelous fabrics. That's my conception of a woman!'" The odd confession, if genuine, helps to account for several facts about the salon "maha-jarah": his failure to marry, his penchant for models and maidservants, the number of submissive females—captives, concubines, slaves, Ophelia, Desdemona—in his pictures.

The first thoughts for *The Sultan* were sketches of Mornay's outdoor audience at Meknes with Abd-er-Rahman. Other paintings derived from the trip are *Moroccan Military Exercises* (1832), *The Fanatics of Tangier* (1836), *Jewish Wedding in Morocco* (1839), *Jewish Musicians at Mogador* (1847), *Arab Horses Fighting in a Stable* (1860), and *The Arab Tax Collection* (1863). In other words, the North African experience remained vivid in the artist's imagination from the moment of his return to France up to the year of his death.

When we move beyond mere subject matter, we are of course obliged to speculate, since we cannot be sure of the way Delacroix's painting technique and general outlook would have evolved if he had never boarded *La Perle*. But some interesting evidence and some probabilities can be considered.

He accumulated seven albums of annotated sketches. (Two of the three that were not eventually dispersed at auctions are now in the Louvre, and the third is in the Musée Condé at Chantilly.) He also produced a set of watercolors for Mornay, which included such items as a finely observed portrait of the Moroccan minister Amin Bias and a cinematic rendering of a gunpowder gallop at Meknes. It is true that he had been an assiduous sketcher for many years, and it is also true that he remained, as far as important works were concerned, a studio painter to the end of his career—in this respect he was no more revolutionary than his neoclassical rivals. Still, a long period of almost daily eye-on-the-object work in brilliant African sunshine, uninterrupted by composing and finishing sessions in a Paris studio, can be assumed to have had some effect. It can be regarded historically as a prelude to the Impressionists' move outdoors, which finally wrecked the academic system.

It was a period of letting the retina correct the academic rules, and one feels this, I think, in his use of color. Here again one must hedge. Delacroix had learned much, long before 1832, from the palettes of such masters as Rubens and Veronese and from the vibrating brushwork of Constable. He had been initiated into the theory of complementary colors: there is a story of his having given up a visit to the Louvre one day in 1827 because he had made the exciting discovery that his yellow fiacre cast a violet shadow. Even so, it is difficult to believe that without the stimulus of Moroccan hues and tinted reflections, the color harmonies in such paintings as *Women of Algiers* and *The Sultan* would be what they are. These harmonies are not just an anticipation of Impressionism (often they are not that at all). They are the work of a sensibility hit by an awareness of color as a thing in itself—as a legitimate material for composition.

The change was noticed almost immediately. When *Women of Algiers* was exhibited at the Paris Salon of 1834, the critic Gustave Planche wrote: "This capital piece . . . marks a grave moment in the intellectual life of Monsieur Delacroix. . . . The color is brilliant and pure everywhere, but without ever being crude. . . . It is painting and nothing else, painting that is frank, vigorous, vividly accented, with a boldness that is thoroughly Venetian and yet owes nothing to the masters of whom it reminds you."

After visiting the Salon of 1845, Baudelaire was equally enthusiastic about the subtle coloring of *The Sultan,* and he added a compliment for the sober composition: "In spite of the splendor of the tones, this picture is so harmonious it is gray—gray like nature, gray like the atmosphere of summer, when the sunshine spreads over each object a sort of trembling, twilit dustiness. . . . The composition is excellent; it has something unexpected about it because it is true and natural."

These poetic remarks contain a hinted recognition of a paradox. One of the ultimate results of the romantic dream-trip to North Africa and Spain seems to have been a taming of the romantic impulse in Delacroix. In his work after 1832 he frequently conquered his old distaste for reality. He moved away perceptibly, although never entirely, from purely literary inspiration. He deepened his already existing Orientalism into something that almost justified his ironical argument that the glory of ancient Athens and Rome had survived in the stinking, noisy streets of Tangier and Meknes. He employed a richer palette but at the same time a more sober one; he was never to repeat the flamboyance that had led him to refer to *The Death of Sardanapalus* as his "massacre No. 2." And finally, Baudelaire was beside the mark in calling the composition of *The Sultan* "true and natural." It is a classical arrangement of verticals and horizontals that might have been invented by Poussin.

One can argue, of course, that few paintings are more densely romantic than *Women of Algiers*. Perhaps the right conclusion is simply that Delacroix, without breaking the continuity of his art, did some intensive ripening during his time away from France. In a letter from Tangier after his visit to Andalusia, he said as much: "In this short while I have lived twenty times more than in several months in Paris."

Reprinted by Permission of AMERICAN HERITAGE magazine, a division of Forbes, Inc., 1969.

Are We Going to Fez?
Talking Paul Bowles with
Cherie Nutting

By Stephen Aiken

editor's note

....

Of all the material in my files about Paul Bowles, this one reveals the most, even though it is an interview *about* him rather than *with* him.

Freelance photographer CHERIE NUTTING first visited Morocco in 1960 for a day, and says, "The moment I hit Morocco, it struck my heart. I just loved it." In the late 1980s, she met Paul Bowles, who introduced her to her future husband, Bachir Attar, hereditary leader of the Master Musicians of Jajouka. Though no longer married to Attar, Nutting remains very connected to Morocco and spends part of each year there. She is the author of *Yesterday's Perfume: An Intimate Memoir of Paul Bowles* (Clarkson Potter, 2000), and recently acquired Bowles's apartment in Tangier. STEPHEN AIKEN is a writer and artist, as well as director of "234" Gallery at Hannah in Wellfleet, Massachusetts.

Say: "O unbelievers,
I serve not what you serve
and you are not serving what I serve."
                                        —THE KORAN

"I am the wrong direction, the dead nerve-end, the unfinished
scream. One day my words may comfort you, as yours can
never comfort me."
                        —Paul Bowles, NEXT TO NOTHING

Cherie Nutting's East Village studio apartment opens to a narrow hallway. There is a modest darkroom on the left and, stepping straight, a small bathroom. "The plumbing is leaking again," she informs me. The bathroom walls are saloned with mementos—Cherie in a Davy Crockett cap, looking like Scout in the movie *To Kill a Mockingbird,* Cherie in a ballerina tutu, Cherie's mother, standing *contrapposto* in a white two-piece, the epitome of late-1950s glamour. There's a psychedelic painting of a knife and heart by Mohamed Mrabet, the Moroccan storyteller, and of course, pictures of Paul Bowles, which prove to be everywhere. Passing the niche kitchen, Cherie opens the refrigerator door. Inside, it looks like an igloo, with something snowed in that may be mayonnaise. I realize I should have brought some take-out with the bag of beer. Our shoes left at the door, we settle down on big Moroccan pillows. My only concern is the sweltering heat. "How is it a numbing sixteen degrees outside and blood temperature in here?" I ask. "You could open the window," she offers, "but the gates are broken. Just pretend you're in the desert!"

It is the frantic week before *Yesterday's Perfume* goes to the printer. Cherie's book chronicles, in photographs and diaristic writing, the thirteen years she spent with Paul Bowles in Morocco. Having just returned from the office of her editor at Random House, Roy Finamore, she is contemplating the economic demands of the publishing industry and how her project resists standardization. Its 264 pages include contributions from Peter Beard and Bruce Weber and previously unpublished writings by Bowles. She is sorting paste-ups. It's a "This is going in, this is coming out, what do you think of this?" kind of conversation. I'm boggled, but form some idea of the overall picture. The great achievement of *Yesterday's Perfume* will be its presenting of Bowles, who died in November 1999, in a new light. Because Bowles chose to remain abroad in his modest Tangier apartment for over fifty years, he is often perceived in this country as standoffish and taciturn. Nutting presents Bowles as a warm and upbeat personality surrounded by a circle of talented friends. Call him the "last existentialist" if you must, as long as that assessment does not preclude having fun.

I've known Cherie for over twenty years. When we first met we learned we had Morocco in common. I had traveled in Tunisia, Algeria, and Morocco, yet an important ingredient was missing in my North African experience. I had yet to read "the book." It wasn't until Cherie gave me the book and I read it that I was, shall I say, initiated. The book was Bowles's *The Sheltering Sky*. Out of print for years, the post–World War II novel was being rediscovered by a cadre of readers at the beginning of the post-Vietnam era. It tapped that same spirit-weary nerve in a new generation looking for anywhere that was not *here*. Anywhere, or better yet nowhere, to shed their Americanness, like the skin of a snake let roll down a desert dune. Bowles derived his title from a popular World War I tune, "Down Among the Sheltering Palms." Because in the Sahara there is only the sky, Bowles omitted the palms, leaving the fine fabric of the sky. Bowles presented the new conditions of modernity, ground rules for the infidel: the sky is the thin membrane between life and death, the traveler's final frontier, and the last obstacle to repose. Those who retreat to the oases of this alien world learned that becoming one with the other is impossible. All that is left to the living is madness or flight. En route to Ceylon, shortly after reading reviews of *The Sheltering Sky*, Bowles stopped in Djibouti and photographed the enamel sign that marked the residence of the great nineteenth-century poet-traveler Arthur Rimbaud. Bowles's novel certainly heeded Rimbaud's marvelous revolutionary cry: *"Il faut être absolument moderne."* (We have to be absolutely modern.)

STEPHEN AIKEN: You first visited Morocco as a child.

CHERIE NUTTING: Yes. My mother and I sailed on the SS *Constitution* in 1960. Oddly enough, I was to learn that Jane Bowles would make the crossing on the same ship, one month later. We were on our way to Spain; however, our first port of call was Casablanca. At the captain's suggestion, we took a bus to Rabat. My mother was now accompanied by a German count, who was loving looking at her. She was tall and gorgeous. In the casbah, all eyes were on my mother's blond hair. At the time I thought that Morocco was in the desert, but of course the Moroccan coast is far from the Sahara. So when the bus passed a spot that looked like the desert, I took a photograph of the landscape, which I later called "The False Desert." That was my first brief experience of Morocco, land of illusions. I always kept this little snapshot with me, thinking that one day I would return.

SA: You went on to Spain?

CN: For a few years we lived in Spain, mostly in Barcelona, where I attended the Marymount International School. I returned to Spain in 1970 and found it a very different place. Franco was still hanging on, but much of the unique flavor of the country had faded.

These were the hippie days. I was traveling with my girlfriend, Stacey, and we decided to go south and take the ferry across the Strait of Gibraltar to Tangier.

SA: Two young American women alone in the casbah.

CN: Oh yes, the hustlers were all over us. Stacey wanted to leave the next day, but I convinced her to stay. We traveled south to Essaouira. One night we got high and Stacey began talking about wanting to get married and settle down. I was absolutely against this idea. I said, "No!" she should stay with me in Morocco. Well, we left for Marrakesh, and there at the American Express office, I met a guy named Meko, and we were married practically the next day.

SA: American Express—I should say so! I thought we were on the Marrakesh Express.

CN: Later we opened a store in Provincetown called Marrakesh Imports.

SA: When did you become aware of Paul Bowles?

CN: Toward the end of our marriage, my ex-husband gave me a copy of *The Sheltering Sky*. "This book was written for you," he said, and he was right. It had an enormous impact on me.

SA: And shortly after, you got the notion to write to Bowles?

CN: Yes, I was having these dreams with strange images of birds swooping and smashing into my head. A short time after this, a good friend, Al DiLauro, died. It was such a shock. He was older than me, but so young at heart. I thought the dreams were a warning.

SA: Al DiLauro, the artist from New York and Provincetown. He did that wonderful series of landscape collages, each with an artificial daffodil placed in the scene.

CN: They had artificial daffodils at his funeral, and I saved two. He loved daffodils because they heralded spring and his return to Provincetown.

SA: In this letter to Paul Bowles, did you write about the dream?

CN: It was the story of my life—in about ten pages. I sent two photos with it. One was of my masculine side, which I called "Scout," I look like an Indian with a headdress. The other was of my feminine side, which I called "Alma," sitting next to my altar in a negligee. I told him it was in my destiny that we should meet!

SA: A ten-page letter from a stranger, and he wrote you back?

CN: Yes. I never expected it. He even invited me to visit him in Tangier.

SA: So you started packing?

CN: Yeah, I went via Spain, stopping in Málaga to pay tribute to Jane Bowles. She is buried in the Cemetery San Miguel. In my hand I carried Al's artificial daffodil to place on her grave. I took away a film canister of earth and a bouquet of white plastic forget-me-nots as gifts for Paul.

SA: In Tangier you had some difficulty locating Bowles's apartment.

CN: Yes, Paul's directions were vague, and the taxi driver was of little help and left me in what looked like the middle of nowhere. I was lost, and it was starting to rain. Then I saw it—the 1966 golden Mustang that I had read about in Jay McInerney's article on Paul in *Vanity Fair.*

SA: He did like to travel in style.

CN: And never lightly, always ten or twelve valises. He liked to have lots of things to wear, I guess.

SA: He wasn't exactly trying to blend in.

CN: No, in the 1950s, he would arrive in little desert towns with his driver, Temsamany, dressed in a cap and chauffeur's outfit. He owned a Jaguar then.

SA: Back to your first meeting. I've read Bowles's description of his apartment in the Immuebe Itesa as being "visually neutral."

CN: Well, it was visually dark—there were no lights in the hallways. When I found the bell and rang it, there was no sound. Just when I knocked, the door pulled open onto a chain-lock, and there was Paul peering out. I said, "I am Cherie Nutting," and the door slammed shut. He was just unlatching the chain—he did let me in.

SA: Did you have your camera?

CN: Of course, I flashed a picture the moment the door opened! His first vision of me was with a camera in front of my face.

SA: Eventually you spent some time living in the same building.

CN: Yes. I lived below him in Jane Bowles's old apartment, number 15. He was above me in number 20. It was nice. We could knock to say goodnight to each other. I would go bang, bang and he would go bang, bang, bang.

SA: It sounds like the Count of Monte Cristo. What about his hypersensitivity to sound?

CN: He had a very particular sleeping arrangement. He liked the head of his bed to face north. He wore a mask and earplugs and locked himself in his room. And then there was this machine he had constructed beside his bed. It was a fan precariously balanced with a coat hanger and a piece of string linked to a *taifor,* which is a low, metal Moroccan table.

SA: I like this, it's very Duchampian. Tell me more.

CN: Once I touched it by mistake, and he almost had a heart attack, telling me that it was all placed so that the sound was the exact same frequency as the dogs that howled all night in the street. If it moved even slightly, the frequency would change.

SA: Bowles said he thought of his childhood self as a "registering consciousness." He fantasized that there was an audience behind his eyes, much like in a theater. He constructed elaborate imaginary diaries in code and, a little later, practiced the surrealistic method of automatic writing. He seemed to be looking for a way to describe the world from outside of himself.

CN: What you're talking about was very evident in his relationship with Mrabet.

SA: Bowles translated Mrabet's tales from Darija Arabic, the unwritten language spoken in Morocco, and brought them to publication.

CN: Mrabet and Bowles also had a language of their own invention. They conversed in symbols. Mrabet's everyday speech had an abstract quality. He spoke in parables. Paul loved Mrabet's concept of the world as a dual reality. Moroccans can be very direct, but more often they speak in a contradictory, circular fashion. Paul uses that funny quote in his book *The Spider's House.*

SA: I have it right here, an old Moroccan saying:

> You tell me you are going to Fez.
> Now if you say you are going to Fez
> That means you are not going.

But I happen to know that you are going to Fez.
Why have you lied to me, you who are my friend?

CN: It was so much fun trying to decipher what those two were talking about. As an only child, I had my own secret club, so I knew a little bit about the business. I was president and sole member of the Golden Eagles. I had a cash box for the dues, but no one ever answered the roll call. I alone spoke the secret language.

SA: On two memorable occasions, you introduced me to Bowles in Morocco. One thing I found very interesting was the way he responded to the words one spoke, not always to their implied meaning. At no one's real expense, he seemed to be able to reflect casual speech back, and get a good laugh out of the absurdities inherent in the language.

CN: Yes, here is an example. He was angry with me for something, and Paul rarely tells you directly when he's angry. He is subtle, so one has to look and listen closely. He's very hard to read. Well, I walked into the room one day and came right out with it. "Paul, are you mad at me?" "*Mad?*" he questioned, "Only dogs are mad, of course I'm not mad!" He was "angry," but we worked it out later.

SA: *Yesterday's Perfume* is difficult to classify. How would you explain it?

CN: Well, the first thing you have to understand is that the book is very personal and subjective. In this sense, it is not strictly about Paul Bowles. It's more of an autobiography of my relationship with Paul. With photography, with text, and other materials, I've recorded our responses to one another. It's a memoir of a time and a place, a time and a place that is already racing away from me. When I first met Paul, he was elderly but still seemed fairly young, and I was a young woman. Now I'm a middle-aged woman, and Paul is gone. Simply put, we went through some of life's changes together.

SA: In one portrait from the book, we can see in Bowles's eyes twin images of you, the photographer, bent over your tripod, looking through the lens at us or, more appropriately, at Bowles. We are somehow sandwiched in an instant between you two. Possession and the transmutation of identities are relevant themes in Bowles's writing. How would you describe your relationship with Bowles?

CN: It was a love affair of the heart, and although we were physically very affectionate, it wasn't consummated in the sexual sense. Paul had been married and very devoted to his wife Jane. They were unique individuals in a special relationship. Paul, for one, hated to be labeled—gay, straight, or bisexual, there was no one quite like him. When Jane died, Paul said, "All the fun is over." Still, I think we had a little fun.

SA: Let's talk a little more about *The Sheltering Sky*. As Bowles tells it he drew from his experience with the drug *majoun* in writing the death scene of his protagonist, Port Moresby. It is one of the most memorable scenes I have ever read. What exactly is *majoun*?

CN: *Majoun* is made from the female cannabis plant. It's mixed into a paste with honey and dates and eaten. It can be quite strong. Port, in *The Sheltering Sky*, dies from typhoid. Paul had typhoid years earlier, and with the memory of that experience and the *majoun*, he worked out much of the death scene. But don't get the wrong idea, Paul wasn't much of a drug taker, nor was he a drinker. He smoked a bit of *kif* and that was all.

SA: In the late 1980s, the celebrities were again turning up in Bowles's milieu. Bertolucci was in Tangier to film *The Sheltering Sky,* along with John Malkovich and Debra Winger. The Rolling Stones were back in town. It must have been very exciting. But the real star for me was your second husband, Bachir Attar.

CN: I met Bachir in Paul's apartment. He is the hereditary leader of the Master Musicians of JaJouka. JaJouka is an ancient music tradition with sources from pre-Islamic times. The Stones came to Morocco because of Bachir. They wanted to record a track with him for their album *Steel Wheels.* Bachir is a hero and a credit to his country, for he has saved his music and brought it to the Western world.

SA: I still have the album—*The Pipes of Pan*—that Brian Jones recorded with Bachir's father. You could make a case for it being the first album of the world music genre.

CN: That was made in 1969. Brian died shortly before the Stones released the record in 1970. Bachir and I rereleased it in 1995. Paul had very little interest in rock music, yet Mick brought the BBC to his apartment to film an interview.

SA: Bowles made his last trip to the States in 1995.

CN: For the Jonathan Sheffer performance of his music with the Eos Orchestra.

SA: Yes, Bowles the composer. There was an "Evening with Paul Bowles" at the New School for Social Research. He was interviewed by the composer Phillip Ramey. They were a perfect team. The audience was awestruck with Bowles's sharp wit. Ramey had all the right cues. They worked the room like George Burns and Gracie Allen.

CN: That's what Paul loved about Phillip. Phillip was able to do that with people, draw them out. Paul can just sit and say nothing at times. He chose people like Phillip and Mrabet and me to create a commotion. He liked to be entertained by a scene, as long as he felt he wasn't involved, but of course, he always was.

SA: You last saw Paul in August 1999.

CN: Yes, he was fading. His body was falling apart, his eyesight, his hearing, yet his brain was perfectly sharp. We said a just-in-case goodbye, but I really thought I'd see him for his birthday on the thirtieth of December. I guess he didn't want to have anything to do with this new millennium. Abdelouahid, who looked after him for many years, said, "The last thing he wanted to hear before he died was the sound of the cicadas." So Abdelouahid went out with a recorder and taped their music for him.

This piece originally appeared in the annual issue of *Provincetown Arts,* a nonprofit press for artists and poets, volume 15, 2000/2001. Copyright © 2000 by Stephen Aiken. Reprinted with permission of the author.

Paula Wolfert's Pursuit of Flavor

BY PEGGY KNICKERBOCKER

∽

editor's note

No book on Morocco would be complete without mention of Paula Wolfert, who, in addition to being a cookbook author and food writer, has served as an unofficial Moroccan cultural attaché to the United States.

PEGGY KNICKERBOCKER writes about food for a variety of publications, and is the author of *Olive Oil: From Tree to Table* (Chronicle, 1997) and, with Reed Hearon, *The Rose Pistola Cookbook* (Broadway, 1999).

For over a quarter century, food writer Paula Wolfert's quest for flavor has drawn her across the Mediterranean, from Berber villages in the Atlas Mountains of Morocco to the plains of Slavic Macedonia, from the far reaches of the Ionian Islands and Sicily through southwestern France and Catalonia. She has knocked on hundreds of back doors in obscure towns, searching for the cook who best executes a particular dish. Her adventures and findings are compiled in five (now six) serious and sensuous cookbooks filled with scholarly information about unpretentious food and regional folklore.

Moroccan *tagines,* Lebanese *kibbeh,* and French *daubes* were not always part of Wolfert's repertoire. In fact, when she married her first husband, she literally could not boil water. Following a few unsuccessful attempts at recipes from *Glamour Girl After Five,* a wedding gift from her mother, she signed up for cooking classes at Dione Lucas's Cordon Bleu cooking school and immediately found her calling. Wolfert ended up leaving her college studies to work full time with Lucas in return for classes.

In 1959 her husband's job took the couple to Morocco, the beginning of a ten-year sojourn abroad. It was an exotic and exciting time for this young woman from Brooklyn. They socialized with co-expatriates Jane and Paul Bowles, William Burroughs, and Tennessee Williams; and little by little Wolfert became fascinated with the richly flavored local dishes and Mediterranean ingredients.

It wasn't until more than a decade later that she decided to write a Moroccan cookbook at the urging of her second husband, the Edgar-winning crime novelist William Bayer. They moved to Tangier in 1971 and stayed for five years, during which time she wrote *Couscous and Other Good Food from Morocco* (1973) and *Mediterranean Cooking* (1976). Both books were enthusiastically received by an entire generation of curious cooks who were hungry for unfamiliar ethnic fare. The year that the Moroccan book came out, Williams-Sonoma did a brisk business selling couscous cookers at Christmas.

Although Wolfert was criticized early on for including hard-to-find ingredients in the name of authenticity, she's remained relentlessly adamant about their use. "Ingredients from a given region have amalgamated gracefully over the years, and if you change them, you simply won't get an authentic taste," she says. "When people return from their travels they want to replicate what they have tasted. It is my job, as a food writer, to explain how to integrate unusual tastes. Most of the ingredients are now readily available, at least by mail order. But you have to be romanced into searching them out. That's part of the fun."

No matter how unusual or common a recipe may be, Wolfert's criteria for including it in a book have always been brutally simple: "Would I like to eat this dish again? Am I absolutely in love with it?"

"My life seems to revolve around finding new recipes—food with plenty of flavor that lingers in the mouth," she says. "Such food appeals to all my senses; every nuance has a meaning. To me, good food is memory. One time or another, I've had a fling with each of the recipes in my books."

France Beckons

Wolfert set out to write *The Cooking of South-West France* (1983) in the late 1970s after traveling around the region in search of the perfect cassoulet and discovering "a magnificent peasant cookery in the process of being updated." Wolfert explains that "southwest France is very much part of the Mediterranean. Most French food isn't very forceful; it's delicate, complex, and built on subtlety. But the southwest employs robust ingredients—truffles, peppers, *cepes* and chicken and goose fat; hardly subtle ingredients." It's Wolfert's style of cooking: country food with layers of taste, simple dishes that showcase the natural affinities of ingredients (as opposed to the wild experimentation that she disdains in certain restaurant dishes and fusion foods).

In order to convince readers not to be put off by the region's reputation for high-fat dishes. Wolfert describes how to use animal fats as a flavoring agent, the way one might use a cinnamon stick in a red wine fruit compote. If she uses good duck or pork fat in a stew, she simmers it all very gently so that the fat mingles with the wine and juices but does not bind with them; then she chills the stew in the refrigerator and skims off all the fat, leaving behind just its flavor, soluble in liquid, to impart what she calls big taste.

A More Healthful Way to Eat

Without ever sacrificing flavor or changing the nature of a dish, Wolfert has been addressing current concerns about the benefits of a balanced, healthful diet. In fact, in the revised edition of *Mediterranean Cooking* (1994), she replaced sixty of the heavier or overly complex dishes with over seventy-five new, more health-conscious recipes.

Wolfert claims to have had a culinary epiphany at a conference in Spain sponsored by Oldways Preservation and Exchange Trust, an international food-issues think tank. In the midst of dissertations on the healthful aspects of the Mediterranean diet, she realized that the hearty meat-driven meals needed to be rethought.

"I turned my plate around: I magnified and minimized it," Wolfert explains. In doing so, she expanded her repertoire to include more greens and grains and diminished the use of meat, cream, and butter. She traveled across the Euphrates and came back with a new daily routine that even gets her eating vegetables in the morning in what she calls her Biblical Breakfast Burrito. As a result, she's lost over thirty pounds, slowly—a pound a month over the past couple of years. At fifty-seven, Wolfert looks amazing, especially for a woman who would rather eat wood chips than exercise.

"I've reversed the emphasis, but I haven't really given up anything," Wolfert explains. "The ingredients I use are still delicious. It doesn't take extra work to eat five to ten servings of vegetables and fruits a day, and I get so many compliments I must be doing something right." (Don't worry: Wolfert has hardly become a smug abstainer. She still indulges in a good cassoulet and was even seen eating a juicy hotdog on the Fourth of July.)

In her first book many recipes called for half a pound of meat per person; in *The Cooking of the Eastern Mediterranean* (1994) and *Mediterranean Grains and Greens* (1998), most call for far less and in many cases none at all. When meat is used, Wolfert is full of tricks to maximize its flavor while cutting fat. Many dishes use inexpensive lamb parts, particularly shanks and neck bones. "These cuts give intense, incredible flavor. I run after dishes that use inexpensive meat not because I'm cheap but because I think less expensive meats cook better and taste better in the stew dishes of the Mediterranean."

Recently, Wolfert has found a new talent as a television personality; she sold thousands of cookbooks on the QVC channel in just twelve minutes. But despite her success as a salesperson, she'll probably continue to follow her muse around the Mediterranean.

"I'll spend the rest of my life doing this, and I will never finish," she laments. "I'll probably do a book on garlic and olive oil and maybe another on fruits and vegetables of the Mediterranean. There are so many more villages to explore, each with a great cook with a great undiscovered secret."

Bibliothèque

Paul Bowles

One can scarcely utter the name of Paul Bowles without also uttering Morocco. He was—and remains—so synonymous, so ubiquitous, so one with the country that it is sometimes easy to forget that Bowles was one of the most talented human beings of our time (or any time, for that matter). Before my husband began to read Bowles's books, he accused me of spending too much time "just reading about expatriates . . . and what do they really know about Morocco?" Some of them know quite a bit, but the vast majority of them will never be as knowledgeable as Bowles. In his book *Tangier: City of the Dream*, author Iain Finlayson relates the time Mohammed Tazzi—the son of the last *mendoub* of Tangier and grandson of the first—discovered the work of Bowles. Tazzi was studying in Paris, and along with his fellow students at the Maison du Maroc, he read *A Life Full of Holes* by Driss ben Hamed Charhadi (nom de plume: Larbi Layachi), which was translated from Maghrebi dialect into French by Bowles. The story is an oral autobiography told by Charhadi, a young working-class Tangerino. Tazzi noted that "this book affected us profoundly because it told of someone from the working class who for once had achieved the dignity of a book, and this was absolutely absorbing—simultaneously, the old books were stripped of their sanctity, debunked, for us, and one could hear Charhadi's experience." Finlayson continues: "Meeting later with Bowles himself, in Tangier, Tazzi was impressed that 'men like him understand the soul of Tangier much more than others.' Tazzi is impatient with the idea that, as a stranger, Bowles—and other foreigners—cannot truly comprehend Moroccan thought. Bowles himself, rather mordantly, has said that 'thought is not a word one can use in connection with Morocco,' not only implying that rational thought and Morocco are a contradiction in terms but also expressing his own bewilderment when confronted with its paradoxes and seeming illogicalities."

The Dream at the End of the World: Paul Bowles and the Literary Renegades in Tangier, Michelle Green, Bloomsbury Publishing, London, 1992; Harper Perennial. This is an incredibly wild ride of a book, authored by a senior writer for *People.* Green documents the world that a motley crew of international expatriates created for themselves in Tangier and all over Morocco. It wasn't always pretty—in fact, at times one could call it a nightmare rather than a dream—but Tangier's status as a free-money market where one could live quite inexpensively and decadently made life seem like a dream; even after independence, which wiped out Tangier's status as an international zone, the new restrictions only partly curtailed the daily lives of the expats, among whom were William Burroughs, Allen Ginsberg, Jack Kerouac, Timothy Leary, Barbara Hutton, Susan Sontag, Truman Capote, and Malcolm Forbes.

Yesterday's Perfume: An Intimate Memoir of Paul Bowles, Cherie Nutting with Paul Bowles, Clarkson Potter, 2000. A highly unique book, written as dated journal entries mixed in with some of Bowles's previously unpublished writings, Nutting's photographs, and contributions by friends Peter Beard, Ned Rorem, and Bruce Weber. Nutting became a special friend of Bowles (she first met him in Tangier in 1986) and was fortunate to spend time with him for much of the later months of his life. (She spent the summer of 1999 in Tangier, and Bowles passed away that year in November.) I was not always captivated by some of Nutting's entries, and I regret that she did not reveal more about her relationship with Bachir, "the true heir to the mantle of Jajouka music"; but certainly some of her images and the dialogue she relates are remarkably memorable and often quite helpful in understanding Moroccans. In one entry dated March 20, 1987, Nutting is talking with Bowles about the house she is hoping to have built on Mohammed Mrabet's land. Bowles comments that it seemed like Mrabet was less interested in building Nutting's house than in building a staff for his animals. When Nutting asks if he means she may never get her house, Bowles replies, "No, I don't mean that. I mean that it might not be the house that you envisaged, but I believe Mrabet cares for you and might not take advantage and you'll get it—eventually. He's like a baby with money;

many Moroccans are the same. One thousand dollars is the same as a hundred thousand to him, he has no conception of its value. He's not a farmer or a contractor as he thinks he is, and the house may not be as great as he dreams it will be. So be very strong with him, keep a list, which will be difficult as you'll be away. I'll try to keep tabs on him if I can, but Mrabet is tough to deal with. He'll hate this, but you should have a notary say you invested ten thousand dollars, and do it now because you've given almost nothing and so have the leverage—and isn't leverage what life's all about? At least in Morocco it is." There are fifteen entries—including some epigrams—by Bowles, the most interesting of which, to me, are "The Interview" and "Tangier." This is a beautiful collage for fans of Bowles, Morocco, and the literary community of Tangier.

Artists

The following are definitive volumes (both are comprehensive catalogs that accompanied museum exhibitions) and are worth an effort to find. However, they are not *catalogues raisonnés*—they represent only the artist's oeuvre in Morocco. For definitive books covering the full range of Delacroix's and Matisse's work, see the *"Musées, Jardins, et Monuments" Bibliothèque* in my *Paris* edition.

Delacroix in Morocco, Maurice Serullaz, Maurice Arama, Lee Johnson, Arlette Serullaz, prologues by Edmonde Charles-Roux and Tahar ben Jelloun, Flammarion, 1994. Published in conjunction with the exhibition of the same name at the Institut du Monde Arabe, Paris (27 September 1994–15 January 1995).

Matisse in Morocco: The Paintings and Drawings, 1912–1913, Jack Cowart, Pierre Schneider, John Elderfield, Albert Kostenevich, Laura Coyle, Harry N. Abrams, 1990. Published in conjunction with the exhibition of the same name at the National Gallery of Art, Washington, D.C. (18 March–3 June 1990); the Museum of Modern Art, New York (20 June–4 September 1990); the State Pushkin Museum of Fine Arts, Moscow (28 September–20 November 1990); and the State Hermitage Museum, Leningrad (15 December–15 February 1991).

MAROC

Des Belles Choses
(Good Things and Favorite Places)

"In Morocco you go into a bazaar to buy a wallet and somehow find yourself being propelled toward the back room to look at antique brass and rugs. In an instant you are seated with a glass of mint tea in your hand and a platter of pastries in your lap, while smiling gentlemen modeling ancient caftans and marriage robes parade in front of you, the salesman who greeted you at the door having completely vanished. Later on you may once again ask timidly to see the wallets, which you noticed on display near the entrance. Likely as not, you will be told that the man in charge of wallets is at the moment saying his prayers, but that he will soon be back, and in the meantime would you not be pleased to see some magnificent jewelry from the court of Moulay Ismail? Business is business and prayers are prayers, and both are a part of the day's work."

—Paul Bowles, THEIR HEADS ARE GREEN
AND THEIR HANDS ARE BLUE

The *Riad* Thing

By Sophy Roberts

As I noted in the "Accommodations" entry in *Renseignements Pratiques*, staying at a Moroccan *riad* is one of the unique pleasures of Morocco. *Roud* (plural for *riad*) are traditional homes of serene beauty, built around internal courtyards, and they are typically hidden away in the medinas of Morocco's oldest cities. *Roud* are now becoming quite popular and are being converted into bed-and-breakfast accommodations for discerning travelers. Here is a good guide to twenty *roud* in Fez, Essaouira, and Marrakesh, some of which do not cost a sultan's ransom.

Note that at the time of publication, $1.00 (U.S.) was equivalent to £0.7005.

SOPHY ROBERTS is a frequent contributor to the British edition of *Condé Nast Traveller,* where this piece originally appeared in February 2001.

Riad Enija, Marrakech

Since opening in spring 1999, Enija has become one of the most desirable of the Moroccan B&Bs, and although relatively expensive, it shows no signs of falling from grace. This has a lot to do with the consistently high quality of service, the good, digestible food (light pastas, salads, and grilled meats), and its location just three minutes' walk from the Djemaa El Fna, the medina's main square. There are nine suites, built around an unusually pretty garden courtyard, all with en-suite bathrooms and most with dressing rooms or private verandas. Decor is different in each, the style like a colorful medley of Trisha Guild, London boutiques, Morocco, and India, with paper lampshades, lots of silk, and silvery details from tassels on the floor cushions to delicate wall sconces. In the rooms, the bed is always the central feature, whether it's a brass four-poster wrapped in lime-green muslin or a wrought-iron Gothic extravaganza. There isn't much else—a fuchsia chair, a rail for your clothes, a vase of flowers, an outsize mirror—but the rooms don't feel sparse. This is because there is so much colour, from red ceilings to blue-and-white-tiled floors. Some of the more feminine decor won't suit everyone, so you'd be well advised to request a specific room. A few pointers: of the courtyard rooms, the Chameleon Suite gets the better light; the Harem Suite, which is a twin, has a fabulous roof terrace; and the Blue Room, the most sober of them all, is the coolest in summer.

Rahba Laktima, *9 Derb Mesfioui (044.44.09.26; fax: 044.27.00). Doubles £149–£190, including breakfast.*

Dar Zellij, Marrakech

Dar Zellij, a four-suite *riad,* is not a glamorous place: cushions are plump but plain; beds are comfortable but no more than mattresses; not all the bathrooms are en suite. But the fact that architect Jean Nouvel stays here has to mean something, and indeed the main salon, which dates back to the seventeenth century, is quite awesome. Its high wooden ceiling is painted with tiny geometrical motifs in red, ochre, and green; hand-carved plaster cornicing lines the upper walls; and the original floor has been restored to create a spectacular mosaic of hand-chipped glazed tiles. What's more, the ground-floor suite is easily the most beautiful room in all of Marrakech, yet costs less than £100 a night.

Sidi Ben Slimane, *1 Kaa Essour (044.38.26.27). Doubles £76–£95, including breakfast.*

Villa Maroc, Essaouira

Villa Maroc is an old favourite. A 22-room guest house occupying two eighteenth-century *riads* with a roof terrace overlooking the city's ramparts, it is painted in the town's signature style of white-washed walls and chalky-blue Majorelle window surrounds. A languorous retreat, it has pots of geraniums, wrought-iron candle-sticks, open fires, excellent food, and a gently buzzing scene at night (which attracts guests from other *riads*). Unfortunately, rooms can be hard to come by, and service has recently become rather complacent.

10 Rue Abdallah ben Yassin (044.47.31.47; fax: 0.47.28.06). Doubles £39–£63, including breakfast, based on two people sharing.

Riad Malika, Marrakech

This eclectic, 12-room *riad* is owned by a French architect with a penchant for chairs—not just any old chairs, but magnificent white, chrome, and black-leather originals by Saarinen, Jacobsen, and Le Corbusier. Like the rest of the elegant clutter that fills the rooms—Art Deco ornaments, Breuer lamps, leather-studded trunks—these have all been sourced in junk shops. Of the six rooms and seven suites, the prettiest is the family room overlooking the courtyard, with its open fire and bathroom behind a stained-glass screen; but if you're into the retro thing, go for the Royal Suite, with its gold flute lighting. Obviously Riad Malika is not to everyone's taste, but for design aficionados it's an absolute gem.

29 Derb Arset Aouzal, Bab Doukkala (telephone/fax: 044.38.54.51). Doubles £63–£98.

Riad Kaiss, Marrakech

Unlike many of the converted *riads,* this new *maison d'hôte* follows an intelligent design that maximizes guest privacy without com-promising the building's original layout. (It also makes the most of the roof terrace space and spectacular views out toward the Atlas Mountains.) Riad Kaiss is owned by a French hotel architect, and it shows. There are eight rooms, all with bathrooms, built around two interconnected courtyards. The best suites are on the top floor of the shared wall. (Light comes in from both sides and what breeze there is blows through.) The style is traditional Moroccan—earth-red walls, fountains in the courtyard, stained-glass windows—executed with impeccable attention to detail. (The jade mosaic *zellige* tiling and painted beamed ceilings are exquisite.) But there is also something quaintly French about the place, from the neat, linen-sheeted beds to the little painted armoires. More significantly, it is clean and efficient, run as professionally as any French *gîte*—something that is often ignored by other *riads,* which tend to rely too much on "character."

65 Derb Jdid, Riad Zitoune Kedim (tel/fax: 044.44.01.41). Doubles £50–£98, including breakfast.

Riad El Cadi, Marrakech

Riad El Cadi is like a small palace. Opened in spring 2000 as a B&B, it dates back to the fourteenth century. (The stone foundations now sit below street level.) But it has been well protected by its location at the point where three narrow alleys end, and by its discreet appearance: the high, windowless walls are unprepossessing, and the front door anonymous. Inside, however, it is a veritable museum (and much of what is displayed does in fact go on loan to major exhibitions), curated by owner Herwig Bartels, former German ambassador to Rabat and an avid collector of early Islamic and Byzantine art. On the walls hang fifteenth-century carpet fragments, early Ottoman kilims, and five-hundred-year-old Berber doors; sixteenth-century Iznik pottery lurks in a corner; an early Roman capital poses as a bedside table. There are 12 rooms spread out over four interconnecting houses—Le Grand Patio, La Douiriya, Le Riad de l'Oranger (good for couples who like their privacy), and Riad du Palmier, which has a small swimming pool. There is also a scarlet *hammam,* a huge roof terrace, and a conference room for twenty-two people. With three doubles and one single, Le Grand Patio is the main house, and the prettiest of the four. At the center of its court-yard lies a sixteenth-century basin surrounded by orange, lemon, and grapefruit trees. Off this is a blushed-pink dining room deco-rated in *tadelakt* style, a traditional technique combining pigment and lime, polished to give walls a marble sheen. There is also a grand salon flanked by a pair of tall ochre, gold, and green wooden doors. It is decorated with some of the best pieces in the collection, includ-ing a stunning eighth-century Jordanian carving and fifth-century Byzantine mosaic. These artifacts are teamed with simple furni-ture—an old teak table, a well-used cream sofa. Indeed, for all the priceless detail, it is the deliberate understatement, uncluttered spaces, white walls, and museum-quality lighting that give this house a refinement somehow lost in those *riads* that come too heavily bedecked in stucco and tiles.

59 Derb El Cadi, Azbezt (044.37.86.55; fax: 044.37.84.78). Doubles £70–£133, including breakfast. Minimum stay three nights.

Riad Noga, Marrakech

The thing about Riad Noga is that you could stay here twice and have a very different experience each time, since it is made up of two interconnected houses. The original house, built around a verdant courtyard, is the prettier, with pale pink sun-bleached walls, climb-ing vines, orange and olive trees, and wooden birdcages hanging in the branches. Its two bedrooms, which are surprisingly cool, are furnished with antiques, painted wardrobes, and bowls of rose petals. It is a sleepy spot, serene and slightly peeling at the edges—in deliberate contrast to the second house, done up in much bolder colors, which opened last May. Here the style is modern Moroccan: the five rooms are painted and tiled in yellow, white, and red and come with modem ports, satellite TVs and hi-fi systems. But it is the communal areas that are the best part: a three-tiered roof terrace and capacious jade-green swimming pool. With this much space, Riad Noga is an excellent choice for guests who like to keep themselves to themselves.

78 Derb Jdid, Douar Graoua (044.44.33.86; fax: 044.44.19.41). Doubles £73–£106, including breakfast.

Dar El Hanaa, Marrakech

Opened last May, Dar El Hanaa is hidden away down the far end of a winding alley deep in the souk. It is fantastically quiet apart from the call of the muezzin from the nearby Ben Youssef Mosque. There are seven rooms, all with en-suite showers, built around a small courtyard of orange trees. The furnishings are simple—four posters swathed in burnt-red cotton—with a Moroccan-style snug bedecked in cushions. On the roof terrace there is a *hammam*, sun loungers, and a rattan woven tent—pretty enough as long as the *riad* isn't full, but too small to serve as communal areas when it is.

16 Derb Ouaihah, Sidi Abdelaziz (telephone/fax: 044.42.99.77). Doubles £51–£95, including breakfast.

Maison Mnabha, Marrakech

In terms of value for money, Maison Mnabha is much the best place to stay in Marrakech, with bed and breakfast starting at £35 a night for single occupancy. Located in the kasbah, the city's eight-hundred-year-old imperial enclave, it is one half of an old *riad*—in other words, it has no courtyard—run by two English brothers. The four rooms are comfortable without being fancy, but the main salon is magnificent, with a seventeenth-century painted wooden ceiling, intricately carved walls and pillars, tasselled curtains, delicate silk cushions, and grandiose stained-glass archways.

32 Derb Mnabha, Kasbah (044.38.13.25; fax: 044.38.99.93). Doubles from £55, including breakfast.

Dar Kawa, Marrakech

Dar Kawa is completely unexpected, a stark, gray-and-white, contemporary affair, utterly at odds with its old rough-walled exterior. While retaining the original central courtyard of the classic *riad* design, Dar Kawa manages to be refreshingly different, decorated as it is with brushed-steel furniture and dark woods, mauves and purples and with brilliant white Egyptian cotton. It only sleeps 10, but Dar Ouali, the *riad* next door, is also available for rent—it's nothing special, but fine for an overflow of teenagers.

102 Rue Dar el Bacha (044.42.80.79). Costs £221–£518, including breakfast, based on sole occupancy for parties of two to ten.

The Tea House, Essaouira

The Tea House, a charming place located in Essaouira's old *mellah,* feels spookily deserted, like the *Marie Celeste.* It's as if the rose petals scattered on the floor were there when the family of Jewish tea merchants left more than one hundred years ago. Decor is delicate and pretty, a deliberate effect created by the English owner, who has spent the last couple of years renovating the two-hundred-year-old *riad* to create something that looks as if it has never changed. A sweet, musty smell hangs in the air; the paint is cracked; salt from the sea air has crystallised on the peeling walls; the embroidered cushions are fraying at the edges; smoke has marked the stone around the fire; the peppermint-green doors are chipped; the pink terrace is bleached by the sun. Both of the two-bedroom apartments—one on the first floor, the other on the second, overlooking a small central courtyard—are filled with antiques sourced from flea markets: a nineteenth-century colonial brass bed, a free-standing bath, a tapestry from Fès. In the salons, which still have the original shutters, there are old, time-worn tamarisk-wood tables, nineteenth-century Baghdad stained glass, and, in the corner, a crystal mirror from Murano that is blackening at the sides. It feels like a secret chanced upon, which it is.

7 Derb Laalouj La Skala (telephone/fax: 044.78.53.43). Doubles £40, including breakfast.

Dar Mouassine, Marrakech

Mouassine is the closest thing Marrakech has to a fashionable enclave. In the last couple of years there have been several new openings in this up-and-coming neighborhood in the northern end of the medina: Le Tobsil, the restaurant set to eclipse Yacout, the city's best restaurant; Ministro del Gusto, a surprisingly hip boutique full of *objêts d'art;* and, since April 2000, Dar Mouassine, an improbably chic guest house. It is owned by a young couple from Paris, with a sort of Boho-*Vogue* style. (Carole must be the only woman in Marrakech to negotiate the souk in kitten heels.) The *riad* is relatively small, with five bedrooms built around a black-and-white-tiled courtyard. What shade there is comes from the squat palms and high walls surrounding the plunge pool. (Quite something for a *riad* of this size in a city where pools are rare.) There is also a roof terrace with a silk-swathed rattan pavilion. Off the courtyard there are two salons—a cushion-stuffed snug with an impressive video library (Eric works in film), and a second sitting room with an open fire and an eclectic collection of French jazz. It is dark and sultry, a winter hideout—quite unlike the bedrooms, which are flooded with light. This has much to do with the interior style, which is more contemporary than traditional Moroccan. The cushions and drapes are made from orange and fuchsia Rajasthani silks, and the walls are sleek and white in preference to the "aged" look. The rooms are uncluttered: antique leather pouffes, fresh flowers crammed into vases, four-posters wrapped in wisps of muslin. This is not a place for children—the stairs are dangerously steep—but it makes a stylish hangout for thirty-somethings who are looking for somewhere central but quiet.

148 Derb Snane, Mouassine (telephone/fax: 044.44.52.87). Doubles £38–£70, including breakfast.

Dar Zina, Marrakech

This five-room *riad* is ideal for families. The main suite is spectacular, with crushed-velvet amber curtains, a painted ceiling, private terrace, and wide bed. On the ground floor there is another double, and upstairs is a third room that sleeps three. The patio isn't huge, but like the rest of the *riad,* there is a thankful absence of things for children to break. There is also a roof terrace and a salon with satellite TV. Gourmets take note: the owner, who cooks the evening *tajine,* used to be head chef at Le Pavilion, one of Marrakech's top restaurants.
38 Derb Assabane, Riad Larousse (telephone/fax: 044.38.52.42). Doubles £57–£83, including breakfast.

Riad Al Madina, Essaouira

In a former incarnation, Riad Al Madina was the hotel of choice for Jimi Hendrix, Leonard Cohen, and Frank Zappa, but you'd be lucky to find a rock star staying here now. The 27-room *riad,* though newly renovated, is a little rough at the edges these days (thin mattresses and poor air circulation in the mezzanine rooms), but it does have by far the most attractive courtyard in Essaouira—tiled and pillared, with a delicate stone fountain at its centre and comfortable armchairs tucked away in one corner.
9 Darb Laaouj al-Attarin (telephone/fax: 044.47.57.27). Doubles £42–£55, including breakfast.

Palazzo Desdemona, Essaouira

Palazzo Desdemona is not strictly a *riad*—the inner courtyard has been lost in the conversion—but as Essaouira's newest privately owned B&B, it deserves a mention. It consists of two houses, making a total of 15 rooms, with a windy terrace looking out towards the Atlantic. The style is light, airy, and simple, with untreated wooden four-posters, safari-style loungers, white walls and pale-stone arches. Ineffably tasteful, it is owned by an Italian film director who also owns Auberge Tangaro, a chic, low-key guesthouse in the nearby village of Diabet. A great alternative to the well-visited Villa Maroc.

12–14 Rue Youssef el Fassi (telephone/fax: 044.47.22.27). Doubles £44–£76, including breakfast.

La Maison Bleue, Fes

From a busy square teeming with cafés, you enter La Maison Bleue through tall wooden doors and find yourself in a remarkable building: a 1915 Andalucian-style *riad* with a glass-covered courtyard decorated top to bottom with blue mosaic tiling, stucco cornicing, and hand-carved cedar and plaster. This atrium is flanked by three salons, where rich red divans wrap around the edges and blue velvet drapes are pulled back across the arches. This is where you eat, and even by Morocco's high standards, it is fantastically atmospheric. The traditional food (*tajine,* oranges with cinnamon and orange-flower water, *pastillas* stuffed with almonds) is served on the owners' family silver. The six suites, which overlook the courtyard or bowl of the medina, are all furnished with Moroccan antiques. The best room is Khadija, with its lattice windows, stained glass, brocaded day bed, cushions, and throws. It shares a small roof terrace with Suite Menza, a peaceful haven at the top of the house with a large four-poster and a wall of windows. But should you tire of the silence, there is Riad Maison Bleue, the owners' new B&B, which has a pool.

2 Place de L'Istiqlal Batha (055.63.60.52; fax: 055.74.18.43). Doubles £95–£159, including breakfast.

The charm of Riad El Arsat lies in what has been left unfinished. The high-walled courtyard is more like a secret garden where finches drink unflustered from the mosaic birdbaths and flowers are almost left to go to seed. It is pretty and wild, deliberately unkempt but for the arch-shaped pool, which is kept immaculately clean. But while it feels as though no one has been here for twenty years, Riad El Arsat is professionally run. There are 10 rooms—four in the summer house, six in the winter house on the opposite side of the garden. Both are flanked by Andalucian-style colonnades wrapped in vines and bougainvillaea. Of the suites, the grandest is on the ground floor of the summer house: filled with the smell of roasting almonds, it has French windows decorated with orange, mauve, and peppermint-green glass, a small four-poster covered with antique velvet, and a pink vaulted bathroom. It is just the place for a low-key honeymoon—romantic without being saccharine.

10bis Derb Chemaa, Arset Loughzail (044.38.75.67; fax: 044.38.76.05). Doubles £54, including breakfast.

Dar Sara is the simple option: it's not going to wow you, but it is pretty and unpretentious. There are eight rooms—six doubles, two singles—with whitewashed walls and peacock-blue window surrounds. The look is deliberately sparse: a coloured rug; a piece of abstract art; an old trunk; a cracked urn. Children can play without fear of breakages, while the alcoves and roof terrace are perfect places to disappear with a book. Last August saw the opening of Dar Lalla, an equally well-priced three-room *riad* with a charming salon overhanging the alley, which is being renovated by the same owner, who also owns Dar Zellij (see above).

120 Derb Arset Aouzal, Bab Doukkala (044.38.58.58). Doubles £29–£38, including breakfast.

Riad Al Bartel, Fes

From the outside, with its graffiti-spattered door, the newly opened Riad Al Bartel looks like a deserted squat. But inside is a stunning five-suite B&B, converted and run by a French couple who will break their backs to help you if asked but will otherwise keep out of your way. The building is a 1930s merchant house, and is decorated in the heavily stuccoed Fezzi style, with high ceilings, blue-and-white-tiled walls, a covered courtyard and an inner balcony. The furniture is more eclectic, a mix of French armoires, simple *thuja*-wood chairs, and, in the *tadelakt* bathrooms, brass shower-heads the size of dinner plates. It is great for those travelling with children: a suite connected to a small double enables parents to get away from the noise, and, unlike most of the *riads* in the town, it isn't more like an antique museum than a B&B.
21 Rue Sournas, Ziat (tel/fax: 055.63.70.53). Doubles £31–£57, including breakfast.

Riad Fes, Fes

Riad Fès, the first of the city's big *riad* conversions, opened in January 2001 with 16 suites. Carved plaster ceilings have been meticulously recreated by the architect owner. The bathrooms, which are all en suite, have traditional pink-and-ochre *tadelakt* walls. Service is untested, but if you want somewhere with a pool, consider this over the city's current favourite place to stay, the Sofitel-run Hôtel Palais Jamai.
5 Derb Benslimane Zerbtana (055.62.07.13; fax: 055.62.63.68). Doubles £48–£286, including breakfast.

Sophy Roberts © Traveller/The Condé Nast Publications Ltd.

Des Belles Choses

Granted, it's quite personal, but this is my list—in no particular order and subject to change on any day of the week—of some favorite things to see, do, and buy in Morocco. I am mindful that singling out "bests" and "favorites" inevitably means that something I very much like will be forgotten. Which is why I emphasize that this is by no means a definitive list; rather, these are some wonderful things that I am happy to share with you here in the hope that you might also enjoy them, and that you will reciprocate by sharing your discoveries with me.

A word about shopping: I am not much into acquiring things, so as a general rule shopping is not one of my favorite pastimes; but I enjoy buying gifts for other people, especially when I'm traveling. To borrow a quote from a great little book called *The Fearless Shopper: How to Get the Best Deals on the Planet* (Kathy Borrus, Travelers' Tales, San Francisco, 2000), shopping is "about exploring culture and preserving memory—the sights, sounds, smells, tastes, tempo, and touch of a place." Most of what I purchase, therefore— even for myself—falls into the culinary category, because for me, food and drink are inextricably linked to a place, especially if that place is Morocco. Every time I smell the bags of cumin, *ras el hanout,* and cinnamon when I open my pantry, I am instantly transported back to the souk where I bought it (and the bags are double-wrapped, by the way; all the spices I saw in Morocco are much more potent than those I buy in the States). A bottle of argan oil isn't just a type of cooking oil—it's a reminder of the time when a young boy came running over to our car, pointing to the goat on top of an argan tree. (Argan trees, by the way, do not grow anywhere else in the world.) To quote again from Kathy Borrus, "I am surrounded— not by things but history and culture and memory." I have found that even *hypermarchés* in Morocco sell beautifully packaged items of yummy stuff that in the United States is either hard to find, expensive, or both.

And a word about stores: I have a particular knack for "discovering" shops that a year or so later end up in books and articles; therefore, as it would be redundant to list some of my favorite retailers that are also featured in the books under "Shopping/*Les Souvenirs*" in the *Bibliothèque* that follows, I have only mentioned them if I had something extra to say about their wares. And you might want to adopt my motto of "When in doubt, buy it now." I learned years ago that the likelihood of being able to retrace my steps past a particular merchant *when it was open* was slim. If you spy some yummy *cornes de gazelles* or sesame cookies in the window of a *pâtisserie* or a piece of Fez blue pottery that has your name all over it, *allez* (go) and get it, for Muhammad's sake. One has regrets only for the roads not taken, or in this case the *objet* not purchased! Visitors should be aware that, in general, most shops are open every day except Sunday, from about nine o'clock to one and again from about three to seven. Shops in the medina, however, are sometimes closed on Friday but not on Sunday.

~*Thé à la menthe* or *naa-naa,* taken anywhere in Morocco, but served properly, in a teapot and poured into a glass from some height. And a nice, silver teapot to take home! (Teapots can be found easily in the souks of every city and town; search carefully for a distinctive one.)

~La Baraka (on the main—only—road to Ait-Benhaddou; 04.4.89.03.05; fax: 04.4.88.62.73), Ait-Benhaddou. La Baraka is one of those simple but comfortable places where one could plant oneself for a number of days, or longer. It's an *auberge,* café, and restaurant as well as the official center of the little village across from the monument everyone has come to see, Ait-Benhaddou. Rooms upstairs are spartan but immaculately clean, and the bathrooms are all modern. The top-floor rooms open onto a terrace with a great view of the kasbah. Meals are served either inside or outside on the terrace, a portion of which is given over to a tent. Lots of international visitors stop here, and all are received warmly. Ask for Brahim Boulkaid, and if he isn't there already, someone will find him for you. Don't even think about walking over to Ait-Benhaddou without him—he was the official guide for Hillary Rodham Clinton when she visited (and he has the official letter to prove it) and is extremely knowledgeable about the history of the kasbah and its construction. He knows everyone, naturally, and speaks English well. He will also, if you're interested, show you the

collection of carpets he keeps in a room at his house that are made by the local women of the village. This is not a hard sell—he sells primarily to dealers—and the rugs are varied and beautiful. It would be worth your while to look at them if you're at all interested. Back across the street at La Baraka, people are drinking mint tea in the shade . . . as I said, this is a real hangout kind of place, very hard to say good-bye.

~The Art Deco architecture of Casablanca.

~Jzenzar: Décoration d'Intérieur et Florale; Artisanat, Antiquités, Créations (20 Rue Attarine, 044.78.36.63), Essaouira.

This lovely little shop, overseen by Saada Julahiane, has the most beautiful and distinctive selection of tea glasses I have seen anywhere in Morocco. Rather than the attractive but plain glasses sold in any souk anywhere, the glasses here are hand-painted in a variety of colors and patterns. Wrapped well in your luggage, they are a perfect souvenir, for yourself or for a fan of festive drinks. (Tea glasses are good for more than just tea!)

~The trays laden with rounds of dough delicately carried by women or young girls through the medinas to the neighborhood baker. Each loaf is indented with each family's bread stamp. Michael Field, in *A Quintet of Cuisines*, related that his guide in Fez pointed out one particular baker who "has worked here for fifty years, and never has he mistaken one family's bread for another. Of this he is very proud."

~Villa Maroc (10 Rue A. Ben Yasine; 044.47.61.47; fax: 044. 47.67.58; e-mail: villa.maroc@casanet.net.ma), Essaouira. My Moroccan friend Nadia told me that the very first thing I should do when planning my trip to Morocco was to secure a reservation at Villa Maroc and plan the rest of my itinerary around it. She said that if I couldn't get a room (there aren't many, and they fill up *fast*), I shouldn't spend the night at all and just visit for the day from Marrakesh. I followed Nadia's advice, and I tend to agree with her (although I really like Essaouria, and the Hotel Riad Al Madina— 9 Rue Attarine, 044.47.57.27; fax: 044.47.66.96—is a worthy substitute for Villa Maroc if it's fully booked). I had been advised to request a room off the terrace or on the third floor, but truthfully, *any* room at Villa Maroc is wonderful, and you will be grateful for any one of them. It's an exceptional value, and it includes dinner and breakfast. (Note that dinner is a preset menu.) Before dinner, guests gather upstairs in the small bar area. It may, at first, be difficult to ascertain the protocol, but essentially it is simply this: the staff will not escort you to your table until you're ready and get up to say so. Some guests prefer to sit and linger over numerous cock-tails, and the staff will not rush you along. Breakfast is different: you show up in the same spot and are shown to your table right away. A very good thing is also the little Villa Maroc gift shop down-stairs, to the right of the reception desk. Those wonderfully attractive plates and bowls and mini *tagines* are all for sale, at prices that are more expensive than you could bargain for in the souk but still a good value. In addition, it offers bottles of the delicious argan oil and a few other Moroccan culinary specialties.

~The *thuya*-wood picture frames purchased from one of the woodcarvers below the *sqala,* Essaouira. (I happen to be particu-larly fond of the carver whose tiny shop is next to last on the right side, at the very end of the alley.) Most of the frames do not have glass, by the way, but the wood is extremely beautiful. Typically the woodcarvers do not bargain, since you are buying straight from the source, but they do offer a good price if you are purchasing a num-ber of items. I also particularly like the wooden pencil or pen boxes; each carver has a selection of unique items. And each will usually polish each item you choose.

~Every inch of Chefchaouen (sometimes spelled Chaouen). The word means "see the peaks," and until the Spanish claimed it in 1926, the village was completely off-limits to non-Muslims. In *Mediterranean Vernacular,* authors Atvoshenko and Grundy note that when the Spanish arrived (they were actually putting down an uprising by the Berber leader Abd el Krim), "they found the inhab-itants employing craft skills in their everyday businesses which had totally disappeared in the outside world over four hundred years before."

~The lavender soap sold in all the souks called Taous. (It's a square, ivory-colored bar wrapped in clear cellophane with a pur-ple logo.) Taous isn't as strongly scented as lavender soap in France, but it's awfully nice, and inexpensive, and with a square ceramic soap dish—from Fez, for example—it makes a great, easy-to-transport gift.

~Jai Chater Rachid (*guide touristique;* No. 8 Guerniz, Derb Bouak; 055.63.68.04; cell phone: 061.20.20.84), Fez. This may be the most important tip in this entire book. Rachid is a exceptional tour guide, and I enthusiastically recommend his services for at least part of one's visit to Fez. He came recommended by the staff at La Maison Bleue (see below), speaks English very well, and is very knowledgeable about the history, current events, and architecture of Fez. He is also familiar with many American writers on Morocco and is simply very accommodating and pleasant to be with. He is popular, however, so you may want to arrange a date with him in advance of your arrival.

~La Maison Bleue (2 Place de L'Istiqlal, Batha; 055.63.60.52; e-mail: maisonbleue@fesnet.net.ma; website: www.maisonbleue.com), Fez. La Maison Bleue is actually a *restaurant gastronomique* and a *maison d'hôte;* in the same gorgeous building as the premier restaurant are some suites, but the Maison Bleue *riad* is not very far away, with equally beautiful rooms and a little restaurant of its own. The *directeur général,* Mehdi El Abbadi, and his superb staff are extremely helpful and welcoming. The main restaurant is magnificent, and even if you don't take a meal there, you should ask to see the room; and you might want to consider making a dinner reservation, as it will probably be one of the best meals of your life, and there are only fourteen tables. The restaurant has long been considered one of the best in Morocco, but it received a special honor about six years ago when a cookbook that was almost five hundred years old was discovered in a library. Under the directive of Hassan II, a competition was held among a number of restaurants in Morocco to create a meal using some of the recipes from this rare book. La Maison Bleue was awarded first prize, and the cook— then and now—was the owner's sister. My husband and I stayed at the *riad,* which in some ways I preferred to the more grand and original inn. The *riad* has an inviting swimming pool in the central courtyard, and its location, near the Bab Boujeloud, is ideal. The little touches at the *riad* are what make it special: the friendly staff, the most beautifully embroidered sheets I've ever seen, the olive oil soap and terra-cotta disk for massaging tired feet in the bathroom, and breakfast on the terrace—and what a breakfast! On any given day, breakfast can consist of the following: rice pudding sweetened with orange-flower water, assorted breads both sweet and savory, jams, hard-boiled eggs, pound cake, coffee, assorted pastries, orange juice, and cumin and salt for sprinkling on anything you like. Highly recommended.

~Any souk, but especially the souk in Fez, followed by Marrakesh.

~Restaurant Asmae (4 Derb Jeniara; 055.74.12.10; fax: 055.63.36.24), Fez. This large restaurant, hidden down a side street in the medina, is a festive place whose *patron* gives a warm welcome. It's filled at lunchtime with tourists, but the foreigners take nothing away from the delicious meal, which, with nineteen individual dishes, makes an Indian *thali* look like a beggar's banquet. As always, the vast array of salads are, to me, the most impressive (these can include lentils, radishes, spinach, carrots, cooked cabbage, zucchini, prepared in infinite ways, and olives), although I had a good version of *pastilla* here, too. Fruit is, of course, the only acceptable follow-up to a meal this big, and—best of all—you're still in the heart of the *medina,* so you don't have to waddle very far to continue the day's explorations.

~Dar Zaouia (4 Derb Jeniara Blida; 055.635.512; fax: 055.633.624), Fez. For a look at antique and modern carpets from all over Morocco, this is a good place to come. It's actually a women's cooperative and is housed in a beautiful old building in the medina on several floors. (There's a rooftop terrace, too.) There is no pressure to buy here, and it's away from the noise and bustle of the street. Prices at cooperatives tend to start higher than in the souk, so if you see something you like, be prepared to take the time to bargain. These are all of very high quality.

~Dar al Hadara (24 Oued Sowafine, Douh.; telephone/fax: 055.74.02.92; cell phone: 061.63.42.34; e-mail: feshadara@wanadoo.net.ma; website: www.perso.wanadoo.net.ma/feshadara), Fez. Naomi Seffar and her family are doing something very special at this *riad,* which I learned about from my friend Jo Ann H. *Dar al Hadara* translates as "cultural experience," and indeed it is more than just a beautiful place to rest your tired feet: it's like staying in a family's home, where you are made to feel like the most important guest. The *riad* itself is magnificent—it's included on a tour of traditional houses during the Fez Music Festival—and the complex is actually several *roud* built around a courtyard with an *orangerie* and a vegetable garden. There are plans for artisan workshops so that guests (and visitors) will have the opportunity to observe the artisans at work in a quiet, open, and airy space. The Seffar family has a vision, and it is one to be commended.

~Chez Benzakour (1–2 Souk Heina; e-mail: BENZAKOUR2001@yahoo.fr), Fez. I looked in all the pottery stalls in the Fez medina—I never made it to the potter's quarter on the other side of town—and decided on this one as the place to make my purchases of Fez blue pottery. I had already, wisely, visited the Dar Batha museum (Musée des Arts et Traditions), and so I was able to recognize that the wares here were of high quality. The young *patron* is also exceptionally kind and eager to make a deal that works out for both parties. It would really be impossible to walk away from his stock empty-handed.

~Argan oil. Two brands I bought are Saveurs du Maroc and Arganati, the first of which is exported to the United States. Argan oil is simply delicious, and deserves wider appreciation. Like olive oil, it is quite labor intensive to make, but more so: all the fruit from an argan tree—averaging about 250 pounds—yields enough seeds for a single liter of oil. In Morocco, argan oil is used mainly as a finishing touch for *tagines* and occasionally couscous, according to an article Florence Fabricant wrote for *The New York Times* (January 3, 2001). But some New York chefs are starting to use it more liberally; it has a very nutty taste and I like it best used alone in salads and drizzled on vegetables. Amalon, an argan paste that is delicious spread on toast, can also be purchased in Morocco as well as at some specialty stores in the States.

~The Koutoubiya Mosque, Marrakesh. A beautiful structure— with beautiful adjoining gardens—and a comforting one to use as a landmark. As Edith Wharton wrote, "The Koutoubya would be magnificent anywhere; in this flat desert it is grand enough to face the Atlas. The Almohad conquerors who built the Koutoubya and embellished Marrakech dreamed a dream of beauty that extended from the Guadalquivir to the Sahara; and at its two extremes they placed their watch-towers. The Giralda watched over civilized ene- mies in a land of ancient Roman culture; the Koutoubya stood at the edge of the world, facing the hordes of the desert."

~Trésor du Sud (Rue El Moissine, no. 49; 44.04.39), Marrakesh. This tiny *bijouterie* (jewelry shop) in the Marrakesh souk stands out for its distinctive quality pieces, both antique and new, which is why dealers and collectors are sometimes found inside examining beautiful things from all over Morocco. Don't let the fact that col- lectors come here turn you away: there are many good value items that will not break your budget. *Patron* Benhatoum Essaid is knowl- edgeable and kind and speaks English. It was from him that I learned about the significance of the number seven. I had wanted to buy some plain silver bangles for a friend, but he wouldn't allow me to break up a set of seven. Seven, it seems, holds a special value to Marrakchis. As Justin McGuinness explains in the Footprint Guide,

"The city has seven spiritual masters, the *seb'atu rijal*. A Berber tale runs that in the beginning were seven brothers born of the same mother at the same time—and who all died at the same time. When they were born, they were presented to the prince of the city on a silver plate in the form of 'seven fried fish.' In the seventeenth century, the powerful Alaouite sultan Moulay Ismail, keen to remove any threats to his rule, is said to have promoted the cult of seven saints in Marrakech—to counterbalance the cult of seven saints in the Regrega region which had led to the overthrow of the preceding dynasty, the Saadians." Additionally, the Marrakchis say their city has seven gates opening onto the cemeteries protecting the town.

~Afternoon tea at La Maison Arabe, Marrakesh. (I have yet to have again, all at once, the unbelievably delicious Moroccan sweets as served here. I think the kitchen should box up the assortment and sell them); and breakfast at La Maison Arabe; and simply being at La Maison Arabe, which has earned its justifiably famous reputation. It's a tranquil, beautifully appointed *maison d'hôte* that is a short, ten-minute walk from the Djemaa el Fna. The inn has a shuttle to take guests to its refreshing pool (a very good thing on a very hot day in Marrakesh), and upon request a Moroccan cooking course for small groups can be arranged. A *great* article to read that I was unable to include here is "Moroccan Secret" by Heather Smith MacIsaac (*Travel & Leisure,* September 1998) with a dozen color photographs of La Maison Arabe, "the perfect hotel." I generally tire of articles about hotels, but this is one of the few that is interesting to read, perhaps because the history and fine details of La Maison Arabe are truly interesting. (The article is also worth tracking down for the shopkeepers recommended by Jacqueline Foissac, who has lived in Marrakesh for over thirty years and is Yves Saint Laurent's decorator.) La Maison Arabe's owner, Fabrizio Ruspoli, stopped at nothing when he undertook to renovate the hotel. (It was once a legendary restaurant.) "People travel a long way for something different," he has said. "I didn't just want to redefine comfort. I wanted the experience to be richer." And it is. (1 Derb Assehbe Bab Doukkala, Marrakesh medina; 044.38.70.10; fax: 044.38.72.21; maisonarabe@cybernet.net.ma; website: www.lamaisonarabe.com)

~La Maison du Thé (angle de la Rue Ibn Aicha et Med El Beqal; 06.1.6.75.58.86), Marrakesh. A quiet and relaxing *salon de thé,* restaurant, and *magasin de thé* in Gueliz, with an enormous choice of quality teas, located not far from the Jardin Majorelle.

~Riad Enija (Derb Mesfioui, no. 9), Marrakesh. The Riad Enija has been referred to as the most luxurious hotel in Morocco. I'm not certain this is absolutely true, but the over-four-hundred-year-old former residence of a silk trader is certainly among the most luxurious places to stay in the world. It has only nine uniquely appointed rooms, none of which has the trappings of our (dubious) progressive times (television and telephone). You'd be hard pressed to name another place that is so synonymous with *serenity.* Some rooms, each one completely different from the others, are suites big enough for a family. The *patrons,* Ursula Haldimann and Bjorn Conerdings, created a promotional postcard that I think perfectly depicts Enija: a simple color photograph of a teal, gold-handled vase filled with light pink roses, set on a white stone surface in front of a Moroccan arabesque window grill. On the reverse of the card is a map—quite helpful initially, until you realize that the *riad* is only a few minutes' walk from the Café de France on the Place Djemaa el Fna. (044.44.09.26 or 44.44.00.14; fax: 044.44.27.00; www.riadenija.com)

~Pâtisserie des Princes (32 Bab Agnaou), Marrakesh. This is definitely a royal *pâtisserie,* with a fabulous array of uncommonly delicious Moroccan sweets. The shop also has boxed assortments of treats, at varying prices, that make great gifts. (And because the confections are not typically perishable, you don't have to worry about them melting on the plane.)

~Dar al Assad (Dabachi, Derb Hajra, no. 29; tel/fax: 044. 42.70.65), Marrakesh. This lovely and calm *maison d'hôte* is just a five-minute walk from the Djemaa el Fna (and is actually quite close to the Riad Enija, above). The *patrons*, Yves Maussion and Daniel Bainvel, are charming and helpful, and they have stocked a particularly good little library off the central courtyard with books (in French) on Morocco. Breakfast is a real treat at Dar al Assad and can include local melons, yogurt, flaky croissants, delicious jams, and fresh orange juice. Brush up on your French because Yves and Daniel do not speak much English.

~Jardin Majorelle et Musée d'Art Islamique (off Avenue Ya'qub al-Mansur), Marrakesh. One of the jewels of Morocco, and the world. Though the Majorelle isn't very large—it was, after all, the home and garden of painter Jacques Majorelle—the rewards of lingering are great. Don't miss the small museum of Islamic art, which houses some exquisite objects. I am as crazy for the famous Majorelle blue as thousands of other visitors, but as Justin McGuinness notes in his Footprint Guide, "Sensitive souls tempted to try Majorelle Garden blue in decorating schemes back home in northern climes should beware—the result depends on bright sunlight filtered by lush vegetation."

~Yacout (79 Sidi Ahmed Soussi; 044.38.29.29; fax: 044. 38.29.00), Marrakesh. As revealed in the articles in *Saveurs Marocains,* the food at Yacout does not stray from the path of traditional Moroccan cuisine. It's very, very good but is not innovative. However, the real reason to come here is for the decor and the experience. I do not think you will be disappointed.

~The Menara Gardens (Avenue de la Menara), Marrakesh. Everyone raves about the view toward the Atlas from here, and the reflecting pool, but I did not find it so impressive. The reason to come here is to do what the Moroccans do: picnic and relax in the olive grove, which surrounds the pavilion.

~Au Minaret Mouassine (56 Fhel Chidmi Mouassine; 044. 44.13.57; cell phone: 061.72.96.78), Marrakesh. You will, of course, pass by or even enter more than a few carpet shops in the Marrakesh souk, but I am partial to this one. I am not implying that you will find the prices here any better than elsewhere, but this was one of the few shops that had a particular type of rug I was looking for: the red wool and straw style from the Ourika Valley (this weaving is unique to the Ourika Valley, so I thought it a good purchase as it is only woven in that part of Morocco). Anyway, once I was inside this shop, I not only found good versions of what I was looking for but a kind and funny staff, especially Hajib. In addition to old and modern rugs, it offers some pottery pieces and a few other Moroccan items.

~La Mamounia (Avenue Bab Jdid; 44.44.44.09; fax: 44.44.49.40; www.mamounia.com), Marrakesh. I know it's really, really famous and really, really expensive, but La Mamounia is positively, as Winston Churchill said, "one of the most lovely spots in the whole world." I would add that it is among only five or ten of the most special places to stay in the universe. Some say it is overpriced, but that is for you to decide. The gardens—which were in existence long before the hotel was built—were originally a wedding gift from the sultan Sidi Mohamed Ben Abdellah, who reigned in the eighteenth century, to his fourth son, Moulay Mamoun. Besides the flowers, lemon trees, palm trees, roses, and banana trees, there are olive trees (which are harvested in the fall) and orange trees (which are picked for four months a year). The gardens, on almost twenty acres, require thirty-four full-time gardeners. Though staying here is a splurge, La Mamounia, too, offers low-season rates. If you do stay, you might be interested in a book entitled *Mamounia, Marrakech, Maroc* (André Paccard Éditions Atelier 74, 1987). It's in French, but that won't matter a bit if you can't read it. Even if you just stop by for a quick look at the hotel, you might want this *luxe livre,* as you can't very well walk around taking photos of it all. My favorite part of the book is the last chapter, "L'Art Traditionnel Marocain à la Mamounia," which details the *zelliges,* fountains, woodwork, stone carvings, marble, metal, gardens, birds, and even the uniforms of each staff member.

~The drive from Marrakesh to Ouarzazate, over the High Atlas Mountains. I have a short list of great drives of the world, and this is on it. The Atlas is like no other range I've seen, and this route almost always offers a view of Toubkal, the highest mountain in North Africa. According to Moroccan lore, Atlas was a Greek god living in the Mediterranean. He was a Titan (just as in Greek mythology) busy fighting other giants. One day he lost a battle and decided to hide along the African shoreline. He was so gigantic, of course, that when he lay down to sleep, his head was tucked into Tunisia and his feet stretched all the way down to Marrakesh. This position was so nice that he never woke up again and became a mountain. Snow fell on Atlas regularly, for a few months of the year, but he could always feel his feet happily ensconced in the desert.

~The neatly arranged pyramids of spices in any souk.

~Comptoir Darna (Avenue Echouada, Hivernage, Marrakesh, 04.43.77.02). For dinner, tapas, and lounge music. A hip, young crowd frequents this outpost of its sister establishment in Paris. As always with mod crowds, *Comptoir* may no longer be "in" when this book is published, although there certainly aren't a great number of nightclubs serving alcohol opening in Morocco. There really isn't another place like *Comptoir,* and I think it will be "in" for a long time.

~El Badi Palace and especially the minbar from the Koutoubia Mosque displayed in a small gallery on the far side of the palace (separate admission charge). This minbar, referred to as a "masterpiece of Islamic art" by Susan Searight in the Maverick guide, is very fragile (it dates from 1137 in Cordoba, where it was made) and in 1996 a U.S./Moroccan team began restoration work (the U.S. was represented by the Metropolitan Museum of Art in New York). It is quite beautiful, and I would never have known about it had Searight not enthused about it in her book. As she notes, "It is impossible to do justice to what the director of the Metropolitan Museum of Art calls 'one of the marvels of its age and one of the finest works of art ever produced by the craftsmen and artists of the Moslem world.'"

~Hotel Riad Salam (Avenue Mohammad V, 044.88.22.06/fax: 044.88.27.66), Ouarzazate. This hotel, created from two kasbah-like structures, is a great place to unwind and relax in the south. Ask for one of the rooms on the second floor with private terraces that overlook the large and inviting pool, complete with a small bar.

When I visited, there were no Americans in sight, just some French and British tourists. The hotel is close to everything you'd want to do in and around Ouarzazate, and the staff also helps arrange trips to the desert and beyond.

· Bibliothèque

Classics

The Arabian Nights: Tales From a Thousand and One Nights, translated, with a preface and notes, by Sir Richard F. Burton, introduction by A. S. Byatt, Modern Library, New York, 2001; *The Arabian Nights,* translated by Husain Haddawy, edited by Muhsin Mahdi, Everyman's Library, New York, 1992. From the original set of stories known as *The Arabian Nights* (or as A. S. Byatt notes in the introduction to the Modern Library edition, "a thousand nights and one night," as translated from Arabic) there evolved two separate versions, a Syrian and an Egyptian. Of these two, the Syrian version is the oldest existing manuscript and can be found at the Bibliothèque Nationale in Paris. As it is the oldest (fourteenth century), it is considered by some therefore to be closest to the "original" collection of tales. The Everyman's Library translation is based on this Syrian edition, while the Modern Library edition is based on a later one. The Burton translation is widely considered to be the more definitive of the two, although I leave that for the reader to decide. Haddawy believes that Burton was working with such an inferior version that his version was "no more than a literary Brighton Pavilion." A. S. Byatt, again in her introduction to the Burton translation, refers to Haddawy's translation as "scholarly and elegant" but says that "the most accessible complete translation remains Burton's extraordinary translation." I have not compared them side by side, but it is true that Haddawy translated only parts of the collection while Burton translated the entire thing. (His original translation ran to sixteen volumes; this Modern Library edition reproduces the Modern Library edition from 1932, for which no less a personage than Random House founder Bennet Cerf chose the most famous and representative stories from Burton's multivolume set.) The Modern Library edition is paperback, while the Everyman's edition is hardcover; whichever volume you read—or reread—there is no other work of fiction as appropriate or as entertaining. The fact that the tales do not derive from Morocco is irrelevant (although it seems many of the magicians in the tales were Moroccan); reflective travelers will see that indeed the tales and their morals are prevalent throughout Moroccan life and deserve some quality time with your eyes and and your thoughts.

Arabian Nights: Four Tales from a Thousand and One Nights, Marc Chagall, introduction by Norbert Noris, Prestel, 1988; original color lithographs published in 1948, together with reproductions of the relevant pen-and-ink drawings, by Pantheon Books in an edition of 111 copies entitled *Four Tales From the Arabian Nights.* This is a beautiful companion volume to the timeless tales of *The Arabian Nights;* in fact, I can't imagine a finer companion than Chagall. The four tales presented here are from the Burton translation and include "The Ebony Horse," "Julnar the Sea-Born and Her Son King Badr Basim of Persia," "Abdullah the Fisherman and Abdullah the Merman," "Kamar Al-Zaman and the Jeweller's Wife." As Noris notes in the introduction, "We know that the tales come from a wide variety of cultures—India and Persia, Egypt and Mesopotamia, Syria and Arabia—and that in the course of centuries they merged into a single work welded together by the Arabic language and the Islamic faith. Few people know that many tales deriving from Hebrew culture also found their way into the collection or that other stories from the traditions and legends of that culture became so strongly assimilated into the Islamic-Arabian world that their origin is scarcely recognizable." Chagall was enchanted by the tales, and this finely printed book is a treasure. It's out of print but is worth every effort to track down. (Try Hacker Books in New York—see "Bookstores" in *Renseignements Pratiques* for details).

Fiction, Short Stories, and Mysteries

~A note about the many titles listed here by Paul Bowles: I have not included every single edition published because each entry would be too cumbersome. Many of Bowles's books were originally published in London by Peter Owen, and readers should know that the American editions of these same books are not always identical. Some titles are no longer in print in hardcover but are still available in paperback; some are in print in the U.K. and are readily available there but not here; still others are out of print altogether. With diligence, one should be able to find every Bowles book published, and I think the effort would be worthwhile.

Corruption, Tahar Ben Jelloun, New Press, 1996.

For Bread Alone, Mohammed Choukri, translated by Paul Bowles, I. B. Tauris, 2000.

A Hundred Camels in the Courtyard, Paul Bowles, City Lights Books, San Francisco, 1962. As readers of my other books know, I don't critique works of fiction, not because I don't have favorites, but because I feel it's more important for readers to recognize the wealth and diversity of companion reading available. I cannot resist describing what Bowles has done with this particular work. In 1960 he had the idea to construct stories "whose subject matter would consist of disparate elements and unrelated characters taken directly from life and fitted together as in a mosaic." He then listed some episodes he'd heard about or witnessed over the previous year and decided to use *kif* as the device to weave them together. I found it to be a brilliant collection, and I will never get out of my head the three statements told to him by a *kif*-smoker from Marrakesh: "The eye wants to sleep, but the head is no mattress"; "The earth trembles and the sky is afraid, and the two eyes are not brothers"; and "A pipe of *kif* before breakfast gives a man the strength of a hundred camels in the courtyard." It's only ninety pages long, making it a great bring-along.

The Lemon, Mohammed Mrabet, translated by Paul Bowles, City Lights Books, San Francisco, 1986.

Let It Come Down, Paul Bowles, Black Sparrow Press, Santa Rosa, California, 1981.

Look and Move On, Mohammed Mrabet, translated by Paul Bowles, Dufour Editions, 1989, hardcover; Black Sparrow Press, Santa Rosa, California, 1976, paperback.

Love with a Few Hairs, Mohammed Mrabet, translated by Paul Bowles, George Braziller, 1968, hardcover; City Lights Books, San Francisco, 1992, paperback.

M'Hashish, Mohammed Mrabet, translated by Paul Bowles, City Lights Books, San Francisco, 1969.

Midnight Mass, Paul Bowles, Black Sparrow Press, Santa Rosa, California, 1983.

Mrs. Pollifax and the Whirling Dervish, Dorothy Gilman, Doubleday, 1990.

Points in Time, Paul Bowles, Ecco Press, 1990.

The Road to Fez, Ruth Knafo Setton, Counterpoint, 2001.

The Sacred Night, Tahar Ben Jelloun, Johns Hopkins University Press, 2000.

The Sand Child, Tahar Ben Jelloun, Johns Hopkins University Press, 2000.

The Shadow Spy, Nicholas Luard, Macmillan, 1990.

The Sheltering Sky, Paul Bowles, originally published by The Ecco Press, 1949. Vintage International edition, 1990 (paperback); anniversary edition published by The Ecco Press, 2000 (hardcover).

The Spider's House, Paul Bowles, with a preface by the author, Black Sparrow Press, Santa Rosa, California, 1999; originally published by Random House, 1955. Once again, I'm making an exception with this Bowles novel because it is a masterpiece, and more than any other work—fiction or nonfiction—conveys the true essence of Morocco and Moroccans. (It's also one of the best books I've ever read, though I am less than enamored with the ending.) Bowles

states in the preface that "I wanted to write a novel using as backdrop the traditional daily life of Fez, because it was a medieval city functioning in the twentieth century. If I had started it only a year sooner, it would have been an
entirely different book. I intended to describe Fez as it existed at the moment
of writing about it, but even as I started to write, events that could not be
ignored had begun to occur there. I soon saw that I was going to have to write,
not about the traditional pattern of life in Fez, but about its dissolution. For
more than two decades I had been waiting to see the end of French rule in
Morocco. Ingenuously I had imagined that after Independence the old manner
of life would be resumed and the country would return to being more or less
what it had been before the French presence. The detestation on the part of the
populace of all that was European seemed to guarantee such a result. What I
failed to understand was that if Morocco was still a largely medieval land, it
was because the French themselves, and not the Moroccans, wanted it that
way." *All* of Bowles's books are well crafted, engrossing reads, but if I was only
going to recommend one, it would be this. *De rigueur.*
Tangier, William Bayer, Dutton, 1978.

Art Styles, Moroccan Crafts, Islamic Art and Architecture

Arts and Crafts of Morocco, James F. Jereb, Chronicle Books, 1996, paperback;
originally published by Thames and Hudson, London, 1995, hardcover. This
book is considered to be the authoritative edition among Moroccan retailers
and importers I've met here in the United States. With individual chapters on
textiles, jewelry, leatherwork, woodwork, metalwork, and ceramics, as well as
particularly good chapters on beliefs, symbols, tattoos, ceremonies, and the
celebration of life and death, it is truly an indispensable book for anyone interested in these artisan traditions. Certainly one's ability to bargain successfully
for crafts in the souks is partially based on one's knowledge of how and why
the items are made, and this book is perhaps the best resource available. As the
author notes, Morocco's artistic traditions can be divided into two distinct
areas of activity: rural and urban. Weaving, jewelry, embroidery, pottery,
woodwork, and leatherwork are all rural arts, while the artistic tradition of the
urban environment—which was developed in the imperial cities as well as in
Essaouira and Tetouan—"is determined by a strict set of aesthetic canons
found throughout the Moslem world: in general, it is more concerned with
scripture, puritanism and devotion." To explain further, rural men and women
are not professional artisans, and the traditions they carry on are primarily util-
itarian (weaving and pottery, for example). Urban artisans earn a full-time living from the works they create, and while in centuries past they filled orders

for the sultans, today they work mostly for wealthier Moroccans and tourists. Sometimes the rural and urban traditions interact, and the rich diversity that this mingling has produced is explored well in the text and illustrations. The final chapter, "Collecting Moroccan Arts and Crafts," is especially helpful and includes not only all sorts of tips on finding particular items and bargaining but—wisely—a list of museums in the States and abroad that have collections of items from the Maghreb. Readers who live close to Indianapolis, Austin, Washington, Honolulu, New York, Philadelphia, and New Mexico, for example, have opportunities to look at and learn about Moroccan arts before departing. And should you decide to fly to Paris en route to Morocco, the Musée des Arts d'Afrique et d'Océanie has "the most representative collection of jewelry, ceramics, woodwork and textiles on display in Europe." (You could add a visit to l'Institut du Monde Arabe and the Paris mosque *hammam* for a really complete visit.) *De rigueur.*

From the Far West: Carpets and Textiles of Morocco, edited by Patricia L. Fiske, W. Russell Pickering, and Ralph S. Yohe, The Textile Museum, Washington, D.C., 1980. In English and French, this outstanding book features color and black-and-white photographs and carpets from all across Morocco. Plus, there's an extremely handy lexicon of textile terms in English, French, and the Berber dialect of Tamazight. An excellent, excellent resource.

Islamic Arts, Jonathan Bloom and Sheila Blair, Phaidon Press Limited, London, 1997. This comprehensive volume is part of the paperback Art and Ideas series. Filled with color photos, its chapters cover mosques, mansions, and mosaics; pots, pans, and pitchers; *madrasas* and *muqarnas;* penmen and painters; warps, wefts, and pile; velvets and carpets; and more. It provides a few good maps of the Islamic world as it appeared at different times throughout history, as well as a glossary, a listing of major dynasties, a chart of key dates, and a good bibliography. Morocco is actually not widely represented in the book; still, this good, general overview allows for much contrasting and comparing of styles and colors with other Muslim nations.

Noble Dreams, Wicked Pleasures: Orientalism in America, 1870–1930, Holly Edwards, with essays by Brian T. Allen, Steven C. Caton, Zeynep Celik, and Oleg Grabar, Princeton University Press, in association with The Sterling and Francine Clark Art Institute, 2000; published on the occasion of the exhibition of the same name at The Sterling and Francine Clark Art Institute, Williamstown, Massachusetts (6 June–4 September 2000); the Walters Art Gallery, Baltimore, Maryland (1 October–10 December 2000); Mint Museum of Art, Charlotte, North Carolina (3 February–23 April 2001). Edwards, who was also the curator of this exhibition, is an Islamic art historian by training. In her preface, she notes that for this show she defined the "Orient" as it was most often conceived in the late nineteenth century—the accessible but still

exotic regions bordering the Mediterranean Sea, including the Levant (referring to the countries bordering the eastern shores of the Mediterranean, and to
the sun rising in the east—note the French verb *se lever* and the Spanish
lavarse) and North Africa. "Representations of Ancient Egypt, India, Tibet,
and even Persia were difficult to incorporate into the exhibition without losing
conceptual clarity. Each of these regions and cultural traditions invoked different and tangential questions." Once she decided to narrow the geographic
focus, she realized she still faced a wide and varied mountain of material ranging from paintings to movies, decorative arts, and advertising; she decided to
concentrate on the *theme* of the show rather than on one *medium*. Therefore,
she did not set out to present a definitive study of Orientalist painting; rather,
the exhibit explores several aspects of the "oriental" phenomenon in American
art and popular culture. I applaud Edwards's broad approach, as I rarely see
the point of examining something in a vacuum. This book is fascinating and
includes one of my most favorite paintings: *Fumée d'ambre gris* by John Singer
Sargent, to my mind one of the top ten paintings in the entire collection of the
Clark Institute. Other artists represented include Louis Comfort Tiffany,
Hiram Powers, Frederick Edwin Church, Edwin Lord Weeks, Maxfield
Parrish, William Merritt Chase, and Frederick Arthur Bridgman.

The Orientalists: Painter-Travellers, Lynne Thornton, ACR PocheCouleur, ACR
Edition Internationale, Paris, 1994. According to author Thornton, "There was
no school of Orientalist painting; the pictures were linked thematically rather
than stylistically." But for lack of a better category in this bibliography, I have
included Orientalism as a "style," and I would consider it a great omission
from a work on Morocco if Orientalism were absent. The word *Orientalist*
refers both to someone who is a bit of an expert on all facets of the Orient—
languages, history, customs, religions—as well as someone who is a Western
painter of the Oriental world. In the nineteenth century, Western painters
(mostly from France and Britain) set out eagerly for what they called the
Orient: the north coast of Africa, Arabia, and the Levant, to the Ottoman
Empire. Spain (because of its Arab history) and Venice (because of its historical connections to Constantinople) were also popular destinations, as they
were seen as gateways to the Orient. Eventually, Orientalism became an official category in the Paris Salon, and when it became all the rage, even artists
who had never set foot in the Near East or North Africa began to bring touches
of the exotic to their work. Best known of these was Ingres, and the best known
of his canvases in this style are *Great Odalisque* (in the Louvre), *Odalisque and
Slave* (in the Fogg Museum of Art, Cambridge, Massachusetts), and *Turkish
Bath* (also in the Louvre). The longevity of Orientalism is impressive: it can be
loosely established as beginning with Napoleon's Egyptian campaign in 1798
and running through the 1870s. (American Orientalism began and ended a lit-

tle later.) Some of the painter-travelers featured in this little book (appropriately named *PocheCouleur* as it's small enough to fit a pocket—*poche*) include Léon Belly, Maurice Bompard, Frederick Arthur Bridgman (though born in America, he moved to France), Frank Dillon, Eugène Flandin, Mariano Fortuny y Marsal, Eugène Fromentin, Jean-Léon Gérôme, Edward Lear, David Roberts, Horace Vernet, and Félix Ziem.

Picturing the Middle East: A Hundred Years of European Orientalism, Gerald Ackerman, Julia Ballerini, Eric Zafran, Ilene Susan Fort, Mary Harper, and James Thompson, published on the occasion of the exhibition of the same name at the Dahesh Museum, New York, 17 October 1995–27 January 1996. The title of this exhibition (which was wonderful) and this book (which began as a series of papers presented at a symposium) is somewhat misleading, as its scope is larger than our current definition of the Near or Middle East. The six essays presented are all enlightening, even if they are not specific to Morocco. Two are devoted to two "undisputed masterpieces of the nineteenth century": Delacroix's *Women of Algiers in Their Apartment* and Ingres's *The Turkish Bath,* both in the Louvre. I especially like the opening essay, "Why Some Orientalists Traveled to the East: Some Sobering Statistics," for the refreshing refrain by Gerald Ackerman: "Instead of endowing painters with a set of insidious colonialist or imperialist motives, one should acknowledge their sympathy and love for the lands and peoples they visited, and recognize that their limited understanding was gained through sincere effort despite great cultural differences. Many worked for the preservation of these cultures, their arts, and their monuments. Some even used the integrity of native crafts as a model for reviving the craft tradition of the West. These young men and women were, of course, saddled with both naivete and some insurmountable prejudices, but for the most part their hearts were in the right place. One should not mistake attitudes for motives." As the authors collectively note, it's important not to over-analyze Orientalism, or we'll completely miss its real artistic merit and real enjoyment. To echo Ackerman's observation above, it would seem impossible for the European painters to completely remove themselves from the conventions of their own environment; but the best of them successfully captured the appearance, romantic and otherwise, of a fascinating part of the world. Whether or not they fully grasped the intricacies of a culture and religion so different from their own is still being debated.

A Practical Guide to Islamic Monuments in Morocco, Richard Parker, published under the sponsorship of The Aga Khan Program for Islamic Architecture at Harvard University and the Massachusetts Institute of Technology, The Baraka Press, Charlottesville, Virginia, 1981. I had never heard of this book until I read the *Maverick Guide to Morocco,* which is entirely vexing as it is not only outstanding but is the only book of its kind. The descriptive copy on the back cover serves as a better review than I could write: "A guide for the person who wants to know more about the wonderful monuments of the Moroccan dynasties than he will find in the usual guidebook, or learn from the tourist guide. It includes practical directions on how to find them, readable descriptions and explanations of their significance, and useful survival information." It also features dozens of black-and-white and color photos, floor plans, a glossary of related terms, and a chapter on Algeria, because, as Parker states, "one must cross the border into Algeria to get a complete picture of Moroccan religious architecture." (Unfortunately, even though Algerians permit non-Muslims to enter mosques, it is no longer so easy to cross the Algerian border. Parker himself is an Arabic specialist who has served as ambassador to Algeria, Lebanon, and Morocco. He wrote a similar book on Islamic monuments in Cairo, which I do not have but am eager to find. Positively a must-have, and *de rigueur.*

The Splendour of Islamic Calligraphy, Abdelkebir Khatibi and Mohammed Sijelmassi, Thames and Hudson, 2001. Originally published in hardcover, this new paperback edition is an excellent companion volume to Parker's *Islamic Monuments.* The authors live in Morocco and are widely considered to be authorities on Islamic art and culture. They lecture and write extensively on all aspects of Islamic arts, and this book has been hailed as "the most beautifully illustrated study ever produced on the subject." Outstanding examples of a variety of scripts—Maghrebi included—are featured in illustrated manuscripts, paintings, and other works of art.

Design and Decorating

Morocco: Design from Casablanca to Marrakesh, photographs by Lisl Dennis, and text by Landt Dennis, Clarkson Potter, 1992, hardcover; revised, paperback edition entitled *Living in Morocco: Design From Casablanca to Marrakesh,* by Thames and Hudson, 2001. This was the book that really put Morocco on the map for a great number of North Americans when it first appeared a decade ago. I was distressed to learn that by the fall of 2000 the original hardcover was out of print, but happily we now have the revised paperback edition. Every corner of Morocco is featured in this book, presenting a full range of habitats as well as the folk arts of textiles, rugs, leather, pottery, and *thuya* wood. The "Shoppers' Guide" at the back of the book—with the names of stores and souks in the United States and Morocco—is a fabulous resource. The paperback edition features a more extensive and updated shopper's guide, and some chapters from the hardcover book have been replaced with new ones (La Mamounia and Yves St. Laurent and Pierre Bergé's house in Marrakesh, and the Tishka Hotel, are new to the paperback). *De rigueur.*

Moroccan Interiors, Lisa Lovatt-Smith, edited by Angelika Muthesius, Taschen, 1995. Another book in the beautiful Interiors series (other volumes include Paris, London, Provence, and Tuscany), this book features the Moroccan residences of Yves Saint Laurent and Pierre Bergé, Jacqueline Foissac, Florence and Bernard Lévy, Vanessa and Frederick Vreeland, Bill Willis, Bert Flint, and David Herbert, among others, as well as an excellent chapter on Islamic architecture in Morocco.

Morocco Modern, Herbert Ypma, Stewart, Tabori and Chang, New York, 1996; Thames and Hudson, London, 1996. Another volume in the World Design Series (other volumes include *Paris Flea Market, Pacific Island,* and *London Minimum,* all conceived and authored by Ypma), this book examines the artisan traditions that still inform modern design as it's practiced today in Morocco, in five chapters, by highlighting just a few well-chosen examples (including the wonderful Villa Maroc in Essaouira). The last chapter, "Virtuosi," focuses on the work of architect Charles Boccara, "nicknamed 'the master' for his singular life-long devotion to the development of an appropriate modern architecture for Morocco." Most helpful are the final two pages of the book: sources for such *belles choses* as a can of Blue Kasbah paint (like the blue at the Jardin Majorelle in Marrakesh), old tin tea containers, tiles, *tagines,* pottery, lanterns, and mosaics.

Gardens

Majorelle: A Moroccan Oasis, Pierre Bergé and Madison Cox, photographs by Claire de Virien, Vendôme Press, Paris, 1999. I still cannot get over the special color of blue found on the buildings, urns, pools, and fountains at the Jardin Majorelle in Marrakesh. This little book, in the Small Books of Great Gardens series (other volumes include Ninfa, Alhambra, and Apremont), is a mini–Majorelle blue portfolio, better than any photographs you could take of your own (with apologies to professional shutterbugs). In addition to the text—about the garden and about painter Jacques Majorelle—there is a plan of the garden and a few photos of Majorelle and some of his paintings.

Antique and Rare

The Classic Mediterranean, John Bancroft Devins, American Tract Society, 1910. A beautifully printed book with a chapter on Morocco. Some of the text—like the following passage—is the reason I like to read these out-of-print, period books: "To-day, with England dominating Egypt and the Soudan, France is having the upper hand in Morocco. Germany does not like this arrangement, and there may be a change in the not too distant future."

I have been unable to find a book exclusively devoted to the shops and souks of Morocco, but *The Fearless Shopper: How to Get the Best Deals on the Planet* (by Kathy Borrus, Travelers' Tales, San Francisco, 2000) is an excellent resource, and Morocco is covered in the "Africa and the Middle East" chapter. Author Borrus is a former assistant director, merchandise manager, and buyer for the Smithsonian Institution Museum Shops. She has a knack for recognizing a good value and offers great advice in the chapters entitled "Bargaining 101," "Advanced Bargaining," and "Bazaars, Souks and Third World Markets." Shipping items home and on-line shopping are addressed, and Borrus also provides a size and comparison chart and a nineteen-page list of resources and references. This book is not just for travelers, however, and my favorite chapter might be "Fair Trade," in which she quotes someone as saying, "When you buy a product, you're endorsing a way of doing business." *De rigueur.*

~Some good shopping vocabulary words to know are *soldes* (sales); *moitié-prix* (half-price); *deuxième choix* (seconds); *tout doit disparaître!* (everything must go!); and *je regarde* (I'm just looking, thank you; useful for any type of shopping or browsing).

~If you return home and realize that, *mon dieu,* you so regret not buying those bowls from Safi or that lantern in Marrakesh, worry not: here are a few companies that import a variety of Moroccan crafts, and there are many more besides (please write and let me know of retailers and wholesalers in your part of the country): The Edge of the World—one of the greatest names for a Moroccan company (251 East 32nd Street, Suite 2F, New York, New York 10016; 212-779-3751; fax: 689-3781). Farid Najjar, originally from Casablanca, imports a multitude of items ranging from lanterns and mosaic tables to painted furniture, ceramics, and scented water bottles. If you are interested in viewing these crafts or talking about them in greater detail, please telephone Farid in New York. *Thé à la Menthe* (147 Albert Palace Mansion, Lurline Gardens, London SW11 4DJ, England; phone and fax: 011.44.207.622.7918; e-mail: N.NASSIF@ukonline.co.uk; website: www.alamen-the.com). Nadia Nassif is the creative force behind *Thé à la Menthe,* an innovative company based in Casablanca that designs, produces, and exports a unique selection of handcrafted furniture and ornamental items from Morocco. (See "Traveling to the Source," *Travel & Leisure,* October 2000 for a profile of Nadia.) Nadia will take a silver Berber bracelet, for example, and fashion it into a candleholder, or even a coaster for a bottle of wine. She has *thuya* wood carvers from Essaouira make frames to accommodate beautiful old travel posters for Morocco. In New York, ABC Carpet and Home, Portico Bed and Bath, and Felissimo regularly carry items from *Thé à la Menthe,* including mosaic tables, wrought-iron chairs, lanterns, straw carpets, and chairs. Inquire about other retail stores around the United States that carry the line via e-mail or the Internet. Requests for customized designs and decorating are happily accepted. (Nadia has done up entire rooms and apartments.) Adam Imports (22 West Bryan Street, Suite 383, Savannah, Georgia 31401; 912-355-6490/fax: 912-234-7573; www.adamimports.com). This company imports unique handcrafted treasures from Morocco and other places around the world. From Morocco are bags, baskets, lamps, lanterns, wood crafts, mirrors, pottery, furniture, rugs, and accessories. Also, www.MedinaShop.com offers a selection of carpets, jewelry, fashion, leather, pottery, wood, metal, and wicker items. I found it a little hard to see some of the items clearly, even when enlarged, but the products seem to be authentic and attractive. There is also a section called "Ali's Good Deals" that features marked-down items and opportunities for bargaining!

Travel Anthologies, Journals, and Other Good Things

Seaside Interiors, Diane Dorrans Saeks, edited by Angelika Taschen, Taschen, 2000. Only two of these to-die-for interiors are Moroccan (one on the North Atlantic coast, the other in Tangier), but who cares? This entire book—one in the Interiors series—is gorgeous and particularly irresistible.

Traveler's Journal (Peter Pauper Press), *Voyages* (Chronicle Books), and the *Lonely Planet Travel Journal* are my current favorite journals. The first two are spiral-bound, which I like because the pages lie flat. *Traveler's Journal* features five clear plastic sleeves at the back for ticket stubs, photos, receipts, and the like (brilliant). *Voyages*—a bigger journal, measuring about 8½ by 11 inches—features an elastic band that wraps around the book from top to bottom (not quite as good as plastic sleeves, but the band helps to keep loose stuff inside). The *best* part about it, however, is the large envelope at the very back, which allows one to put all sorts of important papers inside, including one's *passport and credit cards*. Nobody but nobody wants to steal someone's little journal, and as long as you're not somebody who forgets your belongings, this is a great option for a money belt. The Lonely Planet journal is different from each of these by being rather sleek-looking, with a black, faux-leather cover measuring approximately 4 by 4 inches. Pages are lined on one side and blank on the reverse, and at the back of the book is a ton of essentials: twelve pages of maps of the world, calendars for 1999–2002, address pages, useful websites, clothing and footwear sizes, international dialing codes, metric/imperial conversions, a time zone conversion wheel (very nifty), and a pocket inside the back cover for all the loose ephemera one accumulates.

Additional Credits

The journey has just begun! Don't miss the other books in **Barrie Kerper's Collected Traveler** series—each one a rich source of literary delight and practical travel advice.

Paris: The Collected Traveler
0-609-80444-8. $16.00 paper
(Canada: $24.00)

Central Italy: The Collected Traveler
0-609-80443-X. $16.00 paper
(Canada: $24.00)

Provence: The Collected Traveler
0-609-80678-5. $16.00 paper
(Canada: $24.00)